Supercook

Marshall Cavendish London & New York

Contents

Volume 22

This edition published 1982

© Marshall Cavendish Ltd 1978, 1977, 1976, 1975, 1974, 1973, 1972
58 Old Compton Street, London W1V 5PA

Printed and bound in Singapore by Times Printers Sdn. Bhd.

ISBN (for set) 0 85685 534 0
ISBN (this volume) 0 85685 556 1
Library of Congress catalog card number 78 – 52319

Zihufitanejo	2997	Zrazi s Kashie	3022	Zune Ricotta and Cherry Tartlets	3053
Zindo Vando	2997	Zsa Zsa's Meatball Goulasch	3024	Zungeru Peanut Pork	3054
Zinfandel Beef	2998	Zubia Cod with Alioli Sauce	3025	Zunita Gâteau	3055
Zingara Sauce	2998	Zubov Calf's Liver Stroganov	3025	Zupanja Red Snapper Bake	3055
Zingarella Stew	2999	Zubrick Pork and Spiced Plums	3025	Zuppa di Anguille	3058
Zingari Gipsy-Style Spaghettini		Zubrowka Cocktail	3026	Zuppa di Aragosta	3058
Omelet	2999	Zubrowka Fruit Cocktail	3026	Zuppa di Cozze	3058
Zinnia's Chicken with Tarragon,		Zucca Cheese Loaf	3026	Zuppa a Due Colori	3059
Whisky and Cream	2999	Zucca alla Parmigiana	3027	Zuppa di Fagioli Fiorentina	3059
Zippy Avocado Hors d'Oeuvre	2999	Zuccherini	3028	Zuppa di Fontina	3059
Zippy Savoury Scramble	3000	Zucchero e Formaggio alla Crema	3028	Zuppa Inglese I	3059
Zip-Zap Lunchtime Snack	3000	Zucchini all'Agrodolce	3028	Zuppa Inglese II	3060
Zirje Island Fish Kebabs	3001	Zucchini con Aneto	3030	Zuppa di Pollo	3060
Zite with Italian Sausage Sauce	3001	Zucchini e Cavolfiore	3030	Zuppa di Verdura	3061
Zite with Meatballs and Tomato		Zucchini in Dolce	3030	Zuppa di Vongole e Pancotto	3061
Mushroom Sauce	3002	Zucchini al Formaggio	3030	Zuppa di Zucchini	3063
Zite with Port	3002	Zucchini con Fritelle	3032	Zurich Fruit Crumble	3063
Znojemsky Goulasch	3002	Zucchini con Mandorle	3032	Zurich Hazelnut Biscuits [Cookies]	3063
Zoar's Crispy Apple Bake	3006	Zucchini alla Marinara	3033	Zurich Lamb Delight	3064
Zocca Bananas	3006	Zucchini Orientali	3033	Zurich Roast Pork	3064
Zodiac Cake	3006	Zucchini e Peperoni	3033	Zurich Veal and Parsnip Pie	3065
Zoe's Delight	3007	Zucchini, Pomodori e Finocchio	3036	Zuriga Salmon Trout with	
Zofe Spinach Soup	3007	Zucchini Ripieni	3036	Mushroom Mayonnaise	3065
Zoftic Mixed Vegetables	3007	Zucchini Ripieni di Salsiccie	3036	Zurov Lamb	3066
Zogno Veal Cutlets	3007	Zucchini in Stufato	3037	Zute Salad	3066
Zogno Vegetarian Pasta	3008	Zucchini in Sufflè	3037	Zutian Sardine Flan	3066
Zola Chicken	3008	Zuccotash Sweet Potato and		Zuyder Chicken Breasts with	
Zoll Fruit Loaf	3009	Marshmallow Bake	3038	Tarragon and Sour Cream	3067
Zoller Pumpkin Soup	3009	Zuccotto I	3038	Zuzu Spiced Chicken Breasts	3067
Zoltan's Chicken Breasts	3011	Zuccotto II	3038	Zvengli's Poached Eggs	3068
Zomba Salt Cod and Avocado	3011	Zuccotto Torrone	3040	Zveno Tea Soufflé	3068
Zombie Cocktail	3012	Zuckerman Duck with Olives	3041	Zverovo Steamed Meat Loaf	3069
Zombie's Secret	3012	Zuera Tropical Sundae	3041	Zvettl Wine Cream Soup	3069
Zonder Sweetcorn and Petis Pois		Zug Pork Chops	3042	Zvezdochki	3070
Hors d'Oeuvre	3012	Zug Sausage and Leek Casserole	3042	Zvolen Caraway Seed Soup with	
Zonza Champagne Soup	3013	Zuger Zee Scramble	3043	Dumplings	3071
Zonza Stuffed Spare Rib	3013	Zuidhorn Kipper Pie	3043	Zwartberg Mountain Cassoulet	3071
Zoom-Zoom Sausage Toadstools	3014	Zuidhorn Liver and Rice	3044	Zwetschgenknödeln	3072
Zoondam Pork Ratatouille	3014	Zujar Chicken Liver Casserole	3044	Zwetschgenkuchen	3072
Zoose Pears	3014	Zujar Tomato Soufflés	3045	Zwickau Stuffed Fillet of Beef	3074
Zoo-Time Sandwiches	3014	Zuki Fruit Tartlets	3046	Zwickle Capon in Pastry	3074
Zopperelli Figs in Red Wine	3016	Zula Avocado Hors d'Oeuvre	3046	Zwieback Refrigerator Cheesecake	3074
Zora's Peach Dessert	3016	Zula Tangy Salad	3046	Zwieback mit Rhabarber	3076
Zoradora Dessert	3016	Zulcan Gammon and Gooseberries	3046	Zwieback mit Schwarzen	
Zorba's Meatballs	3016	Zulia Persimmon Flan	3047	Johannisbeeren	3076
Zorba's Tipsy Cake	3016	Zulinka Rum and Chocolate Soufflé	3048	Zwiebelfleisch	3077
Zorin's Lamb with Lemon Sauce	3018	Zulla Fish Pie	3049	Zwiebelkuchen	3077
Zorrell Cheese and Ham Rolls	3018	Zullah's Pasta, Sausage and Bean		Zwingle Spaghetti with Crabmeat	3079
Zossen Oxtail	3018	Salad	3049	Zwolle Orange Turkey	3079
Zouar Banana Ice-Cream	3018	Zulu Beef Pot	3050	Zyman Roast Beef	3079
Zouzou's Crêpes	3020	Zulu Beef Stew	3050	Zyrenia Noodle and Prune Bake	3080
Zoytinyagli Pirasa	3020	Zumar Scallops in Port	3050		
Zraza	3021	Zummah Rabbit Stew	3052		
Zrazi eze Ribi	3022	Zundy Teddy Bear Cake	3053	INDEX	3081

Supercook

The weights and measures equivalents are approximate only.

USEFUL TERMS FROM THE EUROPEAN COOK'S KITCHEN

Foreign Terms — American equivalents

Foreign Terms	American equivalents
bacon rashers	bacon slices
demerara sugar	pale brown granulated sugar
fillet steak	filet mignon
heatproof baking dish	flameproof casserole
icing	frosting
kitchen paper	paper towels
minced meat	ground meat
pastry case	pie crust
salad cream	salad dressing
to grill	to broil
to whisk	to beat
veal escalopes	veal scallops
single cream	light cream
double cream	heavy, whipping cream
cake tin	cake pan
frying pan	skillet
greaseproof paper	waxed paper
sieve	strainer
tea towel	dish towel
starter	appetizer
entree	main course
pudding	dessert

Foreign ingredients — American equivalents

Foreign ingredients	American equivalents
aubergine	eggplant
bicarbonate of soda	baking soda
biscuit	cookie
castor sugar	super fine sugar
cornflour	cornstarch
chutney	relish
cos lettuce	romaine lettuce
courgettes	zucchini
digestive biscuits	graham-cracker
double cream	heavy whipping cream
gammon slice	ham steak
haricot beans	dry white beans
icing sugar	confectioners sugar
marrows	large zucchini, or squash
Martini	vermouth
pancake	crêpe
plain flour	all-purpose flour
potato chips	French fries
potato crisps	potato chips
prawns	shrimp
salt beef	corned beef
scone	baking powder biscuit
single cream	light cream
sorbet	sherbert
sprats	smelts
spring onion	scallion
sultana	raisin
treacle	molasses
tunny fish	tuna fish
wholemeal flour	whole-grain flour

MEASUREMENT CONVERSIONS
Solid Measures

(1 ounce = 28.352 metric grams, but for convenience it is usually calculated, as in this chart, 1 ounce = 30 grams)

½ ounce = 15 grams	3½ ounces = 100 grams
1 ounce = 30 grams	1 pound, 1½ ounces = 500 grams
2 ounces = 60 grams	2 pounds, 3 ounces = 1,000 grams
2½ ounces = 75 grams	(1 kilogram)

Liquid measures

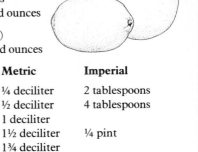

1 American cup = 8 fluid ounces
1 British Imperial cup = 10 fluid ounces

1 pint = 16 fluid ounces (2 cups)
1 British Imperial pint = 20 fluid ounces

fluid oz.	American	Metric	Imperial
1	2 tablespoons	¼ deciliter	2 tablespoons
2	¼ cup	½ deciliter	4 tablespoons
4	½ cup	1 deciliter	
5	²/₃ cup	1½ deciliter	¼ pint
6	¾ cup	1¾ deciliter	
8	1 cup (½ pint)	2¼ deciliter	
10	1¼ cups	2¾ deciliter	½ pint
16	2 cups (1 pint)	4½ deciliter	
20	2½ cups	5½ deciliter	1 pint
32	4 cups (1 quart)	9 deciliter	
36	4½ cups	1 liter	1⅓ pint, plus 1 ounce

Frequently-used measurements

	American	Metric	Imperial
butter	1 tablespoon	15 grams	½ ounce
	½ cup	25 grams	4 ounces
	1 cup	250 grams	1 pound
all-purpose flour	¼ cup	35 grams	1¼ ounces
	½ cup	75 grams	2½ ounces
	1 cup	142 grams	5 ounces
self-raising flour	¼ cup	30 grams	1 ounce
	½ cup	60 grams	2 ounces
	1 cup	120 grams	4 ounces
raisins	1 cup	156 grams	5½ ounces
rice	1 cup	240 grams	8 ounces
brown sugar	1 tablespoon	10 grams	⅓ ounce
	½ cup	90 grams	3 ounces
	1 cup	180 grams	6 ounces
super fine sugar	1 tablespoon	15 grams	½ ounce
	½ cup	120 grams	4 ounces
	1 cup	240 grams	8 ounces

This is the guide to the amount of skill needed for each recipe.

Easy   **Needs special care**   **Complicated**

 This is an estimated guide to the dish's cost, which will, of course, vary with the season.

Inexpensive   **Reasonable**   **Expensive**

This is an indication of the amount of time needed for preparing and cooking the dish.

Less than 1 hour   **1 hour to 2½ hours**   **Over 2½ hours**

Zihufitanejo
CRABMEAT SALAD

An appetizing first course from Central America, Zihufitanejo (thee-hoof-eet-an-ay-ho) is a delicious mixture of crabmeat, olives, tomatoes and onions, garnished with lettuce and advocado.

6-8 SERVINGS

1 lb. crabmeat, shell and
cartilage removed
juice of 2 lemons
2 fl. oz. [¼ cup] olive oil
4 medium-sized tomatoes, thinly
sliced
4 spring onions [scallions], trimmed
and finely chopped
4 oz. [1⅓ cups] stoned black olives
½ teaspoon dried marjoram
¼ teaspoon cayenne pepper
½ teaspoon salt
¼ teaspoon black pepper
4 fl. oz. [½ cup] dry white wine
1 lettuce, outer leaves discarded,
washed and separated into leaves
1 avocado, peeled, stoned and
thinly sliced

Place the crabmeat in a medium-sized bowl, pour over the lemon juice and set aside for 1 hour.

Place the crabmeat in a strainer and press down on the meat with the back of a wooden spoon. Discard the liquid extracted.

Return the crabmeat to the bowl and add the olive oil, tomatoes, spring onions [scallions], olives, marjoram, cayenne, salt, pepper and wine. Carefully mix the ingredients together until they are thoroughly combined.

Arrange the lettuce leaves around the edge of a serving platter and spoon the crabmeat mixture into the centre. Garnish with the slices of avocado and serve at once.

Zindo Vando
MEAT AND FISH STEW

This spicy and unusually-flavoured stew comes from French West Africa, where meat and fish are often combined. Serve Zindo Vando (seen-doh vahn-doh) with fried plantain and yams or boiled rice.

6 SERVINGS

2 lb. boned shin of beef, cut into
1-inch cubes
10 fl. oz. [1¼ cups] beef stock
1 teaspoon salt
1 teaspoon cayenne pepper
1 teaspoon paprika
2 garlic cloves, finely chopped
2 fl. oz. [¼ cup] vegetable oil
1 medium-sized onion, chopped

An exotic and spicy dish from French West Africa, Zindo Vando is ideal to serve for an informal supper party.

8 oz. prawns or shrimps, peeled
4 tomatoes, blanched, peeled and
chopped
1 tablespoon tomato purée
10 oz. frozen leaf spinach,
7 oz. canned tuna fish, drained
and coarsely flaked
2 eggs, scrambled

Place the beef, stock, salt, cayenne, paprika and garlic in a large saucepan. Set the pan over moderate heat and bring the liquid to the boil. Reduce the heat to low and simmer for 30 minutes. Remove the pan from the heat and set aside.

In a large frying-pan, heat the oil over moderate heat. When the oil is hot, add the onion and fry, stirring occasionally, for 8 to 10 minutes or until it is golden. Add the prawns or shrimps, tomatoes and tomato purée and cook for a further 10 minutes, stirring occasionally. Remove the pan from the heat and stir the prawn or shrimp mixture into the meat mixture.

Place the saucepan over low heat and simmer for 20 minutes, stirring occasionally. Increase the heat to moderate. Add the spinach and tuna fish and bring the mixture to the boil. Reduce the heat

to low and simmer the stew for a further 20 minutes or until the cooking liquid has reduced by about one-third. Remove the pan from the heat and stir in the scrambled eggs.

Pour the stew into a warmed serving bowl and serve at once.

Zinfandel Beef

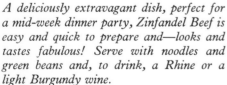

A deliciously extravagant dish, perfect for a mid-week dinner party, Zinfandel Beef is easy and quick to prepare and—looks and tastes fabulous! Serve with noodles and green beans and, to drink, a Rhine or a light Burgundy wine.

6 SERVINGS

1 x 3 lb. fillet of beef
1 tablespoon canned green peppercorns, drained and crushed
2 teaspoons salt
½ teaspoon grated nutmeg
4 oz. [½ cup] butter
2 medium-sized onions, finely chopped
2 small green peppers, white pith removed, seeded and finely chopped

3 oz. button mushrooms, wiped clean and sliced
8 fl. oz. [1 cup] canned beef consommé
4 fl. oz. [½ cup] dry sherry
4 tablespoons tomato purée
1 teaspoon black pepper
1 teaspoon finely grated orange rind
1 oz. [2 tablespoons] beurre manié

Place the beef on a flat working surface and, using a sharp knife, cut it into ½-inch thick slices. Rub the green peppercorns, 1 teaspoon of salt and the nutmeg into both sides of each slice.

In a frying-pan large enough to take the beef slices in one layer, melt 3 ounces [⅜ cup] of butter over moderately high heat. When the foam subsides, add the beef slices to the pan and fry them for 2 minutes on each side. Reduce the heat to moderately low and fry them for a further 2 minutes on each side. This will produce rare steaks; double the times for well-done steaks. Using a large fork, remove the meat slices from the frying-pan and arrange them in a warmed serving dish. Keep warm while you make the sauce.

Impress your friends with this luxurious dinner party dish. Zinfandel Beef is superb served with white wine.

Add the remaining butter to the frying-pan. When the foam subsides, add the onions and green peppers and fry, stirring occasionally, for 5 to 7 minutes or until the onions are soft and translucent but not brown. Stir in the mushrooms and continue to cook for a further 3 minutes. Pour in the consommé and sherry and add the tomato purée, the remaining salt, the black pepper and orange rind. Bring the liquid to the boil, stirring constantly. Stir in the beurre manié, a little at a time, until the sauce thickens a little. Remove the pan from the heat and pour the sauce into a warmed sauceboat.

Serve the beef slices at once, with the sauce.

Zingara Sauce

This sauce is delicious served with thinly sliced veal or beef or simply prepared

white fish. It may also be served as an accompaniment to buttered pasta.

2 PINTS [5 CUPS]

1 oz. [2 tablespoons] butter

4 oz. cooked ham, cut into julienne strips

½ teaspoon cayenne pepper

4 oz. mushrooms, wiped clean, stalks removed and cut into julienne strips

2 black truffles, cut into julienne strips

1½ pints [3¾ cups] Tomato Sauce

2 fl. oz. [¼ cup] Madeira

In a medium-sized frying-pan, melt the butter over moderate heat. When the foam subsides, add the ham, cayenne and mushrooms, reduce the heat to low and fry gently for 3 to 5 minutes or until the mushrooms are cooked.

Add the truffles and tomato sauce, increase the heat to moderate and, stirring constantly, bring the sauce to the boil. Add the Madeira and continue to cook, stirring, for a further 2 minutes. Remove the pan from the heat.

Transfer the sauce to a warmed sauce-boat and serve immediately.

Zingarella Stew

This delicious stew makes a marvellous and economical family lunch or supper dish served with piping hot baked potatoes. If you prefer, chicken may be substituted for the rabbit.

4 SERVINGS

1 oz. [2 tablespoons] bacon fat

6 large carrots, scraped and sliced

2 large onions, thinly sliced

4 oz. mushrooms, wiped clean and sliced

4 streaky bacon slices, rinds removed and chopped

1 x 4 lb. rabbit, cleaned and cut into 4 serving pieces

1 tablespoon chopped fresh parsley

1 teaspoon salt

1 teaspoon black pepper

10 fl. oz. [1¼ cups] milk

10 fl. oz. [1¼ cups] chicken stock

1 oz. [2 tablespoons] butter

2 tablespoons flour

In a large saucepan, melt the bacon fat over moderate heat. When it is hot, add the carrots and fry, stirring occasionally, for 5 minutes. Add the onions, mushrooms and bacon pieces and fry, stirring occasionally, for a further 5 minutes.

Add the rabbit pieces, parsley, salt and pepper and pour over the milk and stock. Reduce the heat to low and bring the

liquid to just under boiling point. Cover and simmer the stew for 1½ hours or until the rabbit is very tender when pierced with the point of a sharp knife.

Remove the pan from the heat. Using a slotted spoon, remove the rabbit pieces and vegetables from the pan and place them on a warmed serving dish Keep hot.

Strain the cooking liquid into a bowl and reserve it.

In a medium-sized saucepan, melt the butter over moderate heat. Remove the pan from the heat and, with a wooden spoon, stir in the flour to make a smooth paste. Gradually add the reserved cooking liquid, stirring constantly and being careful to avoid lumps. Return the pan to the heat and cook, stirring constantly, for 2 to 3 minutes or until the sauce is thick and smooth.

Remove the pan from the heat and pour the sauce over the rabbit pieces and vegetables. Serve at once.

Zingari Gipsy-Style Spaghettini Omelet

This recipe is an excellent way to use up leftover cooked pasta and makes a meal in itself. Serve with a mixed salad and lots of light red wine, such as Valpolicella.

4 SERVINGS

1½ lb. cooked spaghettini

15 fl. oz. [1⅞ cups] Bolognese Sauce

6 eggs, well beaten

½ teaspoon salt

½ teaspoon black pepper

1 oz. [2 tablespoons] butter

2 tablespoons chopped fresh parsley

Place the spaghettini and sauce in a large mixing bowl and, using two forks, toss the ingredients until they are well combined.

Add the eggs, salt and pepper and stir the mixture thoroughly.

In a large, heavy frying-pan or omelet pan, melt the butter over low heat. When the foam subsides, pour the spaghettini mixture into the pan and cook for 3 minutes. Increase the heat to moderate and leave the ingredients to cook, without stirring, for 8 minutes. (Even if you do smell an aroma of burning spaghettini do continue to cook for the 8 minutes — the slightly charcoal-flavoured oùtside adds to the deliciousness of the dish!)

Remove the pan from the heat. Place a heated serving dish over the pan and invert the two. The omelet will slip out easily.

Using a sharp kitchen knife, cut the omelet into quarters. Sprinkle with the parsley and serve at once.

Zinnia's Chicken with Tarragon, Whisky and Cream

A marvellous, rich-tasting dish, Zinnia's Chicken with Tarragon, Whisky and Cream is perfect for a dinner party served with rice and a green salad. Serve it with a well-chilled Gewürztraminer for a really special meal.

4 SERVINGS

1 x 4 lb. chicken, cut into 4 serving pieces

2 teaspoons salt

2 oz. [¼ cup] butter

3 tablespoons olive oil

4 fresh tarragon sprigs

4 chicken livers

4 fl. oz. [½ cup] whisky

8 fl. oz. double cream [1 cup heavy cream]

Rub the chicken pieces with the salt.

In a large saucepan, melt the butter with the oil over moderate heat. When the foam subsides, add the chicken pieces and fry for 2 minutes on each side. Reduce the heat to moderately low and add the tarragon. Cover the pan and fry the chicken, turning occasionally, for 15 minutes.

Add the chicken livers and whisky. Re-cover the pan and cook for a further 15 to 20 minutes or until the chicken is tender when pierced with the point of a sharp knife. Pour over the cream and cook, stirring occasionally, for 2 to 3 minutes or until the cream is hot but not boiling.

Remove the pan from the heat and transfer the mixture to a warmed serving dish Serve at once.

Zippy Avocado Hors d'Oeuvre

This quick and easy dish really lives up to its name, as it takes very little time to prepare. Serve it as a refreshing first course for a summer dinner party or as a light lunchtime snack.

6 SERVINGS

8 fl. oz. [1 cup] canned consommé

2 tablespoons dry sherry

¼ teaspoon Tabasco sauce

4 teaspoons lemon juice

3 large avocados, halved and stoned

½ teaspoon cayenne pepper

In a medium-sized mixing bowl, beat the consommé, sherry, Tabasco sauce and half the lemon juice together. Place the mixture in the refrigerator to chill until

it is set.

Brush the avocado halves with the remaining lemon juice.

Remove the consommé mixture from the refrigerator and break it up gently with a fork. Spoon the mixture into the avocado halves. Sprinkle over the cayenne, and chill in the refrigerator until they are required.

Zippy Savoury Scramble

A delicious, spicy lunch or supper dish, Zippy Savoury Scramble is very quick to make and may be served on hot buttered toast.

4 SERVINGS

1 oz. [2 tablespoons] butter
1 onion, finely chopped
10 lambs' kidneys, cleaned, prepared and quartered
2 oz. mushrooms, wiped clean and chopped
1 tablespoon flour
5 fl. oz. [⅝ cup] home-made beef stock
½ teaspoon Tabasco sauce
1 tablespoon tomato purée
2 tablespoons chopped fresh parsley
1 teaspoon salt
½ teaspoon black pepper
8 eggs, lightly beaten

In a large saucepan, melt the butter over moderate heat. When the foam subsides, add the onion and fry, stirring occasionally, for 5 to 7 minutes or until it is soft and translucent but not brown. Add the kidneys and mushrooms and fry, stirring occasionally, for 3 minutes. Stir in the flour and cook for 1 minute. Remove the pan from the heat and gradually stir in the stock, Tabasco sauce and tomato purée. Return the pan to the heat and cook, stirring constantly, for 2 minutes. Reduce the heat to low and simmer for 20 minutes.

Stir in the parsley, salt and pepper. Remove the pan from the heat and stir in the eggs, beating with a wooden spoon until the ingredients are thoroughly combined. Return the pan to low heat. Stir for 3 to 5 minutes or until the eggs are set.

Remove the pan from the heat and serve at once.

Zip-Zap Lunchtime Snack

This Zip-Zap Lunchtime Snack really can be prepared and cooked within thirty minutes. It is a delicate soufflé-like combination of prawns or shrimps, eggs and cheese on hot buttered bread.

2 SERVINGS

Zip-Zap Lunchtime Snack is the ideal dish to make when a visitor arrives unexpectedly. Serve with a crisp green salad and a glass of cold lager.

4 tablespoons mayonnaise
2 tablespoons single [light] cream
2 teaspoons lemon juice
¼ teaspoon salt
¼ teaspoon freshly ground black pepper
½ teaspoon paprika
8 oz. prawns or shrimps, shelled
2 large slices brown bread, buttered
6 oz. [1½ cups] Emmenthal cheese, grated
4 egg whites, stiffly beaten
2 tomatoes, quartered

Preheat the oven to fairly hot 400°F (Gas Mark 6, 200°C).

In a medium-sized mixing bowl, place the mayonnaise, cream, lemon juice, salt, pepper, paprika and 6 ounces of the prawns or shrimps. Using a wooden spoon, carefully mix the ingredients together and then spoon them on to the slices of bread. Set aside.

In a small mixing bowl, carefully fold the cheese into the egg whites and spread it over the prawn or shrimp mixture.

Place the 2 slices of bread on a baking

sheet and place the baking sheet in the oven. Cook for 15 to 20 minutes or until the egg white has set and is golden brown on top.

Remove the baking sheet from the oven and transfer each slice of bread to a warmed serving plate. Garnish with the remaining prawns or shrimps and the tomato quarters and serve immediately.

Zirje Island Fish Kebabs

Yugoslavia has a productive fishing industry and fish dishes are popular, especially among people living near the coast. Zirje (seer-jay) Island Fish Kebabs is a delicious way to serve fish. Serve piping hot accompanied by spiced rice.

4 SERVINGS

1½ lb. fresh tuna fish, bones and skin removed, cut into 2-inch cubes
2 medium-sized onions, quartered
4 tomatoes, quartered
8 oz. mushrooms, wiped clean
1 green pepper, white pith removed, seeded and cut into 1-inch squares
4 fl. oz. [½ cup] dry white wine
3 tablespoons olive oil
½ teaspoon salt
½ teaspoon paprika
4 bay leaves
1 lemon, quartered
2 tablespoons chopped fresh parsley

Thread the fish cubes on to 4 skewers, alternating them with the onions, tomatoes, mushrooms and green pepper squares.

In a large shallow dish, combine the wine, olive oil, salt and paprika. Lay the skewers in the dish and leave to marinate at room temperature for 2 hours, turning occasionally.

Preheat the grill [broiler] to high.

Remove the kebabs from the marinade. Place them in the rack of the grill [broiler] pan and place the pan under the grill [broiler]. Grill [broil] the kebabs for 5 to 7 minutes, turning the skewers frequently, or until the fish flakes easily when tested with a fork.

Remove the skewers from under the heat. Add a bay leaf and a lemon quarter to the end of each skewer. Lay the

---

Zirje Island Fish Kebabs are excellent and taste even better than they look!

---

skewers on a warmed serving plate and sprinkle over the parsley. Serve at once.

Zite with Italian Sausage Sauce

Zite is a long, tubular type of pasta, which goes particularly well with sturdy meat and tomato sauces. If zite is unobtainable then macaroni or spaghetti may be used instead. Serve Zite with Italian Sausage Sauce with crusty bread and butter and a mixed salad and, to drink, a robust Barolo wine.

4 SERVINGS

1 teaspoon salt
1 lb. zite
SAUCE
2 oz. [¼ cup] butter
1 tablespoon olive oil
2 small onions, finely chopped
3 courgettes [zucchini], trimmed and sliced
1 garlic clove, crushed
1 red pepper, white pith removed, seeded and chopped
28 oz. canned peeled Italian tomatoes
3 tablespoons tomato purée
½ teaspoon salt

1 teaspoon black pepper
1 teaspoon dried basil
1 lb. hot Italian sausages
8 oz. sweet Italian sausages
4 oz. [1 cup] Parmesan cheese,
    grated

First make the sauce. In a large saucepan, melt 1 ounce [2 tablespoons] of the butter with the oil over moderate heat. When the foam subsides, add the onions, courgettes [zucchini], garlic and pepper and fry, stirring occasionally, for 5 to 7 minutes or until the onions are soft and translucent but not brown.

Add the tomatoes with the can juice, the tomato purée, salt, pepper and basil and stir well to mix. Bring the liquid to the boil, reduce the heat to low and simmer the sauce for 15 minutes. Stir in the hot and sweet sausages, cover the pan and simmer the mixture for 30 minutes.

Meanwhile, half-fill a large saucepan with water and add the salt. Set the pan over moderately high heat and bring the water to the boil. When the water boils, add the zite to the pan. Reduce the heat to moderate and cook the zite for 10 to 15 minutes or until it is 'al dente' or just tender. Remove the pan from the heat and drain the zite in a colander.

Transfer the zite to a large serving bowl and add the remaining butter and 1 ounce [¼ cup] of the grated cheese. Using two large spoons, gently toss the zite until all the strands are well coated.

Stir the remaining grated cheese into the sauce and continue stirring until it has melted. Remove the pan from the heat and pour the sauce over the zite. Serve at once.

Zite with Meatballs and Tomato Mushroom Sauce

Serve Zite with Meatballs and Tomato Mushroom Sauce as a main meal with lots of crusty bread, green salad and red wine.

4 SERVINGS

1 teaspoon salt
1 lb. zite
1 oz. [2 tablespoons] butter
MEATBALLS
1½ lb. beef or pork, minced [ground]
2 slices white bread, soaked in
    4 tablespoons milk for 5 minutes
2 teaspoons grated lemon rind
2 oz. [⅔ cup] dried breadcrumbs
1 large egg
2 garlic cloves, crushed
1 teaspoon salt
1 teaspoon black pepper
1½ teaspoons dried oregano

2 fl. oz. [¼ cup] olive oil
8 oz. Italian sausages, cut into
    1-inch lengths
SAUCE
3 tablespoons olive oil
1 large onion, thinly sliced
2 garlic cloves, crushed
4 oz. mushrooms, wiped clean and
    sliced
4 oz. fresh peas, weighed after
    shelling
28 oz. canned peeled Italian
    tomatoes
6 fl. oz. [¾ cup] red wine
5 oz. tomato purée
½ teaspoon salt
1 teaspoon black pepper
1 teaspoon dried oregano
4 oz. Mozzarella cheese, thinly
    sliced

First make the meatballs. In a large mixing bowl, combine all the meatball ingredients except the oil and sausages, beating well with a fork until they are well mixed. Shape the mixture into walnut-sized balls. Place the balls in a large shallow plate and chill them in the refrigerator for 30 minutes.

Meanwhile, make the sauce. In a large saucepan, heat the oil over moderate heat. When the foam subsides, add the onion and garlic and fry, stirring occasionally, for 5 to 7 minutes or until the onion is soft and translucent but not brown. Add the mushrooms and peas and fry, stirring occasionally, for 3 minutes. Add the tomatoes with the can juice, the wine, tomato purée, salt, pepper and oregano and stir well to mix. Bring the liquid to the boil over moderately high heat, stirring occasionally. Reduce the heat to low, cover the pan and simmer the sauce for 30 minutes. Remove the pan from the heat.

In a large frying-pan, heat the oil over moderate heat. When the oil is hot, add the meatballs, a few at a time, and fry, turning occasionally, for 5 to 8 minutes or until they are lightly and evenly browned. Using a slotted spoon, transfer the cooked meatballs to the saucepan containing the sauce. Brown the remaining meatballs and the sausage pieces in the same way. Return the saucepan to low heat and simmer the mixture for a further 30 minutes.

Add the cheese slices to the pan and continue to simmer for a further 10 to 15 minutes or until the cheese has melted.

Meanwhile, half-fill a large saucepan with water and add the teaspoon of salt. Set the pan over moderately high heat and bring the water to the boil. When the water boils, add the zite to the pan. Reduce the heat to moderate and cook the

zite for 10 to 15 minutes or until the zite is 'al dente' or just tender. Remove the pan from the heat and drain the zite in a colander.

Transfer the zite to a large serving bowl and add the butter. Using two large spoons, gently toss the zite until all the strands are well coated. Remove the pan containing the sauce and meatballs from the heat. Pour the mixture over the zite and serve at once.

Zite with Port

The addition of port turns this delicious recipe into a really special lunch or supper. Serve it with grilled [broiled] tomatoes and a green salad and, to drink, a mellow Chianti.

4 SERVINGS

1 teaspoon salt
1 lb. zite
8 oz. [2 cups] Gruyère cheese,
    grated
8 oz. mushrooms, wiped clean and
    sliced
1 teaspoon salt
½ teaspoon black pepper
1½ oz. [3 tablespoons] butter,
    melted
12 fl. oz. [1½ cups] port

Preheat the oven to fairly hot 400°F (Gas Mark 6, 200°C).

Half-fill a large saucepan with water and add the salt. Set the pan over moderately high heat and bring the water to the boil. When the water boils, add the zite to the pan. Reduce the heat to moderate and cook the zite for 10 to 15 minutes or until the zite is 'al dente' or just tender. Remove the pan from the heat and drain the zite in a colander.

Place half the zite in a shallow, oven-proof dish. Sprinkle over half the cheese, the mushrooms, salt and pepper. Spread over the remaining zite and sprinkle with the remaining cheese. Pour over the butter and port. Place the dish in the oven and cook for 20 minutes.

Remove the dish from the oven and serve at once.

Znojemsky Goulasch
HUNGARIAN GOULASCH WITH GHERKINS

The gherkins in Znojemsky Goulasch (zoh-

A deliciously filling dish, Zite with Meatballs and Tomato Mushroom Sauce is an inexpensive family meal.

Zoa

Three mouthwatering dishes; Zoar's Crispy Apple Bake — a combination of apples, mint and cinnamon, Zocca Bananas — bananas coated with Drambuie flavoured syrup and a pretty Zodiac Cake.

yem-ski goo-lah-sh) *give it an interesting texture and flavour. Serve it as a filling family supper or informal dinner party dish with mashed potatoes and buttered carrots and a full bodied red wine, such as Bull's Blood.*

6 SERVINGS

4 tablespoons vegetable oil
4 large onions, finely chopped
1½ tablespoons paprika
3 lb. chuck steak, trimmed of excess fat and cut into 1-inch cubes
8 fl. oz. [1 cup] red wine
8 fl. oz. [1 cup] beef stock
1 teaspoon salt
1 teaspoon freshly ground black pepper
2 tablespoons flour
8 large gherkins, cut into julienne strips

Preheat the oven to moderate 350°F (Gas Mark 4, 180°C).

In a large, flameproof casserole, heat the oil over moderate heat. When the oil is hot, add the onions and fry, stirring occasionally, for 8 to 10 minutes or until they are golden. Remove the casserole from the heat and add the paprika, stirring until the onions are thoroughly coated. Add the steak, wine, stock, salt and pepper. Return the casserole to the heat and bring the liquid to the boil. Remove the casserole from the heat, cover, place it in the oven and cook for 1 hour.

Remove the casserole from the oven. With a large spoon, skim off the surface fat, reserving 2 tablespoons. Place the reserved fat in a small bowl and add the flour, stirring until the mixture forms a smooth paste. Pour the mixture into the casserole and stir well to blend.

Return the casserole to the oven and cook for a further 40 to 45 minutes or until the beef is tender when pierced with the point of a sharp knife. Remove the casserole from the oven and, using a slotted spoon, remove the beef from the casserole. Place it on a warmed serving dish and keep hot.

Skim off any excess fat from the cooking liquid. Add the gherkins to the liquid and set the casserole over moderate heat. Heat for 2 minutes.

Remove the casserole from the heat and pour the sauce and gherkins over the beef. Serve at once.

Zoar's Crispy Apple Bake

A simple and delicious dessert which will delight both children and adults, Zoar's Crispy Apple Bake may be served with ice-cream or whipped cream.

6 SERVINGS

1 teaspoon butter
4 oz. [1 cup] flour
8 oz. [1 cup] sugar
1 teaspoon bicarbonate of soda [baking soda]
1 egg, beaten
2 teaspoons ground cinnamon
3 teaspoons finely chopped fresh mint
4 medium-sized cooking apples, peeled, cored and cut into thin wedges
1 tablespoon soft brown sugar

Preheat the oven to moderate 350°F (Gas Mark 4, 180°C). Using the butter, grease a 9- x 9-inch ovenproof dish and set aside.

Place the flour, sugar and soda in a medium-sized mixing bowl and, using a fork, mix the ingredients together. Make a well in the centre of the mixture and add the egg. Continue to mix the ingredients for 6 to 8 minutes or until the mixture resembles fine breadcrumbs.

In a large mixing bowl, stir the cinnamon and mint leaves together and add the apples. Using two wooden spoons, toss the apples until they are evenly coated with the cinnamon mixture.

Arrange the apple slices in the prepared dish and sprinkle the flour mixture over the apples. Scatter the soft brown sugar over the top.

Place the dish in the oven and bake for 40 to 50 minutes or until the top is crisp and golden brown. Remove the dish from the oven and cover with aluminium foil. Set aside to cool slightly.

Remove the foil and serve immediately.

Zocca Bananas

A super dessert, Zocca Bananas is just the dish for a special dinner party. Serve this delicious dessert with lots of vanilla ice-cream.

4 SERVINGS

6 large bananas
juice of ½ lemon
4 oz. [½ cup] sugar
6 fl. oz. [¾ cup] water
2 fl. oz. [¼ cup] Drambuie
2 tablespoons chopped toasted almonds

Remove and discard the banana skins.

Squeeze over the lemon juice and set aside.

In a medium-sized saucepan, dissolve the sugar in the water over low heat. Add the bananas to the pan and poach them for 5 minutes. Using a slotted spoon, transfer the bananas to a medium-sized decorative serving dish. Pour over the Drambuie and set aside to cool.

Increase the heat to moderately high and bring the syrup to the boil. Cook the syrup, without stirring, until it reaches 225°F (107°C) on a sugar thermometer or until a small amount, cooled, will form a long thread between your thumb and index finger. Remove the pan from the heat and pour the syrup over the bananas.

Sprinkle the almonds over the top and set aside for 5 minutes before serving.

Zodiac Cake

This is an ideal cake to make for a birthday party or indeed any party. It is decorated with the signs of the zodiac so that each guest can choose his own zodiac sign. If you know your guests' particular signs and you find there are two Leos or three Capricorns, you can decorate the cake accordingly, if you wish.

If you are not an expert on piping the signs straight on to the cake then trace them from a book. Place the tracing on top of the cake and, using a pin, mark out the design. Remove the tracing paper and pipe over the marked-out design.

12 SERVINGS

2 x 9-inch Génoise Sponges
FILLING
Buttercream Icing, made with 3 oz. [⅜ cup] unsalted butter, 12 oz. icing sugar [3 cups confectioners' sugar] etc.
ICING
1½ lb. [3 cups] sugar
15 fl. oz. [1⅞ cups] water
12 oz. icing sugar [3 cups confectioners' sugar]

Cut the domed top from one cake and discard it. Spread this cake with the buttercream icing and place the second cake on top, dome side up. Set aside.

To make the icing, in a medium-sized saucepan, dissolve the sugar in the water over low heat, stirring constantly. Increase the heat to moderate, cover the pan and bring the syrup to the boil. Continue boiling until the syrup registers 215°F to 220°F (102°C to 104°C) on a sugar thermometer or until a small amount of the mixture, cooled, will form a short thread between your thumb and index finger.

Remove the pan from the heat and allow the syrup to cool slightly.

Place the icing [confectioners'] sugar in a medium-sized mixing bowl and, with a wooden spoon, gradually beat in the syrup. Continue beating until the icing is thick and smooth.

Place the bowl over a pan of simmering water and set the pan over low heat. Stir until the icing is warm and of a spreading consistency.

Pour half of the icing on to the centre of the cake and spread it out quickly with a flat-bladed knife dipped in hot water.

Once the cake is covered with the icing, clean the blade of the knife and, holding it vertically against the side of the cake, smooth the sides by drawing the blade carefully against the icing.

Clean the blade of the knife again and, holding it horizontally, draw the blade carefully across the icing on top of the cake to make it smooth. Set the cake aside until the icing has set.

Fill a forcing bag, fitted with a plain writing nozzle, with the remaining icing (add a few drops of food colouring, if you prefer the decoration to be of a different colour) and mark 12 dividing lines on the surface of the cake. Using the forcing bag, pipe the required zodiac signs into the divisions. Set the cake aside and allow the icing to set.

Zoe's Delight

Zoe's Delight is a fabulous and easy-to-make dessert which combines spicy apple purée, rum and rum-flavoured cream.

4-6 SERVINGS

3 lb. cooking apples, peeled, cored, cooked and kept hot
1½ teaspoons ground cinnamon
3 tablespoons dark rum
1 tablespoon butter
10 fl. oz. double cream [1¼ cups heavy cream]
1 tablespoon soft brown sugar
1 teaspoon cinnamon sugar

Beat the apples into a thick purée, then stir in half of the cinnamon, 2 tablespoons of the rum and the butter, stirring until the butter has dissolved. Spoon the purée into a large decorative serving bowl and place it in the refrigerator to chill for 30 minutes.

In a large mixing bowl, beat the cream with a wire whisk or rotary beater until it forms stiff peaks. With a metal spoon, fold in the remaining cinnamon, the remaining rum and the sugar and continue to beat until the mixture becomes very thick again.

When the apple purée is cold, remove the bowl from the refrigerator and, using a metal spoon, swirl the cream mixture into the purée, bringing the mixture up into decorative peaks.

Sprinkle over the cinnamon sugar and serve at once.

Zofe Spinach Soup

An adaptation of a traditional Ghanaian dish, Zofe Spinach Soup is easy to make and full of health-giving vitamins. Serve this nutritious soup with lots of crusty French bread and butter and Cheddar cheese for a filling and unusual family supper.

6 SERVINGS

2 oz. [¼ cup] butter
2 large onions, finely chopped
1 large potato, finely chopped
1 garlic clove, crushed
1 green chilli, seeded and finely chopped
2 lb. frozen chopped spinach, thawed and drained
1 lb. okra, trimmed and sliced
2 bay leaves, crumbled
4 oz. desiccated coconut [1 cup shredded coconut], soaked in 1 pint [2½ cups] hot water for 10 minutes
2 pints [5 cups] beef stock
1 teaspoon salt
1 teaspoon freshly ground black pepper
1 teaspoon sugar
GARNISH
6 crab claws, cooked, shelled and kept hot

In a large saucepan, melt the butter over moderate heat. When the foam subsides, add the onions, potato and garlic and fry, stirring occasionally, for 5 to 7 minutes or until the onions are soft and translucent but not brown. Stir in the chilli, spinach, okra and bay leaves and fry, stirring frequently, for 5 minutes. Pour over the coconut mixture and beef stock. Season the mixture with the salt, pepper and sugar.

Increase the heat to high and bring the liquid to the boil. Reduce the heat to low, cover the pan and simmer the soup for 35 minutes. Remove the pan from the heat and pour the soup through a large fine strainer held over a large mixing bowl. Using the back of a wooden spoon, push the ingredients through the strainer until only a dry pulp is left. Discard the pulp in the strainer. Alternatively, blend all the ingredients in an electric blender for 30 seconds or until the mixture forms a thick purée.

Spoon the soup into a large, warmed tureen or individual soup bowls. Garnish with the crab claws and serve immediately.

Zoftic Mixed Vegetables

This really different vegetable dish may be served as part of a vegetarian meal or as an accompaniment to roast meat or poultry.

6 SERVINGS

1 oz. [2 tablespoons] butter
1 small onion, finely chopped
1 lb. frozen peas
14 oz. canned artichoke hearts, drained and halved
8 oz. button mushrooms, wiped clean, stalks removed and discarded
1 teaspoon salt
½ teaspoon white pepper
½ teaspoon paprika
4 fl. oz. [½ cup] sour cream

In a large saucepan, melt the butter over moderate heat. When the foam subsides, add the onion and fry, stirring occasionally, for 5 to 7 minutes or until it is soft and translucent but not brown. Add the peas, artichoke hearts, mushrooms, salt, pepper and paprika. Reduce the heat to low and cook the mixture, stirring frequently, for 10 minutes. Stir in the sour cream and cook for a further 3 minutes. Remove the pan from the heat.

Spoon the vegetables into a warmed serving dish and serve immediately.

Zogno Veal Cutlets

An impressive veal recipe from Italy, Zogno Veal Cutlets make an ideal dish to serve at a dinner party. Croquette potatoes, sautéed courgettes [zucchini] and a chilled bottle of Verdicchio Bianco wine would be the perfect accompaniments.

4 SERVINGS

4 veal cutlets
2 oz. [¼ cup] butter
1 tablespoon beurre manié
2 tablespoons brandy
2 fl. oz. double cream [¼ cup heavy cream]
MARINADE
1 small onion, finely chopped
1 garlic clove, crushed
1 tablespoon finely chopped fresh basil or 1½ teaspoons dried basil
2 tablespoons canned green peppercorns, drained and crushed
8 fl. oz. [1 cup] red wine
2 fl. oz. [¼ cup] brandy
1 teaspoon salt

Zogno Veal Cutlets is the perfect dish to serve at a formal dinner party with lots of chilled white wine.

1 teaspoon sugar
½ teaspoon black pepper

First prepare the marinade. In a large shallow dish, mix all the marinade ingredients together. Add the veal cutlets and set aside to marinate for 1 hour. Remove the cutlets from the marinade and pat dry with kitchen paper towels. Reserve the marinade.

Preheat the oven to moderate 350°F (Gas Mark 4, 180°C).

In a large flameproof casserole, melt the butter over moderate heat. When the foam subsides, add the cutlets and fry, turning frequently, for 6 to 8 minutes or until they are lightly browned all over.

Pour over the reserved marinade and bring the contents of the casserole to the boil. Cover the casserole and transfer it to the centre of the oven. Cook the cutlets for 45 minutes to 1 hour or until they are cooked through and tender.

Remove the casserole from the oven and, using a slotted spoon, transfer the cutlets to a warmed serving dish. Set aside and keep hot.

Place the casserole over low heat and gradually add the beurre manié, a little at a time, stirring constantly. Cook the sauce for 2 to 3 minutes or until it is smooth and fairly thick.

Meanwhile, in a small saucepan heat the brandy over low heat. When the brandy is warm, ignite it. When the flames have died down, add the cream to the brandy. Pour the brandy and cream mixture into the sauce.

Remove the casserole from the heat and pour the sauce over the cutlets. Serve immediately.

Zogno Vegetarian Pasta

Pasta comes in many shapes and sizes and is eaten all over the world with a multitude of sauces. This dish, simple as it is, is one of the most delicious and nourishing and can be made from any type of pasta. Serve with freshly chopped fennel, tomato and lettuce heart salad.

4 SERVINGS

8 oz. [1⅓ cups] shelled almonds
1 pint [2½ cups] boiling water
1 teaspoon sea salt
3 tablespoons olive oil
1 tablespoon salt

1 lb. fresh tagliatelle or other pasta
1 garlic clove, crushed
2 tablespoons chopped fresh parsley
4 oz. [1 cup] plus 1 tablespoon Parmesan cheese, grated
1 teaspoon black pepper
8 fl. oz. single cream [1 cup light cream]

Preheat the oven to fairly hot 375°F (Gas Mark 5, 190°C).

Place the almonds in a medium-sized mixing bowl and pour over the boiling water. Set aside for 10 minutes. Strain off the water and retain the blanched almonds. Remove the skins by pinching the skin at the rounder end. Place the almonds in a shallow, ovenproof dish and place the dish in the oven. Bake for 25 minutes or until they are golden brown. Remove the dish from the oven and sprinkle over the sea salt.

Fill a large saucepan with water, add the olive oil and salt and place the pan over moderate heat. Bring the water to the boil. Reduce the heat to moderately low and add the tagliatelle. Cook for 10 to 12 minutes or until the pasta is 'al dente' or just tender. Remove the pan from the heat. Drain the pasta in a colander, then return it to the pan.

Add the garlic, parsley, 4 ounces [1 cup] of the cheese, the pepper and cream. Using two large spoons, toss the ingredients together until they are well combined. Add the almonds and continue to toss the ingredients until the almonds are completely absorbed into the mixture.

Transfer the mixture to a heated serving dish, sprinkle with the remaining cheese and serve immediately.

Zola Chicken

An unusual way of presenting chicken, Zola Chicken tastes fabulous. Serve with sautéed potatoes and a crisp green salad.

4 SERVINGS

1 x 4 lb. chicken, cleaned, with the liver reserved and finely chopped
1 teaspoon salt
½ teaspoon black pepper
4 oz. chicken liver pâté
6 large flat mushrooms, wiped clean with the stalks discarded
2 oz. [¼ cup] butter, melted

STUFFING

1 tablespoon butter
1 large onion, finely chopped
2 oz. [1 cup] fresh white breadcrumbs
½ teaspoon salt
¼ teaspoon black pepper

½ teaspoon dried marjoram
1 egg
2 tablespoons single [light] cream

Preheat the oven to moderate 350°F (Gas Mark 4, 180°C).

Rub the chicken, inside and out, with the salt and pepper. Using a sharp knife, carefully loosen the skin around the breastbone of the chicken. Run the knife under the skin, separating it from the flesh but being careful not to tear the skin. Using a palette knife or spatula, spread the pâté over the breast of the chicken. Cover the pâté with the mushrooms. Set aside while you prepare the stuffing.

In a medium-sized frying-pan, melt the butter over moderate heat. When the foam subsides, add the onion and fry, stirring occasionally, for 5 to 7 minutes or until it is soft and translucent but not brown. Add the reserved chicken liver and fry, stirring frequently, for 5 minutes. Remove the pan from the heat and transfer the mixture to a medium-sized mixing bowl. Add the breadcrumbs, salt, pepper, marjoram, egg and cream. Beat the ingredients together until they are thoroughly combined.

Spoon the stuffing into the cavity of the chicken and secure with a trussing needle and string. Place the chicken in a large roasting tin and pour over the

Zoll Fruit Loaf is a wholesome tea-bread which is surprisingly easy to make. Serve with lots of butter.

melted butter. Place the tin in the centre of the oven and bake the chicken for 1¼ to 1½ hours or until it is thoroughly cooked and tender.

Remove the chicken from the oven and transfer it to a warmed serving dish. Serve immediately.

Zoll Fruit Loaf

This is an unusual teabread in that the ingredients are boiled before they are baked. It is a very simple recipe and tastes delicious sliced and spread with butter.

ONE 2-POUND LOAF

2 oz. [¼ cup] plus 1 teaspoon butter, cut into pieces
8 oz. [1 cup] sugar
8 fl. oz. [1 cup] milk
6 oz. [1 cup] sultanas or seedless raisins
8 oz. [2 cups] self-raising flour
1 egg, lightly beaten

Preheat the oven to moderate 350°F (Gas Mark 4, 180°C).

With the teaspoon of butter, lightly

grease a 2-pound loaf tin and set aside.

Put the sugar, milk, sultanas or seedless raisins and the remaining butter in a medium-sized saucepan and place the pan over moderate heat. Gradually bring the mixture to the boil, stirring occasionally. Remove the pan from the heat and set aside.

When the mixture has cooled, stir in the flour, a little at a time, until it is incorporated. Add the egg and beat all the ingredients in the pan until they are thoroughly mixed. Spoon the mixture into the prepared loaf tin and place it in the oven. Bake for 1¼ hours or until a skewer inserted into the centre of the loaf comes out clean.

Remove the loaf tin from the oven and leave the loaf in the tin for 10 minutes. Turn the loaf out on to a wire rack to cool completely before serving.

Zoller Pumpkin Stew

A delightful dish from South America, Zoller Pumpkin Stew looks fabulous and tastes even better. Serve with salted popcorn, a mixed salad and a bottle of red wine.

6-8 SERVINGS

1 very large pumpkin
6 oz. [¾ cup] butter
8 oz. [1 cup] sugar

A colourful and spicy dish, Zoller Pumpkin Stew is ideal to serve at an informal dinner party.

1 lb. salt pork, cut into 1-inch cubes

2 tablespoons vegetable oil

2 lb. chuck steak, cut into 1-inch cubes

1 x 3 lb. chicken, cleaned and chopped into 2-inch pieces

2 onions, finely chopped

2 garlic cloves, crushed

1 green chilli, finely chopped

16 oz. canned peeled tomatoes

10 fl. oz. [1¼ cups] beef stock

1 lb. sweet potatoes, peeled and cut into 1-inch cubes

4 corn on the cobs, cut into 1-inch lengths

4 large courgettes [zucchini], trimmed and cut into 1-inch lengths

8 spring onions [scallions], trimmed and cut into 2-inch lengths

1 large green pepper, white pith removed, seeded and cut into 1-inch pieces

1 tablespoon finely chopped fresh thyme or 1½ teaspoons dried thyme

1 teaspoon salt

1 teaspoon black pepper

8 oz. frozen prawns or shrimps, thawed and drained

GARNISH

8 unpeeled fresh prawns or shrimps

Preheat the oven to moderate 350°F (Gas Mark 4, 180°C).

Using a sharp knife, cut a slice approximately 1-inch thick from the side of the pumpkin to form a lid. Using a spoon, scrape out and discard the seeds and pulp from the lid and shell of the pumpkin.

Grease the inside of the pumpkin with 4 ounces [½ cup] of the butter. Sprinkle 2 ounces [¼ cup] of the sugar into the pumpkin, shaking out any excess. Cover with the lid. Place the pumpkin on a large flat baking sheet and place in the centre of the oven. Bake the pumpkin for 35 to 40 minutes or until it is just tender.

Meanwhile, in a large, heavy-based saucepan, fry the salt pork over moderate heat, stirring constantly, for 6 to 8 minutes or until the pork is golden brown all over and has rendered most of its fat. Using a slotted spoon, transfer the pork to a large plate and set aside. Pour the oil into the saucepan. When the oil is hot, add the remaining sugar and reduce the heat to low. Melt the sugar, stirring constantly. When the oil and sugar mixture

is golden brown, add the beef and chicken pieces and fry, turning frequently, for 6 to 8 minutes or until the beef and chicken pieces are golden brown all over. Using a slotted spoon, transfer the beef and chicken to the same plate as the pork. Set aside.

Add the remaining butter to the pan. When the foam subsides, add the onions, garlic and chilli and fry, stirring occasionally, for 5 to 7 minutes or until the onions are soft and translucent but not brown. Add the tomatoes with the can juice and the beef stock to the pan. Return the pork, beef and chicken to the pan. Increase the heat to high and bring the contents of the pan to the boil. Reduce the heat to low, cover the pan and simmer for 40 minutes. Uncover and add the sweet potatoes, corn, courgettes [zucchini], spring onions [scallions], green pepper, thyme, salt, pepper and prawns or shrimps. Cover the pan and cook for a further 15 minutes.

Remove the pumpkin from the oven, remove the lid and set aside for 5 minutes. Remove the pan from the heat and spoon the stew into the pumpkin. Cover the pumpkin with the lid and return it to the centre of the oven. Bake for a further 10 minutes.

Remove the baking sheet from the oven. Transfer the pumpkin to a serving platter. Remove the lid and garnish with the unpeeled prawns or shrimps. Serve immediately.

Zoltan's Chicken Breasts

This delicious dish combines boned chicken breasts, cream of celery soup and cheese and makes the perfect Sunday lunch or mid-week supper dish. Serve with puréed potatoes and Brussels sprouts and, to drink, some well-chilled Hungarian Riesling.

6 SERVINGS

6 chicken breasts, skinned and boned

1½ teaspoons salt

1 teaspoon black pepper

2 teaspoons paprika

3 oz. [⅜ cup] butter

4 oz. button mushrooms, wiped clean and sliced

20 oz. canned condensed cream of celery soup

4 oz. [1 cup] Gruyère cheese, grated

Rub the chicken breasts all over with the salt, pepper and paprika and set aside.

In a large, shallow flameproof casserole, melt the butter over moderate heat. When the foam subsides, add the mushrooms

and fry, stirring occasionally, for 3 minutes. Add the chicken breasts and fry for 5 minutes on each side. Stir in the soup, reduce the heat to low and simmer the mixture for 15 minutes or until the chicken pieces are cooked through.

Meanwhile, preheat the grill [broiler] to moderately high.

Remove the casserole from the heat and sprinkle over the grated cheese. Place the casserole under the grill [broiler] and grill [broil] for 5 minutes or until the top of the mixture is brown and bubbling.

Remove the casserole from under the heat and serve the chicken mixture at once, straight from the casserole.

Zomba Salt Cod and Avocado

A really unusual hors d'oeuvre, Zomba Salt Cod and Avocado is simply delicious served with Melba Toast and a bottle of well-chilled white wine.

6 SERVINGS

2 tablespoons olive oil

1 onion, finely chopped

1 garlic clove, crushed

12 oz. salt cod, washed, soaked in cold water overnight, drained and coarsely chopped

3 ripe avocados, flesh scooped out and coarsely chopped, with shells reserved

1 tablespoon lemon juice

1 tablespoon dry sherry

½ teaspoon salt

¼ teaspoon freshly ground black pepper

⅛ teaspoon hot chilli powder

4 tablespoons double [heavy] cream

Preheat the oven to moderate 350°F (Gas Mark 4, 180°C).

In a large frying-pan, heat the oil over moderate heat. When the oil is hot, add the onion and garlic and fry, stirring occasionally, for 5 to 7 minutes or until the onion is soft and translucent but not brown. Add the salt cod and fry, stirring frequently, for 6 to 8 minutes or until the fish flakes easily when tested with a fork. Remove the pan from the heat and set aside to cool for 5 minutes.

Transfer the mixture to a medium-sized mixing bowl. Add the avocados, lemon juice, sherry, salt, pepper, chilli powder and cream. Using a fork, beat the ingredients together until they are thoroughly combined. Spoon the mixture back into the avocado shells and transfer the shells to a large baking sheet. Place the baking sheet in the centre of the oven and cook for 15 minutes.

Remove the glass from the refrigerator and add the ice cubes. Pour over the rum mixture and decorate with the cherry. Serve at once.

Zombie's Secret

This is an unusual dessert from Haiti and its name belies how delicious it is.

6 SERVINGS

2 avocados, stoned, peeled and cut into 1-inch cubes
2 bananas, peeled and sliced
3 oz. firm cream cheese, cubed
2 tablespoons grated coconut
2 tablespoons sugar
1 teaspoon ground cinnamon
2 tablespoons strong black coffee
10 fl. oz. double cream [1¼ cups heavy cream], stiffly whipped

In a large, deep serving dish, combine the avocados, bananas and cream cheese.

In a bowl, mix together the coconut, sugar and cinnamon. Sprinkle the coconut mixture over the fruit and place the dish in the refrigerator to chill.

Stir the coffee into the cream and pour it over the avocado mixture and serve.

Zonder Sweetcorn and Petits Pois Hors d'Oeuvre

This delicious dish is a combination of sweetcorn, petits pois, red pepper, onion and spicy mayonnaise. Serve as an unusual first course to a special meal.

4 SERVINGS

10 oz. canned sweetcorn, drained
10 oz. canned petits pois, drained
1 large red pepper, white pith removed, seeded and sliced
2 hard-boiled eggs, thinly sliced
4 fl. oz. [½ cup] mayonnaise
⅛ teaspoon Tabasco sauce
2 teaspoons mixed pickle or chutney
1 medium-sized onion, thinly sliced and pushed out into rings

Place the sweetcorn, petits pois, red pepper and eggs in a medium-sized serving bowl. In a small bowl, combine the mayonnaise, Tabasco sauce and pickle or chutney. Spoon the dressing over the vegetable mixture and, using two large spoons, carefully toss the ingredients to mix well.

Arrange the onion rings decoratively over the mixture and place the bowl in the refrigerator to chill for 15 minutes before serving.

Remove the baking sheet from the oven. Transfer the avocados to individual serving plates and serve immediately.

A drink with a kick— Zombie Cocktail will conjure up visions of tropical beaches and swaying palm trees!

Zombie Cocktail

This potent mixture of light rum, dark rum, lime and pineapple juice is so-called because it is considered to be powerful enough to keep the zombies, or 'walking dead' of the West Indies going! It certainly isn't for the weak in heart but its effect can be lessened by adding water and more ice cubes.

1 SERVING

2 fl. oz. [¼ cup] light rum
2 fl. oz. [¼ cup] dark rum
3 tablespoons lime juice
2 tablespoons pineapple juice
1 teaspoon sugar
2 ice cubes
1 Maraschino cherry

Chill a medium-sized cocktail glass in the refrigerator for 30 minutes.

Meanwhile, place all of the ingredients, except the ice cubes, in a cocktail shaker or screw-top jar. Cover and shake the mixture vigorously for about 1 minute.

Zonza Champagne Soup

This must surely be one of the most luxurious soups in the world! It looks exquisite and tastes wonderful and, if Champagne proves too expensive, any dry sparkling white wine may be used instead. Serve the soup with very hot Melba Toast.

4 SERVINGS

2 pints [5 cups] chicken consommé
   juice of $\frac{1}{2}$ lemon
1 lb. salmon, cubed
2 teaspoons chopped fresh dill
2 teaspoons chopped fresh chives
2 teaspoons chopped fresh parsley
12 fl. oz. [$1\frac{1}{2}$ cups] Champagne

Pour the chicken consommé into a medium-sized saucepan and set the pan over moderately high heat. Bring the consommé to the boil and add the lemon juice. Drop the salmon cubes into the consommé and boil for 5 minutes.

Using a slotted spoon, remove the salmon cubes from the consommé and place them in a warmed soup tureen. Pour over the consommé. Sprinkle over the dill, chives and parsley and keep hot.

Pour the Champagne into the saucepan. Heat until it just reaches boiling point, then pour it into the soup. Serve immediately.

Zonza Stuffed Spare Rib

A tasty and economical family dish, Zonza Stuffed Spare Rib is ideal to serve as a family supper. Ice-cold lager and mashed potatoes would be the ideal accompaniments.

4 SERVINGS

1 large sheet barbecue spare ribs
1 teaspoon salt
$\frac{1}{2}$ teaspoon black pepper
6 fl. oz. [$\frac{3}{4}$ cup] tomato ketchup
2 fl. oz. [$\frac{1}{4}$ cup] Worcestershire sauce
2 tablespoons prepared English
   mustard
10 fl. oz. [$1\frac{1}{4}$ cups] beef stock
STUFFING
4 slices streaky bacon, rinds
   removed and finely chopped
2 oz. [$\frac{1}{4}$ cup] butter
2 onions, finely chopped
1 lb. chicken livers, trimmed and
   coarsely chopped
1 tablespoon dried sage
6 oz. [3 cups] fresh white
   breadcrumbs, soaked in cold
   water and squeezed dry
2 eggs, lightly beaten

Preheat the oven to hot 425°F (Gas Mark 7, 220°C).

First prepare the stuffing. In a large frying-pan, fry the bacon over moderate

Delicious Zonza Champagne Soup is well worth the expense involved!

heat, stirring constantly, for 6 to 8 minutes or until it is golden brown all over and has rendered most of its fat. Add the butter to the pan. When the foam subsides, add the onions and chicken livers and fry, stirring constantly, for 5 to 7 minutes or until the onions are soft and translucent but not brown.

Remove the pan from the heat and transfer the mixture to a medium-sized mixing bowl. Add the sage, breadcrumbs and eggs. Beat the ingredients together until they are thoroughly combined. Set aside.

Season the spare ribs with the salt and pepper and place them on a working surface. Spoon the stuffing on to one end of the ribs. Pull the ribs around the stuffing and secure the two ends together with trussing thread or string. Transfer the ribs to a large roasting tin, place in the centre of the oven and roast for 15 minutes.

Meanwhile, in a medium-sized saucepan, combine the ketchup, Worcestershire sauce, mustard and beef stock. Place the pan over moderate heat and bring the contents to the boil, stirring constantly. Remove the pan from the heat and pour the sauce over the ribs.

Reduce the heat to warm 325°F (Gas Mark 3, 170°C). Continue to roast the ribs for a further 1¼ hours or until the ribs are thoroughly cooked.

Remove the tin from the oven and transfer the ribs and sauce to a warmed serving dish. Serve at once.

Zoom-Zoom Sausage Toadstools

Baked beans and sausages are very popular with children and this tasty dish combines both. It looks attractive too and would be ideal to serve for a children's party.

4 SERVINGS

1 oz. [2 tablespoons] butter, melted
1 teaspoon salt
1 teaspoon black pepper
2 lb. potatoes, cooked, mashed and kept hot
14 oz. canned baked beans, heated through and drained
1 lb. sausages, grilled [broiled]
4 oz. large button mushrooms, wiped clean, stalks removed and the caps grilled [broiled]

Beat 1 tablespoon of the butter, the salt and pepper into the potatoes and arrange them over the bottom of a large, shallow serving dish. Cover with the baked beans.

Cut the sausages in half and set them, cut sides down, into the beans and potatoes so that they stand upright. Cover each sausage piece with a mushroom cap. Brush the mushroom caps with the remaining melted butter and serve at once.

Zoondam Pork Ratatouille

Zoondam Pork Ratatouille is an adaptation of a Belgian recipe and may be served with mashed potatoes or fried rice for a superb lunch or supper.

4 SERVINGS

2 lb. pork fillets, cut into 2-inch cubes
2 teaspoons salt
1 teaspoon black pepper
2 fl. oz. [¼ cup] olive oil
1 large onion, finely chopped
2 garlic cloves, crushed
1 large red pepper, white pith removed, seeded and chopped
1 large green pepper, white pith removed, seeded and chopped
3 large courgettes [zucchini], trimmed and sliced
1 small aubergine [eggplant], chopped and dégorged

14 oz. canned peeled tomatoes
4 fl. oz. [½ cup] dry white wine
2 teaspoons grated lemon rind
14 oz. canned white haricot beans, drained

Rub the pork cubes with the salt and pepper and set aside.

In a large flameproof casserole, heat the oil over moderate heat. When the oil is hot, add the onion, garlic, peppers, courgettes [zucchini], aubergine [eggplant] and tomatoes with the can juice. Fry, stirring and turning occasionally, for 8 to 10 minutes or until the onion is soft. Add the pork, pour over the white wine and stir in the lemon rind. Bring the liquid to the boil.

Reduce the heat to low and simmer the mixture for 1 hour. Add the haricot beans and simmer for a further 30 minutes or until the pork is very tender when pierced with the point of a sharp knife.

Remove the casserole from the heat and serve at once.

Zoose Pears

Zoose Pears are scrumptious accompanied by a well-chilled white Loire wine, such as Sancerre.

4 SERVINGS

4 small ripe pears
  the juice of 1 lemon
4 oz. Gorgonzola cheese
1 oz. [2 tablespoons] unsalted butter, softened
4 tablespoons crushed pistachio nuts

Using a sharp knife, peel the pears and core them. Using a pastry brush, brush the lemon juice over the pears and set them aside.

In a medium-sized mixing bowl, cream the cheese and butter with a kitchen fork until they are soft and creamy.

Using a small teaspoon, fill the hollow cores of the pears with the cheese mixture.

Place the crushed pistachio nuts on a plate and roll the pears in the nuts until they are well covered, shaking off any excess.

Place the pears on a serving dish and place the dish in the refrigerator. Chill for 2 hours before serving.

Zoo-Time Sandwiches

These enormous sandwiches are both delicious and nourishing and are ideal to take

on family outings — whether it's to the zoo or the seaside! Eat them with potato crisps [chips] and plenty of cold lemonade or beer.

4 SERVINGS

8 thin slices brown bread, buttered on one side
4 tablespoons peanut butter
4 thick slices mature Cheddar cheese
2 large tomatoes, very thinly sliced
½ teaspoon salt
½ teaspoon black pepper

4 thin slices white bread, buttered on both sides
4 lettuce leaves, washed and shaken dry
4 teaspoons mayonnaise
4 slices cooked chicken breast
1 tablespoon yeast extract

Lay 4 slices of the brown bread, buttered side up, on a flat surface. Spread them generously with the peanut butter. Place the cheese slices on top of the peanut butter and distribute the tomato slices evenly over the cheese. Sprinkle over half the salt and pepper, then carefully place the slices of white bread over the tomatoes.

Place a lettuce leaf over each piece of white bread and place a teaspoon of mayonnaise in the centre of each leaf.

Two super recipes which the children will love, Zoo-Time Sandwiches and Zoom-Zoom Sausage Toadstools are both fun to make and delicious to eat.

Place a slice of chicken breast on each piece of lettuce and sprinkle over the remaining salt and pepper. Spread the yeast extract thinly over the remaining slices of brown bread and then press them firmly, yeast extract side down, on to the chicken.

Using a sharp knife, carefully cut each sandwich diagonally into 2 pieces. Secure the sandwiches with cocktail sticks and wrap them in greaseproof or waxed paper, or aluminium foil, to keep them fresh until they are required.

Zopperelli Figs in Red Wine

Although extremely simple and quick to prepare, this sophisticated dessert tastes superb and is ideal to serve at the end of a summer dinner party.

4 SERVINGS

2 tablespoons soft brown sugar
1 pint [2½ cups] red wine
1-inch strip of lemon rind
1 tablespoon clear honey
12 firm fresh figs

Put all the ingredients, with the exception of the figs, in a large saucepan and place over moderate heat. Bring the liquid to the boil and reduce the heat to low. Add the figs and simmer the mixture for 10 minutes.

Remove the pan from the heat and carefully transfer the contents to a serving bowl. Allow the mixture to cool to room temperature and either serve immediately or place in the refrigerator until required.

Zora's Peach Dessert

Zora's Peach Dessert is marvellously easy to prepare and delicious to eat!

3 SERVINGS

14 oz. canned peach halves, drained
1 tablespoon soft brown sugar
5 fl. oz. [⅝ cup] yogurt
1 tablespoon butter
4 tablespoons medium oatmeal
1 tablespoon clear honey

Put the peach halves into a medium-sized mixing bowl and, using a fork, mash them to a smooth purée. Beat in the brown sugar, then the yogurt, beating until the mixture is well blended. Place the bowl in the refrigerator to chill for 15 minutes.

Meanwhile, in a small saucepan, melt the butter over moderate heat. When the foam subsides, add the oatmeal and fry, stirring constantly, for 3 minutes or until it is lightly toasted. Stir in the honey and remove the pan from the heat. Set the mixture aside until the oatmeal has cooled.

Remove the bowl from the refrigerator and spoon the oatmeal mixture on top. Serve at once.

Zoradora Dessert

This delicious dessert is quite elegant enough to serve at a dinner party, yet so easy to make that it is ideal for a family lunch.

6 SERVINGS

6 oz. strawberries, hulled and washed
6 bananas, peeled and mashed
12 fl. oz. [1½ cups] yogurt
1 tablespoon sugar
juice of ½ lemon
5 fl. oz. double cream [⅝ cup heavy cream], lightly whipped
3 egg whites, stiffly beaten

Place 4 ounces of the strawberries in a large serving bowl and mash them with a fork. Add the bananas and stir in the yogurt, sugar and lemon juice. Using a wooden spoon, beat in the cream and stir until all the ingredients are thoroughly combined. Using a metal spoon, fold in the egg whites until the mixture is well blended.

Halve the remaining strawberries and use them to decorate the top of the dessert. Chill in the refrigerator until ready to serve.

Zorba's Meatballs

A subtle blend of lamb, beef, garlic and spices with a creamy Mozzarella cheese filling makes Zorba's Meatballs a dish with a difference. Serve with boiled rice and a crisp green salad.

6 SERVINGS

1 lb. lean lamb, minced [ground]
1 lb. lean beef, minced [ground]
1 small onion, finely chopped
1 garlic clove, crushed
4 slices white bread, soaked in cold water and squeezed dry
2 eggs, lightly beaten
1 teaspoon salt
½ teaspoon sugar
1 teaspoon black pepper
1 teaspoon ground coriander
8 oz. Mozzarella cheese, cut into 1-inch cubes
2 fl. oz. [¼ cup] olive oil
SAUCE
1 tablespoon olive oil
1 small onion, finely chopped
1 garlic clove, crushed
14 oz. canned peeled tomatoes
3 tablespoons tomato purée
2 fl. oz. [¼ cup] water
1 teaspoon salt
½ teaspoon sugar
½ teaspoon black pepper
1 tablespoon finely chopped fresh mint or 1½ teaspoons dried mint

First prepare the sauce. In a large flame-proof casserole, heat the oil over moderate heat. When the oil is hot, add the onion and garlic and fry, stirring constantly, for 5 to 7 minutes or until the onion is soft and translucent but not brown. Stir in the tomatoes with the can juice, tomato purée, water, salt, sugar, pepper and mint. Increase the heat to high and bring the contents of the casserole to the boil. Reduce the heat to low, cover the casserole and simmer the sauce for 15 minutes.

Meanwhile, in a large mixing bowl, combine the lamb, beef, onion, garlic, bread, eggs, salt, sugar, pepper and coriander. Using a wooden spoon, mix the ingredients together until they are thoroughly combined. Spoon 2 tablespoons of the mixture into the palm of your hand and pat it fairly flat. Place a cube of cheese in the centre of the meat mixture and fold the mixture around the cheese, to form a ball about the size of an egg. Set aside. Repeat this process until all the meat mixture and cheese are used up.

In a large frying-pan, heat half of the oil over moderate heat. When the oil is hot, add the meatballs, a few at a time, and fry, turning frequently, for 6 to 8 minutes or until they are golden brown all over. Using a slotted spoon, transfer the meatballs to a plate. Continue frying the remaining meatballs in the same way, adding more oil when necessary, until all the meatballs are browned.

Add the meatballs to the sauce and simmer for 15 to 20 minutes or until the meatballs are completely cooked. Remove the casserole from the heat and serve immediately, straight from the casserole.

Zorba's Tipsy Cake

This delicious chocolate and vanilla cake, rich with sherry and orange-flavoured liqueur and filled with cream, is an adaptation of a traditional Greek recipe. Serve as a dessert.

4-6 SERVINGS

6 oz. [¾ cup] butter
6 oz. [¾ cup] castor sugar
3 eggs
6 oz. [1½ cups] flour
1 teaspoon baking powder
2 oz. dark [semi-sweet] cooking chocolate, melted
1 teaspoon very finely grated orange rind
¾ teaspoon vanilla essence
½ teaspoon very finely grated lemon rind
2 fl. oz. [¼ cup] sherry

A deliciously rich and tempting dessert, Zorba's Tipsy Cake is fabulous served with lots of whipped cream.

3 tablespoons orange-flavoured
   liqueur
FILLING
10 fl. oz. double cream [1¼ cups
   heavy cream]
 4 tablespoons apricot jam
 2 tablespoons slivered almonds

Preheat the oven to fairly hot 375°F (Gas
Mark 5, 190°C). Line the bottom and

sides of a 6-inch cake tin with greaseproof
or waxed paper and set aside.

   In a large mixing bowl, cream the
butter and sugar together with a wooden
spoon until the mixture is light and
fluffy. Add the eggs, one by one, absorb-
ing each one before adding the next.
Gradually sift the flour and baking
powder into the mixture, beating constantly until the mixture is smooth.

   Transfer half of the mixture to a
second mixing bowl. With a metal spoon,
fold the chocolate and orange rind into
one mixture and the vanilla essence and
lemon rind into the other.

   Place alternate tablespoons of each
mixture in the prepared tin, swirling it
slightly to give the desired 'marbled'
effect. When all the batter has been
added, make swirling patterns on the top

of the cake with a flat-bladed knife.

Place the cake in the oven and bake for 45 minutes or until a skewer inserted into the centre comes out clean.

Remove the cake from the oven and allow it to cool in the tin for 5 minutes. Turn the cake out on to a wire rack. Remove and discard the greaseproof or waxed paper and allow the cake to cool completely.

Meanwhile, making the filling. In a medium-sized mixing bowl, beat the cream with a wire whisk or rotary beater until it forms stiff peaks. With a metal spoon, fold in the jam and almonds stirring to mix well.

With a sharp knife, cut the cake in half, horizontally, and place the bottom half on a large serving plate. Generously spread half the filling over the top. Cover with the remaining cake half. Pour over the sherry and orange-flavoured liqueur and set aside for 15 minutes or until they have soaked into the cake. Decorate the top and sides with the remaining cream mixture and serve immediately.

Zorin's Lamb with Lemon Sauce

Zorin's Lamb with Lemon Sauce is a variation on a traditional recipe from Greece where the addition of lemon to meat dishes is very popular. Ask your butcher to cut through the lamb as it requires a very sharp knife.

6 SERVINGS

1 x 4 lb. leg of lamb, cut at 1-inch intervals down through the bone but not through the meat below
4 garlic cloves, cut into slivers
2 tablespoons vegetable oil
1½ teaspoons salt
1 teaspoon black pepper
2 egg yolks
2 fl. oz. [¼ cup] lemon juice
8 fl. oz. [1 cup] chicken stock
1 lb. broad beans, cooked
½ teaspoon dried thyme

Preheat the oven to moderate 350°F (Gas Mark 4, 180°C).

Place the lamb on a working surface and insert the slivers of garlic between the slices in the lamb. Pour the oil over the lamb and rub 1 teaspoon of the salt and ½ teaspoon of the pepper into the surface.

Place the lamb on a rack in a roasting tin and place it in the oven.

Roast for 1½ hours, basting occasionally, or until the lamb is tender when pierced with the point of a sharp knife.

Meanwhile, in a small mixing bowl,

combine the egg yolks, lemon juice and chicken stock and set aside.

Take the lamb out of the oven, remove and discard the garlic slivers and completely cut through the meat. Transfer the slices to a warmed serving dish and keep warm while you make the sauce. Skim off and discard any fat from the cooking juices remaining in the roasting tin and then pour them into the egg yolk mixture. Pour the mixture into a large saucepan and place over low heat. Add the beans to the pan and stir in the remaining salt, pepper and the thyme. Cook the mixture, stirring occasionally, for 8 to 10 minutes or until the sauce has thickened.

Pour the sauce over the lamb slices and serve immediately.

Zorrell Cheese and Ham Rolls

Zorrell Cheese and Ham Rolls may either be served as a light luncheon, accompanied by new potatoes and French beans or, in greater quantities, as part of a buffet table at a party.

2 SERVINGS

4 oz. [½ cup] Ricotta cheese
2 tablespoons mayonnaise
2 tablespoons chopped walnuts
1 celery stalk, trimmed and finely chopped
¼ teaspoon salt
¼ teaspoon black pepper
4 thin slices Gruyère cheese, about 4- x 6-inches
4 thin slices cooked ham
1 teaspoon prepared French mustard

Place the ricotta cheese, mayonnaise, walnuts, chopped celery, salt and pepper in a medium-sized mixing bowl. Using a wooden spoon, mix all the ingredients together and set aside.

Place the slices of cheese on a flat working surface and lay the ham slices on top of them. Spread the mustard thinly over the ham. Spoon a quarter of the ricotta cheese mixture on to each slice of ham. Carefully roll the ham and cheese up around the cheese mixture to form a cylinder and secure with cocktail sticks.

Place the rolls on a serving plate and serve immediately.

Zossen Oxtail

Oxtail prepared by this method makes an extremely satisfying, filling and nourishing dish. Serve with baked potatoes.

6 SERVINGS

2 tablespoons vegetable oil
1 oxtail, trimmed and cut into pieces
8 shallots, peeled
4 medium-sized carrots, scraped and sliced
4 heads of fennel, trimmed and sliced
4 celery stalks, trimmed and finely chopped
4 fl. oz. [½ cup] Pernod
3 pints [7½ cups] beef stock
½ teaspoon salt
½ teaspoon black pepper
4 oz. [½ cup] pearl barley
4-inch strip of orange rind

Preheat the oven to cool 300°F (Gas Mark 2, 150°C).

In a large frying-pan, heat the oil over moderate heat. When the oil is hot, add the oxtail pieces and fry them, turning occasionally, for 5 minutes or until they are evenly browned. Using tongs or a slotted spoon, transfer the oxtail pieces to a large ovenproof casserole.

Add the shallots, carrots, fennel and celery to the casserole. Pour over the Pernod and shake the casserole vigorously. Pour over the stock and stir well to mix. Stir in the salt and pepper.

Cover the casserole with aluminium foil and a heavy lid. Place the casserole in the oven and cook for 4 hours or until the meat is very tender and comes away from the bones. Remove the casserole from the oven and set aside to cool completely.

Place the casserole in the refrigerator to chill for at least 8 hours or overnight.

Remove the casserole from the refrigerator and remove and discard the fat that has risen to the surface.

Preheat the oven to moderate 350°F (Gas Mark 4, 180°C).

Add the pearl barley and orange rind to the casserole. Place the casserole in the oven and heat it for 30 minutes or until the contents are very hot.

Remove the casserole from the oven and remove and discard the orange rind. Serve immediately.

Zouar Banana Ice-Cream

This is a light-textured banana ice-cream which makes a refreshing end to a rich meal. It is extremely quick and easy to make.

An unusual and succulent dinner party dish, Zorin's Lamb with Lemon Sauce may be served either sliced or whole, with the sauce served separately.

6 SERVINGS

3 bananas, peeled and sliced
5 fl. oz. [⅝ cup] sour cream
2 teaspoons lemon juice
1 teaspoon sugar
3 egg whites, stiffly whipped

Place the bananas, sour cream, lemon juice and sugar in a strainer set over a large bowl and, with the back of a wooden spoon, rub the ingredients through the strainer until they form a purée. Alternatively, place all the ingredients, except the egg whites, in the jar of an electric blender and blend them until they form a purée.

Using a metal spoon, fold in the egg whites. Spoon the mixture into a freezer tray and place it in the frozen food storage compartment of the refrigerator for 2 hours.

Remove the ice-cream from the refrigerator and beat it vigorously with a fork. Return it to the compartment of the refrigerator for 30 minutes or until the ice-cream has set. It is now ready to serve.

Zouzou's Crêpes

An exquisite hors d'oeuvre, Zouzou's Crêpes is a mouth-watering concoction of crêpes stuffed with Roquefort cheese and béchamel sauce.

A sophisticated hors d'oeuvre, Zouzou's Crêpes just melt in your mouth!

6 SERVINGS

8 fl. oz. [1 cup] béchamel sauce
1 egg yolk
5 oz. Roquefort cheese, crumbled
¼ teaspoon salt
½ teaspoon black pepper
8 oz. [2 cups] Crêpe Batter, (Savoury)
1 oz. [2 tablespoons] butter, melted
2 fl. oz. [¼ cup] brandy, warmed

To make the filling, pour the béchamel sauce and egg yolk into a medium-sized mixing bowl and, with a wire whisk or rotary beater, beat them together until they are well blended. Stir in the crumbled cheese, salt and pepper and beat well to blend. Place the bowl in the refrigerator to chill for 1 hour.

Fry the crêpes according to the instructions in the basic recipe.

Lay the crêpes out flat and put about 2 tablespoons of the filling in the centre of each one. Fold the crêpes in half, then in quarters to enclose the filling.

Arrange the crêpes on the bottom of a chafing dish or large, shallow baking dish. Pour over the melted butter. Pour over the warmed brandy and ignite. Shake the dish gently until the flames have died away. Serve at once.

Zoytinyagli Pirasa
LEEK AND BACON RISOTTO

This delightful dish is a perfect mid-week lunch or supper for the family. Serve Zoytinyagli Pirasa (tsoy-ting-yah-glee pee-rah-sah) with a mixed salad and, to drink, some ice-cold lager.

4 SERVINGS

1 lb. streaky bacon slices, rinds removed and chopped
2 fl. oz. [¼ cup] vegetable oil
4 leeks, green part only, cleaned and chopped
1 lb. [2⅔ cups] long-grain rice, washed, soaked in cold water for 30 minutes and drained
14 oz. canned peeled tomatoes
1 teaspoon salt
1 teaspoon black pepper
½ teaspoon cayenne pepper
½ teaspoon ground cumin
1 teaspoon finely grated lemon rind
1½ pints [3¾ cups] chicken stock
2 lemons, thinly sliced
1 tablespoon chopped fresh mint

In a large flameproof casserole, fry the bacon pieces over moderate heat for 6 to 8 minutes or until they are crisp and brown and have rendered most of their fat. With a slotted spoon, transfer the bacon pieces to a plate and set aside.

Add the vegetable oil to the casserole and heat it over moderate heat. When the oil is hot, add the leeks and fry, stirring occasionally, for 12 minutes. Stir in the rice and fry, stirring frequently, for 5 minutes. Add the tomatoes with the can juice, salt, pepper, cayenne, cumin and lemon rind and stir well to mix. Pour over the chicken stock and bring the liquid to the boil.

Return the bacon pieces to the casserole, reduce the heat to low and simmer the mixture for 15 to 20 minutes or until the rice is cooked and tender and all the liquid has been absorbed.

Remove the casserole from the heat and garnish the mixture with the lemon slices and mint. Serve at once.

Zraza

STUFFED BEEF ROLLS IN MUSHROOM SAUCE

Zraza (scrazza) is a traditional Russian recipe in which a piece of meat, either whole or minced [ground] is first stuffed and then cooked. In this particular recipe we have used thin slices of beef, stuffed them and then cooked them in the oven in creamy mushroom sauce.

4 SERVINGS

4 large slices of rump steak, pounded very thin
1 garlic clove, halved
½ teaspoon salt
½ teaspoon black pepper
2 oz. [¼ cup] butter

A classic Russian dish, Zraza should be served with creamed potatoes, a green salad and some white wine.

1 tablespoon chopped fresh parsley
SAUCE
1 oz. [2 tablespoons] butter
1 medium-sized onion, finely chopped
8 oz. mushrooms, wiped clean and coarsely chopped
1 tablespoon flour
10 fl. oz. single cream [1¼ cups light cream]
¼ teaspoon salt
¼ teaspoon black pepper
½ teaspoon paprika

3021

STUFFING

2 oz. [1 cup] fresh white
  breadcrumbs
1 teaspoon finely grated lemon
  rind
1 small onion, very finely chopped
1 teaspoon chopped fresh sage or
  ½ teaspoon dried sage
1 tablespoon chopped fresh parsley
1 egg yolk

Preheat the oven to moderate 350°F (Gas Mark 4, 180°C).

First make the sauce. In a medium-sized frying-pan, melt the butter over moderate heat. When the foam subsides, add the onion to the pan and fry, stirring occasionally, for 5 to 7 minutes or until it is soft and translucent but not brown. Add the mushrooms, reduce the heat to low and fry, stirring occasionally, for 12 to 15 minutes or until the mushrooms are very tender. Remove the pan from the heat and, using a wooden spoon, carefully stir in the flour to make a smooth paste. Gradually add the cream, stirring constantly. Return the pan to the heat, stir in the salt, pepper and paprika and cook, stirring constantly, for 2 to 3 minutes or until the sauce is smooth and fairly thick. Remove the pan from the heat and set aside.

Rub the steaks all over with the garlic halves and discard the garlic. Sprinkle with the salt and pepper and set aside while you prepare the stuffing.

To make the stuffing, in a medium-sized mixing bowl, combine all the stuffing ingredients and, using a wooden spoon, mix them together until they form a paste.

Form the stuffing into 4 sausage shapes and place one on each steak. Roll up the meat Swiss [jelly] roll style and secure the rolls with string or cocktail sticks.

In a large frying-pan, melt 1½ ounces [3 tablespoons] of the butter over moderate heat. When the foam subsides, add the rolls and fry them for 2 minutes on each side or until they are lightly browned.

Using two forks, remove the rolls from the pan and transfer them to a large plate.

Using the remaining butter, grease a deep, ovenproof serving dish. Place the beef rolls in the dish and pour over the reserved mushroom sauce.

Place the dish in the oven and cook for 25 to 30 minutes or until the rolls are tender when pierced with the point of a sharp knife.

Remove the dish from the oven, sprinkle over the parsley and serve immediately, straight from the dish.

Zrazi eze Ribi
FISH BAKED IN CREAM

This mild-flavoured fish dish is popular in Poland where it is sometimes prepared with sole fillets instead of the haddock we have used here. Zrazi eze Ribi (scrazz is ribi) may be served with glazed carrots and lemon wedges and a well-chilled Riesling wine.

4 SERVINGS

4 medium-sized onions, thinly
  sliced
4 eggs, stiffly beaten
6 oz. [3 cups] fresh breadcrumbs
8 fl. oz. [1 cup] milk
4 x 8 oz. haddock fillets
½ teaspoon salt
½ teaspoon black pepper
½ teaspoon dill seeds
3 oz. [1 cup] dried breadcrumbs
  sufficient vegetable oil for
  deep-frying
8 fl. oz. single cream [1 cup light
  cream]
2 tablespoons chopped fresh dill
1 teaspoon black pepper
  grated rind of 1 orange

Place the onions, 3 eggs, the fresh breadcrumbs and milk in a large mixing bowl. Using a fork, stir the mixture together until all the ingredients are combined. Cover the bowl and place it in the refrigerator to chill for 1 hour.

Preheat the oven to moderate 350°F (Gas Mark 4, 180°C).

Place the haddock on a floured working surface and sprinkle it with the salt, pepper and dill seeds.

Remove the bowl from the refrigerator and, using a metal spoon, divide the mixture into 8 pieces. With a flat-bladed knife, spread the breadcrumb mixture over the haddock fillets.

Beat the remaining egg and place it in a shallow dish. Place the dried breadcrumbs in a second dish.

Dip each fillet in the egg, then in the breadcrumbs, shaking off any excess.

Fill a large deep-frying pan one-third full with vegetable oil. Place the pan over moderate heat and heat the oil until it reaches 350°F on a deep-fat thermometer or until a small cube of stale bread dropped into the oil turns light brown in 55 seconds.

Using a slotted spoon, place 2 fillets in the oil and fry them for 5 minutes or until they are golden brown.

Using the slotted spoon, remove the fillets from the oil and drain them on kitchen paper towels. Place them on a warmed ovenproof serving dish and keep them warm while you fry and drain the remaining fillets in the same way.

Pour over the cream and sprinkle over the dill and pepper.

Place the dish in the oven for 15 to 20 minutes or until the cream begins to bubble.

Remove the dish from the oven and sprinkle over the grated orange rind.

Serve immediately.

Zrazi s Kashie
POLISH STUFFED HAMBURGERS

Unusual is a good word to describe this tasty dish which originated in Poland and spread, during the course of history, throughout the Slav countries of eastern Europe. Zrazi s Kashie (scrazz-zi-skashi) are a type of flattened stuffed hamburger. They are stuffed with mincemeat and cooked with sour cream. Serve with thin lemon wedges.

8 SERVINGS

2 lb. beef, minced [ground]
4 oz. [1 cup] cooked semolina
2 medium-sized onions, thinly
  sliced
½ teaspoon salt
½ teaspoon black pepper
8 fl. oz. [1 cup] beef stock
1 oz. [¼ cup] flour
  sufficient vegetable oil for
  deep-frying

FILLING

4 oz. [½ cup] Mincemeat I
½ teaspoon ground cinnamon
2 oz. mushrooms, wiped clean
  and sliced
1 tablespoon butter, softened

SAUCE

16 fl. oz. [2 cups] sour cream
2 tablespoons chopped fresh dill
1 teaspoon black pepper
1 tablespoon grated orange rind

Place the beef, semolina, onions, salt, pepper and stock in a medium-sized mixing bowl. Using a fork, mix the ingredients together until they are well blended. Place the bowl in the refrigerator to chill for 30 minutes.

Meanwhile, make the filling. In a medium-sized mixing bowl, combine the mincemeat, cinnamon, mushrooms and butter. Divide the mixture into 8 pieces. Place the meat pieces on a plate and chill in the refrigerator for 30 minutes.

Remove the beef mixture from the refrigerator. Sprinkle a working surface

---

A really unusual and tasty Polish dish, Zrazi s Kashie is ideal to serve at an informal supper party.

with a little flour. Using well floured hands, roll each portion into a round ball and, using a knife, cut each ball in half. Flour a rolling pin and roll the halved balls into rounds ½-inch thick.

Place the filling in the centre of half of the rounds and place the remaining rounds on top.

With well floured fingers, press the meat edges together, so that the filling makes the meat form a dome in the centre. Set aside.

Preheat the oven to moderate 350°F (Gas Mark 4, 180°C).

Fill a large deep-frying pan one-third full with the vegetable oil. Place the pan over moderate heat and heat the oil until it reaches 350°F on a deep-fat thermometer or until a small cube of stale bread dropped into the oil turns light brown in 55 seconds.

Using a slotted spoon, place 2 of the meat rounds in the oil. Fry for 5 minutes or until they are golden brown. Using the slotted spoon, remove the meat rounds from the oil and place them on kitchen paper towels to drain. Continue frying the remaining meat rounds in the same way.

Place the cooked rounds on a warmed ovenproof serving dish. Pour over the sour cream and place the dish in the oven to cook for 20 minutes.

Remove the dish from the oven and sprinkle over the dill, pepper and grated orange rind. Serve immediately.

Zsa Zsa's Meatball Goulasch

This delicious goulasch makes an invigorating dinner or supper dish. Serve with mashed potatoes and a mixed salad and, to drink, some Egri Bikaver.

4 SERVINGS

2 fl. oz. [¼ cup] vegetable oil
2 medium-sized onions, finely chopped
1 garlic clove, crushed
2 carrots, scraped and sliced
4 oz. button mushrooms, wiped clean and thinly sliced
1½ tablespoons paprika
12 fl. oz. [1½ cups] beef stock
4 fl. oz. [½ cup] red wine
½ teaspoon salt
1 teaspoon black pepper
½ teaspoon dried dill
1 teaspoon caraway seeds
4 large potatoes, peeled and

Zsa Zsa's Meatball Goulasch may be made the night before you wish to serve it and is just as good the next day.

quartered
2 teaspoons cornflour [cornstarch], mixed with 1 tablespoon water
10 fl. oz. [1¼ cups] sour cream
MEATBALLS
1 lb. beef, minced [ground]
1 lb. lean pork, minced [ground]
2 garlic cloves, crushed
1 teaspoon salt
1 teaspoon black pepper
1 teaspoon dried dill
½ teaspoon cayenne pepper
4 slices rye bread, crusts removed and soaked for 5 minutes in 3 tablespoons milk
1 egg
1 teaspoon grated orange rind

First make the meatballs. In a large mixing bowl, beat all the meatball ingredients together until they are thoroughly blended. Using your hands, shape the mixture into small balls. Put all the balls on a large plate or baking sheet, cover them with foil or plastic wrap and put them in the refrigerator to chill for 30 minutes.

In a large flameproof casserole, heat the oil over moderate heat. When the oil is hot, add the onions, garlic and carrots and fry, stirring occasionally, for 5 to 7 minutes or until the onions are soft and translucent but not brown. Stir in the mushrooms and paprika and mix well. Fry the mixture, stirring occasionally, for a further 3 minutes. Pour in the stock and wine and add the salt, pepper, dill and caraway seeds. Bring the liquid to the boil.

Remove the meatballs from the refrigerator and remove and discard the foil or wrap. Add the meatballs to the casserole and bring the liquid back to the boil. Reduce the heat to low, cover and simmer the mixture for 1 hour.

Uncover the casserole and add the potatoes. Re-cover and simmer the mixture for a further 20 minutes or until the potatoes and meatballs are cooked through. Uncover the casserole and stir in the cornflour [cornstarch] mixture and the sour cream. Cook, stirring constantly, for a further 2 to 3 minutes or until the sauce has thickened and is hot but not boiling.

Remove the casserole from the heat and serve at once, straight from the casserole.

Zubia Cod with Alioli Sauce

An adaptation of a traditional Spanish recipe, Zubia Cod with Alioli Sauce is simply superb served with a well-chilled white wine and lots of crusty bread and butter.

4 SERVINGS

1½ pints [3¾ cups] fish stock
10 fl. oz. [1¼ cups] dry white wine
 2 onions, quartered
 2 leeks, trimmed, cleaned and cut into 2-inch lengths
 2 celery stalks, trimmed and cut into 1-inch lengths
 4 potatoes, peeled and cut into quarters
 4 carrots, scraped and cut into 1-inch lengths
 1 teaspoon salt
 ½ teaspoon white pepper
 bouquet garni, consisting of 4 parsley sprigs, 1 thyme spray and 1 bay leaf tied together
 2 lb. cod fillets, skinned
10 fl. oz. [1¼ cups] Alioli Sauce

In a large saucepan, combine the fish stock, white wine, onions, leeks, celery, potatoes, carrots, salt, pepper and bouquet garni. Place the saucepan over high heat and bring the contents of the pan to the boil. Boil for 10 minutes. Add the cod and reduce the heat to low. Cover the pan and simmer the fish for 15 minutes or until the flesh flakes easily when tested with a fork.

Remove the pan from the heat. Using a slotted spoon, transfer the fish and vegetables to a warmed serving dish. Serve immediately, accompanied by the alioli sauce.

Zubov Calf's Liver Stroganov

This easy-to-prepare dish is based on the classic Beef Stroganov and is equally tasty and just as elegant for a dinner party dish. Serve with buttered noodles or puréed potatoes and green beans.

4-6 SERVINGS

1½ lb. calf's liver, thinly sliced
1½ teaspoons salt
 1 teaspoon black pepper
 2 teaspoons paprika
 4 oz. [½ cup] butter
 6 oz. button mushrooms, wiped clean and sliced
 2 fl. oz. [¼ cup] dry white wine
10 fl. oz. [1¼ cups] sour cream
 ½ teaspoon caraway seeds

Lay the liver slices on a flat working surface and rub them with 1 teaspoon of salt and half the pepper and paprika.

Roast pork whose flavour is complemented by spicy plums, Zubrick Pork and Spiced Plums is delicious.

Using a sharp knife, cut the slices into strips.

In a large frying-pan, melt the butter over moderate heat. When the foam subsides, add the mushrooms and fry, stirring occasionally, for 3 minutes. With a slotted spoon, transfer the mushrooms to a plate.

Add the liver strips to the pan and fry, turning and stirring occasionally, for 2 to 3 minutes or until they are cooked through. Stir in the white wine, the remaining salt, pepper and paprika and mix well.

Return the mushrooms to the pan and stir in the sour cream and caraway seeds. Cook for a further 1 to 2 minutes or until the sauce is heated through.

Remove the pan from the heat and transfer the mixture to a warmed serving dish. Serve at once.

Zubrick Pork and Spiced Plums

A most unusual dish, Zubrick Pork and Spiced Plums is a delicious combination which can be eaten hot or cold. When

Zubrowka Cocktail

Zubrowka is a popular Eastern European type of vodka but if it is not available, this delicious drink is just as successful with British or American-type vodka.

1 SERVING

3 fl oz. [⅜ cup] Zubrowka vodka
6 fl. oz. [¾ cup] grapefruit juice
2 teaspoons Campari
2 ice cubes

Place a large cocktail glass in the refrigerator to chill for 30 minutes.

Remove the glass from the refrigerator and pour in the vodka, grapefruit juice and Campari. Using a long-handled spoon, stir until the liquids are well blended.

Add the ice cubes and serve the cocktail at once.

Zubrowka Fruit Cocktail

If you don't have Zubrowka vodka, any other type may be substituted. Serve this refreshing dessert with lots of whipped cream.

4 SERVINGS

6 fresh figs, sliced
2 large ripe peaches, stoned and sliced
2 bananas, peeled and sliced
12 large white grapes, halved and seeded
1 tablespoon soft brown sugar
1 teaspoon very finely grated lemon rind
2 fl. oz. [¼ cup] Zubrowka vodka

Arrange the fruit decoratively in a large, shallow serving dish. Sprinkle over the sugar and lemon rind and pour over the vodka. Place the dish in the refrigerator to chill for 30 minutes, basting the fruit with the vodka from time to time.

Remove the dish from the refrigerator and serve at once.

Zucca Cheese Loaf

Zucca Cheese Loaf could either be served as a rich first course at a dinner party or, accompanied by a salad, as a summer luncheon dish.

ONE 1-POUND LOAF

1 teaspoon vegetable oil
4 oz. Dolcelatte cheese, crumbled
6 oz. cream cheese
½ teaspoon paprika
¼ teaspoon prepared French mustard
½ teaspoon Tabasco sauce

---

served hot, *Pommes de Terre Soufflées* make an exceedingly good vegetable accompaniment. Served cold, the addition of a green salad is all this dish needs.

8 SERVINGS

1 x 5 lb. boned loin of pork, trimmed of excess fat, skin scored for crackling
1 teaspoon salt
½ teaspoon black pepper
2 garlic cloves, peeled and cut in 2 pieces
28 oz. canned red plums, stoned
8 juniper berries
2 tablespoons prepared French mustard

Preheat the oven to fairly hot 375°F (Gas Mark 5, 190°C).

Place the pork on a flat working surface. Rub the surface of the crackling with the salt and pepper.

Using a sharp knife, make four insertions in the pork and press a garlic piece into each one. Place the pork in a roasting tin, place the tin in the oven and roast the

A refreshing and unusual fruit dessert with quite a kick to it, Zubrowka Fruit Cocktail makes a delightful ending to a special dinner party.

---

pork for 2 hours. Increase the heat to hot 425°F (Gas Mark 7, 220°C) and continue to roast for a further 20 minutes or until the pork is cooked and the juices run clear when the pork is pierced with the point of a sharp knife.

Ten minutes before the end of the cooking time, place the plums with the can juice in a medium-sized saucepan. Add the juniper berries and mustard and set the pan over low heat. Bring the mixture to the boil, stirring constantly. Remove the pan from the heat and keep warm.

Remove the roasting tin from the oven and transfer the meat to a large, warmed serving dish. Discard the cooking juices.

Strain the plums and discard the cooking juice. Arrange the plums decoratively around the meat and serve immediately.

½ green pepper, white pith removed, seeded and very finely chopped
4 fl. oz. [½ cup] mayonnaise
4 fl. oz. double cream [½ cup heavy cream]
½ oz. gelatine, dissolved in 2 tablespoons of hot water
2 oz. cooked ham, cut into thin strips
2 oz. red-peppered sausage, very thinly sliced
½ red pepper, white pith removed, seeded and thinly sliced horizontally into rings
6 stuffed olives, halved

Grease a 1-pound loaf tin with the vegetable oil and place the tin, upside-down, on kitchen paper towels to drain.

Using the back of a wooden spoon, rub the cheese through a fine wire strainer into a medium-sized mixing bowl. Beat in the cream cheese, paprika, mustard, Tabasco sauce and green pepper. Fold the mayonnaise and cream into the mixture and then stir in the dissolved gelatine.

Place the bowl in the refrigerator for 10 minutes or until the mixture is on the point of setting. Remove the bowl from the refrigerator and place it in a larger bowl filled with iced water.

Spoon one-third of the cheese mixture

A colourful and appetizing-looking Italian dish, Zucca Cheese Loaf has a marvellous flavour and tastes just as good as it looks.

into the loaf tin. Place the loaf tin in the refrigerator for 10 minutes or until the cheese mixture has set. Carefully arrange the strips of ham over the top so that they form a smooth layer. Spoon half of the remaining cheese mixture over the top and return the loaf tin to the refrigerator for a further 10 minutes or until the cheese mixture has set.

Remove the loaf tin from the refrigerator and arrange the slices of sausage carefully over the top to form a smooth layer. Spoon the remaining cheese mixture over the top and, using a flat-bladed knife, smooth over the surface. Place the loaf tin in the refrigerator and leave to chill for 1 hour or until the mould has set completely.

Remove the loaf tin from the refrigerator and quickly dip the bottom into hot water. Invert a serving plate over the tin, reverse the two and turn the cheese loaf out on to the plate. The loaf should slide out easily.

Garnish the loaf with the red pepper rings and halved olives and either serve immediately or chill in the refrigerator until required.

Zucca alla Parmigiana

PUMPKIN PARMA-STYLE

A tasty Italian dish, Zucca alla Parmigiana (zoo-kah ah-lah pahr-mee-ja-nah) makes a delicious supper served with a green salad and a chilled Soave wine.

4 SERVINGS

2 oz. [¼ cup] plus 1 teaspoon butter
2 eggs, lightly beaten
2 oz. [⅔ cup] dry breadcrumbs
2 lb. pumpkin flesh, cut into slices
1 oz. [¼ cup] Parmesan cheese, grated

SAUCE

2 tablespoons olive oil
1 onion, finely chopped
1 garlic clove, crushed
14 oz. canned peeled tomatoes
2 teaspoons tomato purée
1 tablespoon chopped fresh basil
1 tablespoon chopped fresh parsley
1 teaspoon sugar
1 teaspoon salt
½ teaspoon black pepper

First make the sauce. In a medium-sized saucepan, heat the oil over moderate heat. When the oil is hot, add the onion and garlic and fry, stirring occasionally, for 5 to 7 minutes or until the onion is soft and translucent but not brown. Stir in the tomatoes with the can juice, the tomato

purée, basil, parsley, sugar, salt and pepper. Bring the mixture to the boil, reduce the heat to low and simmer the sauce for 10 minutes.

Meanwhile, using the teaspoon of butter, grease an ovenproof dish. Set aside.

Preheat the oven to moderate 350°F (Gas Mark 4, 180°C). Place the eggs on one plate and the breadcrumbs on another. Dip the pumpkin slices in the eggs, then in the breadcrumbs, shaking off any excess.

In a large frying-pan, melt the remaining butter over moderate heat. When the foam subsides, fry the pumpkin slices, a few at a time, for 5 minutes, turning once until they are golden brown. Using a slotted spoon, transfer the slices to the prepared dish.

Pour over the sauce and sprinkle with the cheese. Place the dish in the oven and bake for 30 minutes or until the cheese is golden brown.

Remove the dish from the oven and serve immediately.

Zuccherini
ITALIAN CHOCOLATE MOUSSE IN CHOCOLATE CUPS

Tempting, melt-in-the-mouth chocolate cups filled with delectable chocolate mousse, Zuccherini (zoo-kair-ee-nee) make a wonderful dessert for a special dinner party. They look particularly attractive decorated with slices of crystallized orange or mandarin orange slices.

6 SERVINGS

6 oz. dark [semi-sweet] cooking
   chocolate
FILLING
2 oz. dark [semi-sweet] cooking
   chocolate
1 tablespoon strong black coffee
2 eggs, separated
2 teaspoons orange-flavoured
   liqueur
10 Macaroons, crushed
5 fl. oz. double cream [⅝ cup heavy
   cream], stiffly whipped

Break the 6 ounces of chocolate into small pieces and place them in a small heatproof bowl. Place the bowl over a saucepan of boiling water set over moderate heat and stir the chocolate with a wooden spoon until it has melted. Remove the pan from the heat and the bowl from the pan.

With the back of a teaspoon, coat the insides of 12 paper cake cases with the chocolate. Lay the cases, upside down, on a plate and place them in the refrigerator to chill overnight.

To make the filling, break the 2 ounces of chocolate into small pieces and place them in a large heatproof bowl. Place the bowl over a saucepan of boiling water set over moderate heat and pour in the coffee. Stir with a wooden spoon until the chocolate has melted. Remove the pan from the heat and the bowl from the pan. Stir in the egg yolks and orange-flavoured liqueur.

In a medium-sized mixing bowl, beat the egg whites with a wire whisk or rotary beater until they form stiff peaks. Using a metal spoon, carefully fold the egg whites into the chocolate mixture. Set aside and allow to cool.

Remove the cake cases from the refrigerator. Carefully peel the paper cases away from the chocolate cups and discard them. Divide the crushed macaroons among the chocolate cups. Spoon the chocolate mixture into the chocolate cups and place them in the refrigerator to chill for 30 minutes.

Place a little whipped cream on the top of each chocolate cup and chill until you are ready to serve them.

Zucchero e Formaggio alla Crema
SUGAR AND CREAM CHEESE DESSERT

Zucchero e Formaggio alla Crema (zoo-ker-oh ay for-maj-oh ah-lah cray-mah) is a delicious Italian dessert which would make a superb end to any dinner party. Serve it with an elegant and extravagant Sauternes wine, such as a Château d'Yquem.

6 SERVINGS

4 oz. [½ cup] plus 1 teaspoon butter,
   melted
8 oz. [2 cups] crushed Brandy Snaps
½ teaspoon ground ginger
1 lb. full fat cream cheese, such as
   Petit Suisse
2 oz. [¼ cup] castor sugar
4 fl. oz. single cream [½ cup light
   cream]
2 tablespoons lemon juice
½ teaspoon ground cinnamon
½ oz. gelatine, dissolved in
   2 tablespoons hot water
15 oz. canned apricot halves,
   drained
4 tablespoons preserved ginger,
   drained and finely chopped
15 fl. oz. double cream [1⅞ cups heavy
   cream]
2 oz. [⅓ cup] soft brown sugar

With the teaspoon of butter, lightly grease a 9-inch loose-bottomed cake tin. Set aside.

In a medium-sized mixing bowl, com-
bine the crushed brandy snaps, the remaining melted butter and ground ginger with a wooden spoon. Line the base of the cake tin with the mixture, pressing it firmly against the bottom of the tin with your fingers or with the back of the wooden spoon. Set aside.

In a medium-sized mixing bowl, beat the cream cheese and sugar together with the wooden spoon until the mixture is smooth and creamy. Stir in the single [light] cream, lemon juice and cinnamon. Beat in the dissolved gelatine mixture and, using a large spoon, spoon the cheese mixture on to the biscuit [cookie] base. Place the tin in the refrigerator to chill for 30 minutes or until the mixture has set.

Preheat the grill [broiler] to high. Remove the cake tin from the refrigerator. Arrange the apricot halves over the cheese mixture and sprinkle the preserved ginger over the apricots.

Using a flat-bladed knife, spread the double [heavy] cream over the top. Sprinkle the brown sugar over the cream and place the cake tin under the grill [broiler]. Grill [broil] the top for 1 to 2 minutes or until the sugar has caramelized. Remove the cake tin from the grill [broiler], slide the dessert out of the tin and serve immediately.

Zucchini

Zucchini is the Italian word for courgettes meaning, literally, 'little marrows'. In America, too, courgettes are called zucchini. For further information see the information entry for COURGETTE.

Zucchini all'Agrodolce
COURGETTES IN SOUR-SWEET SAUCE

Zucchini all'Agrodolce (zoo-kee-nee all agroh-dol-chay) is an unusual way of serving courgettes [zucchini]. This vegetable dish makes an excellent accompaniment to cold meats or it may be served as a first course on its own.

6 SERVINGS

6 large courgettes [zucchini],
   trimmed and blanched
3 tablespoons olive oil
1 garlic clove
½ teaspoon salt
½ teaspoon black pepper
½ teaspoon ground cinnamon
1 tablespoon soft brown sugar

Zucchero e Formaggio alla Crema and Zuccherini are two absolutely scrumptious Italian desserts which make a superb ending to a dinner party.

2 tablespoons white wine vinegar
2 tablespoons water
2 oz. [½ cup] slivered almonds

Cut the courgettes [zucchini] into 4 or more strips lengthways.

In a large saucepan, heat the oil over moderate heat. When the oil is hot, add the garlic to the pan and fry, stirring frequently, for 2 to 3 minutes or until it is lightly browned. With a slotted spoon, remove the garlic clove and discard it.

Add the courgette [zucchini] strips, salt, pepper, cinnamon, sugar and vinegar to the pan. Pour in the water, cover the pan and cook for 10 to 12 minutes or until the courgette [zucchini] strips are lightly browned.

Add the almonds to the pan and cook for a further 2 to 3 minutes or until the almonds are lightly browned. Remove the pan from the heat, transfer the courgette [zucchini] mixture to a warmed serving dish and serve immediately.

Zucchini con Aneto
COURGETTES WITH DILL SAUCE

Zucchini con Aneto (zoo-kee-nee con an-ay-toh) is a combination of sautéed courgettes [zucchini] and a creamy sauce flavoured with dill. Serve as a first course or as a vegetable accompaniment.

6-8 SERVINGS

1 oz. [2 tablespoons] butter
2 lb. courgettes [zucchini], trimmed, thinly sliced and dégorged
1 tablespoon flour
8 fl. oz. single cream [1 cup light cream]
1 tablespoon lemon juice
1 teaspoon sugar
1 tablespoon chopped fresh dill
½ teaspoon salt
⅛ teaspoon white pepper

In a large saucepan, melt the butter over moderate heat. When the foam subsides, add the courgettes [zucchini] to the pan. Reduce the heat to low, cover and simmer the courgettes [zucchini] for 8 to 10 minutes or until they are translucent but still firm.

Remove the pan from the heat and, with a wooden spoon, stir in the flour to make a smooth paste. Gradually add the cream and lemon juice, stirring constantly. Return the pan to moderate heat and cook, stirring constantly, for 2 to 3 minutes or until the sauce is thick and smooth. Stir in the sugar, dill, salt and pepper. Continue cooking for 4 to 5 minutes, stirring occasionally, or until the courgettes [zucchini] are tender.

Remove the pan from the heat and transfer the courgette [zucchini] mixture to a warmed serving dish. Serve immediately.

Zucchini e Cavolfiore
COURGETTES AND CAULIFLOWER WITH TURMERIC

An unusual and exceptionally tasty way to serve vegetables, Zucchini e Cavolfiore (zoo-kee-nee ay kavol-fee-or-ay) adds colour and spice to almost all meat and poultry dishes.

6 SERVINGS

6 medium-sized courgettes [zucchini], trimmed, sliced and dégorged
1 medium-sized cauliflower, trimmed and broken into flowerets
6 fl. oz. [¾ cup] olive oil
2 tablespoons turmeric
1 teaspoon salt

Preheat the oven to fairly hot 375°F (Gas Mark 5, 190°C).

Set a saucepan of boiling, salted water over moderate heat and add the courgettes [zucchini] and the cauliflower. Boil for 3 minutes. Drain the vegetables and set them aside.

Pour the oil into a roasting tin. Set the tin over moderate heat and heat the oil until it is very hot. Remove the tin from the heat and stir in the turmeric and salt. Using a wooden spoon, stir in the courgettes [zucchini] and cauliflower and stir well until the vegetables are thoroughly coated with the oil mixture. Place the roasting tin in the oven and roast the vegetables, turning them in the oil from time to time, for 30 minutes or until they are just tender.

Remove the tin from the oven, drain off the excess oil and transfer the vegetables to a warmed serving dish. Serve at once.

Zucchini in Dolce
COURGETTE CAKE

You may think this cake should be savoury, but — surprisingly — it is sweet and rather like a banana bread. Serve Zucchini in Dolce (zoo-kee-nee in dol-chay) with tea or coffee.

ONE 2-POUND CAKE

1 lb. courgettes [zucchini], trimmed and grated
8 fl. oz. [1 cup] vegetable oil
12 oz. [1½ cups] sugar
3 eggs, well beaten

10 oz. [2½ cups] flour
1½ teaspoons baking powder
1 teaspoon bicarbonate of soda [baking soda]
1½ teaspoons ground cinnamon
1 teaspoon grated nutmeg
1 teaspoon salt
6 oz. [1 cup] walnuts, chopped

Preheat the oven to moderate 350°F (Gas Mark 4, 180°C). Line a 2-pound loaf tin with greaseproof or waxed paper and set aside.

In a large mixing bowl, combine the courgettes [zucchini], oil, sugar and eggs. Set aside.

Sift the flour, baking powder, soda, cinnamon, nutmeg and salt into a medium-sized mixing bowl. Gradually stir the flour mixture into the courgette [zucchini] mixture. Add the walnuts and mix well.

Spoon the mixture into the loaf tin. Place the tin in the oven and bake for 1¼ hours or until a skewer inserted into the centre of the cake comes out clean.

Remove the tin from the oven and allow the cake to cool in the tin for 15 minutes. Then turn it out on to a wire rack and peel off the greaseproof or waxed paper. Allow the cake to cool completely before serving.

Zucchini al Formaggio
COURGETTES WITH CHEESE

An appetizing dish, Zucchini al Formaggio (zoo-kee-nee ahl for-mah-joh) may be served on its own as a light vegetarian meal or as a vegetable accompaniment to plain roast meat, especially beef or lamb.

3-4 SERVINGS

1 oz. [2 tablespoons] butter
1 tablespoon vegetable oil
4 shallots, thinly sliced and pushed out into rings
1 garlic clove, crushed (optional)
1 lb. courgettes [zucchini], trimmed and sliced
4 medium-sized tomatoes, chopped
2 tablespoons finely chopped fresh parsley
1 tablespoon prepared French mustard
3 tablespoons sour cream
1 bay leaf
4 oz. [1 cup] Parmesan cheese, grated

Preheat the oven to fairly hot 375°F (Gas Mark 5, 190°C).

In a medium-sized, shallow flameproof casserole, melt the butter with the oil over moderate heat. When the foam sub-

Zucchini in Dolce is an unusual sweet cake which, surprisingly, contains courgettes [zucchini].

sides, add the shallots and the garlic, if you are using it. Fry, stirring occasionally, for 3 to 4 minutes or until the shallots are soft and translucent but not brown.

Add the courgettes [zucchini] and fry, stirring frequently, for 5 minutes. Stir in the tomatoes, parsley, mustard, sour cream and bay leaf and cook for 5

minutes, stirring occasionally.

Remove the casserole from the heat and remove and discard the bay leaf.

Sprinkle over the Parmesan cheese and place the casserole in the centre of the oven. Cook for 20 to 30 minutes or until the top is golden brown and the courgettes [zucchini] are tender when pierced with the point of a sharp knife.

Remove the casserole from the oven and serve immediately.

Zucchini con Frittelle

COURGETTE PANCAKES

An unusual lunch dish, Zucchini con Frittelle (zoo-kee-nee con free-tell-ay) may be accompanied by Bean Sprout Salad. They may also be made very small (about 1-inch in diameter) and served as cocktail party appetizers.

2-3 SERVINGS

3 medium-sized courgettes [zucchini], trimmed
1 egg, lightly beaten
2 garlic cloves, crushed
1 teaspoon salt
½ teaspoon black pepper
4 tablespoons grated Parmesan cheese
2 oz. [½ cup] flour
2 oz. [¼ cup] butter
4 tablespoons olive oil
2 tablespoons soy sauce

Coarsely grate the courgettes [zucchini] on to several layers of kitchen paper towels. Wrap the towels around the grated courgettes [zucchini] and squeeze to remove the excess moisture.

Transfer the courgettes [zucchini] to a medium-sized mixing bowl. Stir in the egg, garlic, salt, pepper and cheese. Sift in the flour and mix well. The batter should have a slightly thick, dropping consistency, so add more flour if necessary.

In a large frying-pan, melt one-quarter of the butter with 1 tablespoon of the oil over moderate heat. When the foam subsides, drop large spoonfuls of the batter into the pan, well spaced (the pancakes should be about 3-inches in diameter). Fry the pancakes for about 1 minute. With a palette knife or spatula, turn the pancakes over and fry the other sides for 1 minute or until they are golden brown.

Transfer the pancakes to a warmed serving dish. Set aside and keep warm while you fry the remaining pancakes in the same way, using the remaining butter and oil.

When all the pancakes have been cooked, sprinkle over the soy sauce and serve.

Zucchini con Mandorle

COURGETTES WITH ALMONDS

Zucchini con Mandorle (zoo-kee-nee con man-dor-lay) is an Italian dish, usually eaten cold, which is a delicious accompaniment to cold meat dishes.

Zucchini con Fritelle are delicious crispy pancakes, ideal for supper.

4-6 SERVINGS

2 fl. oz. [¼ cup] olive oil
2 medium-sized onions, sliced
1 lb. courgettes [zucchini], trimmed, thinly sliced and dégorged
2 teaspoons lemon juice
2 fl. oz. [¼ cup] dry white wine
4 oz. [1 cup] blanched slivered almonds, toasted
¼ teaspoon salt
¼ teaspoon black pepper

In a large frying-pan, heat the oil over moderate heat. When the oil is hot, add the onions and fry, stirring occasionally, for 8 to 10 minutes or until they are golden brown. Add the courgettes [zucchini] to the pan and fry, stirring and turning frequently, for 10 to 12 minutes or until they are tender. Add the lemon juice and wine to the pan and reduce the heat to low. Stir in the almonds, salt and pepper and continue to cook for 1 minute, stirring constantly.

Remove the pan from the heat and transfer the contents to a serving dish. Set aside to cool completely before serving.

Zucchini alla Marinara

COURGETTES STUFFED WITH PRAWNS OR
SHRIMPS AND TOMATOES

*A sustaining hors d'oeuvre, Zucchini alla
Marinara (zoo-kee-nee ah-la mah-rin-
ah-rah) makes a delectable start to any
extra special meal.*

8 SERVINGS

8 medium-sized courgettes
  [zucchini], trimmed
4½ teaspoons salt
1½ oz. [3 tablespoons] butter
1 shallot or spring onion [scallion],
  trimmed and finely chopped
1 garlic clove, crushed
4 tomatoes, blanched, peeled,
  seeded and coarsely chopped
5 tablespoons grated Parmesan
  cheese
½ teaspoon cayenne pepper
¼ teaspoon white pepper
8 oz. frozen prawns or shrimps,
  thawed
10 fl. oz. [1¼ cups] béchamel sauce,
  kept hot

Using a sharp knife, slice the courgettes
[zucchini] in half lengthways and carefully
hollow out the flesh, leaving boat-shaped
shells. Reserve the shells and finely chop
the flesh. Place the flesh in a small
mixing bowl.

Sprinkle ½ teaspoon of salt into each
shell and drain them on kitchen paper
towels, hollow side down, for 20 minutes.

Preheat the oven to hot 425°F (Gas
Mark 7, 220°C) and lightly grease a large,
fairly shallow baking dish with 1 tablespoon of butter.

In a large frying-pan, heat the remaining butter over moderate heat. When the
foam subsides, add the shallot or spring
onion [scallion] and garlic and fry, stirring
occasionally, for 3 to 4 minutes or until
they are soft and translucent but not
brown. Add the courgette [zucchini] flesh,
the chopped tomatoes, 1 tablespoon of
Parmesan cheese, the cayenne, the remaining salt and the pepper and cook for
3 minutes, stirring occasionally. Stir in
the prawns or shrimps and cook for
2 minutes.

Arrange the drained courgette [zuc-
chini] shells on the bottom of the baking
dish, skin side down, and spoon a little
of the tomato and prawn or shrimp mixture into each of them. Pour the béchamel
sauce over the shells and sprinkle the
remaining cheese over the top.

Place the baking dish in the centre of
the oven and cook for 15 to 20 minutes or
until the cheese has melted and is slightly
bubbly. Remove the dish from the oven
and serve immediately.

Zucchini Orientali

ORIENTAL STUFFED COURGETTES

*A simple dish which is popular throughout
the Middle Eastern countries, Zucchini
Orientali (zoo-kee-nee ory-en-tah-lee) may
be served as either a substantial first course
or as a light lunch with crusty bread.*

4 SERVINGS

4 large courgettes [zucchini],
  trimmed and blanched
8 oz. minced [ground] beef
1 teaspoon chopped fresh dill
½ teaspoon chopped fresh marjoram
½ teaspoon salt
¼ teaspoon freshly ground black
  pepper
1 small onion, finely chopped
2 tablespoons long-grain rice,
  washed, cooked for 10 minutes
  and drained
2 fl. oz. [¼ cup] tomato juice
1 oz. [2 tablespoons] butter
1 tablespoon tomato purée
2 teaspoons finely chopped fresh
  basil or 1 teaspoon dried basil
8 fl. oz. [1 cup] water

Cut the courgettes [zucchini] in half,
lengthways. With a teaspoon, scoop the
flesh out of each half, leaving a ¼-inch
shell. Discard the flesh. Set the courgette
[zucchini] halves aside.

In a medium-sized mixing bowl, combine the meat, dill, marjoram, salt,
pepper, onion and rice. Stir in 1 tablespoon of the tomato juice and mix
the ingredients together until they are
thoroughly combined. Very carefully
spoon the stuffing into the courgette
[zucchini] halves.

In a flameproof casserole, large enough
to take the courgettes [zucchini] in one
layer, melt half the butter over moderate
heat. When the foam subsides, remove
the casserole from the heat. Place the
courgettes [zucchini] in the casserole,
stuffing uppermost.

In a small mixing bowl, combine the
remaining tomato juice, the tomato purée,
basil and water. Spoon the tomato mixture over the courgettes [zucchini].Cut the
remaining butter into 8 pieces and place
one piece on each courgette [zucchini]
half. Return the casserole to moderate
heat and bring the liquid to the boil.
Cover the casserole, reduce the heat to
low and simmer for 30 minutes or until
the courgettes [zucchini] are tender when
pierced with the point of a sharp knife
and the rice is tender. Remove the casserole from the heat.

Transfer the courgettes [zucchini]
to a warmed serving dish and serve
immediately.

Zucchini e Peperoni

COURGETTES BAKED WITH RED PEPPERS

*This is a delicious dish of courgettes
[zucchini], hollowed out, filled with red
pepper and tomato sauce and baked in the
oven. Serve Zucchini e Peperoni (zoo-kee-
nee ay pep-er-oh-nee) either as a light
main course with rice or as a side vegetable
to meat dishes.*

6 SERVINGS

2 red peppers, white pith removed,
  seeded and halved
6 large courgettes [zucchini],
  trimmed and blanched
2 tablespoons plus 1 teaspoon
  olive oil
2 garlic cloves, crushed
6 medium-sized tomatoes,
  blanched, peeled, seeded and
  chopped
½ teaspoon salt
½ teaspoon black pepper
½ teaspoon chopped fresh basil
2 Mozzarella cheeses, thinly sliced

Preheat the grill [broiler] to high.

Place the pepper halves in the grill
[broiler] pan and place the pan under the
grill [broiler]. Grill [broil] for 4 to 5
minutes or until the skin has begun to
blacken and blister. Remove the pan from
the grill [broiler] and leave the peppers
to cool.

Using a sharp knife, slice the courgettes
[zucchini] in half lengthways and carefully
remove the flesh, leaving boat-shaped
shells. Set the shells aside and chop the
flesh. Remove and discard the skins from
the peppers and slice the flesh into thin
strips. Set aside.

In a medium-sized saucepan, heat the
2 tablespoons of oil over moderate heat.
When the oil is hot, add the garlic and
tomatoes to the pan. Stir in the salt,
pepper and basil. Reduce the heat to low,
cover the pan and cook for 15 to 20
minutes or until the tomatoes are soft and
pulpy. Stir in the red peppers and courgettes [zucchini] flesh and set aside.

Preheat the oven to cool 300°F (Gas
Mark 2, 150°C). Using the remaining
teaspoon of oil, grease a shallow, ovenproof baking dish.

Arrange the courgettes [zucchini] shells,
scooped-out side uppermost, in one layer
in the baking dish. Put spoonfuls of the
cooked tomato mixture in each shell.
Arrange the Mozzarella slices over the
top.

Place the baking dish in the oven and
cook for 15 to 20 minutes or until the
cheese has melted and the courgettes
[zucchini] are lightly browned.

Remove the baking dish from the oven

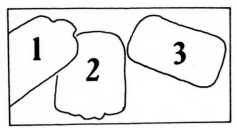

Three delectable and unusual ways with courgettes; Zucchini e Peperoni, Zucchini Orientali and Zucchini Ripieni are filling enough to eat on their own for lunch or supper.

and transfer the courgettes [zucchini] to a warmed serving dish if you are serving them hot, or leave them to cool if you are serving them cold.

Zucchini, Pomodori e Finocchio

COURGETTES, TOMATOES AND FENNEL

This delightful salad, Zucchini, Pomodori e Finocchio (zoo-kee-nee, pom-oh-dory ay fee-nock-ioh) makes a snack meal, served with lots of crusty bread and butter and some well-chilled white wine. Or it makes an ideal accompaniment to grilled [broiled] steaks or chops.

4-6 SERVINGS

4 large courgettes [zucchini], trimmed, sliced, sautéed in butter and cooled
4 large tomatoes, cut into wedges
1 large head of fennel, trimmed and sliced
1 bunch of watercress, washed, shaken dry and chopped
1 medium-sized onion, thinly sliced and pushed out into rings
4 fl. oz. [½ cup] French Dressing

Combine all of the ingredients, except the dressing, in a large serving bowl. Spoon over the French dressing and, using two large spoons, toss the mixture well.

Place the bowl in the refrigerator to chill for 15 minutes before serving.

Zucchini Ripieni

STUFFED COURGETTES

These tasty stuffed courgettes [zucchini] are a regional speciality from Liguria in the north of Italy. Serve Zucchini Ripieni (zoo-kee-nee ree-p'yay-nee) as a vegetable accompaniment to a plain meat dish, especially grilled [broiled] steaks.

6 SERVINGS

½ oz. dried mushrooms
12 medium-sized courgettes [zucchini], trimmed
2 oz. [1 cup] fresh white breadcrumbs, soaked in 4 tablespoons milk
2 eggs, lightly beaten
½ teaspoon salt
1 teaspoon black pepper
1 teaspoon dried oregano
6 oz. [1½ cups] Parmesan cheese, finely grated
2 oz. prosciutto, chopped
2 fl. oz. [¼ cup] olive oil

Place the dried mushrooms in a small mixing bowl, pour over enough water to cover and set aside to soak for 30 minutes. Drain the mushrooms and set aside.

Bring a large saucepan of salted water to the boil over high heat. Add the courgettes [zucchini] and boil for 7 to 8 minutes or until they are just tender when pierced with the point of a sharp knife. Remove the pan from the heat and drain the courgettes [zucchini] in a colander. With a sharp knife, slice the vegetables, lengthways, in half and, using a teaspoon, scoop out the flesh from each half, taking care not to break the skins. Set aside.

With your hands, squeeze any excess moisture out of the breadcrumbs and place them in a medium-sized mixing bowl. Add the reserved courgette [zucchini] flesh, the eggs, salt, pepper, oregano, half the cheese, the prosciutto and the reserved mushrooms. Using your hands, mix all the ingredients together until they are thoroughly combined.

Preheat the oven to fairly hot 400°F (Gas Mark 6, 200°C). Using a pastry brush, coat a shallow ovenproof casserole, large enough to take all the vegetables in one layer, with a little of the oil. Set aside.

Using a teaspoon, spoon a little of the stuffing into each courgette [zucchini] half and sprinkle the remaining cheese over the tops. Place the courgettes [zucchini] in the casserole and sprinkle with the remaining oil.

Place the casserole in the centre of the oven and cook for 15 minutes or until the cheese has melted and the courgettes [zucchini] are golden on top. Remove the casserole from the oven, transfer the courgettes [zucchini] to a warmed serving dish and serve immediately.

Zucchini Ripieni di Salsiccie

COURGETTES STUFFED WITH SAUSAGES

A spicy dish, Zucchini Ripieni di Salsiccie

(zoo-kee-nee ree p'yay-nee dee sahl-see-chay) *may be served with a barbecue sauce and baked potatoes as an ideal lunch or supper dish.*

4-6 SERVINGS

12 large courgettes [zucchini], trimmed
2 teaspoons butter
STUFFING
1½ lb. beef, very finely minced [ground]
6 oz. lean pork, very finely minced [ground]
9 oz. pork fat, very finely minced [ground]
½ tablespoon coriander seeds, roasted and crushed
½ teaspoon black pepper
½ teaspoon grated nutmeg
¼ teaspoon dried sage
¼ teaspoon dried thyme
2 teaspoons salt
½ tablespoon ground allspice
2 fl. oz. [¼ cup] vinegar
6 oz. [3 cups] fresh breadcrumbs
2 eggs, lightly beaten

Preheat the oven to fairly hot 375°F (Gas Mark 5, 190°C).

First make the stuffing. In a large mixing bowl, using a wooden spoon, combine the beef, pork and pork fat. Add the remaining stuffing ingredients, apart from the breadcrumbs and eggs, and beat until the mixture is well blended.

Place the stuffing in a large saucepan and set the pan over low heat. Simmer, stirring occasionally, for 9 to 10 minutes or until the meat is lightly browned. Remove the pan from the heat and add the breadcrumbs and eggs, beating to mix well.

Meanwhile, prepare the courgettes [zucchini]. Using a sharp knife, cut a ¼-inch slice from one end of each courgette [zucchini]. Set aside. Using an apple corer, scoop out and discard the centre of each courgette [zucchini].

Spoon the stuffing into the centre of the courgettes [zucchini] and replace the ends, securing them with cocktail sticks.

Lightly grease a baking sheet with the butter and place the courgettes [zucchini] on the sheet. Put the baking sheet in the centre of the oven and cook for 35 to 40 minutes or until the courgettes [zucchini] are tender when pierced with the point of a sharp knife.

Remove the baking sheet from the oven. Transfer the stuffed courgettes [zucchini] to a warmed serving dish and serve immediately.

Zucchini in Sufflè is a light soufflé which makes a splendid lunch dish.

Zucchini in Stufato
STEWED COURGETTES

Zucchini in Stufato (zoo-kee-nee in stoo-fah-toh) are equally good hot or cold and may be reheated without problems. Courgettes [zucchini] cooked in this way are excellent with veal or lamb chops.

4-6 SERVINGS

2 tablespoons olive oil
2 large onions, sliced and pushed out into rings
2 garlic cloves, crushed
1 lb. courgettes [zucchini], trimmed and cut into ½-inch slices
8 oz. tomatoes, blanched, peeled, seeded and chopped
1 teaspoon coriander seeds, crushed
½ teaspoon dried basil
2 teaspoons chopped fresh parsley

In a medium-sized saucepan, heat the oil over moderate heat. When the oil is hot, reduce the heat to low and add the onions and garlic and fry, stirring occasionally, for 8 to 10 minutes or until the onions are golden brown.

Add the courgettes [zucchini], toma-toes, coriander, basil and parsley to the pan and cook for 25 to 30 minutes or until the courgettes [zucchini] are tender when pierced with the point of a sharp knife.

Remove the pan from the heat, transfer the courgette [zucchini] mixture to a warmed serving dish and serve immediately.

Zucchini in Sufflè
COURGETTE SOUFFLE

Like most vegetable soufflés, Zucchini in Sufflè (zoo-kee-nee in soo-flay) is an extremely light and fluffy main course dish. Serve with a vegetable salad and some chilled white wine.

4 SERVINGS

1½ oz. [3 tablespoons] butter
4 tablespoons olive oil
8 medium-sized courgettes [zucchini], trimmed, blanched and sliced
½ teaspoon salt
1 teaspoon freshly ground black pepper
1 garlic clove, crushed
2 oz. [⅔ cup] fine dry breadcrumbs
4 egg yolks
3 oz. [¾ cup] plus 1 tablespoon Parmesan cheese, grated
1 tablespoon prepared French mustard
2 tablespoons flour
4 fl. oz. single cream [½ cup light cream]
6 egg whites, stiffly beaten
1 tablespoon finely chopped fresh parsley

Using 1 tablespoon of the butter, grease a 2½-pint [1½-quart] soufflé dish and set aside.

In a large frying-pan, heat the olive oil over moderate heat. When the oil is hot, add the courgettes [zucchini] to the pan and fry them, stirring occasionally, for 10 minutes.

Raise the heat to moderately high and stir in the salt, half the pepper, the garlic and breadcrumbs. Remove the pan from the heat and toss the courgette [zucchini] slices gently. Transfer the mixture to a fine wire strainer held over a medium-sized mixing bowl. Using the back of a wooden spoon, rub the ingredients through the strainer. Discard any pulp remaining in the strainer. Alternatively, place the courgette [zucchini] mixture in

the jar of an electric blender and blend to a fine purée.

Place the purée in the refrigerator to chill for 1 hour.

Preheat the oven to very hot 450°F (Gas Mark 8, 230°C.)

Meanwhile, in a medium-sized mixing bowl, beat the egg yolks, 3 ounces [¾ cup] of the cheese, the remaining pepper and the mustard together with a wooden spoon until the ingredients are thoroughly combined. Set aside.

In a small saucepan, melt the remaining butter over moderate heat. Remove the pan from the heat and, using a wooden spoon, stir in the flour to form a smooth paste. Gradually add the cream, stirring constantly and being careful to avoid lumps. Return the pan to the heat and cook, stirring constantly, for 2 to 3 minutes or until the mixture thickens. Remove the pan from the heat and set aside to cool.

When the mixture is cool, stir in the egg yolk mixture. Remove the purée from the refrigerator and stir 8 fluid ounces [1 cup] of the purée into the sauce. Discard any remaining purée or set aside for future use. With a metal spoon, gently fold in the beaten egg whites. Transfer the mixture to the prepared soufflé dish and sprinkle the top with the remaining cheese. Place the dish in the centre of the oven and cook for 10 minutes.

Reduce the heat to fairly hot 400°F (Gas Mark 6, 200°C) and continue to cook for 20 minutes or until the soufflé has risen and is golden brown on top.

Remove the soufflé dish from the oven. Sprinkle over the chopped parsley and serve immediately.

Zuccotash Sweet Potato and Marshmallow Bake

Zuccotash Sweet Potato and Marshmallow Bake is a popular American vegetable accompaniment to hot cooked ham.

4 SERVINGS

1 oz. [2 tablespoons] plus 1 teaspoon
   butter
1½ lb. sweet potatoes, baked
¾ teaspoon salt
2 teaspoons clear honey
   juice of 1 orange
2 eggs, well beaten
4 oz. marshmallows

Preheat the oven to moderate 350°F (Gas Mark 4, 180°C).

Using the teaspoon of butter, grease a large flameproof serving dish and set aside.

Place the sweet potatoes, salt, honey,

the remaining butter, the orange juice and eggs in a large mixing bowl. Using a fork, blend the ingredients together until they form a smooth purée. Transfer the mixture to the serving dish. Place the dish in the oven and cook for 20 minutes.

Preheat the grill [broiler] to moderate.

Remove the dish from the oven and arrange the marshmallows decoratively over the surface of the mixture.

Place the dish under the grill [broiler] and grill [broil] until the marshmallows are dark golden brown.

Remove the dish from under the heat and serve immediately.

Zuccotto I

ITALIAN PUMPKIN-SHAPED CREAM AND
SPONGE DESSERT

Zuccotto (zoo-kot-oh) is a well-known Italian dessert which resembles a pumpkin in shape. Serve this rich, spectacular-looking dessert at a special dinner party.

8-10 SERVINGS

1 pint double cream [2½ cups
   heavy cream], beaten until stiff
1 oz. [¼ cup] plus 2 tablespoons
   icing [confectioners'] sugar
2 oz. [½ cup] hazelnuts, toasted
8 oz. fresh cherries, halved and
   stoned
4 oz. dark [semi-sweet] dessert
   chocolate, finely chopped or
   grated
2 fl. oz. [¼ cup] brandy
2 fl. oz. [¼ cup] orange-flavoured
   liqueur
2 x 8-inch Chocolate Sponge
   Cakes, sliced in 2 horizontally
2 tablespoons cocoa powder

In a small mixing bowl, combine the cream and 1 ounce icing sugar [¼ cup confectioners' sugar]. Using a large metal spoon, fold in the hazelnuts, cherries and chocolate. Chill the bowl in the refrigerator.

In a small mixing bowl, mix together the brandy and orange-flavoured liqueur and set aside.

Line a 2-pint [1½-quart] pudding basin with three-quarters of the sponge, cutting it into pieces with a sharp knife so that it fits the shape of the basin. Sprinkle the brandy mixture over the sponge lining.

Remove the cream mixture from the refrigerator and spoon it into the sponge case. Use the remaining sponge to cover it. Chill the basin in the refrigerator for 2 hours.

Remove the basin from the refrigerator. Run a knife around the edge of the pudding to loosen it. Invert a serving

plate over the basin and, holding the two firmly together, reverse them. The zuccotto should slide out easily.

Sprinkle half of the remaining icing [confectioners'] sugar neatly over one-quarter of the pudding. Sprinkle half the cocoa powder over a second quarter, then repeat this over the other half of the pudding so that the zuccotto has 4 alternating segments of colour.

Serve immediately.

Zuccotto II

ITALIAN PUMPKIN-SHAPED CREAM AND
SPONGE DESSERT

This is another version of the rich Italian dessert, Zuccotto (zoo-kot-oh). Serve it on an attractive dish, sprinkled with finely chopped pistachio nuts.

8-10 SERVINGS

1 teaspoon butter
1½ pints double cream [3¾ cups
   heavy cream]
2 oz. [¼ cup] sugar
3 oz. [½ cup] pistachio nuts,
   blanched, toasted and chopped
3 oz. [¾ cup] almonds, blanched,
   toasted and chopped
4 oz. dark [semi-sweet] dessert
   chocolate, grated
1 x 9-inch Sponge Cake, thinly
   sliced
3 tablespoons brandy
3 tablespoons green Chartreuse

Cut out a piece of greaseproof or waxed paper large enough to line a 2-pint [1½-quart] pudding basin. Grease the paper with the butter and line the pudding basin with the paper. Set the basin aside.

In a large mixing bowl, using a wire whisk or rotary beater, beat the cream until it forms stiff peaks. Using a metal spoon, fold in the sugar, pistachio nuts, almonds and chocolate.

Sprinkle the sponge cake slices with the brandy and Chartreuse. Line the pudding basin with half of the sponge cake slices. Fill the centre with the cream mixture and place the remaining sponge cake slices on top to cover the cream mixture completely.

Place the basin in the refrigerator to chill for 2 hours.

Remove the basin from the refrigerator. Dip the bottom quickly into hot water and place a serving dish, inverted, over the top. Reverse the two giving a sharp

Zuccotto I is a really sumptuous pumpkin-shaped dessert as it is filled with lots of fruit and cream.

shake. The zuccotto should slide out easily.

Remove the greaseproof or waxed paper and serve the zuccotto immediately.

Zuccutto Torrone
ITALIAN CHOCOLATE-FLAVOURED DESSERT

This quick and easy-to-prepare dessert is of Mediterranean origin and is like a chocolate and nut soft nougat. Zuccutto Torrone (zoo-koo-tóh taw-roh-ney) remains good and rich to eat until the last crumb has gone! Serve with cream.

6-8 SERVINGS

½ teaspoon butter, melted
6 oz. [1½ cups] cocoa powder
6 oz. [¾ cup] butter
6 oz. [1 cup] ground almonds
6 oz. [¾ cup] sugar
2 tablespoons water
2 eggs, well beaten
6 oz. plain biscuits [1½ cups plain cookies], broken into almond-sized pieces

Grease a 1-pound loaf tin with the melted butter and set aside.

Place the cocoa and butter in a large mixing bowl and, using a kitchen fork,

blend the mixture together until it forms a thick paste. Stir in the ground almonds.

Place the sugar in a small saucepan, add the water and place the saucepan over moderate heat. Stir constantly until the sugar has dissolved. Remove the pan from the heat and pour the dissolved sugar over the ingredients in the mixing bowl, stirring until they are well blended. Stir in the eggs, then the broken biscuits [cookies]. Stir gently until the cocoa mix-

---

Zuckerman Duck with Olives is a really succulent and tasty way to serve duck for a special family meal.

ture coats the biscuits [cookies] well.

Transfer the mixture to the prepared loaf tin and, using the back of a wooden spoon, press the ingredients down into the tin, smoothing over the top. Cover the tin with aluminium foil and place the tin in the refrigerator for 24 hours.

Remove the tin from the refrigerator and quickly dip the bottom into boiling water. Place a chilled serving dish over the tin and invert the two, giving a sharp shake. The torrone should slide out easily.

Serve immediately.

Zuckerman Duck with Olives

This is a perfect way to serve duck for a dinner party because it does away with difficult carving. Serve with boiled new potatoes and baby carrots.

4 SERVINGS

1 x 5 lb. duck, cut into 4 serving pieces, giblets reserved
1½ pints [3¾ cups] water
2 celery stalks, trimmed and sliced
3 carrots, scraped and sliced
2 teaspoons salt
3 large onions, sliced
2 rosemary sprigs or 1 teaspoon dried rosemary
2 bay leaves
4 lean bacon slices, rinds removed
2 oz. [¼ cup] butter
1½ oz. [⅓ cup] flour
1 tablespoon mushroom ketchup
3 fl. oz. [⅜ cup] port or Madeira
1 teaspoon canned green peppercorns, drained
1 teaspoon lemon juice
12 green olives, stoned

Preheat the oven to hot 425°F (Gas Mark 7, 220°C).

Place the giblets, water, celery, 1 carrot and 1 teaspoon of salt in a saucepan and set the pan over high heat. Bring the liquid to the boil, reduce the heat to low and simmer for 30 minutes. Remove the pan from the heat and strain and reserve the stock.

Meanwhile, arrange the remaining carrots, the onions, rosemary and bay leaves in a roasting tin. Lay the duck pieces over the vegetables and cover each piece with a slice of bacon. Place the tin in the oven and roast for 20 minutes.

Remove the roasting tin from the oven and, using a slotted spoon, transfer the duck pieces to a large, warmed casserole. Keep warm.

Reduce the oven temperature to moderate 350°F (Gas Mark 4, 180°C).

Strain off and discard the fat from the vegetables and bacon. Pour the giblet stock into the tin and set the tin over moderate heat. Stir well with a wooden spoon, scraping the drippings from the bottom of the tin. Boil the mixture until it has reduced by about one-third. Pour the liquid into a bowl through a strainer. Reserve the liquid. Remove and discard the rosemary sprigs and bay leaves and reserve the remaining vegetables and bacon.

In a large saucepan, melt the butter over moderate heat. Remove the pan from the heat and, with a wooden spoon, stir in the flour to make a smooth paste. Gradually pour in the reserved cooking liquid, stirring constantly. Return the pan to the heat and cook, stirring constantly, for 2 to 3 minutes or until the sauce is thick and smooth. Stir in the mushroom ketchup, port or Madeira, the remaining salt, the peppercorns and lemon juice. Remove the pan from the heat and pour the sauce over the duck portions. Stir in the reserved vegetables and bacon.

Cover the casserole and place it in the oven. Cook for a further 20 to 30 minutes or until the duck is tender. Remove the casserole from the oven. Stir the olives into the sauce and serve the duck at once, straight from the casserole.

Zuera Tropical Sundae

A delicious combination of coconut ice-cream, guavas, passion fruit and pineapple makes Zuera Tropical Sundae a really special dessert.

8 SERVINGS

½ small pineapple, peeled, cored and finely chopped
4 fl. oz. [½ cup] rum
1½ pints [3¾ cups] coconut ice-cream
14 oz. canned guavas, drained and finely chopped
14 oz. canned passion fruit or the flesh of 8 fresh passion fruit
8 fl. oz. double cream [1 cup heavy cream], stiffly whipped
2 oz. desiccated coconut [½ cup shredded coconut], lightly toasted
8 Brandy Snaps

Place 8 tall sundae glasses in the refrigerator to chill for 30 minutes.

Place the pineapple in a medium-sized

Zuera Tropical Sundae is a delicious concoction of exotic fruits and rum which evokes the Caribbean sunshine.

Zug

mixing bowl and pour over the rum. Set aside for 30 minutes.

Remove the glasses from the refrigerator and divide the pineapple and rum among the glasses. Using an ice-cream scoop or large spoon, divide half of the ice-cream equally among the glasses. Top with a layer of guavas. Cover the guavas with the remaining ice-cream. Spoon over the passion fruit.

Decorate the top of each glass with the cream and sprinkle over the coconut. Place a brandy snap on the top of each glass and serve immediately.

Zug Pork Chops

This delicious dish combines succulent pork chops with a juniper-flavoured wine sauce, served with a garnish of potatoes, onion and bacon. Serve with a mixed salad and some well-chilled Alsatian white wine.

4 SERVINGS

4 large pork chops
1 teaspoon salt
1 teaspoon black pepper
2 oz. [¼ cup] butter
4 fl. oz. [½ cup] dry white wine
10 juniper berries, crushed
1 tablespoon beurre manié
GARNISH
1 tablespoon butter
1 medium-sized onion, finely chopped
6 lean bacon slices, grilled [broiled] until crisp and crumbled
2 lb. potatoes, cooked, drained, mashed and kept hot

Rub the pork chops all over with the salt and pepper.

In a large frying-pan, melt the butter over moderate heat. When the foam subsides, add the pork chops and fry them for 5 minutes on each side or until they are well browned all over.

Pour over the wine and add the juniper berries. Bring the liquid to the boil, reduce the heat to moderately low and continue cooking the chops for 20 to 30 minutes or until they are thoroughly cooked and tender.

Meanwhile, prepare the garnish. In a medium-sized frying-pan, melt the butter over moderate heat. When the foam subsides, add the onion and fry, stirring occasionally, for 5 to 7 minutes or until it is soft and translucent but not brown. Remove the pan from the heat and stir in the crumbled bacon. Stir in the mashed potatoes and beat well to blend. Return the pan to moderate heat and cook, stirring constantly, for 2 to 3 minutes or until the mixture is heated through.

Remove the pan from the heat and arrange the potato mixture on a large, warmed serving dish.

Remove the pork chops from the frying-pan and arrange them decoratively over the potato mixture. Keep warm while you finish off the sauce. Raise the heat to moderately high and boil the pan juices for 5 minutes. Stir in the beurre manié, a little at a time, until the sauce thickens slightly and is smooth.

Remove the pan from the heat and pour the sauce over the pork chops. Serve at once.

Zug Sausage and Leek Casserole

 ① ✕

This delicious, economical dish is an adaptation of a traditional Swiss recipe. Serve, as a warming family supper, with a mixed salad and some beer.

6-8 SERVINGS

4 oz. [½ cup] butter or margarine
5 large leeks, trimmed, cleaned and cut into 1-inch lengths
1½ lb. sausages, halved
1 teaspoon salt
1½ teaspoons black pepper
1 teaspoon dried thyme
6 tablespoons flour
1 pint [2½ cups] milk
6 oz. [1½ cups] Emmenthal cheese, grated
2 teaspoons Worcestershire sauce
1 teaspoon dry mustard
5 oz. tomato purée
1 lb. small macaroni, cooked and drained

Preheat the oven to moderate 350°F (Gas Mark 4, 180°C).

In a large frying-pan, melt 2 ounces [¼ cup] of the butter or margarine over moderate heat. When the foam subsides, add the leeks and sausages and fry, stirring and turning occasionally, for 8 to 10 minutes or until the leeks are golden brown. Remove the pan from the heat and stir in the salt, pepper and thyme. Set aside.

In a medium-sized saucepan, melt the remaining butter or margarine over moderate heat. Remove the pan from the heat and, using a wooden spoon, stir in the flour to form a smooth paste. Gradually add the milk, stirring constantly and being careful to avoid lumps. Return the pan to the heat and cook, stirring constantly, for 2 to 3 minutes or until the sauce is thick and smooth. Add 4 ounces [1 cup] of the grated cheese and cook, stirring constantly, until it has dissolved into the sauce. Remove the pan from the

heat and stir in the Worcestershire sauce, mustard and tomato purée.

Put half of the cooked macaroni into a large, ovenproof baking dish. Cover with the sausage and leek mixture and top with the remaining macaroni. Pour over the cheese sauce and sprinkle over the remaining grated cheese. Place the dish in the oven and cook the mixture for 20 to 30 minutes or until the top is brown and bubbling.

Remove the dish from the oven and serve at once.

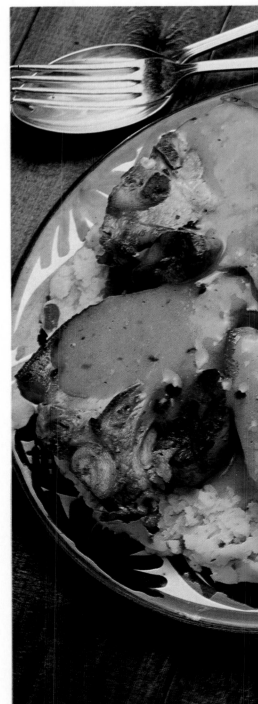

Zug Pork Chops and Zug Sausage and Leek Casserole are tasty and filling.

Zuger Zee Scramble

These luscious baked potatoes topped with Gruyère cheese make a marvellous lunch or supper dish and really need no accompaniment other than a green salad.

6 SERVINGS

- 6 large potatoes, baked in their jackets and kept hot
- 2 teaspoons salt
- 4 oz. [½ cup] butter
- 12 eggs, lightly beaten
- 1 teaspoon black pepper
- 6 spring onions [scallions], trimmed and finely chopped
- 12 oz. Gruyère cheese, thinly sliced

Preheat the grill [broiler] to high.

With a sharp knife, slice three-quarters of the way through the potatoes, lengthways and gently open them out so that they form a V-shape. Sprinkle the insides of the potatoes with half the salt. Set aside and keep warm.

In a medium-sized saucepan, melt the butter over moderate heat. When the foam subsides, add the eggs, the remaining salt and the pepper and cook, stirring constantly, for 3 to 4 minutes or until the mixture thickens. Remove the pan from the heat and stir in the spring onions [scallions]. Continue cooking, stirring constantly until the mixture is creamy. Remove the pan from the heat and divide the scrambled eggs among the potatoes. Lay a slice of cheese over each one.

Place the potatoes in the grill [broiler] pan and place the pan under the grill [broiler]. Grill [broil] for 1 to 2 minutes or until the cheese is bubbling and golden. Remove the pan from under the heat and serve at once.

Zuidhorn Kipper Pie

This pie is a warming mixture of kippers and baked beans topped with mashed potatoes and cheese. Serve for supper with lots of cold milk or beer.

Zui

4 SERVINGS

1 oz. [2 tablespoons] butter
1 medium-sized onion, finely
 chopped
1 lb. kipper fillets, skinned and
 cut into 1-inch pieces
14 oz. canned baked beans
3 tablespoons tomato ketchup
1½ tablespoons Worcestershire sauce
1 teaspoon dry mustard
½ teaspoon salt
2 hard-boiled eggs, sliced
2 lb. potatoes, cooked and mashed
2 oz. [½ cup] Cheddar cheese, grated

Preheat the oven to fairly hot 375°F (Gas
Mark 5, 190°C).

In a medium-sized saucepan, melt the
butter over moderate heat. When the
foam subsides, add the onion and fry,
stirring occasionally, for 5 to 7 minutes
or until it is soft and translucent but not
brown. Add the kipper fillets and baked
beans and fry, stirring occasionally, for a
further 3 to 5 minutes or until they are
heated through. Remove the pan from the
heat and stir in the tomato ketchup,
Worcestershire sauce, mustard and salt.

Spoon the mixture into a medium-sized
baking dish. Cover the mixture with egg
slices, then with the potatoes, bringing the
potatoes up into decorative swirls with a
flat-bladed knife. Sprinkle over the cheese.

Place the dish in the oven and bake the
pie for 20 minutes or until the top is
brown and bubbling.

Remove the dish from the oven and
serve the pie at once.

Zuidhorn Liver and Rice

*This delicious dish is a Dutch adaptation of
a traditional Indonesian dish and makes a
sustaining and festive main course for a
dinner party. Serve with lots of ice-cold
lager or well-chilled Rhine wine.*

6-8 SERVINGS

1 lb. [2⅔ cups] long-grain rice,
 washed, soaked in cold water for
 30 minutes and drained
2 pints [5 cups] water
1 teaspoon salt
3 tablespoons peanut oil
3 eggs, lightly beaten
4 spring onions [scallions], trimmed
 and chopped
3 oz. button mushrooms, wiped
 clean and sliced
1 canned pimiento, drained and
 finely chopped
1 red chilli, finely chopped
2 garlic cloves, crushed
2-inch piece fresh root ginger,
 peeled and very finely chopped

2 tablespoons soy sauce
LIVER
4 tablespoons soy sauce
4 tablespoons beef stock
1 tablespoon wine vinegar
2 tablespoons water
1 teaspoon salt
1 teaspoon black pepper
1 large garlic clove, crushed
4-inch piece fresh root ginger,
 peeled and very finely chopped
2 teaspoons cornflour [cornstarch]
3 lb. lamb's liver, thinly sliced
2 fl. oz. [¼ cup] peanut oil
2 celery stalks, trimmed and
 finely chopped
12 oz. bean sprouts

First prepare the liver. In a large, shallow
dish, combine the soy sauce, beef stock,
vinegar, water, salt, pepper, garlic, half
of the ginger and the cornflour [corn-
starch]. Beat the mixture to mix well.
Place the liver slices in the mixture and
baste well. Set aside to marinate for 45
minutes, basting frequently.

Meanwhile, prepare the rice. Put the
rice in a large saucepan. Pour over the
water and add the salt. Bring the water
to the boil over high heat. Cover the pan,
reduce the heat to very low and simmer
for 15 minutes or until the rice is tender
and has absorbed all the liquid. Remove
the pan from the heat and set aside.

In a small frying-pan, heat 1 tablespoon
of the oil over moderate heat. When the
oil is hot, add the eggs and fry for 3
minutes on each side or until they are set
in a thin omelet. Remove the pan from
the heat. Slide the omelet on to a plate
and cut it into thin strips about 2-inches
long and ½-inch wide. Set aside.

Preheat the oven to very cool 250°F
(Gas Mark ½, 130°C).

In a large frying-pan, heat the remaining oil over moderate heat. When the oil
is hot, add the spring onions [scallions],
mushrooms, pimiento, chilli, garlic and
ginger and fry, stirring occasionally, for
3 to 4 minutes or until the spring onions
[scallions] are soft and translucent but not
brown. Stir in the cooked rice, soy sauce
and omelet strips and fry, stirring occasionally, for 3 minutes or until all the
ingredients are warmed through.

Remove the pan from the heat and
transfer the mixture to a warmed, ovenproof serving dish. Place in the oven and
keep hot while you cook the liver.

In a large frying-pan, heat the oil over
moderate heat. When the oil is hot, add
the remaining ginger and fry, stirring
constantly, for 2 minutes. Increase the
heat to moderately high and add the liver
slices and marinade to the pan. Fry,
stirring and turning occasionally, for 6

minutes. Stir in the celery and bean
sprouts and continue to fry, stirring and
turning occasionally, for a further 3
minutes or until the liver is cooked
through. Remove the pan from the heat.

Remove the serving dish from the oven
and arrange the liver slices decoratively
over the rice. Spoon over the sauce and
vegetables and serve at once.

Zujar Chicken Liver Casserole

*A very quick-to-make and deliciously light
dish, this Spanish chicken liver casserole is
excellent served for lunch or dinner with
rice and French beans.*

4-6 SERVINGS

4 oz. [½ cup] butter
2 garlic cloves, crushed
4 medium-sized onions, thinly
 sliced
1½ lb. chicken livers
1 teaspoon salt
1 teaspoon black pepper
2 bay leaves
1 teaspoon chopped fresh sage
12 oz. mushrooms, wiped clean and
 sliced
2 oz. [½ cup] flour
4 fl. oz. [½ cup] chicken stock
4 fl. oz. [½ cup] Madeira
1 teaspoon lemon juice
2 hard-boiled eggs, finely chopped

In a large, deep-sided frying-pan, melt
half the butter over moderate heat. When
the foam subsides, add the garlic and
onions and fry, stirring occasionally, for
5 to 7 minutes or until the onions are soft
and translucent but not brown. Add the
chicken livers, salt, pepper, bay leaves
and sage and fry, stirring constantly, for
5 minutes. Add the mushrooms and fry,
stirring occasionally, for a further 3
minutes. Remove the pan from the heat
and set aside.

In a small saucepan, melt the remaining butter over moderate heat. Remove
the pan from the heat and, with a wooden
spoon, stir in the flour to make a smooth
paste. Gradually add the stock, Madeira
and lemon juice, stirring constantly.
Return the pan to the heat and cook,
stirring constantly, for 2 to 3 minutes or
until the sauce is thick and smooth.
Remove the pan from the heat and pour
the sauce over the chicken liver mixture.
Stir with a wooden spoon until the livers
are well coated with the sauce.

Return the pan to moderate heat and
cook, stirring occasionally, for 5 minutes.
Remove and discard the bay leaves and
pour the mixture into a warmed serving

dish. Sprinkle over the chopped eggs and serve at once.

Zujar Tomato Soufflés

A really attractive and unusual dish, Zujar Tomato Soufflés make a wonderful lunch time treat or they may be served as an hors d'oeuvre.

6 SERVINGS

6 very large or 12 medium-sized
   tomatoes
1 oz. [2 tablespoons] butter
1 oz. [¼ cup] flour
2 tablespoons double [heavy] cream

2 tablespoons grated Parmesan
   cheese
¼ teaspoon grated nutmeg
½ teaspoon dry mustard
1 teaspoon salt
½ teaspoon black pepper
4 egg yolks
5 egg whites, stiffly beaten

Preheat the oven to hot 425°F (Gas Mark 7, 220°C).

Cut the tomatoes in half and, using a teaspoon, scoop out the seeds and pulp. Place the seeds and pulp in a small saucepan and set the pan over low heat. Simmer for 3 minutes. Remove the pan from the heat and strain the tomato pulp

A Dutch dish with an exotic Indonesian flavour, Zuidhorn Liver and Rice makes a marvellous party dish.

through a strainer into a small bowl. Discard the dry pulp remaining in the strainer.

In a small saucepan, melt the butter over moderate heat. Remove the pan from the heat and, with a wooden spoon, stir in the flour to make a smooth paste. Gradually add the puréed tomato pulp and the cream, stirring constantly. Return the pan to low heat and stir for 2 minutes. Stir in the cheese, nutmeg, mustard, salt and pepper. Remove the pan from the

Mouth-watering fruit tarts in crisp pastry, Zuki Fruit Tartlets are quite irresistible!

heat and leave the sauce to cool for 5 minutes.

Stir in the egg yolks, one at a time, beating until they are well blended. Using a metal spoon, gently fold in the egg whites.

Pat the insides of the tomatoes dry with kitchen paper towels. Spoon the egg mixture into the tomato halves. Place the tomatoes on a baking sheet and place them in the oven for 5 minutes.

Reduce the oven temperature to fairly hot 400°F (Gas Mark 6, 200°C). Continue to cook the tomatoes for 15 to 20 minutes or until they are golden brown on top.

Remove the baking sheet from the oven. Using two spoons, transfer the tomatoes to a warmed serving dish and serve at once.

Zuki Fruit Tartlets

These pretty little fruit tartlets taste wonderfully refreshing and are delicious with tea or coffee or as a dessert.

16 TARTLETS

2 teaspoons butter
1 lb. [4 cups] Shortcrust Pastry II
16 green grapes, peeled, seeded and halved
16 black grapes, peeled, seeded and halved
16 strawberries, hulled, washed and halved
3 oz. canned mandarin oranges, drained
3 oz. canned black cherries, drained and stoned
3 fl. oz. [⅜ cup] Apricot Glaze
3 fl. oz. [⅜ cup] Redcurrant Glaze

Preheat the oven to fairly hot 400°F (Gas Mark 6, 200°C). With the butter, lightly grease 16 patty tins. Set aside.

On a lightly floured surface, roll out the dough to ⅛-inch thick. With a 3-inch pastry cutter cut out 16 circles. Place the circles in the patty tins, taking care not to stretch the dough. Decorate the rims of the dough shells with the prongs of a fork.

Place the patty tins in the oven and bake blind for 20 minutes or until the pastry is golden brown. Remove the tins from the oven and, with a flat-bladed knife, gently lift the tarts out of the tins. Place them on a wire rack and allow them to cool completely.

Mix all the fruit together in a bowl. Spoon a little of the fruit into each pastry shell. Glaze half the tartlets with the apricot glaze and half with the redcurrant glaze and allow the glazes to cool before serving.

Zula Avocado Hors d'Oeuvre

This delicious dish is marvellously easy to prepare — especially if you can buy ready-made taramasalata. Serve as a first course to a Greek meal or as a light summer lunch, accompanied by Pita and some well-chilled Retsina.

4-8 SERVINGS

4 avocados
8 oz. ready-made taramasalata (or make the *Supercook* recipe for Taramasalata, using 8 oz. cod's roe, 2 slices of white bread, etc.)

Halve and stone the avocados and arrange them on individual serving plates. Spoon the taramasalata into the hollows and serve at once.

Zula Tangy Salad

A colourful and unusual salad, Zula Tangy Salad is the perfect accompaniment to any cold meat.

4 SERVINGS

4 tomatoes, sliced
4 oranges, peeled, white pith removed, seeded and sliced
4 oz. pickled walnuts, drained and thinly sliced
8 oz. bean sprouts
4 fl. oz. [½ cup] French Dressing

In a medium-sized salad bowl, combine the tomatoes, oranges, pickled walnuts and bean sprouts. Pour over the French dressing and, using two large spoons, toss the ingredients together.

Serve immediately.

Zulcan Gammon and Gooseberries

Zulcan Gammon and Gooseberries is an inexpensive and spicy dish of grilled [broiled] gammon steaks with a piquant sauce. Serve for lunch or dinner with sautéed sweet potatoes and a mixed salad.

4 SERVINGS

1¼ lb. canned gooseberries
1 oz. [2 tablespoons] butter
1 small onion, thinly sliced
½ teaspoon dried sage
1 teaspoon prepared French mustard

½ teaspoon cornflour [cornstarch], dissolved in 1 teaspoon gooseberry juice
4 large gammon steaks
½ teaspoon salt
¼ teaspoon black pepper

Preheat the grill [broiler] to moderate.

Drain the gooseberries, reserving 3 fluid ounces [⅜ cup] of the can juice. Set the gooseberries aside.

In a medium-sized saucepan, melt the butter over moderate heat. When the foam subsides, add the onion and fry, stirring occasionally, for 5 to 7 minutes or until it is soft and translucent but not brown. Add the drained gooseberries, sage and mustard and fry, stirring frequently, for 6 minutes. Stir in the reserved gooseberry juice and the cornflour [cornstarch] mixture and continue to cook, stirring constantly, until the sauce is thick and hot.

Remove the pan from the heat and keep warm while you cook the gammon steaks.

Rub the gammon all over with the salt and pepper. Place them under the grill [broiler] and grill [broil] for 5 minutes on each side.

Remove the steaks from the heat and transfer them to a heated serving dish. Pour over the gooseberry sauce and serve at once.

Zulia Persimmon Flan

This unusual flan is easy to make and even easier to eat! Serve as a satisfying dessert after a fairly light meal or as a sumptuous snack with freshly percolated coffee.

4-6 SERVINGS

6 oz. crushed ginger biscuits [1½ cups crushed ginger cookies]
2 oz. [¼ cup] unsalted butter, melted
2 tablespoons brandy or peach brandy
½ teaspoon ground ginger
FILLING
6 fl. oz. [¾ cup] white wine
2 oz. [¼ cup] sugar
1 teaspoon very finely grated lemon rind
½ teaspoon ground ginger
4 persimmons, sliced
½ oz. gelatine, dissolved in 2 tablespoons hot water
10 fl. oz. double cream [1¼ cups heavy cream], stiffly beaten
2 tablespoons chocolate vermicelli

In a medium-sized mixing bowl, combine the crushed biscuits [cookies], melted butter, brandy or peach brandy and ginger and, using a fork, beat well to blend. Spoon the mixture into an 8-inch

The unusual flavour of persimmons makes Zulia Persimmon Flan a delicious and special dessert.

flan tin and, using your fingers, spread it out to line the bottom and sides. Place the tin in the refrigerator to chill for 30 minutes.

Meanwhile, make the filling. Pour the white wine into a medium-sized saucepan and add the sugar, lemon rind and ginger. Set the pan over moderately high heat and bring the liquid to the boil, stirring constantly until the sugar dissolves. Boil the mixture, without stirring, for 5 minutes. Reduce the heat to low and add the persimmons to the pan. Simmer the mixture, stirring occasionally, for 10 minutes.

Stir the gelatine into the mixture, remove the pan from the heat and set aside to cool slightly. Pour the mixture into the flan case and place the flan tin in the refrigerator for 2 hours or until it has completely set.

Remove the flan from the refrigerator and, using a flat-bladed knife, spread the cream over the filling, bringing it up into decorative swirls with a flat-bladed knife or a fork.

Sprinkle over the chocolate vermicelli and serve at once.

Zulinka Rum and Chocolate Soufflé

  ① ⊠ ⊠

This superbly rich soufflé combines the flavours of chocolate, rum and orange marmalade. Serve it on its own or with whipped cream for a delectable and warming dessert.

4 SERVINGS

1 oz. [2 tablespoons] plus 1 teaspoon butter

4 oz. dark [semi-sweet] cooking chocolate, broken into small pieces

2 tablespoons water

8 fl. oz. single cream [1 cup light cream]

2 fl. oz. [¼ cup] milk

¼ teaspoon vanilla essence

3 fl. oz. [⅜ cup] dark rum

3 tablespoons sugar

1½ oz. [⅓ cup] flour

2 tablespoons chunky orange marmalade, with the chunks finely chopped

5 egg whites

4 egg yolks

Preheat the oven to hot 425°F (Gas Mark 7, 220°C). Using the teaspoon of butter, grease a medium-sized soufflé dish and set it aside.

Place the chocolate pieces and the water in a small heatproof bowl set over a saucepan half-filled with boiling water. Set the pan over moderately low heat and simmer, stirring occasionally, for 5 minutes or until the chocolate has melted and is smooth. Remove the pan from the heat and set aside.

Pour the cream, milk, vanilla essence and rum into a small saucepan and add the sugar. Set the pan over moderately low heat. Cook, stirring constantly, until the sugar has dissolved. Remove the pan from the heat and set aside.

In a medium-sized saucepan, melt the remaining butter over moderate heat. Remove the pan from the heat and, using a wooden spoon, stir in the flour to make a smooth paste. Gradually add the cream mixture, stirring constantly and being careful to avoid lumps.

Return the pan to the heat and cook the sauce, stirring constantly, for 4 minutes or until it is smooth and very thick. Stir in the melted chocolate and the marmalade and cook for a further 1 minute, stirring constantly. Remove the pan from the heat and set the sauce aside to cool to lukewarm.

Place the egg whites in a large mixing bowl and, using a wire whisk or rotary beater, beat them until they form stiff peaks.

Using a wooden spoon, beat the egg yolks, one at a time, into the cooled sauce. With a metal spoon, gently but thoroughly fold in the egg whites.

Spoon the mixture into the prepared soufflé dish and place the dish in the centre of the oven. Reduce the oven temperature to moderate 350°F (Gas Mark 4, 180°C). Cook for 20 to 25 minutes or until the soufflé is well risen but still slightly soft in the centre.

Remove the dish from the oven and serve immediately.

Zulla Fish Pie has a delicate, smoked flavour which makes it an unusual lunch or supper dish. Serve it with a chilled white wine.

Zulla Fish Pie

The smoked cheese and fish in this pie combine to give it a subtle flavour. Zulla Fish Pie makes an excellent lunch or supper dish. Serve with mashed potatoes and peas.

4-6 SERVINGS

2 oz. [¼ cup] plus 1 teaspoon butter
8 oz. mushrooms, wiped clean and sliced
1½ lb. frozen leaf spinach, cooked and drained
2 lb. smoked haddock fillets, cooked, drained, skinned and flaked
1 teaspoon salt
6 large tomatoes, blanched, peeled and sliced
SAUCE
2 oz. [¼ cup] butter
2 oz. [½ cup] flour
16 fl. oz. [2 cups] milk
½ teaspoon salt
½ teaspoon black pepper
2 oz. [½ cup] smoked cheese, grated
1 tablespoon finely chopped fresh parsley

½ teaspoon cayenne pepper

Preheat the oven to moderate 350°F (Gas Mark 4, 180°C).

In a medium-sized frying-pan, melt the 2 ounces [¼ cup] of butter over moderate heat. When the foam subsides, add the mushrooms and fry, stirring occasionally, for 3 minutes. Remove the pan from the heat.

With the remaining teaspoon of butter, grease an ovenproof casserole. Lay the spinach in the bottom of the casserole. Spread the haddock over the spinach and the mushrooms over the haddock. Sprinkle with half the salt. Place the tomatoes over the mushrooms and sprinkle with the remaining salt. Set the casserole aside while you make the sauce.

In a small saucepan, melt the butter over moderate heat. Remove the pan from the heat and, with a wooden spoon, stir in the flour to make a smooth paste. Gradually add the milk, stirring constantly. Return the pan to the heat and cook, stirring constantly, for 2 to 3 minutes or until the sauce is thick and smooth. Stir in the salt, pepper, cheese

and parsley and cook for a further 2 minutes or until the cheese has melted.

Remove the pan from the heat. Pour the sauce over the ingredients in the casserole. Sprinkle over the cayenne. Place the casserole in the oven and cook for 30 minutes. Remove the casserole from the oven and serve at once.

Zullah's Pasta, Sausage and Bean Salad

An unusual and filling dish, Zullah's Pasta, Sausage and Bean Salad is ideal to serve if unexpected guests drop in for supper (providing you have a well-stocked larder!) Lots of crusty French bread and butter and a bottle of red wine would be the ideal accompaniments.

6 SERVINGS

14 oz. canned French beans, drained
4 tomatoes, sliced

Zullah's Pasta, Sausage and Bean Salad is both colourful and filling.

8 oz. pork luncheon meat, diced
2 medium-sized onions, thinly
    sliced and pushed out into rings
14 oz. canned red kidney beans,
    drained
8 frankfurter sausages, cooked,
    drained, cooled and cut into
    ½-inch lengths
4 oz. [1 cup] black olives
8 oz. pasta shells, cooked, drained
    and cooled
1 small chorizo sausage, thinly
    sliced
½ cucumber, peeled and thinly
    sliced
4 oz. beetroots [beets], cooked,
    peeled and sliced
4 tablespoons chopped mustard
    and cress
DRESSING
1 teaspoon sugar
1 teaspoon salt
½ teaspoon black pepper
1 teaspoon prepared French
    mustard
1 garlic clove, crushed
2 fl. oz. [¼ cup] red wine vinegar
8 fl. oz. [1 cup] olive oil

Arrange the French beans in the bottom
of a large salad bowl. Place the sliced
tomatoes around the side of the bowl.
Continue making layers with the luncheon
meat, one of the onions, the kidney
beans, frankfurter sausages, olives and
half of the pasta shells. Cover the pasta
shells with the remaining onion rings, the
chorizo sausage, cucumber and beetroots
[beets]. Cover the beetroots [beets] with
the remaining pasta shells and the
mustard and cress. Set aside.

In a small mixing bowl, combine all
the dressing ingredients. Using a fork,
beat the ingredients together until they
are thoroughly combined.

Pour the dressing over the salad and
serve immediately.

Zulu Beef Pot

*A hot, spicy stew, Zulu Beef Pot makes an
unusual dish for an informal dinner party.
Serve it with boiled rice and salad and top
it with sliced bananas.*

6-8 SERVINGS
2 green peppers, white pith
    removed, seeded and finely
    chopped
2 green chillis, finely chopped
2 garlic cloves, finely chopped
1-inch piece fresh root ginger,
    peeled and thinly sliced
1 teaspoon turmeric
½ teaspoon ground cardamom

2 teaspoons salt
1 teaspoon black pepper
5 fl. oz. [⅝ cup] red wine
2 oz. [¼ cup] butter
3 fl. oz. [⅜ cup] vegetable oil
3 lb. sirloin steak, boned and cut
    into strips
2 large onions, finely chopped
6 green tomatoes, chopped
1 red or yellow pepper, white pith
    removed, seeded and cut into
    strips

Purée the chopped green peppers, chillis,
garlic and ginger in an electric blender or
food mill. Stir in the turmeric, cardamom,
salt, pepper and wine and set aside.

In a large, deep frying-pan, melt the
butter with the oil over moderate heat.
When the foam subsides, add the beef
strips and fry, stirring and turning
constantly, for 2 to 3 minutes or until the
meat is browned all over. Using a slotted
spoon, transfer the meat to a warmed
serving dish and keep hot.

Add the onions and tomatoes to the pan
and fry, stirring occasionally, for 3 to 5
minutes. Add the red or yellow pepper
and continue to fry for 2 to 4 minutes or
until the onions are soft and translucent
but not brown. Return the meat to the
pan. Pour in the pepper purée and stir
well to mix.

Fry the mixture for a further 5 minutes. Remove the pan from the heat and
transfer the mixture to a warmed serving
dish. Serve immediately.

Zulu Beef Stew

*This warming, sustaining dish is an adapta-
tion of a southern African recipe. Serve
with a mixed salad and lots of beer or
chilled lager.*

4 SERVINGS
2 lb. lean stewing beef, cut into
    2-inch cubes
2 oz. [½ cup] seasoned flour, made
    with 2 oz. [½ cup] flour, 1 teaspoon
    salt, ½ teaspoon black pepper
    and 1 teaspoon cayenne pepper
2 fl. oz. [¼ cup] peanut oil
3 medium-sized onions, thinly
    sliced
1 garlic clove, crushed
14 oz. canned peeled tomatoes
15 fl. oz. [1⅞ cups] stout
3 oz. [½ cup] dried apples
1 teaspoon salt
1 teaspoon black pepper
½ teaspoon cayenne pepper
½ teaspoon dry mustard
1½ lb. sweet potatoes, peeled and
    chopped

4 oz. leaf spinach, trimmed and
    chopped

Preheat the oven to warm 325°F (Gas
Mark 3, 170°C).

Roll the beef cubes in the seasoned
flour, shaking off any excess.

In a large flameproof casserole, heat
the oil over moderate heat. When the oil
is hot, add the onions and garlic and fry,
stirring occasionally, for 5 to 7 minutes or
until the onions are soft and translucent
but not brown. Add the beef cubes and
fry, stirring and turning occasionally, for
5 to 8 minutes or until they are lightly
and evenly browned.

Add the tomatoes with the can juice
and pour over the stout. Bring the liquid
to the boil and stir in the apples, salt,
pepper, cayenne and mustard.

Cover the casserole and place it in the
oven. Cook the mixture for 1½ hours.
Remove the cover and stir in the sweet
potatoes. Return the casserole to the
oven, cover and cook for a further 45
minutes. Stir in the spinach, cover and
cook for a further 15 minutes or until the
meat is tender when pierced with the
point of a sharp knife.

Remove the casserole from the oven
and serve at once.

Zumar Scallops in Port

*Zumar Scallops in Port are ideal to serve at
a dinner party. Accompany this rich dish
with boiled rice and a crisp green salad.*

4 SERVINGS
16 scallops, halved
    juice of 1 lemon
3 oz. [¾ cup] seasoned flour, made
    with 3 oz. [¾ cup] flour, ½ teaspoon
    salt and ½ teaspoon black pepper
2 oz. [¼ cup] butter
1 medium-sized onion, finely
    chopped
8 oz. mushrooms, wiped clean and
    thinly sliced
4 fl. oz. [½ cup] port
5 fl. oz. single cream [⅝ cup light
    cream]
½ teaspoon salt
½ teaspoon black pepper
1 tablespoon chopped fresh parsley

Place the scallop halves in a medium-
sized mixing bowl and pour over the
lemon juice, stirring to coat them well.
Set aside for 5 minutes.

---

*Zulu Beef Pot is hot and spicy and
very delicious for an informal lunch
or dinner party!*

Place the seasoned flour on a plate and dip the scallop halves in it, one by one, coating them thoroughly and shaking off any excess.

In a large, flameproof casserole, melt the butter over moderate heat. When the foam subsides, add the onion to the casserole and fry, stirring occasionally, for 5 to 7 minutes or until it is soft and translucent but not brown. Add the mushrooms to the casserole and fry for 3 minutes. Using a slotted spoon, transfer the onion and mushrooms to a plate and keep them warm.

Add the scallop halves to the casserole and fry them, turning frequently, for 5 minutes or until they are lightly browned all over. Pour the port over the scallops and bring the mixture to the boil, scraping the bottom of the casserole to remove any sediment. Reduce the heat to low and simmer for 6 to 8 minutes or until the liquid has thickened slightly.

Return the onion and mushrooms to the casserole and stir in the cream, salt and pepper. Cook for a further 2 minutes or until the cream is warmed through.

Remove the casserole from the heat, sprinkle over the parsley and serve immediately, straight from the casserole.

Zummah Rabbit Stew

A delicious country stew, Zummah Rabbit Stew is an excellent supper party dish. Accompany it with a full-bodied Burgundy wine or a well-chilled white wine such as Vouvray.

4 SERVINGS

1 x 4 lb. rabbit, cleaned and cut into serving pieces
2 oz. [¼ cup] butter
½ teaspoon salt
½ teaspoon white pepper
½ teaspoon dried thyme
½ teaspoon dried rosemary
1 tablespoon prepared French mustard
1 tablespoon cornflour [cornstarch], dissolved in 2 tablespoons single [light] cream
4 fl. oz. [½ cup] port
3 oz. [½ cup] sultanas or seedless raisins
3 oz. [½ cup] currants

MARINADE
16 fl. oz. [2 cups] dry white wine
4 fl. oz. [½ cup] olive oil
10 oz. dried prunes
2 garlic cloves, crushed

1 teaspoon salt
½ teaspoon freshly ground black pepper
1 medium-sized onion, thinly sliced
1 carrot, scraped and thinly sliced

GARNISH
1 tablespoon chopped fresh parsley
6 crescent-shaped Croûtons

First prepare the marinade. Place all the marinade ingredients in a large, shallow bowl and stir well to blend. Add the rabbit pieces and marinate them at room temperature, basting occasionally, for at least 6 hours.

Remove the rabbit pieces from the marinade and pat them dry with kitchen paper towels. Reserve the marinade.

In a large, deep frying-pan, melt the butter over moderate heat. When the foam subsides, add the rabbit pieces to the pan and fry them, turning occasionally with tongs, for 8 to 10 minutes or until they are lightly and evenly browned.

Add the marinade to the pan and bring the liquid to the boil, stirring occasionally. Stir in the salt and pepper. Reduce the heat to low, cover the pan and simmer

Zummah Rabbit Stew transforms a homely dish into a splendid main course suitable for a supper party. Serve it with red or white wine.

the rabbit for 1 to 1¼ hours or until it is very tender when pierced with the point of a sharp knife.

Remove the pan from the heat and transfer the rabbit pieces to a heated serving dish. Keep warm while you prepare the sauce.

Strain the cooking liquids into a medium-sized saucepan and, using tongs, remove the cooked prunes and add them to the saucepan. Discard any pulp left in the strainer. Place the pan over moderate heat and bring the liquid to the boil. Stir in the thyme and rosemary. Reduce the heat to low and add the mustard and the cornflour [cornstarch] mixture, stirring gently. Add the port, sultanas or seedless raisins and currants and simmer gently for 10 minutes.

Pour the sauce over the rabbit in the heated serving dish. Sprinkle with chopped parsley and arrange the croûtons around the sides of the serving dish

Serve immediately.

Lots of Chocolate Buttercream Icing and light sponge cake make this delightful Zundy Teddy Bear Cake the perfect centrepiece for a party.

---

board. These will form the bear's legs. Arrange the two smaller rolls so that the iced sides lie upright against the sides of the bear's body. These will form the bear's arms. Spread a little icing over one side of the whole reserved slice and place it in the centre of the bear's face to form its snout. Spread a little icing over the cut edges of the halved slice and place them, iced side down, on top of the large roll to form the bear's ears.

Using a flat-bladed knife, spread the remaining buttercream icing over the bear to completely cover it, roughing up the surface with the blade of the knife to give a fur-like appearance. Take care to mould the icing carefully to accentuate the bear-shape of the cake.

Use 9 of the sweets [candies] to form the nose, eyes and paws, and the remaining 3 sweets [candies] for buttons.

The cake is now ready to serve.

Zune Ricotta and Cherry Tartlets

These delicious little tartlets make a dessert with a difference — or serve them as an extra-special snack treat with lots of fresh milk.

16 TARTLETS

2 teaspoons butter
1 lb. [4 cups] Shortcrust Pastry II
FILLING
8 oz. Ricotta cheese
3 oz. cream cheese
3 tablespoons sugar
1 egg, lightly beaten
$\frac{1}{8}$ teaspoon salt
　finely grated rind of 1 orange
1 tablespoon fresh orange juice
14 oz. canned stoned Morello
　cherries, with 2 fl. oz. [$\frac{1}{4}$ cup] of
　the can juice reserved and mixed
　with 2 teaspoons cornflour
　[cornstarch]

Preheat the oven to moderate 350°F (Gas Mark 4, 180°C). Using the butter, lightly grease 16 patty tins.

On a lightly floured surface, roll out the dough to $\frac{1}{8}$-inch thick. With a pastry cutter, cut out 16 circles. Place the circles in the patty tins, taking care not to stretch the dough. Place the patty tins in the oven and bake blind for 12 to 15 minutes or until the pastry is pale gold and firm to the touch.

Zundy Teddy Bear Cake

This super cake is ideal for a children's birthday party. Simple to prepare and assemble, its final appearance is novel and attractive and is sure to delight everybody.

8 SERVINGS

4 x 3-inch bought chocolate Swiss
　[jelly] rolls
1 lb. Buttercream Icing,
　chocolate-flavoured
1 x 9-inch Swiss [Jelly] Roll with
　Cream Filling
12 coloured sweets [candies]

Using a sharp knife, cut a $\frac{1}{2}$-inch slice off the ends of two of the small Swiss [jelly] rolls. Cut one of the slices in half, leave the other slice whole and set them aside.

Spread 1 teaspoon of the buttercream icing over one end of the large Swiss [jelly] roll and stand it upright, iced end down, on a cake board. This will form the body and head of the bear. Spread $\frac{1}{2}$ teaspoon of the buttercream icing along one end and one side of each of the four small Swiss [jelly] rolls. Arrange the two slightly longer rolls so that the iced ends are attached to the base of the bear's body and the iced sides are flat against the cake

Meanwhile, in a medium-sized mixing bowl, beat the ricotta, cream cheese, sugar, egg, salt, orange rind and orange juice together until they are well blended. Remove the patty tins from the oven and spoon the filling into the dough cases so that they are two-thirds full.

Place the patty tins on a baking sheet and put the sheet in the oven. Bake the tartlets for 30 minutes. Remove the sheet from the oven and spoon the cherries over the top of the cheese filling. Sprinkle a little of the reserved cherry juice mixture over each filling. Return the baking sheet to the oven and bake the tartlets for a further 6 to 8 minutes or until the filling is firm and set and the pastry is golden brown.

Remove the baking sheet from the oven and allow the tartlets to cool in the tins for 10 minutes. Run a sharp knife around the edges of the patty tins to loosen the pastry and turn the tartlets out on to a wire rack to cool completely before serving.

Zungeru Peanut Pork

This is a variation on a traditional West African recipe, where the popularity of the combination of pork and peanuts is well established.

Zungeru Peanut Pork is a mouth-watering dish from West Africa, combining succulent loin of pork with a delicious layer of crushed peanuts.

4-6 SERVINGS

1 x 4 lb. boned loin of pork, trimmed of excess fat
1 teaspoon salt
½ teaspoon black pepper
12 oz. [3 cups] shelled peanuts
2 tablespoons peanut oil
1 tablespoon water
8 oz. cooked ham, very thinly sliced

Preheat the oven to fairly hot 375°F (Gas Mark 5, 190°C).

Rub the pork all over with half the salt and pepper and place it, fat side down, on a working surface. Set aside.

Place the peanuts, peanut oil, water and the remaining salt and pepper in the jar of an electric blender. Blend the mixture for 20 seconds or until the peanuts have formed a thick paste which still has small pieces of whole nut in it. Alternatively, place the peanuts in a mortar and crush them into small pieces. Empty the crushed peanuts into a small bowl and, using the back of a wooden spoon, gradually beat in the peanut oil, water and the remaining salt and pepper until the mixture forms a crunchy paste.

Spoon three-quarters of the peanut mixture on to the pork. With a flat-bladed knife, spread the peanut mixture to within 1-inch of the edge of the meat. Arrange the slices of ham over the peanut mixture.

Roll up the meat tightly and tie securely, with trussing string, at 1-inch intervals.

Place the meat on a rack in a roasting tin and roast for 2 to 2½ hours, or 30 to 35 minutes per pound depending on the thickness of the cut, or until the juices run clear when the meat is pierced with the point of a sharp knife.

Five minutes before the end of the roasting time, remove the roasting tin from the oven. Remove and discard the string. Spread the remaining peanut mixture over the top of the pork and return the roasting tin to the oven. Increase the heat to hot 425°F (Gas Mark 7, 220°C) and roast for 5 minutes or until the peanuts on the outside of the pork have formed a golden-brown crust.

Remove the tin from the oven and transfer the pork to a warmed serving dish. Serve immediately.

This delightful dish, Zupanja Red Snapper Bake with vegetables and herbs is ideal for a dinner party.

Zunita Gâteau

This impressive dessert cake is ideal to serve at a dinner party.

6-8 SERVINGS

1 teaspoon butter
1 tablespoon grated orange rind
10 oz. [2½ cups] Choux Pastry
2 oz. [½ cup] chopped almonds
2 tablespoons sugar
14 fl. oz. [1¾ cups] Crème Pâtissière
½ teaspoon almond essence
14 oz. canned apricot halves,
    drained, 6 reserved and the
    remainder coarsely chopped

Preheat the oven to hot 425°F (Gas Mark 7, 220°C). Using the teaspoon of butter, lightly grease a large baking sheet. Set aside.

In a large mixing bowl, beat the orange rind into the choux pastry. Place heaped tablespoonfuls of the mixture, one against another, in the shape of a ring, on the prepared baking sheet. Sprinkle the almonds over the top of the dough ring and place it in the oven. Bake for 25 to 30 minutes or until the pastry ring is puffed up and light golden. Sprinkle the sugar over the ring and bake the pastry for a further 5 minutes or until the sugar has melted and the ring is golden brown. Remove the sheet from the oven and set aside to cool completely.

When the ring is cool, carefully cut it in two, crosswise. Pull out any excess dough from the inside of the two ring halves. Set aside.

In a medium-sized mixing bowl, combine the crème pâtissière, almond essence and the chopped apricots. Using a wooden spoon, beat the ingredients together until they are thoroughly combined.

Spoon the mixture into one half of the ring and place the remaining apricot halves decoratively over the mixture. Place the other ring over the apricot halves.

Transfer the ring to a serving dish and serve immediately.

Zupanja Red Snapper Bake

This delicious Yugoslavian dish has a delicate flavour and makes a change to serve at a dinner party. The vegetable sauce may be puréed if you prefer. Serve the fish with a well-chilled Yugoslavian Riesling.

6 SERVINGS

2 fl. oz. [¼ cup] olive oil
2 large onions, finely chopped
2 garlic cloves, finely chopped
2 celery stalks, trimmed and finely
    chopped
1 green pepper, white pith
    removed, seeded and finely
    chopped
1 lb. leaf spinach, washed, shaken
    dry and chopped
4 carrots, scraped and thinly sliced
2 tablespoons chopped fresh
    parsley
1 tablespoon chopped fresh dill
1 lb. canned peeled tomatoes
8 fl. oz. [1 cup] dry white wine
2 teaspoons salt
1 teaspoon black pepper
1 x 6 lb. red snapper, cleaned
    juice of 1 lemon
1 oz. [2 tablespoons] butter, cut into
    small pieces

Preheat the oven to fairly hot 400°F (Gas Mark 6, 200°C).

In a large frying-pan, heat the oil over moderate heat. When the oil is hot, add the onions and garlic and fry, stirring occasionally, for 5 to 7 minutes or until the onions are soft and translucent but

Zup

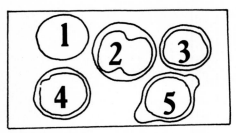

Five fabulous soups from Italy; 1 Zuppa di Cozze, 2 Zuppa di Fontina, 3 Zuppa di Aragosta, 4 Zuppa di Fagioli Fiorentina and 5 Zuppa di Anguille—each one is a meal in itself!

not brown. Add the celery, green pepper, spinach, carrots, parsley and dill and fry, stirring occasionally, for 5 minutes. Stir in the tomatoes with the can juice, the wine, $1\frac{1}{2}$ teaspoons of the salt and the pepper. Increase the heat to high and bring the liquid to the boil. Reduce the heat to low, cover the pan and simmer for 15 minutes. Remove the pan from the heat and pour the vegetables into a large, flameproof baking dish or fish kettle. Set aside.

Sprinkle the fish with the remaining salt and the lemon juice. Lay the fish on top of the vegetable mixture. Dot the butter over the fish. Cover the baking dish with greaseproof or waxed paper or a lid. Place the dish in the oven and cook for 30 to 35 minutes or until the fish is tender but still firm.

Transfer the fish to a warmed serving dish and keep hot.

Set the baking dish or kettle over high heat and bring the vegetable mixture to the boil. Continue to boil for 6 to 8 minutes or until the sauce becomes thick. Remove the dish or kettle from the heat and pour the sauce over the fish. Serve immediately.

Zuppa

Zuppa (*zoo-pah*) is the Italian name for soups and thin stews.

It is also sometimes used to describe a traditional Italian trifle-like dessert.

Zuppa di Anguille
EEL SOUP

This Italian soup is almost like a stew in texture and makes a meal on its own when served with hot, crusty rolls and a salad. Zuppa di Anguille (zoo-pah dee ang-gwee-lay) should be made from small eels, but if they are not available, use large, skinned ones. Serve the soup garnished with hot fresh toast.

4-6 SERVINGS

2 lb. small eels, washed, dried and cut into rounds
2 large onions, thinly sliced
1 large carrot, scraped and thinly sliced
2 celery stalks, trimmed and sliced
2 tablespoons chopped fresh parsley
1 teaspoon grated lemon rind
2 garlic cloves, finely chopped
2 teaspoons salt
1 teaspoon black pepper
3 tablespoons tomato purée
1 tablespoon wine vinegar

Cover the bottom of a large saucepan with a layer of eels. Place a layer of onions, carrot, celery, parsley, lemon rind and garlic over the eels. Continue to layer the eels and vegetables in the same way, ending with a layer of vegetables. Pour over enough water to cover the ingredients. Add the salt and pepper.

Set the pan over moderate heat and bring the liquid to the boil. Reduce the heat to low, cover the pan and simmer for 15 minutes. Stir in the tomato purée and vinegar. Cover the pan again and simmer for a further 25 to 30 minutes or until the eels are tender.

Remove the pan from the heat and pour the soup into a warmed tureen. Serve at once.

Zuppa di Aragosta
CRAYFISH SOUP

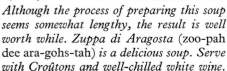

Although the process of preparing this soup seems somewhat lengthy, the result is well worth while. Zuppa di Aragosta (zoo-pah dee ara-gohs-tah) is a delicious soup. Serve with Croûtons and well-chilled white wine.

8 SERVINGS

3 pints [$7\frac{1}{2}$ cups] Court Bouillon
1 medium-sized onion, thinly sliced
1 medium-sized carrot, scraped and finely chopped
$\frac{1}{2}$ teaspoon salt
$\frac{1}{4}$ teaspoon black pepper
1 teaspoon paprika
16 large crayfish, shelled
8 oz. [3 cups] cooked long-grain rice
  bouquet garni, consisting of 4 parsley sprigs, 1 thyme spray and 1 bay leaf tied together
2 fl. oz. [$\frac{1}{4}$ cup] brandy
4 fl. oz. [$\frac{1}{2}$ cup] white wine
4 egg yolks, beaten
1 oz. [2 tablespoons] butter
2 tablespoons finely chopped fresh tarragon

Pour the court bouillon into a large saucepan. Add the onion, carrot, salt, pepper, paprika, 8 crayfish, the rice and bouquet garni. Place the pan over moderate heat and bring the liquid to the boil. Reduce the heat to low and simmer gently for 20 minutes.

Meanwhile, in a small saucepan, warm the brandy over low heat. Remove the pan from the heat.

Place the remaining crayfish in a large soup tureen. Pour over the brandy and ignite. Stir with a wooden spoon until the flames die away. Pour over the white wine and set aside.

Remove the saucepan from the heat and strain the liquid into a large mixing bowl. Discard the bouquet garni. Using the back of a wooden spoon, press the remaining pulp through the strainer into the liquid. Discard any dry pulp remaining in the strainer. Alternatively, blend the mixture with a little of the liquid in an electric blender.

Transfer the mixture to a large saucepan and return the pan to moderate heat. Bring the liquid to the boil. Reduce the heat to low and simmer for 10 minutes. Remove the pan from the heat.

Place 6 fluid ounces [$\frac{3}{4}$ cup] of the hot liquid in a medium-sized mixing bowl. Add the egg yolks and butter and stir for 4 minutes. Pour the mixture into the saucepan and continue to stir for 2 minutes. Return the pan to moderate heat and bring the liquid to the boil. Reduce the heat to low and simmer, stirring constantly, for 3 minutes. Remove the pan from the heat.

Pour the soup over the crayfish mixture in the soup tureen. Sprinkle with the tarragon and serve immediately.

Zuppa di Cozze
MUSSEL SOUP

Zuppa di Cozze (zoo-pah dee cot-zay) makes an excellent first course served by itself or as a light main course served with crisp buttered rolls and a chilled white wine. Remember to provide a plate for the empty mussel shells.

4 SERVINGS

2 tablespoons olive oil
1 medium-sized onion, sliced
1 celery stalk, trimmed and chopped
2 garlic cloves, crushed
$\frac{1}{2}$ teaspoon salt
$\frac{1}{2}$ teaspoon black pepper
1 teaspoon dried basil
$\frac{1}{2}$ teaspoon dried oregano
$1\frac{1}{2}$ lb. tomatoes, blanched, peeled, seeded and chopped

6 fl. oz. [¾ cup] dry white wine
10 fl. oz. [1¼ cups] water
2½ quarts mussels, scrubbed
2 tablespoons chopped fresh
  parsley

In a large saucepan, heat the oil over moderate heat. When the oil is hot, add the onion, celery and garlic to the pan and fry, stirring occasionally, for 5 to 7 minutes or until the onion is soft and translucent but not brown. Add the salt, pepper, basil and oregano to the pan and cook for a further 1 minute. Add the tomatoes to the pan and cook for 5 minutes, stirring frequently. Pour in the wine and the water and bring the liquid to the boil. Reduce the heat to low and simmer for 10 minutes or until the tomatoes are pulpy. Increase the heat to high, add the mussels and cook, shaking the pan occasionally, for 8 to 10 minutes or until the shells open.

With a slotted spoon, transfer the mussels to a warmed soup tureen or individual soup bowls. Remove and discard approximately half of the shells. Set the mussels aside and keep warm.

Strain the cooking liquid into a bowl, pushing down on the vegetables with the back of a wooden spoon to extract all the juices. Return the liquid to the saucepan. Place the pan over high heat and bring the liquid to the boil. Boil for 2 minutes. Remove the pan from the heat, pour the liquid over mussels, sprinkle over the parsley and serve immediately.

Zuppa a Due Colori
TWO-COLOURED SPONGE PUDDING

Zuppa a Due Colori (zoo-pah ah doo-ay koh-loh-ree) is a regional speciality of Italy. This rich dessert is well worth the time and care required in its preparation.

6 SERVINGS

1 x 8-inch Chocolate Sponge Cake,
  cut into thin slices
4 fl. oz. [½ cup] chocolate-flavoured
  liqueur
1 x 7-inch Sponge Cake, cut into
  thin slices
4 fl. oz. [½ cup] rum
12 fl. oz. [1½ cups] Crème Pâtissière
10 fl. oz. double cream [1¼ cups
  heavy cream], stiffly whipped
2 oz. dark [semi-sweet] cooking
  chocolate, grated
4 oz. [1 cup] flaked hazelnuts,
  toasted

CHOCOLATE CREAM
1 lb. dark [semi-sweet] cooking
  chocolate, broken into pieces
1 oz. [2 tablespoons] butter

2 fl. oz. [¼ cup] rum
5 eggs, lightly beaten

First make the chocolate cream. In a medium-sized heatproof mixing bowl set over a saucepan half-filled with boiling water, melt the chocolate, with the butter and rum, over low heat, stirring occasionally until the mixture is smooth. Using a wire whisk or rotary beater, beat in the egg yolks, one at a time, and, beating constantly, cook the cream for 12 to 15 minutes or until it begins to thicken. Remove the pan from the heat and remove the bowl from the pan.

Place half of the chocolate sponge slices in a layer in the bottom of a deep, glass serving bowl. Pour over half of the chocolate-flavoured liqueur. With a flat-bladed knife, spread half of the chocolate cream over the sponge. Place half of the plain sponge slices over the cream. Sprinkle the sponge with half of the rum. Spoon all of the crème pâtissière over the sponge and continue to make layers in this way ending with the plain sponge.

Place the pudding in the refrigerator to chill for 1 hour. Remove the pudding from the refrigerator, spoon over the double [heavy] cream, sprinkle over the grated chocolate and hazelnuts and serve immediately.

Zuppa di Fagioli Fiorentina
BEAN SOUP FLORENCE-STYLE

This soup is almost a meal in itself. Thick and nourishing and simple to prepare, Zuppa di Fagioli Fiorentina (zoo-pah dee faj-ee-oh-lee f'yor-ehn-tee-nah) is traditionally served with a bowl of grated Parmesan cheese to sprinkle over the soup as desired. For a delicious extra touch pour 2 tablespoons of dry sherry into each serving.

6 SERVINGS

10 oz. dried white haricot beans,
  soaked overnight and drained
4 oz. large macaroni, broken into
  4-inch pieces
1 lb. bacon hock, sliced into 1-inch
  cubes
1 large onion, sliced
1 large garlic clove, crushed
4 medium-sized tomatoes,
  quartered
3 pints [7½ cups] vegetable stock
bouquet garni, consisting of 4
  parsley sprigs, 1 thyme spray and
  1 bay leaf tied together
¼ teaspoon salt
½ teaspoon black pepper
2 oz. button mushrooms, wiped
  clean and finely chopped

2 tablespoons finely chopped fresh
  parsley

Place all the ingredients in a large saucepan and set the pan over high heat. Bring the liquid to the boil, stirring frequently. Reduce the heat to low and simmer the soup for 1½ to 2 hours or until the beans are cooked.

Taste the soup and add more seasoning if necessary.

Ladle the soup into individual bowls and serve immediately.

Zuppa di Fontina
BREAD AND CHEESE SOUP

Zuppa di Fontina (zoo-pah dee fawn-tee-nah) consists of layers of fried bread and Fontina cheese in home-made beef stock. This soup is very filling, takes little time to prepare and may be served either as a first course or on its own as a luncheon.

4-6 SERVINGS

3 oz. [⅜ cup] butter
12 slices French bread
12 slices Fontina cheese
3 pints [7½ cups] home-made beef
  stock, boiling

In a large frying-pan, melt the butter over moderate heat. When the foam subsides, add the bread slices and fry them for 3 to 4 minutes on each side or until the bread is crisp and golden. Remove the pan from the heat and transfer the bread to kitchen paper towels to drain.

Preheat the oven to moderate 350°F (Gas Mark 4, 180°C).

Lay the bread slices on the bottom of an ovenproof soup tureen or individual ovenproof serving bowls and top with the cheese slices.

Pour the boiling stock over the bread and cheese and place the tureen or serving bowls in the oven for 10 minutes or until the cheese has nearly melted.

Remove the tureen or serving bowls from the oven and serve the soup immediately.

Zuppa Inglese I
ENGLISH TRIFLE I

Although the true origin of the name Zuppa Inglese (zoo-pah ing-glay-say) is not known, this dessert does bear a great resemblance to an English trifle. This delicious dessert consists of layers of Marsala-soaked sponge and Zabaglione and it would make an ideal ending to a special dinner party.

6 SERVINGS

2 x 7-inch Sponge Cakes, sliced
  across in half
18 fl. oz. [2¼ cups] Zabaglione,
  cooled
8 fl. oz. [1 cup] Marsala
16 fl. oz. double cream [2 cups
  heavy cream], stiffly whipped
18 Maraschino cherries

Place one half of a sponge, cut side
uppermost, on a serving plate. Sprinkle
over one quarter of the Marsala. Spread
one third of the zabaglione over the
sponge. Continue making layers in this
way until all the ingredients are used up
ending with a layer of sponge.

Using a flat-bladed knife, spread the
cream over the top and sides of the trifle.
Arrange the cherries decoratively over the
surface and place the trifle in the refrigerator to chill for 1 hour before serving.

Zuppa Inglese II
ENGLISH TRIFLE II

This fabulous Zuppa Inglese II (zoo-pah
ing-glay-say) *is truly a compliment to
English cooking! It makes a superb ending
to a fairly light meal.*

8-10 SERVINGS

1 teaspoon butter
4 oz. [⅔ cup] mixed glacé fruit,
2 tablespoons brandy
3 tablespoons cornflour [cornstarch]
5 oz. [⅝ cup] sugar
14 fl. oz. [1¾ cups] milk, hot
6 egg yolks, lightly beaten
1 teaspoon vanilla essence
5 fl. oz. double cream [⅝ cup heavy
  cream], stiffly whipped
4 fl. oz. [½ cup] rum
1 x 7-inch Sponge Cake, cut across
  into 4 slices
6 oz. Meringue Suisse

With the butter, grease a medium-sized
baking sheet and set aside.

Place the glacé fruit in a small bowl
and pour over the brandy. Set aside for 1
hour.

Place the cornflour [cornstarch] and
sugar in a medium-sized saucepan and
gradually stir in 12 fluid ounces [1½ cups]
of the milk, stirring constantly and being
careful to avoid lumps. Set the pan over
moderate heat and cook the custard,
stirring constantly, until it is thick and
smooth. Remove the pan from the heat.

Preheat the oven to very hot 450°F
(Gas Mark 8, 230°C).

In a large mixing bowl, combine the
egg yolks and the remaining milk. Using
a wooden spoon, slowly stir the hot

custard into the egg yolk mixture until
the mixture is thoroughly combined.
Return the mixture to the pan. Set the
pan over low heat and cook, stirring constantly, until the custard becomes thick.
Add the vanilla essence. Remove the pan
from the heat, pour the custard back into
the bowl and chill in the refrigerator until
it is cold.

Remove the custard from the refrigerator and fold in the cream. Sprinkle the
rum over the sponge cake slices. Sandwich the slices of sponge cake together
with the custard and place the cake on the
prepared baking sheet. Spread the glacé
fruit over the top layer of the cake.
Secure the layers with wooden cocktail
sticks or skewers.

Using a spatula, spread the meringue
mixture over the top and sides of the cake
to cover it completely. Remove and
discard the cocktail sticks or skewers.
Place the baking sheet in the oven and
bake for 4 to 5 minutes or until the
meringue is lightly browned. Remove the
baking sheet from the oven and allow the
cake to cool completely.

*Serve Zuppa Inglese II as a fab-
ulously rich dessert accompanied by
some liqueur and coffee.*

Using two fish slices, transfer the cake
to a serving dish and cut it into wedges
before serving.

Zuppa di Pollo
CHICKEN SOUP

Zuppa di Pollo (zoo-pah dee pol-loh) *is a
delicate chicken soup from the Piedmont
region of Italy. It is an ideal first course for
a dinner party and may be made several
hours in advance and then reheated. Serve
it with Croûtons and a chilled Italian white
wine.*

8 SERVINGS

2 tablespoons olive oil
12 spring onions [scallions], trimmed
  and finely chopped
6 slices lean bacon, rinds removed
  and chopped

½ teaspoon dried tarragon
1 x 3 lb. chicken, skinned, boned and cut into thin strips
6 fl. oz. [¾ cup] dry white wine
2 pints 14 fl. oz. [6¾ cups] home-made chicken stock
3 oz. [¾ cup] Parmesan cheese, grated

In a large saucepan, heat the oil over moderate heat. When the oil is hot, add the spring onions [scallions], bacon and tarragon to the pan and fry, stirring occasionally, for 3 to 5 minutes or until the bacon is lightly browned.

Add the chicken strips to the pan and continue frying for a further 6 to 8 minutes, stirring occasionally, or until the chicken strips are lightly browned.

Add the white wine and enough chicken stock just to cover the chicken strips. Reduce the heat to low and simmer the chicken for 20 to 30 minutes or until the chicken is tender when pierced with the point of a sharp knife. Pour the remaining stock into the pan, increase the heat to high and bring the liquid to the boil, stirring frequently. Remove the pan from the heat and ladle the soup into a warmed soup tureen.

Sprinkle over the cheese and serve immediately.

Zuppa di Verdura
GREEN VEGETABLE SOUP

Zuppa di Verdura (zoo-pah dee vehr-doo-rah) *is a thick vegetable soup from Tuscany with a rich, appetizing green colour. This is an ideal soup to make during the summer when fresh vegetables are plentiful.*

6 SERVINGS

2 tablespoons olive oil
2 leeks, trimmed, cleaned and chopped
2 tablespoons flour
2 pints [5 cups] chicken stock, boiling
½ teaspoon salt
½ teaspoon black pepper
½ teaspoon celery seeds
¼ teaspoon dried rosemary
6 large lettuce leaves, washed and shaken dry
1 lb. spinach, washed and trimmed
1 bunch watercress, washed and shaken dry
8 oz. fresh shelled or frozen and thawed peas
2 mint sprigs
2 tablespoons chopped fresh parsley

In a large saucepan, heat the oil over moderate heat. When the oil is hot, add the leeks to the pan and fry, stirring occasionally, for 5 to 7 minutes or until they are soft and translucent but not brown.

Remove the pan from the heat. With a wooden spoon, stir in the flour to make a smooth paste. Gradually stir in the chicken stock, being careful to avoid lumps. Stir in the salt, pepper, celery seeds and rosemary.

Return the pan to the heat and bring the soup to the boil, stirring constantly. Add the lettuce, spinach, watercress, peas and mint to the pan and bring the soup back to the boil. Boil for 2 minutes. Reduce the heat to low, cover the pan and simmer the soup for 20 to 25 minutes or until the vegetables are very tender.

Remove the pan from the heat. Ladle the soup into the jar of an electric blender, a little at a time, and blend until the soup is smooth and creamy. Alternatively, pour the soup through a fine wire strainer held over a large bowl. Using the back of a wooden spoon, rub the vegetables through a strainer until only a dry pulp is left. Discard the pulp in the strainer.

Return the soup to the saucepan. Return the saucepan to moderate heat and, stirring occasionally, bring the soup to the boil.

Remove the pan from the heat. Taste the soup and add more seasoning if necessary. Pour the soup into a warmed soup tureen or individual soup bowls. Sprinkle over the parsley and serve at once.

Zuppa di Vongole e Pancotto
CLAM AND BREAD SOUP

This superb soup might be better described as a thin stew rather than a thick soup. Serve Zuppa di Vongole e Pancotto (zoo-pah dee vawn-goh-lay ay pan-cot-toh) *with mixed salad and well-chilled white wine for a filling lunch or supper.*

4 SERVINGS

4 fl. oz. [½ cup] olive oil

1 onion, finely chopped
3 garlic cloves, crushed
6 tomatoes, blanched, peeled, seeded and chopped
6 fl. oz. [¾ cup] white wine
16 fl. oz. [2 cups] fish stock
2½ lb. frozen or canned clams, thawed or drained
1 teaspoon salt
1 teaspoon black pepper
1 tablespoon chopped fresh basil
1 oz. [2 tablespoons] butter, softened
4 slices French or Italian bread, toasted

In a large saucepan, heat the oil over moderate heat. When the oil is hot, add the onion and 2 garlic cloves and fry, stirring occasionally, for 5 to 7 minutes or until the onion is soft and translucent but not brown. Stir in the tomatoes and cook, stirring occasionally, for a further 3 minutes or until they have pulped slightly.

Pour over the wine and fish stock and bring the liquid to the boil. Reduce the heat to low and simmer the mixture for 20 minutes, stirring occasionally. Stir in the clams, salt, pepper and basil and continue to simmer the mixture for a further 15 minutes.

Meanwhile, in a small mixing bowl, combine the remaining garlic and the butter, beating well to blend. Generously spread the butter over the toasted bread and place one slice on the bottom of each of 4 warmed serving bowls. Remove the pan from the heat and ladle the soup over the bread. Serve at once.

Zuppa di Zucchini
COURGETTE SOUP

This delightful and unusual soup makes an ideal first course for a dinner party. Or serve Zuppa di Zucchini (zoo-pah dee zoo-kee-nee) with lots of crusty bread and some well-chilled white wine for a satisfying lunch.

4 SERVINGS
2 oz. [¼ cup] butter
12 spring onions [scallions], trimmed and finely chopped
1 lb. courgettes [zucchini], trimmed and coarsely grated
1 medium-sized potato, peeled and coarsely grated
1 pint [2½ cups] chicken stock

Zurich Fruit Crumble is a wholesome and colourful winter dessert which is perfect to serve for a family dinner with plenty of cream or custard.

8 fl. oz. [1 cup] white wine
¼ teaspoon grated nutmeg
½ teaspoon dill seeds
2 oz. [½ cup] Parmesan cheese, grated

In a large saucepan, melt the butter over moderate heat. When the foam subsides, add the spring onions [scallions], courgettes [zucchini] and potato to the pan and fry, stirring occasionally, for 3 to 4 minutes or until the spring onions [scallions] are soft and translucent but not brown. Add the stock and wine to the pan and stir in the nutmeg and dill. Bring the mixture to the boil. Reduce the heat to low and simmer for 20 to 25 minutes or until the vegetables are very tender when pierced with the point of a sharp knife.

Stir in the cheese and cook for a further 1 to 2 minutes or until the cheese begins to melt.

Remove the pan from the heat and pour the soup into a warmed soup tureen or small individual bowls. Serve immediately.

Zurich Fruit Crumble

This sustaining dish makes a nourishing winter dessert. Serve hot with whipped cream or custard.

6 SERVINGS
10 fl. oz. [1¼ cups] water
8 fl. oz. [1 cup] white wine
5 oz. [⅝ cup] sugar
4 oz. [⅔ cup] dried apricots, soaked overnight and drained
4 oz. [⅔ cup] dried figs, soaked overnight and drained
4 oz. [⅔ cup] dried peaches, soaked overnight and drained
4 oz. [⅔ cup] dried prunes, soaked overnight and drained
4 oz. [⅔ cup] dried pears, soaked overnight and drained
4 oz. [⅔ cup] dried apples, soaked overnight and drained
2 oz. [½ cup] shelled pistachio nuts
2 oz. [½ cup] shelled Brazil nuts
3 oz. desiccated coconut [¾ cup shredded coconut]
3 oz. [¾ cup] flour
3 oz. [⅜ cup] butter, softened

Pour the water and wine into a large saucepan and set the pan over moderate heat. Add 2 ounces [¼ cup] of the sugar and stir until it has dissolved. When the sugar has completely dissolved, add the dried fruits and nuts. Increase the heat to high and bring the mixture to the boil, stirring constantly. Reduce the heat to low and simmer for 20 minutes. Taste the

syrup and add more sugar if desired.
Preheat the oven to moderate 350°F (Gas Mark 4, 180°C).

Remove the pan from the heat and, using a slotted spoon, transfer the fruits and nuts to a large ovenproof dish. Set aside.

In a medium-sized mixing bowl, combine the coconut, flour, butter and the remaining sugar. Using your fingertips, rub the ingredients together until the mixture resembles fine breadcrumbs.

Cover the fruit mixture with the crumble mixture and place the dish in the centre of the oven. Bake for 20 to 30 minutes or until the crumble is cooked and golden brown.

Remove the dish from the oven and serve immediately.

Zurich Hazelnut Biscuits [Cookies]

These delicious, crispy biscuits [cookies] from Switzerland make a marvellous treat.

20 BISCUITS [COOKIES]
2 oz. [¼ cup] unsalted butter, softened
4 oz. [1 cup] flour
1 egg, lightly beaten
6 oz. [1 cup] ground hazelnuts
3 oz. [⅜ cup] sugar
2 tablespoons apricot jam, slightly warmed
20 whole hazelnuts, blanched
ICING
3 oz. dark [semi-sweet] cooking chocolate
2 tablespoons sugar
4 tablespoons water
1 teaspoon butter

Preheat the oven to cool 300°F (Gas Mark 2, 150°C).

Place the butter and flour in a large mixing bowl and beat them together with a wooden spoon until they are well blended. Using a metal spoon, fold in the egg, hazelnuts and sugar and mix well.

Place the dough on a lightly floured surface and roll it out to ⅛-inch thick. Using a 1-inch pastry cutter, cut the dough into 40 rounds. Place the rounds on a baking sheet and bake in the oven for 20 to 25 minutes or until the biscuits [cookies] are lightly browned. Remove the baking sheet from the oven and allow the biscuits [cookies] to cool.

Meanwhile, make the icing. In the top of a double boiler, melt the chocolate over low heat. Remove the boiler from the heat. In a small saucepan set over high heat, combine the sugar and water and boil, stirring constantly, until the mixture

forms a thick syrup. Remove the pan from the heat and pour the syrup on to the chocolate. Stir well to blend. Stir in the butter. Set aside.

Sandwich pairs of the biscuits [cookies] together with the apricot jam. Using a palette knife, spread the icing over the top of each biscuit [cookie] and place a whole hazelnut in the centre of each one. Allow the icing to cool before serving.

Zurich Lamb Delight

A deliciously refreshing stew from Switzerland, Zurich Lamb Delight is excellent to serve at a summer dinner party accompanied with new potatoes or buttered noodles and a green vegetable. Serve it with a well-chilled Fendant wine.

6 SERVINGS

3 lb. leg of lamb, cubed
1½ teaspoons salt
2 fl. oz. [¼ cup] olive oil
2 lemons, thinly sliced
3 teaspoons ground cinnamon
2 teaspoons canned green peppercorns, drained
1 teaspoon saffron threads, mixed with 1 tablespoon stock
15 fl. oz. [1⅞ cups] beef stock, hot
2 tablespoons chopped fresh mint

Rub the lamb cubes all over with the salt.

In a large flameproof casserole, heat the oil over moderate heat. When the oil is hot, add the lamb cubes and fry, turning occasionally, for 6 to 8 minutes or until they are golden brown all over. Place the lemon slices over the meat and sprinkle over the cinnamon and peppercorns. Add the saffron mixture and stock. Reduce the heat to low, cover the pan and simmer for 1 hour or until the lamb is tender when pierced with the point of a sharp knife.

Remove the casserole from the heat, sprinkle over the mint and serve at once.

Zurich Roast Pork

Zurich Roast Pork is the ideal dish to serve for a family Sunday luncheon. Serve with roast potatoes and Broccoli with Almonds, and to drink, a chilled bottle of Riesling.

6-8 SERVINGS

1 x 4 lb. knuckle end half leg of pork, scored
3 garlic cloves, crushed
1 teaspoon salt
1 teaspoon freshly ground black pepper
½ teaspoon ground cinnamon

Serve Zurich Lamb Delight with lots of chilled white wine.

½ teaspoon ground nutmeg
2 lb. canned pineapple rings, can juice reserved
1 teaspoon vegetable oil
2 tablespoons sugar

Preheat the oven to fairly hot 375°F (Gas Mark 5, 190°C).

Place the pork on a working surface and rub it all over with the garlic, salt and pepper, cinnamon and nutmeg. Using a very sharp long knife, carefully slide the knife between the fat and the flesh of the pork, without breaking the skin.

Stuff the pineapple rings into the cavity between the flesh and the fat. Secure the skin with wooden cocktail sticks. Transfer the meat to a large roasting tin and pour over the oil. Pour the reserved pineapple juice over the meat.

Place the tin in the centre of the oven and roast for 3 hours, basting occasionally. Sprinkle over the sugar and increase the temperature to hot 425°F (Gas Mark 7, 220°C). Roast the pork for a further 20 minutes or until the juice that runs out of the pork is clear when the meat is pierced with the point of a sharp knife and the skin is crisp and golden brown.

Remove the tin from the oven. Transfer the pork to a large warmed serving dish and serve immediately.

Zurich Veal and Parsnip Pie

This unusual pie is topped with a lid, not of pastry, but of parsnips which gives it an unusual flavour. Serve with baked potatoes and creamed spinach.

4 SERVINGS

3 oz. [⅜ cup] butter
1½ lb. parsnips, peeled and cut into rounds
2 large onions, chopped
2 lb. stewing veal, cubed
2 teaspoons salt
½ teaspoon black pepper
½ teaspoon grated nutmeg
5 fl. oz. double cream [⅝ cup heavy cream]
5 fl. oz. [⅝ cup] medium-dry sherry

Preheat the oven to fairly hot 400°F (Gas Mark 6, 200°C).

Using 1 ounce [2 tablespoons] of the butter, generously grease an ovenproof baking dish. Line the bottom and sides of the dish with the largest parsnip rounds.

Reserve enough large parsnip rounds to make a lid for the pie. Place the remaining parsnip rounds, the onions, veal, salt, pepper and nutmeg in a large mixing bowl and stir well until they are thoroughly combined. Spoon the mixture into the baking dish.

In a small bowl, combine the cream and sherry. Pour the liquid over the meat mixture and lay the reserved parsnip rings over to form a lid. Dot the top of the pie with the remaining butter. Place the dish in the oven and bake for 1 hour.

Remove the dish from the oven and serve immediately.

Zuriga Salmon Trout with Mushroom Mayonnaise

An unusual and tasty way of serving salmon trout, Zuriga Salmon Trout with Mushroom Mayonnaise is the ideal dish to serve for a small luncheon party, accompanied by boiled new potatoes and a crisp green salad.

4 SERVINGS

1 x 3 lb. salmon trout, cleaned and with the head and tail left on
2 pints [5 cups] Court Bouillon
8 oz. mushrooms, wiped clean and finely chopped
juice of 1 lemon
12 fl. oz. [1½ cups] mayonnaise

A simple yet sophisticated dish, Zuriga Salmon Trout with Mushroom Mayonnaise is really delicious.

2 garlic cloves, crushed
½ teaspoon black pepper
8 lemon slices

Wash the salmon trout under cold running water and pat it dry with kitchen paper towels. Transfer the fish to a large saucepan or fish kettle. Pour over the court bouillon and place the pan or fish kettle over moderate heat. Bring the liquid to the boil. Reduce the heat to low, cover and simmer the fish for 5 minutes. Remove the pan or fish kettle from the heat and set aside to cool. When the cooking liquid is completely cold, remove the fish from the pan or kettle and discard the cooking liquid. Carefully remove the skin from the body of the fish, leaving it on the head and tail. Transfer the fish to a decorative serving plate and set aside while you prepare the mayonnaise.

In a medium-sized saucepan, combine the mushrooms and lemon juice. Cover the pan and place it over low heat. Simmer the mushrooms gently for 5 minutes, shaking the pan from time to time. Remove the pan from the heat and transfer the mushrooms to a medium-sized mixing bowl. Set aside to cool completely. When cold, add the mayonnaise, garlic and pepper. Using a wooden spoon, beat the ingredients together until they are thoroughly combined.

Garnish the fish with the lemon slices. Spoon the mayonnaise into a sauceboat and serve immediately, with the fish.

Zurov Lamb

A sophisticated and unusual dinner party dish, Zurov Lamb is absolutely delightful served with boiled new potatoes, a crisp green salad and a bottle of light red wine, such as Beaujolais Villages.

4 SERVINGS

4 slices streaky bacon
4 noisettes of lamb, approximately 2½-inches thick
½ teaspoon salt
½ teaspoon freshly ground black pepper
6 oz. [¾ cup] butter
3 oz. Stilton cheese

Preheat the oven to very hot 450°F (Gas Mark 8, 230°C).

Wrap a slice of bacon around each noisette and secure it firmly with trussing string or a wooden cocktail stick. Season the noisettes with the salt and pepper and set aside. In a heatproof casserole, melt 3 ounces [¾ cup] of the butter over high heat. When the foam subsides add the noisettes and fry, for 1 minute on each side, turning once.

Remove the casserole from the heat and transfer the casserole to the centre of the oven. Roast the noisettes for 12 to 15 minutes, this will produce rare meat. For well done meat, roast for a further 5 minutes.

Meanwhile, in a small mixing bowl, beat the remaining butter and cheese together until they are thoroughly combined. Remove the noisettes from the oven and transfer the noisettes on to a warmed serving dish. Place the butter mixture on top of the noisettes and serve.

Zute Salad

A super crunchy salad combining sweet and savoury ingredients, Zute Salad is just the dish to serve as part of a vegetarian meal.

4 SERVINGS

1 lb. fresh beansprouts, washed and drained
4 oz. red cabbage, finely shredded
4 celery stalks, trimmed and finely sliced
4 oz. unsalted peanuts
3 bananas, cut into ¼-inch slices
6 fl. oz. [¾ cup] French Dressing

Combine all the salad ingredients in a large salad bowl and pour over the French dressing. Using two large forks, toss all the ingredients together to coat them thoroughly. Serve immediately.

Zutian Sardine Flan

A delicious dish for unexpected guests, Zutian Sardine Flan is super served with a crisp green salad, baked potatoes in their jackets and a bottle of full-bodied red wine.

4-6 SERVINGS

1 x 9-inch Flan Case, made with shortcrust pastry
10 oz. canned sardines, drained
2 tablespoons finely chopped fresh parsley
1 tablespoon finely chopped fresh basil
2 large Spanish [Bermuda] onions, finely chopped.
8 oz. canned peeled tomatoes, drained and finely chopped
1 teaspoon salt
1 teaspoon sugar
1 teaspoon freshly ground black

Two unusual and imaginative chicken recipes, Zuzu Spiced Chicken Breasts and Zuyder Chicken Breasts with Tarragon and Sour Cream are superb.

pepper
1 tablespoon butter, melted
6 anchovies
12 black olives
4 eggs, lightly beaten
8 fl. oz. single cream [1 cup light cream]

Preheat the oven to moderate 350°F (Gas Mark 4, 180°C).

Place the flan case on a baking sheet.

Arrange the sardines in the bottom of the case, heads facing inwards. Sprinkle over the parsley, basil, onions, tomatoes, salt, sugar, pepper and butter. Arrange the anchovies and olives decoratively over the top of the mixture. Pour over the beaten eggs and the cream. Place the flan in the centre of the oven and bake for 25 to 30 minutes or until the mixture is firm to the touch.

Remove the flan from the oven and set aside to cool completely before serving.

Zuyder Chicken Breasts with Tarragon and Sour Cream

This marvellous combination of succulent chicken breasts cooked with a fragrant sauce is a perfect lunch or supper dish. Serve with mashed potatoes and a well-chilled white wine. Fresh tarragon should be used if it is available if not, 1½ teaspoons of dried tarragon may be substituted.

4 SERVINGS
4 large chicken breasts, skinned and boned
1 teaspoon salt
1½ teaspoons black pepper
3 oz. [⅜ cup] butter
3 tablespoons flour
10 fl. oz. [1¼ cups] home-made chicken stock
1 tablespoon chopped fresh tarragon
4 fl. oz. [½ cup] sour cream
3 tablespoons grated Parmesan cheese

Rub the chicken breasts all over with half the salt and half the pepper.

In a large frying-pan, melt 2 ounces [¼ cup] of the butter over moderate heat. When the foam subsides, add the chicken breasts and fry, turning occasionally, for 5 to 8 minutes or until they are lightly and evenly browned. Remove the chicken from the pan and set aside.

Add the remaining butter to the pan. When the foam subsides, remove the pan from the heat and, using a wooden spoon, stir in the flour to form a smooth paste. Gradually add the chicken stock and tarragon, stirring constantly and being careful to avoid lumps. Return the pan to moderate heat and cook, stirring constantly, for 2 to 3 minutes or until the sauce is smooth and thick.

Return the chicken breasts to the pan, reduce the heat to low and simmer the breasts for 20 to 30 minutes or until they are tender when pierced with the point of a sharp knife. Using tongs, transfer the chicken breasts to a warmed serving dish. Set aside and keep warm while you finish off the sauce.

Stir the sour cream and 2 tablespoons of grated cheese into the sauce and cook, stirring constantly, for 2 minutes or until the cream and cheese have been absorbed and the sauce is hot but not boiling.

Remove the pan from the heat and pour the sauce over the chicken breasts. Sprinkle over the remaining grated cheese and serve at once.

Zuzu Spiced Chicken Breasts

Zuzu Spiced Chicken Breasts make an excellent supper dish. Serve with buttered

noodles, sprinkled with oregano and — a bottle of well-chilled dry white wine.

4 SERVINGS

3 oz. [⅜ cup] butter
2 tablespoons clear honey
1 garlic clove, crushed
1 teaspoon ground ginger
½ teaspoon salt
½ teaspoon black pepper
4 chicken breasts, skinned
3 tablespoons sesame seeds

Preheat the oven to fairly hot 400°F (Gas Mark 6, 200°C).

In a large frying-pan, melt the butter over moderate heat. When the foam subsides, add the honey and, stirring constantly, fry for 3 minutes. Add the garlic, ginger, salt and pepper.

Increase the heat to moderately high and add the chicken breasts. Fry for 4 minutes on each side or until the chicken breasts are golden brown all over.

Transfer the chicken to an ovenproof baking dish and sprinkle over the sesame seeds. Pour over the cooking juices and place the dish in the oven for 25 to 30 minutes or until the chicken is tender and the juices run clear when it is pierced with the point of a sharp knife.

Remove the dish from the oven and serve immediately.

Zvengli's Poached Eggs

A favourite dish of Zvengli, the famous German theologian, Zvengli's Poached Eggs makes an ideal supper snack or luncheon dish.

Just the dish if unexpected guests turn up at lunch-time, Zvengli's Poached Eggs are delicious served with crusty French bread and butter.

4 SERVINGS

1½ lb. fresh broccoli, trimmed, cooked, puréed and kept warm
1 oz. [2 tablespoons] butter
1 teaspoon salt
½ teaspoon black pepper
1 teaspoon lemon juice
4 eggs, poached
2 oz. [½ cup] dry breadcrumbs
2 oz. [½ cup] freshly grated Parmesan cheese

Preheat the grill [broiler] to high.

Arrange the broccoli in a heat proof serving dish. Dot over half the butter and sprinkle over the salt, pepper and lemon juice. Arrange the eggs on the broccoli and cover the eggs with the breadcrumbs and cheese. Dot over the remaining butter.

Place the dish under the grill [broiler] for 5 minutes or until the top is golden brown. Remove the dish from under the grill [broiler] and serve immediately.

Zveno Tea Soufflé

A very light, delicately flavoured soufflé, Zveno Tea Soufflé is inexpensive to make and is perfect to serve at a dinner party. Scatter a few chopped pistachio nuts over the top before serving.

6 SERVINGS

1 oz. [2 tablespoons] plus 1 teaspoon butter
1 oz. [¼ cup] flour
3 tablespoons milk
6 fl. oz. [¾ cup] strong tea, strained
2 oz. [¼ cup] sugar
4 egg yolks
5 egg whites, stiffly beaten

With the teaspoon of butter, grease a 2-pint [1½-quart] soufflé dish.

Preheat the oven to fairly hot 400°F (Gas Mark 6, 200°C).

In a medium-sized saucepan, melt the remaining butter over moderate heat. Remove the pan from the heat and, with a wooden spoon, stir in the flour to make a smooth paste. Gradually add the milk, stirring constantly. Pour in the tea and add the sugar. Return the pan to the heat and cook, stirring constantly, for 2 to 3 minutes or until the sauce is thick and smooth. Remove the pan from the heat and set aside to cool slightly. Beat in the egg yolks, one by one. With a metal spoon, fold the egg whites into the mixture.

Pour the mixture into the prepared soufflé dish, place the dish in the oven and bake for 40 minutes or until the soufflé has risen and is golden brown.

Remove the dish from the oven and serve at once.

Zverovo Steamed Meat Loaf

This delicious meat loaf makes an economical and sustaining family meal. Serve with Brussels sprouts and a mixed salad.

4 SERVINGS

1½ lb. lean pork, minced [ground]
14 oz. canned peeled tomatoes, drained
4 oz. frozen green beans, thawed and drained
6 oz. small macaroni, cooked and drained
1 garlic clove, crushed
1 teaspoon salt
1 teaspoon black pepper
2 tablespoons tomato purée
½ teaspoon dried thyme
1 egg, lightly beaten
2 teaspoons butter

In a large mixing bowl, combine all the ingredients except the butter, beating well to blend.

Using 1 teaspoon of the butter, lightly grease a 2-pint [1½-quart] pudding basin. Spoon the mixture into the pudding basin — the mixture will not completely fill the basin but it will rise slightly during cooking.

Cut out a circle of greaseproof or waxed paper about 4-inches wider in diameter than the rim of the basin. Grease the paper with the remaining butter. Cut out a circle of aluminium foil the same size as the paper circle.

Put the greaseproof or waxed paper circle and the foil circle together, the buttered side of the greaseproof or waxed paper away from the foil and, holding them firmly together, make a 1-inch pleat across the centre. Place the pleated paper and foil circle, foil uppermost, over the pudding basin. With a piece of string,

---

A nourishing and economical family dish, Zverovo Steamed Meat Loaf should be served with lots of lager.

securely tie the paper and foil circle around the rim of the basin.

Place the basin in a large saucepan and pour in enough boiling water to come about two-thirds of the way up the sides of the basin. Cover the pan and place it over low heat. Steam the loaf for 2 hours, adding more boiling water as necessary.

When the loaf has finished steaming, lift the basin out of the water. Remove the foil and paper circles. Turn the loaf out on to a serving dish and serve.

Zvettl Wine Cream Soup

Sweet soups make a refreshing and unusual start to a dinner party and can also form part of a nourishing diet for invalids. Serve this soup with puff pastry crescents or Croûtons.

4 SERVINGS

4 fl. oz. [½ cup] water
8 fl. oz. [1 cup] white wine
2 tablespoons sugar

3 cloves
3 cinnamon sticks
8 fl. oz. single cream [1 cup light cream]
2 egg yolks, well beaten

Pour the water and wine into a large saucepan and add the sugar, cloves and cinnamon. Set the pan over moderate heat and bring the mixture to the boil. Reduce the heat to low and simmer for 10 minutes.

Meanwhile, in a small saucepan set over moderately low heat, heat the cream until it is hot but not boiling. Place the egg yolks in a soup tureen, remove the saucepan from the heat and pour the cream on to the egg yolks, stirring constantly.

Remove the pan containing the wine mixture from the heat and strain the liquid into the tureen, stirring constantly.

Delightful Zvettl Wine Cream Soup, flavoured with cinnamon, is sweet and makes a pleasant and unusual change as a start to a meal.

Discard the contents of the strainer.
Serve the soup at once.

Zvezdochki

RUSSIAN STAR-SHAPED BISCUITS [COOKIES]

Zvezdochki (svehz-dau-kee) *are delicious additions to a petits-fours tray or serve them as a snack with tea or coffee.*

36 BISCUITS [COOKIES]

4 eggs, well beaten
6 oz. [¾ cup] sugar
1 teaspoon vanilla essence
8 oz. [1 cup] unsalted butter, melted
12 oz. [3 cups] self-raising flour
1 teaspoon icing [confectioners'] sugar

Preheat the oven to moderate 350°F (Gas Mark 4, 180°C).

Place the eggs in a large mixing bowl and add the sugar and vanilla essence. Using a wire whisk, blend them together. Gradually add the butter, then fold in the

This tasty, unusual dish, Zwartberg Mountain Casserole is a meal in itself, served with lots of buttered rolls.

flour until the mixture becomes quite firm. Place the mixture in the refrigerator to chill for 1 hour.

Remove the mixture from the refrigerator. Turn the dough out on to a lightly floured board or marble slab and, using a floured rolling pin, roll out to ¼-inch thick.

Using a small star-shaped pastry cutter, cut out 36 dough shapes. Place the dough shapes on a baking sheet and place the sheet in the oven. Bake for 10 to 12 minutes or until the biscuits [cookies] are golden brown. Remove the sheet from the oven and, using a flat-bladed knife, transfer the biscuits [cookies] to a wire rack to cool slightly.

Sprinkle a little icing [confectioners'] sugar over the biscuits [cookies] to dust them lightly. Allow to cool completely.

Serve immediately or store in an airtight tin until required.

Zvolen Caraway Seed Soup with Dumplings

This most unusual Balkan soup makes a pleasant first course served with hot crusty rolls and butter.

4-6 SERVINGS

2 pints [5 cups] home-made beef stock
1½ tablespoons caraway seeds
1 oz. [2 tablespoons] butter
1 oz. [¼ cup] flour
2 fl. oz. [¼ cup] water
DUMPLINGS
1 egg, lightly beaten
3 tablespoons flour
½ teaspoon salt
½ teaspoon black pepper

Pour the stock and caraway seeds into a large saucepan and set the pan over high heat. Bring the stock to the boil. Reduce the heat to low and simmer for 30 minutes.

Meanwhile, make the dumplings. In a small bowl, using a fork, beat together the egg, flour, salt and pepper. The batter should be of a dropping consistency. Add a little more flour if it is too thin.

In a small saucepan, melt the butter over moderate heat. Remove the pan from the heat and, with a wooden spoon, stir in the flour to make a smooth paste. Gradually add the water, stirring constantly. Return the pan to the heat and cook, stirring constantly, for 2 to 3 minutes or until the sauce is smooth. Set aside.

Strain the stock into a large bowl, discarding the caraway seeds. Return the stock to the pan and stir in the sauce until it is well blended. Return the pan to low heat and, when the soup comes to the boil, add the dumpling batter, a teaspoon at a time. Simmer for 5 minutes. Remove the pan from the heat and pour the soup and dumplings into a warmed tureen. and serve at once.

Zwartberg Mountain Cassoulet

This is an excellent dish to serve as a winter main course. Italian boiling sausages can be bought at most Italian delicatessens.

8 SERVINGS

6 oz. salt pork, cut into 1-inch cubes
6 shallots, peeled
4 carrots, scraped and cut into 1-inch slices
bouquet garni, consisting of 4 parsley sprigs, 1 thyme spray and 1 bay leaf tied together
2 lb. dried green flageolet beans, soaked overnight and drained
1½ lb. Italian pepper boiling sausages
6 garlic cloves
1 teaspoon canned green peppercorns, drained
3 fl. oz. [⅜ cup] vegetable oil
8 fl. oz. [1 cup] dry white wine
1½ pints [3¾ cups] beef stock
2 tablespoons chopped fresh parsley

Preheat the oven to warm 325°F (Gas Mark 3, 170°C).

In a medium-sized flameproof casserole, fry the salt pork over moderate heat for 5 to 8 minutes or until it has rendered most of its fat. Add the shallots, carrots, bouquet garni, beans, sausages, garlic, peppercorns and vegetable oil.

Mix the ingredients together, then pour over the wine and beef stock. Bring the liquid to the boil and remove the casserole from the heat.

Cover the casserole and place it in the oven. Cook the mixture for 3 hours.

Remove the casserole from the oven. Remove and discard the bouquet garni. Sprinkle over the parsley and serve immediately.

Zwetschgenknödeln

PLUM DUMPLINGS

These sweet dumplings are a very popular German dessert. Serve Zwetschgenknödeln (zwet-shen-k'ner-del'n) with Crème à la Vanille.

4-6 SERVINGS

¼ oz. fresh yeast
2 tablespoons plus ¼ teaspoon sugar
3 tablespoons warm water
10 oz. [2½ cups] flour
2 teaspoons ground cinnamon
¼ teaspoon salt
4 fl. oz. [½ cup] lukewarm milk
1 oz. [2 tablespoons] butter, melted
12 small blue plums, halved and stones removed
3 tablespoons cinnamon sugar
COOKING LIQUID
1 oz. [2 tablespoons] butter
2 tablespoons sugar
4 fl. oz. [½ cup] milk

Crumble the yeast into a small bowl and mash in the ¼ teaspoon of sugar with a kitchen fork. Add the water and cream the water and yeast together. Set the bowl aside in a warm, draught-free place for 15 to 20 minutes or until the yeast mixture is puffed up and frothy.

Sift the flour, cinnamon, salt and remaining sugar into a warmed, large mixing bowl. Make a well in the centre and pour in the yeast, milk and melted butter. Using your fingers or a spatula, gradually draw the flour mixture into the liquid. Continue mixing until all the flour mixture is incorporated and the dough comes away from the sides of the bowl.

Turn the dough on to a lightly floured board or marble slab and knead it for about 5 minutes, reflouring the surface if the dough becomes too sticky. The dough should be elastic and smooth.

Rinse, thoroughly dry and lightly grease the large mixing bowl. Shape the dough into a ball and return it to the bowl. Cover the bowl with a clean, damp cloth and set it in a warm, draught-free place. Leave it for 1 hour or until the dough has risen and almost doubled in bulk.

Turn the risen dough out of the bowl on to a floured surface and knead it for about 4 minutes. Divide the dough into 12 equal pieces and roll out each piece into a small circle about 3-inches in diameter. Re-form whole plums with two halves and place one in the centre of each circle. Sprinkle over a little of the cinnamon sugar and enclose each plum completely with the dough.

Place the balls on a baking sheet, cover with a clean cloth and return the sheet to a warm place for 45 minutes to 1 hour or until the balls have almost doubled in size.

To prepare the cooking liquid, in a large saucepan, melt the butter over moderate heat. When the foam subsides, stir in the sugar and milk. Bring the liquid to the boil. Carefully place the dumplings in one layer in the pan.

Cover the pan tightly, reduce the heat to very low and simmer for 20 to 25 minutes or until the dumplings have absorbed all the liquid. Remove the pan from the heat. Transfer the dumplings to a warmed serving dish and serve at once.

Zwetschgenkuchen

PLUM FLAN

Zwetschgenkuchen (zwet-shen-koo-ken) is a plum flan from Germany. It is unlike most other fruit flans in that the pastry and the plums are baked together. Serve it either hot or cold with Crème à la Vanille or ice-cream. Blue plums are nearly always used in German cooking, but other varieties of plums may be substituted.

4-6 SERVINGS

1 x 9-inch Flan Case, made with rich shortcrust pastry, uncooked
2 lb. blue plums, halved and stones removed
6 oz. [¾ cup] castor sugar
1 teaspoon ground cinnamon
½ teaspoon ground allspice
2 oz. [½ cup] slivered almonds, toasted

Preheat the oven to fairly hot 400°F (Gas Mark 6, 200°C). Place the flan case on a baking sheet.

Arrange the plum halves decoratively, cut sides down, on the flan case and set aside.

In a small mixing bowl, combine the sugar, cinnamon and allspice. Sprinkle the sugar mixture evenly over the plums. Place the baking sheet in the oven and bake the flan for 35 to 40 minutes or until the pastry is crisp and golden and the plums are tender.

Remove the baking sheet from the oven, sprinkle the almonds over the plums and serve the flan at once if you are serving it hot, or set aside to cool completely if serving cold.

An excellent dessert to serve on any occasion Zwetschgenkucken is traditionally made with small blue plums but if these are not available other varieties may be used instead.

Zwickau Stuffed Fillet of Beef

Zwickau Stuffed Fillet of Beef is an unusual but delicious way of cooking beef, consisting of spicy continental sausage meat, mixed with mushrooms, cooked inside a flattened fillet of beef.
Home-made stock is an essential ingredient for this recipe and the time and effort involved in the preparation is well worth it for the end results.

6 SERVINGS

1 x 3 lb. fillet of beef
1 garlic clove
½ teaspoon salt
½ teaspoon freshly ground black pepper
3 bacon slices
6 fl. oz. [¾ cup] red wine
4 fl. oz. [½ cup] home-made beef stock
1 tablespoon beurre manié
STUFFING
1 tablespoon butter
2 oz. mushrooms, wiped clean and coarsely chopped
1 medium-sized spicy continental sausage, skinned
½ teaspoon salt
½ teaspoon freshly ground black pepper
1 egg yolk, lightly beaten
1 tablespoon chopped fresh parsley or 2 teaspoons dried parsley

Preheat the oven to very hot 450°F (Gas Mark 8, 230°C).

Place the beef on a working surface and, using a sharp knife, make two deep incisions down the middle of the meat, taking care not to cut right through. Using a rolling pin or wooden meat mallet, beat the beef until it has been flattened into an oblong shape. Rub the meat all over with the garlic clove, salt and pepper and set aside while you make the stuffing.

In a small frying-pan, melt the butter over moderate heat. When the foam subsides, add the mushrooms to the pan and fry for 2 to 3 minutes or until they are cooked.

Remove the pan from the heat and transfer the mushrooms to a medium-sized mixing bowl. Add the sausage meat, salt, pepper, egg yolk and parsley. Stir all the ingredients together until they are thoroughly combined.

Spoon the stuffing down the centre of the beef, fold the two edges of the beef over the stuffing and secure with cocktail sticks or trussing string to form a sausage shape.

Place the bacon slices over the beef and

secure the roll with trussing string.

Place the beef on a rack in a roasting tin and roast for 40 to 45 minutes or until the meat is tender when pierced with the point of a sharp knife.

When the meat is cooked, remove the roasting tin from the oven and, using two large forks, transfer the beef to a warmed serving plate. Remove and discard the string, bacon and cocktail sticks and keep the beef warm while you make the sauce.

Remove and discard the fat on the surface of the cooking juices remaining in the roasting tin. Pour the cooking juices into a medium-sized saucepan and place over moderate heat. Add the wine and stock to the pan, increase the heat to high and bring the mixture to the boil. Reduce the heat to low, add the beurre manié, a little at a time, and cook, stirring constantly, for a further 5 minutes or until the sauce has thickened.

Pour the sauce into a warmed sauceboat and serve immediately with the beef.

Zwickle Capon in Pastry

An elegant dinner party dish, Zwickle Capon in Pastry is attractive to present and marvellous to taste. Serve with sautéed potatoes and Broccoli with Almonds, and a chilled bottle of white wine, such as Liebfraumilch.

4-6 SERVINGS

1 x 5 lb. capon, roasted for 30 minutes and cooled
1 teaspoon salt
½ teaspoon freshly ground black pepper
1 lb. [2 cups] Duxelles
2 oz. [¼ cup] plus 1 tablespoon Beurre d'Ail, softened
8 slices prosciutto
10 oz. [2½ cups] Shortcrust Pastry 1

Preheat the oven to moderate 350°F (Gas Mark 4, 180°C).

Season the capon with the salt and pepper. Spoon the duxelles mixture into the cavity of the bird and close the opening with a needle and trussing string.

Using a sharp knife, separate the skin from the breast of the bird, being careful not to pierce the skin. Spread the 2 ounces [¼ cup] of beurre d'ail under the skin of the capon. Cover the capon with the slices of prosciutto. Set aside.

On a lightly floured surface, roll the dough out until it is approximately ⅛-inch thick. Place the capon in the centre of the dough and pull the dough over and around the bird so that it is

Zwieback Refrigerator Cheesecake is surprisingly simple to make.

completely encased.

Transfer the parcel to a large baking sheet. Brush the top of the dough with the remaining beurre d'ail.

Place the baking sheet in the centre of the oven and bake for 35 to 45 minutes or until the pastry is golden brown.

Remove the baking sheet from the oven. Transfer the capon to a warmed serving dish and serve immediately.

Zwieback

The word zwieback (*svee-bak*) in German means literally 'twice-baked' and, is the name given to a rusk-like sweet bread which may be bought, sliced, from most bakeries or delicatessen shops.

Zwieback Refrigerator Cheesecake

A delicious and easy-to-prepare cheesecake, Zwieback Refrigerator Cheesecake may be served as a dessert or as a snack with coffee or tea. It is also ideal for freezing — allow at least 3 hours to thaw out at room temperature before serving.

4-6 SERVINGS

14 zwieback, crushed
3 oz. [⅜ cup] butter, melted
½ teaspoon ground allspice
3 egg yolks
3 oz. [⅜ cup] castor sugar
¾ oz. gelatine, softened in 2 tablespoons hot water
1 lb. cream cheese
½ teaspoon vanilla essence
2 teaspoons grated lemon rind
15 fl. oz. [1⅞ cups] sour cream
8 oz. raspberries or blackberries, hulled and washed

In a large mixing bowl, combine the crushed zwieback, butter and allspice. Line the bottom of an 8-inch cake tin with a removable base with the mixture and place the tin in the refrigerator to chill for 30 minutes or until it is set.

In a medium-sized heatproof bowl, beat the egg yolks and sugar together with a wooden spoon until they are light and smooth. Place the bowl in a saucepan half-filled with hot water and set the pan over low heat. Cook the mixture, stirring constantly, for 5 minutes. Stir in the gelatine mixture and cook, stirring constantly, until the mixture has completely dissolved. Remove the pan from the heat and the bowl from the pan.

Place the cream cheese in a large mixing bowl and gradually add the egg mixture, stirring constantly and being careful to avoid lumps (if the mixture does go lumpy, push it through a strainer). Add the vanilla essence, lemon rind and sour cream and stir to blend thoroughly. Spoon the mixture into the cake tin, smoothing over the top with a knife.

Place the cake tin in the refrigerator and chill for 1 to 1½ hours or until the cheese mixture is set. Remove the tin from the refrigerator and remove the cake from the tin. Place the cake on a serving dish. Arrange the fruit decoratively over the top and serve.

Zwieback mit Rhabarber
RUSKS WITH RHUBARB

Zwieback mit Rhabarber (svee-bak mit ra-bar-bah) is a German dessert consisting of contrasting layers of crispy rusks, tart rhubarb and double [heavy] cream. It is very simple to make and may be prepared well in advance. If zwieback are not obtainable, rusks make a perfectly good substitute.

6 SERVINGS

An unusual combination of blackcurrants and zwieback make Zwieback mit Schwarzen Johannisberren that something special.

6 zwieback
1 lb. rhubarb, cooked and strained
10 fl. oz. double cream [1¼ cups heavy cream], stiffly whipped
1 tablespoon cinnamon sugar

Place the zwieback in a layer along the bottom of a serving dish. Spoon the rhubarb evenly over the zwieback. Spread the cream over the rhubarb with a flat-bladed knife.

Sprinkle the cinnamon sugar over the cream and place the dish in the refrigerator for 1 hour or until it is chilled.

Zwieback mit Schwarzen Johannisbeeren
RUSKS WITH BLACKCURRANTS

The combination of tart blackcurrants with crunchy zwieback is delicious. Serve Zwieback mit Schwarzen Johannisbeeren (svee-bak mit shvart-sen yo-hann-iss-beer-en) hot with lots of whipped cream.

4-6 SERVINGS

3 oz. [⅜ cup] plus 1 teaspoon butter, cut into small pieces
2 oz. [½ cup] flour
8 fl. oz. [1 cup] milk
3 egg yolks
2 tablespoons sugar
12 oz. canned blackcurrants, drained
3 egg whites, stiffly beaten
8 zwieback, crushed

With the teaspoon of butter, grease a 1½-pint [1-quart] ovenproof serving dish.

Preheat the oven to warm 325°F (Gas Mark 3, 170°C).

In a small saucepan, melt 2 ounces [¼ cup] of the butter over moderate heat. Remove the pan from the heat and, with a wooden spoon, stir in the flour to make a smooth paste. Gradually add the milk, stirring constantly. Return the pan to the heat and cook, stirring constantly, for 2 to 3 minutes or until the sauce is thick and smooth. Remove the pan from the heat and pour the sauce into a medium-sized mixing bowl.

With a fork, gradually beat the egg yolks and sugar into the sauce. Stir in the blackcurrants and, using a metal spoon, fold in the egg whites.

Spoon half of the blackcurrant mixture into the dish. Sprinkle half of the crushed zwieback over the blackcurrant mixture. Continue making layers in this way until all the ingredients are used up, finishing with a layer of zwieback.

Dot the remaining butter over the surface and place the dish in the oven. Bake for 40 to 45 minutes or until the top is crisp and golden brown.

Remove the dish from the oven and serve immediately.

Zwiebelfleisch
BEEF WITH ONIONS

Zwiebelfleisch (zwee-behl-flysh) is a traditional German dish of fried beef and onions. Although raw beef is more frequently used in this recipe, cooked beef is sometimes substituted. Serve Zwiebelfleisch with boiled potatoes and fresh green beans.

4 SERVINGS

1 oz. [2 tablespoons] butter
2 lb. fillet of beef, cut into strips
2 large onions, thinly sliced
1 garlic clove, crushed
½ teaspoon dried oregano
½ teaspoon salt

Zwiebelfleisch takes moments to prepare and tastes superb!

½ teaspoon black pepper
10 fl. oz. [1¼ cups] beef stock, hot
4 fl. oz. [½ cup] sour cream
1 tablespoon chopped fresh parsley

In a large, heavy-based frying-pan, melt the butter over moderate heat. When the foam subsides, add the beef to the pan and fry, turning occasionally, for 4 to 6 minutes or until it is lightly browned on all sides. Using a slotted spoon, remove the beef from the pan and set it aside on a plate.

Add the onions and garlic to the pan and fry, stirring occasionally, for 8 to 10 minutes or until the onions are golden brown.

Stir in the oregano, salt and pepper. Add the stock to the pan. Return the beef to the pan and bring the liquid to the boil. Reduce the heat to low and simmer for 8 to 10 minutes or until the beef is cooked and tender. Stir in the sour cream.

Remove the pan from the heat and transfer the contents to a warmed serving dish. Sprinkle the parsley over the top and serve immediately.

Zwiebelkuchen
GERMAN ONION TART

In Germany, Zwiebelkuchen (zwee-behl-koo-ken) is available hot, fresh from the bakers' shops. However, it is also delicious eaten cold with a tossed green salad.

4-6 SERVINGS

1 x 9-inch Flan Case, made with shortcrust pastry, baked blind and cooled
1 oz. [2 tablespoons] butter
3 medium-sized onions, thinly sliced
2 eggs, lightly beaten
6 fl. oz. single cream [¾ cup light cream]
1 teaspoon caraway seeds
1 teaspoon salt
½ teaspoon black pepper

Preheat the oven to fairly hot 375°F (Gas Mark 5, 190°C).

Place the flan case on a large baking sheet and set aside.

In a large frying-pan, melt the butter over moderate heat. When the foam subsides, add the onions and fry, stirring occasionally, for 5 to 7 minutes or until they are soft and translucent but not

Zyman Roast Beef is a relatively inexpensive dish which is perfect for a special family occasion.

brown. Remove the pan from the heat and set aside.

In a medium-sized mixing bowl, lightly beat the eggs and cream together with a fork. Stir in the caraway seeds, salt and pepper. Add the onions and mix well.

Pour the mixture into the flan case. Place the baking sheet in the centre of the oven and bake the tart for 35 to 40 minutes or until the filling has risen and is golden brown.

Remove the baking sheet from the oven. Transfer the tart to a serving dish and serve immediately, if you are serving it hot.

Zwingle Spaghetti with Crabmeat

This is a family dish with a difference, since the crabmeat gives the spaghetti a rather exotic flavour. Serve it with a tossed green salad.

4 SERVINGS

2 oz. [¼ cup] butter
2 onions, finely chopped
8 oz. mushrooms, wiped clean and sliced
8 oz. spaghetti, cooked, drained and kept hot
8 oz. crabmeat, shell and cartilage removed
10 oz. canned condensed tomato soup
1 teaspoon salt
½ teaspoon black pepper
6 oz. [1½ cups] Parmesan cheese, grated
10 fl. oz. [1¼ cups] tomato juice

With 2 teaspoons of the butter, grease a large, ovenproof casserole.

Preheat the oven to moderate 350°F (Gas Mark 4, 180°C).

In a medium-sized frying-pan, melt the remaining butter over moderate heat. When the foam subsides, add the onions and fry, stirring occasionally, for 4 minutes. Add the mushrooms and fry for a further 1 to 3 minutes or until the onions are soft and translucent but not brown. Remove the pan from the heat and set aside.

In a large mixing bowl, combine the mushroom and onion mixture with the spaghetti, crabmeat, soup, salt, pepper and 4 ounces [1 cup] of the cheese. Stir well to mix thoroughly, then pour in the tomato juice. Transfer the mixture to the prepared casserole and sprinkle over the remaining cheese.

Place the casserole in the oven and cook for 35 to 40 minutes or until the cheese is golden and bubbling.

Remove the casserole from the oven and serve at once.

Zwolle Orange Turkey

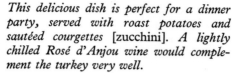

This delicious dish is perfect for a dinner party, served with roast potatoes and sautéed courgettes [zucchini]. A lightly chilled Rosé d'Anjou wine would complement the turkey very well.

8 SERVINGS

1 x 8 lb. turkey, oven-ready
3 oz. [⅜ cup] butter
2 small garlic cloves, crushed
finely grated rind of 1 orange
¼ teaspoon cayenne pepper
STUFFING:
2 tablespoons vegetable oil
2 medium-sized onions, finely chopped
1 lb. sausage meat
4 oz. [1⅓ cups] cooked rice
3 teaspoons finely grated orange rind
2 tablespoons brandy
1½ teaspoons salt
2 teaspoons black pepper
1 teaspoon dried thyme
2 eggs, lightly beaten
3 tablespoons sultanas or seedless raisins, soaked in orange juice for 20 minutes and drained

Preheat the oven to very hot 450°F (Gas Mark 8, 230°C).

First make the stuffing. In a medium-sized frying-pan, heat the oil over moderate heat. When the oil is hot, add the onions and fry, stirring occasionally, for 5 to 7 minutes or until they are soft and translucent but not brown. Stir in the sausage meat and fry, stirring frequently, for 5 minutes or until it loses its pinkness. Remove the pan from the heat and spoon the mixture into a large mixing bowl. Add all of the remaining stuffing ingredients to the bowl and stir to blend well.

Spoon the mixture into the stomach cavity of the turkey and secure the cavity with trussing needle and string or a skewer.

In a small mixing bowl, beat the butter, garlic, orange rind and cayenne together until they are thoroughly blended. Using a flat-bladed knife, spread the butter mixture over the turkey.

Place the turkey in a roasting tin and place the tin in the oven. Roast the turkey for 10 minutes. Reduce the oven temperature to warm 325°F (Gas Mark 3, 170°C) and continue roasting for a further 3 hours, basting occasionally. To test if the turkey is cooked, pierce the thigh with the point of a sharp knife, if the juices that run out are clear, the turkey is cooked.

Remove the tin from the oven. Remove and discard the string or skewer. Transfer the turkey and cooking juices to a warmed serving dish and serve at once.

Zyman Roast Beef

A fabulous dish for a special family meal, Zyman Roast Beef is delightful served with roast potatoes, minted peas and green beans.

8-10 SERVINGS

1 x 10 lb. aitchbone of beef
1 teaspoon salt
1 teaspoon black pepper
1 tablespoon beurre manié
2 tablespoons double [heavy] cream
MARINADE
4 garlic cloves, crushed
1 large onion, finely chopped
1 lb. mushrooms, wiped clean and thinly sliced
8 fl. oz. [1 cup] Madeira
8 fl. oz. [1 cup] red wine

Season the beef with the salt and black pepper. Set aside.

In a large roasting tin, combine the garlic, onion, mushrooms, Madeira and wine. Place the beef in the tin and set aside in a cool place to marinate for 24 hours, basting occasionally.

Preheat the oven to hot 425°F (Gas Mark 7, 220°C).

Place the roasting tin in the centre of the oven and braise for 20 minutes. Reduce the heat to moderate 350°F (Gas Mark 4, 180°C) and braise for a further 2½ hours. This will produce rare beef; braise for a further 30 minutes for well-done beef. Remove the tin from the oven and transfer the beef to a warmed serving dish. Set aside and keep warm while you finish the sauce.

Strain the contents of the roasting tin into a medium-sized saucepan. Discard the contents of the strainer. Place the pan over high heat and bring the mixture to the boil. Boil for 10 minutes or until the mixture has reduced by one-third. Reduce the heat to low and stir in the beurre manié, a little at a time. Cook for a further 2 to 3 minutes or until the sauce is smooth and fairly thick. Stir in the cream.

Remove the pan from the heat and pour the sauce into a warmed sauceboat. Serve immediately, with the beef.

Zyrenia Noodle and Prune Bake

An unusual, warming pudding for a cold winter's day, Zyrenia Noodle and Prune Bake may be served with lots of whipped cream. Apricots may be substituted for the prunes if you prefer a slightly sharper flavour.

4-6 SERVINGS

2 oz. [¼ cup] butter, cut into small pieces

6 oz. wide noodles or lasagne, cooked in unsalted water and drained

1 lb. prunes, stoned, stewed and cooking liquid reserved

4 oz. [½ cup] sugar

1 tablespoon ground cinnamon

3 oz. [1 cup] dried breadcrumbs or 2 oz. [1 cup] fresh breadcrumbs

Preheat the oven to moderate 350°F (Gas Mark 4, 180°C).

An unusual combination of pasta and prunes. Zyrenia Noodle and Prune Bake is a delicious dessert which may be served hot or cold.

With 2 teaspoons of the butter, grease a deep, ovenproof baking dish. Lay one-third of the noodles in the dish and cover with one-quarter of the remaining butter and half the prunes. In a small bowl, combine the sugar and cinnamon and sprinkle half the mixture over the prunes. Continue making layers in this way, ending with a layer of noodles. Pour the reserved prune juice over the mixture and sprinkle over the breadcrumbs and the remaining butter.

Place the dish in the oven and bake for 20 to 30 minutes or until the breadcrumbs are golden brown. Remove the dish from the oven and serve immediately.

Supercook

Indexes

Marshall Cavendish London & New York

The Indexes

How to Use the Index

The Index is divided for your convenience into three completely separate sections. **The General Index** (page 3083) acts as a simple page reference listing all the recipes in alphabetical order. **The Thematic Index** (page 3113) lists the recipes under classified headings such as Meat, Soups, Salads etc. (A page guide to these main entries is provided). This Index serves as a handy reference when planning a dinner party—you can see at a glance what starters, main courses and desserts are offered in Supercook. **The International Index** (page 3163) provides a reference to the recipes according to their country and/or area of origin. The origins of many dishes are often difficult to determine accurately. Sometimes recipes originate in one place but are popularised in another, with the result that the latter becomes the commonly held place of origin. In such instances the classification used here is the *most commonly held* view.

For example: Hungarian Fish Soup **8**–990

is listed in the General Index under "H"; the Thematic Index under "Soups" and the International Index under "Hungary".

All references in the index indicate both the volume number in bold type and then the page number in normal type.

Thus the example: Hungarian Fish Soup **8**–990 indicates that the recipe is to be found on page 990 in Volume 8.

General Index

A

Abalone Chinese-Style **1**–1
Abbacchio Brodettato **1**–3
Adam and Eve Pudding **1**–4
Adrak Chutney **1**–4
Agneau à la Bonne Femme **1**–5
   en Brochette **1**–5
   à la Hongroise **1**–**6**
   aux Tomates **1**–6
Agurkai su Rukescia Grietne **1**–6
Agurkesalat **1**–7
Aïgo Bouïdo **1**–7
Aïgo Sau **1**–8
Aiguillette de Boeuf **1**–9
Aillade **1**–9
Aïoli *see* Alioli Sauce
Ajja **1**–9
Albóndigas **1**–9
   Soup **1**–10
Ale Berry **1**–10
   Posset **1**–11
Alebele **1**–10
Alexander Torte **1**–11
Alioli Sauce **1**–12
Alivenci **1**–12
Allemande Sauce **1**–12
Allspice Veal Roll **1**–14
Allumettes **1**–17
Almejas à la Marinera **1**–17
Almond (*info*) **1**–20
   Apples **1**–20
   Biscuits **6**–785
   Black Cherry Aspic Salad, and **1**–20
   Blanched **1**–18
   Broccoli, with **2**
   Cakes **1**–129
   Cherry Cake **1**–20
   Chicken **1**–20
   Chocolate Cake **3**–404
   Cookies **1**–21
   Crabmeat, with **4**–472
   Cream Soup **20**–2661
   Cream with Strawberries **3**–359
   Crêpes **4**–496
   Crescent Biscuits **10**–1298
   Crunchies **1**–21
   Cucumber Salad Dressing, and **1**–22
   Curry Sauce **1**–22
   Custard Sauce **1**–23
   Filling **6**–739
   Italian Cheese Pudding **8**–1036
   Layer Cake **10**–1298
   Meringue Cake **4**–554
   Pastry **14**–1827
   Soufflé **17**–2352
   Sweets **5**–658; **19**–2580
Almondine Sauce **1**–23
Almundigoes *see* Albóndigas
Alouettes sans Têtes **1**–24
Alu Makhala **8**–1089
Ambrosia **1**–25
Anchovy (*info*) **1**–29
   Butter **1**–29

Garlic Dip **1**–105
Hors d'Oeuvre **1**–29
Niçoise **1**–30
Rolls **1**–29
Anchoyade **1**–29
   à la Niçoise **1**–30
Andalousian Beefsteaks **1**–30
   Chicken **1**–31
Angelica Candies **1**–32
   Tart **1**–32
Angélique Confite **1**–32
Angel Cake **1**–32
Angels on Horseback **1**–32
Anguilla Marinate **1**–34
Anguilles au Vert **1**–34
Anise Fork Biscuits **1**–35
Aniseed Carrots **1**–35
Apfelbettelmann **1**–38
Apfelkuchen **1**–38
Apfelstrudel **1**–38
Äppel-Fläsk **1**–40
Äppelformar **1**–40
Apple (*info*) **1**–20
   Almond **1**–20
   Amber **1**–41
   Apricot Dessert **14**–1862
   Aspic **1**–80
   Bacon, with *see* Äppel-Fläsk
   Baked **1**–42
   Baked in Brandy and Vermouth **14**–1864
   Batter Pudding **7**–855
   Bread Pudding **1**–42
   Bristol **1**–42
   Brown Betty **1**–43
   Burgundy Wine, with **14**–1862
   Butter **1**–43
   Caramel Mould **14**–1864
   Charlotte **1**–44
   Chutney **4**–422
   Cucumber Salad, and **1**–45
   Drink, Hot **7**–972
   Dumplings **1**–45
   Flambé **1**–47
   Florentine **1**–46
   Fritters **1**–47
   German *see* Apfel
   Hat **1**–48
   Hungarian **8**–987–8
   Meringue Topping, with **14**–1864
   Mousse à la Chantilly **1**–48
   Omelet **12**–1583
   Pancakes **1**–45
   Pie **1**–26, 40, 48
   Pork Casserole, and **1**–48
   Potato Stuffing, and **1**–49
   Rice Flan, and **14**–1864
   Rice Pudding, and **1**–49
   Sauce **1**–50
   Scandinavian Almond **17**–2272
   Snow **1**–50
   Sonning **1**–50
   Soup **21**–2900
   Sponge Pudding, and **1**–4
   Strudel **1**–38, 133

Turnovers **1**–51
Applesauce Cake **1**–50
Apricot (*info*) **1**–51
   Bars **5**–577
   Bourdaloue Tart **1**–52
   Brandy, in **1**–52
   Cake **6**–783
   Condé **1**–52
   Gammon, with **1**–57
   Glaze **1**–57
   Granville **1**–54
   Jam **1**–54
   Jam with Almonds **1**–56
   Liqueur **9**–1243
   Loaf **14**–1958
   Pudding **1**–56
   Salad **1**–56
   Tart **1**–57, 126
   Water Ice **17**–2349
Arabian Stewed Lamb **1**–59
Aragosta Fra Diavolo **1**–59
Aranygaluska **1**–59
Arbroath Smokies **1**–3
Archbishop Punch **1**–60
Ardei cu Untdelemn **1**–60
   Umplutzi cu Orez **1**–61
Armenian Dried Fruit Dessert **9**–1148
Arnavut Cigeri **1**–62
Arni Psito **1**–62
Arroz con Pollo **1**–65
Artichoke (*info*) **1**–66
   Boiled **1**–66
   Braised with Mixed Vegetables **1**–69
   Dill Sauce, with **1**–69
   à la Grecque **1**–70
   Hearts à l'Allemande **1**–73
   Hearts in Butter **1**–73
   Hearts with Cream **6**–731
   Hearts with Herbs **1**–74
   Hearts, Marinated **21**–2946
   Heart, Salad **16**–2210
   Heart Soufflé **1**–68
   Heart with Vegetables and Ham **6**–732
   à la Provençale **1**–70
   Stuffed with Pork and Almonds **1**–70
   Stuffed with Prawns and Mayonnaise **1**–72
   Veal and Peppers, with **1**–72
Ashe Reste **1**–74
Asparagus (*info*) **1**–75
   au Beurre **1**–75
   Cream Soup **1**–76
   Eggs, with **1**–76
   au Gratin **1**–76
   Hot, with Orange **20**–2736
   Polonaise **1**–78
   Quiche **15**–2022
   Sour Cream, with **1**–78
   Timbale **1**–78
Aspic **1**–79
   Apple **1**–80
   Avocado **1**–92
   Basil and Tomato **1**–127
   Braised Beef **2**–202
   Chicken Liver **3**–396

Asynpoeding 1–81
Athenian Walnut Cake 1–81
Atholl Brose 1–82
Aubergine (*info*) 1–82
  Basquaise 5–635
  Boston 5–635
  Brazilian 2–238
  Casserole 5–636
  Curried *see* Bharta; Turkari Baingan;
    Wengyachen
  Farcies 1–82
  Fiesta 5–636
  Flan 5–636
  Fritters 1–83
  Gratinées 1–84
  Grilled 1–84
  Hors d'Oeuvres 11–1482; 16–2160
  Hungarian Style 5–637
  Mustard Dressing 11–1478
  New Haven Baked 11–1498
  Parmesan 5–638
  Pizza 14–1830
  Rice, with 20–2762
  Salad 1–85
  Sautéed 1–86
  Shrimps, with 11–1526
  Soufflé 1–86
  Stuffed *see* Dolma
  Sweet and Sour Sauce, in 3–318
  Tomatoes and Onions, with 8–1016
  à la Tunisienne 1–87
  à la Turque 1–87
  Vol au Vent 20–2717
Augolemono Soup 1–88
Aurore Sauce 1–88
Austrian Boiled Beef 1–89
  Cabbage 1–89
  Cherry Strudel 9–1149
  Coffee Cake 1–89
  Iced Blackberry Soup 8–1101
  Jam Doughnuts 1–89
  Pudding 1–90
  Yeast Cake 7–893
Aviyal 1–91
Avocado (*info*) 1–92
  Aspic 1–92
  Chicken Soup 1–92
  Chicken Supreme 1–92
  Courgette Salad, and 1–92
  Dip 1–94; 7–889
  Herb Salad Dressing 1–94
  Ice-Cream 14–1936
  Jellied Consommé, with 1–94
  Salt Cod, with 22–3011
  Soup 1–95
Azerbaijan Pilaff 1–95

B

Baba aux Fraises 1–98
  au Rhum 1–98
Bacalhau 1–98
Bacon (*info*) 1–98
  Apples and Onions, with 1–40
  Baked 1–102
  Boiled 1–102
  Dumplings 1–102
  Egg Pie, and 1–102
  Liver Rolls, and 1–103
  Whole-Wheat Scones 1–103
Badami Gosht 1–104
Badminton Cup 1–105
Bagna Cauda 1–105
Baked Alaska 1–105
Bakewell Tart 1–107
Baking Powder Biscuits 1–107
Balkan Champagne Cup 1–108
  Chicken Pilaff 1–108
Baltimore Stuffing 12–1653
Bamboo Shoots with Mushrooms 1–108
  Pork, with 1–109
Banana (*info*) 1–109
  Baked 1–110; 8–1022
  Baked in Orange Juice 1–110

  Baked with Custard 1–110
  Beauharnais 1–110
  Brazil Nut Cake 2–239
  Caribbean 1–110
  Cream Pie 1–110
  Creole 1–112
  Fried 1–113
  Fritters 1–113
  Ice-Cream 22–3018
  Italian 8–1035
  Orange, with 1–113
  Pudding 1–113
  Raspberry Cream, and 1–114
  Sherry, with 1–114
  Teabread 21–2913
  Walnut Loaf 1–114
Banbury Cakes 1–115
Banghali Polo 1–105
Bangra Masala 1–115
Baps 1–116
Bara Brith 1–116
Barbecue Sauce 1–117
Barbecued Beef, Chinese Style 1–117
  Chicken 1–117
  Duck 1–117
  Fish 1–119
  Lamb 1–119
  Pork 1–120
  Prawns 1–120
  Shrimps 1–120
  Spareribs 1–121
  Veal Chops 1–122
Barley Bread 1–122
  Country Soup 1–123
  Mushroom Casserole, and 1–125
  Vegetable Soup 9–1176
Barm Brack 1–125
Barquettes aux Abricots 1–126
Basil Baked Tomatoes 1–127
  Tomato Aspic, and 1–127
Bass Baked in Lemon and Mushroom Sauce
  1–128
  Braised 2–228
Batatas à Portuguêsa 1–128
Bath Buns 1–128
  Chap 1–128
Bâtonnets aux Amandes 1–129
Battenberg Cake 1–129
Batter Pudding 1–131
  Crêpe 4–494
Bauernsuppe 1–133
Bavarian Chocolate Cream 1–134
  Cream 1–133; 10–1323
  Cream, with Caramelized Almonds 1–135
  Cream, with Marrons Glacé 1–135
  Orange Cream 1–135
  Strudel 1–133
Bavarois 1–133
  au Chocolat 1–134
  Clermont 1–135
  à l'Orange 1–135
  Praline 1–135
Bean (*info*) 1–136
  Bacon Soup, and 1–638
  Baked, Italian-Style 5–668
  Boston Baked 2–212
  Broad 2–263
  Brown, Egyptian 5–638
  Butter 3–281
  Curd and Crabmeat 1–139
  French *see* French Beans
  Green *see* Green Beans
  Kidney *see* Kidney Beans
  Lima *see* Lima Beans
  Red *see* Red-Bean
  Refried *see* Frijoles Refritos
  Runner *see* Runner Bean
  Salad 1–139
  Spanish, and Sausage Soup 5–668
  Soup 2–179
  Vegetable Soup, and 12–1632
Bean Sprout (*info*) 1–139
  Ginger, with 1–140
  Green Peppers, with 1–140
  Salad 1–140

Béarnaise Sauce 2–141
Béchamel Sauce 2–141
Beef *see also* Boeuf; Entrecote; Steak
  (*info*) 2–142
  Austrian Boiled 1–89
  Barbecued, Chinese Style 1–117
  Bean Casserole, and 2–144
  Boiled 2–191; 2–205
  Boiled and Dumplings 2–205
  Boiled Italian, Chicken and Sausage 2–206
  Boiled, Lemon Sauce, with 16–2124
  Braised 2–229; 5–662, 663
  Braised, in Red Wine 10–1306
  Braised Ribs of 2–230
  Braised Round of 2–230
  Brazil 2–146
  Brisket with Jelly 2–262
  Burgers 2–279
  Cabbage, with 2–146
  Capers, with 2–146
  Casserole 2–147
  Cheese Roll, and 2–147
  Chick Peas, with 2–148
  Clove Casserole, and 6–817
  Coffee and Wine Sauce, in 2–146
  Collops 4–440
  Curry 5–579
  Dumplings 2–148; 2–205
  Goulash, Hungarian 2–204
  Ground Rice, in 10–1368
  Indonesian, in Cheese Sauce 8–1022
  Leg of, in Fruit Sauce 9–1170
  Loaf 2–149
  Madeira Casserole, and 2–149
  Marinated 20–2738
  Marjoram Ring 2–150
  Minced Pie, Spicy 2–190
  Minced in Red Wine Sauce 2–169
  Olives, with 2–150
  Piquant 13–1819
  Planters' 14–1840
  Pork Stew, and 8–1061
  Potato Curry, and 6–823
  Red-Cooked with Star Anise 8–986
  Red Wine, in 18–2429
  Ribbons 15–2108
  Rice Stew, and 5–573
  Roll 2–150
  Roll, German stuffed 16–2173
  Roll, Grilled 2–226
  Roll in Piquant Sauce 13–1793
  Roll, Stuffed 1–24
  Roll Stuffed with Anchovies 12–1639
  Roll Stuffed with Bacon 12–1565
  Roll, Stuffed in Mushroom Sauce 22–3021
  Roll with Tomato Sauce 11–1419
  Sauerkraut Rolls, and 11–1494
  Sliced, Quick-fried with Oyster Sauce 7–923
  Sour Cream Sauce, in 2–151
  Spiced Lemon and Caper Sauce, with 2–151
  Spices, with 19–2600
  Stew 2–153, 154; 8–1100
  Stew, with Dumplings 6–780
  Stew, Sweet and Sour 5–660
  Stew, with Tomatoes, Mushrooms and
    Olives 4–547
  Stir-fried, with Broccoli 18–2412
  Stock 2–154
  Stroganov 2–154
  Tea 2–154
  Tomato Pie, and 2–155
  Wellington 2–156
Beefsteak and Kidney Pudding 2–152
Beer Soup 2–157
  Vegetable Soup, and 12–1568
Beetroot (*info*) 1–158
  Apple Salad, and 2–158
  Boiled 2–158
  Cream Sauce, with 2–158
  Harvard 7–932
  Jellied Soup 8–1064
  Onion Salad, and 2–159
  Orange Salad, and 2–159
  Orange Sauce, in 2–159
  Pickled 8–1026

Pickles 2–159
Piquante 2–160
Soup Ukrainian 2–211
Sour Cream, in 2–160
Beignets, d'Ananas 2–160
au Fromage 2–160
Soufflé 2–160
Belgian Chicken Stew 20–2749
Fish Stew 20–2747
Bergamot Sauce 2–162
Bergens Fiskesuppe 2–162
Berlin Stew 2–162
Berliner Eintopf 2–162
Berry Soup 9–1128
Torte 2–163
Besugo al Horno 2–164
Beurre d'Ail 2–164
Bercy 2–164
au Citron 2–164–6
composée 2–164
de Crevettes à Froid 2–166
de Crustacées 2–166
d'Estragon 2–166
Marchand de Vins 2–166
de Moutarde 2–166
Nantais 2–167
Noir 2–167
à l'Oeuf 2–167
Bharta 2–168
Bien me Sabe de Coco 2–171
Bife à Portuguesa 2–168
Biff à la Lindström 2–169
Bifteck Haché au Vin Rouge 2–169
Marchand de Vins 2–170
Sauté Bercy 2–170
Sauté au Beurre 2–171
Bigos 8–993
Bircher Muesli 2–172
Bird's Nest Soup 2–172
Chicken and Mushroom, with 6–735
Birnbrot 2–172
Birnensuppe 2–173
Biryani 2–174
Biscuit Crust 2–175
Bishop's Bread 2–176
Bisque d'Homard 2–176
Bistecca alla Fiorentina 2–177
alla Pizzaiola 2–177
Bitkis 2–178
Bitokes 2–178
Black Bun 13–1696
Black-Bean Casserole 2–178
Smoked Meats, with 5–683
Soup 2–178
Blackberry see also Bramble
Apple Pie, and 2–180
Bounce 2–180
Fool 2–180
Iced Soup 8–1101
Black-Bottom Parfait 2–181
Pie 2–182
Blackcurrant and Apple Pie 5–573
Gin 20–2694
Liqueur 9–1248
Black-Forest Cherry Cake 2–182
Black-Pepper Cookies 2–184
Blanquette de Veau 2–184
Blinis 2–186
Bloody Mary 2–186
Blotake 2–186
Blueberry Crumble 2–188
Muffins 2–188
Blumenkohlsuppe 2–188
Bobtie 2–190
Boerenkaas Soep 2–190
Boeuf Bouilli à la Diable 2–191
Bouilli Froid à la Parisienne 2–191
Bourgeois 2–193
Bourguignonne 2–193
Braisé Prince Albert 2–194
à la Catalane 2–196
Chinois 2–197
à la Cuillère 2–197
Daniell 2–198
en Daube 2–198

Martignes 2–200
à la Mode 2–200
Printanier 2–202
à la Russe 2–203
à la Vinaigrette 2–203
Bogrács Gulyás 2–204
Bolivian Cream 10–1305
Bollito Misto 2–206
Bolognese Sauce 2–206
Bombe Coppelia 2–206
Framboises 2–208
Marie-Claire 2–208
Bookmaker's Sandwich 2–209
Borani Esfanaj 2–209
Bordelaise Sauce 2–210
Bordure de Pommes de Terre 2–210
Boston Baked Beans 2–212
Brown Bread 2–212
Boti Kebabs 2–212
Bouchées aux Fruits de Mer 2–218
au Jambon 2–219
Newburg 2–219
Parmentier au Fromage 2–219
Bouillabaisse 2–220
de Cabillaud 2–222
Bouillon 2–222
Boules de Neige au Chocolat 2–223
Bourbon-glazed Ham 2–224
Bourride 2–225
Boxty 2–225
Bracinolia di Manzo 2–226
Ripiene 2–226
Brain (info) 2–227
Baked with Eggs 2–227
Breaded 2–228
Butter, in 2–227
Bramborové Knedliky 2–233
Bramble Jelly 2–232
Bramborova Polevka 2–233
Bran Nut Muffins 2–233
Brandied Cherries 2–233
Peaches 13–1712
Brandy Alexander Pie 2–234
Butter 2–235
Cocktail 2–236
Egg Cake 13–1693
Peach 13–171
Punch 2–236
Snaps 2–236
Bratwurst in Sour Cream Sauce 2–237
Brawn 2–238
Brazilian Aubergines 2–238
Black Beans and Smoked Meats 5–683
Macaroons 2–236
Rice 2–239
Swiss Roll 2–239
Brazil Nut Banana Cake 2–239
Cake 2–240
Chive Spread 2–240
Piecrust 2–240
Stuffing 2–240
Bread, Bara Brith 1–116
Bishop's 2–176
Butter Pudding, and 2–250
Genoese 12–1670
German Dried Fruit 8–996
Honey Dessert, and 19–2523
Middle-Eastern 14–1826
Mozzarella 8–1038
Name-Day 9–1172
Plaited 18–2424
Quick 2–247; 15–2026
Salad 5–678
Sauce 2–251
Soda 8–1031; 11–1496, 1520; 17–2336
Sourdough 16–2236; 17–2361
Sticks 2–252
Swedish Rye 2–248
Sweet 2–249
Wheat Germ 20–2775
Wholewheat 2–250
Breadcrumb Dumplings 2–251
Stuffing 2–251
Breaded Swordfish Steaks with Piquant Tomato
Sauce 8–1018

Breakfast Buns 2–253
Bream (info) 2–253
Baked, with Potatoes 2–164
Bananas, with 4–548
Fennel in White Wine, with 4–549
Rice, with 4–550
Stuffed, with Spinach 4–548
Tomatoes, with 4–550
Brèdes de Chou 2–253
de Cresson 2–253
Bremen Sweet Bread 2–254
Bremer Küchen 2–254
Bridge Rolls 2–254
Brie Cheese Croquettes 2–256
Brill with Aubergine 2–256
Courgette, with 2–257
à la Duglére 2–258
Brioche 2–258
aux Fraises avec Moussades Framboises
2–260
Mousseline 2–262
Strawberries and Raspberry Cream Filling,
with 2–260
Brisket of Beef with Jelly 2–262
Broad Beans à la Crème 2–263
Soup 2–263
Vinaigrette 2–263
Broccoli (info) 2–264
Almonds, with 2–264
Black Olives, with 2–264
Capers, with 2–264
Cheese Sauce, with 2–265
Chinese-Style 2–265
Cream Soup 14–1916
Green Peppers, with 2–265
à la Polonaise 2–266
Purée 15–1990
Salad 2–264
Soufflé 2–266
Brochettes Amalti 2–267
Italiennes 2–267
de Porc 2–267
de Rognons et Foie de Monton 2–268
de Veau aux Champignons 2–268
Brodet Dubrovna 2–269
Bronx Cocktail 2–269
Brown Baked Potato Slices 2–276
Butter Sauce 2–267
Chaudfroid Sauce 2–269
Chicken Fricassée 2–270
Sauce Diable 2–271
Sauce, with Red Wine and Shallots 17–2246
Stock 2–272
Sugar Tart 2–272
Browned Baked Eggs 7–922
Brownies 2–270
Brunswick Stew 2–272
Brussels Sprouts 2–272
Bacon, with 2–273
Chestnuts, with 2–275
Creole 2–275
Grapes, with 2–275
Ham, with 2–275
Mould 2–275
Polanaise 2–276
Bubble and Squeak 2–277
Bublanina 2–277
Buchteln 2–278
Buckwheat Stew 8–1112
Burbridge Pudding 7–891
Burgers in Red Wine 2–279
Butter, Apple 1–43
Biscuits 3–281
Brandy 2–235
Coconut Biscuits 3–281
Cream 4–488
Sauces 2–164–7
Butter-Beans Ménagère 3–281
Buttercream Icing 3–282
Orange 4–554
Buttermilk Doughnuts 3–282
Pie 3–283
Scones 3–283
Butterscotch 3–284
Brownies 2–270

C

Cabbage (info) 3–284
  Beef-Stuffed 2–203
  Braised in Stock 3–284
  Brèdes 2–253
  Cheese 3–416
  Kärdia 8–1107
  Lamb Hot-Pot, and 3–285
  Orange Juice, in 3–284
  Penang 13–1734
  Pepper Salad, and 3–286
  Pineapple Salad 3–286
  Potato Soup with Sausage, and 3–299
  Red-Braised 8–986
  Rolls 3–286
  Rolls, Stuffed 7–846
  Salad 3–286
  Sausage Casserole, and 3–287
  Soup 3–287
  Sour Cream, in 3–288
  Sour-Sweet 3–342
  White Wine, in 3–288
Cabillaud à la Boulangère 3–288
  Gratiné 3–288
  Provençal 3–289
Cabinet Pudding 3–290
Caesar Salad 3–290
Café Brûlot 3–292
Cailles avec Raisins en Timbale 3–292
Calàmares en su Tinta 3–296
Calamari Ripeni 3–296
Calderete de Jerez 3–297
Caldo de Congrio 3–297
  Haba 3–298
  Tlalpeño 3–298
  Verde 3–299
Calf's Brains Braised 3–349
  Purée in Scallop Shells 8–1098
Calf's Foot Jelly 3–300
  Tuscan Style 21–2974
Calf's Liver with Apples and Onion Rings 3–300
  Cream Sauce, with 8–1099
  Devilled 4–558
  Mustard and Cream Sauce, with 3–300
  Parmesan Cheese, with 5–680
  Sauté 3–301
  Storganov, Zubov 22–3025
  Tomatoes, Mushrooms and Onions, with 5–680
  Tyrolean Style 18–2503
  Wine, with 5–680
Calf's Tongue with Madeira Sauce 12–1548
  Slices with Mushroom Sauce 8–1099
Camembert Biscuits 6–784
  Croquettes 3–303
Canapés du Crab 3–303
  des Crevettes 3–303
  aux Ecrivisses 3–304
  aux Epinards 3–304
  Piquants 3–304
  aux Sardines 3–305
Canard Braisé avec Choucroute 3–306
  Braisé au Chou Rouge 3–306
  à l'Orange 3–307
Canary Island Chicken 3–308
  Pudding 3–308
Candied Angelica 1–32
  Fruits 3–309
Caneton à l'Alsacienne 3–311
  aux Cerises 3–309
  aux Navets 3–310
Canja 3–311
Cannelloni 3–312
  con Pollo e Prosciutto 3–313
  di Manzo e Spinace 3–313
Cantaloup Surprise 3–314
Cantonese Roast Pork 3–314; 17–2296
Cape ai Ferri 3–315
Cape-Cod Salad 3–315
Caper Sauce 3–316
Capon with Mushrooms and Bacon 8–1105
  8–1105

Pastry, in 22–3074
  Russian Style 3–316
Caponata 3–318
Caramel 3–319, 320
  Apricots 3–320
  Custard 4–490
  Icing 3–320
  Pudding 8–1100
  Sauce 3–320
  -Topped Cake 19–2526
Caragheen 8–1030
Caraway Knots 3–320
  Potatoes 9–1179
  Seed Biscuits 3–322
  Seed Soup with Dumplings 22–3071
  Seed Sponge Cake 3–322
Carbonnade de Boeuf à la Flamande 3–323
  à la Provençale 3–324
Cardamom Biscuits 3–324
  Honey Dressing 3–325
Carottes à l'Algerienne 3–327
  aux Champignons 3–328
  à la Crème 3–328
  au Neige 3–328
  au Raisins 3–328
  Vichy 3–329
Carp (info) 3–329
  Baked 18–2509
  Black Sauce, with 3–329
  Jewish-Style 8–1109
  Paprika Sauce, in 8–1108
  Red Wine Sauce, with 3–326
  Steamed in White Wine 12–1656
  White Wine, in 3–326
Carpe Mâtelote 3–326
Carpetbag Steak 3–330
Carré d'Agneau au Cidre 3–331
Carrot (info) 3–331
  Bacon, and 3–337
  Baked Puréed 3–328
  Braised in Butter and Cream Sauce 3–328
  Cake 3–332
  Flan 6–721
  Glazed 3–328
  Halva 6–781
  Mushrooms, with 3–328
  Onions, with 3–332
  Onions with Raisins in Wine Sauce, and 3–328
  Radish Salad, and 3–333
  Soufflé 3–333
  Soup 3–333; 14–1918
Cassata alla Siciliana 3–334
Cassolettes de Carottes au Jambon 3–337
Cassoulet Gascogne 3–336
  de Languedoc 3–335
Catalan Fish Soup 3–337
  Sole 9–1233
  Soup 5–658
Castilian Omelet 3–338
  Soup 3–339
Cat's Tongue Biscuits 9–1207
Cauliflower (info) 3–339
  Cheese 3–339
  Cream Soup 14–1917
  Italian Sauce, with 3–339
  Loaf 12–1658
  Mexicana 3–340
  Mustard Sauce, with 3–340
  Polonaise 3–340
  Salad 3–340
  Shrimp Sauce, with 3–418
  Soup 2–188
  Spicy 7–843
  Tomatoes and Cheese, with 3–417
  Vinaigrette 3–341
Caviar, Red Dip 15–2078
  Sour Cream Soup, and 21–2897
Cavolo in Agrodolce 3–342
Celeriac (info) 3–342
  Braised 3–342
  Salad 3–343
  Stuffed 3–343
Celeri-rave Braisé 3–343
  à la Paysanne 3–343

Vinaigrette 3–343
Céleris Amandines 3–344
  Braisés au Lard 3–344
  à la Grecque 3–344
Celery (info) 3–344
  Almonds, with 3–344
  Bacon, with 3–345
  Braised 3–345
  Creamed 3–346
  Far East 5–675
  Fritters 3–346
  Fruit Salad 17–2286
  Greek Style 3–344
  Jugged 8–1085
  Red Caviar, with 3–346
  Tarragon, with 3–346
  Vinaigrette 3–347
Cenci 3–347
Cerdo à la Aragonesa 3–348
Cervelles Braisés 3–349
Cevap 3–348
Cevapcici 3–348
Ceviche 3–350
Cha Chang Mein 10–1369
Chablis Chicken 3–377
Chamonix 3–350
Champ 3–351
Champagne Chicken 3–353
  Cup, Balkan 1–108
  Punch 8–110
  Soup 22–3013
Champignons au Beurre 3–353
  à Blanc 3–353
  Fareis 3–354
  Grillés 3–354
  au Madère 3–354
  Pyramide 3–355
  Sautés à la Crème 3–355
Channa Dhal 3–356
Chao-Chieh-Ts'ai 2–265
Chapatti 3–357
Charlotte, Cheese 3–365
  au Chocolat 3–357
  aux Fraises 3–359
  aux Framboises 3–358
  Russe 3–359
Chartreuse de Pommes 3–360
Chasseur Sauce 3–360
Chaudfroid Sauce, Brown 2–269
  Chicken 3–378
  White 3–361
Cheddar Spread 3–361
Cheeps 3–361
Cheese (info) 3–362
  Asparagus, with 1–76
  Bacon Quiche, and 15–2023
  Balls, Deep-Fried 18–2503
  Beef Roll, and 2–147
  Biscuits 6–784
  Bread 9–1126
  Brie Croquettes 2–256
  Camembert Croquettes 3–303
  Charlotte 3–365
  Chive Spread, and 3–365
  Cocktail Snacks 1–28
  Devilled 4–558
  Farmer's Soup 2–190
  Fritters 2–160
  Ham Soufflé, and 3–360
  Hungarian Dip 8–988
  Logs 3–366
  Omelet 12–1581
  Onion Pie, and 3–366
  Pancakes 8–1111
  Pastry 7–857
  Pie 4–506
  Potato Sticks 2–219
  Quenelles 15–2016
  Savouries 5–564
  Soufflé 3–366
  Soup 3–368; 8–1111
  Soured Cream Soufflé, and 1–12
  Spinach Crêpes, and 11–1441
  Spread 3–368
  Straws 3–368

Strudel **8**–1110
Toasties **3**–368
Cheesecake **8**–1111
Cheesy Snacks **3**–368
Chef's Salad **3**–369
Chelsea Buns **3**–369
Cherry (info) **3**–370
  Austrian, Strudel **9**–1149
  Compôte **3**–370
  -Filled Crêpes **9**–1150
  Flan **9**–1150
  Ice-Cream, with **9**–1149
  Italian **8**–1036
  Jubilee **3**–371
  Pie **3**–371
  Salad **3**–372
  Soup **3**–372; **8**–989
  Tapioca **3**–372
Chervil Avocado Salad **3**–373
  Leek Soup, and **3**–373
  Soup **9**–1161
Chestnut (info) **3**–373
  Braised **10**–1325
  Cake **6**–893
  Chocolate Dessert, and **12**–1663
  Compôte **3**–374
  Dessert **10**–1327
  Mould **10**–1327
  Pudding **19**–2529
  Sauce **3**–374
  Sausage Stuffing, and **3**–374
  Soufflé **10**–1327
  Soup **3**–375
Chicken (info) **3**–375
  Almond and Raisins, with **11**–1450
  Apricots, with **14**–1946
  Baby, Cooked with Butter and Lemon **14**–1957
  Baby, with Ginger **14**–1956
  Balkan Pilaff **1**–108
  Barbecued **1**–117
  Basil, with **14**–1949
  Belgian Stew **20**–2749
  Boiled **3**–379
  Calvados and Apple Sauce, with **14**–1946
  Chablis **3**–377
  Chaudfroid **3**–378
  Cherry Sauce, in **14**–1942
  Circassian **4**–424
  Coriander and Mint, with **4**–569
  Cream and Mushroom Sauce, with **14**–1945
  Croquettes **4**–506
  Curry **3**–379; **5**–572
  Danish Casserole **4**–533
  Danos **4**–532
  Devilled **4**–558
  Drumsticks, Shanghai-Style **5**–578
  Edna's **5**–604
  English-Style **3**–379
  Flan **18**–2483
  Florentine **3**–380
  Fricassée **6**–752
  Garlic and Almonds, with **14**–1858
  Ginger, with **3**–380
  Grilled Devilled **14**–1945
  Ham and Mushroom Crêpes **4**–500
  Ham Paste, and **3**–381
  Herbs, with **3**–381; **14**–1858
  Hyères **8**–999
  Grahamstown **7**–859
  Grilled, with Soy Sauce **7**–881
  Juniper **3**–381
  Kiev **3**–382
  à la King **3**–382
  Leek Pie, and **3**–382
  Lemon Jelly, with **20**–2714
  Long-Simmered in White Wine **12**–1656
  Macaroni, and Artichoke Heart Salad **16**–2210
  Mango **10**–1300
  Marbled **10**–1312
  Marengo **3**–390
  Marinated and Baked **18**–2495
  Marinated Spiced **18**–2474
  Marsala and Clove **10**–1330
  Maryland **10**–1336

Mayonnaise **3**–384
Moulds **4**–534
Mousse **3**–384
Mozzarella **11**–1441
Murray **11**–1451
Mushroom Soup, and **8**–1093
Mushrooms, with **14**–1942
Olives, with **8**–1062
Paprikash **3**–384
Peach Sauce, with **9**–1130
Peaches and Orange-Flavoured Liqueur, with **14**–1946
  Penang **13**–1734
Pickled **13**–1778
Pilau **19**–2544
Poached with Broccoli **14**–1943
Prawn and Asparagus, with **9**–1185
Prawn or Shrimps and Wine, with **14**–1944
Pulao **3**–385
Quick-Fried Cubes, with Walnuts **7**–972
Red-Cooked **7**–985
Rice, with **1**–65
Rice and Cherries, with **3**–387
Riviera **3**–387
Roast with Canapés **4**–446
Russian, Blinis **8**–1106
Rustom's **16**–2192
Salad, with Avocados and Russian Dressing **3**–388
Salad, with Bean Sprouts and Olives **3**–388
Salad, with Sour Cream Dessing **3**–389
San Marino **3**–390
Satay **8**–1022
Sauté **3**–390
Sautéed with Basil **14**–1949
Sautéed in Chasseur Sauce **14**–1951
Sautéed in Madeira-Flavoured Cream Sauce **14**–1948
Sautéed with Potatoes and Artichoke Hearts **14**–1950
Siena **3**–392
Sindhi **17**–2320
Soufflé **3**–392
Soy Sauce and Sake, in **8**–1117
Spanish-Style **3**–392
Spring Vegetable Soup with Dumplings, and **3**–393
Stewed in Red Wine **4**–444
Stock **3**–393
Sultan **3**–393
Sweet Red Wine, in **3**–394
Tamale Pie **3**–395
Tarragon, Whisky and Cream, with **22**–2999
Terrine **18**–2497
Tetzazzini **3**–395
Tomato and Cinnamon Sauce, with **9**–1169
Tunisian Casserole **19**–2561
Valentine **3**–396
Vol-au-Vent **20**–2719
Wine and Brandy, with **14**–1942
Wine, Tomatoes and Mushrooms, with **14**–1856
Yogurt **11**–1450
Chicken Breasts, Flambéed **18**–2444
  Ham, with **18**–2444
  Ham and Cheese, with **14**–1856
  en Papillote **3**–377
  Pâté, with **18**–2445
  Spiced **22**–3066
  Tarragon, with **3**–377
  Tarragon and Sour Cream, with **22**–3066
Chicken Liver Aspic **3**–396
  Bacon and Sage, with **5**–680
  Casserole **22**–3044
  Flan **6**–721
  Ham and Sherry, with **3**–396
  Hors d'Oeuvres **9**–1247
  Pasta, with **18**–2464
  Risotto **3**–398
  Stuffed Crêpes **4**–496
  Sweet and Sour Sauce, with **3**–398
  Water Chestnuts, with **3**–398
  Wine, in **3**–398
Chick-Peas (info) **3**–399
  Balls **5**–674

Catalan **3**–399
Curried **3**–356
Greek Soup **15**–2098
Paste **8**–985
Whole **8**–1091
Chico **13**–1752
Chicory (info) **3**–399
  Braised **3**–400
  Cheese and Ham, with **3**–400
  Eggs, and **3**–401
  Stuffed with Cream Cheese **5**–646
  Tomato Salad, and **3**–401
Children's Cake **9**–1142
Chilli con Carne **3**–401; **10**–1385
  Soya Protein **17**–2365
  Spaghetti **10**–1386
Chinese Cabbage in Cream Sauce **11**–1467
  Chicken and Ham **21**–2948
  Fried Rice **3**–402
Ching-Chiao-Ch'ao niu-jou **3**–402
Chiopino **3**–404
Chive and Brazil Nut Spread **2**–240
Chocolate, Almond Cake **3**–404
  Biscuits **3**–406
  Bread and Butter Pudding **21**–2882
  Cake **16**–2198
  Cake with Almonds and Rum **6**–806
  Cherry Tart **3**–406
  Chiffon Pie **3**–407
  Chip Cookies **3**–408
  Cinnamon Biscuits **3**–408
  Cream **4**–490
  Cream Pie **3**–409
  Cream Slices **16**–2122
  Custard, Individual **13**–1765
  Custard in a Sponge Finger Mould **3**–357
  Eggless Cake **5**–632
  Fried Bread **3**–409
  Gateau **18**–2487
  Hazelnut Cake **3**–406
  Ice-Cream **8**–1004
  Italian Mousse **22**–3028
  Icing **3**–409
  Lazy Cake **9**–1214
  Loaf **8**–1037
  Mocha Pudding **3**–409
  Mousse **8**–1057
  Mushroom Cake **3**–410
  Nougat **19**–2523
  Peppermint Sandwich Cake **3**–410
  Pineapple Rings **3**–412
  Pudding **3**–412; **11**–1410
  Rich Cake **16**–2116
  Rum Fondue, and **3**–412
  Rum Truffles **3**–413
  Sauce **3**–413
  Soufflé **3**–413
  Sour Cream Cake, and **3**–414
  Sponge Cake **3**–415
  Steamed Pudding **17**–2273
  Swiss Roll **3**–415
Chokladkaka **3**–416
Chorizo Patties **3**–418
Chou au gratin **3**–416
Choucroute Garnie **3**–416
Chou-fleur en Casserole **3**–417
  Sauce Crevette **3**–418
Chou-Rouge à la Flamande **3**–418
  à la Limousine **3**–418
Choux Pastry **3**–418
  Gâteau **15**–2095
  Puffs **3**–418
Chow Barg Choy **6**–755
Chow Mein **10**–1368
Christmas Bread **20**–2721
  Cake **3**–420; **4**–421
  German Sweet Bread **18**–2415
  Ham **8**–1086
  Honey Rice Pudding **9**–1183
  Manitoba Poppy Seed Roll **10**–1304
  Mincemeat Pies **10**–1398
  Phoenician Honey Cakes **13**–1773
  Pudding **4**–421
  Swedish Crullers **9**–1154
  Venison Saddle **16**–2142

Wassail Bowl **20**–2740
White Cake **20**–2783
Xmas Cheer **21**–2897
Yorkshire Gingerbread **21**–2935
Yule Log **21**–2957
Chutney (*info*) **4**–422
  Apple **4**–422
  Date and Banana **4**–422
  Ginger **1**–4
  Gooseberry **7**–850
  Lemon and Mustard Seed **9**–1229
  Mango **10**–1300
  Mint **11**–1402
  Nectarine **11**–1486
  Pear **13**–1719
  Tomato **18**–2473
  Tomato, Pepper and Apple **4**–422
Cider Cup **4**–423
Cinnamon Butter **4**–423
  Danish Pastry Filling **4**–531
  Flavoured Layer Cake **8**–1104
  Fried **4**–423
Circassian Chicken **4**–424
Clafoutis aux Cerises **4**–424
  aux Pommes **4**–424–5
  aux Prunes **4**–425
Clam (*info*) **4**–426
  Baked with Potatoes and Sweetcorn **12**–1667
  Bread Soup, and **22**–3061
  Chowder **4**–426
  Hors d'Oeuvres **21**–2964
  Sake Flavoured **7**–919
  Sake and Soy Sauce Flavoured **7**–919
  Stuffed **12**–1667
  Tomato and Garlic Sauce, in **1**–17
Cock-Leeckie **4**–427
Cockle Soup **4**–428
Cocoa Hazelnut Candy **16**–2162
Coconut (*info*) **4**–429
  Barfi **4**–429
  Chutney **11**–1476
  Cookies **4**–430
  Cream Pie **4**–430
  Custard Cakes **15**–2034
  -Filled Dessert Pancakes **1**–10
  Fudge **4**–429
  Ice-Cream **19**–2544
  Jamaican Sauce **8**–1050
  Pyramids **17**–2307
  Rice **4**–430
  Turnovers **11**–1477
Cod (*info*) **4**–432
  Alioli Sauce, with **22**–3025
  Asparagus, with **9**–1163
  Bake **4**–433
  Balls **4**–434
  Fillets with Caper Sauce **5**–693
  Green Peppers, Anchovies and Black Olives, with **3**–289
  Potatoes and Onions, with **3**–288
  Roc Paste **8**–2479
  Soup **2**–222
  Tomato, Parsley and Almond Sauce, in **10**–1382
  White Sauce, in **3**–288
Coda di Bue con Sedano **4**–432
Coddle **4**–434
Coeur à la Crème **4**–435
Coffee Bread **4**–436
  Buttercream Cake **6**–804
  Cakes **4**–437
  Cream **21**–2944
  Crumble **4**–438
  Ice-Cream **8**–1005
  Iced **8**–1008
  Refrigerator Cake **15**–2091
  Rum Ice-Cream **2**–206
  Soufflé **17**–2353
  Spiced with Cognac **3**–292
Colcannon **4**–438
Coleslaw with Caraway **4**–438
  Dressing **4**–439
Collops of Beef **4**–440
Compôte of Dried Fruits **4**–441
  de Poires **4**–441

Conger Eel Stew **3**–297
Consommé Brunoise **4**–442
  aux Champignons **4**–442
  Demidoff **4**–442
  Madrilène **4**–442
  Petite Marmite **13**–1758
Côntrefilet Braisé Chipolata **4**–443
Convent Eggs **4**–444
Coquilettes Farcies **4**–447
Coquilles Saint-Jacques
  à l'Ail **4**–448
  à la Crème **4**–449
  Gratinées **4**–449
  aux Tomates à la Crème **4**–450
Coriander Fruit Crumble **4**–451
Corn Bread **4**–452
  Chowder **4**–452
  on the Cob **4**–452
  Fritters **19**–2522
  Meal Biscuits **4**–453
  Prawn Savoury **4**–453
  Red Peppers, with **4**–454
Corned Beef Hash **4**–454
Cornets de Crème **4**–454
  de Jambon **4**–455
Cornish Custard Cream **4**–456
  Pasties **4**–456
Corvina à la Peruana **4**–457
Costillas à la Mexicana **4**–457
Costoletta di Maiale alla Pizzaiola **4**–458
  alla Modense **4**–458
Costolette di Agnello alla Milanese **4**–458
Côtelettes d'Agneau au Concombre **4**–460
  de Veau en Casserole **4**–460
Côtes-de-Porc Braisées **4**–461
Côtes-de-Veau au Genièvre **4**–461
  aux Herbes **4**–462
  en Papillote **4**–462
Cottage Cheese Soup **4**–464
  Pie **4**–464
Coulis de Tomates Provençale **4**–464
Country Captain **8**–1105
Coupe Jacques **4**–464
Courgettes (*info*) **4**–464
  Almonds, with **22**–3032
  Baked with Aubergines **4**–466
  Cake **22**–3030
  Cauliflower with Turmeric, and **22**–3030
  Cheese, with **4**–467; **22**–3030
  Cooked in Olive Oil with Garlic and Parsley, **4**–467
  Dill Sauce, with **22**–3030
  Grilled **4**–467
  Lemon, Butter and Parsley Sauce, with **4**–467
  Oriental Stuffed **22**–3033
  Pancakes **22**–3032
  Quiche **15**–2022
  Red Peppers, with **22**–3033
  Soufflé **22**–3037
  Soup **22**–3063
  Sour-Sweet Sauce, in **22**–3028
  Stewed **22**–3037
  Stuffed **22**–3036
  Stuffed with Almonds **4**–446
  Stuffed with Prawns or Shrimps and Tomatoes **22**–3033
  Stuffed with Sausages **22**–3036
  Sweetcorn with Goat's Milk Cheese, and **5**–642
  Tomato Casserole, and **4**–468
  Tomatoes and Fennel, with **22**–3036
Court Bouillon **4**–468
Couscous **4**–468, 470
Crab (*info*) **4**–471
  Bake **4**–472
  Bean Curd, with **1**–139
  Canapés **3**–303
Crab Apple Jelly **4**–470
  Preserve **4**–470
Crabmeat with Almonds **4**–472
  Appetizer **4**–472
  Flan **4**–472
  Herbs, with **4**–474
  Mayonnaise **4**–474
  Morney **4**–474

  Salad **4**–474
  Soup **4**–475
  White Chaudfroid Sauce, in **4**–472
Cranberry Conserve **4**–476
  Mousse **4**–476
  Orange Relish, and **4**–477
  Pie **4**–477
  Sauce **4**–471
Crayfish (*info*) **4**–478
  Cooked in Court Bouillon **5**–602
  Scandinavian-Style **4**–478
Cream Butter Sauce **17**–2247
  Mushroom Sauce **17**–2247
  Horns **4**–454
  Puffs **4**–484
Cream Cheese Dressing **4**–478
  Flan **4**–478
Cream of Avocado Soup **4**–479
  Carrot Soup **4**–480
  Celery Soup **4**–480
  Chicken Soup **4**–481–2
  Clam Soup **4**–482
  Cucumber Soup **4**–482
  Green Pea Soup **4**–483
  Lettuce Soup **4**–483
  Mushroom Soup **4**–484
  Shrimp Soup **4**–484
  Watercress Soup **4**–484
Creamed Camembert **4**–485
  Chicken **4**–485
  Chicken Livers **4**–486
  Mushrooms **4**–486
  Peas and Onions **4**–486
  Shrimps **7**–864
  Spinach **4**–487
  Sweetbreads **4**–487
Creamy Cheese **4**–488
  Dip **4**–488
Crème au Beurre **4**–488
  Brulée **4**–488
  Caramel **4**–490
  Chantilly **4**–490
  au Chocolat **4**–490
  aux Fraises **4**–492
  Pâtisserie **4**–492
  Vamilo **4**–492
Creole Chicken **4**–492
  Fruit Salad **16**–2211
  Shrimps **4**–493
Crêpes *see also* Pancakes
  aux Amandes **4**–496
  Batter **4**–493
  à la Confiture **4**–496
  Cheese-Stuffed **11**–1428
  Dutch **6**–725
  d'Epinards **4**–496
  Fourrées Gratinées **4**–496
  Frangipane **4**–498
  au Fruits de Mer **4**–498
  Hungarian **8**–991
  Ice-Cream **8**–1005
  Jam and Sour Cream **12**–1663
  à l'Orange **4**–499
  Plum-Stuffed **16**–2156
  Rolled Stuffed with Bananas **16**–2156
  Suzettes **4**–501
  Suisse **4**–500
Croissants **4**–501
Croquettes aux Crevettes **4**–503
  de Jambon **4**–503
  de Poisson **4**–504
  de Pommes de Terre **4**–504
  de Pommes de Terre et Viande **4**–505
  de Poulet **4**–506
  de Semoule au Sirop **4**–506
Crostata di Ricotta **4**–506
Croustades **4**–507
  aux Oeufs Brouillés **4**–508
  aux Oeufs Durs **4**–508
Crôutes **4**–508
  de Crevettes **4**–509
  Dorées **4**–509
  de Jambon **4**–509
Crowdie **4**–511
Crown Roast of Lamb **4**–511

of Pork with Sausage and Prune Stuffing 4–511
Crudités avec Aioli 4–512
Crumb Flan Crust 4–512
Crumpets 4–513
Crystallized Violets 4–514
Cucumber (*info*) 4–515
  Beer Soup, and 4–515
  Browned 21–2969
  Cream, with 4–515
  Danish Pickled, Salad 1–7
  Dressing 4–515
  Florentine 4–515
  Grape Salad, and 4–515
  Mushrooms in Cream Sauce, and 4–517
  Onion Salad, and 4–517
  Pickled 13–1778
  Pork Soup, and 4–517
  Relish 4–518
  Soup 4–518
  Soured Cream Salad, and 1–6
  Stuffed, with Tuna 4–518
  Tomato Salad, and 4–518
  Yogurt Salad, and 20–2661
Cullen Skink 4–518
Cumberland Rum Butter 4–519
  Sauce 4–519
Cumin Chicken 21–2989
  Meat 21–2987
  Raspberry Buns 4–520
Curd Sugar and Saffron 17–2307
Curried Aubergines 20–2763
  Aubergine Purée 2–168
  Avocado Soup 4–520
  Beef 15–2096
  Chicken with Onions 5–572
  Chick-Peas 3–356
  Eggs 4–521
  Kidneys 7–897
  Lamb 6–2152
  Meat and Potatoes 8–1042
  Minced Meat 9–1128
  Potatoes and Eggs 4–523
  Rice with Chicken 12–1661
  Sauce 17–2247
  Soup 11–1449
Custard Base, Ice-Cream 8–1003–4
  Caramel 4–490
  Glazed Baked 4–489
  Pear Tart, and 4–524
  Tart 4–524; 10–1370
  Tartlets 9–1240
Czechoslovakian Fruit Dumplings 9–1185
  Veal Ragoût 4–52

D

Dadar Djawa 4–526
Daiquiri 4–526
Dakar Shrimp 4–526
Dala'Matishi 4–526
Dalmation Fish Stew 2–269
Damson Cheese 4–527
  Jam 4–528
  Soufflé 4–528
Danish Bacon and Egg Cake 6–718
  Blue Salad 4–528
  Butter Cake 17–2334
  Chicken Casserole 4–533
  Fried Trout 18–2410
  Marzipan 9–1172
  Meat Patties 6–758
  Meatballs with Curry Sauce 9–1159
  Open Sandwiches 4–528
  Pastries 4–530
  Pork 4–532
  Rice and Almond Dessert 16–2129
Danos Chicken 4–532
Dansk Hönse Kässerolle 4–533
  Rôdspätte i Fiôdesovs 4–534
Danwiches 4–528
Daoud Pasha 4–534
Darioles de Volaille 4–534

Darius Casserole 4–535
Darne Montpelier 4–537
  de Saumon à l'Ancienne 4–536
Dartois 4–537
Date (*info*) 4–538
  Apple Pie, and 4–538
  Banana Chutney, and 4–422
  Banana Dessert, and 4–538
  Bars 4–538
  Cake 4–539, 540
  Chutney, Old Fashioned 12–1570
  Fig Pudding 19–2564
  Fudge 4–540
  German Cakes 4–544–545
  Jewels 4–540
  Loaf 4–540
  Marzipan 4–543
  Pudding 4–540
  Raisin Loaf, and 4–542
  Rice Pudding, and 4–542
  Walnut Diamonds, and 4–543
  Walnut Loaf, and 4–544
Dattelkuchen 4–544
Datteltorte 4–545
Daube d'Avignon 4–545
  de Boeuf 4–545
  de Boeuf à la Provençale 4–547
  de Lapin 4–547
  de Mouton 4–548
Daurade aux Bananes 4–548
  Farcie à l'Epinard 4–548
  au Fenouil 4–549
  au Riz 4–550
  aux Tomates 4–550
Deep Dish Peach Pie 4–550
Deep-Fried Cheese Balls 18–2503
  Cheese Sandwiches 11–1440
  Fish and Shellfish 6–762
  Japanese-Style Food 18–2491
  Liver and Kidneys 16–2187
  Meat and Vegetables 6–762
  Pork Slices 16–2187
  Prawns 4–551
  Spiced Fish 18–2470
  Sprats 4–552
  Sweet Crisp Pastries 3–347
  Whitebait 20–2791
  Wholemeal Bread 15–1991
Delaware Pudding 4–552
Delft Cake 4–554
Demi-Glace Sauce 4–555
Derby Biscuits 4–555
Devil Sauce 4–555
Devil's Food Cake 4–556
  Loaf 4–557
Devilled Almonds 1–18
  Boiled Beef 2–191
  Calf's Liver 4–558
  Cheese 4–558
  Chicken 4–558
  Dip 4–558
  Lobster 4–559
  Oranges 4–560
  Pork Chops 4–560
  Pork Ribs 4–560
  Turkey Drumsticks 5–561
Devils on Horseback 4–557
Devonshire Layer Cake 5–561
  Splits 5–562
Dhal Curry 5–562
Dhansak 5–562
Diablotins 5–564
Diamond Cakes with Curry Filling 5–564
Diced Pork on Crackling Rice 9–1181
Dill Dip 5–565
  Piroshki 5–565
  Salad 5–565
Dinde aux Marrons 5–566
Dindings Duck 5–567
Diplomate Pudding 5–568
Djeja M'qalia 5–569
Djuveč 5–569
Doboz Torte 5–569
Dolmadakia 5–570
Donegal Mussel Soup 5–572

Dopyaza Chicken 5–572
Dos 5–572
Double-Crust Blackcurrant and Apple Pie 5–573
Double Decker Sandwiches 5–573
Doughnuts 5–574
  French 7–857
  Isle of Wight 8–1034
  Jam 5–575
  Neapolitan 21–2992
  Sour Cream, with 5–576
  Syrup-Coated 9–1160
Dream Fudge 5–576
Dreaming Cake 5–576
Dried Apricot Bars 5–577
  Fruits in Syrup 5–578
Drop Scones 5–578
Drumsticks Shanghai-Style 5–578
Dry Beef Curry 5–579
  Martini 5–579
Dublin Bay Prawns 5–580
Duchess Potatoes 5–581
  Pralinés 5–581
  Pudding 5–581
Duck (*info*) 5–582
  Apricot and Sausage Stuffing, with 5–582
  Barbecued 1–117
  Boned, in Pastry 13–1698
  Braised 3–306
  Braised in Red Wine 5–582
  Curry 5–583
  Dindings 5–582
  Figs, with 5–584
  Grape Casserole, and 5–584
  in a Ring 5–586
  Indian Roast 19–2610
  Marmalade-Coated 12–1627
  Norman-Style 5–584
  Olives, with 22–3041
  Port, with 5–585
  Provençal 5–586
  Roast 3–306
  Spanish Style 5–587
  Terrine 18–2497
Duckling, Braised with Turnips 3–310
  Roast with Apple and Sausage Stuffing 3–311
  Roast with Cherries 3–309
  Sweet and Sour Sauce, in 5–588
Düğün Corbari 5–588
Dulma 5–589
Dumplings, Apple 1–45
  Bacon 1–102
  Baked 7–841
  Boiled Beef, with 2–205
  Breadcrumb 2–251
  Filled with Crabmeat 5–683
  Fruit 9–1185
  Malynka's Lamb 10–1296
  Mushroom Sauce 17–2286
  Plum 22–3072
  Roman-Style 7–842
  Savoury 5–590; 9–1157
  Semolina 7–879
  Spinach 7–842
  Stuffed 9–1174
  Sweet 5–590; 8–1107
  Trentina 19–2543
Dundee Cake 5–590
  Marmalade 5–591
Dušene Zeli 5–592
Dusseldorf Salad 5–592
Dutch Almond Biscuits 5–592
  Crêpes 6–725
  Meat Pancake 6–822
  Split Pea Soup 5–592
  Steak 5–594
Duxelles 5–594

E

Early American Cookies 5–595
East Coast Oyster Casserole 5–595
  Seafood Bake 5–595

East Indian Salad 5–596
Easter Bread 5–596
  Bunnies 5–597
  Cake 5–598
  Festival Bread 5–598
  Halva Cake 5–600
  Lamb 5–601
  Russian Dessert 13–1689
  Soup 5–601
Eastern Cutlets 5–601
Eccles Cakes 5–602
Ecrevisses à la Nage 5–602
Ecuadorian Lamb Stew 5–603
Edna's Chicken 5–604
Edwardian Biscuits 5–604
Eel (info) 5–605
  Batter, in 5–605
  Green Sauce, in 1–34
  Jellied 8–1066
  Marinated 1–34
  Mâtelote Sauce, in 5–605
  Neapolitan-Style 5–606
  Soup 22–3058
  Stew 5–607
  Tomato Sauce, in 5–607
Egg (info) 5–607
  Anchovy Mousse, and 5–610
  Artichokes, in 5–610
  Asparagus, with 1–76
  Bacon Bake, and 5–610
  Bacon Scramble, and 5–611
  Baked with Chicken 5–612
  Baked with Haddock 5–612
  Baked with Mushrooms 5–612
  Baked with Onions 5–613
  Baked Potatoes, in 5–613
  Baked with Sausages, Onions and Peppers 7–980
  Balls 5–614
  Bel Paese 5–614
  Benedict 5–614
  Bread 5–614
  Brown Baked 7–922
  Cabbage Pirog, and 5–615
  Cake 11–1409
  Caper Dressing, and 5–616
  Caviar 5–616
  Cheese Rissoles, and 5–616
  Cheese Soup, and 5–616
  Convent 4–444
  Corn Savoury, and 5–618
  Country Style 12–155
  Cream Cheese Tart, and 5–618
  Creole 5–618
  Croquettes 12–1556
  Cutlets 5–618
  -Drop Soup 5–619
  Essen 5–619
  Flamenco 5–620
  Flip 5–620
  Floradora 6–726
  Foo Yung 5–621
  Hard-Boiled in Pastry 4–508
  Herb Stuffing, with 5–621
  Indian Style 5–621
  Lemon Soup, and 1–88
  Mixed Herbs, with 5–621
  Mousse 21–2964
  Onion Sauce, with 12–1558
  Paprika Sauce, with 12–1557
  Peas and Corn, with 5–624
  Poached, with Cheese Sauce 12–1557
  Poached, in Red Wine 12–1555
  Portuguese, in Tomato Shells 12–1635
  Puffs 5–624
  Quail's 15–2001
  Ratatouille 5–624
  Rum Sauce, and 7–844
  Salad 5–624
  Sardine Hors d'Oeuvres 5–625
  Sauce 5–625
  Sausage and Pepper Casserole 5–625
  Savoury Creamed Lettuce, with 5–626
  Savoury Nest 5–626
  Scrambled, with Chilli 5–638

  Scrambled, in Pastry Shells 4–508
  Sherry, with 5–626
  Shirred 17–2303
  Spicy Scrambled, with Sausage and Green Peppers 1–9
  Spinach, with 12–1557
  Spinach Salad, and 5–626
  Stuffed with Tuna 5–627
  Tarragon Mayonnaise, with 5–628
  Tartlets 5–628
  Tomatoes and Onion, with 5–629
  Vegetable Flan, and 5–629
  White Wine Sauce, in 12–1558
  Yogurt Salad, and 5–630
  Yolk Butter 2–167
Eggah, Courgettes 5–630
  Noodles and Chicken, with 5–630
  Spinach, with 5–630
Egg-Braised, Sliced Chicken 9–1181
  Slice Fish 9–1182
Eggburgers 5–615
Eggless Chocolate Cake 5–632
Eggnog Chiffon Pie 5–633
Egg-Noodles 5–622
  Baked with Spinach 5–622
  Creamy Cheese Sauce, with 5–623
  Pork Sauce, with 5–623
Eggplant see Aubergine
Egyptian Braised Steak 5–638
  Brown Beans 5–638
  Lamb Soup 5–678
Ekuri 5–638
Elderberry and Apple Jelly 5–640
  Pie 5–640
  Wine 21–2843
Elderflower Wine 21–2483
Election Cake 5–641
Elegante 5–642
Ella's Tomato and Potato Pie 5–642
Emincé de Porc au Poirons 5–642
  de Veau 5–643
Empenadas 5–644
Emperor's Pancake 8–1096
Empress Rice Pudding 16–2135
Endive Farcie 5–646
Engadiner Nusstorte 5–646
Entrecôte aux Echalottes 5–647
  à la Lyonnaise 5–648
  Mirabeau 5–648
  au Poivre 5–649
  Steak with Sour Cream 5–692
Epaule d'Agneau Roulée aux Pruneaux 5–649
  de Mouton à la Boulangère 5–650
  de Veau Farcie 5–651
Epinards au Gratin 5–651
  à la Provençale 5–652
Erbsenpuree 5–652
Erwtensoep 5–652
Escabeche 5–652
Escalopes au Calvados 5–653
  Cordon Bleu 5–654
  à la Crème 5–654
  Holstein 5–655
  à l'Hongroise 5–655
  Perigueux 5–656
  à la Provençale 5–656
  de Veau Amandine 5–653
  au Vin Rouge 5–656
Escargots à la Bourguignonne 5–657
Escarole Soup 5–658
Escravaniya 5–658
Escudilla Cataluña 5–658
Eshkaneh 5–659
Espada Abonga 5–659
Essex Meat Layer Pudding 5–660
Essig Flaish 5–660
Esterhazy Steaks 5–664
Estonian Rissoles 5–662
Estouffade à l'Albigeoise 5–663
  de Boeuf 5–662
Estouffat 5–644
Exeter Pudding 5–644
Exmouth Pudding 5–655

F

Fabada 5–666
Foggots 5–666
Fagioli al Forno 5–668
  con Prosciuto 5–668
  con Tonno 5–668
Fairy Cakes 5–668
Faisan en Chartreuse 5–670
  Normand 5–671
  en Oranges 5–671
  au Riz Basquais 5–672
  Souvaroff 5–672
  au Vin Rouge 5–673
Falafel 5–674
Family Fruit Cake 5–674
Fan Tans 5–675
Far East Celery 5–675
Farce Duxelles 5–676
Farfallette Dolci 5–676
Farm Soup 5–676
Farmer's Cheese Soup 2–190
Farshmak 5–677
Fata 5–678
Fattoush 5–678
Faux Soufflé Meringué aux Ananas 5–679
Fegatini di Pollo alla Salvia 5–680
Fegato alla Veneziana 5–680
Fegato-di-Vitello Alla Parmigiana 5–680
  al Pomodoro 5–680
  di Vitello con Vino 5–681
Feijoada 5–683
Feng Kuo 5–683
Fennel with Cheese Sauce 5–684
  Chicory and Tomato Salad, with 8–1026
  Cream Sauce 5–684
  Cucumber Salad, and 5–684
  Greek Style 5–685
Fenouils au Gratin 5–684
  à la Grecque 5–685
Fesenjen 5–686
Fettucine Alfredo 5–686
  alla Romana 5–687
Feuilles de Chou Farcies 5–687
Fig, Carnival 5–688
  Creme de Cacao, with 5–691
  Flavoured Ham 5–688
  Flutter 5–689
  Hazelnut Biscuits, and 5–689
  Nut Sweets, and 5–689
  Preserve 5–690
  Pudding 5–690
  Rice Dessert, and 16–2113
    Salad 16–2211
    Stuffed 5–691
    Tart 5–690
Figos Recheados 5–691
Figues au Cacao 5–691
Filbert and Chocolate Cake 5–692
Filetgulasch mit Saurer Sahne 5–692
Filets de Cabilland aux Capres 5–693
  de Lièvre Chasseur 5–694
  de Maquereaux aux Fines Herbes 5–694
  de Maquereaux Gratinées aux Capres 5–694
  de Maquereaux Sauce Moutarde 5–695
  de Merlan Dieppoise 5–696
  de Sole Cecilia 5–679
  de Sole à la Florentine 5–697
  de Turbot Hermitage 5–697
Filletti di Sogliole Pizzaiola 5–692
Fines Herbes Sauce 5–698
  Vinaigrette 5–700
Finnan Haddie 5–700
Finnish Vegetable Soup 9–1125
Fish and Chips 6–707
  Aspic 6–704
  Belgian, Stew 20–2747
  Baked Greek Style 6–704
  Baked in Sour Cream 6–704
  Balls 6–811
  Balls with Almonds 6–705
  Balls with Fines Herbes Sauce 6–706
  Cakes 6–707
  Catalañ Soup 3–337
  Chowder 6–707

Cream-baked **22**–3022
Cream Soup **20**–2662
Croquettes **4**–507; **6**–708
Dalmatian, Stew **2**–269
Dressing **6**–708
Fillets Mediterranean-Style **6**–698
Fried in Lime Juice **8**–1015
Grilled with Cheese **6**–709
Grilled in Japanese Wine Sauce **7**–881
Kebabs **6**–710; **22**–3001
Leek Flan, and **6**–711
Loaf **6**–711
Mayonnaise **6**–711
Mediterranean Stew **1**–8
Mould **6**–712
Mousse **19**–2586
Mushroom Soup, and **6**–712
Norwegian, Soup **2**–162
Orange Sauce, with **10**–1383
Pickled **5**–652; **8**–1024; **13**–1756
Potato Pie, and **6**–713
Potato Salad, and **6**–713
Prawn Mousse, and **6**–713
Prawns in Wine and Tomato Sauce, and **6**–715
Provençal, Soup **2**–225
Pudding with Prawn Salad **6**–717
Raw Sliced **17**–2324
Russian Pie **9**–1178
Salad **6**–715
Sliced, in Ground Rice **10**–1368
Sliced, in Tomato Sauce **8**–998
Sliced, in Wine Sauce **9**–1245
Soup **2**–220; **8**–990; **16**–2195; **17**–2358; **19**–2599
Spanish Stew **21**–2984
Steaks, in Sweet and Sour Sauce **6**–715
Stew with Peppers **14**–1852
Stock **6**–716
-Stuffed Marrow **6**–716
Wine and Mushrooms, with **6**–716
Yangtze, Soup **7**–978
Fisherman's Lemons **6**–716
Fish-House Punch **6**–709
Fiskebudding med Rejesovs **6**–717
Five Fruit Marmalade **6**–718
Flaeskeaeggekage **6**–718
Flamri de Semoule **6**–718
Flan d'Anana **6**–721
à la Bourguignonne **6**–721
de Carottes **6**–721
Cases **6**–721
Crumb Case **4**–512
Greengage **7**–875
Leek and Bacon **6**–721
Pastry Cases **6**–720
au Potiron Caramelisé **6**–722
Sponge Case **6**–720
Flangarde **6**–722
Flank Steak Stew with Herbs **6**–723
Flapjacks **6**–724
Flemish, Beef Stew with Beer **3**–323
Carrots **6**–724
Cream Cake **6**–802
Flensjes **6**–725
Flim Flam Sauce **6**–726
Floating Island **8**–1016
Floddies **6**–726
Floradora Eggs **6**–726
Florentine Chocolate Dessert **6**–727
Florentines **6**–727
Florida Salad **6**–727
Fløtevafler **6**–728
Flounder see also Plaice
Fillets Baked with Spinach **8**–1102
Pickled **8**–1114
Flour Panade **12**–1668
Flummery **6**–730
Foie de Porc à l'Espagnole **6**–730
Fondant **6**–731
Fonds d'Artichauts à la Crème **6**–731
Mirepoix **6**–732
Fonds Lié **6**–732
Fondue, Bourguignonne **6**–732
Japonais **6**–733

Orientale **6**–734
Suisse **6**–734
Fontina Cheese and Peppers Salad **8**–1026
Forcemeat of Pork **6**–736
Foong Yin Mun Sung **6**–735
Four Cheeses with Rice **15**–2002
Fox Noodles **6**–737
Fraises Romanoff **6**–737
Frangipane **6**–739
Crêpes **4**–498
Frankfurter, Alabama Style **6**–739
Bake **6**–739
Cabbage Salad, and **6**–739
Kranz **6**–739
Stew **6**–740
Fransk Aeblekage **6**–740
French Apple Pudding **4**–424
Beef Stew **4**–545
Bread **6**–747
Cherry Pudding **4**–424
Dressing **6**–748
Onion Soup **6**–748
Orange-Flavoured Cake **15**–2002
Peach Tart **6**–748
Pigeon Stew **16**–2215
Pork Pie **19**–2534
Plum Pudding **4**–425
Potato Salad **6**–749
Provençal Garlic Soup **1**–7
Roast Cake **6**–749
Sponge Cake **2**–175
Toast **6**–750
Vegetable Soup **14**–1920
Yeast Cake **17**–2260
French Bean, Pickled **13**–1780
Salad **6**–746
Tomato Sauce, with **6**–747; **8**–1084
Fresno Salad **6**–750
Friar Tuck Toast **6**–750
Fricadelles à la Crème **6**–751
à l'Hongroise **6**–752
de Veau Smitane **6**–752
Fricassée de Poulet **6**–752
de Veau **6**–754
Fried Aubergines **6**–754
Baked Meat Cakes with Spinach **8**–1082
Chinese Cabbage **6**–755
Fish in Lime Juice **8**–1015
Fish with Vinegar Dressing **11**–1470
Mixed Vegetables **6**–755; **8**–1091
Pheasant in Cream and Brandy Sauce **6**–756
Pineapple and Cucumber, Chinese-Style **6**–756
Rabbit with Hungarian Sauce **6**–757
Rice, Chinese-Style **6**–757
Smelts with Lemon Butter **6**–757
Frijoles Refritos **6**–758
Frikadeller **6**–758
Frittata di Carne e Vegetali **6**–759
di Ricotta con Salsa Rossa **6**–759
Fritter Batter **6**–760
Coated Spinach Leaves **6**–760
Filled with Chicken Livers and Mushrooms **6**–760
Honey Sauce, with **6**–760
Sweet **13**–1766
Fritto di Mare **6**–762
Misto **6**–762
Frogs' Legs with Parsley Butter Sauce **7**–876
Tomatoes and Garlic, with **7**–877
Frosted Walnut Cake **6**–763
Fruit Ambrosia **6**–766
Chicken Salad, and **6**–767
Cream **6**–768
Crêpes **4**–498
Curry **6**–768
Dried, in Syrup **5**–578
Fool **6**–768
Grilled, Salad Packets **7**–882
Kirsch-Soaked **11**–1474
Mixed Nut Cake, and **6**–770
Nut Biscuits, and **6**–771
Pork Casserole, and **6**–712
Pudding **6**–722
Salad **6**–773

Soup **9**–1128
Tart **12**–1546
Uncooked, Soup **19**–2591
Vegetable Salad, and **6**–775
Fruits de Mer en Salade **6**–769
Fudge **6**–775
Coconut **4**–429
Date **4**–540
Dream **5**–565
Fingers **6**–776
Frosting **6**–776
Hansom **7**–922
Layer Cake **6**–776
Sauce **6**–776
Walnut and Coffee **20**–2732
Fusili Noodles with Tomatoes and Cheese **6**–777
Fyldt KalveFars **6**–778
Fyllda Strutar **6**–778

G

Gaisburger Marsch **6**–780
Gajjar Halva **6**–781
Galantine de Faisan **6**–781
de Veau au Vin Blanc **6**–782
Galette aux Abricots **6**–783
Amandines **6**–784
au Camembert **6**–784
de Feuilles **6**–785
au Fromage **6**–785
Nantaises **6**–786
Noisettine **6**–786
Normande **6**–786
Gamberi con Riso **6**–787
Game Chips **6**–788
Pâté **6**–790
Pie **6**–790
Sauce **3**–360
Soup **6**–791
Stew **6**–791
Stock **6**–792
Gammon and Apricot, with **1**–57
Baked with Herbs **6**–792
Gooseberry, with **22**–3046
Pineapple, with **6**–792
Steaks, Rochester **16**–2145
Tarragon Cream Sauce, with **6**–794
Tomato Sauce, with **6**–794
Gänsebraten mit Füllsel **6**–795
Garbanzos à la Mexicana **6**–796
Garbure **6**–796
Garibaldi Biscuits **6**–796
Garides me Saltsa Domates **6**–798
Garlic Bread **6**–798
Butter **2**–164
Dip **6**–798
Mashed Potatoes **6**–799
Mayonnaise **1**–12
Salad **6**–800
Soup **1**–7, **6**–801
Stuffed Eggs **6**–801
Toast **6**–801
Garmi Polo **6**–801
Gâteau Flamand à la Crème **6**–802
aux Fraises et Amandes **6**–803
de Marrons **6**–803
Millefeuille **6**–804
Mocha **6**–804
Noir **6**–806
Noir **8**–806
Noisette **6**–806
à l'Orange **6**–806
St. Honoré **6**–808
Gazpacho **6**–810
Salad **6**–810
Gebratener Pike **6**–811
Geelrys **6**–811
Gefillte Fish **6**–811
Gefüllte Melonen **6**–812
Gefüllter Heilbutt mit Krabben **6**–812
Genevoise Sauce **6**–813
Gengi Tsukeyaki **6**–814

Genoa Cake **6**–815
Genoese Salad **6**–815
  Sweet Bread **12**–1670
Génoise Sponge **6**–816
Georgian Cheese Bread **9**–1126
  Soup **6**–816
German Apple and Custard Tart **1**–38
  Apple Pudding **1**–38
  Beef and Clove Casserole **6**–817
  Caraway Potatoes **9**–1178
  Country Breakfast **6**–818
  Dried Fruit Bread **8**–996
  Liver Strudel **14**–1846
  Nut Pastry Roll **11**–1529
  Peasant Soup **1**–133
  Potato Salad **6**–819
  Sauerkraut in Wine **20**–2755
  Sausage Salad **21**–2880
  Shrimp Bisque **9**–1171
  Spice Cake **6**–819
  Stuffed Beef Rolls **16**–2173
  Style Calves' Brains **6**–819
  Sweet Bread **2**–254, **18**–2415
  Veal Stew with Asparagus **8**–1098
  Wine Jelly **20**–2755
Geschmörte Schweinenfleisch mit Kummel
  6–820
Gevulde Botterkoek **6**–821
Ghanaian Baked Trout **9**–1184
  Stewed Aubergine with Shrimps **11**–1526
Ghiveciu **6**–823
Ghost aur Aloo **6**–823
Ghourounaki Yemisto me Feta **6**–824
Gigot d'Agneau Farci **6**–826
  à la Bretonne **6**–824
  de Porc à la Crème **6**–828
  à la Provençale **6**–827
  au Vin Rouge **5**–827
Ginger and Apple Jam **6**–830
  Baby Chicken, with **14**–1956
  Banana Crêpes, and **6**–830
  Bean Sprouts, with **1**–140
  Cheesecake **6**–852
  Chicken, with **3**–380
  Chutney **1**–4
  Cream Filled Horns **9**–1171
  Cream Wafers **6**–833
  Flapjack **6**–834
  Ice-Cream **8**–1005
  Lemon Flan **6**–834
  Pear Sauce **6**–834
  Pudding **6**–834
  Rhubarb, with **16**–2104
  Sauce **6**–835
  Snap Biscuits **6**–835
  Sponge Cake **6**–836
Ginger Ale Fruit Jelly **6**–829
Ginger Beer **6**–830
Gingerbread **6**–831
  Bites **6**–832
Gingered Beef **6**–836
Giouvetsi **6**–837
Girdle Scones **6**–837
Glacé Icing **6**–837
Glamorgan Sausages **6**–838
Glazed Bacon **6**–838
  Fresh Fruit **13**–1760
  Ham **7**–917
  Onions **6**–839
  Orange **12**–1612
  Orange Rind **6**–839
  Radishes **15**–2045
Glögg **6**–840
Gluhwein **6**–840
Gnocchi al Forno Napoletano **7**–841
  di Patate **7**–842
  alla Romana **7**–842
  Verdi **7**–842
Goan Vinegar Curry **7**–843
Gobi Ki Sabzi **7**–843
Godcakes **7**–844
Gogol Mogol Sauce **7**–844
Golden Biscuits **7**–845
  Gooseberry Bake **7**–845
Golubtsy **7**–846

Goose (*info*) **7**–846
  Apricot and Veal Stuffing, with **7**–846
  Casserole **7**–847
  Liver Pilaf **7**–848
  Michaelmas **10**–1389
  Pâté **7**–849
  Pie **7**–849
  Roast, with Apple and Nut Stuffing **6**–795
  Roast, with Apples and Prunes **6**–778
  Roast, with Chestnut Stuffing **12**–1562
  Roast, with Lemon, Apple and Parsley
    Stuffing **12**–1561
  Roast, with Pork and Olive Stuffing Glazed
    with Honey **8**–999
  Roast, with Sauerkraut Stuffing **13**–1727
  Roast, Stuffed with Onion and Sage **12**–1560
  Roast, Stuffed with Prunes and Goose Liver
    Pâté **12**–1562
  Soup **7**–850
  Stew with Chestnuts **15**–2048
Gooseberry (*info*) **7**–850
  Charlotte **7**–850
  Chutney **7**–850
  Crumble **7**–851
  Curd **7**–852
  Golden Bake **7**–845
  Jam **7**–852
  Kissel **7**–852
  Pie **7**–852
  Sauce **7**–853
  Steffon **7**–853
Gorgonzola Biscuits **7**–854
  Dip **7**–854
Gormeh Sabzi **7**–855
Gouère aux Pommes **7**–855
Gougère **7**–857
Gougnettes **7**–857
Goulasch **7**–857-8; **19**–2537
  Gherkins, with **22**–3002
  Soup **7**–858
Grahamstown Chicken **7**–859
Grand-Veneur Sauce **7**–860
Grape (*info*) **7**–860
  Concentrate Wine **21**–2843
  Grapefruit Salad, and **7**–860
  Tartlets **7**–860
Grapefruit (*info*) **7**–860
  Avocado Salad, and **7**–861
  Barley Water **7**–862
  Grilled **7**–822
  Hot Spiced **7**–977
  Ice-Cream Filled **8**–1005
  Jelly **7**–862
  Marmalade **7**–862
  Orange Salad, and **7**–862
  Trebujena, Cocktail **19**–2541
Gras Double Provençale **7**–864
Gratin de Crevettes **7**–864
  aux Fruits de Mer **7**–865
  de Pommes de Terre à la Dauphinoise **7**–866
  de Pommes de Terre à la Savoyard **7**–866
  de Pommes de Terre et Viande **7**–866
Gravad Lax **7**–867
Greek Bouillabaisse **8**–1096
  Butter Biscuits **9**–1170
  Chick-Pea Soup **15**–2098
  Lamb Kebabs **7**–868
  Lamb Stew **7**–869
  Salad **7**–869
Green Chilli Relish **7**–870
  Goddess Sauce **7**–870
  Grape and Apple Pie **7**–871
  Grasshopper Pie **17**–2259
  Mealie Fritters **7**–872
  Peas with Ham **7**–872
  Pea Soup **7**–872
  Pepper Salad **7**–873
  Peppers Stuffed with Pork and Veal **7**–873
  Rice **7**–874
  Tomato Chutney **7**–874
Green Beans with Apples and Almonds **7**–930
  Cream, with **7**–929
  Onion and Bacon, with **7**–929
  Sour Cream, in **9**–1154
Greengage Flan **7**–875

Jam **7**–875
Grenadine Almond Flan **7**–876
  Walnut Soufflé, and **7**–876
Grenouilles aux Persil **7**–876
  à la Provençale **7**–877
Grey Mullet (*info*) **7**–878
  Béchamel Sauce, with **7**–878
  Martigues **7**–878
  Tomatoes and Capers, with **7**–878
Griessklösschen **7**–879
Griesstorte **7**–880
Grilled Chicken in Soy Sauce **7**–881
  Fish in Japanese Wine Sauce **7**–881
  Fruit Salad Packets **7**–882
  Grapefruit **7**–882
  Sardines Watercress Sauce, with **16**–2240
  Squab in Butter Sauce **7**–882
Ground Almonds **1**–18
Ground Rice Cake **7**–884
  Chilled Pudding **11**–1443
  Pudding **7**–884
Groundnut Stew **7**–883
Grouse (*info*) **7**–884
  Brandy and Cream Sauce, with **7**–885
  Casserole **7**–885
  Soufflé **7**–886
  Stew **7**–887
Grumble Pie **7**–887
Grüne Melone Mousse **7**–887
Gruyère and Mushroom Salad **7**–888
  Omelet **7**–888
  Puffs **7**–888
  Soufflettes **7**–889
Guacamole **7**–889
  Ring **7**–890
Guard's Pudding **7**–891
Guava Jelly **7**–891
  Pie **7**–892
Gugelhopf **7**–893
Guinea Fowls (*info*) **7**–894
  Almond Sauce, with **7**–894
  Casserole **7**–894
  Cherry Sauce, with **13**–1812
  Cream and Wine Sauce, with **7**–894
  Stuffed **13**–1814
Guido's Italian Sausage Rolls **7**–893
Guleh Kambing **7**–895
Gurda Khorma **7**–897
Gurkenbowle **7**–897
Gurkensosse **7**–897
Gus-Khrustalny Cream Pudding **7**–898
Gyuniku Teriyaki **7**–898

H

Habas à la Catalana **7**–898
Haddock (*info*) **7**–900
  Almonds and Lemon, with **7**–900
  Cheesy Topping, with **7**–900
  Cider, with **7**–902
  Morsels **7**–902
  Mustard Sauce, with **7**–902
  Parsley Sauce, with **7**–902
  Poached Eggs, with **7**–903
  Scandinavian, Parcels **16**–2147
  Soufflé **7**–904
  Smoked **1**–3; **5**–700
  Soup **7**–904
Hag Ha'asif Tzimmis **7**–905
Hake (*info*) **7**–906
  Cider Bake, and **7**–906
  Ham and Egg Stuffing, with **7**–907
Half Pay Pudding **7**–907
Halibut (*info*) **7**–907
  Baked with Cream **7**–907
  Bananas, with **7**–908
  Green Pepper, with **21**–2885
  Jellied **8**–1069
  Steaks with Lemon and Chive Butter **7**–908
  Steaks with Tomatoes and Cream **7**–908
  Stuffed **21**–2870
  Stuffed with Shrimps and Crabmeat **6**–812

Halva Cake 5–600
  Gajjar 6–781
Ham (info) 7–910
  Apples, with 19–2534
  Artichoke Heart Mould, and 7–910
  Baked in Pastry 8–1057
  Baked, with Sauerkraut 7–910
  Balls 7–912
  Bourbon-glazed 2–224
  Braised in Madeira 8–1053
  Braised in Red Wine 7–912
  Braised in White Wine 8–1056
  Cabbage and Potatoes, with 7–913
  Champagne Sauce, with 7–913
  Chicken Rolls, and 15–1978
  Cider Sauce, in 7–914
  Cones with Pâté de Foie Gras 4–454
  Cooked in Beer 8–1087
  Croquettes 4–503
  Croûtes 4–509
  Custard 7–915
  Figs, with 7–9
  Fried Rice, with 7–916
  Fritters, with Almonds 7–916
  Glazed 7–916
  Honey Syrup, in 11–1409
  Kidney Kebabs, and 20–2749
  Liscamnor 7–917
  Macaroni, with 17–2273
  Madeira Sauce, with 19–2536
  Melon, with 15–1979
  Mould 18–2502
  Omelet 12–1581
  Pear, with 15–1979
  Peas, with 15–1979
  Rice Salad, and 7–918
  Sauce 7–918
  Shallots, with 8–1054
  Smoked, and Cucumber Soup 19–2557
  Steaks with Barbecue Sauce 7–918
Hamaguri Sakani 7–919
  Shiguri-Ni 7–919
Hamburgers 7–920
  Cooked in Beef Stock 8–1094
  Cream Sauce, with 2–178
  Dill, with 7–920
  French 2–169
  Mint, with 7–920
  Polish Stuffed 22–3022
  Sherry, with 7–921
  Swedish 2–169
Hamilton Chops 7–922
Hamindas 7–922
Handsome Tipsy Cake 7–922
Hansom Fudge 7–922
Hao Yiu Ngiu Jou Pien 7–923
Hapsburg Sole 7–923
Hard Sauce 7–924
Hare (info) 7–924
  Casseroled in Wine and Herb Sauce 7–932
  Fillets in Mushroom and Wine Sauce 5–694
  Hunter's Stew, Yugoslavian 21–2954
  Jänis paisti 8–1058
  Jugged 8–1086
  Onions and Sour Cream, with 7–924
  Pudding 7–925
  Soup 7–925
  Sweet and Sour Sauce, in 7–926
Harengs à la Boulangère 7–927
  à la Meunière 7–927
Haricot Mutton 7–928
Haricots Verts à la Crème 7–929
  à l'Oignon et Lard 7–929
  aux Pommes 7–930
Harira 7–930
Haroset 7–930
Harriet's Orange Pudding 7–932
Harvard Beets 7–932
Hasenpfeffer 7–932
Hash, Aubergine 7–933
  Brown Potatoes 7–934
  Mushroom and Tomato Sauce, with 7–934
Hasselbackspotatis 7–934
Hasty Pudding 7–935
Havrekex 7–935

Hawaiian Chicken 7–936
  Cream Roll 7–937
  Fruit Cocktail 7–937
  Sauce 7–938
  Soup 7–938
Hazelnut Biscuits 18–2391; 22–3063
  Biscuit Cake 6–786
  Cream 7–939
  Macaroon 7–939
  Meringue Cake 6–806; 19–2601
  Sauce 7–940
  Soufflé 7–940
  Toffee 7–940
  Torte 7–941
Heart (info) 7–941
  Fruit·Stuffing, with 7–942
  Stewed in Wine 7–942
Heavy Cake 7–942
Hedgehog Cake 7–943
Herb Bread 7–944
  Bread Crisps 7–945
  Fritters 7–945
  Lemon Sauce, and 7–946
  Omelet 12–1580
  Orange Stuffing, and 7–946
  Pastry 7–946
  Potato Soup, and 7–946
  Sauce 5–700
  Spinach Flan, and 7–946
  Stuffing 7–947
  Vinegar 7–948
Hermits 7–948
Herring (info) 7–949
  Apple Bake, and 7–949
  Baked with Potatoes and Onions 7–927
  Butter Sauce, in 7–927
  Mustard Sauce, with 7–949
  Rolled Oats, in 7–950
  Salad 7–950
  Scandinavian, Baked in Foil 17–2319
  Soused 17–2362
  Spiced 1–115
  Stuffed with Rice 7–950
Herring Roes in Cream Sauce 7–949
  Devilled Sauce, in 7–950
Het Pint 7–951
Hickory Loaf 7–951
Highball 7–952
Himmel und Erde 7–952
Himmelsk Mundfeld 7–953
Hindle Wakes 7–953
Ho Tao Chi Tin 7–972
Hochepot 7–954
Hogs Pudding 7–954
Hollandaise Salad 7–954
  Sauce 7–955
  Soup 7–956
Holstein Flan 7–956
  Sauce 7–957
  Stew 7–957
Homard à l'Americaine 7–958
  Braisé au Vin Blanc 7–958
  à la Crème 7–958
  à l'Ecossaise 7–958
  à la Parisienne 7–960
  Provençale 7–960
Honey Baked Pears 7–961
  Balls 7–961
  Banana Toasts 7–961
  Cake 7–962; 9–1223
  Cream Cheese Pie, and 7–962
  Dressing 7–962
  Fruit Muesli, and 7–963
  Glazed Goose 8–999
  Ginger Pudding 7–964
  Mousse 7–964
  Nut Toffee, and 7–964
  Pecan Flan 7–964
  Polish Drink 9–1176
  Pudding 7–964
  Rice Pudding, and 9–1183
  Spice Cake 7–965
  Sweets 18–2491
  Vinegar Dressing, and 7–965
  Walnut Bars, and 7–965

  Walnut Pudding, and 7–965
  Walnut Torte 5–646
Honeycomb Cream 7–966
  Toffee 7–966
  Pear Salad 7–967
Honeyed Chicken 7–967
  Ham with Bean Sprouts 7–967
Honeymoon Cup 7–968
Hoppelpoppel 7–968
Hoppin' John 7–969
Horse's Neck 7–970
Horseradish and Apricot Sauce 7–971
  Butter 7–971
  Herb Sauce, and 7–971
  Sauce 7–971
  Sour Cream Sauce, and 7–971
  Vinegar 7–971
Hostess Salad 7–972
Hot Apple Drink 7–972
  Buttered Rum 7–973
  Cross Buns 7–973
  Mussel, Hake and Vegetable Salad 16–2210
  Orange Pudding 7–974
  Slaw 7–977
  Sour Soup 7–977
  Spiced Grapefruit 7–977
  Toddy 7–977
  -Water Pastry 7–977
Hot-Pot 7–974
  Beef, Carrots and Potatoes, of 8–995
  Liver, Bacon and Apple, of 7–974
  Rabbit, of 7–974
  Veal, of 7–978
Household Bread 2–247
Huang Yu Tang 7–978
Huckleberry Meringue Pie 7–979
Huevos à la Flamenca 7–980
Hui Mein 10–1368
Huish Cake 7–980
Humbugs 8–982
Hummer mit Dill 8–982
  Ragoût 8–983
Hummersalat 8–984
Hummus bi Tahina 8–985
Hung Shao Chi 8–985
  Chu Jo 8–986
  Ngiu Jou 8–986
  Pai Tsai 8–986
Hungarian Apple Pie 8–987
  Apple Salad 8–988
  Apple Soup 8–988
  Apricot Soup 8–988
  Beef 8–988
  Beef Goulash 2–204
  Cheese Dip 8–988
  Cherry Soup 8–989
  Chocolate Layer Cake 8–989
  Cream Cake 8–989
  Fish Soup 8–990
  Layered Cabbage 8–991
  Layered Crêpes 8–991
  Potato Pie 15–2060
  Sauerkraut and Sausage Soup 8–992
  Strudel 15–2098
  -Style Sauerkraut 8–992
Hunter's Hare Stew 21–2954
  Stew 8–993
  Style Eggs 19–2593
Huntingdon Fidgett Pie 8–994
Huseini Kebabs 8–995
Hush Puppies 8–995
Hussar Meat Loaf 8–995
Hutspot 8–995
Hutzelbrot 8–996
Huysman's Salad 8–996
Hwang Chi Hsia Ren 8–996
  Yu Pien 8–998
Hyères Chicken 8–999
Hymettus Goose 8–999

I

Ibadan Shrimp Salad 8–1000
Icebergs 8–1000
Icebox Biscuits 8–1000
  Cake 8–1001
Ice-Cream see also Bombe
  Bases 8–1003-4
  Cake Dessert 21–2989
  Chocolate 8–1004
  Coffee 8–1005
  Crêpes 8–1005
  Ginger 8–1005
  Grapefruit 8–1005
  Roll 8–1006
  Strawberry 8–1005
Iced Almond Biscuits 6–783
  Asparagus Soup 8–1007
  Beetroot and Meat Soup 9–1154
  Carrot and Orange Soup 8–1007
  Chocolate Dominoes 8–1008
  Coffee 8–1008
  Fruit Soup 8–1009
  Herb Tea 8–1009
  Peaches 8–1010
  Pineapple with Orange Syrup 8–1010
  Raspberry-Filled Pastry Cakes 1–11
  Tea 8–1010
  Zabaglione 8–1010
Icicles 8–1010
Icing see also Frosting
  Glacé 6–837
  Plastic 14–1842
  Sugar Syrup Based 8–1013
Idma Soup 8–1014
Igloo Pudding 8–1014
Ikan Goreng 8–1015
Ile Flottante 8–1016
Imam Bayeldi 8–1016
Immos 8–1018
Impanata di Pesce Spada 8–1018
Imps 8–1019
Incanestrato Cheese with Chicken Livers and
  Noodles 8–1020
Indian Fried Wholemeal Bread 12–1675
  Lime Pickle 8–1020
  Pudding 8–1020
  Roast Duck 19–2610
  Tomato Sauce 18–2474
Individual Cheese and Fish Bakes 8–1021
  Custard Creams 14–1934
Indonesian Baked Banana 8–1022
  Beef in Chinese Sauce 8–1022
  Chicken Satay 8–1022
  Fried Rice 8–1023
  Rice 11–1477
Ingber 8–1024
Ingelegte 8–1024
Ingots 8–1024
Inkfish, Stewed in Red Wine 8–1025
Inlagda Rödbetor 8–1026
Insalata d'Arancia e Lemone 8–1026
  di Finocchio, Cicoria e Pomodoro 8–1026
  di Fontina 8–1026
  di Funghi 8–1026
Instant Yogurt Pudding 8–1026
Iranian Beef Stew 9–1130
  Nut Bread 8–1029
  Prune Soup 8–1030
Involtini alla Contadino 8–1028
  alla Marito 8–1029
  alla Sophia 8–1029
Irish Leek and Oatmeal Broth 8–1030
  Moss Mould 8–1030
  Potato Cakes 8–1031
  Potato Pancakes 2–225
  Soda Bread 8–1031
  Stew 8–1032
  Tipsy Pudding 8–1032
Iscas 8–1033
Ishu Didi 8–1034
Isle of Wight Doughnuts 8–1034
Israeli Deep-Fried Pastries 12–1654
Italian Baked Beans 5–668
  Bananas 8–1035

Boiled Beef 2–206
Braised Lamb 1–3
Breakfast Bread 12–1672
Cheese and Almond Pudding 8–1036
Cherries 8–1036
Chocolate Dessert 22–3040
Chocolate Loaf 8–1037
Chocolate Mousse in Chocolate Cups
  22–3028
Kebabs 18–2383
Meat Loaf 8–1037
Meat Sauce 2–206
Meat Stew 19–2590
Meat and Vegetable Soup 8–1037
Melon Salad 8–1038
Mozzarella Bread 8–1038
Pasta 3–312
Pumpkin-Shaped Dessert 22–3038
  Roast Pork 1–65
  Sauce 8–1039
  Sausages with Haricot Beans 16–2226
  Stuffed Squid 3–296
  Tomato Garlic Sauce 14–1828
  Vegetable Soup 14–1824
Ivanhoe Croûtes 8–1039
Ivory Coast Grill 8–1040

J

Jacqueline's Lemon Wonder Pudding 8–1041
Jaffa Biscuits 8–1041
Jagnjeci But 8–1042
Jal Farazi 8–1042
Jalousie à la Confiture 8–1043
  au Fromage 8–1043
Jam Buns 8–1046
  Coconut Bars 8–1047
  Crêpes 4–496
  Date and Nut Turnovers 8–1047
  Dougnuts 5–575
  Glaze 8–1048
  Greengage 7–875
  Loganberry 9–1259
  Omelet 8–1048
  Roly-Poly 8–1048
  Sauce 8–1048
  Sour Cream Crêpes, and 12–1663
  Tarts 8–1048; 9–1242
  Triangles 8–1049
Jamaican Beans 8–1050
  Casserole 8–1050
  Coconut Sauce 8–1050
  Coffee 8–1050
  Pepper Wine 8–1050
  Pie 8–1052
  Plain Cake 8–1052
  Rum Pudding 8–1052
  Rum Punch 8–1053
  Spice Loaf 8–1053
Jambalaya 8–1054
Jambon Braisé au Madère 8–1055
  Braisé au Vin Blanc 8–1056
  en Croûte 8–1057
  aux Echalottes 8–1055
James's Chocolate Mousse 8–1057
Jamon Con Nabos 8–1058
Jänispaisti 8–1058
Jansson's Temptation 8–1059
Japanese Cakes 8–1059
  Chicken and Oyster Fondue 21–2943
  Grilled Fish in Wine Sauce 7–881
  Sardines 8–1060
  Soup 8–1116
  Steak with Vegetables 6–814
Japonica Jelly 8–1061
Jarret de Boeuf en Daube 8–1061
Javanese Curry 8–1061
  Fish in Soy Sauce 8–1062
  Omelet 4–526
  Pork 8–1062
  Steak 8–1062
Jege Zeitoon 8–1062
Jellied Beetroot Soup 8–1064

Cheesecake 8–1064
Chicken Breasts 8–1065
Cream and Strawberry Flan 8–1065
Eels 8–1066
Eggs 8–1067
Fish Mould 8–1067
Grape and Cheese Salad 8–1067
Halibut 8–1068
Mayonnaise 8–1069
Melon Salad 8–1069
Pork Soup 6–813
Sponge Cakes 8–1069
Veal 8–1070
Jelly Crêpes 8–1072
  Sauce 8–1072
  Tart 8–1073
Jenny Lind Cake 8–1073
Jersey Wonders 8–1074
Jerusalem Artichoke Casserole 8–1074
  au Gratin 8–1075
  Savoury Pie 17–2263
  Soufflé 8–1075
  Soup 8–1076
Jewfish Mexican Style 8–1076
Jewish Noodles 8–1076
  Potato Pancakes 9–1212
  Potato Salad 8–1109
  Stuffed Dumplings 9–1174
Jhinga Kari 8–1076
  Pakoras 8–1076
  Tikka 8–1077
Jiffy Tuna Surprise 8–1078
Jinja Stew 8–1078
John Dory (info) 8–1079
  Cider, in 8–1079
  Marsala, in 8–1079
  Onion and Cream Sauce, with 8–1080
  Provençal Sauce, with 8–1080
Johnnycake 8–1080
Jojamba 8–1080
Jordanian Stuffed Lamb 8–1081
Jordgubbsvisp 8–1082
Jou Ping Hui Por-Ts'ai 8–1082
  Si Chow Ching Ts'ai 8–1082
  Yuan Ts'a Hui
Judge Biscuits 8–1084
Judias Verdes con Salsa di Tomate 8–1084
Jug Jug 8–1084
Jugged Celery 8–1085
  Hare 8–1086
Juleskinke 8–1086
Juliana Cakes 8–1087
Julienne Celery, Potatoes and Green Pepper
  8–1088
  Soup 8–1089
Jumbles 8–1089
Jumping Potatoes 8–1089
Junidessert 8–1090
Juniper Berry Sauce 8–1090
Junipered Pork Chops 8–1090
Junket 8–1090

K

Kabli Channa 8–1091
Kachang Bendi Goreng 8–1091
Kadu Polo 8–1092
Kaeng Chud Kai Hed 8–1093
Kaffeecreme 8–1094
Kahklehtin 8–1094
Kakaria 8–1096
Kaiser Cutlets 8–1095
  Garnele mit Dillsosse 8–1096
Kaiserschmarrn 8–1096
Kakavia 8–1096
Kalamaria Yemista 8–1096
Kalbsfrikassee mit Spargel 8–1098
Kalbshirn in Muscheln 8–1098
Kalbsleber mit Sahne 8–1099
Kalbsreisfleisch 8–1099
Kalbszunge mit Pilzen 8–1099
Kale (info) 8–1100
  Cream Sauce, with 8–1100

Onions and Italian Sausage, with 8–1100
Kalops 8–1100
Kalte Ente 8–1100
Kaltschale 8–1101
Kalve Soubise 8–1102
Kalveschnitzel med Sur Fløte 8–1100
Kalvesuppe med Madeira og Champignoner 8–1102
Kalvetournedos med Asparges 8–1102
Kambala s Shpinafom 8–1102
Kannelagkage 8–1104
Kapaun mit Champignons und Spek 8–1105
Kapitan Curry 8–1105
Karamelrand 8–1106
Karani 8–1106
Kärdia Cabbage 8–1107
Karlstadtklösse 8–1107
Karp po Zydowsku 8–1109
Karpion b'Paprika 8–1108
Kartoffelmos med Aebler 8–1109
Kartoffelsalat 8–1109
Käse Bouillon mit Ei 8–1110
Käsekuchen 8–1111
Käsepfannkuchen 8–1111
Käsespätzle 8–1112
Käsestrudel 8–1110
Kasha Cholent Liver Bake 8–1112
 Mushrooms and Onions, with 8–1113
 Tomatoes and Parmesan Cheese, with 8–1113
Kashoniri 11–1450
Kasseler Rippchen 8–1114
Katerfrühstück 8–1114
Katheryn Cake 8–1115
Katsudon 8–1116
Katushki and Prunes 8–1116
Kawasaki Chicken 8–1116
Kazan Stew 8–1117
Kebab, American Style 8–1118
 Fruit, with 8–1118
 Herb Marinade, in 8–1118
 Italian 18–2383
 Liver 11–1422
 Marinated in Yogurt 8–1118
 Massalan 8–1120
 South African 17–2350
  Soy Sauce and Sherry, with 8–1120
  Spiced Lamb 19–2500
  Veal 8–1120
  Yogurt Marinade 8–1118
 Kedgeree 9–1121; 21–2944
 Kipper 9–1146
Kefta 9–1121
Keftedes 9–1122
Kelaa Almond Pastries 9–1122
Kemah Lamb Cubes 9–1122
Kerkenna Island Hotpot 9–1124
Kesäkeitto 9–1125
Khachapuri 9–1126
Khalva 9–1126
Kheema 9–1128
Khichri 9–1128
Kholodetz 9–1128
Khoresh Bademjan 9–1128
 Holu 9–1130
 Karafs 9–1130
Kichlack 9–1130
Kid, Italian-Style 9–1131
 Tomatoes and Courgettes, with 9–1132
Kidney (info) 9–1134
 Bacon Snacks, and 9–1134
 Bacon with Wine, and 9–1135
 Casserole 9–1136
 Chicken Liver Brochettes, and 2–267
 Creole 16–2153
 Curried 7–897
 Fried with Chillis 9–1136
 In Their Overcoats 9–1140
 Lamb's Liver Brochettes, and 2–268
 Mushroom Croûtes, and 9–1136
 Mustard Sauce, in 9–1138
 Noodles, with 16–2153
 Omelet 12–1585
 Ragout 9–1138
 Sauté 17–2259
 Sautéed and Flambéed 16–2153

 Sausage and Scrambled Egg, with 11–1540
 Savoury Stuffing, with 9–1138
 Sesame Sauce, with 9–1138
 Sherry, with 9–1139; 16–2126
 Sour Cream, with 9–1140
 Sweetcorn, with 9–1140
 White Wine, with 9–1141
Kidney Beans and Brains in Spanish Sauce 9–1132
 Herb Casserole, and 9–1132
 Mexican-Style 9–1133
 Soup 9–1134
Kielbasa Loaf 9–1141
Kim u Chi 9–1141
Kinderkuchen 9–1142
King Crab Louis 9–1143
Kingly Orange Cake 9–1144
Kipper Cakes 9–1144
 Kedgeree 9–1146
 Pâté 9–1146
 Pie 9–1147
Kirovakan Fruit 9–1148
Kirsch with Bananas 9–1149
 Chestnut Cream, and 9–1149
Kirschen mit Eiskrem 9–1149
Kirschenstrudel 9–1149
Kirschkuchen 9–1150
Kirschpfannkuchen 9–1150
Kissel Chocolate 9–1151
 White Wine, with 9–1151
Kizlyar Boby 9–1154
Klenäter 9–1154
Klodnik 9–1154
Klops 9–1154
Klyazma River Soup 9–1155
Knackwurst and Beer Sauce 9–1156
 Lentil Casserole, and 9–1156
Knaidlach 9–1157
Knickerbocker Glory 9–1157
Knishes with Meat and Potato Filling 9–1158
Kødboller med Sellerisauce 9–1159
Koeksusters 9–1160
Koervelsuppa 9–1161
Kofta-Kabab Khatai 9–1161
 Kari 9–1162
Kogt Torsk med Asparges 9–1163
Kohlrabi in Béchamel Sauce 9–1164
 Soup 9–1164
Kokonda 9–1164
Kolduny Litewskie 9–1165
Königsberger Klops 9–1166
Kopfsalat mit Apfelsinen 9–1166
 mit Buttermilch 9–1166
Korean Pickled Cabbage 9–1141
 Vegetable Salad 9–1167
Korma 9–1167
Korsakov Meat and Potato Pie 9–1168
Kotelett mit Pflaumen 9–1168
Kotlety Pozharskie 9–1169
Kotopoulo Kapama 9–1169
Köttbullar 9–1169
K'ou Tse Ngiu Lan 9–1170
Kourambiedes 9–1170
Krabbensuppe 9–1171
Krammerhuse 9–1171
Kransekager 9–1172
Krendel 9–1172
Kreplach 9–1174
Kringles 9–1174
Kromeski with Chicken and Ham 9–1175
Krumkaker 9–1170
Krupnik 9–1176
Kuchen 9–1177
Kugel with Apples 9–1178
Kulebiak Ryba 9–1178
Kümmelkartoffeln 9–1179
Kumquat and Pineapple Salad 9–1179
Kuo Pa Jou Tin 9–1181
 Tieh Chi 9–1181
 Tieh Yu Pien 9–1182
Kurnic 9–1183
Kusa 9–1183
Kutya 9–1183
Kuzuhiki Soup 9–1184
Kyenam 9–1184

Kyllinger med Rejerog Asparges 9–1185
Kynute Ovocné Knedliky 9–1185

L

Labskaus 9–1186
Lady Baltimore Cake 9–1187
 Biscuits 9–1188
Laitues aux Crevettes 9–1188
 au Gratin 9–1188
Lamb (info) 9–1191
 Almonds, with 1–104
 Apples, with 9–1192
 Apricot Pilaff, and 9–1192
 Arabian Stewed 1–59
 Artichokes, with 9–1193
 Aubergine Sauce, with 9–1128
 Baked with Peppers and Cheese 9–1193
 Barbecued 1–119
 Bean Casserole, and 4–535
 Beef Balls, Skewered, and 3–348
 Breasts, with Devil Sauce 9–1194
 Breasts, Stuffed 4–526
 Cabbage Stew, and 9–1194
 Cashew Nut Curry 9–1194
 Cider Sauce, in 3–331
 Coconut, with 17–2293
 Coconut Curry 19–2565
 Country-Style 9–1197
 Curry 7–895; 9–1167
 Easter 5–601
 Ecuadorian, Stew 5–603
 Egyptian Soup 5–678
 Isabella 9–1198
 Italian Braised 1–3
 Jordanian Stuffed 8–1081
 Kebabs 7–868; 17–2297
  Knuckle of 9–1159
 Knuckle of, and Tomato Soup 9–1159
 Languedoc, Pie 9–1207
 Leg of, Adapazari 9–1218
 Leg of, with Coriander and Garlic 9–1219
 Leg of, English Style 9–1219
 Leg of, Marinated in Spiced Yoghurt and Roasted 15–2037
 Leg of, Roast, Coated with Mustard 6–826
 Leg of, Roast, with Haricot Beans 6–827
 Leg of, with Savoury Rice 9–1220
 Leg of, with Wine and Lemon Sauce 9–1220
 Leg of, Yugoslavian 8–1042
 Lemon Sauce, with 22–3018
 Lemon Soup, and 5–588
 Lentils, with 9–1198
 Loin of, with Mushrooms 9–1260
 Loin of, with Peas and Beans 9–1260
 Loin of, with Tomatoes and Potatoes 10–1261
 Marinated, Grilled on Skewers 8–995
 Marinated, Kebabs 8–995
 Mushroom Stew, and 9–1200
 Neck of, with Marjoram and Orange 11–1486
 Patties, Greek-Style 9–1201
 Pilaff 9–1200
 Ragoût 1–5
 Rice, with 9–1201
 Rice and Dill, with 1–105
 Rice Pilaff, and 19–2598
 Saddle 16–2200
 Salad 7–869; 9–1201
 Sauté 17–2257
 Sautéed with Paprika 1–6
 Sherry Sauce, in 21–2944
 Shoulder of, with Potatoes 5–650
 Shoulder of, with Prunes 5–649
 Shoulder of, with Turnips 9–1201
 Skewered 1–5; 2–212
 Soup 7–930
 Spiced Rice, with 2–174
 Steamed 17–2296
 Stew with Bacon and Onions 4–545
 Stew, Greek 7–869
 Stew with Parsley 7–855
 Stew with Sherry 3–297
 Stew with Tomatoes 4–548
 Stew with Vegetables 9–1202

Turkish, Stew and Lemon Soup 5–588
Vegetable Casserole, and 19–2584
Walnut Bake, and 20–2734
Yoghurt, with 21–2931
Lamb Chops, Boned with Aubergine and
Tomato Sauce 11–1506
Boned, with Mushroom Sauce 11–1508
Boned, with Mushrooms and Tomato Sauce
11–1508
Boned, in Pastry Cases with Puréed Peas
11–1506
Boned, with Spaghetti and Tomato Sauce
11–1507
Boned, with Vegetables and Rice 11–1507
Coated in Breadcrumbs and Parmesan
Cheese 4–458
Fruit Sauce with Rice, in 6–801
Pakistani 12–1661
Peveragno 13–1767
Rosemary, with 9–1195
Sweetcorn and Pimentos, with 9–1197
Tomatoes and Herbs, with 9–1197
Victor Hugo 9–1197
Yugoslavian 3–348
Lamb Cutlets in Aspic 9–1198
Cucumber and Onion, in 4–460
New Orleans 11–1499
Lamb's Liver with Cauliflower 9–1202
Peppers, with 1–62
Tomato Sauce, with 9–1202
Lamb's Tongues with Red Wine 9–1204
Lancashire Hot Pot 9–1205
Tea Cakes 9–1205
Langue de Boeuf Braisé 9–1206
Langues de Chats 9–1207
Languedoc Lamb Pies 9–1207
Länttulaatikka 9–1208
Lapin aux Poireaux 9–1208
à la Sauce Moutarde 9–1209
Lapland Loaf 9–1209
Lardy Cake 9–1210
Lasagne 9–1212
Latkes 9–1213
Lauchsalat 9–1214
Layer Cake with Buttercream Filling 6–739
Lazy Chocolate Cake 9–1214·
Lebanon Immos 8–1018
Leek (info) 9–1215
Bacon Rissotto, and 22–3021
Béchamel Sauce, with 9–1215
Cress Soup, and 14–1920
Honey Dressing, with 14–1850
Hungarian-Style 14–1849
Potato Cold Soup, and 20–2685
Salad 9–1214
Sausage Tart, and 9–1216
Shrimp Salad, and 9–1216
Soup 9–1216
Vinaigrette 9–1216
Légumes à la Grecque 9–1221
Nouveaux Flambés 9–1222
Leipziger Allerlei 9–1223
Lekach 9–1223
Lemon and Almond Flan 9–1223
Balm and Orange Drink 9–1224
Biscuits 9–1225
Bread Pudding 9–1225
-Butter Sauce 2–164–6
Cake 9–1226
Chicken 9–1240
Curd 9–1226
Doughnuts 5–579
Egg Soup, and 1–88
Lime Chiffon, and 9–1226
Mackerel 3–350
Manqué 9–1229
Marmalade 9–1228
Meringue Cake 19–2600
Meringue Pie 9–1228
Mustard Seed Chutney, and 9–1229
Posset 9–1230
Salad, and 9–1224
Sauce 1–128; 9–1230
Soufflé 9–1230
Sponge 9–1231

Tapioca Pudding 9–1231
Walnut Buns, and 9–1232
Whip 9–1233
Lemonade 9–1233
Lenguado Catalan 9–1233
Lentil Curry 5–562
Spices, with 16–2234
Vegetable Soup, and 9–1240
Lesco 9–1234
Lettuce (info) 9–1234
Baked with Shrimps 9–1188
Cheese Sauce, with 9–1189
Cos see Romaine
Heart, and Fruit Salad 9–1235
Romaine and Orange Salad 16–2159
Salad with Buttermilk 9–1166
Leverpostej 9–1235
Lightning Orange and Chocolate Cake 9–1236
Lihamurekepiiras 9–1237
Lima Beans with Mushrooms 9–1238
Lime Cream Pie 9–1238
Juice Cordial 9–1238
Marmalade 9–1239
Lin-Moun Chi 9–1240
Linsensuppe 9–1240
Linser 9–1260
Linzertorte 9–1242
Lipauer Cheese 9–1242
Liqueur d'Abricot 9–1243
de Cassis 9–1245
Lithuanian Meat-Filled Pockets 9–1165
Liu Jou-Pien 9–1245
Yu-Pien 9–1245
Liver see also Calf's Liver; Chicken Livers;
Lamb's Liver; Pig's Liver; Ox Liver
(info) 9–1246
Bacon, with 9–1246
Brochettes with Sausage 2–267
Casserole 9–1246
Italian-Style 9–1247
Mousse 9–1248
Mushroom Omelet, and 9–1249
Olive Pâté, and 9–1245
Olives and Mushrooms, with 9–1249
Onions, with 5–680
Oysters, with 9–1250
Pakistani Spiced 12–1662
Pâté 9–1235; 9–1250
Pâté Quenelles 15–2015
Pie 9–1251
Portuguese Marinated, with Red Wine Sauce
8–1038
Sausage, and Egg Spread, 9–1251
Sauté 17–2259
Strudel 14–1846
Stuffing 9–1252
White Wine, in 9–1252
Yu-Tsin Pot Roast 21–2951
Lobster (info) 9–1252
Bisque 2–176
Braised in White Wine 7–958
Brandy Sauce, with 9–1254
Butter 9–1254
Canapés 3–304
Chowder 9–1254
Cold, Stuffed with Vegetables 7–960
Cooked with Garlic, Herbs, Tomatoes
and Wine 7–958
Cream, with 7–958
Curry Sauce, in 9–1254
Devilled 4–449
Devilled Sauce, with 1–59
Dill, with 8–982
Marsala 10–1331
Mayonnaise 9–1254
Mushroom Mousse, and 9–1257
Newburg 9–1257
Salad 8–984; 9–1257
Sauce 9–1258
Stew 8–983
Thermidor 9–1258
Tomatoes, Onions and Garlic, with 7–960
Whisky, with 7–958
Loganberry Jam 9–1259
Lökdolmar 10–1266

Lokshen Pudding 10–1267
Lombo de Porco com Pimentos 10–1267
London Broil with Béarnaise 10–1267
Buns 10–1268
Long Island Bake 10–1268
Clam Sauce 10–1269
Halibut Steaks with Cucumber Sauce 10–1270
Seafood Pilau 10–1270
Lotus Root Salad 10–1272
Lou Jo 10–1272
Loucoumades 6–761
Louisiana Coconut Pie 10–1272
Rice Pudding 10–1272
Snack 10–1272
Luncheon Cake 10–1274
Luxembourg Waffles 6–809
Lvov Black Bread 10–1275

M

Macadamia Nut Pie 10–1275
Macaroni Cheese 10–1276
Herring Salad, and 10–1276
Neapolitan-Style 10–1277
Raisins and Apricots, with 10–1278
Ricotta Pudding, and 10–1278
Macaroon and Apricot Whip 10–1279
Brazilian 2–236
Chocolate, with 10–1280
Grand Marnier, with 10–1280
Hazelnuts, with 10–1281
Pecans, with 10–1281
Tartlets 11–1405
Mackerel (info) 10–1282
Baked Stuffed 17–2290
Fillet, with Caper Sauce 5–694
Fillet Flan 18–2483
Fillet, with Herbs 5–694
Fillet, with Mustard Sauce 5–695
Fillets, Marinated in Lemon Juice
Lemon and Caper Sauce, with 10–1282
Monte's 11–1416
Piquant 21–2895
Soused 17–2363
Soy Sauce, with 10–1282
White Wine Sauce, in 10–1283
Madeira Cake 10–1284
Sauce 10–1285
Madeleines 10–1285
Madras Chicken Curry 10–1286
Madrid Stew 10–1286
Mahasha 10–1287
Mahogany Cake 10–1278
Maids of Honour 10–1288
Maine Cauliflower and Tomato Pickle 10–1289
Pancakes 10–1288
Maitre d'Hotel Butter 10–1290
Maize Pudding 10–1290
Malakoff Sponge Cake 10–1290
Malaysian Fish 10–1290
Grilled Chicken 10–1292
Omelet 10–1292
Pork Chops 10–1293
Mallow Brownies 10–1294
Malt Bread 10–1295
Maluive Poulet 10–1296
Malynka's Lamb Dumplings 10–1296
Ma-Mounia 10–1297
Manchester Tart 10–1298
Mandarin Orange Butter 10–1298
Mandel-Halbmonde 10–1298
Mandletorte 10–1298
Mange-tout Salad 10–1300
Mango Chicken 10–1300
Chutney 10–1300–1
Manhattan Clam Chowder 10–1302
Cocktail 10–1303
Manicotti with Ricotta Stuffing 10–1303
Manitoba Poppy Seed Roll 10–1304
Manjar Blanco 10–1305
Manzo Brasato alla Vino Blanca 10–1305
alla Vino Rosso 10–1306
Maple Bread Pudding 10–1306

Butterscotch **10**–1307
Cocktail **10**–1308
Cream Pie **10**–1308
Orange Mousse, and **10**–1308
Spare Rib Casserole **10**–1309
Syrup Cake **10**–1310
Maraccas Beach Pilau **10**–1310
Marak Perot Car **10**–1311
Marble Cake **10**–1311
Marbled Chicken **10**–1312
Marinara Sauce **10**–1314
Maritozzi Uso Fornaio **10**–1317
Marjoram Vinegar **10**–1318
Marlborough Apple Pie **10**–1318
Marmalade Bars **10**–1320
  Chocolate Cake **10**–1321
  Dundee **5**–591
  Five Fruit **6**–718
  Grapefruit **7**–862
  Pudding **10**–1322
  Sauce **10**–1322
  Tangerine Flan, and **10**–1322
Marquise Alice **10**–1323
  Tartlets **10**–1324
Marrons Braisés **10**–1325
  Charlotte **10**–1327
  Montpélier **10**–1327
  Soufflé **10**–1327
Marrow (info) **10**–1328
  Ginger Jam, and **10**–1328
  Pickle **10**–1328
  Savoury Stuffing, with **10**–1329
  Soup **10**–1330
Marsala Clove Chicken 1330
  Lobster 1331
  Dressing **10**–1332
  Sauce **10**–1332
  So'mores **10**–1332
  Squares **10**–1332
  Tangerine **10**–1334
Marshmallows **10**–1332
Martha Washington Cake **10**–1334
Martinville Soulfood Stew **10**–1335
Maryland Chicken **10**–1336
  Seafood Soup **10**–1337
Marzipan **10**–1337
  Biscuits **10**–1338; **13**–1760
  Danish Cake **9**–1172
  Hazelnuts **10**–1338
  Roll **10**–1340
Mataloe Rice Cakes **10**–1340
Matambre **10**–1341
Matchstick Potatoes **1**–17
Matrimonial Cake **10**–1342
Mattersburg Almond Roll **10**–1342
Matzo Brei **10**–1344
  Chicken and Dill **10**–1344
  Fry **10**–1345
  Fry **10**–1345
  Kugel **10**–1345
Mayonnaise **10**–1346
  Jellied **8**–1069
  Piquant Herb **17**–2246
  Remoulade **15**–2096
  Roquefort **16**–2164
Maze Gohan **10**–1346
Meat and Corn Pie **13**–1692
  Flan **18**–2487
  Fruit Pilau, and **10**–1352
  Glaze **10**–1352
  Mould **8**–1084
  Pastries **5**–644
  Patties **2**–178
  Pickled Herring Patties, and **5**–677
  Potato Croquettes, and **4**–505
  Potato Hot Pot, and **10**–1355
  Pudding **14**–1939
  Quenelles **15**–2017
  Vegetable Stew, and **13**–1776
Meatballs American-Style **10**–1355
  Chop Suey **8**–1084
  Chutney Sauce, with **10**–1356
  Cream, with **10**–1356
  Curry **9**–1162
  Dates and Almonds, with **16**–2194

Enclosed in Spinach **18**–2478
Goulasch **22**–3024
Hot Mexican Sauce, with **10**–1356
Katushi **8**–1116
Lemon Sauce, with **10**–1357
Lemon and Caper Soup, with **9**–1166
Onion Casserole, and **10**–1358
Oriental Sweet and Sour Sauce, in **10**–1358
Pomegranate and Walnut Sauce, with **5**–686
Sherry Sauce, with **10**–1359
Spaghetti, with **17**–2369
Spiced **9**–1122
Spicy Sauce, with **10**–1360
Stew **10**–1361
Stuffed with Cream Cheese **10**–1361
Stuffed with Hard-Boiled Eggs **11**–1476
Swedish **9**–1169
Tabriz **18**–2464
Tomato Sauce, in **1**–6; **10**–1362
Vegetable Stew, and **12**–1574
Yiddish **21**–2924
Yogurt Sauce, in **9**–1161
Meat Loaf **10**–1352, 1354
  Egg, with **9**–1154
  Italian **8**–1037
  New England **11**–1496
  Olive **12**–1572
  Pastry, in **9**–1237
  Piquant **13**–1820
  Steamed **14**–1858
  Tuscan **19**–2581
Medaljer med Fløde **10**–1362
Mediterranean Chicken **10**–1363
  Fish Stew **1**–8
  Seafood Stew **10**–1365
  Veal Stew **10**–1365
Mee Fong Jou **10**–1368
  Ngiu Jou **10**–1368
  Yu Pien **10**–1368
Mein **10**–1368
Melba Sauce **10**–1370
  Toast **10**–1370
Melkeringer **10**–1370
Melktert **10**–1370
Melon (info) **10**–1370
  Avocado Salad, and **10**–1371
  Balls in White Wine **10**–1372
  Cherry Coupe, and **10**–1372
  Cold Pork Salad, and **10**–1375
  Crème Pâtissière and Strawberries, with **10**–1373
  Honeydew, with Blackcurrant Iced Mousse **7**–967
  Honeydew, and Pear Salad **7**–967
  Italian, Salad **8**–1038
  Jellied, Salad **8**–1069
  Mélange **10**–1373
  Mousse **7**–887
  Prawn or Shrimp Cocktail, and **10**–1373
  Stuffed **6**–812
  Water see Watermelon
Melonade **10**–1371
Melted Butter Sauce **10**–1373
Melting Moments **10**–1374
Melton Mowbery Pie **10**–1374
Meringue Almond Layer Cake **10**–1378
  Basket **10**–1378
  Chantilly **10**–1379
  Crown **10**–1380
  Cream Cake with Strawberries **19**–2600
  Cuite **10**–1378
  Italienne **10**–1378
  Leaves **6**–785
  Martinique **10**–1380
  Pancake **10**–1381
  Pineapple Soufflé, and **5**–679
  Poached on Chocolate Custard **2**–223
  Suisse **10**–1378
  Walnut Cake **10**–1381
Merlans Farcis aux Crevettes **10**–1382
Merluza à la Marinera **10**–1382
Mero à la Naranja **10**–1383
Mexican Cheese Squares **15**–2018
  Chicken and Bean Soup **3**–298
  Chicken with Fruit **10**–1384

Chilli con Carne **10**–1385
Chilli Spaghetti **10**–1386
Fruit Drink **10**–1386
Pork Chops **4**–457
Pork Fillets **10**–1386
Pork and Rice **10**–1386
Stuffed Eggs **10**–1388
Stuffed Pancakes **5**–645
Stuffed Peppers **10**–1388
Mi Tse Ho-Tui **11**–1409
Michaelmas Goose **10**–1389
Midsummer Dream **10**–1390
  Soup **10**–1391
Milk Curd **10**–1370
  Punch **14**–1872
Mille-feuille Stuffed with Crab **10**–1392
Millet Bread **10**–1392
Millionaire Salad **10**–1394
Mince Casserole **10**–1393
Minced Beef and Aubergine Casserole **10**–1394
  Chicken **10**–1395
Mincemeat **10**–1396
  Apple Crumble, and **10**–1396
  Apple Flan, and **21**–2958
  Cake **10**–1398
  Pies **10**–1398
  Sauce **10**–1398
Minestrone **10**–1400
Minorcan Vegetable Soup **10**–1401
Mint Ale **11**–1402
  Chutney **11**–1402
  Dressing **11**–1402
  Julep **11**–1402
  Mushroom Soup, and **11**–1403
  Pastries **11**–1404
  Sauce **11**–1404
Mirabelle Soufflé **11**–1405
Miranda's Salad **11**–1405
Mirlitons **11**–1405
Miroton de Boeuf **11**–1406
Montevideo Fish Casserole **11**–1416
Monywa Soup **11**–1416
Morbrad med Aebler og Svesker **11**–1418
Morcon **11**–1419
Morello Cherry Flan **11**–1420
  Sauce **11**–1420
  Yogurt, with **11**–1420
Mornay Sauce **11**–1420
Morue à l'Americaine **11**–1423
Mistress Hill's Cakes **11**–1407
Mixed Seafood Casserole **11**–1409
Mkate Wa Mayai **11**–1409
Mocha Cream Pie **11**–1410
  Katy **11**–1409
Mock Cream **11**–1410
  Turtle Soup **11**–1410
Mohrschokoladedessert **11**–1412
Molasses Crumb Pie **11**–1413
  Hazelnut Pie **11**–1413
  Sponge Cake **11**–1414
  Taffy **11**–1414
Molina Soup **11**–1414
Mombasa Biscuits **11**–1415
Monday Soup **11**–1415
Monk Fish Sauce **21**–2887
Monte's Mackerel **11**–1416
Moravian Loaf **11**–1418
Moroccan Chicken **11**–1421
  Kebabs **15**–2036
  Lamb and Honey Casserole **11**–1422
  Liver Kebabs **11**–1423
  Minced Lamb Kebabs **9**–1121
Mos-bolletjies **11**–1424
Moscari Psito **11**–1424
Mother's Bread Pudding **11**–1426
  Matzo Balls with Chicken Soup **11**–1426
Motley Cake **11**–1426
Moulded Cream Pudding **11**–1428
  Egg Custard **16**–2176
  Peach Salad **11**–1428
Moules au Citron **11**–1429
  Marinières **11**–1429
Moussaka **11**–1430–1
  Fish, with **11**–1431
  Greek-Style **11**–1432

Vegetarian **19**–2656
Mousse Apricot, with Blackberries **11**–1433
　Chocolate **11**–1434
　Frozen Orange **11**–1436
　Ice-Cream Base, for **8**–1004
　Orange and Chocolate **11**–1436
　Raspberry **11**–1436
　Salmon, Frozen **11**–1436
Mousseline au Chocolat **11**–1438
　Sauce **11**–1439
Mouton Farci **11**–1439
Mozzarella in Carozza **11**–1440
　Chicken **11**–1441
　Crespoltini **11**–1441
Muesli **2**–172
Muffins with Apples **11**–1442
　Blueberry **2**–188
　Bran Nut **2**–233
　Cheese, with **11**–1442
　Herbs, with **11**–1443
Muhalabia **11**–1443
Mulberry and Apple Pie **11**–1444
　Jelly **11**–1444
Mulled Wine **11**–1446
Mullet (*info*) **7**–878; **15**–2082
　Andalucian-Style **11**–1446
　Bacon and Peas, with **11**–1447
　Baked in Rock Salt **11**–1447
　Fennel and Wine, with **11**–1447
　Grey, with Béchamel Sauce **7**–878
　Grey, Martigues **7**–878
　Grey, with Tomatoes and Capers **7**–878
　Polynesian-Style **11**–1449
　Red, Baked in Foil **15**–2082
　Red, Baked with Shrimps **15**–2082
　Red, Marinated in Oil and Herbs **15**–2082
　Red, with Mixed Herbs **16**–2171
　Red, with Mushrooms **16**–2171
　Red, with Riviera Sauce **15**–2085
　Small Red in Tomato Sauce **14**–1851
Mulligatawny Soup **11**–1449
Murg Bhuna **11**–1449
Murray Chicken **11**–1451
Mushroom (*info*) **11**–1451
　Asparagus Mayonnaise, and **11**–1452
　Bacon Salad, and **11**–1452
　Celery on Toast, and **11**–1452
　Consommé **4**–442
　Cream and Sherry, with **3**–355
　Creamed **3**–355
　Cucumber, with **11**–1452
　Fish Pie, and **19**–2533
　Grilled **3**–354
　Ham Crêpes, and **11**–1452
　Hungarian-Style **11**–1453
　Ketchup **11**–1454
　Madeira Sauce, with **3**–354
　Marinated **10**–1314
　Mint Salad, and **11**–1454
　Omelet **12**–1578
　Pie **11**–1454
　Purée **11**–1455
　Rice, with **16**–2130
　Rolls **11**–1456
　Salad **8**–1026
　Sandwich Filling **11**–1456
　Sauce **11**–1457
　Sautéed in Butter **3**–353
　Soufflé **17**–2353
　Soup **11**–1457
　Stewed **3**–354
　Stuffed **3**–354
　Stuffing **5**–594, 676
　Tarragon Mayonnaise, with **11**–1458
　Vine Leaves, in **11**–1458
Mussel (*info*) **11**–1458
　Baked with Basil and Tomato **11**–1455
　Beef Pie, and **11**–1460
　Chowder **11**–1460
　Donegal, Soup **5**–572
　Fried in Batter **11**–1460
　Garlic Butter, with **11**–1462
　Hot, Hake and Vegetable Salad **16**–2210
　Lemon Sauce, with **11**–1429
　Mariners' Style **11**–1429

Mustard Butter **2**–166
　Mould with Prawns and Fruit **11**–1463
　Sauce **11**–1464
Mutton Chops Stuffed with Mushrooms and
　Celery **11**–1464
　Pies **11**–1465
　Stew **11**–1479–80
　Stuffed Shoulder, of **11**–1439

N

Nabob's Delight **11**–1466
Nabobeep Salad **11**–1466
Nai-yu-ts'ai-hsin **11**–1467
Najafabad Biscuits **11**–1467
Nakompatoa Forowee **11**–1468
Nalesnik **11**–1468
Namasu Maguro **11**–1469
Name-Day Bread **9**–1172
Nanban Zuke **11**–1470
Nantais Biscuits **11**–1470
Nantes Cakes **11**–1471
Nantwinam Kyewee **11**–1471
Nanymo Squares **11**–1472
Napoleon au Fromage Blanc **11**–1472
Narangas al Kirsch **11**–1474
Narbonne Biscuits **11**–1475
Nargisi Koftas **11**–1476
Nariel Chatni **11**–1476
　Samosas **11**–1477
Nasi Goreng **11**–1477
Nasturtium Buds, Pickled **11**–1477
　Spread **11**–1478
Nasu Karashi Sumiso-ae **11**–1478
Natalie's Dream Dessert **11**–1478
Nautical Stew **11**–1478
Navarin de Mouton **11**–1479
　Printanier **11**–1480
Navets Glacés **11**–1481
　au Gratin **11**–1481
　au Petit Salé **11**–1481
Navy Fruit Cake **11**–1482
Nazkhatun **11**–1482
Neapolitan Beef Stew **11**–1483
　Doughnuts **21**–2992
　Pizzas **11**–1484
　Stuffed Peppers **11**–1485
　Veal Chops **11**–1485
Near Eastern Pork with Peanuts and Grapes
　11–1486
Nectarine Chutney **11**–1488
　Cream Mould **11**–1488
　Pie **11**–1488
　Tartlets **11**–1488
Negroni Cocktail **11**–1490
Neptune's Delight **11**–1491
Nesselrode Pudding **11**–1493
Netherlands Pork **11**–1493
Nettle Soup **11**–1493
Neustadt Rouladen **11**–1494
Nevada Rice Cake **11**–1495
New England Boiled Dinner **11**–1496
　Meat Loaf **11**–1496
　Soda Bread **11**–1496
　Wedding Cake **11**–1496
New Haven Baked Aubergines **11**–1498
New Orleans Barbequed Pork Chops **11**–1499
　Lamb Cutlets **11**–1499
New Potatoes Cooked in Butter **11**–1500
　Sour Cream and Caviar, with **11**–1500
Newcastle Potted Salmon **11**–1501
Newington Snow **11**–1501
Nigerian Fried Yams **8**–1034
　Jollof Rice **11**–1501
Nitzanei-Kruv be'dvash **11**–1502
Njursaute **11**–1502
Nkontomire Fro **11**–1502
Noce de Vitello Farcito **11**–1502
Noisettes d'Agneau Arlésienne **11**–1506
　à la Clamart **11**–1506
　Ismail Bayeldi **11**–1507
　Milanaise **11**–1508
　Monegasque **11**–1508

　au Sauce Champignon **11**–1508
Noisettes de Porc aux Pruneaux **11**–1509
Noix de Veau aux Fruits **11**–1510
Noodles, with Breadcrumbs and Cheese,
　11–1524
　Brown Butter, with **11**–1510
　Cheese, with **8**–1112; **11**–1526
　Cheese and Cream, with **5**–686
　Chinese **10**–1368, 1369
　Crusty **4**–514
　Fettucine *see* Fettucine
　Foy **6**–737
　Fusilli, with Tomatoes and Cheese **6**–777
　Ham, with **11**–1510
　Jewish **8**–1076
　Mushrooms, with **11**–1512
　Onions, with **11**–1524
　Pudding with Apples **11**–1512
　Romano **16**–2160
　Soup **1**–75
　Tomato Soup, with **5**–687
Norfolk Dumplings **11**–1513
　Fruit Chutney **11**–1513
Norma's Breakfast Breads **11**–1514
Normandy Pear Tart **11**–1514
　Pork **11**–1516
Norrländsk Laxsoppa **11**–1516
North Country Cake **11**–1517
Northumberland Puddings **11**–1518
Norwegian Cream **11**–1518
　Cucumber and Potato Soup **11**–1519
　Fish Pudding **11**–1519
　Fish Soup **2**–162
　Rhubarb Dessert **8**–1090
　Soda Bread **11**–1520
　Sponge Cake **2**–186
　Venison Steaks **11**–1520
　Waffles **6**–728
Nougat Ice-Cream **11**–1521
Nougatine Cakes **11**–1522
Nouilles au Gratin **11**–1524
　à la Lyonnaise **11**–1524
Nova Scotia Potato Patties **11**–1524
　Salmon Cream **11**–1524
Noyau Cream **11**–1525
Ntroba Forowee **11**–1526
Nudel mit Käse **11**–1526
Nun's Salad **11**–1527
Nuremburg Chocolate Pudding **11**–1527
　Spice Squares **11**–1528
Nursery Cakes **11**–1529
Nuss Schlagsahne **11**–1531
Nusscreme Torte **11**–1529
Nusspastete **11**–1529
Nut and Apple Cream **11**–1531
　Cauliflower Flan, and **11**–1532
　Cheese Dressing, and **11**–1533
　Chocolate Cookies, and **11**–1533
　Chocolate Sauce, and **11**–1533
　Cream Cheese Balls, and **11**–1533
　Cream Cheese Puffs, and **11**–1534
　Croquettes **11**–1534
　Date Biscuits, and **11**–1535
　Fritters **11**–1535
　Princesses **11**–1537
　Raisin Stuffing, and **11**–1537
　Roll **11**–1537
　Sauce **11**–1538
　Sweet Potato Flan, and **11**–1538
　Waffles **11**–1538
Nutalie Flan **11**–1538
Nutmeg Cream **11**–1539
Nyrer med Karbonadepølser og Røraeg
　11–1540

O

Oat Bread **12**–1541
　-Cakes **7**–935; **12**–1542
　Caraway Bread **12**–1542
Oatmeal Bannocks **12**–1543
　Carrot Soup, and **12**–1543

Cheese Biscuits, and **12**–1543
  Cookies **12**–1545
  Ice-Cream **12**–1545
  Pancakes **12**–1545
  Skirlie **17**–2323
  Stuffing **12**–1545
Oban Kipper Soufflé **12**–1546
O'Brien Potatoes **12**–1546
Obsttorte **12**–1546
Obuasi Peanut Stew **12**–1547
Oca Arrosta Ripiena **12**–1548
Ocean Rolls **12**–1548
Ochsenzunge mit Madeira Sasse **12**–1548
Ocopa Arequipña **12**–1550
October Cobbler **12**–1550
Octopus (*info*) **12**–1551
  Alioli Sauce, with **12**–1552
  Anchovies, with **12**–1552
  Prawn Pilau, and **12**–1552
  Stew **12**–1554
  Tomatoes and Garlic, with **12**–1554
Oeufs Bourguignonne **12**–1555
  Campagnards **12**–1555
  Croquettes **12**–1556
  Espagnole **12**–1557
  Florentine **12**–1557
  à l'Hongroise **12**–1557
  Mornay **12**–1557
  Robert **12**–1558
  Soubise **12**–1558
Ohio Meat Pie **12**–1559
  Pudding **12**–1560
Oie Rôtie à l'Anglaise **12**–1561
  Farcie **12**–1561
  aux Marrons **12**–1562
  aux Pruneaux et Foie Gras **12**–1562
Oil Biscuits **12**–1564
  Chocolate Cake **12**–1564
Oiseaux Sans Têtes **12**–1565
Okra (*info*) **12**–1565
  Bacon, with **12**–1567
  Curried **20**–2665
  Lamb Casserole, and **12**–1567
  Salad **12**–1567
  Tomato Casserole, and **12**–1567
Okroshka **12**–1568
Old English Cider Cake **12**–1568
  Venison Stew **12**–1569
Old Fashioned Cocktail **12**–1569
  Date Chutney **12**–1570
Oliebollen **12**–1270
Olive Meat Loaf **12**–1572
  Pizza **12**–1572
  -Stuffed Eggs **12**–1573
  -Stuffed Pork **12**–1573
  Salad **12**–1573
  Vegetable Mix, and **12**–1574
Olla Podrida **12**–1574
Omelet (Omelette) Americaine **12**–1574
  Arnold Bennett **12**–1578
  Bacon, Onion and Potato **7**–968
  Bonne Femme **12**–1578
  aux Champignons **12**–1578
  Chasseur **12**–1578
  aux Crevettes **12**–1579
  aux Fines Herbes **12**–1580
  Florentine **12**–1580
  aux Fraises **12**–1580
  au Fromage **12**–1581
  Jam **8**–1048
  au Jambon **12**–1581
  Javanese **4**–526
  Liver and Mushroom **9**–1249
  à la Lorraine **12**–1581
  Lyonnaise **12**–1582
  Malaysian **10**–1292
  Meat and Vegetable **6**–759
  Mousseline **12**–1582
  Niçoise **12**–1582
  Normande **12**–1583
  Parmentier **12**–1583
  aux Poire **12**–1583
  Provençale **12**–1584
  au Rhum **12**–1584
  aux Rognons **12**–1585

Ricotta Cheese with Tomato Sauce **6**–759
  aux Rognons **12**–1585
  Soufflé **12**–1585
Onion (*info*) **12**–1587
  Bread **12**–1587
  Cake **19**–2583
  Dip **12**–1588
  Egg and Potato Pie, and **12**–1588
  Egg Spread, and **12**–1590
  Gruel **12**–1590
  Kuchen **12**–1590
  Lemon and Marjoram Sauce, with **12**–1591
  Mackerel Salad, and **12**–1592
  Omelet **12**–1582
  Paprika Dressing, and **12**–1592
  Pickled **13**–1780
  Pie **12**–1593
  Potato Hash, and **12**–1593
  Prunes, and **12**–1594
  Quiche **15**–2024
  Ragoût **12**–1594
  Rings, Deep-Fried **12**–1594
  Smothered with Walnuts **12**–1595
  Soup **12**–1595
  Sour Cream, with **12**–1596
  Stuffed and Baked **12**–1597
  Sweet and Sour Sauce, in **12**–1597
  Sweetcorn Hors d'Oeuvres, and **12**–1598
  Tart **22**–3077
Open Sandwich Gâteaux **12**–1598
Openwork Pastry Cheese Tart **8**–1043
  Jam Tart **8**–1043
Opiekanki z Grochu **12**–1598
Orange (*info*) **12**–1555
  Blossom Cocktail **12**–1601
  Cake **6**–806; **12**–1601
  Cake Fingers **12**–1623
  Caramel Trifle **12**–1602
  Carrot Salad, and **12**–1603
  Celery Salad, and **12**–1603
  Chicken with Rosemary **12**–1603
  Chocolate Biscuits, and **12**–1604
  Chocolate Dessert, and **12**–1604
  Cinnamon, with **12**–1605
  Crêpes **4**–499
  Crêpes Flamed with Orange Liqueur **4**–501
  Curd **12**–1605
  Custard **12**–1606
  Dessert **1**–25
  Devilled **4**–560
  -Flavoured Banana Fritters **12**–1606
  -Flavoured Liqueur **12**–1606
  Flip **12**–1606
  Fondants **12**–1607
  Glacées **12**–1612
  Glaze **12**–1612
  Glazed Pork Chops **12**–1612
  Grapefruit Salad, and **12**–1612
  Honey Butter, and **12**–1612
  Hot, Pudding **7**–794
  Lemon Salad, and **8**–1026
  Liqueur Soufflé **17**–2354
  Mint Sauce, and **12**–1613
  Peach Fondue, and **12**–1613
  Pickle **12**–1614
  Pork Casserole, and **12**–1615
  Rice **12**–1615
  Salad **12**–1616
  Sauce **12**–1616
  Shortbread Biscuits **12**–1616
  Soufflés **12**–1617
  Soufflé-Filled Crêpes **12**–1617
  Sour Cream Sauce, and **12**–1618
  Stuffed with Orange Cream **12**–1618
  Stuffed with Prawns or Shrimps and Rice **12**–1618
  Surprise Pudding **12**–1620
  Walnut Cake **12**–1621
  Wine Cup **12**–1622
Orangeade **12**–1601
Orangenstangerin **12**–1623
Oriental Cake **12**–1625
  Fried Chicken **12**–1626
  Fruit Salad **12**–1625
  Relish **12**–1625

Sauce **12**–1625
Orientalisk Kyckling **12**–1626
Orlando Duck **12**–1627
Oslo Eggs **12**–1628
  Salad **12**–1629
Osso Buco **12**–1630
Ostiones **12**–1630
Otterberg Biscuits **12**–1630
Oublies à la Parisienne **12**–1630
Ouillade **12**–1632
Oven Beef Casserole **12**–1632
  -Braised Beef with Burgundy **12**–1633
Oviedo Beef Stew **12**–1634
Ovos Duros à Portuguesa **12**–1635
Ox-heart Stew **12**–1635
Ox-palate Fricassée **12**–1637
Ox-tongue Braised with Bacon **12**–1637
  Devil Sauce, with **12**–1638
  Horseradish Sauce, with **12**–1638
  Hot Raisin Sauce, with **12**–1638
Oxford Sauce **12**–1638
Oxrullader **12**–1639
Oxtail (*info*) **12**–1640
  Braised **2**–230; **12**–1640
  Casserole **12**–1640
  Celery, with **4**–432
  Grilled **12**–1642
  Ragoût **12**–1642
  Soup **12**–1643
  Stew **7**–954
  Wine Stew, and **15**–2021
Oyster (*info*) **12**–1645
  Avocado Salad, and **12**–1647
  Baked **12**–1630
  Beef, Kidney and Mushroom Pie **12**–1648
  Cheese Sauce, with **12**–1648
  Chowder **12**–1650
  Cocktail **12**–1650
  Fritters **12**–1650
  Grilled **8**–981
  Grilled with Cream Cheese **8**–981
  Kilpatrick **12**–1651
  Marinated **8**–981; **12**–1651
  Meat Sausage, and **12**–1651
  Quenelles **15**–2017
  Rarebit **12**–1652
  Rockefeller **12**–1652
  Shrimp Fricassée, and **12**–1653
  Soup **12**–1654
  Stuffing **12**–1653
  Sweetcorn Stew, and **12**–1653
Oznei Haman **12**–1654

P

Pacific Oyster Soup **12**–1654
Paella **12**–1654
Paglia e Fieno **12**–1656
Pai Chou Chi **12**–1658
  Jou **12**–1658
Pain de Chou Fleur **12**–1658
  Pommes de Terre au Jambon **12**–1659
  Saumon **12**–1660
Pia Chiu Tung Chi **12**–1656
  Li Yu **12**–1656
Pakistani Chicken Tikka **12**–1661
  Lamb Chops **12**–1661
  Pulau **12**–1661
  Spiced Liver **12**–1662
Pakoras **12**–1662
Palacsinken **12**–1663
Palissade aux Marrons **12**–1663
Palm Hearts with Cheese Sauce **12**–1664
  Cocktail **12**–1664
  Salad **12**–1665
Palmiers **12**–1666
Palourdes Farcies **12**–1667
Perdues **12**–1667
Panade à la Farine **12**–1668
Pancakes *see also* Crêpes
  American-Style **12**–1668
  Blueberries, with **12**–1669
  Brie Topped **12**–1669
  Coconut Filled **1**–10

Dutch Meat 6–822
Emperor's 8–1096
Jewish Potato 9–1213
Maine 10–1289
Maple Syrup, with 12–1670
Russian 2–186
Pandolce Genovese 12–1670
Pandowdy 12–1671
Panettone 12–1672
Papanberg Bread 12–1672
Paprika Vegetable and Sausage Stew
12–1674
Wine Sauce 17–2246
Paprikasertésbord 12–1674
Paratha 12–1675
Parfait Judy 12–1677
Paris-Brest 12–1675
Parisian Wafers 12–1630
Parker House Rolls 12–1678
Parkin 12–1679
Parsley Fish Pie 12–1680
Lemon Stuffing, and 13–1681
Potatoes 13–1681
Sauce 13–1681
Parsnip (info) 13–1681
Glazed 13–1682
Onions, with 13–1682
Puréed 13–1682
Salad 13–1682
Soufflé 17–2357
Soup 21–1991
Tomato Soup, and 13–1682
Partridge (info) 13–1684
Cabbage, with 13–1751
Catalan-Style 13–1684
Curried 19–2588
Orange and Vermouth Sauce, with 13–1685
Pears, with 13–1685
Pie 13–1685
Pot Roast 13–1686
Quince, with 15–2082
Stuffed with Mushrooms 13–1687
Terrine 13–1687
White Wine and Vegetables, with 13–1751
Party Cake 13–1688
Pashka 13–1689
Passion Fruit and Banana Cream 13–1689
Pasta 3–312
Green Pea Sauce, with 13–1749
Ham, with 15–1995
Stuffed 4–447
Stuffed in Broth 3–319
Veal and Mushrooms, with 12–1656
Veal and Spinach, with 15–2070
Pastel de Choclo 13–1692
Pastilles Flavoured with Lemon 13–1692
Pastis 13–1693
Pâté en Croûte 13–1698
à Pâté 13–1702
Sucrée 13–1702
Paterson Creek Stew 13–1702
Pastry Bows 3–347
Cake 13–1696
Cake with Apple Purée 6–786
Cases 2–218
Choux 5–418
Cones with Cream and Fruit 6–778
Cream 4–492
Deep-Fried 3–347
Hot Water Crust 7–977
Openwork Tarts see Jalousie
Rich French 13–1702
Rough Puff 16–1712
Shortcrust 17–2306
Strudel 18–2425
Sweet 2–175; 13–1702
Patriotic Pudding 13–1703
Paul's Lemon Pudding 13–1704
Paupiettes de Boeuf à l'Hongroise 13–1704
de Porc 13–1706
de Sole à l'Indienne 13–1707
de Veau 13–1708
Pavlova 13–1709
Pea (info) 13–1710
Croquettes 12–1598

Soup 5–652
Soup with Ham 13–1710
Peach (info) 13–1711
Blackberry Dessert, and 13–1728
Brandy, in 13–1712
Cobbler 13–1712
Champagne Dessert, and 11–1490
Deep-Dish, Pie 4–550
Flan 13–1713
Jam 13–1713
Macaroon Cream Filling, with 13–1728
Marzipan, with 13–1728
Melba 13–1714
Pickle 13–1714
Puffs 13–1714
Raspberry Purée, with 13–1728
Wine 21–1843
Peanut Biscuits 13–1716
Ice-Cream 13–1718
Pork 22–3054
Stew 12–1547
Peanut Butter 13–1716
Biscuits 13–1717
Chicken Stew, and 13–1717
Pear (info) 13–1718
Baked with Cardamon 13–1718
Bread 2–172
Caramel Sauce, with 14–1851
Chicory Salad, and 13–1718
Chutney 13–1719
Condé 13–1721
Ice-Cream and Chocolate Sauce, with
14–1850
Jam 13–1721
Normandy Tart 11–1514
Omelet 12–1583
Paradiso 13–1721
Poached in Red Wine 13–1722
Poached in Vanilla Syrup 4–441
Salad 13–1722
Soup 2–173
Stuffed with Roquefort Cheese 13–1722
Tart Bourdaloue 13–1722
Pease Pudding 13–1724
Pecan Bars 13–1724
Loaf 13–1725
Pie 13–1725
Sour Cream Flan 13–1726
Torte 13–1727
Pecaná Husa se Zelím 13–1727
Pêches Cardinal 13–1728
aux Macarons 13–1728
au Massepain 13–1728
Rafraîchies aux Mûres 13–1728
Peebles Crab Bake 13–1730
Peloponnesian Lamb with Noodles 13–1731
Penang Beef 13–1734
Cabbage 13–1734
Chicken 13–1734
Curry Puffs 13–1734
Pennsylvania Dutch Chicken Corn Soup
13–1735
Mixed Chow-Chow 13–1736
Poultry Stuffing 13–1737
Peperonata 13–1737
Peperoni alla Bagna Cauda 13–1738
Ripieni 13–1738
e Zucchini 13–1739
Peppermint Chocolate Ice-Cream 13–1743
Chocolate Sandwich Cake 3–410
Clouds 13–1744
Creams 13–1745
Fondants 13–1745
Pepperoni Pizza 13–1747
Pepper (info) 13–1740
Corned Beef Hash, and 13–1739
Courgettes, with 13–1739
Garlic and Anchovy Sauce, with 13–1738
Green, Salad 7–873
Green, Stuffed with Pork and Veal 7–873
Green, Stuffed, and Tomato Sauce 1–61
Marinated Salad 2–160
Preserved in Vinegar 13–1743
Red see also Pimiento
Red, and Tomato Stew 13–1737

Red, Purée 15–1990
Sauce 13–1739
Stuffed with Lamb and Rice 13–1743
Stuffed with Tomato, Tuna, Anchovy and
Olive 13–1738
Tomato Omelet, and 13–1815
Zarzar Red, and Onion Soup 21–2984
Perch with Oregano 13–1748
Perciatelli con Piselli 13–1749
Perdices Estofadas 13–1751
Perdrix aux Choux 13–1751
Pernod and Chocolate Cream 13–1752
Persian Fried Rice 13–1752
Onion and Aubergine 13–1753
Onion Soup 5–569
Yogurt Soup 13–1753
Persimmon Flan 22–3047
Peruvian Chowder 13–1756
Pork Stew 13–1756
Seviche 13–1756
Petite Marmite 13–1758
Petits Chaussons au Roquefort 13–1758
Pâtés à la Russe 13–1762
Pots de Champignons 13–1765
Pots de Crème au Chocolat 13–1765
Petits-Fours 13–1758
au Chocolat 13–1760
aux Fruits Glacés 13–1760
au Massepain 13–1760
Petits-Pois au Beurre 13–1762
à la Bonne Femme 13–1762
à Crème 13–1763
aux Oignons 13–1764
Pets de Nonnes 13–1766
Peveragno Lamb Chops 13–1767
Pheasant (info) 13–1768
Almond Butter, in 13–1768
Aspic Jelly, with 6–781
Chestnut Casserole, and 13–1768
Cream, Calvados and Apples, with 5–671
Moulded with Cabbage and Vegetables 5–670
Oranges, with 5–671
Pâté, Country-Style 13–1770
Red Wine, with 5–673
Rice and Red Pepper, with 5–672
Sauerkraut and Apples, with 13–1771
Soup 13–1772
Truffles and Pâté, with 5–672
Philadelphia Pepper Pot 13–1772
Phoenician Honey Cakes 13–1773
Piatto Freddo di Ortaggi 13–1773
Picardy Rice 13–1774
Piccalilli 13–1774
Pichelsteiner 13–1776
Pichones en Mole 13–1776
Pickled Beetroot 8–1026; 13–1777
Chicken 13–1778
Cucumber 13–1778
Eggs 13–1779
Fish 5–652; 8–1024; 13–1756
French Beans 13–1780
Onions 13–1780
Pork Hash 9–1186
Salmon 7–867
Picnic Patties 13–1781
Salad 13–1783
Piedmont Salad 13–1783
Pigeon see also Squab (info) 13–1783
Casserole 13–1784
Cherries, with 13–1784
Chestnuts, with 13–1784
Green Peas, with 13–1786
à la Niçoise 13–1787
à la Normande 13–1787
aux Olives 13–1788
Orange and Wine Sauce, with 13–1789
Pie 13–1791
Stew 16–2215
Pig's Trotters with Breadcrumbs 13–1792
Pikantsas Oxrullader 13–1793
Pike (info) 13–1794
Anchovy Stuffing, with 13–1794
Baked 6–811
Mustard Butter, with 21–2977
Stuffed with Cucumber and Rice 19–2597

Stuffed with Mushrooms and Tomatoes 18–2509
White Wine, with 21–2976
Pilaff Azerbaijan 1–95
Balkan Chicken 1–108
Chicken Liver Ragoût, with 13–1795
à la Grecque 13–1795
Lamb and Almonds, with 13–1796
Nuts and Fruit, with 13–1796
Peppers and Chicken, with 13–1796
Pineapple and Cashew Nuts, with 13–1797
Pimiento Chicken 13–1798
Purée with Rice 15–1990
Pineapple (info) 13–1799
Bavarian Cream 13–1800
Cake 13–1800
Cheesecake 13–1802
Cheese Salad, and 13–1802
Chocolate Rings, and 3–412
Cream 13–1805
Custard 15–2018
Delight 13–1805
Flan 6–720
Fritters 2–160
Fruit Salad 13–1805
Honey Sorbet, and 13–1806
Jam 13–1806
Lettuce Salad, and 13–1806
Liqueur 13–1807
Pork Casserole, and 13–1808
Refrigerator Cake 15–2092
Sauce 13–1808
Shrub 13–1808
Soufflé 13–1808
Turkey Salad, and 13–1811
Upside-Down Cake 13–1811
Walnut Ice-Cream, and 13–1811
Pine-Nut Orange Buns 10–1317
Pink Lady Cocktail 13–1812
Pintades aux Cerises 13–1812
Farcies 13–1814
Pipérade 13–1815
Piquant Dip 13–1820
Stew 14–1822
Pirogen 14–1822
Piroshki 14–1823
Dill 5–565
Pissaladières 14–1824
Pistachio Ice-Cream 14–1824
Pistou 14–1824
Pita 14–1826
Pitcaithly Bannock 14–1827
Pithiviers 14–1827
Pizza alle Asciughe 14–1828
Aubergine, with 14–1830
Canapés 14–1831
Capri 14–1832
ai Funghi 14–1833
Neapolitan 11–1484
Olive 12–1572
Pepperoni 13–1747
al Prosciutto 14–1834
Quattrostagione 15–2002
Pizzaiola Sauce 14–1828
Plaice (info) 11–1834
Anatole 14–1834
Artichoke Sauce, with 14–1836
Baked with Sour Cream and Peppers 14–1838
Fillets in Asparagus Sauce 4–534
Garlic and Tomatoes, with 14–1836
Indonesian-Style 14–1839
Mushrooms, with 14–1836
Pickled 8–1114
Plaintain Chips 14–1839
Sesame Seed Coated 14–1840
Plaited Loaf 18–2424
Planters' Beef 14–1840
Punch 14–1840
Plastic Icing 14–1842
Plate Pie 14–1842
Plön Strudel 14–1846
Plum (info) 14–1846
Apple Marmalade, and 14–1846
Cake 18–1847
Cherry Soup, and 18–1847

Compôte 14–1847
Dumpling 22–3072
Jam 14–1847
-Stuffed Crêpes 14–1848
Poco Albondiga 14–1849
Poireaux à l'Hongroise 14–1849
au Miel 14–1850
Poires Belle Hélène 14–1850
au Caramel 14–1851
Poissons à la Niçoise 14–1851
aux Poivrons 14–1851
Polish Beetroot 14–1853
Bigos 14–1853
Carp 14–1854
Deep-Fried Potato Cakes 15–2044
Honey Drink 9–1176
Jam and Coconut Biscuits 15–1992
Orange and Almond Flan 14–1855
Ravioli 14–1822
Pollo alla Bolognese 14–1856
alla Cacciatora 14–1856
alla Diavola 14–1858
en Pepitoria 14–1858
Poloni 14–1858
Pomarez Pineapple 14–1860
Pomeroy Rolls 14–1861
Pommes et Abricots à l'Ancienne 14–1862
à la Bourguignonne 14–1862
au Cognac 14–1864
Gratinées 14–1864
Grimaldi 14–1864
Normandes 14–1866
Pommes-de-Terre Anna 14–1866
Campagnardes 14–1866
Dauphine 14–1868
Fondantes 14–1868
Galette 14–1869
à la Lyonnaise 14–1869
à la Provençale 14–1869
au Roquefort 14–1870
Sautées au Citron 14–1870
Soufflés 14–1871
Pomodori all Siciliana 14–1871
Ponche de Crème 14–1872
Poona Pilaff 14–1872
Poppy Seed Bread 14–1873
Cake 14–1875
Roll 14–1875
Pork (info) 14–1877
Apricot Bake, and 21–2888
Apricot Salad, and 14–1880
Balls with Ginger 14–1880
Balls in Wine Sauce 14–1881
Barbecued 1–120
Bean Stew, and 5–664
Braised Loin of, with Soured Cream and Caraway Sauce 6–820
Brawn 2–238
Cabbage Casserole, and 17–2302
Cantonese Roast 3–314
Casserole with Lemon 14–1882
Check see Bath Chap
Chinese Roast 3–402
Crown Roast of, with Peaches 21–2944
Curry 14–1890
Fillets, in Cream Sauce 14–1890
Fillets, Korean-Style 14–1892
Fillets, Marinated 10–1316
Fillets, with Red Wine 14–1892
Fillets, Stuffed with Apple 13–1706
Fillets, Wydling, Peppered 21–2886
Fried Rice 14–1893
Ginger and Pineapple, with 14–1894
Goulasch 14–1894
Grapes, with 14–1895
Ground Rice, in 10–1368
Italian Roast 1–65
Loin of, Braised 6–820
Loin of, with Garlic and Vegetables 10–1261
Loin of, with Juniper Berries 10–1262
Loin of, with Oranges and Pineapple 10–1263
Loin of, with Red Peppers 10–1267
Loin of, Stuffed with Apple and Prunes 11–1418

Mixed Vegetables, with 14–1897
Peaches, with 21–2923
Pie 14–1900
Pimentos and Onions, with 5–642
Ratatouille 22–3014
Red-Cooked with Soy Sauce 8–986
Ribs with Juniper Berries 14–1900
Roast California 16–2142
Romanian, Bake 16–2182
Saddle, of 16–2202
Sliced in Wine and Orange Sauce 14–1901
Smoked Fillet of, with Melon 17–2328
Pork Chops with Apples 14–1882
Apricots, with 19–2608
Baked with Cabbage 14–1883
Baked with Cream and Tarragon 14–1884
Barbequed 11–1449
Boned, with Prunes 11–1509
Braised, with Onions and Wine 14–1885
Braised, with Paprika Sauce 12–1674
Cheese, with 14–1885
Cooked in a Piquant Sauce 4–461
Cranberry Sauce, with 14–1886
Devilled 4–560
Juniper 8–1090
Malaysian 10–1293
Marinated 10–1314
Marinated Sweet and Sour 17–2250
Mexican 4–457
Morello Cherries, with 14–1886
Mushroom and Parsley Stuffing, with 14–1887
Mushrooms and Tomatoes, with 14–1888
Mustard Sauce, with 14–1888
Orange Glazed 12–1612
Piquant 14–1821
Pistachio Nut Stuffing, with 14–1889
Planters' 14–1840
Plums, with 9–1169
Rosemary, with 14–1890
Smoked 8–1114
Tomato and Green Pepper Sauce, in 4–458
White Wine and Herbs, in 4–458
Porridge 14–1902
Chocolate Biscuits 14–1902
Port Flip 14–1903
Raspberry Kissel, and 14–1903
Wine Steaks 14–1904
Portuguese Chicken Soup with Lemon 3–311
Custard 14–1908
Eggs in Tomato Shells 12–1635
Fried Potatoes 1–128
Kebabs 14–1908
Marinated Liver with Red Wine 8–1033
Potatoes 14–1908
Steak 2–168
Pot au Feu à la Béarnaise 14–1910
Pot Roast with Brandy 14–1912
Brewer's Gravy, with 14–1913
Garlic and Wine, with 14–1914
Marinated 10–1316
Peppers and Garlic, with 14–1914
Vegetables, with 14–1914
Potage au Brocoli 14–1916
au Chou-Fleur 14–1917
Crécy 14–1918
d'Hiver 14–1918
Parmentier 14–1919
Paysanne 14–1920
de Poireaux et Cresson 14–1920
de Tomate à la Paysanne 14–1921
Potato (info) 14–1921
Baked with Beef Stock and Cheese 7–866
Baked with Blue Cheese 14–1870
Baked with Milk, Cheese and Garlic 7–866
Bean and Tomato Salad 16–2212
Beef Patties Baked with Tomato Sauce, and 7–866
Border 2–210
Bread 14–1925
Cake 14–1869
Casserole 14–1925
Champ 3–351
Cheeps 3–361
Cheese Pie, and 14–1925

Cheese Salad, and **14**–1929
Cheese Sticks **2**–219
Country-Style **14**–1866
Croquettes **4**–504; **14**–1926
Curried **19**–2564
Deep-Fried, Shapes **14**–1868
Duchess **5**–581
Dumplings **2**–233; **7**–842
Egg, and Anchovy Salad **14**–1929
Garlic, with **14**–1869
Fritters **14**–1926; **17**–2273
Ham Loaf, and **12**–1659
Herring Salad, and **14**–1927
Hungarian, Pie **15**–2060
Irish, Pancakes **2**–225
Jumping **8**–1089
Kugel **14**–1927
Matchstick **1**–17
New **11**–1500
Omelet **12**–1581
Olive-Shaped **14**–1868
Onions, with **14**–1869
Peanut and Chilli Sauce, with **12**–1550
Peppers and Olives, with **14**–1927
Portuguese **1**–128
Puffs **14**–1871, 1929
Roast, Fans **7**–934
Salad **14**–1929
Sautéed with Lemon **14**–1870
Scones **14**–1930
Slices, Butter-baked **14**–1866
Soup **2**–233; **14**–1919
Soured **17**–2250
Spices and Mustard, with **14**–1930
Stovies **18**–2418
Stuffed, and Baked **14**–1930
Swiss, Cakes **16**–2167
Poteca **14**–1933
Pots de Crème de Luxe **14**–1934
Potted Cheese **14**–1935
Hare **14**–1935
Herrings **14**–1935
Pork **16**–2124
Shrimps **14**–1936
Tongue **14**–1936
Ponding d'Avocat **14**–1936
aux Fruits Sechés **14**–1938
de Viande **14**–1939
Poulet Brandade **14**–1942
au Brocoli **14**–1943
en Casserole à la Bonne Femme **14**–1942
aux Cerises **14**–1942
aux Champignons **14**–1942
au Crevettes **14**–1944
aux Girolles à la Crème **14**–1945
Frillé à la Diable **14**–1945
à la Normande **14**–1946
aux Pêches **14**–1946
Rôti aux Abricots **14**–1946
Sauté à l'Archiduc **14**–1948
Sauté au Basilic **14**–1949
Sauté à la Bordelaise **14**–1950
Sauté à la Provençale **14**–1951
Pound Cake **14**–1952
Pousse Café Gâteau **14**–1954
Poussins au Gingembre **14**–1956
Pressed, Caucasian-Style **18**–2462
Sautés au Citrons **14**–1956
Povoa Almond Cake **14**–1958
Prague Apricot Loaf **14**–1958
Praline Chocolate Ice-Cream Dessert **15**–1961
Soufflé **15**–1962
Prawn (*info*) **15**–1963
Avocado, and **15**–1963
Avocado Cocktail, and **15**–1966
Chick-Pea Fritters, and **8**–1076
Chow Mein **15**–1966
Coconut Stew, and **19**–2609
Cocktail **15**–1966
Crabmeat Spread, and **15**–1966
Curry **8**–1076; **15**–1967
Deep-Fried **4**–551
Dublin Bay **5**–580
Egg Foo Yung **15**–1968
Fritters **15**–1969

Patties **8**–1077
Piquant **14**–1821
Quenelles **15**–2014
Salad **15**–1970
Sweet and Sour Sauce, in **14**–1971
Tomato Sauce, with **6**–798; **8**–996
Presbyterian **15**–1971
Pretzels **15**–1974
Princess Cakes **15**–1975
Prinsessbakelser **15**–1975
Profiteroles with Ice-Cream and Chocolate
15–1976
Prosciutto Chicken Rolls **15**–1978
Melon **15**–1979
Pear **15**–1979
ai Piselli **15**–1979
Provençal Fish Soup **2**–225
Mushrooms **15**–1980
Prune (*info*) **15**–1980
Apple Maringue Flan, and **15**–1980
Iranian, Soup **8**–1030
Red Wine, in **15**–1981
Sage and Apple Stuffed **16**–2206
Tartlets **19**–2526
Walnut Soufflé, and **15**–1982
Prunella Starkies Indian Cake **15**–1982
Ptarmigans, with Red Cabbage and Wine
15–1982
Puff Pastry Biscuits **12**–1666
Cases **2**–218–9; **20**–2717
Layers with Chantilly and Jam **6**–804
Layers with Cream Cheese Filling **11**–1472
Twists **16**–2199
Puffy Fritters **2**–161
Sweet Biscuits **9**–1130
Pumpkin (*info*) **15**–1985
Caramel Flan, and **6**–722
Lamb Patties with Rice, and **8**–1092
Parma-Style **22**–3027
Pie **15**–1986
Salad **15**–1986
Soup **15**–1987
Punch **15**–1988
Archbishop **1**–60
Brandy **2**–236
German **6**–840
Jamaican Rum **8**–1053
Scandinavian **6**–840
Puntzin **15**–1989
Purée de Brocoli **15**–1990
de Piments an Riz **15**–1990
Puris **15**–1990
Putignano Ham **15**–1992
Puttlingen Biscuits **15**–1992
Pyrishky **15**–1992
Pytt i Panna **15**–1994

Q

Quadrettini con Prosciutto **15**–1995
Quail (*info*) **15**–1995
Cherries, with **15**–1996
Curry Sauce, with **15**–1996
Grapes in a Pastry Case, with **3**–292
Juniper Berries, with **15**–1998
Orange Stuffing, with **15**–1999
Risotto, with **15**–2000
Vegetables, with **15**–2001
Quail's Egg Soup **15**–2001
Quatre Quarts **15**–2002
Quattro Formaggi con Rise **15**–2002
Quattrostagione Pizza **15**–2002
Quebec Butter Tarts **15**–2004
Onion Soup **15**–2005
Split Pea Soup **15**–2008
Quagliette di Vitello **15**–1995
Queen Anne's Custard **15**–2008
Almond Pudding **15**–2008
Cakes **15**–2009
Flan **15**–2009
Mary's Tart **15**–2010
Muffins **15**–2010
Pudding **15**–2011
Puddings, of **15**–2011

Sauce **15**–2012
Soup **15**–2012
Queijadas de Evora **15**–2013
Quenelles **15**–2014
de Crustaces **15**–2014
de Foie Gras **15**–2015
de Fromage **15**–2016
aux Huîtres **15**–2016
de Truite **15**–2017
de Viande **15**–2017
Queretaro Bake **15**–2017
Quesadillas **15**–2018
Quesillo de Piña **15**–2018
Quetchuan Duck **15**–2021
Queue de Boeuf au Vin **15**–2021
Quiche aux Asperges **15**–2022
aux Champignons **15**–2022
aux Courgettes et Tomates **15**–2022
aux Crevettes **15**–2022
Lorraine **15**–2023
aux Oignons **15**–2024
au Thon **15**–2024
aux Trois Fromages **15**–2024
Quick Cassoulet **21**–2982
Crème de Menthe Turkish Delight **15**–2026
Italian-Style Beef **15**–2028
Lamb with Mushrooms **15**–2028
Peach Dessert **15**–2028
Tuna Fish Delight **15**–2029
Quick-Braised Beef and Vegetables **18**–2440
Quick-Fried Beef Slices with Oyster Sauce
7–922
Chicken Cubes with Walnuts **7**–972
Chicken Cubes in White Sauce **15**–2027
Prawns on Crackling Rice **21**–2962
Shredded Pork with Fish **21**–2948
Spinach with Shredded Pork **15**–2027
Quince (*info*) **15**–2029
Apple Sauce, and **15**–2030
Apple Turnovers, and **15**–2030
Compôte **15**–2032
Jelly **15**–2032
Lamb and Honey Stuffing, with **15**–2032
Partridge, with **15**–2032
Sherbert **15**–2033
Soup **15**–2033
Sweets **15**–2033
Water **15**–2033
Quindins **15**–2034
Quin's Loaf **15**–2034
Sauce **15**–2035
Quotban **15**–2036

R

Raan **15**–2037
Rabarberkompott **15**–2037
Rabbit (*info*) **15**–2038
Apricots, with **15**–2038
Broth **15**–2038
Cider, in **15**–2040
Fried in Breadcrumbs **15**–2040
Leek Casserole, and **9**–1208
Mustard Sauce, with **9**–1208
Pie **15**–2040
Stew **4**–547
Sweet and Sour Sauce, in **15**–2043
White Wine, in **15**–2043
Racuchy **15**–2044
Radis Glacés **15**–2045
Radish (*info*) **15**–2044
Celery and Cucumber Salad **15**–2045
Cream, in **15**–2045
Glazed **15**–2045
Ragenka **15**–2046
Ragoût de Boeuf aux Pois-Chiche **15**–2046
de Fruits de Mer **15**–2047
Lamb, of **1**–5
Martiniquais **15**–2048
d'Oie aux Marrons **15**–2048
de Veau **15**–2049
Rahmschnitzel **15**–2050
Raie au Beurre Noir **15**–2050

en Fritot **15**–2050
au Fromage **15**–2051
Railway Pudding **15**–2052
Rainbow Hors d'Oeuvre **15**–2052
Refrigerator Cakes **15**–2053
Raisin Brown Bread **15**–2054
Buns **11**–2056
Celery Sauce, and **15**–2057
Doughnuts **12**–1570
Rolls **15**–2057
Sauce **15**–2058
Turkey Salad, and **15**–2054
Raita **15**–2059
Rakott Burgonya **15**–2060
Ranchers' Eggs **15**–2061
Raspberry (*info*) **15**–2063
Bombe **2**–208
Buns **15**–2063
Cumin Buns **4**–520
Fool **15**–2063
Ice-Cream and Maraschino, with **15**–2063
Iced, Filled Pastry Cases **1**–11
Jam **15**–2064
Lemon Sorbet, and **4**–464
Liqueur **15**–2064
Meringue Delight **15**–2064
Mould **3**–358
Sauce **15**–2064
Rassolnik **15**–2066
Ratafia Biscuits **15**–2067
Trifle **15**–2067
Ratatouille **15**–2067
Rauschenburg Tart **15**–2068
Rava Kheer **15**–2068
Ravigote Butter **15**–2068
Sauce **15**–2068
Ravioli **15**–2068
di Manzo e Spinace **15**–2070
Piedmontese **15**–2072
di Rapallo **15**–2073
Ražnjići **15**–2073
Reading Apples **15**–2074
Rebhühner mit Birnen **15**–2074
Recruitment Apple Pastries **15**–2075
Red Bean Casserole **15**–2076
Lamb Casserole, and **15**–2076
Red-Braised Cabbage **8**–986
Red Cabbage and Bacon Casserole **5**–592
Braised **16**–2150
Red Wine, with **15**–2077
Salad **15**–2077
Red Caviar Dip **15**–2078
Radish Dressing **15**–2078
Red-Cooked Beef with Star Anise **8**–986
Chicken **8**–985
Pork in Soy Sauce **8**–986
Red Flannel Hash **15**–2081
Red Sea Salad **15**–2086
Red Snapper Almond and Walnut Sauce
15–2087
Bake **22**–3055
Oyster Stuffing, with **15**–2087
Red Wine Cup **15**–2087
Sauce **15**–2087
Redcurrant (*info*) **15**–2078
Cheesecake **15**–2078
Cream Biscuits, and **10**–1362
Flan **15**–2079
Frosted **15**–2080
Glaze **15**–2080
Jelly **15**–2080
Raspberry Compôte, and **15**–2081
Wine **20**–2843
Reform Sauce **15**–2089
Refried Beans **6**–758
Refrigerator Coffeecake **15**–2091
Pineapple Cake **15**–2092
Regal Flan **15**–2092
Regina Cake **15**–2094
Religieuse **15**–2095
Remington Salad **15**–2095
Rémoulade Sauce **15**–2096
Renny's Pudding **15**–2097
Rétes **15**–2098
Revythia **15**–2098

Rhine Wine Cup **15**–2100
Rhubarb (*info*) **16**–2164
Apple Crumble, and **16**–2101
Brown Betty **16**–2103
Cake **16**–2103
Compôte **15**–2037
Cream **16**–2103
Cream Flan **18**–2484
Flan **18**–2484
Ginger Compôte, and **16**–2104
Ginger Jam, and **16**–2104
Ginger Roly Poly, and **16**–2105
Norwegian Dessert **8**–1090
Orange Pie, and **16**–2107
Pudding **16**–2107
Rusks, with **22**–3076
Strudel **16**–2107
Ribbon Cakes **16**–2109
Rice (*info*) **16**–2110
Aubergine and Potato, with **16**–2112
Beetroot Salad, and **16**–2113
Brazilian **2**–239
Braised *see* Rissotto
Chicken and Vegetables, with **16**–2137
Chinese Fried **3**–402
Croquettes **16**–2113
Danish, and Almond Dessert **16**–2129
Empress, Pudding **16**–2135
Fig Dessert, and **16**–2113
Indonesian Fried **8**–1023
Lemon, with **16**–2134
Lentils, with **9**–1128
Meat with Chick-Peas, with **16**–2177
Noodles, Pork and Prawn or Shrimps, with
16–2114
Noodles with Spicy Beef **16**–2114
Peach Dessert, and **16**–2136
Peas, with **16**–2130
Picardy **13**–1774
Pudding, Rich **16**–2116
Ring Filled with Fruit **16**–2115
Shrimps, with **6**–786
Spanish **16**–2135
Yellow **6**–811
Rich Biscuits **16**–2116
Brown Sauce **4**–555
Chocolate Cake **16**–2116, 2147
Corn Meal Bread **16**–2116
Lamb Curry **9**–1167
Rum Fruit Cake **16**–2118
Yogurt **15**–2046
Richmond Cake **16**–2119
Ricotta Balls **16**–2120
al Caffé **16**–2120
Flan **16**–2120
Olive Scramble **16**–2121
Rigo Jancsi **16**–2122
Rillettes **16**–2124
Rindfleisch mit Zitronensusse **16**–2124
Riñones al Jerez **16**–2126
Ris de Veau au Beurre Noir **16**–2127
au Coulis de Tomates Provençale **16**–2127
au Fromage **16**–2128
aux Pâtes **16**–2129
Risalamande **16**–2129
Risi e Bisi **16**–2130
Risotto alla Bolognese **16**–2130
con Funghi **16**–2130
con Gamberetti **16**–2131
alla Milanese **16**–2132
con Zucchini **16**–2132
Rissoies de Camarâo **16**–2132
Rissoles, Estonian **5**–662
Portuguese Shrimp **16**–2132
Riverside Apple Flan **16**–2134
Riz au Citron **16**–2134
à l'Espagnole **16**–2135
à l'Impératrice **16**–2135
Melba **16**–2136
Rizotto Corine **16**–2137
aux Fruits de Mer **16**–2138
Roach Fried with Onions and Tomatoes
16–2139
Roast Beef Hash **16**–2142
Potato Fans **7**–934

Robert Sauce **16**–2144
Robin's Cake **16**–2144
Rochester Gammon Steaks **16**–2145
Rock Buns **16**–2145
Rock Salmon with Cayenne Sauce **16**–2146
Rococco Torte **16**–2147
Rodaballo de Fiesta **16**–2147
Rødkaal **16**–2150
Roe (*info*) **16**–2150
Scallop Shells, in **16**–2151
Toast, on **16**–2151
Rogham Gosht **16**–2152
Rognons à la Créole **16**–2153
Sautés et Flambés **16**–2153
Sautés aux Nouilles **16**–2153
Rollade **6**–2155
Rollmops **16**–2158
Roly-Poly with Dried Fruit **16**–2159
Romaine and Orange Salad **16**–2159
Roman Aubergine Hors d'Oeuvre **16**–2160
Beef Stew **18**–2427
Romanian Pork Bake **16**–2182
Sweet Bread **16**–2183
Vegetable Stew **6**–823
Romano Noodles **16**–2160
Roomborstplaat **16**–2162
Roquefort Brandy Spread **16**–2162
Cream Cheese Ring **16**–2162
Dressing **16**–2163
Mayonnaise **16**–2164
Rose Hip Syrup **16**–2164
Rose's Old-Fashioned Vegetable Soup
16–2165
Rosemary Bread **16**–2166
Eggs **16**–2166
Jelly **16**–2167
Rösti **16**–2167
Rothesay Pudding **16**–2168
Rouennaise Sauce **16**–2169
Rougets aux Champignons **16**–2171
aux Fines Herbes **16**–2171
Rough Puff Pastry **16**–2172
Rouladen **16**–2173
Roulades de Boeuf **16**–2173
aux Fraises **16**–2172
de Veau **16**–2174
Royal Icing **16**–2175
Peach Meringue **16**–2176
Pot Roast **17**–2326
Royale **16**–2176
Roz bi Dfeen **16**–2177
Rum Baba **1**–96
Bacardi **1**–98
Bananas **16**–2178
Butter **4**–519; **16**–2178
Chocolate Mousse **16**–2178
Chocolate Soufflé, and **22**–3048
Egg Sauce, and **7**–844
Hot Buttered **7**–973
Macaroon Cream, and **16**–2178
Omelet **12**–1584
Orange Layer Cake, and **16**–2180
Punch **16**–2181
Rich Fruit Cake **16**–2118
Sauce **16**–2181
Trifle **16**–2181
Rumanian *see* Romanian
Run Tsa Chin Kan **16**–2187
Li Chi **16**–2187
Runner Bean and Bacon Salad **16**–2188
Casserole **16**–2188
Mushrooms and Sour Cream Dressing, with
16–2188
Russian Chicken Blinis **8**–1106
Chicken Patties **9**–1169
Chicken Pie **9**–1183
Easter Dessert **13**–1689
Eggs **16**–2188
Fish Bake **16**–2188
Fish Pie **9**–1178
Fruit Mould **16**–2190
Herring and Beetroot Salad **16**–2190
Kidney and Cucumber Soup **15**–2066
Name Day Bread **9**–1172
Pancakes **2**–186

Salad **16**–2191
Salt Beef Mould **21**–2972
Star-Shaped Biscuits **22**–3070
Rustom's Chicken **16**–2192
Rutabaga and Apple Snow **16**–2192
Bake **16**–2192
Rutabiya **16**–2194
Rutland Gooseberry Cream **16**–2194
Rybnaia Solianka **16**–2195
Rye Bread **16**–2196

S

Sablés **16**–2197
Sabzi Pulao **16**–2198
Sachertorte **16**–2198
Sacristans **16**–2199
Saffron Buns **16**–2204
Cake **16**–2204
Rice **16**–2132, 2204
Shortcake **16**–2205
Sag Ghost **16**–2205
Sage and Cheese Bake **16**–2206
Onion Stuffing, and **16**–2206
Pork Fillets **15**–2207
Sago Pudding **16**–2208
Sake-Steamed Chicken **16**–2209
Salade d'Artichauts **16**–2210
Bagration **16**–2210
de Boeuf Côte d'Azur **16**–2210
Chaude Basquaise **16**–2210
de Figues **16**–2211
de Fruits à la Créole **16**–2211
Mimosa **16**–2212
Niçoise **16**–2212
Salami Stuffed Prunes **16**–2213
Sally Lunn **16**–2213
Salmagundy **16**–2214
Salmis de Pigeon **16**–2215
Salmon (info) **16**–2216
Aspic, in **16**–2218
Baked, Steak, with Mushrooms **4**–536
Balls **16**–2220
Cream Sauce, with **16**–2221
Dill Mayonnaise, with **16**–2221
Green Mayonnaise, with **17**–2254
Grilled **4**–537
Hollandaise Sauce, with **16**–2221
Kedgeree, of **9**–1121
Loaf **12**–1660; **16**–2222
Mushroom Patties, and **13**–1762
Pickled **7**–867
Roll **16**–2225
Smoked **17**–2332
Soufflé **17**–2357
Soup **11**–1516
Steaks Florentine **16**–2225
Steaks with Sweetcorn and Mushrooms **16**–2225
Yok Kai Chi Marinated **21**–2932
Salmon Trout and Mushroom Mayonnaise **22**–3065
Salsicce con Fagioli **16**–2226
Salsify Sautéed with Butter and Herbs **16**–2227
Tarragon Sauce, with **16**–2228
Salt Beef Mould **21**–2972
Brisket of Beef **16**–229
Coa Curry **21**–2979
Fish Balls **16**–2229
Fish Stew **16**–2231
Pork and Beef Stew **16**–2231
Pork and Lentil Stew **16**–2231
Salt Cod Casserole **1**–98
Rice and Brandy and Wine Sauce, with **11**–1423
Seasoned **17**–2283
Salted Almonds **1**–18
Fish Fried with Vegetables **11**–1468
Sambal **16**–2232
Sambar **16**–2234
Samosas **16**–2235
San Francisco Sourdough Bread **16**–2236
Sanctuary Pudding **16**–2236

Sand Cake **16**–2237
Sandwich Loaf **16**–2239
Sangria **16**–2239
Sardine (info) **17**–2239
Canapés **3**–305
Cups **16**–2240
Flan **22**–3066
Grilled Watercress Sauce, with **16**–2240
Pâté **21**–2992
Rarebit **17**–2241
Salad **17**–2241
Sandwiches **17**–2242
Satay Ayam **8**–1022
Sate **17**–2242
Sauce Bigarade **17**–2246
Blonde **1**–12
Espagnole **2**–271
Gribiche **17**–2246
Hongroise **17**–2246
à l'Indienne **17**–2247
Ivoire **17**–2247
Normande **17**–2247
Parisienne see Sauce Blonde
Saucisse en Croûte **17**–2248
aux Pommes **17**–2248
à la Purée de Celeri Rave **17**–2249
Sauer Kartoffeln **17**–2250
Sauerbraten **17**–2249
Sauerkraut see also Choucroute
mit Aprikose **17**–2252
Casserole with Dill Cucumbers **17**–2252
Chocolate Cake **17**–2252
Hungarian, and Sausage Soup **8**–992
Potato Bake, and **19**–2585
Wine, with **20**–2755
Sausage and Apple Cake **17**–2254
Apples, with **17**–2248
Bratwurst **2**–237
Broad Bean Casserole, and **7**–898
Cabbage Soup, and **6**–796
Glamorgan **6**–838
Italian, with Haricot Beans **16**–2226
Pastry, in **17**–2248
Puréed Celeriac, with **17**–2249
Rolls **17**–2256
Vegetable Stew, and **9**–1234
Sauté d'Agneau **17**–2257
Sautéed Kidneys with Chipolatas and Wine **17**–2259
Sauterelle **17**–2259
Savarin **17**–2260
aux Cerises **17**–2262
aux Macarons **17**–2262
Savoury Duck see Faggots
Dumplings **9**–1157
Fruit Salad **21**–2901
Scallops (info) **17**–2264
Cream Sauce, in **4**–445
Curry Sauce, with **17**–2265
Garlic and Basil, with **4**–445
Kebabs **17**–2264
Mushrooms in White Wine Sauce and Cheese, and **4**–449
Port, with **22**–3050
Salad **17**–2264
Shrimps, with **17**–2265
Soup **17**–2264
Tomato and Cream Sauce, in **4**–450
Vermouth Sauce, with **17**–2265
Vol au Vent **20**–2719
Scaloppine alla Limona **17**–2268
alla Marsala **17**–2269
alla Romana **17**–2269
Scampi Kebabs **17**–2270
Salad **17**–2270
Scandinavian Almond Apples **17**–2272
Biscuits **9**–1175
Haddock Parcels **16**–2147
Herrings, Baked **17**–2319
Potato Fritters **17**–2273
Punch **6**–840
S-Shaped Biscuits **18**–2397
Strawberry **8**–1082
Veal Escalopes in Sour Cream **8**–1101
Wheat Biscuits **20**–2684

Schokoladenpudding **17**–2273
Schwabische Schneeken **17**–2274
Scones with Cheese **17**–2275
Dried Fruit, with **17**–2275
Sour Cream, with **17**–2278
Wholemeal **17**–2278
Scotch Broth **17**–2278
Eggs **17**–2279
Mist **17**–2279
Pancakes **5**–578
Woodcock **17**–2279
Scrapple **17**–2279
Screwdriver **17**–2280
Sea Bass White Butter Sauce, with **17**–2280
Pie **17**–2281
Seafood Crêpes **4**–498
Mousse **20**–2736
Pie **7**–865
Salad **6**–769
Stew **15**–2047
Seamen's Stew **17**–2282
Seed Cake **17**–2283
Seekh Kebabs **17**–2284
Selkirk Bannocks **17**–2284
Selleriesalat mit Obst **17**–2286
Semmelknodel mit Pilzer **17**–2286
Semolina Cake with Raspberry Cream **7**–880
Croquettes **4**–506
Dumplings **7**–879
Milk Dessert **15**–2068
Pudding **10**–1297; **17**–2287
Pudding, with Strawberry Sauce **6**–718
Semur Banka **8**–1022
Serundeng **17**–2289
Sesame Seed and Aniseed Biscuits **19**–2524
Oatmeal Biscuits, and **17**–2289
Rolls **17**–2290
Salad **17**–2290
Seven Minute Frosting **6**–765
Sevian **17**–2290
Sgombro Ripieno **17**–2290
Shakooti Rassa **17**–2293
Shallot Butter with Red Wine **2**–166
Mushroom Salad, and **17**–2293
Shanghai-Style Drumsticks **5**–578
Shark's Fin Soup **21**–2947
Shashlik **17**–2297
Shellfish Butter **2**–166
Rice, with **16**–2138
Shepherd's Pie **17**–2298
Sherbert **17**–2299
Sherry and Almond Cake **17**–2300
Jelly **17**–2300
Shih-tzu-tou **17**–2302
Shikaree Slices **17**–2302
Shirred Eggs **17**–2303
Shoemaker's Pot **17**–2303
Shoofly Pie **17**–2304
Shortbread **17**–2304
Butter, with Almond and Fruit Filling **6**–821
Shortcake **17**–2304
Savoury **17**–2306
Shortcrust Pastry **17**–2306
Shredded Coconut Pyramids **17**–2307
Shrewsbury Biscuits **17**–2307
Shrikhand **17**–2307
Shrimp see also Prawn
Avocado Surprise, and **17**–2310
Bread Case, in a **4**–509
Butter **2**–166
Canapés **3**–303
Cheese Mould, and **17**–2310
Coralie **17**–2310
Creamed **7**–864
Cress-Stuffed Crêpes, and **17**–2311
Croquettes **4**–503
Curried Avocados, with **17**–2311
Dakar **4**–526
Dill Sauce, with **8**–1096
Egg and Cucumber Ring **17**–2311
Gilbert **17**–2311
German, Bisque **9**–1171
Ibadan, Salad **8**–1000
Omelet **12**–1579
Portuguese Rissoles **16**–2132

Provençale-Style 17–2312
Quiche 15–2022
Seviche 17–2313
Soufflé with Wine Sauce 17–2313
Stir-Fried with Ginger 17–2314
-Stuffed Fish 17–2314
Sweetcorn Soup, and 17–2314
Veal Rolls, and 17–2316
Shrove Tuesday Buns 17–2317
Sicilian Cake with Chocolate Icing 3–334
Sidecar 17–2318
Sill I Kapprock 17–2319
Sillgratin 17–2318
Simnel Cake 17–2320
Sindhi Chicken 17–2321
Singapore, Sling 17–2323
Singin' Hinny 17–2322
Skate (info) 17–2322
Black Butter, with 15–2050
Cheese Sauce, with 15–2051
Deep-Fried 15–2050
Egg and Lemon Sauce, with 17–2322
Skewered Lamb and Beef Balls 3–348
Skirlie 17–2323
Sloe Gin 17–2325
Jelly 17–2325
Slottsteck 17–2326
Smelt Mushrooms and Cheese 17–2327
Smoked Fish Salad 17–2328
Haddock, Baked with Mushrooms 17–2328
Haddock Scramble 17–2329
Salmon Creams 17–2332
Salmon Quiche 16–2332
Salmon Salad 17–2332
Salmon with Scrambled Egg 17–2332
Trout Pâté 17–2333
Smokies Arbroath 1–3
Cream, in 17–2334
Smørkage 17–2334
Snails Garlic Butter, with 5–657
Herb Butter, with 17–2274
Snicker Biscuits 17–2336
Snowball 17–2336
Soda Bread 17–2336
Solöga 17–2346
Sole (info) 17–2340
Bonne Femme 17–2340
Catalan 9–1233
English-Style 17–2341
Fillet of, with Asparagus Tips 5–697
Fillets of, with Butter Sauce 17–2342
Fillets of, with Cheese Sauce 17–2342
Fillets of, with Cream, Tomato and Parsley Sauce 17–2340
Fillets of, in Curry Cream Sauce 13–1706
Fillets of, with Grapes 17–2344
Fillets of, with Herbs 17–2341
Fillets of, with Mushrooms and Wine Sauce 17–2340
Fillets of, with Mussels and Shrimps 17–2343
Hapsburg 7–922
en Goujons 17–2341
Meunière 17–2342
Mornay 17–2342
Normande 17–2342
Red Wine, with 17–2344
Veronique 17–2344
White Sauce, in 17–2345
Solomon Grundy 17–2347
Sommargryta 17–2347
Sonhia 17–2349
Sorbet Glacée aux Abricots 17–2349
Spanish 17–2372
Söta Kakor 17–2351
Soufflé aux Amandes 17–2352
au Café 17–2353
de Champignons 17–2353
d'Epinards et Jambon 17–2354
au Grand Marnier 17–2354
Omelet 12–1585
Omelet with Pastry Cream 17–2357
aux Panais 17–2357
de Saumon 17–2357
Soupe Albigeoise 17–2358
de Poissons 17–2358

Sour Cream Icing 17–2360
Milk Cake 17–2360
Milk Orange Cake 17–2361
Pickle Sauce 17–2361
Sourdough Bread 16–2236; 17–2361
Soured Potatoes 17–2250
Sour-Sweet Cabbage 3–342
Soused Herring 17–2362
Mackerel 17–2363
South African Boiled Pudding 17–2363
Kebabs 17–2350
Soy Sauce Chicken 17–2364
Soya Protein Chilli 17–2365
Sour Cream, with 17–2365
Spaghetti con Aglio, olio e Peperoncino 17–2368
all'Amatriciana 17–2368
Butter and Cheese, with 17–2368
alla Carbonara 17–2368
Fennel Sauce, with 17–2369
Meatballs and Tomato Sauce, with 17–2370
con Salsa Verde 17–2369
alle Vangole 17–2370
Spanish Bean and Sausage Soup 5–666
Chicken 17–2370
Fish Stew 21–2984
Ham and Turnip Stew 8–1058
Omelet 17–2371
Pork Casserole 3–348
Rice 16–2135
Rice, Chicken and Seafood 12–1654
Sorbet 17–2372
Spare-Rib Helene 17–2372
Paprika Sauce, with 17–2375
Seville 17–2376
Southern-Style 17–2372
Stuffed with Kidneys 17–2374
Spice and Nut Cake 17–2376
Spiced Apple Sauce Cake 17–2377
Brisket 21–2959
Beef 17–2379
Chicken with Honey 17–2379
Fish 17–2379
Herrings 1–115
Lamb Kebabs 18–2500
Meatballs 9–1122
Ox Tongue 17–2380
Prawns 17–2349
Rice 18–2381
Rice with Lamb 2–174
Spicy Apple Flan 18–2382
Brown Sauce 2–271
Cauliflower 7–843
Chicken Casserole 18–2383
Chicken Kebabs 12–1661
Chick-Peas 6–796
Fish Salad 9–1164
Minced Beef Pie 2–190
Scrambled Eggs 1–9
Spiedini 18–2383
Spinach (info) 18–2383
Cheese Canpés, and 3–304
Cheese, with 5–651
Crêpes 4–496; 18–2389
Dumplings 7–842
Ham, with 18–2383
Meat, with 16–2205
Mould 18–2500
Omelet 12–1580
Potatoes, with 18–2385
Ring 18–2385
Salad 18–2388
Soufflé 18–2388
Soufflé with Ham 17–2354
Soup 18–2388
Stewed, with Fish 11–1502
Tomatoes and Garlic, with 5–652
Yarmacott, and Apple Soufflé 21–2911
Yogurt Salad, and 2–209
Spiral Biscuits 18–2389
Bread 18–2390
Spitzgebäck 18–2391
Split-Pea Soup 5–592; 18–2392
Vegetable Purée 5–652
Spoleto Pork Fillets 18–2392
Sponge Cake 18–2392

Cakes with Orange and Chocolate Topping 18–2394
Chocolate 3–414
Czech 2–277
Finger Biscuits 18–2394
Flan, Cherry Filled 18–2394
Flan Filled with Pineapple and Chestnut Cream 18–2394
Jellied 8–1069
Liqueur Icing 14–1954
Norwegian 2–186
Venezuelan 2–171
Spotted Dick 18–2396
Sprats Deep-Fried 4–552
Spring Onion and Tomato Soup 18–2397
Spritsar 18–2397
Squab see also Pigeon (info) 18–2397
Chocolate, with 13–1776
Grilled in Butter Sauce 7–883
Pie 18–2398
Squash with Bacon and Spices 18–2399
Soufflé 9–1183
Tomatoes, with 18–2399
Squid see also Inkfish (info) 18–2400
In Its Own Ink 3–296
Italian Stuffed 3–296
Rice-Stuffed 18–2400
Salad 18–2400
Stuffed 8–1096
Stargazey Pie 18–2400
Steak Andalousian 1–30
Barbecue Sauce, with 18–2404
Braised 2–232
Carpetbag 3–330
Chestnut Sauce, with 18–2404
Diane 18–2405
Dutch 5–594
Egyptian 5–638
Entrecôte 5–647
Esterhazy 5–664
Fillet, with Artichokes and Petits Pois 19–2532
Fillet, with Béarnaise Sauce 19–2529
Fillet, with Ham, Mushroom and White Wine Sauce 19–2529
Fillet, with Mushrooms and Wine Sauce 19–2532
Fillet, with Pâté 19–2582
Fillet, with Soy Sauce and Sake 7–898
Flank, Stew with Herbs 6–723
Green Peppercorns, with 18–2406
Japanese, and Vegetables 6–814
Kidney Pie, and 18–2404
Kidney Pudding, and 2–152
Marinated, Grilled 2–177; 18–2494
Marinated Skirt 10–1317
Mixed Herbs, with 18–2405
Mushrooms, with 18–2405
Pastry Cases, in 18–2406
Pepper, with 3–402
Porterhouse, with Red Wine Sauce 14–1905
Porterhouse, with Roquefort Cheese 14–1906
Porterhouse, with Spices 14–1906
Porterhouse, with Watercress Butter 14–1906
Portuguese 2–168
Raglan 18–2407
Red Wine Sauce, with 2–170
Rolled and Stuffed 10–1341
Rump, with Beer and Peppers 16–2184
Rump, with Coriander and Mushrooms 16–2185
Rump, with Mustard and Brandy Sauce 16–2185
Sandwiches 18–2407
Sautéed in Butter 2–171
Stuffed with Chicken Livers 18–2408
Sugared 21–2990
Tartare 18–2409
Tomatoes and Garlic, with 2–177
Wellington 2–156
Steamed Lamb 17–2296
Pudding 18–2409
Sweet Dumplings 8–1107
Stegt Ørred med Fløtdesors 18–2410
Stilton Ham Bake 18–2412

Stollen **18**–2415
Stories **18**–2418
Strawberry (*info*) **18**–2419
  Almond Cake, and **6**–803
  Baba **1**–98
  Charlotte **3**–359
  Cheesecake **3**–359
  Cream **4**–492
  Flan **18**–2419
  Ice-Cream **8**–1005
  Jam **18**–2419
  Omelet **12**–1586
  Orange-Flavoured Liqueur with Crème
    Chantilly, in **6**–737
  Sauce **18**–2419
  Scandinavian, Dessert **8**–1082
  Shortcake **18**–2420
  Soda **18**–2421
  Sponge Roll **16**–2172
  Sundae **18**–2421
  Tartlets **18**–2421
  Torte **18**–2422
  Ziggurat **18**–2422
Stritzel **18**–2424
Strudel, Beef Filled **18**–2427
  Fruit Rolls **18**–2428
  Pastry **18**–2425
Stufatino alla Romana **18**–2427
Stufato alla Genoese **18**–2429
  al Vino Rosso **18**–2429
Stuffed Aubergines, Courgettes and Tomatoes
    5–589
  Beef Rolls **1**–24; **6**–778; **16**–2173
  Breast of Veal **18**–2429
  Cabbage **6**–821; **18**–2430
  Cabbage Leaves **5**–687
  Cabbage Rolls with Sour Cream **7**–846
  Carrots **21**–2975
  Courgettes **21**–1979
  Cucumbers **18**–2430
  Goose, Roast **12**–1548
  Green Peppers **1**–61; **18**–2431
  Melon **6**–812
  Onions **10**–1287; **18**–2432
  Savoury Pastries **16**–2235
  Shoulder of Mutton **11**–1439
  Shoulder of Veal **5**–651
  Tomatoes **18**–2433
  Veal Rolls **2**–226; **16**–2174
Sturgeon, Russian-Style **18**–2433
Succotash **18**–2436
Suckling Pig with Sausage and Apricot Stuffing
    18–2436
  Roast, Stuffed with Feta Cheese **6**–824
Suédois **18**–2437
Suetcrust Pastry **18**–2437
Sugar and Cream Cheese Dessert **22**–3028
Sugared Almonds **1**–18
Sukiyaki **18**–2440
Sultana and Sago Pudding **18**–2440
Summer Casserole **17**–2347
  Pudding **18**–2440
Sun's Eye Hors d'Oeuvre **17**–2346
Suprêmes au Jambon **18**–2445
  Rossini **18**–2445
  de Volaille Flambés **18**–2444
Sussex Hot Pot **18**–2446
Swede (*info*) **18**–2446
  Apple Snow, and **16**–2192
  Bake **16**–2192
  Casserole **9**–1208
Swedish Beef Cakes **18**–2446
  Christmas Bread **20**–2721
  Christmas Crullers **9**–1154
  Gooseberry Pie **18**–2447
  Hamburgers **2**–169
  Hash **15**–1994
  Meat Loaf **18**–2449
  Meatballs **9**–1169
  Rye Bread **2**–248
  Sautéed Kidneys **11**–1502
Sweet Biscuits **17**–2351
  Bread **2**–249
  Cheese Tartlets **15**–2013
  Croûtes **4**–509

Pilaff **21**–2982
Potato Flan **18**–2454
Sweetbreads Braised with Mushrooms and
    Cream **18**–2450
  Brown Butter Sauce, in **16**–2127
  Cheese, with **16**–2128
  Chinese-Style **18**–2450
  Herb-Flavoured Tomato Sauce, with
    16–2127
  Pasta, with **16**–2129
  Vol au Vent **20**–2720
Sweet-and-Sour Beef **18**–2455
  Beef Stew **5**–660
  Carp **18**–2456
  Liver **18**–2457
Sweetcorn (*info*) **18**–2451
  Chicken Soup, and **18**–2452
  Mayonnaise **18**–2452
  Mushroom Croûtes, and **18**–2452
  Rarebit **18**–2452
  Salad **18**–2454
Swiss Brazilian Roll **2**–239
  Potato Cake **16**–2167
  Potatoes **18**–2457
  Roll **18**–2458
  Roll, Cream-Filled **18**–2458
  Steak **18**–2459
  Yeast Cake **14**–1933
Swordfish Cooked with Almonds **5**–659
  Breaded Steaks, with Piquant Tomato Sauce
    8–1018
Syllabub **18**–2459
  Trifle **18**–2460
Syrian Walnut and Orange Pastries **18**–2461
Syrup-Coated Doughnuts **9**–1160
  -Filled Buns **18**–2461

T

Tabaka **18**–2462
Tabboulch **18**–2462
Tabriz Meatballs **18**–2464
Tagliarini con Fegatini **18**–2464
Tagliatelle, con Prosciutto **18**–2465
  Verde with Bacon and Tomatoes **18**–2465
  Verde con Salsa di Tonno **18**–2466
Tajine de Mouton aux Fruits Secs **18**–2467
Tain Cereal **18**–2467
Taiyika Chicken **18**–2467
Takhing Pancakes with Pork Filling **18**–2468
Talairan Rice Salad with Garlic Sausage
    18–2468
Talawa Gosht **18**–2468
Tali Machi **18**–2470
Talmouses **18**–2471
Tamale Casserole **18**–2471
Tamarind Fish **18**–2472
  -Flavoured Mushrooms **18**–2473
  Sauce **18**–2473
Tamatar Bharta **18**–2473
  Chatni **18**–2473
  Machli **18**–2474
  Sas **18**–2474
Tan Mein **10**–1369
Tandoori Murg **18**–2474
Tangerine Stuffing **18**–2476
Tango Cocktail **18**–2476
Tansy Apple Cream **18**–2477
  Cakes **18**–2477
Tapioca with Apples **18**–2477
  Pudding **18**–2478
  Soup **8**–1093
Taraba **18**–2478
Taramasalata **18**–2479
Tarragon Butter **2**–166
  Pâté **18**–2480
  Sauce with Artichokes **18**–2480
  Vinegar **18**–2481
Tartare Sauce **18**–2482
Tarte aux Figues **18**–2482
  aux Filets de Maquereaux **18**–2483
  au Poulet **18**–2483
  à la Rhubarbe **18**–2484

à la Rhubarbe Soufflé **18**–2484
à la Viande **18**–2487
Tauchendorfer Torte **18**–2487
Tea Punch **18**–2490
  Sorbet **18**–2491
  Soufflé **22**–3068
Teddy Bear Cake **22**–3053
Teiglach **18**–2491
Tempura **18**–2491
Tenali Baked Fish **18**–2493
Tendrons de Veau aux Epinards **18**–2493
  au Jardinière **18**–2494
Teriyaki **18**–2495
Terrine de Canard **18**–2497
  Maison **18**–2497
Thayir Curry **18**–2497
Thousand Island Dressing **18**–2498
Three-Cheese Quiche **15**–2024
  -Fruit Sauce **18**–2498
Thrifty Soup **18**–2499
Thyme Stuffing **18**–2500
Tiffany Bake **18**–2500
Tikkah Lamb **18**–2500
Timbale aux Epinards **18**–2500
  de Jambon **18**–2502
  de Mais **18**–2502
Tinga de Cerda y Ternera **18**–2503
Tiraka Tiganita **18**–2503
Tiroler Kalbsleber **18**–2503
Toad in the Hole **18**–2504
Toast Sevilla **18**–2504
Toffee **18**–2505
  Almonds and Chocolate, with **18**–2505
  Apples **18**–2505
  Apples, Chinese-Style **15**–2508
  Cake **18**–2508
  Pudding **18**–2508
  Sauce **18**–2509
Tolona Baked Carp **18**–2509
Töltött Csuka **18**–2509
Tomaszow Roast **18**–2510
Tomato (*info*) **18**–2512
  Aspic **18**–2513
  Basil, with **1**–127
  Cheese Savoury, and **8**–2512
  Chicken Salad, and **18**–2512
  Chutney **18**–2473, 2513
  Consommé **4**–442
  Courgette Soup, and **18**–2513
  Curry **18**–2514
  Filled Choux Pastry Ring **18**–2514
  Fish, with **18**–2414
  French Bean Salad, and **18**–2515
  Mozzarella Salad, and **18**–2515
  Omelet **12**–1574
  Orange Salad, and **18**–2516
  Pie **18**–2516
  Puréed **18**–2473
  Rice **18**–2516
  Salad **18**–2518
  Sauce **18**–2518
  Sauce with Herbs **4**–464
  Soup **18**–2518
  Soup, Peasant-Style **14**–1920
  Stuffed with Anchovies **18**–2510
  Stuffed with Eggs **18**–2510
  Stuffed with Rice **18**–2511
Tongan Salad **18**–2519
Tongue (*info*) **18**–2520
  Braised Beef **9**–1206
  Cherry Sauce, with **18**–2520
  Lamb's, in Red Wine **9**–1204
  Salad **19**–2521
  Vegetable Aspic, and **19**–2521
Topton Biscuits **19**–2522
Torrejas de Maiz Terno **19**–2522
Torrijas **19**–2523
Torrone di Cioccolata **19**–2523
Tortas de Aceite **19**–2524
Tortellini **19**–2524
Tortillas de Chorizo **19**–2526
  Enchiladas **5**–645
Toscakake **19**–2526
Toucy Prune Tartlets **19**–2526
Toulouse Spiced Pâté **19**–2527

Touraine Chestnut Pudding **19**–2529
Tournedos à la Béarnaise **19**–2529
    Chasseur **19**–2529
    à la Clamart **19**–2532
    Rossini **19**–2532
    Sautés aux Champignons **19**–2533
    Vert-Pré **19**–2533
Tourte aux Champignons **19**–2533
    de Porc **19**–2534
Tranches de Jambon à la Normande **19**–2534
    en Piperade **19**–2536
    à la Sauce Madeire **19**–2536
Transparent Icing **19**–2537
Transvaal Braised Lamb **19**–2537
Transylvanian Goulasch **19**–2537
Treacle Biscuits **19**–2538
    Layer Pudding **19**–2538
    Scones **19**–2540
    Sweets **19**–2557
    Tart **19**–2540
Trebujena Grapefruit Cocktail **19**–2541
Trentina Dumplings **19**–2543
Trevose Barley Scones **19**–2543
Trifle **19**–2543; **22**–3059
Trinidad Chicken Pilau **19**–2544
    Coconut Ice-Cream **19**–2544
    Shark and Bakes **19**–2544
Tripe (*info*) **18**–2546
    Beans, and **19**–2546
    Onions, with **19**–2546
    Tomato Casserole, and **19**–2548
    White Wine, in **7**–864
    Wine Sauce, in **3**–301
Tropical Fruit Salad **19**–2549
Trote al Pomidoro **19**–2549
    Sulla Brace **19**–2550
Trout (*info*) **19**–2550
    Almonds, with **19**–2554
    Bacon, with **19**–2550
    Baked in Red Wine **19**–2556
    Baked in Tomato Sauce **19**–2549
    Baked in White Wine **19**–2550
    Butter Sauce, in **19**–2555
    Danish Fried, in Sour Cream Sauce **18**–2410
    Ghanian Baked **9**–1184
    Grilled **19**–2550
    Ham, with **19**–2555
    Horseradish Sauce, in **19**–2551
    Quenelles **15**–2017
    Smoked **17**–2333
Trucial Dainties **19**–2552
Truffles with Almonds **19**–2552
    Coffee, with **19**–2553
    Nuts, with **19**–2553
    Raisins, with **19**–2553
    Rum, with **19**–2553
    Whisky, with **19**–2554
Truites aux Amandes **19**–2554
    au Jambon **19**–2555
    Meunière **19**–2555
    au Vin Rouge **19**–2556
Trumps Creamed Lobster **19**–2557
Tsingshih Soup **19**–2557
Tuloons **19**–2557
Tuna Fish and Apple Salad **19**–2559
    Fish Spread **19**–2559
    Jiffy, Surprise **8**–1078
    Puffs **19**–2559
    Quiche **15**–2024
    Steaks, Provençale-Style **19**–2560
    -Stuffed Tomatoes **19**–2560
    Vegetable Salad, and **11**–1469
Tungpo Honey Apples **19**–2560
Tunisian Chicken Casserole **19**–2561
Turbot (*info*) **19**–2563
    Crabmeat Sauce, with **16**–2147
    Fillets Filled with Crabmeat **5**–697
    à l'Orange **19**–2563
    à la Piémontaise **19**–2563
    Shrimp Sauce, with **19**–2564
    Zara's with Clams **21**–2982
Turdillos **19**–2564
Turkari Allo **19**–2564
    Baingan **19**–2564
    Molee **19**–2565

Turkey (*info*) **19**–2566
    American-Style **19**–2567
    Apricot Stuffing, with **19**–2568
    Cherry Stuffing, with **19**–2568
    Chestnuts, with **5**–566
    Coronation **19**–2571
    Devilled, Drumsticks **19**–2571
    Ham and Mushrooms, with **19**–2571
    Ham Stuffing, with **19**–2571
    Lettuce and Tomato Sandwiches **19**–2572
    Meat Mould **19**–2573
    Orange Sauce, with **19**–2573
    Veal and Rice Stuffing, with **19**–2574
    Walnut Pie, and **19**–2574
    Yankee, Roast **21**–2909
Turkish Delight **15**–2026; **19**–2576
    Lamb Casserole **19**–2577
    Lamb and Lemon Soup **5**–588
Turlough Tarts **19**–2577
Turnips (*info*) **11**–1481
    Date Salad, and **19**–2578
    Fried in Butter **19**–2579
    Pickle **19**–2579
    Potato and Carrot Hash **19**–2579
    Soup **19**–2579
    Tops, Creole-Style **19**–2580
Turron **19**–2580
Tuscan Meat Loaf **19**–2581
Tushikow Chicken **19**–2581
Twelfth Night Cake **19**–2582
Tyler's Custard Pie **19**–2583
Tzibbele Kugel **19**–2583
Tzimmis **19**–2584

U

Uachdar Pudding **19**–2584
Uberbakens Sauerkraut **19**–2585
Uccelli Scappati **19**–2586
Uchaud Fish Mousse with Sole **19**–2586
Ugine Biscuits **19**–2587
Ugli Cocktail **19**–2587
Ukranian Borscht **2**–211
Umabai's Baked Spiced Fish **19**–2587
    Curried Partridges **19**–2588
    Spiced Almond Chicken **19**–2588
Umidio di Carne **19**–2590
Uncooked Fruit Soup **19**–2591
Unleavened Bread Rolls **19**–2593
    Indian Bread **3**–357
Uova alla Cacciatora **19**–2593
Uppingham Pâté **19**–2593
Upside-Down Apple Tart **19**–2594
    Apricot Cake **19**–2594
    Coconut Cake **19**–2596
Urchins **19**–2596
Uunissa Paistettu Hauki **19**–2597
Uvat Fish Soup **19**–2598
Uzbeck Plov **19**–2598

V

Vaca Filete con Especias **19**–2600
Vacherin Chantilly **19**–2600
    au Citron **19**–2600
    aux Noisettes **19**–2601
Valentine Cake **19**–2604
Vanilla Blancmange **19**–2605
    Crisps **19**–2605
    Custard **4**–492
    Khodoletz **19**–2606
    Mousse **19**–2606
    Rusks **19**–2607
    Soufflé **19**–2608
    Sugar **19**–2608
    Whipped Cream **4**–490
Varkenslappen met Abrikozen **19**–2608
Vatapa **19**–2609
Vath **19**–2610
Vatkattu Marjapuro **19**–2611
Vatrushka Pie **19**–2611

Veal (*info*) **19**–2612
    Artichokes, with **19**–2612
    Avocado Salad, and **19**–2613
    Bacon and Mushroom Brochettes **2**–268
    Bean Stew, and **19**–2613
    Benedictine **19**–2613
    Bigos **19**–2613
    Braised in White Wine **19**–2638
    Cake **19**–2626
    Casserole **19**–2639
    Cold with Tuna Fish Sauce **20**–2710
    Cream Sauce, in **2**–185; **20**–2710
    Curried **19**–2639
    Fasano **19**–2622
    Fillet with Basil **19**–2623
    Fricassée **6**–752
    German, Stew with Asparagus **8**–1098
    Ham and Cheese, with **19**–2623
    Ham Pie, and **19**–2624
    Jellied **8**–1070
    Knuckle of **9**–1159
    Knuckle of, with Gherkin Sauce **9**–1159
    Loin of, with Herb Stuffing **10**–1264
    Loin of, with Sage **20**–2709
    Loin of, Vichy **10**–1266
    Mushroom and Liver Stuffing, with **19**–2628
    Neck, of **11**–1486
    Nut and Raisin Stuffing, with **19**–2629
    Olives **19**–2629
    Olives on Skewers **19**–2629
    Orloff **19**–2629
    Oyster and Bacon Pie **19**–2630
    Parsley Sauce, with **19**–2630
    Pâté with Calf's Brains **19**–2632
    Patties **6**–751
    Predmontese **20**–2709
    Pot Roast **19**–2633
    Pork Pâté in Pastry, and **13**–1700
    Rice Casserole, and **8**–1099
    Roast **11**–1424
    Rolls with Mushroom and Ham Stuffing **19**–2633
    Scrambled Egg, with **20**–2710
    Soup with Madeira and Mushrooms **8**–1102
    Spanish-Style **19**–2634
    Spiced Stuffed Shoulder, of **18**–2381
    Stew **15**–2049; **18**–2429
    Stew with Tomatoes, Paprika and Green Peppers **2**–211
    Stock **19**–2634
    Strips in Wine and Cream Sauce **5**–642
    Stroganov **19**–2635
    Stuffed with Italian Hot Sausage **20**–2711
    Stuffed with Kidneys **19**–2636
    Stuffed with Peppers and Sausage **19**–2637
    Stuffed with Meat **11**–1502
    Stuffed Rolls **2**–226
    Tongue Pie, and **19**–2637
    Topside of, with Fruit **11**–1510
    Tournedos with Asparagus **8**–1102
    Vegetables, with **19**–2641
    Watercress, with **19**–2638
    Wednesday **20**–2754
    White Wine, with **6**–782
Veal Chops with Apple Cream Sauce **19**–2618
    Barbecued **1**–122
    Braised in White Wine **19**–2638
    Casseroled **4**–461
    Cooked in Paper Cases **4**–462
    English-Style **19**–2619
    Herbs, with **4**–462
    Juniper, with **4**–461
    Marinated in Coconut Milk **11**–1471
    Neapolitan **11**–1485
    Olive and Tomato Sauce **19**–2619
    Sherry, with **19**–2620
Veal Escalopes with Aubergine and Tomato Sauce **20**–2708
    Anchovies and Egg, with **5**–654
    Calvados Cream and Apples, with **5**–653
    Coated with Ground Almonds **5**–653
    Cream, with **15**–2050
    Cream Sauce, with **5**–654
    Ham and Cheese, with **5**–654
    Lemon Sauce, with **17**–2268

Madeira and Truffle Sauce, in 5–656
Marsala, with 17–2269
Mustard Sauce, with 19–2626
Paprika and Sour Cream, with 5–657
Red Wine, with 5–656
Roman-Style 17–2269
Scandinavian 8–1101
Spanish-Style 19–2621
Stuffed with Cheese and Herbs 8–1029
Tarragon Sauce, with 19–2622
Wine, Tomatoes and Garlic, with 5–656
Veal Kidneys, Braised in Port 19–2625
French Beans, with 19–2625
Gin, with 19–2626
Lemon Sauce, with 19–2626
Pasties 19–2626
Veau Braisé au Vin Blanc 19–2638
à la Chinoise 19–2639
en Cocotte 19–2639
à l'Indienne 19–2639
à la Ménagère 19–2641
Sauté Marengo 19–2641
Vegetable Bharta 19–2641
Casserole 15–2067; 19–2643
Consommé 4–422
Couscous 19–2643
Curry 1–91; 19–2644
Fritters 12–1662
Kitcheri 19–2645
Marinated 9–1221
Marrow Salad 19–2646
Mix 19–2647
Mixed with Brandy 9–1222
Paella 19–2648
Patties 19–2648
Pie 19–1648
Pilaff 16–2198
Pork Salad, and 19–2650
Prawn Curry, and 19–2651
Pulao with Prawns 19–2651
Raw with Garlic Mayonnaise 4–512
Rice 15–1989
Rissoles 19–2652
Romanian Stew 6–823
Salad 20–2714
Savoury 19–2653
Soup 14–1920; 16–2165; 19–2653
Stock 19–2654
Vegetarian Gravy 19–2654
Lentil Loaf 19–2654
Moussaka 19–2656
Nut Bake 19–2657
Nut Rissoles 19–2657
Nut Roast 19–2658
Stew Indian-Style 19–2658
Veiled Country Lass 19–2660
Veldt Bread 19–2660
Vellarikai Pachadi 20–2661
Velouté aux Amandes 20–2661
d'Artois 20–2662
aux Poissons 20–2662
Velvet Crab 20–2664
Cream 20–2664
Raisin Flan 20–2664
Vendai Kai Kari 20–2665
Venetian Cream Sponge 20–2667
Eel Kebabs 20–2667
Venezuelan Chicken 20–2667
Sponge Cake 2–171
Venison (info) 20–2667
Aspic with Maraschino Cherries, in 20–2668
Cumberland Sauce, with 20–2671
Cutlets with Cream and Pepper 20–2808
Goulasch 20–2671
Meat Loaf 20–2671
Norwegian, Steaks 11–1520
Old English, Stew 12–1569
Oregon 12–1624
Pâté 20–2674
Pie 20–2674
Pork Patties 20–2674
Roast Saddle, of 16–2142
Saddle of, with Pepper Sauce 16–2202
Sherry Sauce, with 20–2675
Stew with Chestnuts 20–2676

Venus Pudding 20–2676
Verbena and Apricot Sherbet 20–2678
Verity Cream 20–2678
Vermicelli Dessert 17–2290
Soup 20–2678
Vegetables, Chinese-Style 20–2678
Vermont Corn Bake 20–2680
Maple Dip 20–2680
Vermouth Punch 20–2681
Salad Dressing 20–2681
Verona Veal 20–2681
Vesuvian Surprise 20–2682
Vetekaka med Applen 20–2683
Veteken 20–2684
Vicarage Pudding 20–2684
Vichyssoise 20–2685
Victoria Sandwich 20–2687
Sauce 20–2687
Victorian Orange Buns 20–2687
Victor's Sauce 20–2687
Vienna Cakes 20–2687
Viennese Breaded Chicken Pieces 20–2804
Breaded Veal Escalopes 20–2804
Calf's Liver 20–2804
Chestnut Cake 20–2688
Chocolate Cake 20–2689
Croquettes 20–2689
Fingers 20–2690
Fresh Pea Soup 20–2690
Fruit Custard 20–2692
Jam Puffs 2–278
Raspberry Pudding 20–2693
Steaks 20–2804
White Wine and Soda Cup 20–2806
Viking Apple Pudding 20–2693
Villeroy Sauce 20–2694
Vin Chaud 20–2694
Vinaigrette Beef 2–203
Vinbarsbrännvin 20–2694
Vindaloo with Chicken 20–2695
Vine Leaves and Apricots 20–2698
Mushrooms, with 20–2698
Stuffed 20–2698
Wrapped in Grey Mullet 20–2698
Vinegar Cake 20–2699
Egg Sauce, and 20–2699
Goan, Curry 7–843
Marjoram 10–1318
Pudding 1–81
Sauce 20–2699
Sesame Seed Fish 20–2699
Vinegared Beef and Beans 20–2700
Vinita Biscuits 20–2702
Vintage Pâté 20–2703
Violet Creams 20–2704
Crystallized 4–514
Virgin Island Salt Cod Stew 20–2704
Virginia Chicken Salad 20–2704
Crab Patties 20–2707
Vitalise Milk Shake 20–2707
Vitello con Melanzane 20–2708
alla Piemontese con Tartufi 20–2709
con Salvia 20–2709
all Siciliana 20–2710
Tonnata 20–2710
Con Uova 20–2711
Vincenzo 20–2711
Vodka Fruit Cocktail 22–3026
Ice-Cream 20–2714
Martini 20–2714
Voedzaam Salade 20–2714
Volaille en Escabèche 20–2714
Vol-au-Vent 20–2717
d'Aubergines 20–2717
d'Eté 20–2718
de Pétoncles 20–2719
de Poulet et Champignons 20–2719
de Ris de Veau 20–2720
Volcanoes 20–2720
Volendam Canapés 20–2721
Vortlimpor 20–2721
Vulci Cheese Savoury 20–2723

W

Waffles 20–2724
Fruit 20–2724
Ham 20–2724
Luxembourg 6–809
Wake Island Pastry Cases with Egg and Asparagus 20–2726
Walnut Banana Loaf 1–114
Cake, Athenian 1–81
Cauliflower 20–2726
Cheese and Artichoke Heart Salad 20–2728
Cherry Buns, and 20–2728
Chicken Omelet, and 20–2729
Coffee Biscuits, and 20–2730
Coffee Fudge, and 20–2730
Cream Cheese Biscuits, and 20–2731
Custard 9–1126
Fruit Bread 20–2732
Fudge Cake 20–2732
Gingerbread 20–2734
Honey Sweets, and 20–2734
Lamb Bake, and 20–2734
Liver Stuffing, and 20–2734
Pastry 20–2734
Rice Salad, and 20–2735
Rum Caramels, and 20–2735
Warmer Malteser Spargel 20–2736
Warsaw Liqueur 20–2736
Washington Marinated Beef 20–2738
Wasps' Nests 20–2738
Wassail Bowl 20–2740
Waterbul 20–2741
Watercress and Almond Soup 20–2741
Avocado Mayonnaise, and 20–2742
Bredes 2–253
Fennel, Cucumber and Tomato Salad 20–2742
Pork Soup, and 20–2743
Sauce 20–1743
Soup 20–2744
Watermelon and Banana Salad 20–2745
Cocktail 20–2746
Fizz 20–2746
Fruit Bowl 20–2746
Provençal Wine, with 20–2747
Soup 20–2747
Waterzooi de Brochet 20–1747
de Poulet 20–2749
Wecksnappspiess 20–2749
Wedding Cake 11–1496; 20–2750
Salad 20–2752
Wednesday Veal 20–2754
Weingelee 20–2755
Weinkraut 20–2755
Welcome Soup 20–2756
Welfordian Steaks 20–2756
Wellington 20–2757
Roast Lamb 20–2758
Welsh Cakes 20–2759
Rarebit 20–2759
Stew 20–2760
Wen Welsh Duck 20–2760
Wengi Bhat 20–2762
Wengyachen Bharit 20–2763
Wensley Dale Marrow 20–2764
Wessex Ham 21–2959
Lamb 20–2764
Lamb Cutlets 20–2764
West African Beef and Fruit Curry 20–2766
Chicken 10–1296
Fish and Avocado Spread 20–2766
West Country Junket 20–2767
West Indian Avocadoes 20–2767
Chicken Casserole 20–2768
Pepperpot 20–2768
Pilau 20–2768
Western Burgers 20–2770
Fruit and Vegetable Stew 20–2770
Omelet 20–2770
Quick-Fried Chicken, Shrimps and Peas 20–2770
Quick-Fried Eggs with Peas and Shrimps 20–2771
Sandwiches 20–2772

Westphalian Chicken **20**–2773
Weston Eggs **20**–2772
Wexford Stuffed Lamb **20**–2774
Wheat Fruit Dessert **20**–2775
   Tomato Salad **18**–2462
Wheat-Germ Bread **20**–2775
   Lamb Casserole **20**–2776
Whipped Avocado Dessert **20**–2778
   Berry Pudding **19**–2611
   Cheese Croûtes **20**–2778
Whiskey Sour **20**–1778
Whisky and Chocolate Mousse **20**–2779
   Coffee Soufflé, and **20**–2780
   Mac **20**–2780
   Pecan Cake **20**–2780
   Sauce **20**–2781
White Bean Soup with Ham and Sausage **3**–298
   Butter Sauce **2**–167
   Cabbage in Sour Cream Sauce **20**–2781
   Chicken Curry **20**–2782
   Christmas Cake **20**–2783
   Cut Chicken **20**–2785
   Fish Curry **20**–2785
   Fish Fondue **20**–2785
   Fish Pie **20**–2786
   Grape and Ginger Syllabub **20**–2786
   Hatter Stew **20**–2786
   Lady **20**–2787
   Meat Casserole **20**–2788
   Mountain Frosting **6**–765
   Peach Cream **20**–2789
   Peaches with Caramelized Sugar **20**–2789
   Port Sorbet **20**–2789
   Pumpkin Halva **20**–2790
   Russian Cocktail **20**–2790
   Sauce **2**–167
Whitebait (info) **20**–2790
   Breadcrumb Fritters, and **20**–2791
   Deep-Fried **20**–2791
White-cooked Chicken **12**–1658
   Pork **12**–1658
Whiting (info) **20**–2794
   Apple Sauce, with **20**–2794
   Cheese and Breadcrumbs, with **20**–2794
   Colbert **20**–2794
   Courgettes, with **20**–2795
   Fennel, with **20**–2795
   Fillets with Prawns and Mussels **5**–696
   Italian-Style **20**–2795
   Mould **20**–2797
   Mushroom Sauce, in **20**–2797
   Provençal-Style **20**–2797
   Red Wine Sauce, in **20**–2798
   Stuffed with Shrimps **10**–1382
Whitstable Fish Soup **20**–2799
Whitsun Lamb **20**–2800
Wholemeal Bread **2**–250; **20**–2801
   Muffins **20**–2082
   Teabread **20**–2082
Wholewheat Bread **2**–250
Widdecombe Duck **20**–2083
Wienerbackhendl **20**–2804
Wienerleber **20**–2804
Wienerrostbraten **20**–2804
Wienerschnitzel **20**–2804
Wienerspritz **20**–2806
Wienerwurst Noodle Casserole **20**–2806
   Risotto **20**–2806
Wieprza Stew **20**–2807
Wigs **20**–2807
Wild Duck, with Grapefruit Sauce **20**–2808
Wild Rice Casserole **20**–2810
   Meat Loaf with Barbecue Sauce **20**–2810
   Mushrooms, with **20**–2811
   Pork Pilaff, and **20**–2811
   Stuffing **20**–2812
Wildbretkoteletten **20**–2808
Wildspitzer Fish Casserole **20**–2812
Wilhelmine Fruit Salad **20**–2813
   Sole **20**–2815
Willapa Bay Spoon Bread **20**–2815
Williamsburg Lamb **20**–2815
Willow Lake Spinach **20**–2815
Wilted Cumber **20**–2816
   Lettuce Salad **20**–2816

Wiltshire Ham **20**–2817
   Lardy Cake **20**–2818
Wimple Rabbit Casserole **20**–2821
Winchester Nut Bread **20**–2821
Windermere Soup **20**–2822
Windsor Cream Soup **20**–2823
   Hors d'Oeuvre **20**–2824
   Pastries **20**–2824
   Salad Americana **20**–2826
   Soup **20**–2826
Windward Island **20**–2826
Windy City Beef Stew **20**–2828
Wine Baked Pork **21**–2844
   Beef Stew **21**–2844
   Biscuits **21**–2845
   Bread and Cheese Casserole **21**–2846
   Consommé **20**–2846
   Cup, Warmed **20**–2694, 2736
   Dessert **21**–2847
   Fruit Jellies, and **21**–2847
   Jelly **20**–2755; **21**–2847
   Pepper Sauce, and **7**–860
   Salad Dressing **21**–2848
Winnetka Rarebit **21**–2848
Winnipeg Dipper **21**–2848
Winnsboro Bean Rarebit **21**–2848
Winter Beef Party Stew **21**–2848
   Compôte **21**–2848
   Crumble **21**–2849
   Fish Crêpes **21**–2851
   Lamb Stew **21**–2851
   Poussins with Watercress Stuffing **21**–2851
   Prawns **21**–1852
   Soup **21**–2853
   Vegetable Soup **14**–1918
   Warmer **21**–2853
Winterthur Lobster **21**–2854
Wisconsin Ham Crumble **21**–2855
Wladimir Chicken Breasts **21**–2856
   Turbot **21**–2897
Wonton Almonds and Dates **21**–2859
   Dough **21**–2858
   Pork **21**–2859
   Pork and Shrimps **21**–2859
   Soup **21**–2860
Wood Pigeons (info) **21**–2864
   Irish-Style **21**–2864
   Russian-Style **21**–2865
   Steamed **21**–2961
Woodcock Casserole **21**–2861
   Claret, in **21**–2863
Woodland Picnic Sandwich **21**–2863
Woosung Crabmeat Soup **21**–2865
Worcester Beef Croûte **21**–2866
   Sauce **21**–2866
Working Man's Bake **21**–2867
Wotan's Delight **21**–2868
Wow-Wow Relish **21**–2868
Wraby Ginger Chicken **21**–2868
Wrangell Stuffed Halibut **21**–
Wrangler's Gammon Bake **21**–2870
Wrasse Baked in Seaweed **21**–2871
Wreking Spiced Kidneys **21**–2872
Wrexham Mackerel, Orange and Mustard **21**–2872
   Rice Croquettes **21**–2872
Wrighton Pie **21**–2873
Wrotham Stuffed Eggs **21**–2873
Wrotherham Hot-Pot **21**–2874
Wry Banana Fluff **21**–2874
Wuchow Chicken Mandarin **21**–2874
Wuki Chicken **21**–2876
Wunderbar Macaroon Cake **21**–2877
Wunnumminlake Chicken Bouilli **21**–2877
Wuntho Crabmeat Soup **21**–2877
Wurst Ratatouille **21**–2878
   Sweet and Sour Sauce **21**–2879
Wurstel Sausage in Aspic **21**–2880
Wurstsalat **21**–2880
Wurtemburg Sole with Nuts **21**–2880
Wurzburg Chocolate Bread and Butter Pudding **21**–2882
Würzsauerkraut **21**–2882
Wyandotte Sweetcorn and Tomato Bake **21**–2882

Wye Cottage Cheese Salad **21**–2882
   Cream Pudding **21**–2883
   Valley Lamb **21**–2884
Wykeham Mushrooms **21**–2885
Wykehamist Halibut Steaks **21**–2885
Wyllin Glen Trout **21**–2887
Wymering Soufflé with Monk Fish Sauce **21**–2887
Wyndham Pork and Apricot Bake **21**–2888
Wynns Green Beef **21**–2888
Wynyard Mousse **21**–2889
Wyoming Beef Ribs **21**–2889
   Chicken Hash **21**–2889
   Cranberry Bread **21**–2890
   Devilled Steaks **21**–2890
   Parsley Soup **21**–2891
   Viking Salad **21**–2892
Wytcherley Pork Chops **21**–2892
Wytfontein Salad **21**–2893
Wyviss Porridge Apples **21**–2893
   Sugar and Spice Cakes **21**–2894
Wyvern Eggs **21**–2894

X

Xanadu Orange Delight **21**–2895
Xareu Portuguese **21**–2895
Xato **21**–2897
Xavier Consommé en Gelée **21**–2897
Xmas Cheer **21**–2897
Xuxu **21**–2898

Y

Y Mwd Leeks **21**–2899
Yablonchini Apple Soup **21**–2900
Yahm Chompu **21**–2901
Yakhni Pulao **21**–2903
Yakutsk Choux Puffs **21**–2904
Yale Chilli **21**–2905
Yam Cheese Sauce **21**–2905
   Chips **21**–2905
   Fried **8**–1034
   Fritters **21**–2907
   Oranges, with **21**–2907
   Yogurt, with **21**–2907
Yangchow Noodles **21**–2907
Yangtse Fish Soup **7**–978
Yankee Bean Soup **21**–2908
   Stuffed Corn **21**–2908
   Turkey, Roast **21**–2909
Yarborough Beef Ring **21**–2910
Yarm Stuffed Artichokes **21**–2910
Yarmacott Spinach and Apple Soufflé **21**–2911
Yarmouth Bloater Paste **21**–2912
   Soup **21**–2913
Yarrow Banana Teabread **21**–2913
Yazan Cranberry Flan **21**–2914
Yeaman's Spiced Potatoes **21**–2914
Yeast Buckwheat Pancakes **21**–2916
   Cake with Apples **20**–2683
Yelverton Blackberry Jelly **21**–2916
Yellow Lentil Soup **21**–2917
   Rice **6**–811; **21**–2917
   Soup **21**–2919
   Split Pea Purée **21**–2919
Yellowman **21**–2917
Yemeni Chick-Pea Soup **21**–2919
   Lamb Casserole **21**–2920
Yerevan Lamb Pilaff **21**–2920
Yetminster Stuffed Pork **21**–2921
Yi'allaq Meringue Dessert **21**–2923
Yiddish Chopped Liver with Green Peppers **21**–2923
   Meatballs **21**–2924
Yieldtree Potatoes with Shallots **21**–2925
Yingkow Stuffed Pineapple **21**–2925
Yogurt and Avocado Soup **21**–2926
   Banana Raita, and **21**–2926
   Chicken **21**–2926
   Chicken Barley Soup, and **21**–2928

Crumb Cake **21**–2928
Cucumber Salad, and **21**–2929
Curd Cheese **21**–2929
Curry **18**–2497
Dip **21**–2929
Dressing **21**–2929
Instant Pudding **8**–1026
Orange Jelly, and **21**–2929
Rich **15**–2046
Salad **15**–2059
Soup **21**–2929
Yok Kai Chi Marinated Salmon **21**–2932
Yolande's Choux Puff Pyramid **21**–2932
Yolk of Egg Italian-Style **21**–2932
Yom Tov Deep-Fried Fish **21**–2933
Yonkers Pear Delight **21**–2933
York Castle Chocolate Tart **21**–2934
Ham Cones **21**–2934
Rolls **21**–2934
Yorkshire Cheesecakes **21**–2935
Christmas Gingerbread **21**–2935
Giblet Pie **21**–2935
Ham Pie **21**–2935
Lamb Hot Pot **21**–2938
Meat Pudding **21**–2938
Pancakes **21**–2938
Ploughboy **21**–2938
Pudding **21**–2940
Rarebit **21**–2940
Savoury Meatballs **21**–2941
Yorktown Pork Fillets **21**–2941
Yoseabe **21**–2943
Yoshida Scampi Skewers **21**–2943
Young Man's Fancy **21**–2943
Youngstown Lamb in Sherry Sauce **21**–2944
Yoxford Crown Roast of Pork with Peaches **21**–2944
Ypres Coffee Cream **21**–2944
Ysa Kedgeree **21**–2944
Yssolde Red Fruit Dessert **21**–2946
Yssingeaux Marinated Artichoke Hearts **21**–2946
Yu Chi-Tang **21**–2947
Hsiang Jou Si **21**–2948
-Lang-Chi **21**–2949
Savoury Toast **21**–2950
-Tsin Liver Pot Roast **21**–2951
Yucatan Fish with Tomato Chilli Sauce **21**–2951
Stuffed Peppers **21**–2951
Yueng Chow Rice **21**–2952
Yugoslavian Barbecued Beef **21**–2953
Hunter's Hare Stew **21**–2954
Rice Pudding **21**–2954
Shoulder of Lamb **21**–2954
Veal and Pork Kebabs **15**–2073
Veal Sandwiches **21**–2954
Yule Log **21**–2957
Mincemeat and Apple Flan **21**–2958
Yuletide Pudding **21**–2958
Spiced Brisket **21**–2959
Wessex Ham **21**–2959
Yulla Brown Onion Soup with Port **21**–2960
Yummy Meat and Vegetable Pie **21**–2960
Yun Yook **21**–2961
Yungchow Fruit Surprise **21**–2962
Yunnan Quick Fried Prawns on Crackling Rice **21**–2962
Yuri's Chicken Puffs **21**–2963
Yvetot Clam Hors d'Oeuvre **21**–2964
Yvonne's Egg Mousse **21**–2964

Z

Zabaglione **21**–2966
alla Creole **21**–2966
Iced **8**–1010
Orientale **21**–2968
Zabon's Salad **21**–2968
Zacatecas Browned Cucumber **21**–2969
Zafra Potato Crunch **21**–2969
Zafran Paella **21**–2969
Zagreb Chicken Casserole **21**–2970
Zahna Meat Medley **21**–2970

Zalovnoye s Solonine **21**–2972
Zambesi Vegetarian Salad **21**–2973
Zambian Cheese and Sardine Fritters **21**–2973
Zampa di Vitello alla Toscana **21**–2974
Zanahorias Rillenas **21**–2975
Zandam Bread Bake **21**–2975
Zandar Marinate Poussins **21**–2976
Zander im Ofen Gebacken mit Weisswein **21**–2976
Schnitte mit Senfbutter **21**–2977
Zany Stuffed Drumsticks **21**–2978
Zanzibar Salt Cod Curry **21**–2979
Zapata Veal **21**–2979
Zapellitos Rellenos **21**–2979
Zapponeta Pasta Shells with Mussels **21**–2981
Zara Ice-Cream Dessert **21**–2981
Zara's Turbot with Clams **21**–2982
Zarda **21**–2982
Zardov Quick Cassoulet **21**–2982
Zaria Beef **21**–2982
Zarzar Red Pepper and Onion Soup **21**–2984
Zarzuela **21**–2984
Zebra Meringue Torte **21**–2984
Zeebrugge Crabmeat and Lettuce Mould **21**–2986
Zeera Gosht **21**–2987
Murg **21**–2989
Zelimander **21**–2989
Zell Pilau **21**–2989
Zena's Sugared Steak **21**–2990
Zenda Sausage Snacks **21**–2991
Zenith Pear and Carrot Soufflé **21**–2991
Zennor's Country Parsnip Soup **21**–2991
Zeppole **21**–2992
Zermatt Sardine Pâté **21**–2992
Zesty Layer Cake **21**–2993
Zetland Baked Lamb **21**–2994
Fish Balls **21**–2994
Zhukov Boiled Beef Dinner with Horseradish Sauce **21**–2994
Zihuatanejo Fish Salad **21**–2996
Zihufitanejo **22**–2997
Zindo Vando **22**–2997
Zinfandel Beef **22**–2998
Zingarella Stew **22**–2999
Zingari Gipsy-Style Spaghetti Omelet **22**–2999
Zinnia's Chicken with Tarragon, Whisky and Cream **22**–2999
Zippy Avocado Hors d'Oeuvre **22**–2999
Savoury Scramble **22**–3000
Zip-Zap Lunchtime Snack **22**–3000
Zirje Island Fish Kebabs **22**–3001
Zite Italian Sausage Sauce **22**–3001
Meatballs with Tomato Mushroom Sauce **22**–3002
Port, with **22**–3002
Znojemsky Goulasch **22**–3002
Zoar's Apple Bake **22**–3007
Zocca Bananas **22**–3006
Zodiac Cake **22**–3006
Zoe's Delight **22**–3007
Zofe Spinach Soup **22**–3007
Zoftic Mixed Vegetables **22**–3007
Zogno Veal Cutlets **22**–3007
Vegetarian Pasta **22**–3008
Zola Chicken **22**–3008
Zoll Fruit Loaf **22**–3009
Zoller Pumpkin Stew **22**–3009
Zoltan's Chicken Breasts **22**–3011
Zomba Salt Cod and Avocado **22**–3011
Zombie Cocktail **22**–3012
Zombie's Secret **22**–3012
Zonder Sweetcorn and Petits Pois **22**–3012
Zonza Champagne Soup **22**–3013
Stuffed Spare Rib **22**–3013
Zoom-zoom Sausage Toadstools **22**–3014
Zoondam Pork Ratatouille **22**–3014
Zoose Pears **22**–3014
Zoo Time Sandwiches **22**–3014
Zopparelli Figs in Red Wine **22**–3016
Zora's Peach Dessert **22**–3016
Zoradora Dessert **22**–3016
Zorba's Meatballs **22**–3016
Tipsy Cake **22**–3016
Zorin's Lamb with Lemon Sauce **22**–3018

Zorrell Cheese and Ham Rolls **22**–3018
Zossen Oxtail **22**–3018
Zouar Banana Ice-Cream **22**–3018
Zou Zou's Crêpes **22**–3020
Zoytinyagli Pirasa **22**–3020
Zraza **22**–3021
Zrazi eze Ribi **22**–3022
s Kashie **22**–3022
Zsa Zsa's Meatball Goulasch **22**–3024
Zubia Cod with Aioli Sauce **22**–3025
Zubov Calf's Liver Stroganov **22**–3025
Zubrick Pork and Spiced Plums **22**–3025
Zubrowka Cocktail **22**–3026
Fruit Cocktail **22**–3026
Zucca Cheese Loaf **22**–3026
alla Parmigiana **22**–3027
Zuccherini **22**–3028
Zucchero Formaggio alla Crema **22**–3028
Zucchini *see also* Courgettes
all' Agrodolce **22**–3028
con Aneto **22**–3030
e Cavolfiore **22**–3030
in Dolce **22**–3030
al Formaggio **22**–3030
con Frittelle **22**–3032
con Mandorle **22**–3032
alla Marinara **22**–3033
Orientali **22**–3033
e Peperoni **22**–3033
Pomodori e Finocchio **22**–3036
Ripieni **22**–3036
Ripieni di Salsiccie **22**–3036
in Stufato **22**–3037
in Sufflé **22**–3037
Zuccotash Sweet Potato and Marshmallow Bake **22**–3038
Zuccotto **22**–3038
Torrone **22**–3040
Zuckerman Duck with Olives **22**–3041
Zuera Tropical Sundae **22**–3041
Zug Pork Chops **22**–3042
Sausage and Leek Casserole **22**–3042
Zuger Zee Scramble **22**–3043
Zuidhorn Kipper Pie **22**–3043
Liver and Rice **22**–3044
Zujar Chicken Liver Casserole **22**–3044
Tomato Soufflé **22**–3045
Zuki Fruit Tartlets **22**–3046
Zula Avocado Hors d'Oeuvre **22**–3046
Tangy Salad **22**–3046
Zulcan Gammon and Gooseberries **22**–3046
Zulia Persimmon Flan **22**–3047
Zulinka Rum and Chocolate Soufflé **22**–3048
Zulla Fish Pie **22**–3049
Zullah's Pasta, Sausage and Bean Salad **22**–3049
Zulu Beef Pot **22**–3050
Beef Stew **22**–3050
Zumar Scallops in Port **22**–3050
Zummah Rabbit Stew **22**–3052
Zundy Teddy Bear Cake **22**–3053
Zune Ricotta and Cherry Tartlets **22**–3053
Zungeru Peanut Pork **22**–3054
Zunita Gâteau **22**–3055
Zupanja Red Snapper Bake **22**–3055
Zuppa di Anguille **22**–3058
di Aragosta **22**–3058
di Cozze **22**–3058
a Due Colori **22**–3059
di Fagioli Fiorentina **22**–3059
di Fontina **22**–3059
Inglese **22**–3059
di Pollo **22**–3060
di Verdura **22**–3061
di Vongole e Pancotto **22**–3061
di Zucchini **22**–3063
Zurich Fruit Crumble **22**–3063
Hazelnut Biscuits **22**–3063
Lamb Delight **22**–3064
Roast Pork **22**–3064
Veal and Parsnip Pie **22**–3065
Zuriga Salmon Trout with Mushroom Mayonnaise **22**–3065
Zurov Lamb **22**–3066
Zute Salad **22**–3066

Thematic Index

A Guide to the Index

Aspic	3113
Biscuits [Cookies]	3113
Bread and Rolls	3114
Butter	3114
Cakes and Gateaux - Large	3115
Cakes - Small	3116
Cereals	3116
Cheese and Cheese Dishes	3116
Cheesecake	3117
Chocolate	3117
Chutneys, Pickles and Relishes	3117
Coffee	3118
Condiments	3118
Cookery Terms	3118
Curries, Indian and Pakistani Dishes	3119
Desserts - Hot	3119
Desserts - Cold	3120
Dips	3123
Drinks - Alcoholic	3123
Drinks - Non-Alcoholic	3124
Dumplings - Savoury	3124
Dumplings - Sweet	3124

Eggs (including Meringues, Omelets and Soufflés)	3124
Fish	3125
Fondues	3129
Fritters	3129
Fruit	3129
Game	3133
Garnishes	3134
General Information	3134
Herbs and Spices	3134
Honey	3135
Hors d'Oeuvres	3135
Icing, Frosting and Glazing	3136
Jams, Jellies and Preserves	3136
Kebabs	3136
Kitchen Utensils	3136
Meat	3136
Milk	3143
Nuts	3143
Offal	3144
Pancakes and Crêpes - Savoury	3145
Pancakes and Crêpes - Sweet	3145
Pasta	3145
Pastry	3146

Pâté and Terrine	3146
Pies - Savoury	3146
Pies - Sweet	3147
Pizza	3147
Poultry	3147
Rice	3149
Salads	3149
Sandwiches and Fillings	3150
Sauces and Dressings - Savoury	3150
Sauces - Sweet	3151
Scones, Muffins and Waffles	3151
Shellfish	3151
Snails	3153
Soups	3153
Stock	3154
Stuffing	3154
Sugar and Syrup	3154
Sweets [Candies]	3154
Tarts and Flans - Savoury	3155
Tarts and Flans - Sweet	3155
Tea	3155
Vegetables	3155
Yoghurt	3162

ASPIC

Aspic (info) 1–79
Almond and Black Cherry Aspic Salad 1–20
Aspic I 1–79
Aspic II 1–80
Aspic de Pommes (Apple Aspic) 1–80
Avocado Aspic 1–92
Basil and Tomato Aspic 1–127
Calf's Foot Jelly 3–300
Chicken Livers in Aspic 3–396
Fish Aspic 6–704
Gelatine (info) 6–813
Gelée d'Avignon (Jellied Pork Soup) 6–813
Jellied Chicken Breasts 8–1065
Jellied Eels 8–1066
Jellied Eggs 8–1066
Jellied Fish Mould 8–1067
Jellied Grape and Cheese Salad 8–1067
Jellied Halibut 8–1068
Jellied Mayonnaise 8–1068
Jellied Melon Salad 8–1069
Jellied Veal 8–1070
Jelly [Gelatin] (info) 8–1071
Lamb Cutlets in Aspic 9–1198
Salmon in Aspic 16–2218
Tomato Aspic 18–2512
Tongue and Vegetable Aspic 18–2521
Venison in Aspic with Maraschino Cherries 20–2668
Volaille en Escabèche (Chicken in Lemon Jelly [Gelatin]) 20–2714
Wurstel Sausage in Aspic 21–2880

BISCUITS [Cookies]

Biscuit (info) 2–175
Almond Cookies 1–21
Almond Crunchies 1–21
Anise Fork Biscuits [Cookies] 1–35
Bath Oliver (info) 1–129
Black Pepper Cookies 2–184
Brandy Snaps 2–236
Brazilian Macaroons 2–236
Butter Biscuits [Cookies] 3–281
Butter Coconut Biscuits [Cookies] 3–282
Caraway Seed Biscuits 3–322
Cardamon Biscuits [Cookies] 3–324
Cheese Straws 3–368
Chocolate Biscuits [Cookies] 3–406
Chocolate Chip Cookies 3–408
Chocolate Cinnamon Biscuits [Cookies] 3–408
Coconut Cookies 4–430
Cookie (info) 4–444
Corn Meal Biscuits 4–453
Cracknel (info) 4–475
Date and Walnut Diamonds 4–543
Derby Biscuits [Cookies] 4–555
Duchess Pralinés 5–581
Dutch Almond Biscuits [Cookies] 5–592
Early American Cookies 5–595
Easter Bunnies 5–597
Edwardian Biscuits [Cookies] 5–604
Fig and Hazelnut Biscuits [Cookies] 5–689
Flapjacks 6–724
Florentines 6–727
Fruit and Nut Biscuits [Cookies] 6–771
Galettes Amandines (Iced Almond Biscuits [Cookies]) 6–784

Galettes au Camembert (Camembert Biscuits 6–784
Galettes de Feuilles (Meringue Leaves) 6–785
Galettes au Fromage (Cheese Biscuits) 6–785
Galettes Nantaises (Almond Biscuits [Cookies]) 6–785
Garibaldi Biscuits [Cookies] 6–796
Gingerbread Bites 6–832
Ginger and Cream Wafers 6–833
Ginger Snap Biscuits [Cookies] 6–835
Golden Biscuits [Cookies] 7–845
Gorgonzola Biscuits 7–854
Havrekex (Oat Cakes) 7–935
Hazelnut Macaroons 7–939
Hermits 7–948
Husbands (info) 8–995
Icebox Biscuits [Cookies] 8–1000
Icicles 8–1010
Jaffa Biscuits [Cookies] 8–1041
Jersey Wonders 8–1074
Judge Biscuits [Cookies] 8–1084
Jumbles 8–1089
Kichlach (Puffy Sweet Biscuits) 9–1130
Klenäter (Swedish Crullers) 9–1154
Kourambiedes (Greek Biscuits [Cookies]) 9–1170
Krammerhuse (Ginger Cream-Filled Horns) 9–1171
Kringles (Rich Butter Biscuits [Cookies]) 9–1174
Krumkaker (Scandinavian Biscuits [Cookies]) 9–1175
Lady Biscuits [Cookies] 9–1188
Langues de Chats (Sweet Biscuits [Cookies]) 9–1207

Lemon Biscuits [Cookies] 9–1225
Macaroons (info) 10–1279
Macaroons 10–1279
Macaroons with Chocolate 10–1280
Macaroons with Grand Marnier 10–1280
Macaroons with Hazelnuts 10–1281
Macaroons with Pecans 10–1281
Mandel-Halbmonde (Almond Crescent Biscuits [Cookies]) 10–1298
Marmalade Bars 10–1320
Marshmallow So'mores 10–1332
Marshamallow Squares 10–1332
Marzipan Biscuits [Cookies] 10–1338
Matrimonial Cake 10–1342
Medaljer med Fløde (Cream and Redcurrant Biscuits [Cookies]) 10–1362
Melting Moments 10–1374
Mombasa Biscuits [Cookies] 11–1415
Najafabad Biscuits [Cookies] 11–1467
Nantais Biscuits [Cookies] 11–1470
Nanymo Squares 11–1472
Narbonne Biscuits [Cookies] 11–1475
Nursery Cakes 11–1529
Nut and Chocolate Cookies 11–1533
Nut and Date Biscuits [Cookies] 11–1535
Oatcakes 12–1542
Oatmeal and Cheese Biscuits 12–1543
Oatmeal Cookies 12–1545
Oil Biscuits [Cookies] 12–1564
Orange and Chocolate Biscuits [Cookies] 12–1604
Orange Shortbread Biscuits [Cookies] 12–1616
Otterberg Biscuits [Cookies] 12–1630
Oublie (info) 12–1630
Oublies à la Parisienne (Parisian Wafers) 12–1630
Palmiers (Puff Pastry Biscuits [Cookies]) 12–1666
Peanut Biscuits [Cookies] 13–1716
Peanut Butter Biscuits [Cookies] 13–1717
Petits Fours (info) 13–1758
Petits Fours au Massepain (Marzipan Biscuits [Cookies]) 13–1760
Petticoat Tails 13–1766
Pitcaithly Bannock 14–1827
Porridge and Chocolate Biscuits [Cookies] 14–1902
Pretzel (info) 15–1974
Pretzels 15–1974
Puttlingen Biscuits [Cookies] 15–1992
Pyrizhky (Polish Jam and Coconut Biscuits [Cookies]) 15–1992
Ratafia (info) 15–2067
Ratafia Biscuits [Cookies] 15–2067
Rich Biscuits [Cookies] 16–2116
Rusk (info) 16–2188
Sablés (French Egg Biscuits [Cookies]) 16–2197
Sacristans (Puff Pastry Twists) 16–2199
Sesame Seed and Oatmeal Biscuits [Cookies] 17–2289
Shortbread 17–2304
Shortcake 17–2304
Shrewsbury Biscuits [Cookies] 17–2307
Snicker Biscuits 17–2336
Söta Kakor (Sweet Biscuits [Cookies]) 17–2351
Spiral Biscuits 18–2389
Spitzgebäck (Hazelnut Biscuits [Cookies]) 18–2391
Sponge Finger Biscuits [Cookies] 18–2394
Spritsar (Scandinavian 'S' Shaped Biscuits [Cookies]) 18–2397
Topton Biscuits [Cookies] 19–2522
Tortas de Aceite (Sesame Seed and Aniseed Biscuits [Cookies] 19–2524
Treacle Biscuits [Cookies] 19–2538
Ugine Biscuits [Cookies] 19–2587
Urchins 19–2596
Vanilla Crisps 19–2605
Vanilla Rusks 19–2607
Veteken (Scandinavian Wheat Biscuits) 20–2684
Viennese Fingers 20–2690
Vinita Biscuits [Cookies] 20–2702
Wafers (info) 20–2724
Walnut and Coffee Biscuits [Cookies] 20–2730
Walnut and Cream Cheese Biscuits [Cookies] 20–2731

Wasps' Nests 20–2738
Water Biscuit [Cracker] (info) 20–2741
Wine Biscuits [Cookies] 21–2845
Zurich Hazelnut Biscuits [Cookies] 22–3063
Zvezdochki (Russian Star-Shaped Biscuits [Cookies]) 22–3070

BREAD AND ROLLS

Bread (info) 2–240
Banana Walnut Loaf 1–114
Baps 1–116
Barley Bread 1–122
Barm Brack (Irish Fruit Loaf) 1–125
Birnbrot (Pear Bread) 2–172
Boston Brown Bread 2–212
Bread Making (info) 2–241
American White Bread 2–246
Household Bread 2–247
Quick Bread 2–247
Swedish Rye Bread 2–248
Sweet Bread 2–249
Wholewheat Bread 2–250
Breadcrumbs (info) 2–251
Bread Sticks 2–252
Bremer Küchen (Bremen Sweet Bread) 2–254
Bridge Rolls 2–254
Brioche (info) 2–258
Brioche I 2–258
Brioche II 2–260
Brioche aux Fraises avec Moussade Framboises (Brioche with Strawberries and Raspberry Cream Filling) 2–260
Brioche Mousseline 2–262
Caraway Knots 3–320
Chapatti (Unleavened Indian Bread) 3–357
Cinnamon Fried Bread 4–423
Coffee Bread 4–436
Corn Bread 4–452
Crispbread (info) 4–501
Croissants 4–501
Croûtes 4–508
Date Loaf 4–540
Date and Raisin Loaf 4–542
Date and Walnut Loaf 4–544
Devil's Loaf 4–557
Dough (info) 5–574
Easter Bread 5–596
Easter Festival Bread 5–598
Egg Bread 5–614
Fan Tans 5–675
French Bread 6–747
Garlic Bread 6–798
Grissini (info) 7–883
Herb Bread 7–944
Herb Bread Crisps 7–945
Hickory Loaf 7–951
Hot Cross Buns 7–973
Hutzelbrot (German Dried Fruit Bread) 8–996
Iranian Nut Bread 8–1029
Irish Soda Bread 8–1031
Italian Mozzarella Bread 8–1038
Jamaican Spice Loaf 8–1053
Jenny Lind Cake 8–1073
Johnnycake 8–1080
Khachapuri (Georgian Cheese Bread) 9–1126
Kipfel (info) 9–1144
Kissing Crust (info) 9–1151
Krendel (Russian Name-Day Bread) 9–1172
Lapland Loaf 9–1209
Leaven (info) 9–1215
Lvov Black Bread 10–1275
Malt Bread 10–1294
Manitoba Poppy Seed Roll 10–1304
Maritozzi Uso Fornaio (Pine Nut and Orange Buns) 10–1317
Matzo (info) 10–1344
Melba Toast 10–1370
Millet Bread 10–1392
Moravian Loaf 11–1418
Mos-bolletjies (Raisin Buns) 11–1424
Naan (info) 11–1466
New England Soda Bread 11–1496
Norma's Breakfast Breads 11–1514

Norwegian Soda Bread 11–1520
Oat Bread 12–1541
Oat and Caraway Bread 12–1542
Onion Bread 12–1587
Onion Kuchen 12–1590
Pandolce Genovese (Genoese Sweet Bread) 12–1670
Panettone (Italian Breakfast Bread) 12–1672
Papanberg Bread 12–1672
Paratha (Indian Fried Wholemeal Bread) 12–1675
Parker House Rolls 12–1678
Pecan Loaf 13–1725
Perth Treacle Loaf 13–1755
Pita (Middle Eastern Bread) 14–1826
Pizza (info) 14–1828
Pomeroy Rolls 14–1861
Poppy Seed Bread 14–1875
Poppy Seed Roll 14–1875
Potato Bread 14–1925
Prague Apricot Loaf 14–1958
Proving (info) 15–1980
Pumpernickel (info) 15–1985
Puris (Deep-Fried Wholemeal [Wholewheat] Bread) 15–1991
Quick Bread 15–2026
Quin's Loaf 15–2034
Raisin Brown Bread 15–2054
Raisin Rolls 15–2057
Rich Corn Meal Bread 16–2116
Rosemary Bread 16–2166
Rumanian Sweet Bread 16–2183
Rye Bread 16–2196
San Francisco Sourdough Bread 16–2236
Selkirk Bannocks 17–2284
Sesame Seed Rolls 17–2290
Shrove Tuesday Buns 17–2317
Soda Bread 17–2336
Sourdough Bread 17–2361
Spiral Bread 17–2390
Stollen (German Sweet Bread) 18–2415
Strizel (Plaited Loaf) 18–2424
Unleavened Bread (info) 19–2593
Unleavened Bread Rolls 19–2593
Veldt Bread 19–2660
Vortlimpor (Swedish Christmas Bread) 20–2721
Walnut Fruit Bread 20–2732
Wheat Germ Bread 20–2775
Wholemeal [Wholewheat] Bread I 20–2801
Wholemeal [Wholewheat] Bread II 20–2802
Wholemeal [Wholewheat] Teabread 20–2802
Willapa Bay Spoon Bread 20–2815
Winchester Nut Bread 20–2821
Wyoming Cranberry Bread 21–2890
Yarrow Banana Teabread 21–2913
York Rolls 21–2934
Zoll Fruit Loaf 22–3009
Zwieback (info) 22–3074

BUTTER

Butter (info) 2–280
Anchovy Butter 1–29
Beurres Composés (info) 2–164
Beurre d'Ail (Garlic Butter) 2–164
Beurre Bercy (Butter with Shallots and Wine) 2–164
Beurre au Citron (Hot Lemon-Butter Sauce) 2–164
Beurre au Citron (Cold Lemon Butter) 2–166
Beurre de Crevettes à Froid (Cold Shrimp Butter) 2–166
Beurre de Crustacés (Shellfish Butter) 2–166
Beurre d'Estragon (Tarragon Butter) 2–166
Beurre Manié (info) 2–166
Beurre Marchand de Vins (Shallot Butter with Red Wine) 2–166
Beurre de Moutarde (Mustard Butter) 2–166
Beurre Nantais (White Butter Sauce) 2–167
Beurre Noir (Brown Butter Sauce) 2–167
Beurre à l'Oeuf (Egg Yolk Butter) 2–167
Brandy Butter 2–235
Cinnamon Butter 4–423
Cocoa Butter (info) 4–429

Crème au Beurre (Butter Cream) **4**–488
Crème au Beurre Mousseline **4**–489
Crème au Beurre Meringuée **4**–489
Cumberland Rum Butter **4**–519
Drawn Butter **5**–576
Ghee (info) **6**–822
Horseradish Butter **7**–971
Kneaded Butter (info) **9**–1157
Lobster Butter **9**–1254
Maître d'Hôtel Butter **10**–1290
Mandarin Orange Butter **10**–1298
Nut Butter **11**–1532
Orange Butter **12**–1601
Peanut Butter **13**–1716
Rum Butter **16**–2178
Shortening (info) **17**–2307

CAKES AND GATEAUX—LARGE

Cakes (info) **3**–294
Almond Cherry Cake **1**–20
Angel Cake **1**–32
Applesauce Cake **1**–50
Athenian Walnut Cake **1**–81
Austrian Coffee Cake **1**–89
Baba (info) **1**–96
Baba au Rhum **1**–96
Baba aux Fraises **1**–98
Baklava (info) **1**–107
Bara Brith **1**–116
Battenberg Cake **1**–129
Bien me Sabe de Coco (Venezuelan Sponge Cake) **2**–171
Biscuit Fin au Beurre (French Sponge Cake) Cake) **2**–175
Bishop's Bread **2**–176
Black Bun *see* Pastry Cake **13**–1696
Black Forest Cherry Cake **2**–182
Blotkake (Norwegian Sponge Cake) **2**–186
Brazilian Swiss [Jelly] Roll **2**–239
Brazil Nut Banana Cake **2**–239
Brazil Nut Cake **2**–240
Bublanina (Sponge Cake with Cherries) **2**–277
Cake Mix (info) **3**–294
Cake Making (info) **3**–294
Caraway Seed Sponge Cake **3**–322
Cardamon Cake **3**–324
Carrot Cake **3**–332
Cassata (info) **3**–334
Cassata alla Siciliana (Sicilian Cake with Chocolate Icing) **3**–334
Cheesecakes *see* Cheesecake
Chocolate Almond Cake **3**–404
Chocolate Cake with Hazelnuts **3**–406
Chocolate Mushroom Cake **3**–410
Chocolate Peppermint Sandwich Cake **3**–410
Chocolate and Sour Cream Cake **3**–414
Chocolate Sponge Cake **3**–414
Chocolate Swiss [Jelly] Roll **3**–415
Chokladkaka **3**–416
Christmas Cake I **3**–420
Christmas Cake II **4**–421
Date Cake **4**–539
Dattelkuchen (Date Cake) **4**–544
Datteltorte **4**–545
Delft Cake (Almond Meringue Layer Cake with Orange Buttercream Filling) **4**–554
Devil's Food Cake **4**–556
Devonshire Layer Cake **5**–561
Doboz Torte (Hungarian Chocolate Layer Cake) **5**–569
Dreaming Cake **5**–576
Dundee Cake **5**–590
Easter Cake I **5**–598
Easter Cake II **5**–598
Easter Halva Cake **5**–600
Eggless Chocolate Cake **5**–632
Election Cake **5**–641
Family Fruit Cake **5**–674
Filbert and Chocolate Cake **5**–692
Frankfurter Kranz (Layer Cake with Buttercream Filling) **6**–739

Frosted Walnut Cake **6**–763
Fruit and Mixed Nut Cake **6**–770
Fudge Layer Cake **6**–776
Galette (info) **6**–783
Galette aux Abricots (Apricot Cake) **6**–783
Galette Noisettine (Hazelnut Biscuit Cake) **6**–786
Galette Normande **6**–786
Gâteau (info) **6**–802
Gâteau Flamand à la Crème (Flemish Cream Cake) **6**–802
Gâteau aux Fraises et Amandes (Strawberry and Almond Cake) **6**–803
Gâteau de Marrons (Chestnut Cake) **6**–803
Gâteau Mille-feuille (Layers of Puff Pastry with Crème Chantilly and Jam) **6**–804
Gâteau Mocha (Coffee Buttercream Cake) **6**–804
Gâteau Noir (Chocolate Cake with Almonds and Rum) **6**–806
Gâteau Noisette (Hazelnut and Meringue Cake) **6**–806
Gâteau à l'Orange (Orange Cake) **6**–806
Genoa Cake **6**–815
Génoise Sponge **6**–816
German Spice Cake **6**–819
Gevulde Botterkoek (Butter Shortbread with Almond and Fruit Filling) **6**–821
Gingerbread **6**–831
Ginger Flapjack **6**–834
Ginger Sponge Cake **6**–836
Griesstorte (Semolina Cake with Raspberry Cream Filling) **7**–880
Ground Rice Cake **7**–884
Gugelhopf (Austrian Yeast Cake) **7**–893
Handsome Tipsy Cake **7**–922
Hawaiian Cream Roll **7**–937
Heavy Cake **7**–942
Hedgehog Cake **7**–943
Honey Cake **7**–962
Honey Spice Cake **7**–965
Huish Cake **7**–980
Hungarian Cream Cake **8**–989
Icebox Cake **8**–1001
Independence Cake (info) **8**–1020
Jamaican Plain Cake **8**–1052
Jamaican Spice Loaf **8**–1053
Jelly Roll (info) **8**–1072
Jenny Lind Cake **8**–1073
Kannellagkage (Cinnamon-Flavoured Layer Cake) **8**–1104
Kinderkuchen (Children's Cake) **9**–1142
Kingly Orange Cake **9**–1144
Kransekager (Danish Marzipan Cake) **9**–1172
Kuchen (Rich Yeast Cake) **9**–1177
Lady Baltimore Cake **9**–1187
Lardy Cake **9**–1210
Lazy Chocolate Cake **9**–1214
Lekach (Honey Cake) **9**–1223
Lemon Cake **9**–1226
Lemon Manqué **9**–1228
Lightning Orange and Chocolate Cake **9**–1236
Luncheon Cake **10**–1274
Madeira Cake **10**–1284
Mahogany Cake **10**–1287
Malakoff Sponge Cake **10**–1290
Mandeltorte (Almond Layer Cake) **10**–1298
Maple Syrup Cake **10**–1310
Marble Cake **10**–1311
Marmalade Chocolate Cake **10**–1321
Martha Washington Cake **10**–1334
Marzipan Roll **10**–1340
Matrimonial Cake **10**–1342
Mattersburg Almond Roll **10**–1342
Meringue Almond Layer Cake **10**–1378
Meringue Walnut Cake **10**–1381
Mincemeat Cake **10**–1398
Mkate Wa Mayai (Egg Cake) **11**–1409
Molasses Sponge Cake **11**–1414
Motley Cake **11**–1426
Mousseline au Chocolat (Rich Chocolate Cake) **11**–1438
Navy Fruit Cake **11**–1482
Nevada Rice Cake **11**–1495
New England Wedding Cake **11**–1496

North Country Cake **11**–1517
Nusscreme Torte (Nut and Cream Cake) **11**–1529
Nut Roll **11**–1537
Oil Chocolate Cake **12**–1564
Old English Cider Cake **12**–1568
Orange Cake **12**–1601
Orange Walnut Cake **12**–1621
Oriental Cake **12**–1625
Paris-Brest (Choux Pastry Ring Filled with Crème Pâtissière) **12**–1677
Parkin **12**–1679
Party Cake **13**–1688
Pastis (Rich Egg and Brandy Cake) **13**–1693
Pastry Cake **13**–1696
Pecan Torte **13**–1727
Pineapple Cake **13**–1800
Plum Cake **14**–1847
Poppy Seed Cake **14**–1875
Poteca (Swiss Yeast Cake) **14**–1933
Pound Cake **14**–1952
Pousse Café Gâteau (Sponge Cake with Liqueur-Flavoured Icing) **14**–1954
Povoa Almond Cake **14**–1958
Prunella Starkie's Indian Plum Cake **15**–1982
Quatre Quarts (French Orange-Flavoured Cake) **15**–2002
Raisin Cake **15**–2056
Refrigerator Coffeecake **15**–2091
Refrigerator Pineapple Cake **15**–2092
Regina Cake **15**–2094
Religieuse (Choux Pastry Gâteau) **16**–2103
Rhubarb Cake **16**–2103
Rich Chocolate Cake **16**–2116
Rich Rum Fruit Cake **16**–2118
Richmond Cake **16**–2119
Rigo Jancsi (Chocolate Cream Slices) **16**–2122
Robin's Cake **16**–2144
Rococo Torte (Rich Chocolate Cake) **16**–2146
Rotterdam Crumb Cake **16**–2168
Rum and Orange Layer Cake **16**–2180
Sachertorte (Chocolate Cake) **16**–2198
Saffron Cake **16**–2204
Sally Lunn **16**–2213
Sand Cake **16**–2237
Sauerkraut Chocolate Cake **17**–2252
Savarin (French Yeast Cake) **17**–2260
Savarin Aux Cerises (French Yeast Cake with Cherries) **17**–2262
Savarin aux Macarons (French Yeast Cake with Macaroons) **17**–2262
Scotch Bun (info) **17**–2279
Seed Cake **17**–2283
Sherry and Almond Cake **17**–2300
Simnel Cake **17**–2320
Singin' Hinny **17**–2322
Smørkage (Danish Butter Cake) **17**–2334
Sour Milk Cake **17**–2360
Sour Milk Orange Cake **17**–2361
Spice and Nut Cake **17**–2376
Spiced Applesauce Cake **17**–2377
Sponge Cakes **18**–2392
Stollen (German Sweet Bread) **18**–2415
Swiss [Jelly] Roll **18**–2458
Swiss [Jelly] Roll with Cream Filling **18**–2458
Tauchendorfer Torte (Chocolate Gâteau) **18**–2487
Toffee Cake **18**–2508
Toscakake (Caramel-Topped Cake) **19**–2526
Twelfth Night Cake **19**–2582
Upside-Down Apricot Cake **19**–2594
Upside-Down Coconut Cake **19**–2596
Valentine Cake **20**–2604
Venetian Cream Sponge **20**–2667
Vetekaka med Applen (Yeast Cake with Apples) **20**–2683
Victoria Sandwich **20**–2687
Viennese Chestnut Cake **20**–2688
Vinegar Cake **20**–2699
Walnut Fudge Cake **20**–2732
Walnut Gingerbread **20**–2734
Wedding Cake I **20**–2750
Wedding Cake II **20**–2750
Whisky and Pecan Cake **20**–2780
White Christmas Cake **20**–2783

Thematic

Wiltshire Lardy Cake 20-2818
Yorkshire Christmas Gingerbread 21-2935
Yule Log I 21-2957
Yule Log II 21-2957
Zesty Layer Cake 21-2993
Zodiac Cake 22-3006
Zorba's Tipsy Cake 22-3016
Zucchini in Dolce (Courgette Cake) 22-3030
Zundy Teddy Bear Cake 22-3053
Zunita Gâteau 22-3055

CAKES—SMALL

Alexander Torte (Iced Raspberry-Filled Pastry
    Cakes) 1-11
Aranygaluska (Hungarian Buns) 1-59
Austrian Jam Doughnuts 1-89
Baba (info) 1-96
Baba au Rhum 1-96
Baklava (info) 1-107
Banbury Cakes 1-115
Bannocks (info) 1-116
Bath Buns 1-128
Bâtonnets aux Amandes (Almond Cakes) 1-129
Breakfast Buns 2-253
Brownies (Chocolate Nut Squares) 2-270
Buttermilk Doughnuts 3-282
Butterscotch Brownies 3-284
Chelsea Buns 3-369
Coffee Cakes 4-437
Cruller (info) 4-512
Cumin and Raspberry Buns 4-520
Date Bars 4-538
Date Cakes 4-540
Devonshire Splits 5-562
Diamond Cakes with Cherry Filling 5-564
Doughnuts I 5-574
Doughnuts II 5-574
Doughnuts with Jam 5-575
Doughnuts with Lemon 5-576
Doughnuts with Sour Cream 5-576
Dried Apricot Bars 5-577
Eccles Cakes 5-602
Fairy Cakes 5-668
Godcakes 7-844
Gougnettes (French Doughnuts) 7-857
Hot Cross Buns 7-973
Iced Chocolate Dominoes 8-1008
Ingots 8-1024
Isle of Wight Doughnuts 8-1034
Jam Buns 8-1046
Jam and Coconut Bars 8-1047
Japanese Cakes 8-1059
Jellied Sponge Cakes 8-1069
Juliana Cakes 8-1087
Koeksusters (Syrup-Coated Doughnuts) 9-1160
Lancashire Tea Cakes 9-1205
Lemon and Walnut Buns 9-1232
London Buns 10-1268
Madeleines 10-1285
Maids of Honour 10-1288
Mallow Brownies 10-1294
Mistress Hill's Cakes 11-1407
Nantes Cakes 11-1470
Nougatines (info) 11-1522
Nougatine Cakes 11-1522
Nuremburg Spice Squares 11-1528
Oliebollen (Raisin Doughnuts) 12-1570
Orange Yeast Buns 12-1622
Orangenstangerln (Orange Cake Fingers)
    12-1623
Petits Fours (info) 13-1758
Petits Fours (Small Iced Cakes) 13-1758
Phoenician Honey Cakes 13-1773
Prinsessbakelser (Princess Cakes) 15-1975
Queen Cakes 15-2009
Quindins (Coconut Custard Cakes) 15-2034
Rainbow Refrigerator Cakes 15-2053
Raisin Rolls 15-2057
Raspberry Buns 15-2063
Ribbon Cakes 16-2109
Rock Buns 16-2145
Saffron Buns 16-2204
Shredded Coconut Pyramids 17-2307

Sponge Cakes with Orange and Chocolate
    Topping 18-2394
Syrup-Filled Buns 18-2461
Tansy Cakes 18-2477
Victorian Orange Buns 20-2687
Vienna Cakes 20-2687
Walnut and Cherry Buns 20-2728
Welsh Cakes 20-2759
Wigs 20-2807
Wyviss Sugar and Spice Cakes 21-2894
Yorkshire Cheesecakes 21-2935
Zeppole (Neapolitan Doughnuts) 21-2992

CEREALS

Cereal (info) 3-348
Barley (info) 1-122
Barley Water (info) 1-125
Barley Wine (info) 1-125
Bircher Muesli 2-172
Bran (info) 2-233
Buckwheat (info) 2-278
Corn (info) 4-451
Cornflour [Cornstarch] (info) 4-455
Couscous (info) 4-468
Couscous I 4-468
Couscous II 4-470
Crowdie or Crowdy (info) 4-511
Flour (info) 6-729
Gluten (info) 6-840
Graham Flour (info) 7-859
Groats (info) 7-883
Hominy (info) 7-961
Honey and Fruit Muesli 7-963
Indian Corn (info) 7-1020
Kasha (info) 8-1112
Maize (info) 10-1290
Malt (info) 10-1294
Masa (info) 10-1340
Mamaliga (info) 10-1297
Millet (info) 10-1392
Oat (info) 12-1541
Oatmeal (info) 12-1543
Pearl Barley (info) 13-1724
Polenta (info) 14-1842
Popcorn (info) 14-1873
Porridge (info) 14-1902
Porridge 14-1902
Rye (info) 16-2196
Sago (info) 16-2208
Scrapple 17-2279
Semolina (info) 17-2287
Skirlie (Oats) 17-2323
Sorghum (info) 17-2350
Tain Cereal 18-2467
Tamale (info) 18-2471
Tapioca (info) 18-2477
Wheat (info) 20-2775
Wheatgerm (info) 20-2775
Wholemeal [Wholewheat] Flour 20-2801

CHEESE AND CHEESE DISHES

Cheese (info) 3-362
Alivenci (Cheese and Soured Cream Soufflé)
    1-12
Amuse-Gueules au Fromage (Cheese Cocktail
    Snacks) 1-28
Appenzell (info) 1-40
Beef and Cheese Roll 2-147
Beignets au Fromage (Cheese Fritters) 2-160
Bel Paese (info) 2-161
Blue Dorset (info) 2-188
Boerenkaas Soep (Farmer's Cheese Soup) 2-190
Bouchées Parmentier au Fromage (Potato
    Cheese Sticks) 2-219
Boursin (info) 2-225
Bresse Bleu (info) 2-254
Brick Cheese (info) 2-254
Brie Cheese (info) 2-256
Brie Cheese Croquettes 2-256

Caccio-Cavallo (info) 3-290
Caerphilly (info) 3-290
Camembert (info) 3-303
Camembert Croquettes 3-303
Canapés aux Epinards (Spinach and Cheese
    Canapés) 3-304
Canapés Piquants 3-304
Cauliflower Cheese 3-339
Cheddar Cheese (info) 3-361
Cheddar Spread 3-361
Cheesecake *see next heading*
Cheese Charlotte 3-365
Cheese and Chive Spread 3-365
Cheese and Ham Soufflé 3-365
Cheese Logs 3-366
Cheese and Onion Pie 3-366
Cheese Soufflé 3-366
Cheese Soup 3-368
Cheese Spread 3-368
Cheese Straws 3-368
Cheese Toasties 3-368
Cheshire Cheese (info) 3-373
Chou au Gratin (Cheese Cabbage) 3-416
    Cabbage) 3-416
Cottage Cheese (info) 4-463
Cottage Cheese Soup 4-464
Courgettes Gratinées à la Milanaise
    (Courgettes [Zucchini] Baked with Cheese)
    4-467
Cream Cheese (info) 4-478
Cream Cheese Dressing 4-478
Cream Cheese Flan 4-478
Creamed Camembert 4-485
Creamy Cheese 4-488
Creamy Cheese Dip 4-488
Crostata di Ricotta (Cheese Pie) 4-506
Crowdie or Crowdy (info) 4-511
Crowdie 4-511
Cucumber and Cheese Salad 4-515
Danish Blue Cheese (info) 4-528
Danish Blue Salad 4-528
Devilled Cheese 4-558
Diablotins (Cheese Savouries) 5-564
Double Gloucester Cheese (info) 5-573
Dunlop Cheese (info) 5-592
Edam Cheese (info) 5-603
Eggs Bel Paese 5-614
Egg and Cheese Rissoles 5-616
Egg and Cream Cheese Tart 5-618
Egg Noodles with Creamy Cheese Sauce 5-623
Emmenthal (info) 5-643
Endive Farcie (Chicory [French or Belgian
    Endive] Leaves Stuffed with Cream Cheese)
    5-646
Epinards au Gratin (Spinach with Cheese)
    5-651
Feta (info) 5-686
Fondue Suisse 6-734
Frittata di Ricotta con Salsa Rossa (Ricotta
    Cheese Omelet with Tomato Sauce) 6-759
Fusilli Noodles with Tomatoes and Cheese
    6-777
Galettes au Camembert (Camembert Biscuits)
    6-784
Galettes au Fromage (Cheese Biscuits) 6-785
Ghourounaki Yemisto me Feta (Roast Suckling
    Pig Stuffed with Feta Cheese) 6-824
Glamorgan Sausages 6-838
Gloucester Cheese (info) 6-840
Gorgonzola (info) 7-854
Gorgonzola Biscuits 7-854
Gorgonzola Dip 7-854
Gouda (info) 7-855
Gougère (Cheese Pastry) 7-857
Gratin de Pommes de Terre à la Dauphinoise
    (Potatoes baked with Milk, Cheese and
    Garlic) 7-866
Gratin de Pommes de Terre à la Savoyarde
    (Potatoes baked with Beef Stock and Cheese)
    7-866
Greek Salad 7-869
Gruyère (info) 7-887
Gruyère and Mushroom Salad 7-888
Gruyère Omelet 7-888
Gruyère Puffs 7-888
Gruyère Soufflettes 7-889

Haddock with Cheesy Topping 7–900
Harzé (info) 7–932
Harzkäse (info) 7–932
Havarti (info) 7–935
Herkimer Cheese (info) 7–948
Honey and Cream Cheese Pie 7–962
Hungarian Cheese Dip 8–988
Incanestrato Cheese (info) 8–1019
Incanestrato Cheese with Chicken Livers and Noodles 8–1020
Individual Cheese and Fish Bakes 8–1021
Insalata di Fontina (Fontina Cheese and Peppers Salad) 8–1026
Italian Cheese and Almond Pudding 8–1036
Italian Mozzarella Bread 8–1038
Jalousie au Fromage (Openwork Pastry Cheese Tart) 8–1043
Jellied Grape and Cheese Salad 8–1067
Jerusalem Artichokes au Gratin 8–1075
Käsestrudel (Cheese Strudel) 8–1110
Käse Bouillon Mit Ei (Cheese Soup with Egg) 8–1110
Käsepfannkuchen (Cheese Pancakes) 8–1111
Käsespätzle (Egg Noodles with Cheese) 8–1112
Khachapuri (Georgian Cheese Bread) 9–1126
Kreplach (Jewish Stuffed Dumplings) 9–1174
Kümmelkäse (info) 9–1179
Laitues au Gratin (Lettuces with Cheese Sauce) 9–1189
Lancashire Cheese (info) 9–1205
Leicester Cheese (info) 9–1223
Limburger Cheese (info) 9–1238
Liptauer Cheese (info) 9–1242
Macaroni Cheese 10–1276
Macaroni and Ricotta Pudding 10–1278
Manchego (info) 10–1298
Manicotti with Ricotta Stuffing 10–1303
Maroilles (info) 10–1323
Marquise Tartlets 10–1324
Mozzarella (info) 11–1440
Mozzarella in Carozza (Deep-Fried Cheese Sandwiches) 11–1440
Mozzarella Chicken 11–1441
Mozzarella Crespoltini (Cheese and Spinach Crêpes) 11–1441
Munster (info) 11–1449
Nalesniki (Crêpes Stuffed with Cheese) 11–1468
Napoleon au Fromage Blanc (Puff Pastry Layers with Cream Cheese Filling) 11–1472
Neufchâtel Cheese (info) 11–1494
Noekkelost (info) 11–1503
Normandy Cheese Spread 11–1514
Nouilles au Gratin (Noodles with Breadcrumbs and Cheese) 11–1524
Nut and Cream Cheese Balls 11–1534
Nut and Cream Cheese Puffs 11–1534
Omelette au Fromage (Cheese Omelet) 12–1581
Omelette à la Lorraine (Bacon, Cheese and Cream Omelet) 12–1581
Oysters with Cheese Sauce 12–1648
Pancakes with Brie Topping 12–1669
Parmesan Cheese (info) 12–1679
Petits Chaussons au Roquefort (Pastry Turnovers with Roquefort Cheese) 13–1758
Pineapple and Cheese Salad 13–1802
Pirogen (Polish Ravioli) 14–1822
Port-Salut (info) 14–1904
Potted Cheese 14–1935
Processed Cheese (info) 15–1976
Provolone (info) 15–1980
Quattro Formaggi con Riso (Four Cheeses with Rice) 15–2002
Quenelles de Fromage (Cheese Quenelles) 15–2016
Quiche Lorraine (Cheese and Bacon Quiche) 15–2023
Quiche aux Trois Fromages (Three-Cheese Quiche) 15–2024
Raclette (info) 15–2043
Rarebit (info) 15–2061
Ricotta Cheese (info) 16–2119
Ricotta Balls 16–2120
Ricotta al Caffè (Ricotta Cheese with Coffee) 16–2120
Ricotta Flan 16–2120

Ricotta and Olive Scramble 16–2121
Ris de Veau au Fromage (Sweetbreads with Cheese) 16–2128
Roquefort Cheese (info) 16–2162
Roquefort and Brandy Spread 16–2162
Roquefort and Cream Cheese Ring 16–2162
Roquefort Dressing 16–2163
Roquefort Mayonnaise 16–2164
Roquefort Mousse 16–2164
Sage and Cheese Bake 16–2206
Samsoe Cheese (info) 16–2235
Stilton (info) 18–2411
Stilton Ham Bake 18–2412
Sweetcorn Rarebit 18–2452
Talmouses (Savoury Tartlets) 18–2471
Tilsiter Cheese (info) 18–2500
Tiraka Tiganita (Deep-Fried Cheese Balls) 18–2503
Tomato and Mozzarella Salad 18–2515
Uppingham Pâté 19–2593
Vulci Cheese Savoury 20–2723
Walnut and Cream Cheese Biscuits [Cookies] 20–2731
Welsh Rarebit 20–2759
Wensleydale Cheese (info) 20–2763
Whipped Cheese Croûtes 20–2778
Wine, Bread and Cheese Casserole 21–2846
Winnetka Rarebit 21–2848
Wye Cottage Cheese Salad 21–2882
Wynyard Mousse 21–2889
Yogurt Curd Cheese 21–2929
Yorkshire Rarebit 21–2940
Zambian Cheese and Sardine Fritters 21–2973
Zandam Bread Bake 21–2975
Zorell Cheese and Ham Rolls 22–3018
Zouzou's Crêpes 22–3020
Zucca Cheese Loaf 22–3026
Zucchero e Formaggio alla Crema (Sugar and Cream Cheese Dessert) 22–3028
Zuppa di Fontina (Bread and Cheese Soup) 22–3059

CHEESECAKE

Berry Torte 2–163
Cheesecake 3–368
Crostata di Ricotta (Cheese Pie) 4–506
Ginger Cheesecake 6–832
Jellied Cheesecake 8–1064
Käsekuchen (Cheesecake) 8–1111
Pineapple Cheesecake 13–1802
Redcurrant Cheesecake 15–2078
Strawberry Cheesecake 18–2419
Yorkshire Cheesecakes 21–2935
Zwieback Refrigerator Cheesecake 22–3074

CHOCOLATE

Chocolate (info) 3–404
Bavarois au Chocolat (Chocolate Bavarian Cream) 1–134
Boules de Neige au Chocolat (Poached Meringues on Chocolate Custard) 2–223
Charlotte au Chocolat (Chocolate Custard in a Sponge Finger Mould) 3–357
Chocolate Almond Cake 3–404
Chocolate Biscuits [Cookies] 3–406
Chocolate Cake with Hazelnuts 3–406
Chocolate Caraque (info) 3–406
Chocolate Cherry Tart 3–406
Chocolate Chiffon Pie 3–407
Chocolate Chip Cookies 3–408
Chocolate Cinnamon Biscuits [Cookies] 3–408
Chocolate Cream Pie 3–409
Chocolate Fried Bread 3–409
Chocolate Icing I 3–409
Chocolate Icing II 3–409
Chocolate Mocha Pudding 3–409
Chocolate Mushroom Cake 3–410
Chocolate Peppermint Sandwich Cake 3–410
Chocolate Pineapple Rings 3–412
Chocolate Pudding 3–412
Chocolate and Rum Fondue 3–412

Chocolate Rum Truffles 3–413
Chocolate Sauce 3–413
Chocolate Soufflé 3–413
Chocolate and Sour Cream Cake 3–414
Chocolate Sponge Cake 3–414
Chocolate Swiss [Jelly] Roll 3–415
Chokladkaka 3–416
Cocoa (info) 4–429
Crème au Chocolat (Chocolate Cream) 4–490
Devil's Food Cake 4–556
Eggless Chocolate Cake 5–632
Filbert and Chocolate Cake 5–692
Florentine Chocolate Dessert 6–727
Gâteau Noir (Chocolate Cake with Almonds and Rum) 6–806
Ice-Cream, Chocolate-Flavoured 8–1004
Italian Chocolate Loaf 8–1037
James's Chocolate Mousse 8–1057
Kinderkuchen (Children's Cake) 9–1142
Kingly Orange Cake 9–1144
Kissel with Chocolate 9–1151
Lazy Chocolate Cake 9–1214
Lightning Orange and Chocolate Cake 9–1236
Macaroons with Chocolate 10–1280
Marmalade Chocolate Cake 10–1321
Mocha Cream Pie 11–1410
Mohrschokoladedessert (Chocolate Pudding) 11–1412
Mousse au Chocolat (Chocolate Mousse) 11–1434
Mousse à l'Orange et au Chocolat (Orange and Chocolate Mousse) 11–1436
Mousseline au Chocolat (Rich Chocolate Cake) 11–1438
Natalie's Dream Dessert 11–1478
Nuremburg Chocolate Pudding 11–1527
Nut and Chocolate Cookies 11–1533
Nut and Chocolate Sauce 11–1533
Oil Chocolate Cake 12–1564
Orange and Chocolate Biscuits [Cookies] 12–1604
Orange and Chocolate Dessert 12–1604
Palissade aux Marrons (Chestnut and Chocolate Dessert) 12–1663
Pernod and Chocolate Cream 13–1752
Petits Fours au Chocolat (Little Chocolate Balls) 13–1760
Petits Pots de Crème au Chocolat (Individual Chocolate Custards) 13–1765
Praline and Chocolate Ice-Cream Dessert 15–1961
Rich Chocolate Cake 16–2116
Rigo Jancsi (Chocolate Cream Slices) 16–2122
Rococo Torte (Rich Chocolate Cake) 16–2146
Rum Chocolate Mousse 16–2178
Sachertorte (Chocolate Cake) 16–2198
Sauerkraut Chocolate Cake 17–2252
Schokoladenpudding (Chocolate Steamed Pudding) 17–2273
Tauchendorfer Torte (Chocolate Gâteau) 18–2487
Torrone di Cioccolata (Chocolate Nougat) 19–2523
Truffles, Sweets [Candies] (info) 19–2552
Viennese Chocolate Dessert 20–2689
Wasps' Nests 20–2738
Whisky and Chocolate Mousse 20–2779
York Castle Chocolate Tart 21–2934
Zuccherini (Italian Chocolate Mousse in Chocolate Cups) 22–3028
Zuccutto Torone (Italian Chocolate-Flavoured Dessert) 22–3040
Zulinka Rum and Chocolate Soufflé 22–3048

CHUTNEYS, PICKLES AND RELISHES

Adrak Chutney (Ginger Chutney) 1–4
Beetroot Pickles 2–159
Capers (info) 3–316
Chutney (info) 4–422
Chutney I 4–422
Chutney II 4–422
Chutney III 4–422
Cranberry and Orange Relish 4–477

Thematic

Cucumber Relish **4**–518
Gooseberry Chutney **7**–850
Green Chilli Relish **7**–870
Green Tomato Chutney **7**–874
Indian Lime Pickle **8**–1020
Jamaican Pepper Wine **8**–1050
Ketchup (info) **9**–1126
Kim U Chi (Korean Pickled Cabbage) **9**–1141
Lemon and Mustard Seed Chutney **9**–1229
Maine Cauliflower and Tomato Pickle **10**–1289
Mango Chutney I **10**–1301
Mango Chutney II **10**–1302
Marrow Pickle **10**–1328
Mint Chutney **11**–1402
Mushroom Ketchup **11**–1454
Nariel Chatni (Coconut Chutney) **11**–1476
Nasturtium Buds, Pickled **11**–1477
Nectarine Chutney **11**–1488
Norfolk Fruit Chutney **11**–1513
Old Fashioned Date Chutney **12**–1570
Orange Pickle **12**–1614
Old Fashioned Date Chutney **12**–1570
Orange Pickle **12**–1614
Oriental Relish **12**–1625
Peach Pickle **13**–1714
Pear Chutney **13**–1719
Pennsylvania Dutch Mixed Chow-Chow **13**–1736
Piccalilli **13**–1774
Pickle (info) **13**–1777
Pickled Beetroot [Beets] **13**–1777
Pickled Cucumbers I **13**–1778
Pickled Cucumbers II **13**–1779
Pickled French Beans **13**–1780
Pickled Onions **13**–1780
Pickled Walnuts **13**–1780
Pickling Brine **13**–1780
Pickling Spice (info) **13**–1781
Relish (info) **15**–2095
Tamatar Chatni (Indian Tomato Chutney) **18**–2473
Tomato Chutney **18**–2513
Turnip Pickle **19**–2579
Wow-Wow Relish **21**–2868

COFFEE

Coffee (info) **4**–436
Café Brûlot **3**–292
Caffeine (info) **3**–292
Coffee Cakes **4**–437
Coffee Crumble **4**–438
Ice-Cream, Coffee-Flavoured **8**–1005
Iced Coffee I **8**–1008
Iced Coffee II **8**–1008
Jamaican Coffee **8**–1050
Kaffeecreme (Coffee Cream) **8**–1094
Mocha (info) **11**–1410
Mocha Cream Pie **11**–1410
Mocha Katy **11**–1410
Soufflé au Café (Coffee Soufflé) **17**–2353
Whisky and Coffee Soufflé **20**–2780
Ypres Coffee Cream **21**–2944

CONDIMENTS

Condiments (info) **4**–441
Caper (info) **3**–316
Celery Salt (info) **3**–346
Celery Seed (info) **3**–346
Herb Vinegar **7**–948
Horseradish Vinegar **7**–971
Marjoram Vinegar **10**–1318
Monosodium Glutamate (info) **11**–1416
Mustard (info) **11**–1462
Pepper (info) **13**–1739
Salt (info) **17**–2282
Seasoned Salt **17**–2283
Tarragon Vinegar **18**–2481
Vinegar (info) **20**–2699
Wine Vinegar (info) **21**–2848

COOKERY TERMS

Abaisse **1**–1
Acidify **1**–4
Acidulate **1**–4

Aiguillette de Boeuf **1**–9
Aillade **1**–9
Al Dente **1**–10
Algérienne, à l' **1**–12
Allemande, à l' **1**–12
Allumettes **1**–16
Alsacienne, à l' **1**–24
Américaine, à l' **1**–25
Ancienne, à l' **1**–25
Andalouse, à l' **1**–30
Anglaise, à l' **1**–34
Animelle **1**–34
Appareil **1**–40
Archiduc, à l' **1**–60
Arlésienne, à l' **1**–61
Armoricaine **1**–62
Assiette Anglaise **1**–80
Athénienne, à l' **1**–82
Au Beurre **1**–87
Au Beurre Noir **1**–87
Au Blanc **1**–87
Au Brun **1**–87
Au Four **1**–87
Au Gras **1**–87
Au Gratin **1**–87
Au Jus **1**–88
Au Lait **1**–88
Au Maigre **1**–88
Au Naturel **1**–88
Au Rouge **1**–89
Au Vert **1**–91
Bake Blind (Pre-Bake) **1**–105
Baking **1**–107
Ballotine **1**–108
Bard **1**–122
Barquettes **1**–125
Basquaise, à la **1**–128
Baste **1**–128
Batuto **1**–133
Beat **2**–141
Beignet **2**–160
Bénédictine, à la **2**–161
Bigarade, à la **2**–171
Bind **2**–172
Blanch **2**–184
Blanquette **2**–185
Blend **2**–185
Au Bleu **2**–186
Boil **2**–205
Bonne Femme, à la **2**–209
Bordelaise, à la **2**–210
Bourgeoise, à la **2**–224
Bourguignonne, à la **2**–224
Brabançonne, à la **2**–226
Braise **2**–228
Bretonne, à la **2**–254
Broiling **2**–269
Browning **2**–271
Brush **2**–272
Carbonnade **3**–323
Carte, à la **3**–333
Chasseur, à la **3**–360
Chateau **3**–361
Chaudfroid **3**–361
Chining **3**–402
Clarify **4**–426
Coddling **4**–434
Colbert, à la **4**–438
Condé **4**–441
Creaming **4**–488
Crécy, à la **4**–488
Crème, à la **4**–488
Crystallize **4**–514
Darne **4**–535
Daube **4**–545
Deep-Frying **4**–552
Déglacer **4**–552
Dégorge **4**–552
Devil **4**–555
Dice **5**–565
Dieppoise, à la **5**–565
Diplomate, à la **5**–568
Dredge **5**–577
Dressing **5**–577
Emincer **5**–642
Estouffade **5**–662
Etoufée **5**–664
Faisandage **5**–673
Farci **5**–676
Fermière, à la **5**–686

Feuilleton **5**–687
Financière **5**–698
Fines Herbes **5**–698
Flake **6**–718
Flamande, â la **6**–718
Flamber **6**–718
Florentine, à la **6**–726
Flouring **6**–730
Flute **6**–730
Fold **6**–731
Forestière, à la **6**–736
Frappé **6**–740
Frascati, à la **6**–741
Fricandeau **6**–752
Fricassée **6**–752
Fritot **6**–759
Frothing **6**–765
Frying **6**–775
Glaçage **6**–837
Glaze **6**–838
Godard, à la **7**–844
Gratin, au **7**–864
Grésiller **7**–878
Grill [Broil] **7**–880
Grind **7**–883
Harlequin **7**–930
Hongroise, à l' **7**–968
Imperiale, à l' **8**–1019
Infusion **8**–1024
Italienne, à l' **8**–1039
Jardinière, à la **8**–1061
Khoresh **9**–1128
Knead **9**–1157
Larding **9**–1210
Liaison **9**–1236
Lorraine, à la **10**–1270
Lucullus, à la **10**–1274
Macédoine **10**–1282
Macerate **10**–1282
Madrilène **10**–1286
Maître d'Hotel, à la **10**–1290
Marinade **10**–1312
Marinière, à la **10**–1317
Masking **10**–1340
Melt **10**–1373
Meunière, à la **10**–1384
Mirabeau, à la **11**–1404
Mirepoix **11**–1405
Mode, à la **11**–1412
Mornay, à la **11**–1420
Mousse **11**–1433
Mousseline **11**–1438
Nantua, à la **11**–1471
Nap **11**–1472
Niçoise, à la **11**–1501
Nivernaise, à la **11**–1502
Normande, à la **11**–1514
Norvégienne, à la **11**–1518
Panade **12**–1668
Parboil **12**–1677
Pare **12**–1677
Parisienne, à la **12**–1678
Parmentier **12**–1679
Paysanne, à la **13**–1710
Périgourdine, à la **13**–1751
Persillade **13**–1753
Piemontaise, à la **13**–1783
Planking **14**–1839
Plucking **14**–1846
Poaching **14**–1848
Pot Roast **14**–1912
Princesse, à la **15**–1975
Printanière, à la **15**–1976
Provençale, à la **15**–1980
Proving **15**–1980
Purée **15**–1990
Ragoût **15**–2046
Ramekins **15**–2061
Réchauffé **15**–2074
Reduce **15**–2087
Refresh **15**–2090
Render **15**–2097
Roasting **16**–2140
Roux **16**–2175
Rubbing In **16**–2177
Salé **16**–2213
Salmis **16**–2215
Salpicon **16**–2226
Au Sang **16**–2239
Sauté **17**–2256

Scald **16**–2264
Scallop **17**–2264
Shred **17**–2307
Sift **17**–2318
Simmer **17**–2319
Skim **17**–2323
Soaking **17**–2336
Steaming **18**–2410
Stewing **18**–2410
Stir-Frying **18**–2413
Timbale **18**–2500
Trussing **19**–2557
Tyrolienne, à la **19**–2583
Whip **20**–2778
Whisk **20**–2778
Zakuski **21**–2972

CURRIES, INDIAN AND PAKISTANI DISHES

Curry (info) **4**–523
Almond Curry Sauce **1**–22
Aviyal (Vegetable Curry) **1**–91
Badami Gosht (Lamb with Almonds) **1**–104
Bharta (Curried Aubergine Purée) **2**–168
Biryani (Spiced Rice with Lamb) **2**–174
Channa Dhal (Curried Chick Peas) **3**–356
Chicken Curry **3**–378
Chicken Pulao **3**–385
Curried Eggs **4**–521
Curried Potatoes and Peas **4**–523
Dhal Curry **5**–562
Dhansak (Chicken with Lentils and Vegetables) **5**–562
Dopyaza Chicken (Curried Chicken with Onions) **5**–572
Dry Beef Curry **5**–579
Duck Curry **5**–582
Fruit Curry **6**–768
Ghost aur Aloo (Beef and Potato Curry) **6**–823
Goan Vinegar Curry **7**–843
Gobi Ki Sabzi (Spicy Cauliflower) **7**–843
Guleh Kambing (Lamb Curry) **7**–895
Gurda Khorma (Curried Kidneys) **7**–897
Jal Farazi (Curried Meat and Potatoes) **8**–1042
Javanese Curry **8**–1061
Jhinga Kari (Prawn or Shrimp Curry) **8**–1076
Jinja Stew **8**–1078
Kapitan Curry **8**–1105
Kheema (Curried Minced [Ground] Meat) **9**–1128
Kofta Kari (Meatball Curry) **9**–1162
Korma (Rich Lamb Curry) **9**–1167
Lamb and Cashew Nut Curry **9**–1194
Madras Chicken Curry **10**–1286
Murg Bhuna (Fried Chicken) **11**–1449
Murg Kashmiri (Chicken with Almonds and Raisins) **11**–1450
Murgi Dahi (Chicken in Yogurt) **11**–1450
Pakistani Chicken Tikka (Spicy Chicken Kebabs) **12**–1661
Pakistani Lamb Chops **12**–1661
Pakistani Pulau (Curried Rice with Chicken) **12**–1661
Pakistani Spiced Liver **12**–1662
Pakoras (Vegetable Fritters) **12**–1662
Penang Curry Puffs **13**–1734
Poona Pilaff **14**–1872
Pork Curry **14**–1890
Pork Korma (Braised Sliced Pork) **14**–1896
Pork Vindaloo (Pork Vinegar Curry) **14**–1901
Prawn or Shrimp Curry I **15**–1967
Prawn or Shrimp Curry II **15**–1967
Prawn or Shrimp Curry III **15**–1968
Quails in Curry Sauce **15**–1996
Raan (Leg of Lamb Marinated in Spiced Yogurt and Roasted) **15**–2037
Rendang (Curried Beef) **15**–2096
Roghan Gosht (Curried Lamb) **16**–2152
Sag Gohst **16**–2205
Sambal (info) **16**–2232
Sambal I **16**–2232
Sambal II **16**–2232
Sambal III **16**–2233
Sambal IV **16**–2233
Sambar **16**–2234
Scallops with Curry Sauce **17**–2265
Seekh Kebabs (Minced [Ground] Meat Kebabs) **17**–2284

Shakooti Rassa (Lamb with Coconut) **17**–2293
Sindhi Chicken **17**–2320
Stuffed Green Peppers Indian-Style **18**–2431
Stuffed Tomatoes Indian-Style **18**–2433
Talawa Gosht (Deep-Fried Lamb and Potatoes) **18**–2468
Tali Machee (Deep-Fried Fish) **18**–2470
Tamatar Bharta (Puréed Tomatoes) **18**–2473
Tamatar Machli (Tomato Fish) **18**–2474
Tandoori Murg (Spiced Chicken) **18**–2474
Thayir Kari (Yogurt Curry) **18**–2497
Tikkah Kabab (Spiced Lamb Kebabs) **18**–2500
Tomato Curry **18**–2514
Turkari Aloo (Curried Potatoes) **19**–2564
Turkari Baingan (Curried Aubergines [Eggplant]) **19**–2564
Turkari Molee (Lamb and Coconut Curry) **19**–2565
Umabai's Baked Spiced Fish **19**–2587
Umabai's Curried Partridges **19**–2588
Umabai's Spiced Almond Chicken **19**–2588
Vath (Indian Roast Duck) **19**–2610
Veau à l'Indienne (Curried Veal Stew) **19**–2639
Vegetable Bharta **19**–2641
Vegetable Curry **19**–2644
Vegetable Kitcheri **19**–2645
Vegetables and Prawn or Shrimp Curry **19**–2651
Vegetable Pulao with Prawns or Shrimps **19**–2651
Vegetarian Stew Indian-Style **19**–2658
Vellarikai Pachadi (Cucumber and Yogurt Salad) **20**–2661
Vendai Kai Kari (Curried okra) **20**–2665
Vindaloo with Chicken **20**–2695
Wengi Bhat (Aubergines [Eggplants] and Rice) **20**–2762
Wengyachen Bharit (Curried Aubergines [Eggplants]) **20**–2763
West African Beef and Fruit Curry **20**–2766
West Indian Chicken Casserole **20**–2768
White Chicken Curry **20**–2782
White Fish Curry **20**–2785
Yogurt and Banana Raita **21**–2926
Yogurt Chicken **21**–2926
Zanzibar Salt Cod Curry **21**–2979
Zeera Gosht (Cumin Meat) **21**–2987
Zeera Murg (Cumin Chicken) **21**–2989

DESSERTS—HOT

Adam and Eve Pudding (Apple and Sponge Pudding) **1**–4
Alebele (Coconut Filled Pancakes) **1**–10
Alivenci (Cheese and Soured Cream Soufflé) **1**–12
American Apple Pie **1**–26
Apfelbettelmann (Apple Pudding) **1**–38
Apfelkuchen (Apple and Custard Tart) **1**–38
Apfelstrudel **1**–38
Äppelformar (Small Apple Pies) **1**–40
Apple Amber **1**–41
Apples, Baked **1**–42
Apple Bread Pudding **1**–42
Apple Brown Betty **1**–43
Apple Charlotte **1**–44
Apple Dumplings **1**–45
Apple-Filled Pancakes **1**–45
Apple Florentine **1**–46
Apple Flambé **1**–47
Apple Fritters **1**–47
Apple Hat **1**–48
Apple Pie **1**–48
Apple and Rice Pudding **1**–49
Apple Sonning **1**–50
Apple Turnovers **1**–51
Apricot Condé **1**–52
Apricot Pudding **1**–56
Apricot Tart **1**–57
Asynpoeding (Vinegar Pudding) **1**–81
Austrian Pudding **1**–90
Baked Alaska **1**–105
Bakewell Tart **1**–107
Bananas, Baked **1**–109
Bananas Baked with Custard **1**–110
Bananas Baked in Orange Juice **1**–110
Bananas Beauharnais (Bananas Baked in Rum and Cream) **1**–110
Bananas Caribbean **1**–110
Bananas, Fried **1**–113

Banana Fritters **1**–113
Bananas with Orange **1**–113
Bananas in Sherry **1**–114
Batter Pudding **1**–131
Bavarian Strudel (Apple Filled Pastry) **1**–133
Beignets d'Ananas (Pineapple Fritters) **1**–160
Beignets Soufflés (Puffy Fritters) **1**–160
Blackberry and Apple Pie **2**–180
Blinis (Russian Pancakes) **2**–186
Blueberry Crumble **2**–188
Bread and Butter Pudding **2**–250
Brown Sugar Tart **2**–272
Buttermilk Pie **3**–283
Canary Pudding **3**–308
Cherries Jubilee **3**–371
Cherry Pie **3**–371
Cherry Tapioca **3**–372
Chocolate Cherry Tart **3**–406
Chocolate Fried Bread **3**–409
Chocolate Pudding **3**–412
Chocolate and Rum Fondue **3**–412
Chocolate Soufflé **3**–413
Christmas Pudding **3**–421
Clafoutis (info) **4**–424
Clafoutis aux Cerises (French Cherry Pudding) **4**–424
Clafoutis aux Pommes (French Apple Pudding) **4**–424
Clafoutis aux Prunes (French Plum Pudding) **4**–425
Coffee Crumble **4**–438
Coriander Fruit Crumble **4**–451
Cranberry Pie **4**–477
Crème Brulée (Glazed Baked Custard) **4**–489
Crêpe (info) **4**–494
Crêpe Batter (Sweet) **4**–494
Crêpes aux Amandes (Almond Crêpes) **4**–496
Crêpes à la Confiture (Jam Crêpes) **4**–496
Crêpes Frangipane (Crêpes with Almond Cream and Chocolate) **4**–498
Crêpes aux Fruits (Fruit Crêpes) **4**–498
Crêpes à l'Orange (Orange Crêpes) **4**–499
Crêpes Suzettes (Crêpes Flamed with Orange Liqueur) **4**–501
Croquettes de Semoule au Sirop (Semolina Croquettes) **4**–506
Croûtes Dorées (Sweet Croûtes) **4**–509
Custard and Pear Tart **4**–524
Damson Soufflé **4**–528
Date and Apple Pie **4**–538
Date Pudding **4**–541
Deep-Dish Peach Pie **4**–550
Delaware Pudding **4**–552
Double-Crust Blackcurrant and Apple Pie **5**–573
Duchess Pudding **5**–581
Dumpling (info) **5**–590
Dumplings (Sweet) **5**–590
Elderberry Pie **5**–640
Exeter Pudding **5**–664
Faux Soufflé Meringué aux Ananas (Meringue and Pineapple Soufflé) **5**–679
Fig Carnival **5**–688
Fig Flutter **5**–689
Fig Pudding **5**–690
Flan (info) **6**–719
Flan d'Ananas (Pineapple Flan) **6**–721
Flangnarde (Baked Custard) **6**–722
Flensjes (Dutch Crêpes) **6**–725
Fransk Aeblekage (Apple and Almond Pudding) **6**–740
French Toast **6**–750
Fritters with Honey Sauce **6**–761
Fruit Pudding **6**–772
Frumenty (info) **6**–775
Galette aux Abricots (Apricot Cake) **6**–783
Ginger and Banana Crêpes **6**–830
Ginger Pudding **6**–834
Golden Gooseberry Bake **7**–845
Gooseberry Crumble **7**–851
Gooseberry Kissel **7**–852
Gooseberry Pie **7**–852
Gooseberry Steffon **7**–853
Gouère aux Pommes (Apple Batter Pudding) **7**–855
Green Grape and Apple Pie **7**–871
Grilled [Broiled] Fruit Salad Packets **7**–882
Ground Rice Pudding **7**–884
Grumble Pie **7**–887
Guard's Pudding **7**–891
Guava Pie **7**–892

Thematic

Gus-Khrustalny Cream Pudding 7–898
Half Pay Pudding 7–907
Hasty Pudding 7–935
Hazelnut Soufflé 7–940
Honey-Baked Pears 7–961
Honey and Banana Toasts 7–961
Honey Ginger Pudding 7–964
Honey Pudding 7–964
Hot Orange Pudding 7–974
Huckleberry Meringue Pie 7–979
Hungarian Apple Pie 8–987
Hungarian Apple Soup 8–988
Hungarian Layered Crêpes 8–991
Ice-Cream Crêpes 8–1005
Indian Pudding II 8–1020
Indonesian Baked Bananas 8–1022
Instant Yogurt Pudding 8–1026
Jam, Date and Nut Turnovers 8–1047
Jam Omelet 8–1048
Jam Roly-Poly 8–1048
Jamaican Rum Pudding 8–1052
Jelly Crêpes 8–1072
Kaiserschmarrn (Emperor's Pancakes) 8–1096
Karlstadtklösse (Steamed Sweet Dumplings) 8–1107
Käsestrudel (Cheese Strudel) 8–1110
Kebabs with Fruit 8–1118
Khalva (Walnuts in Custard) 9–1126
Kirschpfannkuchen (Cherry-Filled Crêpes) 9–1150
Kissel (info) 9–1151
Kissel with White Wine 9–1151
Kugel with Apples 9–1178
Kynute Ovochné Knedliky (Czechoslovakian Fruit Dumplings) 9–1185
Lemon Bread Pudding 9–1225
Lemon Meringue Pie 9–1228
Lemon Soufflé—Hot 9–1231
Lemon Sponge 9–1231
Lemon Tapioca Pudding 9–1231
Lokshen Pudding 10–1266
Louisiana Rice Pudding 10–1272
Macadamia Nut Pie 10–1275
Macaroni with Raisins and Apricots 10–1278
Macaroni and Ricotta Pudding 10–1278
Maine Pancakes 10–1289
Maize Pudding 10–1290
Ma-Mounia (Semolina Pudding) 10–1297
Maple Bread Pudding 10–1306
Marlborough Apple Pie 10–1319
Marmalade Pudding 10–1322
Marron Soufflé (Chestnut Soufflé) 10–1327
Matzo Fry 10–1345
Matzo Kugel 10–1345
Meringue Pancakes 10–1381
Mincemeat and Apple Crumble 10–1396
Mirabelle Soufflé 11–1405
Mohrschokoladedessert (Chocolate Pudding) 11–1412
Mother's Bread Pudding 11–1426
Mulberry and Apple Pie 11–1444
Nectarine Pie 11–1488
Noodle Pudding with Apples 11–1512
Northern Lights 11–1518
Northumberland Puddings 11–1518
Nuremburg Chocolate Pudding 11–1527
Nut Fritters 11–1535
Nut and Sweet Potato Flan 11–1538
Nutalie Flan 11–1538
Oatmeal Pancakes 12–1545
October Cobbler 12–1550
Ohio Pudding 12–1560
Omelette aux Fraises (Strawberry Omelet) 12–1580
Omelette Normande (Apple Omelet) 12–1583
Omelette aux Poires (Pear Omelet) 12–1583
Omelette au Rhum (Rum Omelet) 12–1584
Orange Custard 12–1606
Orange-Flavoured Banana Fritters 12–1606
Orange and Peach Fondue 12–1613
Orange Soufflés 12–1617
Orange Soufflé-Filled Crêpes 12–1617
Orange Surprise Pudding 12–1620
Oznei Haman (Israeli Deep-Fried Pastries) 12–1654
Palacsinken (Jam and Sour Cream Crêpes) 12–1663
Pancake (info) 12–1668
Pancakes with Blueberries 12–1669
Pancakes with Maple Syrup 12–1670
Pandowdy 12–1671

Patriotic Pudding 13–1703
Peach Cobbler 13–1712
Peach Flan 13–1713
Peach Puffs 13–1714
Pears Paradiso 13–1721
Pets de Nonnes (Sweet Fritters) 13–1766
Pineapple Soufflé 13–1808
Pineapple Upside-Down Cake 13–1811
Plum-Stuffed Crêpes 14–1848
Pommes et Abricots à l'Ancienne (Apple and Apricot Dessert) 14–1862
Pommes au Cognac (Apples Baked in Brandy and Vermouth) 14–1864
Pommes Grimaldi (Apple and Rice Flan) 14–1864
Pommes Normandes (Apple and Caramel Mould) 14–1866
Port and Raspberry Kissel 14–1903
Pouding aux Fruits Sèches (Dried Fruit Pudding) 14–1938
Praline Soufflé 15–1962
Prune and Apple Meringue Flan 15–1981
Prune and Walnut Soufflé 15–1982
Pumpkin Pie 15–1986
Queen's Almond Pudding 15–2008
Queen Anne's Custard 15–2008
Queen of Puddings 15–2011
Queen's Pudding 15–2011
Quesillo de Piña (Pineapple Custard) 15–2018
Quince and Apple Turnovers 15–2030
Rabarberkompott (Rhubarb Compôte) 15–2037
Railway Pudding 15–2052
Recruitment Apple Pastries 15–2074
Rhubarb and Apple Crumble 16–2101
Rhubarb Brown Betty 16–2103
Rhubarb and Ginger Roly-Poly 16–2105
Rhubarb and Orange Pie 16–2107
Rhubarb Pudding 16–2107
Rice and Fig Dessert 16–2113
Rich Rice Pudding 16–2116
Ricotta Balls 16–2120
Rolled Crêpes Stuffed with Bananas 16–2156
Roly-Poly (info) 16–2159
Roly-Poly with Dried Fruit 16–2159
Rothesay Pudding 16–2168
Royal Peach Meringue 16–2176
Sago Pudding 16–2208
Sanctuary Pudding 16–2236
Scandinavian Almond Apples 17–2272
Schokoladenpudding (Chocolate Steamed Pudding) 17–2273
Semolina Pudding 17–2287
Semolina Pudding with Fruit and Nuts 17–2287
Soufflé (info) 17–2352
Soufflé aux Amandes (Almond Soufflé) 17–2352
Soufflé au Café (Coffee Soufflé) 17–2353
Soufflé au Grand Marnier (Orange Liqueur Soufflé) 17–2354
Soufflé Omelet with Pastry Cream 17–2357
South African Boiled Pudding 17–2363
Spotted Dick 18–2396
Steamed Pudding 18–2409
Strudel Fruit Rolls 18–2427
Sultana and Sago Pudding 18–2440
Swedish Gooseberry Pie 18–2447
Tansy Apple Cream 18–2477
Tapioca with Apples 18–2477
Tapioca Pudding 18–2478
Tarte à la Rhubarbe (Rhubarb Flan) 18–2484
Tarte à la Rhubarbe Soufflé (Rhubarb Cream Flan) 18–2484
Toffee Apples Chinese-Style 18–2508
Toffee Pudding 18–2508
Torrijas (Bread and Honey Dessert) 19–2523
Treacle Layer Pudding 19–2538
Treacle Tart I 19–2540
Treacle Tart II 19–2540
Tungpo Honey Apples 19–2560
Turdillos (Date and Fig Dumplings) 19–2564
Tyler's Custard Pie 19–2583
Uachdar Pudding 19–2584
Upside-Down Apple Tart 19–2594
Upside-Down Apricot Cake 19–2594
Upside-Down Coconut Cake 19–2596
Vanilla Soufflé 19–2608
Vatrushka Pie 19–2611
Vicarage Pudding 20–2684
Viennese Raspberry Pudding 20–2693
Walnut Fudge Cake 20–2732
Waterbul (Pastry Roll) 20–2741

White Peaches with Caramelized Sugar 20–2789
Wine Dessert 21–2847
Winter Compôte 21–2849
Winter Crumble 21–2849
Wontons with Almonds and Dates 21–2858
Wrighton Pie 21–2873
Wry Banana Fluff 21–2874
Wurzburg Chocolate Bread and Butter Pudding 21–2882
Wyviss Porridge Apples 21–2893
Yugoslavian Rice Pudding 21–2954
Zabaglione (info) 21–2966
Zabaglione (Italian Egg Yolk and Wine Dessert) 21–2966
Zabaglione Orientale (Italian Egg Yolk Dessert with Orange-Flavoured Liqueur) 21–2968
Zarda (Sweet Pilaff) 21–2982
Zoar's Crispy Apple Bake 22–3006
Zulinka Rum and Chocolate Soufflé 22–3048
Zurich Fruit Crumble 22–3063
Zwetschgenknödeln (Plum Dumplings) 22–3072
Zwetschgenkuchen (Plum Flan) 22–3072
Zwieback mit Schwarzen Johannisbeeren (Rusks with Blackcurrants) 22–3076
Zyrenia Noodle and Prune Bake 22–3080

DESSERTS—COLD

Almond Apples 1–20
Ambrosia (Orange Dessert) 1–25
Angelica Tart 1–32
Apfelkuchen (Apple and Custard Tart) 1–38
Apfelstrudel 1–38
Apple Amber 1–41
Apples, Baked 1–42
Apple Bread Pudding 1–42
Apples Bristol 1–42
Apple Mousse à la Chantilly 1–48
Apple Snow 1–50
Apple Sonning 1–50
Apple Turnovers 1–51
Apricot Bourdaloue Tart 1–52
Apricots in Brandy 1–52
Apricot Condé 1–52
Apricots Granville 1–54
Apricot Pudding 1–56
Apricot Tart 1–57
Aspic de Pommes (Apple Aspic) 1–80
Athenium Walnut Cake 1–81
Austrian Coffee Cake 1–89
Baba au Rhum 1–96
Baba aux Fraises 1–98
Baked Alaska 1–105
Bakewell Tart 1–107
Bananas Baked with Custard 1–110
Banana Cream Pie 1–110
Bananas Creole 1–112
Banana Pudding 1–113
Banana and Raspberry Cream 1–114
Bavarian Strudel (Pastry Filled with Apples) 1–133
Bavarois (Bavarian Cream) 1–133
Bavarois au Chocolat (Chocolate Bavarian Cream) 1–134
Bavarois Clermont (Bavarian Cream with Marrons Glacés) 1–135
Bavarois à l'Orange (Orange Bavarian Cream) 1–135
Bavarois Praline (Bavarian Cream with Caramelized Almonds) 1–135
Berry Torte 2–163
Bien me sabe de coco (Venezuelan Sponge Cake) 2–171
Blackberry and Apple Pie 2–180
Blackberry Fool 2–180
Black Bottom Parfait 2–181
Black Bottom Pie 2–182
Blancmange (info) 2–184
Blueberry Crumble 2–188
Bombe (info) 2–206
Bombe Coppelia (Coffee and Rum Ice-Cream Filled with Praline) 2–206
Bombe Framboises (Moulded Ice-Cream with Raspberries) 2–208
Bombe Marie-Claire (Moulded Vanilla Ice-Cream with Apricot Filling) 2–208
Boules de Neige au Chocolat (Poached Meringues on Chocolate Custard) 2–223

Brandy Alexander Pie 2–234
Brazil Nut Banana Cake 2–239
Brioche aux Fraises avec Moussade Framboises (Brioche with Strawberries and Raspberry Cream Filling) 3–260
Brown Sugar Tart 3–272
Cabinet Pudding 3–290
Cantaloupe Surprise 3–314
Caramel Apricots 3–320
Cassata (info) 3–334
Chamonix 3–350
Charlotte (info) 3–357
Charlotte au Chocolat (Chocolate Custard in a Sponge Finger Mould) 3–357
Charlotte aux Framboises (Raspberry Mould) 3–358
Charlotte aux Fraises (Almond Cream with Strawberries) 3–359
Charlotte Russe 3–359
Chartreuse de Pommes (Apple Mould with Redcurrant Sauce) 3–360
Cheesecakes see Cheesecake
Cherry Compôte 3–370
Cherry Pie 3–371
Chestnut Compôte 3–374
Chocolate Almond Cake 3–404
Chocolate Cake with Hazelnuts 3–406
Chocolate Cherry Tart 3–406
Chocolate Chiffon Pie 3–407
Chocolate Cream Pie 3–409
Chocolate Mocha Pudding 3–409
Chocolate Peppermint Sandwich Cake 3–410
Chocolate Pineapple Rings 3–412
Coconut Cream Pie 4–430
Coeur à la Crème 4–435
Coffee Crumble 4–438
Compôte (info) 4–441
Compôte of Dried Fruits 4–441
Compôte de Poires (Pears Poached in Vanilla Syrup) 4–441
Coriander Fruit Crumble 4–451
Cornish Custard Cream 4–456
Coupe Jacques (Raspberry and Lemon Sorbet with Fresh Fruit) 4–464
Cranberry Mousse 4–476
Cream Cheese Flan 4–478
Cream Puffs 4–485
Crème Brulée (Glazed Baked Custard) 4–489
Crème Caramel (Baked Caramel Custard) 4–490
Crème au Chocolat (Chocolate Cream) 4–490
Crème aux Fraises (Strawberry Cream) 4–492
Custard (info) 4–523
Custard Tart 4–524
Date and Banana Dessert 4–538
Date Jewels 4–540
Date and Rice Pudding 4–542
Delft Cake (Almond Meringue Layer Cake with Orange Buttercream Filling) 4–554
Diplomate Pudding 5–568
Dried Fruits in Syrup 5–578
Eggnog Chiffon Pie 5–633
Engadiner Nusstorte (Honey and Walnut Torte) 5–646
Fig Carnival 5–688
Fig Tart 5–690
Figues au Cacao (Figs in Crème de Cacao) 5–691
Flamri de Semoule (Semolina Pudding with Strawberry Sauce) 6–718
Flan (info) 6–719
Flan d'Ananas (Pineapple Flan) 6–721
Flan au Potiron Caramelisé (Pumpkin and Caramel Flan) 6–722
Flangnarde (Baked Custard) 6–722
Florentine Chocolate Dessert 6–727
Flummery 6–730
Fool (info) 6–735
Fraises Romanoff (Strawberries in Orange-Flavoured Liqueur with Crème Chantilly) 6–737
Frankfurter Kranz (Layer Cake with Buttercream Filling) 6–739
Fransk Aeblekage (Apple and Almond Pudding) 6–740
French Apricot Pudding 6–745
French Peach Tart 6–749
Frosted Walnut Cake 6–763
Fruit Ambrosia 6–766
Fruit Cream 6–768

Fruit Fool 6–768
Fruit Salad 6–773
Fruit Salad with Kirsch 6–773
Fyllda Strutar (Pastry Cones with Cream and Fruit) 6–778
Gajjar Halva (Carrot Dessert) 6–781
Galette aux Abricots (Apricot Cake) 6–783
Galette Noisettine (Hazelnut Biscuit Cake) 6–786
Galette Normande (Rich Pastry Filled with Apple Purée) 6–786
Gâteau (info) 6–802
Gâteau Flamande à la Crème (Flemish Cream Cake) 6–802
Gâteau aux Fraises et Amandes (Strawberry and Almond Cake) 6–803
Gâteau de Marrons (Chestnut Cake) 6–803
Gâteau Mille-feuille (Layers of Puff Pastry with Crème Chantilly and Jam) 6–804
Gâteau Mocha (Coffee Buttercream Cake) 6–804
Gâteau Noir (Chocolate Cake with Almonds and Rum) 6–806
Gâteau Noisette (Hazelnut and Meringue Cake) 6–806
Gâteau à l'Orange (Orange Cake) 6–806
Gâteau St. Honoré (Caramel-Coated Choux Puffs, Pastry Cream and Crème Chantilly on a Pastry Base) 6–808
Gefüllte Melonen (Stuffed Melon) 6–812
Gevulde Botterkoek (Butter Shortbread with Almond and Fruit Filling) 6–821
Ginger Ale Fruit Jelly [Gelatin] 6–829
Ginger Lemon Flan 6–834
Gooseberry Charlotte 7–850
Gooseberry Kissel 7–852
Gooseberry Pie 7–852
Grape Tartlets 7–860
Grapefruit Jelly [Gelatin] 7–862
Greengage Flan 7–875
Grenadine Almond Flan 7–876
Grenadine and Walnut Soufflé 7–876
Ground Rice Pudding 7–884
Grüne Melone Mousse (Green Melon Mousse) 7–887
Guava Pie 7–892
Handsome Tipsy Cake 7–922
Harriet's Orange Pudding 7–932
Hasty Pudding 7–935
Hawaiian Cream Roll 7–937
Hazelnut Torte 7–941
Himmelsk Mundfeld (Fruit Salad with Madeira Sauce) 7–953
Honey-Baked Pears 7–961
Honey and Cream Cheese Pie 7–962
Honey and Fruit Muesli 7–963
Honey Mousse 7–964
Honey Pecan Flan 7–964
Honey and Walnut Pudding 7–965
Honeycomb Cream 7–966
Honeydew Melon with Blackcurrant Iced Mousse 7–967
Huckleberry Meringue Pie 7–979
Hungarian Apple Soup 8–988
Hungarian Cherry Soup 8–989
Hungarian Cream Cake 8–989
Icebergs 8–1000
Icebox Cake 8–1001
Ice-Cream (info) 8–1002
Ice-Cream, Custard Base 8–1003
Ice-Cream, Custard Base for 'Still-Frozen' 8–1004
Ice-Cream, Mousse Base 8–1004
Ice-Cream, Chocolate-Flavoured 8–1004
Ice-Cream, Coffee-Flavoured 8–1005
Ice-Cream, Ginger-Flavoured 8–1005
Ice-Cream, Strawberry-Flavoured 8–1005
Ice-Cream Crêpes 8–1005
Ice-Cream Filled Grapefruit 8–1005
Ice-Cream Roll 8–1006
Iced Coupes (info) 8–1009
Iced Peaches 8–1010
Iced Pineapple with Orange Syrup 8–1010
Iced Soufflés (info) 8–1010
Iced Zabaglione 8–1010
Igloo Pudding 8–1014
Ile Flottante (Floating Island) 8–1016
Indian Pudding I 8–1020
Indian Pudding II 8–1020
Instant Yogurt Pudding 8–1026
Irish Moss Mould 8–1030

Irish Tipsy Pudding 8–1032
Italian Cheese and Almond Pudding 8–1036
Italian Cherries 8–1036
Italian Chocolate Loaf 8–1037
Jacqueline's Lemon Wonder Pudding 8–1041
Jalousie (info) 8–1043
Jalousie à la Confiture (Openwork Pastry Jam Tart) 8–1043
Jamaican Pie 8–1052
James's Chocolate Mousse 8–1057
Jellied Cream and Strawberry Flan 8–1065
Jelly [Gelatin] (info) 8–1071
Jelly Tart 8–1073
Jordgubbsvisp (Scandinavian Strawberry Dessert) 8–1082
Junidessert (Norwegian Rhubarb Dessert) 8–1090
Junket 8–1090
Kaffeecreme (Coffee Cream) 8–1094
Kaltschale (Austrian Iced Blackberry Soup) 8–1101
Kannellagkage (Cinnamon-Flavoured Layer Cake) 8–1104
Karamelrand (Caramel Pudding) 8–1106
Katheryn Cake 8–1115
Kirovakan Fruit (Armenian Dried Fruit Dessert) 9–1148
Kirsch with Bananas 9–1149
Kirsch and Chestnut Cream 9–1149
Kirschen mit Eiskrem (Cherries with Ice-Cream) 9–1149
Kirschenstrudel (Austrian Cherry Strudel) 9–1149
Kirschkuchen (Cherry Flan) 9–1150
Kissel (info) 9–1151
Kissel with Chocolate 9–1151
Knickerbocker Glory 9–1157
Krammerhuse (Ginger Cream-Filled Horns) 9–1171
Kugel with Apples 9–1178
Kutya (Honey and Rice Pudding) 9–1183
Lemon and Lime Chiffon 9–1226
Lemon Meringue Pie 9–1228
Lemon Posset 9–1230
Lemon Soufflé—Cold 9–1230
Lemon Whip 9–1233
Lime Cream Pie 9–1238
Linzertorte (Jam Tart) 9–1242
Louisiana Coconut Pie 10–1272
Louisiana Rice Pudding 10–1272
Macadamia Nut Pie 10–1275
Macaroni with Raisins and Apricots 10–1278
Macaroni and Ricotta Pudding 10–1278
Macaroon and Apricot Whip 10–1279
Maize Pudding 10–1290
Malakoff Sponge Cake 10–1290
Ma-Mounia (Semolina Pudding) 10–1297
Manchester Tart 10–1298
Mandeltorte (Almond Layer Cake) 10–1298
Manjar Blanco (Bolivian Cream) 10–1305
Maple Cream Pie 10–1300
Maple and Orange Mousse 10–1308
Marak Perot Car (Cold Fruit Soup) 10–1311
Marlborough Apple Pie 10–1319
Marmalade and Tangerine Flan 10–1322
Marquise Alice (Bavarian Cream Dessert) 10–1323
Marron Charlotte (Chestnut Mould) 10–1327
Marrons Montpélier (Chestnut Dessert) 10–1327
Marshmallow and Tangerine Pudding 10–1334
Martha Washington Cake 10–1334
Melkeringer (Milk Curd) 10–1370
Melktert (Custard Tart) 10–1370
Melon Balls in White Wine 10–1372
Melon and Cherry Coupe 10–1372
Melon Mélange 10–1372
Melons Pâtissière aux Fraises (Melon with Crème Pâtissière and Strawberries) 10–1373
Meringues (info) 10–1378
Meringue Cuite 10–1378
Meringue Italienne 10–1378
Meringue Suisse 10–1378
Meringue Almond Layer Cake 10–1378
Meringue Basket 10–1379
Meringue Chantilly 10–1379
Meringue Crown 10–1379
Meringue Martinique 10–1380
Midsummer Dream 10–1390
Mocha Cream Pie 11–1410

Thematic

Mocha Katy 11–1410
Molasses (info) 11–1413
Molasses Crumb Pie 11–1413
Molasses Hazelnut Pie 11–1413
Molasses Sponge Cake 11–1414
Morello Cherry Flan 11–1420
Morello Cherries with Yogurt 11–1420
Moulded Cream Pudding 11–1428
Mousse (info) 11–1433
Mousse aux Abricots (Apricot Mousse) 11–1433
Mousse aux Abricots et aux Mûres (Apricot
  Mousse with Blackberries) 11–1434
Mousse au Chocolat (Chocolate Mousse)
  11–1434
Mousse aux Framboises (Raspberry Mousse)
  11–1435
Mousse à l'Orange et au Chocolat (Orange and
  Chocolate Mousse) 11–1436
Mousse à l'Orange Glacée (Frozen Orange
  Mousse) 11–1436
Muhalabia (Chilled Ground Rice Pudding)
  11–1433
Mulberry and Apple Pie 11–1444
Nabob's Delight 11–1466
Naranjas al Kirsch (Fruit Soaked in Kirsch)
  11–1474
Natalie's Dream Dessert 11–1478
Neapolitan Ice-Cream 11–1483
Nectarine Cream Mould 11–1488
Nectarine Pie 11–1488
Nectarine Tartlets 11–1489
Neige de Pêches au Champagne (Peach and
  Champagne Dessert) 11–1490
Nesselrode Pudding 11–1493
Newington Snow 11–1501
Normandy Pear Tart 11–1514
Northumberland Puddings 11–1518
Norwegian Cream 11–1518
Nougat Ice-Cream 11–1521
Noyau Cream 11–1525
Nuremburg Chocolate Pudding 11–1527
Nuss Schlagsahne (Nut Cream) 11–1531
Nut and Apple Cream 11–1531
Nut Apple Jellies [Gelatins] 11–1531
Nut Roll 11–1537
Nutalie Flan 11–1538
Oatmeal Ice-Cream 12–1545
Obsttorte (Fruit Tart) 12–1546
Orange Caramel Trifle 12–1602
Orange and Chocolate Dessert 12–1604
Oranges with Cinnamon 12–1605
Orange Custard 12–1606
Oranges Glacées 12–1612
Orange Rice 12–1615
Oranges Stuffed with Orange Cream 12–1618
Oriental Fruit Salad 12–1625
Palissade aux Marrons (Chestnut and Chocolate
  Dessert) 12–1665
Parfait (info) 12–1677
Parfait Judy 12–1677
Paris-Brest (Choux Pastry Ring Filled with
  Crème Pâtissière) 12–1677
Paskha (Russian Eastern Dessert) 13–1689
Passion Fruit and Banana Cream 13–1689
Paul's Lemon Pudding 13–1704
Pavlova 13–1709
Peach Flan 13–1713
Peach Melba 13–1714
Peach Puffs 13–1714
Peanut Ice-Cream 13–1718
Pears Baked with Cardamom 13–1718
Pear Condé 13–1721
Pears Poached in Red Wine 13–1722
Pear Tart Bourdaloue 13–1722
Pecan Pie 13–1725
Pecan and Sour Cream Flan 13–1726
Pecan Torte 13–1727
Pêches Cardinal (Fresh Peaches with
  Raspberry Purée) 13–1728
Pêches aux Macarons (Peaches with Macaroon
  Cream Filling) 13–1728
Pêches au Massepain (Peaches with Marzipan)
  13–1728
Pêches Refraîchies aux Mûres (Peach and
  Blackberry Dessert) 13–1728
Peppermint and Chocolate Ice-Cream 13–1743
Pernod and Chocolate Cream 13–1752
Perth Tart 13–1755
Petits Pots de Crème au Chocolat (Individual
  Chocolate Custards) 13–1765

Pineapple Bavarian Cream 13–1800
Pineapple Cream 13–1805
Pineapple Delight 13–1805
Pineapple Flan 13–1805
Pineapple Fruit Salad 13–1805
Pineapple and Honey Sorbet 13–1806
Pineapple Upside-Down Cake 13–1811
Pineapple and Walnut Ice-Cream 13–1811
Pistachio Ice-Cream 14–1824
Plum Compôte 14–1847
Poires Belle Hélène (Pears with Ice-Cream and
  Chocolate Sauce) 14–1850
Poires au Caramel (Pears with Caramel Sauce)
  14–1851
Polish Orange and Almond Flan 14–1855
Pomarez Pineapple 14–1860
Pommes à la Bourguignonne (Apples in
  Burgundy Wine) 14–1862
Pommes au Cognac (Apples Baked in Brandy
  and Vermouth) 14–1864
Pommes Gratinées (Apples with Meringue
  Topping) 14–1864
Pommes Normandes (Apple and Caramel
  Mould) 14–1866
Port and Raspberry Kissel 14–1903
Portuguese Custard 14–1908
Pots de Crème au Luxe (Small Custard
  Creams) 14–1934
Pouding d'Avocat (Avocado Ice-Cream)
  14–1936
Praline and Chocolate Ice-Cream Dessert
  15–1961
Profiteroles (info) 15–1976
Profiteroles with Ice-Cream and Chocolate
  15–1976
Prunes in Red Wine 15–1981
Queen's Almond Pudding 15–2008
Queen Anne's Custard 15–2008
Queijadas de Evora (Sweet Cheese Tartlets)
  15–2013
Quesillo de Piña (Pineapple Custard) 15–2018
Quick Peach Dessert 15–2028
Quince and Apple Turnovers 15–2030
Quince Compôte 15–2032
Rabarberkompott (Rhubarb Compôte)
  15–2037
Raspberry Fool 15–2063
Raspberries with Ice-Cream and Marashino
  15–2063
Raspberry and Meringue Delight 15–2064
Ratafia Trifle 15–2067
Rauschenburg Tart 15–2068
Rava Kheer (Semolina and Milk Dessert)
  15–2068
Redcurrant and Raspberry Compôte 15–2081
Refrigerator Pineapple Cake 15–2092
Regal Flan 15–2092
Regina Cake 15–2094
Renny's Pudding 15–2097
Rhubarb Cream 16–2103
Rhubarb and Ginger Compôte 16–2104
Rhubarb Strudel 16–2107
Rice Ring Filled with Fruit 16–2115
Rich Rice Pudding 16–2116
Ricotta al Caffè (Ricotta Cheese with Coffee)
  16–2120
Ricotta Flan 16–2120
Risalamande (Danish Rice and Almond Dessert)
  16–2129
Riz a l'Impératrice (Empress Rice Pudding)
  16–2135
Riz Melba (Rice and Peach Dessert) 16–2136
Roulade aux Fraises (Strawberry Sponge Roll)
  16–2172
Rum Bananas 16–2178
Rum Chocolate Mousse 16–2178
Rum and Macaroon Cream 16–2178
Rum Trifle 16–2181
Russian Fruit Mould 16–2190
Rutland Gooseberry Cream 16–2194
Saffron Shortcake 16–2204
Salade de Figues (Fresh Fig Salad) 16–2211
Salade de Fruits à la Créole 16–2211
Sauterelle (Green Grasshopper Pie) 17–2259
Savarin (French Yeast Cake) 17–2260
Savarin aux Cerises (French Yeast Cake with
  Cherries) 17–2262
Savarin aux Macarons (French Yeast Cake with
  Macaroons) 17–2262
Sevian (Vermicelli Dessert) 17–2290

Sherbet (info) 17–2299
Sherbet 17–2299
Sherry Jelly [Gelatin] 17–2300
Shoofly Pie 17–2304
Shrikhand (Curd with Sugar and Saffron)
  17–2307
Sorbet (info) 17–2349
Sorbet Glacée aux Abricots (Apricot Water Ice)
  17–2349
Spanish Sorbet 17–2372
Spicy Apple Flan 18–2382
Sponge Flan with Cherry Filling 18–2395
Sponge Flan Filled with Pineapple and
  Chestnut Cream 18–2395
Strawberry Flan 18–2419
Strawberry Shortcake 18–2420
Strawberry Sundae 18–2421
Strawberry Torte 18–2422
Strawberry Ziggurat 18–2422
Strudel Fruit Rolls 18–2427
Suèdoise (Fruit Jelly [Gelatin] Mould) 18–2437
Summer Pudding 18–2442
Sundae (info) 18–2443
Syllabub 18–2459
Syllabub Trifle 18–2460
Tarte aux Figues (Fig Flan) 18–2482
Tarte à la Rhubarbe (Rhubarb Flan) 18–2482
Tea Sorbet 18–2491
Toffee Pudding 18–2508
Torrijas (Bread and Honey Dessert) 19–2523
Touraine Chestnut Pudding 19–2529
Treacle Tart I 19–2540
Treacle Tart II 19–2540
Trifle I 19–2543
Trifle II 19–2543
Trinidad Coconut Ice-Cream 19–2544
Tropical Fruit Salad 19–2549
Tyler's Custard Pie 19–2583
Ugli Cocktail 19–2587
Uncooked Fruit Soup 19–2591
Upside-Down Apple Tart 19–2594
Upside-Down Apricot Cake 19–2594
Upside-Down Coconut Cake 19–2596
Vacherin (info) 19–2600
Vacherin Chantilly (Meringue and Cream Cake
  with Strawberries) 19–2600
Vacherin au Citron (Lemon Meringue Cake)
  19–2600
Vacherin aux Noisettes (Hazelnut Meringue
  Cake) 19–2601
Vanilla Blancmange 19–2605
Vanilla Kholodetz 19–2606
Vanilla Mousse 19–2606
Vatkattu Marjapuuro (Whipped Berry Pudding)
  19–2611
Vatrushka Pie 19–2611
Veiled Country Lass 19–2660
Velvet Cream 20–2664
Velvet Raisin Flan 20–2664
Venus Pudding 20–2676
Verbena and Apricot Sherbert 20–2678
Verity Cream 20–2678
Vesuvian Surprise 20–2682
Vicarage Pudding 20–2684
Viennese Chestnut Cake 20–2688
Viennese Chocolate Dessert 20–2689
Viennese Fruit Custard 20–2692
Viking Apple Pudding 20–2693
Vine Leaves and Apricots 20–2698
Vodka Ice-Cream 20–2714
Water Ice (info) 20–2741
Watermelon and Banana Salad 20–2745
Watermelon Cocktail 20–2746
Watermelon Fruit Bowl 20–2746
Watermelon with Provençal Wine 20–2747
Watermelon Shells Filled with Fruit 20–2747
Watermelon Soup 20–2747
Wedding Salad 20–2752
Weingelee (German Wine Jelly [Gelatin] with
  Fruit) 20–2755
West Country Junket 20–2767
West Indian Avocados 20–2767
Wheat and Fruit Dessert 20–2775
Whipped Avocado Dessert 20–2778
Whisky and Chocolate Mousse 20–2779
Whisky and Coffee Soufflé 20–2780
White Grape and Ginger Syllabub 20–2786
White Peach Cream 20–2789
White Port Sorbet 20–2789
Wilhelmine Fruit Salad 20–2813

Wine and Fruit Jellies [Gelatins] **21**–2847
Winnipeg Dipper **21**–2848
Winter Compôte **21**–2849
Wissant Pears with Ginger **21**–2855
Wrighton Pie **21**–2873
Wunderbar Macaroon Cream **21**–2877
Wye Cream Pudding **21**–2883
Xanadu Orange Delight **21**–2895
Yazoo Cranberry Flan **21**–2914
Yelverton Blackberry Jelly [Gelatin] **21**–2916
Yi'allaq Meringue Dessert **21**–2923
Yogurt Crumb Cake **21**–2928
Yogurt and Orange Jelly [Gelatin] **21**–2929
Yolande's Choux Puff Pyramid **21**–2932
Yolk of Egg Italian-Style **21**–2932
Yonkers Pear Delight **21**–2933
York Castle Chocolate Tart **21**–2934
Young Man's Fancy **21**–2943
Ypres Coffee Cream **21**–2944
Ysolde Red Fruit Dessert **21**–2946
Yule Mincemeat and Apple Flan **21**–2958
Yuletide Pudding **21**–2958
Yungchow Fruit Surprise **21**–2962
Zabaglione (info) **21**–2966
Zabaglione (Italian Egg Yolk and Wine
    Dessert) **21**–2966
Zabaglione alla Creole (Italian Egg Yolk
    Dessert with Rum and Cream) **21**–2966
Zara Ice-Cream Dessert **21**–2981
Zebra Meringue Torte **21**–2984
Zelimander (Ice-Cream and Cake Dessert)
    21–2989
Zocca Bananas **22**–3006
Zoe's Delight **22**–3007
Zombie's Secret **22**–3012
Zoose Pears **22**–3014
Zopperelli Figs in Red Wine **22**–3016
Zora's Peach Dessert **22**–3016
Zoradora Dessert **22**–3016
Zorba's Tipsy Cake **22**–3016
Zouar Banana Ice-Cream **22**–3018
Zubrowka Fruit Cocktail **22**–3026
Zuccherini (Italian Chocolate Mousse in
    Chocolate Cups) **22**–3028
Zucchero e Formaggio alla Crema (Sugar and
    Cream Cheese Dessert) **22**–3028
Zuccotto I (Italian Pumpkin-Shaped Cream and
    Sponge Dessert) **22**–3038
Zuccotto II (Italian Pumpkin-Shaped Cream
    and Sponge Dessert) **22**–3038
Zuccutto Torrone (Italian Chocolate-
    Flavoured Dessert) **22**–3040
Zuera Tropical Sundae **22**–3041
Zuki Fruit Tartlets **22**–3046
Zulia Persimmon Flan **22**–3047
Zunita Gâteau **22**–3055
Zuppa (info) **22**–3058
Zuppa a Due Colori (Two-Coloured Sponge
    Pudding) **22**–3059
Zuppa Inglese I (English Trifle) **22**–3059
Zuppa Inglese II (English Trifle) **22**–3060
Zveno Tea Soufflé **22**–3068
Zwieback mit Rhabarber (Rusks with
    Rhubarb) **22**–3076

DIPS

Dip (info) **5**–568
Avocado Dip I **1**–94
Avocado Dip II **1**–94
Bagna Cauda (Anchovy and Garlic Dip) **1**–105
Creamy Cheese Dip **4**–488
Devilled Dip **5**–558
Dill Dip **5**–565
Garlic Dip **6**–798
Gorgonzola Dip **7**–854
Guacamole (Avocado Dip) **7**–889
Hungarian Cheese Dip **8**–988
Onion Dip **12**–1588
Piquant Dip **13**–1820
Red Caviar Dip **15**–2078
Vegetable Savoury **19**–2653
Vermont Maple Dip **20**–2680
Yogurt Dip **21**–2929

DRINKS—ALCOHOLIC

Absinthe (info) **1**–4
Advocaat (info) **1**–4
Ale (info) **1**–10
Alcohol (info) **1**–10
Ale Berry **1**–10
Ale Posset (info) **1**–11
Alicante Wines (info) **1**–12
Alsatian Wines (info) **1**–24
Anisette (info) **1**–36
Apéritif (info) **1**–36
Apple Brandy (info) **1**–42
Apricot Brandy (info) **1**–52
Aquavit (info) **1**–59
Archbishop **1**–60
Armagnac (info) **1**–61
Aromatic Bitters (info) **1**–62
Arrack (info) **1**–63
Asti Spumante (info) **1**–81
Atholl Brose (info) **1**–82
Australian Wines (info) **1**–89
Austrian Wines (info) **1**–91
Bacardi Rum (info) **1**–98
Badminton Cup **1**–105
Balkan Champagne Cup **1**–108
Banyuls (info) **1**–116
Barley Wine (info) **1**–125
Barsac (info) **1**–126
Beaujolais (info) **2**–141
Beaune (info) **2**–141
Beer (info) **2**–157
Benedictine (info) **2**–161
Beverage (info) **2**–168
Bishop (info) **2**–175
Bitters (info) **2**–178
Blackberry Bounce **2**–180
Blackcurrant Liqueur (info) **2**–182
Black Velvet (info) **2**–184
Blanc de Blancs (info) **2**–184
Bloody Mary **2**–186
Bordeaux Wines (info) **2**–209
Bourbon (info) **2**–224
Bourgueil (info) **2**–224
Brandy (info) **2**–234
Brandy Blazer **2**–235
Brandy Cocktail **2**–236
Brandy Punch **2**–236
Bristol Milk (info) **2**–263
Bronx **2**–269
Burgundy Wines (info) **2**–279
Café Brûlot **3**–292
Calvados (info) **3**–303
Canadian Whisky (info) **3**–303
Cassis (info) **3**–334
Chablis (info) **3**–350
Champagne (info) **3**–353
Chartreuse (info) **3**–360
Cherry Brandy (info) **3**–370
Chianti (info) **3**–375
Chilean Wines (info) **3**–401
Cider (info) **4**–422
Cider Cup **4**–423
Clos de Vougeot (info) **4**–426
Clover Club Cocktail **4**–427
Cobbler (info) **4**–427
Cocktails (info) **4**–428
Cognac (info) **4**–438
Cointreau (info) **4**–438
Collins **4**–439
Crème de Cacao (info) **4**–490
Crème de Menthe (info) **4**–492
Cypriot Wines (info) **4**–524
Daiquiri **4**–526
Decanting (info) **4**–550
Drambuie (info) **5**–576
Dry Martini **5**–579
Egg Flip II **5**–620
Egg Flip III **5**–621
Elixir (info) **5**–642
Entre Deux Mers (info) **5**–649
Est ! Est ! ! Est ! ! ! (info) **5**–661
Fendant (info) **5**–683
Feuillette (info) **5**–687
Fiasque (info) **5**–687
Fish House Punch **6**–709
Flips (info) **6**–726
Fortified Wines (info) **6**–736
Frascati (info) **6**–740
Gin (info) **6**–828
Glögg (Scandinavian Punch) **6**–840
Gluhwein **6**–840
Goldwasser (info) **7**–846
Grand Marnier (info) **7**–859
Graves (info) **7**–867
Greek Wines (info) **7**–869
Grenache (info) **7**–875
Grog (info) **7**–883
Gurkenbowle (Cucumber Punch) **7**–897
Halb und Halb (info) **7**–907
Haut-Brion (info) **7**–935
Heather Ale (info) **7**–942
Hermitage (info) **7**–948
Het Pint **7**–951
Highball (info) **7**–952
Hippocras (info) **7**–954
Hock (info) **7**–954
Honeymoon Cup **7**–968
Horse's Neck **7**–970
Hot Apple Drink **7**–972
Hot Buttered Rum **7**–973
Hot Toddy **7**–977
Hungarian Wines (info) **8**–992
Irish Whiskey (info) **8**–1033
Israeli Wines (info) **8**–1035
Italian Wines (info) **8**–1039
Jamaican Coffee **8**–1050
Jamaican Rum Punch **8**–1053
Jeroboam (info) **8**–1076
Jingle (info) **8**–1078
Julep (info) **8**–1087
Kahlua (info) **8**–1095
Kalte Ente (Champagne Punch) **8**–1100
Kir (info) **9**–1148
Kirsch (info) **9**–1148
Krupnik (Polish Honey Drink) **9**–1176
Kümmel (info) **9**–1179
Kumyss (info) **9**–1181
Kvass (info) **9**–1184
Lacrima Christi (info) **9**–1186
Lafite (info) **9**–1188
Lager (info) **9**–1188
Lamb's Wool (info) **9**–1205
Latour (info) **9**–1214
Liebfraumilch (info) **9**–1236
Liqueur (info) **9**–1243
Liqueur d'Abricot (Apricot Liqueur) **9**–1243
Liqueur de Cassis (Blackcurrant Liqueur)
    9–1245
Loire Wines (info) **10**–1264
Mâcon Wines (info) **10**–1283
Madeira (info) **10**–1284
Magnum (info) **10**–1287
Malmsey (info) **10**–1294
Manhattan Cocktail **10**–1303
Maple Cocktail **10**–1308
Maraschino (info) **10**–1311
Marc (info) **10**–1312
Marsala (info) **10**–1330
Mateus (info) **10**–1342
Mead (info) **10**–1347
Médoc Wines (info) **10**–1368
Mint Julep **11**–1402
Moselle Wines (info) **11**–1425
Mulled Wine **11**–1446
Negroni **11**–1490
Negus (info) **11**–1490
Noyau (info) **11**–1524
Nuits St. Georges (info) **11**–1527
Old Fashioned Cocktail **12**–1569
Orange Blossom Cocktail **12**–1601
Orange-Flavoured Liqueur **12**–1606
Orange Wine Cup **12**–1621
Orvieto Wines (info) **12**–1628
Ouzo (info) **12**–1632
Pastis (info) **13**–1693
Peach Brandy **13**–1711
Pernod (info) **13**–1752
Perry (info) **13**–1752
Pineapple Liqueur **13**–1807
Pineapple Shrub **13**–1808

Pink Lady **13**–1812
Planter's Punch **14**–1840
Pomerol (info) **14**–1861
Ponche de Crème (Milk Punch) **14**–1872
Port (info) **14**–1902
Port Flip **14**–1903
Porter (info) **14**–1905
Portuguese Wines (info) **14**–1910
Posset (info) **14**–1910
Pouilly Fuissé (info) **14**–1939
Pouilly Fumé (info) **14**–1939
Pousse Café (info) **14**–1954
Presbyterian **15**–1971
Proof (info) **15**–1976
Pulque (info) **15**–1985
Punch (info) **15**–1988
Punch I **15**–1988
Punch II **15**–1988
Punch III **15**–1989
Punch IV **15**–1989
Purl (info) **15**–1991
Quassia-Amara **15**–2002
Quince Water **15**–2033
Raspberry Liqueur **15**–2064
Ratafia (info) **15**–2067
Red Wine Cup **15**–2087
Retsina (info) **15**–2098
Rhine Wines (info) **15**–2099
Rhine Wine Cup **15**–2100
Rhône Wines (info) **15**–2100
Rice Wine (info) **16**–2115
Riesling (info) **16**–2121
Rum (info) **16**–2177
Rum Punch **16**–2181
Rumfustian (info) **16**–2184
Rusty Nail **16**–2192
Sack (info) **16**–2199
St. Emilion (info) **16**–2208
Sake (info) **16**–2208
Sangria **16**–2239
Sauternes (info) **17**–2260
Schnapps (info) **17**–2273
Scotch Mist **17**–2279
Scotch Whisky (info) **17**–2279
Screwdriver **17**–2280
Sherry (info) **17**–2300
Shrub (info) **17**–2318
Sidecar **17**–2318
Singapore Sling **17**–2322
Sloe Gin **17**–2325
Snowball **17**–2336
Spanish Wines (info) **17**–2372
Spirits (info) **18**–2391
Stout (info) **18**–2418
Strega (info) **18**–2424
Tavel (info) **18**–2488
Tea Punch **18**–2490
Tokay Wines (info) **18**–2509
Traminer (info) **20**–2534
United States Wines (info) **20**–2591
Valpolicella (info) **20**–2604
Verdicchio (info) **20**–2678
Vermouth (info) **20**–2681
Vermouth Punch **20**–2681
Vin Chaud (Warmed Wine Cup) **20**–2694
Vinbarsbrännvin (Blackcurrant Gin) **20**–2694
Vinho Verde (info) **20**–2701
Vodka (info) **20**–2711
Vodka Martini **20**–2714
Warmed Wine Cup **20**–2736
Warsaw Liqueur **20**–2736
Wassail Bowl **20**–2740
Watermelon Fizz **20**–2746
Whiskey Sour **20**–2778
Whisky (info) **20**–2778
Whisky Mac **20**–2780
White Lady **20**–2787
White Russian **20**–2790
Wienerspritz (Wine and Soda Cup) **20**–2806
Wine (info) **21**–2829
Wine—Home-made **21**–2840
Xmas Cheer I **21**–2897
Xmas Cheer II **21**–2898
Yugoslavian Wines (info) **21**–2956
Zombie Cocktail **22**–3012
Zubrowka Cocktail **22**–3026

DRINKS—NON-ALCOHOLIC

Barley Water (info) **1**–125
Beverage (info) **2**–168
Cocoa (info) **4**–429
Coffee (info) **4**–436
Cola (info) **4**–438
Cordial (info) **4**–450
Egg Flip I **5**–620
Ginger Ale **6**–829
Ginger Beer **6**–830
Grapefruit Barley Water **7**–862
Grenadine (info) **7**–875
Hawaiian Fruit Cocktail **7**–937
Hot Apple Drink **7**–972
Hydromel (info) **8**–999
Iced Coffee I **8**–1008
Iced Coffee II **8**–1008
Iced Herb Tea **8**–1009
Iced Tea **8**–1010
Lemon Balm and Orange Drink **9**–1224
Lemonade **9**–1233
Lime Juice Cordial **9**–1238
Malted Milk **10**–1295
Maté (info) **10**–1342
Melonade **10**–1371
Mexican Fruit Drink **10**–1386
Milk (info) **10**–1391
Milkshake (info) **10**–1391
Chocolate Milkshake **10**–1391
Banana Milkshake **10**–1391
Raspberry or Strawberry Milkshake **10**–1391
Coffee Milkshake **10**–1391
Mineral Water (info) **10**–1400
Mint Ale **11**–1402
Mocha (info) **11**–1410
Nectar (info) **11**–1487
Oolong (info) **12**–1598
Orangeade **12**–1601
Orange Flip **12**–1606
Orange Pekoe (info) **12**–1614
Orgeat (info) **12**–1624
Prairie Oyster **14**–1960
Quince Sherbet **15**–2033
Quinine Water **15**–2034
Rose Hip Syrup **16**–2164
Soda Water **17**–2337
Strawberry Soda **18**–2421
Tea (info) **18**–2488
Tisane (info) **18**–2504
Tonic Water (info) **19**–2522
Vitalise Milk Shake **20**–2707
Water (info) **20**–2741

DUMPLINGS—SAVOURY

Dumpling (info) **5**–590
Bacon Dumplings **1**–102
Bramborové Knedliky (Potato Dumplings) **2**–233
Breadcrumb Dumplings **2**–251
Dumplings (Savoury) **5**–590
Feng Kuo (Dumplings Filled with Crabmeat) **5**–683
Gnocchi (info) **7**–841
Gnocchi al Forno Napoletana (Baked Dumplings with Tomato Sauce) **7**–841
Gnocchi di Patate (Potato Dumplings) **7**–842
Gnocchi alla Romana (Dumplings Roman-Style) **7**–842
Gnocchi Verdi (Spinach Dumplings) **7**–842
Griessklösschen (Semolina Dumplings) **7**–879
Hodgil (info) **7**–954
Knaidlach (Savoury Dumplings) **9**–1157
Kreplach (Jewish Stuffed Dumplings) **9**–1174
Malynka's Lamb Dumplings **10**–1296
Norfolk Dumplings **11**–1513
Quenelle (info) **15**–2014
Quenelles **15**–2014
Quenelles de Crustacés (Prawn or Shrimp Quenelles) **15**–2014
Quenelles de Foie Gras (Liver Pâté Quenelles) **15**–2015

Quenelles de Fromage (Cheese Quenelles) **15**–2016
Quenelles aux Huîtres (Oyster Quenelles) **15**–2016
Quenelles de Truite (Trout Quenelles) **15**–2017
Quenelles de Viande (Meat Quenelles) **15**–2017
Semmelknodel mit Pilzer (Dumplings with Mushroom Sauce) **17**–2286

DUMPLINGS—SWEET

Dumpling (info) **5**–590
Apple Dumplings **1**–45
Dumplings (Sweet) **5**–590
Karlstadtklösse (Steamed Sweet Dumplings) **8**–1107
Kynute Ovocné Knedliky (Czechoslovakian Fruit Dumplings) **9**–1185
Norfolk Dumplings **11**–1513
Trentina Dumplings **19**–2543
Turdillos (Sweet Date and Fig Dumplings) **19**–2564
Zwetschgenknödeln (Plum Dumplings) **22**–3072

EGGS

Eggs (info) **5**–607
Ajja (Spicy Scrambled Eggs with Sausage and Green Peppers) **1**–9
Albumin (info) **1**–10
Bacon and Egg Pie **1**–102
Chicory and Eggs **3**–401
Coddling (info) **3**–434
Convent Eggs **3**–444
Croustades aux Oeufs Brouillés (Scrambled Eggs in Pastry Shells) **4**–508
Croustades aux Oeufs Durs (Hard-Boiled Eggs in Pastry Shells) **4**–508
Curried Eggs **4**–521
Egg and Anchovy Mousse **5**–610
Eggs in Artichokes **5**–610
Egg and Bacon Bake **5**–610
Egg and Bacon Scramble **5**–611
Eggs Baked with Chicken and Tomatoes **5**–612
Eggs Baked with Chicken Livers and Mushrooms **5**–612
Eggs Baked with Creamed Mushrooms **5**–612
Eggs Baked with Haddock **5**–612
Eggs Baked with Onions **5**–613
Eggs in Baked Potatoes **5**–613
Egg Balls **5**–614
Eggs Bel Paese **5**–614
Eggs Benedict **5**–614
Egg Bread **5**–614
Eggburgers **5**–615
Egg and Cabbage Pirog **5**–615
Egg and Caper Dressing **5**–616
Eggs Caviar **5**–616
Egg and Cheese Rissoles **5**–616
Egg and Cheese Soup **5**–617
Egg and Corn Savoury **5**–617
Egg and Cream Cheese Tart **5**–618
Eggs Creole **5**–618
Egg Cutlets **5**–618
Egg-Drop Soup **5**–619
Eggs Essen **5**–619
Eggs Flamenco **5**–620
Egg Foo Yung **5**–621
Eggs with Herb Stuffing **5**–621
Eggs Indian-Style **5**–621
Eggs with Mixed Herbs **5**–621
Egg Noodles **5**–622
Egg Noodles Baked with Spinach **5**–622
Egg Noodles with Creamy Cheese Sauce **5**–623
Egg Noodles with Pork Sauce **5**–623
Eggs with Peas and Corn **5**–624
Egg and Potato Pie **5**–624
Egg Puffs **5**–624
Egg Ratatouille **5**–624
Egg Salad **5**–624
Egg and Sardine Hors D'Oeuvre **5**–625
Egg Sauce **5**–625

Egg, Sausage and Pepper Casserole **5**–625
Eggs with Savoury Creamed Lettuce **5**–626
Eggs in a Savoury Nest **5**–626
Eggs with Sherry **5**–626
Egg and Spinach Salad **5**–626
Eggs Stuffed with Ham and Herbs **5**–627
Eggs Stuffed with Tuna **5**–627
Eggs with Tarragon Mayonnaise **5**–628
Egg Tartlets **5**–628
Eggs with Tomatoes and Onion **5**–629
Egg and Vegetable Flan **5**–629
Egg and Yogurt Salad **5**–630
Ekuri (Scrambled Eggs with Chilli) **5**–638
Flaeskeaeggekage (Danish Bacon and Egg Cake) **6**–718
Floradora Eggs **6**–726
Garlic Stuffed Eggs **6**–801
Hamindas (Brown Baked Eggs) **7**–922
Huevos a la Flamenca (Eggs Baked with Sausages, Onions and Pepper) **7**–980
Hundred-Year-Old Eggs (info) **8**–985
Iced Zabaglione **8**–1010
Jellied Eggs **8**–1066
Käse Bouillon mit Ei (Cheese Soup with Egg) **8**–1110
Lapwing Eggs (info) **9**–1210
Liver Sausage and Egg Spread **9**–1251
Matzo Brei (Scrambled Eggs and Matzo) **10**–1344
Matzo Chicken and Dill Casserole **10**–1344
Mexican Stuffed Eggs **10**–1388
Nyrer Med Karbonadepølser og Røraeg (Kidneys with Sausage and Scrambled Eggs) **11**–1540
Oeufs Bourguignonne (Eggs Poached in Red Wine) **12**–1555
Oeufs Campagnards (Country-Style Eggs) **12**–1555
Oeuf Croquettes (Egg Croquettes) **12**–1556
Oeufs Espagnole (Spanish-Style Eggs) **12**–1556
Oeufs Florentine (Eggs with Spinach) **12**–1557
Oeufs à l'Hongroise (Eggs with Paprika Sauce) **12**–1557
Oeufs Mornay (Poached Eggs and Ham with Cheese Sauce) **12**–1557
Oeufs Robert (Eggs in White Wine Sauce) **12**–1558
Oeufs Soubise (Eggs with Onion Sauce) **12**–1558
Olive-Stuffed Eggs **12**–1573
Onion, Egg and Potato Pie **12**–1588
Oslo Eggs **12**–1628
Ovos Duros à Portuguesa (Eggs in Tomato Shells) **12**–1635
Pickled Eggs **13**–1779
Quail Egg Soup **15**–2001
Ranchers Eggs **15**–2061
Ricotta and Olive Scramble **16**–2121
Rosemary Eggs **16**–2166
Royale (Moulded Egg Custard) **16**–2176
Russian Eggs **16**–2188
Scotch Eggs **17**–2279
Shirred Eggs **17**–2303
Smoked Haddock Scramble **17**–2329
Smoked Salmon with Scrambled Egg **17**–2332
Uova alla Cacciatora (Hunter's Style Eggs) **19**–2593
Western Quick-Fried Eggs with Petits Pois and Shrimps **20**–2771
Weston Eggs **20**–2772
Wrotham Stuffed Eggs **21**–2873
Wywern Eggs **21**–2894
Yaitsa Kraschenie (Russian Coloured Eggs, info) **21**–2902
Yvonne's Egg Mousse **21**–2964
Zippy Savoury Scramble **22**–3000
Zuger Zee Scramble **22**–3043
Zvengli's Poached Eggs **22**–3068

Meringues

Meringues (info) **10**–1378
Baked Alaska **1**–105
Chamonix **3**–350

Delft Cake (Almond Meringue Layer Cake with Orange Buttercream Filling) **4**–554
Easter Cake I **5**–598
Faux Soufflé Meringué aux Ananas (Meringue and Pineapple Soufflé) **5**–679
Hazelnut Torte **7**–941
Huckleberry Meringue Pie **7**–979
Icicles **8**–1010
Igloo Pudding **8**–1014
Kisses (info) **9**–1151
Lemon Manqué **9**–1228
Lemon Meringue Pie **9**–1228
Meringue Cuite **10**–1378
Meringue Italienne **10**–1378
Meringue Suisse **10**–1378
Meringue Almond Layer Cake **10**–1378
Meringue Basket **10**–1379
Meringue Chantilly **10**–1379
Meringue Crown **10**–1380
Meringue Martinique **10**–1380
Meringue Pancakes **10**–1381
Meringue Walnut Cake **10**–1381
Midsummer Dream **10**–1390
Nut Meringues **11**–1535
Pavlova **13**–1709
Raspberry and Meringue Delight **15**–2064

Omelets

Castilian Omelet **3**–338
Dadar Djawa (Javanese Omelet) **4**–526
Eggah (info) **5**–630
Eggah with Courgettes [Zucchini] **5**–630
Eggah with Noodles and Chicken **5**–630
Eggah with Spinach **5**–632
Frittata di Carne e Vegetali (Vegetable and Meat Omelet) **6**–759
Frittata di Ricotta con Salsa Rossa (Ricotta Cheese Omelet with Tomato Sauce) **6**–759
Gruyère Omelet **7**–888
Hoppelpoppel (Egg Omelet with Bacon, Onion and Potato Slices) **7**–968
Jam Omelet **8**–1048
Liver and Mushroom Omelet **9**–1249
Malaysian Omelet **10**–1292
Omelette Americaine (Tomato Omelet) **12**–1574
Omelette Arnold Bennett (Omelet with Haddock, Cream and Cheese) **12**–1578
Omelette Bonne Femme (Onion, Mushroom and Bacon Omelet) **12**–1578
Omelette Aux Champignons (Mushroom Omelet) **12**–1578
Omelette Chasseur (Omelet with Mushrooms, Shallots and Wine) **12**–1579
Omelette Clamart (Green Pea Omelet) **12**–1579
Omelette aux Crevettes (Shrimp Omelet) **12**–1579
Omelette aux Fines Herbes (Herb Omelet) **12**–1580
Omelette Florentine (Spinach Omelet) **12**–1580
Omelette aux Fraises (Strawberry Omelet) **12**–1580
Omelette au Fromage (Cheese Omelet) **12**–1581
Omelette au Jambon (Ham Omelet) **12**–1581
Omelette à la Lorraine (Bacon, Cheese and Cream Omelet) **12**–1581
Omelette Lyonnaise (Onion Omelet) **12**–1582
Omelette Mousseline (Omelet with Cream) **12**–1582
Omelette Niçoise (Omelet with Anchovies, Olives, Tomatoes and Onion) **12**–1582
Omelette Normande (Apple Omelet) **12**–1583
Omelette Parmentier (Potato Omelet) **12**–1583
Omelette aux Poires (Pear Omelet) **12**–1583
Omelette Provençale (Tomato, Onion and Garlic Omelet) **12**–1584
Omelette au Rhum (Rum Omelet) **12**–1584
Omelette aux Rognons (Kidney Omelet) **12**–1585
Omelette Soufflé (Soufflé Omelet) **12**–1585
Persian Onion and Aubergine [Eggplant] Omelet **13**–1753
Pipérade (Pepper and Tomato Omelet) **13**–1815
Soufflé Omelet with Pastry Cream **17**–2357
Spanish Omelet **17**–2371

Tortilla (info) **19**–2525
Tortilla de Chorizo (Spanish Omelet with Sausage) **19**–2526
Walnut and Chicken Omelet **20**–2729
Western Omelet **20**–2770
Zingari Gipsy-Style Spaghettini Omelet **22**–2999

Soufflés—Savoury

Soufflé (info) **17**–2352
Alivenci (Cheese and Soured Cream Soufflé) **1**–12
Artichoke Heart Soufflé **1**–68
Aubergine [Eggplant] Soufflés **1**–86
Broccoli Soufflé **2**–266
Carrot Soufflé **3**–333
Cheese and Ham Soufflé **3**–365
Cheese Soufflé **3**–366
Chicken Soufflé **3**–392
Cod's Roe Soufflé **4**–435
Grouse Soufflé **7**–886
Gruyère Soufflettes **7**–889
Haddock Soufflé **7**–904
Jerusalem Artichoke Soufflé **8**–1075
Kusa (Squash Soufflé) **9**–1183
Oban Kipper Soufflé **12**–1546
Shrimp Soufflé with Wine **17**–2313
Soufflé de Champignons (Mushroom Soufflé) **17**–2353
Soufflé d'Epinards et Jambon (Spinach Soufflé with Ham) **17**–2354
Soufflé aux Panais (Parsnip Soufflé) **17**–2357
Soufflé de Saumon (Salmon Soufflé) **17**–2357
Spinach Soufflé **18**–2358
Wymering Soufflé with Monk Fish Sauce **21**–2887
Yarmacott Spinach and Apple Soufflé **21**–2911
Zenith Pear and Carrot Soufflé **21**–2991
Zucchini in Suffle (Courgette Soufflé) **22**–3037
Zujar Tomato Soufflés **22**–3045

Soufflés—Sweet

Soufflé (info) **17**–2352
Apple Soufflé **1**–50
Chocolate Soufflé **3**–413
Damson Soufflé **4**–528
Faux Soufflé Meringue aux Ananas (Meringue and Pineapple Soufflé) **5**–679
Fig Flutter **5**–689
Grenadine and Walnut Soufflé **7**–876
Iced Soufflés (info) **8**–1010
Mirabelle Soufflé **11**–1405
Omelette Soufflé (Soufflé Omelet) **12**–1585
Orange Soufflés **12**–1617
Pineapple Soufflé **13**–1808
Praline Soufflé **15**–1962
Prune and Walnut Soufflé **15**–1982
Soufflé aux Amandes (Almond Soufflé) **17**–2352
Soufflé au Café (Coffee Soufflé) **17**–2353
Soufflé au Grand Marnier (Orange Liqueur Soufflé) **17**–2354
Whisky and Coffee Soufflé **20**–2780
Zulinka Rum and Chocolate Soufflé **22**–3050
Zveno Tea Soufflé **22**–3068

FISH

Fish (info) **6**–701
Alewife (info) **1**–11

Anchovy

Anchovy (info) **1**–29
Anchovy Butter **1**–29
Anchovy Essence (info) **1**–29
Anchovy Rolls **1**–29
Anchoyade (Anchovy Hors d'Oeuvre) **1**–29
Anchoyade à la Niçoise (Anchovy Hors d'Oeuvre) **1**–30
Bagna Cauda (Anchovy and Garlic Dip) **1**–105
Solöga (Sun's Eye Hors d'Oeuvres) **17**–2346
Solomon Grundy **17**–2346

Thematic

Angler Fish (info) 1–34
Barbel (info) 1–122
Barracuda (info) 1–126
Barracouta (info) 1–126

Bass

Bass (info) 1–128
Bass Baked in Lemon and Mushroom Sauce 1–128
Braised Bass 2–228
Jewfish Mexican Style 8–1076
Loup de Mer (info) 10–1273
Sea Bass with White Butter Sauce 16–2280

Bêche-de-Mer (info) 2–142
Bluefish (info) 2–188
Bombay Duck (info) 2–206

Bream [Porgy]

Bream (info) 2–253
Besugo al Horno (Bream Baked with Potatoes) 2–164
Daurade aux Bananes (Bream [Porgy] with Bananas) 5–548
Daurade Farcie à l'Epinard (Bream [Porgy] Stuffed with Spinach) 5–548
Daurade au Fenouil (Bream [Porgy] with Fresh Fennel in White Sauce) 5–549
Daurade au Riz (Bream [Porgy] with Rice) 5–550
Daurade aux Tomates (Baked Bream [Porgy] with Tomatoes) 5–550

Brill

Brill (info) 2–256
Brill with Aubergine [Eggplant] 2–256
Brill with Courgette [Zucchini] 2–257
Brill à la Dugléré (Baked Brill with Tomatoes, Onions and White Wine) 2–258

Carp

Carp (info) 3–329
Carp in White Wine 3–326
Carpe Matelote (Carp with Red Wine Sauce) 3–326
Carp with Black Sauce 3–329
Karpion b'Paprika (Carp in Paprika Sauce) 8–1108
Karp po Zydowsku (Cold Carp Jewish-Style) 8–1109
Pai Chiu Tung Li Yu (Carp Steamed in White Wine) 12–1656
Polish Carp 14–1854
Sweet and Sour Carp 18–2456
Tolona Baked Carp 18–2509

Catfish (info) 3–338
Caviar *see* Roe
Char (info) 3–357

Cod

Cod (info) 4–432
Bacalhau (Salt Cod Casserole) 1–98
Barbecued Fish 1–119
Bergens Fiskesuppe (Norwegian Fish Soup) 2–162
Bouillabaisse de Cabillaud (Cod Soup) 2–222
Brandade de Morue (info) 2–233
Cabillaud à la Boulangère (Cod with Potatoes and Onions) 3–288
Cabillaud Gratiné (Cod in White Sauce) 3–288
Cabillaud Provençal (Cod with Green Peppers, Anchovies and Black Olives) 3–289
Cod Bake 4–433
Cod Balls 4–434
Cod's Roe Pâté 4–434
Cod's Roe Soufflé 4–435
Filets de Cabillaud Sauce aux Capres (Fillets of Cod with Caper Sauce) 5–693
Fish Balls with Almonds 6–705
Fish Balls with Fines Herbes Sauce 6–706

Fish Chowder 6–707
Fish Grilled [Broiled] with Cheese 6–709
Fish and Leek Flan 6–711
Fish and Mushroom Soup 6–712
Fish and Potato Pie 6–713
Fish and Potato Salad 6–713
Fiskebudding med Rejesovs (Fish Pudding with Prawn Sauce) 6–717
Javanese Fish in Soy Sauce 8–1062
Kogt Torsk med Asparges (Cod Baked with Asparagus) 9–1163
Kulebiak z Ryba (Russian Fish Pie) 9–1178
Ling (info) 9–1239
Merluzà a la Marinera (Cod Fillets in Tomato, Parsley and Almond Sauce) 10–1382
Mollina Soup 11–1414
Morue à l'Americaine (Salt Cod with Rice and Brandy and Wine Sauce) 11–1423
Nkontomire Fro (Stewed Spinach with Fish) 11–1502
Norwegian Fish Pudding 11–1519
Parsley and Fish Pie 12–1680
Roe in Scallop Shells 16–2151
Salt Fish Balls 16–2229
Salt Fish Stew 16–2231
Spiced Fish 17–2379
Taramasalata (Cod's Roe Paste) 18–2479
Tenali Baked Fish 18–2493
Umabai's Baked Spiced Fish 19–2587
Virgin Island Salt Cod Stew 20–2704
White Fish Curry 20–2785
Worikambo Salt Cod Hash 21–2867
Zanzibar Salt Cod Curry 21–2979
Zomba Salt Cod and Avocado 22–3011
Zubia Cod with Alioli Sauce 22–3025

Dab (info) 4–526
Devil Fish (info) 4–555

Eel

Eel (info) 5–605
Anguilla Marinate (Marinated Eel) 1–34
Anguilles au Vert (Eels in Green Sauce) 1–34
Caldo de Congrio (Conger Eel Soup) 3–297
Conger Eel (info) 4–441
Eels in Batter 5–605
Eels in Matelote Sauce 5–605
Eels Neapolitan Style 5–606
Eel Stew 5–607
Eels in Tomato Sauce 5–607
Jellied Eels 8–1066
Zuppa di Anguille (Eel Soup) 22–3058

Flounder *see* Plaice
Garfish (info) 6–796

General Fish Dishes

Aïgo-Sau (Mediterranean Fish Stew) 1–8
Bouillabaisse (Fish Soup Served with Pieces of Fish) 2–220
Bourride (Provençal Fish Soup with Garlic Mayonnaise) 2–225
Brodat Dubrovna (Dalmatian Fish Stew) 2–269
Cacciucco (Italian Seafood Stew) 3–290
Catalan Fish Soup 3–337
Croquettes de Poissons (Fish Croquettes) 4–504
Escabeche (Pickled Fish) 5–652
Fillets of Fish Mediterranean Style 5–698
Fish Aspic 6–704
Fish Baked Greek Style 6–704
Fish Baked in Sour Cream 6–704
Fish Cakes 6–707
Fish and Chips 6–707
Fish Croquettes in Hot Sauce 6–708
Fish Loaf 6–711
Fish Mayonnaise 6–711
Fish Mould 6–712
Fish and Prawn Mousse 6–713
Fish Salad 6–715
Fish Steaks in Sweet and Sour Sauce 6–715
Fish Stock 6–716
Fish with Wine and Mushrooms 6–716
Fondue Japonais 6–733

Fritto Misto di Mare (Deep-Fried Fish and Shellfish) 6–762
Gefillte Fish (Fish Balls) 6–811
Gratin aux Fruits de Mer (Seafood Pie) 7–865
Hungarian Fish Soup 8–990
Javanese Fish in Soy Sauce 8–1062
Jellied Fish Mould 8–1067
Kakavia (Greek Bouillabaisse) 8–1096
Kokonda (Spicy Fish Salad) 9–1164
Kulebiak z Ryba (Russian Fish Pie) 9–1178
Malaysian Fish 10–1290
Mediterranean Seafood Stew 10–1365
Montivideo Fish Casserole 11–1416
Nakompatoa Forowee (Salted Fish Fried with Vegetables) 11–1468
Ocean Rolls 12–1548
Russian Fish Bake 16–2188
Rybnaia Solianka (Fish Soup with Cucumbers and Tomatoes) 16–2195
Smoked Fish Salad 17–2328
Soupe de Poissons 17–2358
Tamatar Machli (Tomato Fish) 18–2474
Tempura (Deep-Fried Food Japanese-Style) 18–2491
Uvat Fish Soup 19–2598
Velouté aux Poïssons (Fish Cream Soup) 20–2662
White Fish Fondue 20–2785
White Fish Pie 20–2786
Whitstable Fish Soup 20–2799
Yom Tov Deep-Fried Gefilte Fish 21–2933
Zarzuela I (Spanish Fish Stew) 21–2984
Zarzuela II (Spanish Fish Stew) 21–2984
Zindo Vando (Meat and Fish Stew) 22–2997

Gudgeon (info) 7–892
Gurnet (info) 7–898

Haddock

Haddock (info) 7–900
Aberdeen or Arbroath Smokies (info) 1–3
Barbecued Fish 1–119
Bergens Fiskesuppe (Norwegian Fish Soup) 2–162
Cullen Skink 4–518
Eggs Baked with Haddock 5–612
Finnan Haddie 5–700
Fish Balls with Almonds 6–705
Fish Chowder 6–707
Fish Grilled [Broiled] with Cheese 6–709
Fish and Potato Pie 6–713
Haddock with Almonds and Lemon 7–900
Haddock with Cheesy Topping 7–900
Haddock with Cider 7–902
Haddock Morsels 7–902
Haddock with Mustard Sauce 7–902
Haddock with Parsley Sauce 7–902
Haddock with Poached Eggs 7–903
Haddock Soufflé 7–904
Haddock Soup 7–904
Individual Cheese and Fish Bakes 8–1021
Ivanhoe Croûtes 8–1039
Javanese Fish in Soy Sauce 8–1062
Kedgeree 9–1121
Kulebiak z Ryba (Russian Fish Pie) 9–1178
Mollina Soup 11–1414
Omelette Arnold Bennett (Omelet with Haddock, Cream and Cheese) 12–1578
Röding I Kapprock (Scandinavian Haddock Parcels) 16–2147
Serbian Fish 17–2288
Smoked Haddock Baked with Mushrooms 17–2328
Smoked Haddock Scramble 17–2329
Smokies in Cream 17–2334
Sommargryta (Summer Casserole) 17–2347
Tenali Baked Fish 18–2493
Winter Fish Crêpes 21–2851
Ysa Kedgeree 21–2944
Zetland Fish Balls 21–2994
Zrazi eze Ribi (Fish Baked in Cream) 22–3022
Zulla Fish Pie 22–3049

Hake

Hake (info) **7**–906
Hake and Cider Bake **7**–906
Hake with Ham and Egg Stuffing **7**–907
Salade Chaude Basquaise (Hot Mussel, Hake and Vegetable Salad) **16**–2210

Halibut

Halibut (info) **7**–907
Corvina à la Peruana (Fish Stew) **4**–457
Fish with Prawns in Wine and Tomato Sauce **6**–715
Gefüllter Heilbutt mit Krabben (Halibut Stuffed with Shrimps and Crabmeat) **6**–812
Halibut Baked with Cream **7**–907
Halibut with Bananas **7**–908
Halibut Steaks with Lemon and Chive Butter **7**–908
Halibut Steaks with Tomatoes and Cream **7**–908
Jellied Halibut **8**–1068
Long Island Halibut Steaks with Cucumber Sauce **10**–1270
Moussaka with Fish **11**–1431
Neptune's Delight **11**–1491
Norwegian Fish Pudding **11**–1519
Wrangell Stuffed Halibut **21**–2870
Wykehamist Halibut Steaks with Green Peppercorns **21**–2885

Herring

Herring (info) **7**–949
Bangra Masala (Spiced Herrings) **1**–115
Bismarck Herring (info) **2**–176
Bloater **2**–186
Buckling (info) **2**–278
Düsseldorf Salad **5**–592
Farshmak (Meat and Pickled Herring Patties) **5**–677
Grilled [Broiled] Fish in Japanese Wine Sauce **7**–881
Harengs à la Boulangère (Herrings Baked with Potatoes and Onions) **7**–927
Harengs à la Meunière (Herrings in Butter Sauce) **7**–927
Herring and Apple Bake **7**–949
Herrings with Mustard Sauce **7**–949
Herring Roes in Cream Sauce **7**–949
Herring Roes in Devilled Sauce **7**–950
Herrings in Rolled Oats **7**–950
Herring Salad **7**–950
Herrings Stuffed with Rice **7**–950
Jansson's Temptation **8**–1059
Kipper (info) **9**–1144
Kipper Cakes **9**–1144
Kipper Kedgeree **9**–1146
Kipper Pâté **9**–1146
Kipper Pie **9**–1147
Macaroni and Herring Salad **10**–1276
Oslo Salad **13**–1629
Potato and Herring Salad **14**–1927
Potted Herring **14**–1935
Rollmops **16**–2158
Rollmop Hors d'Oeuvre **16**–2158
Salmagundy **16**–2214
Salt Herring (info) **16**–2231
Sillgratin (Herring and Potato Casserole) **17**–2318
Sill I Kapprock (Scandinavian Herrings Baked in Foil) **17**–2319
Solomon Grundy **17**–2346
Soused Herring **17**–2362
Stargazey Pie **18**–2400
Wyoming Viking Salad **21**–2892
Yarmouth Bloater (info) **21**–2912
Yarmouth Bloater Paste **21**–2912
Yarmouth Bloater Soup **21**–2913
Zuidhorn Kipper Pie **22**–3043

John Dory

John Dory (info) **8**–1079

John Dory in Cider **8**–1079
John Dory in Marsala **8**–1079
John Dory with Onion and Cream Sauce **8**–1080
John Dory with Provençal Sauce **8**–1080
Kipper *see* Herring

Lamprey (info) **9**–1205

Mackerel

Mackerel (info) **10**–1282
Ceviche (Mackerel Fillets Marinated in Lemon Juice) **3**–350
Filets de Maquereaux aux Fines Herbes (Mackerel Fillets with Herbs) **5**–694
Filets de Maquereaux Gratinées aux Capres (Mackerel Fillets with Caper Sauce) **5**–694
Filets de Maquereaux Sauce Moutarde (Mackerel Fillets with Mustard Sauce) **5**–695
Fish Kebabs **6**–710
Ikan Goreng (Fried Fish in Lime Juice) **8**–1015
Mackerel with Lemon and Caper Sauce **10**–1282
Mackerel in Soy Sauce **10**–1282
Mackerel in White Wine Sauce **10**–1283
Monte's Mackerel **11**–1416
Nkontomire Fro (Stewed Spinach with Fish) **11**–1502
Onion and Mackerel Salad **12**–1592
Sgombro Ripieno (Baked Stuffed Mackerel) **17**–2290
Shrimp-Stuffed Fish **17**–2314
Sliced Raw Fish **17**–2324
Soused Mackerel **17**–2363
Tarte aux Filets de Maquereaux (Mackerel Fillet Flan) **18**–2483
Wrexham Mackerel with Orange and Mustard Sauce **21**–2872
Xareu Portuguese (Piquant Mackerel) **21**–2895
Zihuatanejo Fish Salad **21**–2996

Mâtelote (info) **10**–1342

Mero

Mero a la Naranja (Fish with Orange Sauce) **10**–1383

Minnow (info) **11**–1401

Monk Fish

Wymering Soufflé with Monk Fish Sauce **21**–2887

Mullet

Grey Mullet (info) **7**–878
Red Mullet (info) **15**–2082
Grey Mullet with Béchamel Sauce **7**–878
Grey Mullet Martigues **7**–878
Grey Mullet with Tomatoes and Capers **7**–878
Mullet Andalucian-Style **11**–1446
Mullet with Bacon and Peas **11**–1447
Mullet Baked in Rock Salt **11**–1447
Mullet with Fennel and Wine **11**–1447
Mullet Polynesian-Style **11**–1449
Poissons à la Niçoise (Small Red Mullet in Tomato Sauce) **14**–1851
Red Mullets Baked in Foil **15**–2082
Red Mullets Baked with Shrimps **15**–2082
Red Mullets Marinated in Oil and Herbs **15**–2082
Red Mullets with Riviera Sauce **15**–2085
Rougets aux Champignons (Red Mullets with Mushrooms) **16**–2171
Rougets aux Fines Herbes (Red Mullets with Mixed Herbs) **16**–2171
Tamarind Fish **18**–2472
Vine Leaf Wrapped Grey Mullet **20**–2698
Vinegar and Sesame Seed Fish **20**–2699

Octopus

Octopus (info) **12**–1551
Octopus with Alioli Sauce **12**–1552

Octopus with Anchovies **12**–1552
Octopus and Prawn Pilau **12**–1552
Octopus Stew **12**–1554
Octopus with Tomatoes and Garlic **12**–1554

Perch

Perch (info) **13**–1748
Perch with Oregano **13**–1748
Zander Schnitte mit Senfbutter (Pike or Perch Fillets with Mustard Butter) **21**–2977

Pike

Pike (info) **13**–1794
Gebratener Pike (Baked Pike) **6**–811
Pike with Anchovy Stuffing **13**–1794
Quenelles **15**–2014
Töltött Csuka (Pike Stuffed with Mushrooms and Tomatoes) **18**–2509
Uunissa Paistettu Hauki (Baked Pike Stuffed with Cucumber and Rice) **19**–2597
Waterzooi de Brochet (Belgian Fish Stew) **20**–2747
Zander im Ofen Gebacken mit Weisswein (Pike Baked in White Wine) **21**–2976
Zander Schnitte mit Senfbutter (Pike or Perch Fillets with Mustard Butter) **21**–2977

Plaice [Flounder]

Plaice (info) **14**–1834
Dansk Rødspätte i Flødesovs (Plaice [Flounder] Fillets in Creamy Asparagus Sauce) **4**–534
Kambala s Shpinatom (Flounder Fillets Baked with Spinach) **8**–1102
Katerfrühstück (Pickled Plaice or Flounder) **8**–1114
Plaice [Flounder] Anatole **14**–1834
Plaice [Flounder] with Artichoke Sauce **14**–1836
Plaice [Flounder] Baked with Garlic and Tomatoes **14**–1836
Plaice [Flounder] Baked with Mushrooms **14**–1837
Plaice [Flounder] Baked with Sour Cream and Peppers **14**–1838
Plaice [Flounder] Indonesian-Style **14**–1839

Pope (info) **14**–1873
Porgy *see* Bream

Red Snapper

Red Snapper (info) **15**–2086
Red Snapper with Almond and Walnut Sauce **15**–2086
Red Snapper with Oyster Stuffing **15**–2087
Yucatan Fish with Tomato Chilli Sauce **15**–2951
Zupanja Red Snapper Bake **22**–3055

Roach

Roach (info) **16**–2138
Roach Fried with Onions and Tomatoes **16**–2139

Roe

Roe (info) **16**–2150
Caviar (info) **3**–342
Herring Roes in Cream Sauce **3**–342
Herring Roes in Devilled Sauce **7**–950
Milt (info) **10**–1394
Red Caviar (info) **15**–2078
Red Caviar Dip **15**–2078
Red Caviar with Radish Dressing **15**–2078
Roe in Scallop Shells **16**–2151
Roes on Toast I **16**–2151
Roes on Toast II **16**–2151
Taramasalata (Cod's Roe Paste) **18**–2479

Rock Salmon

Rock Salmon (info) **16**–2146
Rock Salmon with Cayenne Sauce **16**–2146

Thematic

Salmon

Salmon (info) **16**–2216
Darne de Saumon à l'Ancienne (Baked Salmon Steak with Mushrooms) **4**–536
Darne de Saumon Montpelier (Grilled [Broiled] Salmon with Herb Butter) **4**–537
Fera (info) **5**–685
Fisherman's Lemons **6**–716
Gravad Lax (Pickled Salmon) **7**–867
Grilse (info) **7**–882
Jinja Stew **8**–1079
Kedgeree of Salmon **9**–1121
King Salmon (info) **9**–1143
Kulebiak z Ryba (Russian Fish Pie) **9**–1178
Mousse de Saumon (Moulded Salmon Mousse) **11**–1436
Newcastle Potted Salmon **11**–1501
Nova Scotia Salmon Cream **11**–1524
Pain de Saumon (Salmon Loaf) **12**–1660
Petits Pâtés à la Russe (Salmon and Mushroom Patties) **13**–1762
Salmon in Aspic **16**–2218
Salmon Balls **16**–2220
Salmon in Cream Sauce **16**–2221
Salmon with Dill Mayonnaise **16**–2221
Salmon with Hollandaise Sauce **16**–2222
Salmon Loaf I **16**–2222
Salmon Loaf II **16**–2223
Salmon Roll **16**–2225
Salmon Steaks Florentine **16**–2225
Salmon Steaks in Mushroom and Cream Sauce **16**–2225
Salmon Steaks with Sweetcorn and Mushrooms **16**–2225
Saumon à la Sauce Verte (Salmon with Green Mayonnaise) **17**–2254
Smoked Salmon Creams **17**–2332
Smoked Salmon Quiche **17**–2332
Smoked Salmon Rolls **17**–2332
Smoked Salmon Salad **17**–2332
Smoked Salmon with Scrambled Egg **17**–2332
Soufflé de Saumon (Salmon Soufflé) **17**–2357
Yachtsman's Delight **21**–2900
Yok Kai Chi Marinated Salmon **21**–2932
Zonza Champagne Soup **22**–3013

Salmon Trout

Salmon Trout (info) **16**–2226
Zuriga Salmon Trout with Mushroom Mayonnaise **22**–3065

Sardine

Sardine (info) **16**–2239
Canapés aux Sardines (Sardine Canapés) **3**–305
Egg and Sardine Hors d'Oeuvre **5**–625
Japanese Sardines **8**–1060
Pilchard (info) **13**–1798
Royan (info) **16**–2177
Sardine Cups **16**–2240
Sardines Grillées au Sauce Cresson (Grilled [Broiled] Sardines with Watercress Sauce) **16**–2240
Sardine Rarebit **17**–2241
Sardine Salad **17**–2241
Sardine Sandwiches **17**–2242
Zambian Cheese and Sardine Fritters **17**–2973
Zermatt Sardine Pâté **21**–2992
Zutian Sardine Flan **22**–3066

Shad (info) **17**–2293

Shark

Shark's Fin (info) **17**–2297
Trinidad Shark and Bakes **19**–2544
Yu-Chi-Tang (Shark's Fin Soup) **19**–2947
Shellfish *see* Shellfish

Skate

Skate (info) **17**–2322

Raie au Beurre Noir (Skate with Black Butter) **15**–2050
Raie en Fritot (Deep-Fried Skate) **15**–2050
Raie au Fromage (Skate in Cheese Sauce) **15**–2051
Skate with Egg and Lemon Sauce **17**–2322

Smelt

Smelt (info) **17**–2327
Fried Smelts with Lemon Butter **6**–757
Smelts with Mushrooms and Cheese **17**–2327

Sole

Sole (info) **17**–2340
Filetti di Sogliole Pizzaiola (Sole Fillets with Tomatoes and Garlic) **5**–692
Filets de Sole Cecilia (Fillets of Sole with Asparagus Tips) **5**–697
Filets de Sole à la Florentine (Sole Fillets with Spinach and Mornay Sauce) **5**–697
Hapsburg Sole **7**–922
Hwang Chi Yu Pien (Sliced Fish in Tomato Sauce) **8**–998
Ingelegte (Pickled Fish) **8**–1024
Kuo Tieh Yu Pien (Egg-Braised Sliced Fish) **9**–1182
Lemon Sole (info) **9**–1230
Lenguado Catalan (Catalan Sole) **9**–1233
Limanade Sole (info) **9**–1238
Liu Yu-Pien (Sliced Fish in Wine Sauce) **9**–1245
Mee Feng Yu Pien (Sliced Fish in Ground Rice) **10**–1368
Paupiettes de Sole à l'Indienne (Fillets of Sole Rolls in Curry Cream Sauce) **13**–1706
Peruvian Seviche (Pickled Fish) **13**–1756
Poissons aux Poivrons (Fish Stew with Peppers) **14**–1852
Sole Bonne Femme (Sole Fillets with Mushroom and Wine Sauce) **17**–2340
Sole Dugléré (Sole Fillets with Cream, Tomato and Parsley Sauce) **17**–2340
Sole English-Style **17**–2341
Sole Fillets Stuffed with Herbs **17**–2341
Sole en Goujons (Deep-Fried Sole Strips) **17**–2341
Sole Meunière (Sole Fillets with Butter Sauce) **17**–2342
Sole Mornay (Sole Fillets with Cheese Sauce) **17**–2342
Sole Normande (Sole Fillets with Mussels and Shrimps) **17**–2343
Sole with Red Wine **17**–2344
Sole Veronique (Sole Fillets with Grapes) **17**–2344
Sole in White Sauce **17**–2345
Tali Machee (Deep-Fried Spiced Fish) **18**–2470
Uchaud Fish Mousse with Sole **19**–2586
Wilhelmine Sole **20**–2815
Wurtemburg Sole with Walnuts **21**–2880

Sprat

Sprat (info) **18**–2396
Deep-Fried Sprats **4**–552

Squid

Squid (info) **18**–2400
Calamares en su Tinta (Squid in its Own Ink) **3**–296
Calamari Ripieni (Italian Stuffed Squid) **3**–296
Inkfish Stew in Red Wine **8**–1025
Kalamaria Yemista (Stuffed Squid) **8**–1096
Squid Salad **18**–2400
Squid Stuffed with Rice **18**–2400

Sterlet (info) **18**–2410

Sturgeon

Sturgeon (info) **18**–2433
Sturgeon Russian-Style **18**–2433

Swordfish

Espada Abouga (Swordfish Cooked with Almonds) **5**–659
Impanata di Pesce Spada (Breaded Swordfish Steaks with Piquant Tomato Sauce) **8**–1018

Tench (info) **18**–2493

Trout

Trout (info) **19**–2550
Kyenam (Ghanaian Baked Trout) **9**–1184
Quenelles de Truite (Trout Quenelles) **15**–2017
Shrimp-Stuffed Fish **17**–2314
Smoked Trout Pâté **17**–2333
Stegt Ørred med Flødesors (Danish Fried Trout in Sour Cream Sauce) **18**–2410
Trote al Pomidoro (Trout Baked in Tomato Sauce) **19**–2549
Trote Sulla Brace (Grilled [Broiled] Trout) **19**–2550
Trout and Bacon **19**–2550
Trout Baked in White Wine **19**–2550
Trout in Horseradish Sauce **19**–2551
Truites aux Amandes (Trout with Almonds) **19**–2554
Truites au Jambon (Trout with Ham) **19**–2555
Truites Meunière (Trout in Butter Sauce) **19**–2555
Truites au Vin Rouge (Trout Baked in Red Wine) **19**–2556
Wyllin Glen Trout **21**–2887

Tuna

Tuna (info) **19**–2559
Albacore (info) **1**–9
Bonito (info) **2**–209
Cucumber Stuffed with Tuna **4**–518
Eggs Stuffed with Tuna **5**–627
Fagioli con Tonno (White Bean and Tuna Salad) **5**–668
Fisherman's Lemons **6**–716
Jiffy Tuna Surprise **8**–1078
Mexican Stuffed Peppers **10**–1388
Namasu Maguro (Tuna and Vegetable Salad) **11**–1469
Peperoni Ripieni (Peppers Stuffed with Tomatoes, Tuna, Anchovies and Olives) **13**–1738
Pizza alle Asciughe (Pizza with Anchovies and Tuna) **14**–1828
Quiche au Thon (Tuna Fish Quiche) **15**–2024
Quick Tuna Fish Delight **15**–2029
Tuna Fish and Apple Salad **15**–2559
Tuna Fish Spread **15**–2559
Tuna Puffs **15**–2559
Tuna Steaks Provençale-Style **15**–2560
Tuna-Stuffed Tomatoes **15**–2560
West African Fish and Avocado Spread **20**–2766
Zirje Island Fish Kebabs **22**–3001

Turbot

Turbot (info) **19**–2563
Filets de Turbot Hermitage (Turbot Fillets Filled with Crabmeat) **5**–697
Nanban Zuke (Fried Fish with Vinegar Dressing) **11**–1470
Rodaballo de Fiesta (Turbot with Crabmeat Sauce) **16**–2147
Turbot à l'Orange (Turbot with Orange) **19**–2563
Turbot à la Piémontaise (Turbot with Vegetable Rice) **19**–2563
Turbot with Shrimp Sauce **19**–2564
Wladimir Turbot **21**–2857
Zara's Turbot with Clams **21**–2982

Whitebait

Whitebait (info) **20**–2790
Whitebait and Breadcrumb Fritters **20**–2791
Whitebait, Deep-Fried **20**–2791

Whiting

Whiting (*info*) **20**–2794
Filets de Merlan Dieppoise (Whiting Fillets with Prawns or Shrimps and Mussels) **5**–696
Merlans Farcis aux Crevettes (Whiting Stuffed with Shrimps or Prawns) **10**–1382
Tourte aux Champignons (Mushroom and Fish Pie) **19**–2533
Whiting in Apple Sauce **20**–2794
Whiting with Cheese and Breadcrumbs **20**–2794
Whiting Colbert **20**–2794
Whiting with Courgettes [Zucchini] **20**–2795
Whiting with Fennel **20**–2795
Whiting Italian-Style **20**–2795
Whiting Mould **20**–2797
Whiting in Mushroom Sauce **20**–2797
Whiting Provençal-Style **20**–2797
Whiting in Red Wine Sauce **20**–2798
Wildspitzer Fish Casserole **20**–2812

Wrasse

Wrasse (*info*) **21**–2871
Wrasse Baked in Seaweed **21**–2871

FONDUES

Fondue (*info*) **6**–732
Chocolate and Rum Fondue **3**–412
Fondue Bourguignonne **6**–732
Fondue Japonais **6**–733
Fondue Orientale **6**–734
Fondue Suisse **6**–734
Orange and Peach Fondue **2**–163
White Fish Fondue **20**–2785
Yosenabe (Japanese Chicken and Oyster Fondue) **21**–2942

FRITTERS

Fritters (*info*) **6**–760
Apple Fritters **1**–47
Aubergine Fritters I **1**–82
Aubergine Fritters II **1**–82
Banana Fritters **1**–113
Beignets d'Ananas (Pineapple Fritters) **2**–160
Beignets au Fromage (Cheese Fritters) **2**–160
Beignets Soufflés (Puffy Fritters) **2**–161
Celery Fritters **3**–346
Fritter Batter I **6**–760
Fritter Batter II **6**–760
Fritter Batter III **6**–760
Fritter-Coated Spinach Leaves **6**–760
Fritters Filled with Chicken Livers and Mushrooms **6**–761
Fritters with Honey Sauce **6**–761
Green Mealie Fritters **7**–872
Ham Fritters with Almonds **7**–916
Herb Fritters **7**–945
Hush Puppies **8**–995
Jhinga Pakoras (Prawn or Shrimp and Chick Pea Fritters) **8**–1076
Matzo Fry **10**–1345
Nut Fritters **11**–1535
Onion Rings, Deep Fried **12**–1594
Orange Flavoured Banana Fritters **12**–1606
Ox Palate Fritters **12**–1637
Oyster Fritters **12**–1650
Pakoras (Vegetable Fritters) **12**–1662
Pets de Nonnes (Sweet Fritters) **13**–1766
Potato Fritters **14**–1926
Prawn or Shrimp Fritters **15**–1969
Puffer (*info*) **15**–1984
Scandinavian Potato Fritters **17**–2273
Torrejas de Maiz Tierno (Fresh Corn Fritters) **19**–2522
Yam Fritters **21**–2907
Zambian Cheese and Sardine Fritters **21**–2973

FRUIT

Fruit (*info*) **6**–766

Apple

Apple (*info*) **1**–40
Adam and Eve Pudding **1**–4
Almond Apples **1**–20
American Apple Pie **1**–26
Apfelbettelmann (German Apple Pudding) **1**–38
Apfelkuchen (German Apple and Custard Tart) **1**–38
Apfelstrudel **1**–38
Äppel-Fläsk (Bacon Cooked with Apples and Onions) **1**–40
Äppelformar (Small Apple Pies) **1**–40
Apple Amber **1**–41
Apples, Baked **1**–42
Apple Bread Pudding **1**–42
Apples Bristol **1**–42
Apple Brown Betty **1**–43
Apple Butter **1**–43
Apple Charlotte **1**–44
Apple and Cucumber Salad **1**–45
Apple Dumplings **1**–45
Apple-Filled Pancakes **1**–45
Apple Florentine **1**–46
Apple Flambé **1**–47
Apple Fritters **1**–47
Apple Hat **1**–48
Apple Mousse à la Chantilly **1**–48
Apple Pie **1**–48
Apple and Pork Casserole **1**–48
Apple and Potato Stuffing **1**–49
Apple and Rice Pudding **1**–49
Apple Sauce **1**–50
Applesauce Cake **1**–50
Apple Snow **1**–50
Apple Sonning **1**–50
Apple Turnovers **1**–51
Aspic de Pommes (Apple Aspic) **1**–80
Chartreuse de Pommes (Apple Mould with Redcurrant Sauce) **3**–360
Clafoutis aux Pommes (French Apple Pudding) **4**–424
Coriander Fruit Crumble **4**–451
Date and Apple Pie **4**–538
Double-Crust Blackcurrant and Apple Pie **5**–573
Elderberry and Apple Jelly **5**–640
Fransk Aeblekage (Apple and Almond Pudding) **6**–740
Gouère aux Pommes (Apple Batter Pudding) **7**–855
Green Grape and Apple Pie **7**–871
Herring and Apple Bake **7**–949
Himmel und Erde (Mashed Potatoes and Apple) **7**–952
Hungarian Apple Pie **8**–987
Hungarian Apple Salad **8**–988
Hungarian Apple Soup **8**–988
Huntingdon Fidgett Pie **8**–994
Kartoffelmos med Aebler (Mashed Potato with Apple Purée) **8**–1109
Marlborough Apple Pie **10**–1319
Mincemeat and Apple Crumble **10**–1396
Pandowdy **12**–1671
Pommes et Abricots à l'Ancienne (Apple and Apricot Dessert) **14**–1862
Pommes à la Bourguignonne (Apples in Burgundy Wine) **14**–1862
Pommes au Cognac (Apples Baked in Brandy and Vermouth) **14**–1864
Pommes Gratinées (Apples with Meringue Topping) **14**–1864
Pommes Grimaldi (Apple and Rice Flan) **14**–1864
Pommes Normandes (Apple and Caramel Mould) **14**–1866
Prune and Apple Meringue Flan **15**–1981
Reading Apples **15**–2074
Recruitment Apple Pastries **15**–2074
Scandinavian Almond Apples **17**–2272
Spicy Apple Flan **18**–2382
Tansy Apple Cream **18**–2477
Tapioca with Apples **18**–2477
Toffee Apples **18**–2505
Toffee Apples Chinese-Style **18**–2508
Tranches de Jambon à la Normande (Ham Slices with Apples) **19**–2534
Tungpo Honey Apples **19**–2560
Upside-Down Apple Tart **19**–2594
Vetekaka med Applen (Yeast Cake with Apples) **20**–2683
Viking Apple Pudding **20**–2693
Wyviss Porridge Apples **21**–2893
Yablonchni Apple Soup **21**–2900
Yarmacott Spinach and Apple Soufflé **21**–2911
Yule Mincemeat and Apple Flan **21**–2958
Zoar's Crispy Apple Bake **22**–3006
Zoe's Delight **22**–3007

Apricot

Apricot (*info*) **1**–51
Apricot Bourdaloue Tart **1**–52
Apricot Brandy (*info*) **1**–52
Apricots in Brandy **1**–52
Apricot Condé **1**–52
Apricot Glaze **1**–54
Apricots Granville **1**–54
Apricot Jam **1**–54
Apricot Jam with Almonds **1**–56
Apricot Pudding **1**–56
Apricot Salad **1**–56
Apricots with Gammon or Ham **1**–57
Apricot Tart **1**–57
Barquettes aux Abricots (Apricot Tarts) **1**–126
Bombe Marie-Claire (Moulded Vanilla Ice-Cream with Apricot Filling) **2**–208
Caramel Apricots **3**–320
Dried Apricot Bars **5**–577
French Apricot Pudding **6**–745
Galette aux Abricots (Apricot Cake) **6**–783
Hungarian Apricot Soup **8**–988
Kynute Ovocné Knedliky (Czechoslovakian Fruit Dumplings) **9**–1185
Liqueur d'Abricot (Apricot Liqueur) **9**–1243
Macaroon and Apricot Whip **10**–1279
Mousse aux Abricots (Apricot Mousse) **11**–1433
Mousse aux Abricots et aux Mûres (Apricot Mousse with Blackberries) **11**–1434
Pommes et Abricots à l'Ancienne (Apple and Apricot Dessert) **14**–1862
Prague Apricot Loaf **14**–1958
Sauerkraut mit Aprikose (Sauerkraut with Apricots) **17**–2252
Upside-Down Apricot Cake **19**–2594
Verbena and Apricot Sherbert **20**–2678
Vine Leaves and Apricots **20**–2698
Wunderbar Macaroon Cream **21**–2877
Ashberry (*info*) **1**–74
Azarole (*info*) **1**–95
Avocado *see* Vegetables

Banana

Banana (*info*) **1**–109
Bananas, Baked **1**–109
Bananas Baked with Custard **1**–110
Bananas Baked in Orange Juice **1**–110
Bananas Beauharnais (Bananas Baked in Rum and Cream) **1**–110
Bananas Caribbean **1**–110
Banana Cream Pie **1**–111
Bananas Creole **1**–112
Bananas, Fried **1**–113
Banana Fritters **1**–113
Bananas with Orange **1**–113
Banana Pudding **1**–113
Banana and Raspberry Cream **1**–114
Bananas in Sherry **1**–114
Banana Walnut Loaf **1**–114
Brazil Nut Banana Cake **2**–239
Date and Banana Dessert **4**–538
Hawaiian Cream Roll **7**–937
Honey and Banana Toasts **7**–961
Indonesian Baked Bananas **8**–1022

Thematic

Italian Bananas 8–1035
Kirsch with Bananas 9–1149
Orange-Flavoured Banana Fritters 12–1606
Passion Fruit and Banana Cream 13–1689
Patriotic Pudding 13–1703
Rolled Crêpes Stuffed with Bananas 16–2156
Rum Bananas 16–2178
Watermelon and Banana Salad 20–2745
Wry Banana Fluff 21–2874
Yarrow Banana Teabread 21–2913
Yogurt and Banana Raita 21–2926
Zocca Bananas 22–3006
Zoradora Dessert 22–3016
Zouar Banana Ice-Cream 22–3018

Barberry (info) 1–122
Bilberry (info) 1–172

Blackberry

Blackberry (info) 2–180
Blackberry and Apple Pie 2–180
Blackberry Bounce 2–180
Blackberry Fool 2–180
Bramble (info) 2–232
Bramble Jelly 2–232
Kaltschale (Austrian Iced Blackberry Soup) 8–1101
Mousse aux Abricots et aux Mûres (Apricot Mousse with Blackberries) 11–1434
October Cobbler 12–1550
Yelverton Blackberry Jelly [Gelatin] 21–2916

Blackcurrant

Blackcurrant (info) 2–182
Blackcurrant Jam 2–182
Blackcurrant Liqueur (info) 2–182
Double-Crust Blackcurrant and Apple Pie 5–573
Honeydew Melon with Blackcurrant Iced Mousse 7–967
Liqueur de Cassis (Blackcurrant Liqueur) 9–1245
Vinbarsbrännvin (Blackcurrant Gin) 20–2694
Zwieback mit Schwarzen Johannisbeeren (Rusks with Blackcurrants) 22–3076

Blueberry

Blueberry (info) 2–188
Blueberry Crumble 2–188
Blueberry Muffins 2–188
Pancakes with Blueberries 13–1669
Yeast Buckwheat Pancakes with Blueberries and Sour Cream 21–2916

Breadfruit (info) 2–251
Bullace (info) 2–278
Cape Gooseberry (info) 3–315
Carob (info) 3–326
Chayote (info) 3–361

Cherry

Cherry (info) 3–370
Bublanina (Sponge Cake with Cherries) 2–277
Cherry Compôte 3–370
Cherry Jam 3–370
Cherries Jubilee 3–371
Cherry Pie 3–371
Cherry Salad 3–372
Cherry Soup 3–372
Cherry Tapioca 3–372
Clafoutis aux Cerises (French Cherry Pudding) 4–424
Hungarian Cherry Soup 8–989
Italian Cherries 8–1036
Kirschen mit Eiskrem (Cherries with Ice-Cream) 9–1149
Kirschenstrudel (Austrian Cherry Strudel) 9–1149
Kirschkuchen (Cherry Flan) 9–1150
Kirschpfannkuchen (Cherry-Filled Crêpes) 9–1150

Melon and Cherry Coupe 10–1372
Morello Cherry (info) 11–1420
Morello Cherry Flan 11–1420
Morello Cherry Sauce 11–1420
Morello Cherries with Yogurt 11–1420
Savarin aux Cerises (French Yeast Cake with Cherries) 17–2262
Sponge Flan with Cherry Filling 18–2395
Zune Ricotta and Cherry Tartlets 22–3053

Chinese Gooseberry (info) 3–402
Citron (info) 4–424
Clementine (info) 4–426
Compôte (info) 4–441

Crab Apple

Crab Apple (info) 4–470
Crab Apple Jelly 4–470
Crab Apple Preserve 4–470

Cranberry

Cranberry (info) 4–475
Cranberry Conserve 4–476
Cranberry Mousse 4–476
Cranberry and Orange Relish 4–477
Cranberry Pie 4–477
Cranberry Sauce 4–477
Yazoo Cranberry Flan 21–2914
Crowberry (info) 4–511
Currant (info) 4–520
Currants (info) 4–520
Custard Apple (info) 4–523

Damson

Damson (info) 4–527
Damson Cheese [Butter] 4–527
Damson Jam 4–528
Damson Soufflé 4–528

Date

Date (info) 4–538
Date and Apple Pie 4–538
Date and Banana Dessert 4–538
Date Bars 4–538
Date Cake 4–539
Date Cakes 4–540
Date Fudge 4–540
Date Jewels 4–540
Date Loaf 4–540
Date Pudding 4–541
Date and Raisin Loaf 4–542
Date and Rice Pudding 4–542
Dates Stuffed with Marzipan 4–543
Date and Walnut Diamonds 4–543
Date and Walnut Loaf 4–544
Dattelkuchen (Date Cake) 4–544
Datteltorte 4–545
Jam, Date and Nut Turnovers 8–1047
Nut and Date Biscuits 12–1535
Oriental Fruit Salad 12–1625

Dried Fruit (info) 5–578

Elderberry

Elderberry (info) 5–640
Elderberry and Apple Jelly 5–640
Elderberry Pie 5–640

Fig

Fig (info) 5–688
Fig Carnival 5–688
Fig-Flavoured Ham 5–688
Fig Flutter 5–689
Fig and Hazelnut Biscuits [Cookies] 5–689
Fig and Nut Sweets [Candies] 5–689
Fig Preserve 5–690
Fig Pudding 5–690
Fig Tart 5–690
Figos Recheados (Stuffed Figs) 5–691

Figues au Cacao (Figs in Crème de Cacao) 5–691
Ham with Figs 7–915
Oriental Fruit Salad 12–1625
Salade de Figues (Fresh Fig Salad) 16–2211
Tarte aux Figues (Fig Flan) 18–2482
Yungchow Fruit Surprise 21–2962
Zopperelli Figs in Red Wine 22–3016

Fruit Kernel (info) 6–769
Fruit Sauce (info) 6–775

General Fruit Dishes

Compôte of Dried Fruits 4–441
Dried Fruits in Syrup 5–578
Fruit Ambrosia 6–766
Fruit Cream 6–768
Fruit Curry 6–768
Fruit Fool 6–768
Fruit Pudding 6–772
Fruit Salad 6–773
Fruit Salad with Kirsch 6–773
Fruit and Vegetable Salad 6–775
Grilled [Broiled] Fruit Salad Packets 7–882
Hawaiian Fruit Cocktail 7–937
Himmelsk Mundfeld (Fruit Salad with Madeira Sauce) 7–953
Honey and Fruit Muesli 7–963
Iced Fruit Soup 8–1009
Jelly Tart 8–1073
Kebabs with Fruit 8–1118
Kholdetz (Berry Soup) 9–1128
Kissel with White Wine 9–1151
Marak Perot Car (Cold Fruit Soup) 10–1311
Naranjas al Kirsch (Fruit Soaked in Kirsch) 11–1474
Noix de Veau aux Fruits (Topside of Veal with Fruit) 11–1510
Pouding aux Fruits Sechés (Dried Fruit Pudding) 14–1938
Suédoise (Fruit Jelly [Gelatin] Mould) 18–2437
Toast Sevilla 18–2504
Tongan Salad 18–2519
Tropical Fruit Salad 19–2549
Ugli Cocktail 19–2587
Uncooked Fruit Soup 19–2591
Waffles with Fruit 20–2724
Weingelee (German Wine Jelly [Gelatin] with Fruit) 20–2755
Western Fruit and Vegetable Stew 20–2770
Wheat and Fruit Dessert 20–2775
Wilhelmine Fruit Salad 20–2813
Wine and Fruit Jellies [Gelatins] 21–2847
Ysolde Red Fruit Dessert 21–2946
Zubrowka Fruit Cocktail 22–3026
Zuki Fruit Tartlets 22–3046
Zurich Fruit Crumble 22–3063

Gooseberry

Gooseberry (info) 7–850
Golden Gooseberry Bake 7–845
Gooseberry Charlotte 7–850
Gooseberry Chutney 7–850
Gooseberry Crumble 7–851
Gooseberry Curd 7–852
Gooseberry Jam 7–852
Gooseberry Kissel 7–852
Gooseberry Pie 7–852
Gooseberry Sauce 7–853
Gooseberry Steffon 7–853
Rutland Gooseberry Cream 16–2194
Swedish Gooseberry Pie 18–2447

Granadilla (info) 7–859

Grape

Grape (info) 7–860
Cucumber and Grape Salad 4–516
Grape and Grapefruit Salad 7–860
Grape Tartlets 7–860
Green Grape and Apple Pie 7–871
Grenache (info) 7–875
Jellied Grape and Cheese Salad 8–1067

Sole Véronique (Sole Fillets with Grapes) **17**–2344
White Grape and Ginger Syllabub **20**–2786

Grapefruit

Grapefruit (*info*) **7**–861
Grape and Grapefruit Salad **7**–860
Grapefruit and Avocado Salad **7**–861
Grapefruit Barley Water **7**–862
Grapefruit Jelly [Gelatin] **7**–862
Grapefruit Marmalade **7**–862
Grapefruit and Orange Salad **7**–862
Grilled [Broiled] Grapefruit **7**–882
Hot Spiced Grapefruit **7**–977
Ice-Cream Filled Grapefruit **8**–1005
Orange and Grapefruit Salad **12**–1612
Trebujena Grapefruit Cocktail **19**–2541

Greengage

Greengage (*info*) **7**–875
Greengage Flan **7**–875
Greengage Jam **7**–875

Guava

Guava (*info*) **7**–891
Guava Jelly **7**–891
Guava Pie **7**–892

Huckleberry (*info*) **7**–979

Japonica

Japonica (*info*) **8**–1060
Japonica Jelly **8**–1061

Jujube (*info*) **8**–1087
Juneberry (*info*) **8**–1089

Juniper Berry

Juniper Berry (*info*) **8**–1090
Juniper Berry Sauce **8**–1090
Junipered Pork Chops **8**–1090
Loin of Pork with Juniper Berries **10**–1262

Kernal (*info*) **9**–1125
Kissel (*info*) **9**–1151

Kumquat

Kumquat (*info*) **9**–1179
Kumquat and Pineapple Salad **9**–1179

Lemon

Lemon (*info*) **9**–1223
Herb and Lemon Sauce **7**–946
Insalata d'Arancia e Limone (Orange and Lemon Salad) **8**–1026
Jacqueline's Lemon Wonder Pudding **8**–1041
Lemon and Almond Flan **9**–1223
Lemon Balm (*info*) **9**–1224
Lemon Biscuits [Cookies] **9**–1225
Lemon Bread Pudding **9**–1225
Lemon Cake **9**–1226
Lemon Curd **9**–1226
Lemon and Lime Chiffon **9**–1226
Lemon Manqué **9**–1228
Lemon Marmalade **9**–1228
Lemon Meringue Pie **9**–1228
Lemon and Mustard Seed Chutney **9**–1229
Lemon Possett **9**–1230
Lemon Sauce **9**–1230
Lemon Soufflé—Cold **9**–1230
Lemon Soufflé—Hot **9**–1231
Lemon Sponge **9**–1231
Lemon Tapioca Pudding **9**–1231
Lemon and Walnut Buns **9**–1232
Lemon Whip **9**–1233
Lemonade **9**–1233
Paul's Lemon Pudding **9**–1704

Lime

Lime (*info*) **9**–1238
Ikan Goreng (Fried Fish in Lime Juice) **8**–1015
Indian Lime Pickle **8**–1020
Lemon and Lime Chiffon **9**–1226
Lime Cream Pie **9**–1238
Lime Juice Cordial **9**–1238
Lime Marmalade **9**–1238

Loganberry

Loganberry (*info*) **9**–1259
Loganberry Jam **9**–1259

Loquat (*info*) **10**–1270
Lychee (*info*) **10**–1275
Macédoine (*info*) **10**–1282
Macerate (*info*) **10**–1282

Mandarin Orange

Mandarin Orange (*info*) **10**–1298
Jamaican Pie **8**–1041
Jellied Sponge Cakes **8**–1069
Mandarin Orange Butter **10**–1298

Mango

Mango (*info*) **10**–1300
Hawaiian Cream Roll **7**–937
Mango Chicken **10**–1300
Mango Chutney I **10**–1301
Mango Chutney II **10**–1302

Mangosteen (*info*) **10**–1302
Medlar (*info*) **10**–1368

Melon

Melon (*info*) **10**–1370
Cantaloup (*info*) **3**–314
Cantaloup Surprise **3**–315
Gefüllte Melonen (Stuffed Melon) **6**–812
Grüne Melone Mousse (Green Melon Mousse) **7**–887
Honeydew Melon (*info*) **7**–967
Honeydew Melon with Blackcurrant Iced Mousse **7**–967
Honeydew Melon and Pear Salad **7**–967
Italian Melon Salad **8**–1038
Jellied Melon Salad **8**–1069
Melonade **10**–1371
Melon and Avocado Salad **10**–1371
Melon Balls in White Wine **10**–1372
Melon and Cherry Coupe **10**–1372
Melon and Cold Pork Salad **10**–1372
Melon Mélange **10**–1372
Melons Pâtissière aux Fraises (Melons with Crème Pâtissière and Strawberries) **10**–1373
Melon and Prawn or Shrimp Cocktail **10**–1373
Oriental Fruit Salad **12**–1625
Prosciutto with Melon **15**–1979
Smoked Fillet of Pork with Melon **17**–2328
Watermelon (*info*) **20**–2745
Watermelon and Banana Salad **20**–2745
Watermelon Cocktail **20**–2746
Watermelon Fizz **20**–2746
Watermelon Fruit Bowl **20**–2746
Watermelon with Provençal Wine **20**–2747
Watermelon Shells Filled with Fruit **20**–2747
Watermelon Soup **20**–2747

Mirabelle

Mirabelle (*info*) **11**–1404
Mirabelle Soufflé **11**–1405

Mostarda (*info*) **11**–1425

Mulberry

Mulberry (*info*) **11**–1444
Mulberry and Apple Pie **11**–1444
Mulberry Jelly **11**–1444

Naartje (*info*) **11**–1466

Nectarine

Nectarine (*info*) **11**–1487
Nectarine Chutney **11**–1488
Nectarine Cream Mould **11**–1488
Nectarine Pie **11**–1488
Nectarine Tartlets **11**–1489
New Zealand Kiwi Fruit (*info*) **11**–1501
Olive *see* Vegetables

Orange

Orange (*info*) **12**–1599
Ambrosia (Orange Dessert) **1**–25
Bavarois à l'Orange (Orange Bavarian Cream) **1**–135
Crêpes à l'Orange (Orange Crêpes) **4**–499
Crêpes Suzettes (Crêpes Flamed with Orange Liqueur) **4**–501
Devilled Oranges **4**–560
Glazed Orange Rind **6**–839
Grapefruit and Orange Salad **7**–862
Harriet's Orange Pudding **7**–932
Herb and Orange Stuffing **7**–946
Hollandaise Sauce with Orange **7**–956
Hot Orange Pudding **7**–974
Icebergs **8**–1000
Iced Carrot and Orange Soup **8**–1007
Iced Pineapple with Orange Syrup **8**–1010
Insalata d'Arancia e Limone (Orange and Lemon Salad) **8**–1026
Jaffa Biscuits [Cookies] **8**–1041
Kingly Orange Cake **9**–1144
Kopfsalat mit Apfelsinen (Lettuce and Orange Salad) **9**–1166
Lemon Balm and Orange Salad **9**–1224
Lightning Orange and Chocolate Cake **9**–1236
Loin of Pork with Oranges and Pineapple **10**–1263
Mousse à l'Orange et Chocolat (Orange and Chocolate Mousse) **11**–1436
Mousse à l'Orange Glacée (Frozen Orange Mousse) **11**–1436
Orangeade **12**–1601
Orange Blossom Cocktail **12**–1601
Orange Butter **12**–1601
Orange Cake **12**–1601
Orange Caramel Trifle **12**–1602
Orange and Carrot Salad **12**–1603
Orange and Celery Salad **12**–1603
Orange Chicken with Rosemary **12**–1603
Orange and Chocolate Biscuits [Cookies] **12**–1604
Orange and Chocolate Dessert **12**–1604
Oranges with Cinnamon **12**–1605
Orange Curd **12**–1605
Orange Custard **12**–1606
Orange-Flavoured Banana Fritters **12**–1606
Orange-Flavoured Liqueur **12**–1606
Orange Flip **12**–1606
Orange-Flower Water (*info*) **12**–1607
Orange Fondants **12**–1607
Orange Garnishes **12**–1608
Orange Glacées (Glazed Oranges) **12**–1612
Orange Glaze **12**–1612
Orange-Glazed Pork Chops **12**–1612
Orange and Grapefruit Salad **12**–1612
Orange and Honey Butter **12**–1612
Orange Marmalade Glaze **12**–1612
Orange and Mint Sauce **12**–1612
Orange and Peach Fondue **12**–1612
Orange Peel, Candied (*info*) **12**–1614
Orange Pickle **12**–1614
Orange and Pork Casserole **12**–1615
Orange Rice **12**–1615
Orange Salad **12**–1616
Orange Sauce **12**–1616

Thematic

Orange Shortbread Biscuits [Cookies] **12**–1616
Orange Soufflés **12**–1617
Orange Soufflé-Filled Crêpes **12**–1617
Orange and Sour Cream Sauce **12**–1618
Oranges Stuffed with Orange Cream **12**–1618
Oranges Stuffed with Prawns or Shrimps and
    Rice **12**–1618
Orange Surprise Pudding **12**–1620
Orange Walnut Cake **12**–1621
Orange Wine Cup **12**–1621
Orange Yeast Buns **12**–1622
Orange Zest (info) **12**–1623
Orangelo (info) **12**–1623
Orangenstangerln (Orange Cake Fingers)
    12–1623
Orlando Duck **12**–1627
Ortanique (info) **12**–1628
Polish Orange and Almond Flan **14**–1855
Seville Orange (info) **17**–2290
Toast Sevilla **18**–2504
Tomato and Orange Salad **18**–2516
Xanadu Orange Delight **21**–2895
Yogurt and Orange Jelly [Gelatin] **21**–2929

Papaya (info) **12**–1673

Passion Fruit

Passion Fruit (info) **13**–1689
Passion Fruit and Banana Cream **13**–1689

Peach

Peach (info) **13**–1711
Deep-Dish Peach Pie **4**–550
French Peach Tart **6**–749
Iced Peaches **8**–1010
Khoresh Holu (Chicken with Peach Sauce)
    9–1130
Knickerbocker Glory **9**–1157
Neige de Pêches au Champagne (Peach and
    Champagne Dessert) **11**–1490
Orange and Peach Fondue **12**–1613
Peach Brandy **13**–1711
Peaches in Brandy **13**–1712
Peach Cobbler **13**–1712
Peach Flan **13**–1713
Peach Jam **13**–1713
Peach Melba **13**–1714
Peach Pickle **13**–1714
Peach Puffs **13**–1714
Pêches Cardinal (Fresh Peaches with
    Raspberry Purée) **13**–1728
Pêches aux Macarons (Peaches with Macaroon
    Cream Filling) **13**–1728
Pêches au Massepain (Peaches with Marzipan)
    13–1728
Pêches Rafraîchies aux Mûres (Peach and
    Blackberry Dessert) **13**–1728
Quick Peach Dessert **15**–2028
Royal Peach Meringue **16**–2176
Vesuvian Surprise **20**–2682
White Peach (info) **20**–2788
White Peaches with Caramelized Sugar
    20–2789
White Peach Cream **20**–2789
Wye Cream Pudding **21**–2883
Yungchow Fruit Surprise **21**–2962
Zora's Peach Dessert **22**–3016

Pear

Pear (info) **13**–1718
Birnbrot (Pear Bread) **2**–172
Birnensuppe (Pear Soup) **2**–173
Compôte de Poires (Pears Poached in Vanilla
    Syrup) **4**–441
Custard and Pear Tart **4**–524
Ginger Pear Sauce **6**–834
Honey-Baked Pears **7**–961
Honeydew Melon and Pear Salad **7**–967
Omelette aux Poires (Pear Omelet) **12**–1583
Pears Baked with Cardamon **13**–1718
Pear and Chicory [French or Belgian Endive]
    Salad **13**–1718

Pear Chutney **13**–1719
Pear Condé **13**–1721
Pear Jam **13**–1721
Pears Paradiso **13**–1721
Pears Poached in Red Wine **13**–1722
Pear Salad **13**–1722
Pears Stuffed with Roquefort Cheese **13**–1722
Pear Tart Bourdaloue **13**–1722
Poires Belle Hélène (Pears with Ice-Cream and
    Chocolate Sauce) **14**–1850
Poires au Caramel (Pears with Caramel Sauce)
    14–1851
Prosciutto with Pear **15**–1979
Rebhühner mit Birnen (Partridges with Pears)
    15–2074
Shoemaker's Pot **17**–2303
Wissant Pears with Ginger **21**–2855
Yonkers Pear Delight **21**–2933
Zenith Pear and Carrot Soufflé **21**–2991
Zoose Pears **22**–3014

Persimmon

Persimmon (info) **13**–1753
Zulia Persimmon Flan **22**–3047

Pineapple

Pineapple (info) **13**–1799
Beignets d'Ananas (Pineapple Fritters) **2**–160
Faux Soufflé Meringué aux Ananas (Meringue
    and Pineapple Soufflé) **5**–679
Flan d'Ananas (Pineapple Flan) **6**–721
Fried Pineapple and Cucumber Chinese-Style
    6–756
Iced Pineapple with Orange Syrup **8**–1010
Kumquat and Pineapple Salad **9**–1179
Pilaff with Pineapple and Cashew Nuts **13**–1797
Pineapple Bavarian Cream **13**–1800
Pineapple Cake **13**–1800
Pineapple Cheesecake **13**–1802
Pineapple and Cheese Salad **13**–1802
Pineapple Cream **13**–1805
Pineapple Delight **13**–1805
Pineapple Flan **13**–1805
Pineapple Fruit Salad **13**–1805
Pineapple and Honey Sorbet **13**–1806
Pineapple Jam **13**–1806
Pineapple and Lettuce Salad **13**–1806
Pineapple Liqueur **13**–1807
Pineapple and Pork Casserole **13**–1808
Pineapple Sauce **13**–1808
Pineapple Shrub **13**–1808
Pineapple Soufflé **13**–1808
Pineapple and Turkey Salad **13**–1811
Pineapple Upside-Down Cake **13**–1811
Pineapple and Walnut Ice-Cream **13**–1811
Pomarez Pineapple **14**–1860
Sponge Flan Filled with Pineapple and
    Chestnut Cream **18**–2395
Wrighton Pie **21**–2873
Yingkow Stuffed Pineapple **21**–2925

Plantain

Plantain (info) **14**–1839
Plantain Chips **14**–1839
Plantain Coated with Sesame Seeds **14**–1840

Plum

Plum (info) **14**–1846
Clafoutis aux Prunes (French Plum Pudding)
    4–425
Kynute Ovoché Knedliky (Czechoslovakian
    Fruit Dumplings) **9**–1185
Mirabelle Soufflé **11**–1405
Plum and Apple Marmalade **14**–1846
Plum Cake **14**–1847
Plum and Cherry Soup **14**–1847
Plum Compôte **14**–1847
Plum Jam **14**–1847
Plum Sauce **14**–1848
Plum-Stuffed Crêpes **14**–1848
Prunelle (info) **15**–1982

Zwetschgenknödeln (Plum Dumplings)
    22–3072
Zwetschgenkuchen (Plum Flan) **22**–3072

Pomegranate (info) **14**–1861
Pomelo (info) **14**–1861
Prickly Pear (info) **15**–1975

Prune

Prune (info) **15**–1980
Iranian Prune Soup **8**–1030
Katheryn Cake **8**–1115
Onion and Prunes **12**–1594
Prune and Apple Meringue Flan **15**–1981
Prunes in Red Wine **15**–1981
Prune and Walnut Soufflé **15**–1982
Sage and Apple Stuffed Prunes **16**–2206
Salami Stuffed Prunes **16**–2213
Toucy Prune Tartlets **19**–2526
Zyrenia Noodle and Prune Bake **22**–3080

Quince

Quince (info) **15**–2029
Quince and Apple Sauce **15**–2030
Quince and Apple Turnovers **15**–2030
Quince Compôte **15**–2032
Quince Jelly **15**–2032
Quince with Lamb and Honey Stuffing **15**–2032
Quince with Partridges **15**–2032
Quince Sherbert **15**–2033
Quince Soup **15**–2033
Quince Sweets [Candies] **15**–2033
Quince Water **15**–2033

Raisin

Raisin (info) **15**–2054
Lokshen Pudding **10**–1266
Raisin Brown Bread **15**–2054
Raisin Cake **15**–2056
Raisin Rolls **15**–2057
Raisin Sauce **15**–2058
Velvet Raisin Flan **15**–2664

Raspberry

Raspberry (info) **15**–2063
Banana and Raspberry Cream **1**–114
Bombe Framboises (Moulded Ice-Cream with
    Raspberries) **1**–208
Broiche aux Fraises avec Moussade Framboises
    (Brioche with Strawberries and Raspberry
    Cream Filling) **2**–260
Charlotte aux Framboises (Raspberry Mould)
    3–358
Crêpes aux Fruits (Fruit Crêpes) **4**–498
Cumin and Raspberry Buns **4**–520
Ile Flottante (Floating Island) **8**–1016
Mousse aux Framboises (Raspberry Mousse)
    11–1435
Port and Raspberry Kissel **14**–1903
Raspberry Buns **15**–2063
Raspberry Fool **15**–2063
Raspberry with Ice-Cream and Maraschino
    15–2063
Raspberry Jam **15**–2064
Raspberry Liqueur **15**–2064
Raspberry and Meringue Delight **15**–2064
Raspberry Sauce **15**–2064
Summer Pudding **18**–2442
Vatkattu Marjapuur (Whipped Berry Pudding)
    19–2611
Viennese Raspberry Pudding **20**–2693

Redcurrant

Redcurrant (info) **15**–2078
Redcurrant Cheesecake **15**–2078
Redcurrant Flan **15**–2079
Redcurrants, Frosted **15**–2080
Redcurrant Glaze **15**–2080
Redcurrant Jelly **15**–2080
Redcurrant and Raspberry Compôte **15**–2081

Rhubarb

Rhubarb (info) **16**–2164
Junidessert (Norwegian Dessert) **8**–1090
Rabarberkompott (Rhubarb Compôte) **15**–2037
Rhubarb and Apple Crumble **16**–2101
Rhubarb Brown Betty **16**–2103
Rhubarb Cake **16**–2103
Rhubarb Cream **16**–2103
Rhubarb and Ginger Compôte **16**–2104
Rhubarb and Ginger Jam **16**–2105
Rhubarb and Ginger Roly-Poly **16**–2105
Rhubarb and Orange Pie **16**–2107
Rhubarb Pudding **16**–2107
Rhubarb Strudel **16**–2107
Tarte à la Rhubarbe (Rhubarb Flan) **18**–2484
Tarte à la Rhubarbe Soufflé (Rhubarb Cream Flan) **18**–2484
Zwieback mit Rhabarber (Rusks with Rhubarb) **22**–3076

Rose Hip (info) **16**–2164
Rowan Berry (info) **16**–2175
Satsuma (info) **17**–2242
Shaddock (info) **17**–2293

Sloe

Sloe (info) **17**–2324
Sloe Gin **17**–2345
Sloe Jelly **17**–2345

Strawberry

Strawberry (info) **18**–2419
Baba aux Fraises **1**–98
Broiche aux Fraises avec Moussade Framboises (Brioche with Strawberries and Raspberry Cream Filling) **2**–260
Charlotte aux Fraises (Almond Cream with Strawberries) **3**–359
Crème aux Fraises (Strawberry Cream) **4**–492
Crêpes aux Fruits (Fruit Crêpes) **4**–498
Flensjes (Dutch Crêpes) **6**–725
Fraises Romanoff (Strawberries in Orange-Flavoured Liqueur with Crème Chantilly) **6**–737
Hungarian Cream Cake **8**–989
Ice-Cream, Strawberry-Flavoured **8**–1005
Ile Flottante (Floating Island) **8**–1016
Jellied Cream and Strawberry Flan **8**–1065
Jordgubbsvisp (Scandinavian Strawberry Dessert) **8**–1082
Knickerbocker Glory **9**–1157
Omelette aux Fraises (Strawberry Omelet) **12**–1580
Strawberry Cheesecake **18**–2419
Strawberry Flan **18**–2419
Strawberry Jam **18**–2419
Strawberry Sauce **18**–2419
Strawberry Shortcake **18**–2420
Strawberry Soda **18**–2421
Strawberry Sundae **18**–2421
Strawberry Tartlets **18**–2421
Strawberry Torte **18**–2422
Strawberry Ziggurat **18**–2422
Zoradora Dessert **22**–3016

Sultanas (info) **18**–2440
Tangelo (info) **18**–2474

Tangerine

Tangerine (info) **18**–2474
Tangerine Stuffing **18**–2476

Tangleberry (info) **18**–2476
Ugli (info) **19**–2587
Youngberry (info) **21**–2943

GAME

Game (info) **6**–788
Capercaillie (info) **3**–316

General Game Dishes

Game Pâté **6**–790
Game Pie **6**–790
Game Soup **6**–791
Game Stew **6**–791
Game Stock **6**–792

Grouse

Grouse (info) **7**–884
Grouse with Brandy and Cream Sauce **7**–885
Grouse Casserole **7**–885
Grouse Soufflé **7**–886
Grouse Stew **7**–887
Moorfowl (info) **11**–1416

Guinea Fowl

Guinea Fowl (info) **7**–894
Guinea Fowls with Almond Sauce **7**–894
Guinea Fowl Casserole **7**–894
Guinea Fowls with Cream and Wine Sauce **7**–894
Pintades aux Cerises (Guinea Fowls with Cherry Sauce) **14**–1812
Pintades Farcies (Stuffed Guinea Fowls) **14**–1814

Hare

Hare (info) **7**–924
Filets de Lièvre Chasseur (Fillets of Hare in a Mushroom and Wine Sauce) **5**–694
Hare with Onions and Sour Cream **7**–924
Hare Pudding **7**–925
Hare Soup **7**–925
Hare in Sweet and Sour Sauce **7**–926
Hasenpfeffer (Hare Casseroled in Wine and Herb Sauce) **7**–932
Jänispaisti **8**–1058
Jugged Hare **8**–1086
Leveret (info) **9**–1235
Potted Hare **14**–1935
Toulouse Spiced Pâté **19**–2527
Yugoslavian Hunters' Hare Stew **19**–2954

Hazel-Hen (info) **7**–938
Moorhen (info) **11**–1418
Ortolan (info) **12**–1628

Partridge

Partridge (info) **13**–1684
Partridges Catalan-Style **13**–1684
Partridges with Orange and Vermouth Sauce **13**–1685
Partridge Pie **13**–1685
Partridge Pot Roast **13**–1686
Partridges Stuffed with Mushrooms **13**–1687
Partridge Terrine **13**–1687
Perdices Estofadas (Partridges with White Wine and Vegetables) **13**–1751
Perdrix aux Choux (Partridges Cooked with Cabbage) **13**–1751
Quince with Partridges **15**–2032
Rebhühner mit Birnen (Partridges with Pears) **15**–2074
Umbai's Curried Partridges **19**–2588

Pheasant

Pheasant (info) **13**–1768
Faisan en Chartreuse (Pheasant Moulded with Cabbage and Vegetables) **5**–670
Faisan Normand (Pheasant with Cream, Calvados and Apples) **5**–671
Faisan en Oranges (Pheasant with Oranges) **5**–671
Faisan au Riz Basquais (Pheasant with Rice and Red Pepper) **5**–672
Faisan Souvaroff (Roast Pheasant with Truffles and Pâté) **5**–672
Faisan au Vin Rouge (Pheasant in Red Wine) **5**–673

Fried Pheasant in Cream and Brandy Sauce **6**–756
Galantine de Faisan (Pheasant with Aspic Jelly) **6**–781
Pheasants in Almond Batter **13**–1768
Pheasant and Chestnut Casserole **13**–1768
Pheasant Pâté, Country-Style **13**–1770
Pheasants with Sauerkraut and Apples **13**–1771
Pheasant Soup **13**–1772

Pigeon

Pigeon (info) **13**–1783
Pigeon Casserole **13**–1784
Pigeons aux Cerises (Pigeons with Cherries) **13**–1784
Pigeons with Chestnuts **13**–1784
Pigeons with Green Peas **13**–1786
Pigeons à la Niçoise (Pigeons Cooked with Garlic, Anchovies and Wine) **13**–1787
Pigeons à la Normande (Pigeons Cooked with Apples and Cider) **13**–1787
Pigeons aux Olives (Pigeons with Olives) **13**–1788
Pigeons with Orange and Wine Sauce **13**–1789
Pigeon Pie I **13**–1791
Pigeon Pie II **13**–1791
Salmis de Pigeons (French Pigeon Stew) **16**–2215

Pintail (info) **13**–1815
Plover (info) **14**–1846

Ptarmigan

Ptarmigan (info) **15**–1982
Ptarmigans with Red Cabbage and Wine **15**–1982

Quail

Quail (info) **15**–1995
Cailles avec Raisins en Timbale (Quails with Grapes in a Pastry Case) **3**–292
Quails with Cherries **15**–1996
Quails in Curry Sauce **15**–1996
Quails with Juniper Berries **15**–1998
Quails with Orange Stuffing **15**–1999
Quails with Risotto **15**–2000
Quails with Vegetables **15**–2001
Quail Egg Soup **15**–2001

Rail (info) **15**–2051
Reindeer (info) **15**–2094
Rook (info) **16**–2162
Ruff (info) **16**–2177
Snipe (info) **17**–2336

Squab

Squab (info) **18**–2397
Grilled [Broiled] Squab with Butter Sauce **7**–882
Pichones en Mole (Squabs with Chocolate) **13**–1776
Squab Pie **18**–2398

Venison

Venison (info) **20**–2667
Hunter's Stew **8**–993
Norwegian Venison Steaks **11**–1520
Old English Venison Stew **12**–1569
Oregon Venison **12**–1624
Roast Saddle of Venison **16**–2142
Saddle of Venison with Pepper Sauce **16**–2202
Venison in Aspic with Maraschino Cherries **20**–2668
Venison Chops with Cream Sauce **20**–2669
Venison Chops with Sour Cream and Horseradish Sauce **20**–2670
Venison with Cumberland Sauce **20**–2671
Venison Goulasch **20**–2671
Venison Meat Loaf **20**–2671
Venison Pâté **20**–2674

Venison Pie 20–2674
Venison and Pork Patties 20–2674
Venison with Sherry Sauce 20–2675
Venison Stew with Chestnuts 20–2676
Wildbretkoteletten (Venison Cutlets with
    Cream and Pepper Sauce) 20–2808

Widgeon (*info*) 20–2804
Wild Boar (*info*) 20–2808

Wild Duck

Wild Duck (*info*) 20–2808
Wild Duck with Grapefruit Sauce 20–2808

Woodchuck (*info*) 21–2861

Woodcock

Woodcock (*info*) 21–2861
Woodcock Casserole 21–2861
Woodcock in Claret 21–2863

Wood Pigeon

Wood Pigeon (*info*) 21–2864
Wood Pigeons Irish-Style 21–2864
Wood Pigeons Russian-Style 21–2865
Yun Yook (Chinese Steamed Wood Pigeons)
    21–2961

GARNISHES

Garnish (*info*) 6–801
Croûtons 4–511
Crystallized Violets 4–514
Egg Balls 5–614
Financière 5–698
Fleuron 6–725
Forestière, à la 6–736
Glazed Orange Rind 6–839
Godard, à la 7–844
Godiveau 7–844
Imperiale, à la 8–1019
Jardinière, à la 8–1061
Jellied Mayonnaise 8–1068
Jewish Noodles 8–1076
Julienne 8–1088
Languedocienne, à la 9–1207
Lorraine, à la 10–1270
Lucullus, à la 10–1274
Mirabeau, à la 11–1404
Niçoise, à la 11–1501
Nivernaise, à la 11–1502
Onion and Prunes 12–1594
Orange Garnishes 12–1608
Princesse, à la 15–1975
Printanière, à la 15–1976
Royale (Moulded Egg Custard) 16–2176
Serundeng (Coconut and Peanut Garnish)
    17–2289
Tyrolienne, à la 19–2583

GENERAL INFORMATION

Acetic Acid 1–4
Acidity 1–4
Agar-agar 1–4
Albumen 1–10
Albumin 1–10
Almond Essence 1–10
Angostura 1–34
Armorcaine 1–62
Aroma 1–62
Aromatic 1–62
Arrowroot 1–65
Asafoetida 1–74
Baking Powder 1–107
Baking Soda 1–107
Barbecue 1–117
Batter 1–131
Bicarbonate of Soda 2–168
Bird's Nest 2–172

Bottling 2–214
Botulinum 2–218
Bouquet 2–224
Brandade de Morue 2–233
Breakfast 2–252
Brewer's Yeast 2–254
Brine 2–258
Brochettes 2–267
Caffeine 3–292
Calcium 3–297
Calories 3–302
Capillaire 3–316
Carafe 3–319
Carbohydrates 3–322
Carbon Dioxide 3–323
Carmine 3–325
Carotene 3–327
Carte, à la 3–333
Casein 3–333
Casserole 3–334
Cassolette 3–337
Chapon 3–357
Charcoal 3–357
Charlotte 3–357
Chine 3–402
Chining 3–402
Coaster 4–426
Cochineal 4–427
Cola 4–438
Corn Oil 4–453
Cornet 4–454
Cream of Tartar 4–485
Croquettes 4–503
Croûtes 4–508
Croûtons 4–511
Crumble 4–512
Crystallize 4–514
Curdling 4–520
Curds 4–520
Curing 4–520
Dandelion 4–528
Dolmas, Dolmades or Dolmadakia 5–572
Dough 5–574
Entrée 5–649
Epergne 5–651
Essence 5–660
Estouffade 5–662
Event 5–664
Ewe 5–664
Extract 5–666
Farina 5–676
Farl 5–676
Fats 5–678
Fecula 5–680
Fermentation 5–686
Flavouring 6–724
Food Additives 6–734
Freezing 6–741
Fricandeau 6–752
Frozen Food 6–765
Gallimaufry 6–787
Gallon 6–787
Gelatine 6–813
Gendarme 6–813
Gill 6–828
Glycerine 7–841
Gristle 7–883
Gum 7–896
Haunch 7–935
Hay Box Cookery 7–938
Hop 7–968
Hotch Potch 7–978
Ichthyophagy 8–1010
Imperial Measures 8–1019
Iron 8–1033
Isinglass 8–1034
Jelly Roll 8–1072
Joint 8–1080
Juice 8–1087
Kickshaw 9–1131
Kissing Crust 9–1151
Kosher Food 9–1168
Krupuk 9–1177
Lactic Acid 9–1186
Lactose 9–1186

Liaison 9–1236
Liquorice 9–1245
Luting Paste 10–1275
Macrobiotic Food 10–1283
Magnum 10–1287
Manioc 10–1304
Margarine 10–1312
Marmite or Petite Marmite 10–1322
Melitot 10–1370
Menu Planning 10–1376
Microwave Cookery 10–1390
Minerals 10–1398
Mould 11–1428
Noggin 11–1503
Nonpareille 11–1510
Nutrition 11–1539
Olive Oil 12–1572
Oven Temperature 12–1634
Palm Kernel Oil 12–1665
Palm Oil 12–1666
Pasteurization 13–1692
Pectin 13–1730
Phosphorus 13–1773
Planking 14–1839
Pope's Eye or Ear 14–1873
Pope's Nose 14–1873
Popovers 14–1873
Potting 14–1935
Preservation 15–1971
Preservatives 15–1971
Pressure Cookery 15–1972
Proof 15–1976
Proteins 15–1979
Puffball 15–1984
Quaich 15–1995
Quick Freezing 15–2027
Raising Agents 15–2059
Raspings 15–2065
Refrigerator 15–2090
Rennet 15–2097
Reveillon 15–2098
Rice Paper 16–2115
Rijsttafel 16–2123
Rissole 16–2133
Rose Water 16–2165
Safflower Oil 16–2202
Salting 16–2232
Saltpetre 16–2232
Sambal 16–2232
Sarsaparilla 17–2242
Savouries 17–2263
Smoking 17–2334
Smörgåsbord 17–2334
Smørrebrød 17–2336
Starch 18–2400
Sterilization 18–2410
Storage of Food 18–2415
Suet 18–2437
Sunflower Oil 18–2443
Taco 18–2464
Tahina 18–2466
Tamale 18–2471
Tartaric Acid 18–2482
Thanksgiving Dinner 18–2497
Timbale 18–2500
Tortilla 19–2525
Truffle 19–2552
Turnover 19–2580
Turtle 19–2580
Tutti Frutti 19–2582
Verjuice 20–2678
Violet 20–2703
Vitamins 20–2707
Waterless Cookery 20–2745
Wax Paper 20–2749
Whale 20–2774
Wrapping 21–2870
Yeast 21–2915
Yucca 21–2952
Zest 21–2992

HERBS AND SPICES

Allspice 1–14
Angelica 1–32
Anise 1–35
Asafoetida 1–74
Balm 1–108
Basil 1–126
Bay Leaves 1–136
Bergamot 2–161
Borage 2–209
Bouquet Garni 2–224
Camomile 3–303
Caraway Seed 3–322
Cardamom 3–324
Cassia 3–334
Catmint [Catnip] 3–338
Cayenne 3–342
Celery Seed 3–346
Chervil 3–373
Chilli 3–402
Chilli Powder 3–402
Chive 3–404
Cinnamon 4–423
Cloves 4–426
Coriander 4–450
Cumin 4–520
Dill 5–565
Epices Composées 5–651
Fennel 5–684
Fenugreek 5–685
Fines Herbes 5–698
Four Spices 6–736
Garam Masala 6–796
Garlic 6–798
Ginger 6–828
Herbs 7–944
Hyssop 8–999
Kentjur 9–1124
Lemon Balm 9–1224
Lemon Thyme 9–1232
Lovage 10–1273
Mace 10–1282
Marjoram 10–1318
Melitot 10–1370
Mint 11–1402
Mixed Spice 11–1409
Mustard 11–1462
Myrtle 11–1465
Nutmeg 11–1539
Oregano 12–1623
Paprika 12–1674
Parsley 12–1679
Pimento 13–1798
Poppy Seed 14–1873
Purslane 15–1992
Rosemary 16–2165
Saffron 16–2202
Sage 16–2206
Savory 17–2263
Sesame Seeds 17–2289
Sorrel 17–2350
Spice 17–2376
Tamarind 18–2472
Tansy 18–2477
Tarragon 18–2479
Thyme 18–2499
Turmeric 18–2577
Verbena 19–2678
Wormwood 20–2868

HONEY

Honey (info) 7–961
Cardamom Honey Dressing 3–325
Honey-Baked Pears 7–961
Honey Balls 7–961
Honey and Banana Toasts 7–961
Honey Cake 7–962
Honey and Cream Cheese Pie 7–962
Honey Dressing 7–963
Honey and Fruit Muesli 7–963
Honey Ginger Pudding 7–964
Honey Mousse 7–964

Honey and Nut Toffees 7–964
Honey Pecan Flan 7–964
Honey Pudding 7–964
Honey Spice Cake 7–965
Honey and Vinegar Dressing 7–965
Honey and Walnut Bars 7–965
Honey and Walnut Pudding 7–965
Honeyed Chicken 7–967
Honeyed Ham with Beansprouts 7–967
Honeymoon Cup 7–968
Hydromel (info) 8–999
Ingots 8–1024
Kutya (Honey and Rice Pudding) 9–1183
Lekach (Honey Cake) 9–1223
Orange and Honey Butter 12–1612
Phoenician Honey Cakes 13–1773

HORS D'OEUVRES

Hors d'Oeuvres (info) 7–970
Amuse-Geules au Fromage (Cheese Cocktail
    Snacks) 1–28
Anchovy Rolls 1–29
Anchoyade (Anchovy Hors d'Oeuvre) 1–29
Anchoyade à la Niçoise (Anchovy Hors
    d'Oeuvre) 1–30
Angels on Horseback 1–32
Antipasto (info) 1–36
Artichokes à la Grecque 1–70
Artichokes à la Provençale 1–70
Asparagus au Beurre 1–75
Aubergine Salad 1–85
Avocado with Jellied Consommé 1–94
Bacon and Liver Rolls 1–103
Beignets au Fromage (Cheese Fritters) 2–160
Bouchées (info) 2–218
Bouchées aux Fruits de Mer (Puff Pastry Cases
    Filled with Mussels and Prawns) 2–218
Bouchées au Jambon (Puff Pastry Cases Filled
    with Ham) 2–219
Bouchées Newburg (Puff Pastry Cases Filled
    with Lobster) 2–219
Bouchées Parmentier au Fromage (Potato
    Cheese Sticks) 2–219
Canapés (info) 3–303
Canapés du Crabe (Crab Canapes) 3–303
Canapés des Crevettes (Shrimp Canapes) 3–303
Canapés aux Ecrevisses (Lobster Canapes)
    3–303
Canapés au Epinards (Spinach and Cheese
    Canapes) 3–304
Canapés Piquants 3–304
Canapés aux Sardines (Sardine Canapes) 3–305
Cape ai Ferri (Grilled [Broiled] Scallops) 3–315
Céleris à la Grecque (Celery Greek-Style) 3–344
Celery with Red Caviar 3–346
Champignons Farcis (Stuffed Mushrooms)
    3–354
Cheese Logs 3–366
Cheese Straws 3–368
Cheese Toasties 3–368
Cheesy Snacks 3–368
Corn on the Cob 4–452
Crabmeat Appetizer 4–472
Crabmeat in White Chaudfroid Sauce 4–472
Crabmeat with Herbs 4–474
Crabmeat Mornay 4–474
Creamed Camembert 4–485
Creamed Mushrooms 4–486
Crudités avec Aioli (Raw Vegetables with Garlic
    Mayonnaise) 4–512
Deep-Fried Prawns 4–551
Devils on Horseback 4–552
Eggs Caviar 4–557
Eggs with Herb Stuffing 5–621
Egg and Sardine Hors d'Oeuvre 5–625
Eggs with Tarragon Mayonnaise 5–628
Eggplant Boston 5–635
Garlic Stuffed Eggs 6–801
Gratin de Crevettes (Creamed Shrimps or
    Prawns) 7–864
Gravad Lax (Pickled Salmon) 7–867
Grenouilles aux Persil (Frogs' Legs with Parsley
    Butter Sauce) 7–876

Grenouilles à la Provençale (Frogs' Legs with
    Tomatoes and Garlic) 7–877
Grilled [Broiled] Grapefruit 7–882
Gruyère Puffs 7–888
Ham Custard 7–915
Ham with Figs 7–915
Herb Bread Crisps 7–945
Hollandaise Salad 7–954
Honeydew Melon and Pear Salad 7–967
Hot Spiced Grapefruit 7–977
Hwang Chi Yu Pien (Sliced Fish in Tomato
    Sauce) 8–998
Ivanhoe Croûtes 8–1039
Jalousie au Fromage (Openwork Pastry Cheese
    Tart) 8–1043
Jambon aux Echalottes (Ham with Shallots)
    8–1054
Japanese Sardines 8–1060
Jellied Chicken Breasts 8–1065
Jellied Eggs 8–1066
Jellied Melon Salad 8–1069
Jhinga Tikka (Prawn or Shrimp Patties) 8–1077
Kidney and Bacon Snacks 9–1134
Laitues aux Crevettes (Lettuce Baked with
    Shrimps) 9–1188
Laitues au Gratin (Lettuce with Cheese Sauce)
    9–1189
Lenguado Catalan (Catalan Sole) 9–1233
Lettuce Heart and Fruit Salad 9–1235
Liver Hors d'Oeuvre 9–1247
Lobster Bouchées 9–1253
Lobster Newburg 9–1257
Mackerel in Soy Sauce 10–1282
Mahasha (Stuffed Onion Skins) 10–1287
Melon and Prawn or Shrimp Cocktail 10–1373
Mexican Stuffed Eggs 10–1388
Mexican Stuffed Peppers 10–1388
Mustard Mould with Prawns or Shrimps and
    Fruit 11–1463
Nazkhatun (Aubergine [Eggplant] Hors
    d'Oeuvre) 11–1482
Newcastle Potted Salmon 11–1501
Njursaute (Swedish Sautéed Kidneys) 11–1502
Nut and Cream Cheese Balls 11–1534
Oeufs Robert (Eggs in White Wine Sauce)
    12–1558
Olive-Stuffed Eggs 12–1573
Onion and Sweetcorn Hors d'Oeuvre 12–1598
Orange and Grapefruit Salad 12–1612
Orange Salad 12–1616
Oranges Stuffed with Prawns or Shrimps and
    Rice 12–1618
Ovos Duros à Portuguesa (Portuguese Eggs in
    Tomato Shells) 12 –1635
Oyster and Avocado Salad 12–1647
Oyster Cocktail 12–1650
Oyster Fritters 12–1650
Oysters Rockefeller 12–1652
Palm Heart Cocktail 12–1664
Pears Stuffed with Roquefort Cheese 13–1722
Petits Chaussons au Roquefort (Pastry
    Turnovers with Roquefort Cheese) 13–1758
Plön Strudel (German Liver Strudel) 14–1846
Prawns or Shrimps and Avocados 14–1963
Prawn or Shrimp and Avocado Cocktail
    15–1966
Prawn or Shrimp Cocktail 15–1966
Prawn or Shrimp Egg Foo Yung 15–1968
Prawn or Shrimp Fritters 15–1969
Putignano Ham 15–1992
Rainbow Hors d'Oeuvre 15–2052
Roe in Scallop Shells 16–2151
Rollmop Hors d'Oeuvre 16–2158
Roman Aubergine Hors d'Oeuvre 16–2160
Russian Eggs 16–2188
Sage and Apple Stuffed Prawns 16–2206
Salami Stuffed Prunes 16–2213
Sardine Cups 16–2240
Scotch Woodcock 17–2279
Selleriesalat mit Obst (Celery and Fruit Salad)
    17–2286
Shrimp and Avocado Surprise 17–2310
Shrimp and Cheese Mould 17–2310
Shrimps Coralie 17–2310
Shrimps with Curried Avocados 17–2311

Thematic

Shrimp, Egg and Cucumber Ring 17–2311
Shrimp Seviche 17–2313
Smoked Salmon Rolls 17–2332
Smoked Salmon with Scrambled Egg 17–2332
Smoked Trout Pâté 17–2333
Solöga (Sun's Eye Hors d'Oeuvre) 17–2346
Spinach Ring 18–2385
Spinach-Stuffed Crêpes 18–2389
Tiraka Tiganita (Deep-Fried Cheese Balls) 18–2503
Tomates Farcies aux Oeufs (Tomatoes Stuffed with Eggs) 18–2510
Tomates Farcies à la Provençale (Tomatoes Stuffed with Anchovies, Breadcrumbs and Garlic) 18–2510
Tomates Farcies aux Riz (Tomatoes Stuffed with Rice) 18–2511
Tomato Aspic 18–2512
Tomato and Mozzarella Salad 18–2515
Tomato and Orange Salad 18–2516
Tomato Salad 18–2516
Trebujena Grapefruit Cocktail 19–2541
Vermont Maple Dip 20–2680
Viennese Croquettes 20–2689
Vine Leaves and Mushrooms 20–2698
Volcanoes 20–2720
Volendam Canapés 20–2721
Watercress and Avocado Mayonnaise 20–2742
West Indian Avocadoes 20–2767
Weston Eggs 20–2772
Whipped Cheese Croûtes 20–2778
Windsor Hors d'Oeuvre 20–2824
Winter Prawns or Shrimps 21–2852
Worcester Beef Croûte 21–2886
Wrotham Stuffed Eggs 21–2873
Wykeham Mushrooms 21–2885
Wywern Eggs 21–2894
Y Mwd Leeks 21–2899
Yakutsk Choux Puffs 21–2904
Yarm Stuffed Artichokes 21–2910
Yok Kai Chi Marinated Salmon 21–2932
York Rolls 21–2934
Yssingeaux Marinated Artichoke Hearts 21–2946
Yvetot Clam Hors d'Oeuvre 21–2964
Yvonne's Egg Mousse 21–2964
Yzeron Alligator Pears 21–2964
Zakuski (info) 21–2972
Zeebrugge Crabmeat and Lettuce Mould 21–2986
Zenda Sausage Snacks 21–2990
Zippy Avocado Hors d'Oeuvre 22–2999
Zomba Salt Cod and Avocado 22–3011
Zonder Sweetcorn and Petits Pois Hors d'Oeuvre 20–3012
Zoose Pears 20–3014
Zorrell Cheese and Ham Rolls 20–3018
Zouzou's Crêpes 20–3020
Zucca Cheese Loaf 20–3026
Zula Avocado Hors d'Oeuvre 20–3046

ICING, FROSTING AND GLAZING

Icing (info) 8–1012
Apricot Glaze 1–54
Buttercream Icing 3–282
Caramel Icing 3–320
Chocolate Icing I 3–409
Chocolate Icing II 3–409
Crème Chantilly (Vanilla-flavoured Whipped Cream) 4–490
Crème Pâtissière (Pastry Cream) 4–492
Fondant (info) 6–731
Fondant 6–731
Frosting I or White Mountain Frosting 6–765
Frosting II or Seven Minute Frosting 6–765
Fudge Frosting 6–776
Glacé Icing 6–837
Glaze (info) 6–838
Icing Based on Sugar Syrup 8–1012
Icing [Confectioners'] Sugar 8–1013
Jam Glaze 8–1048

Marzipan (info) 10–1337
Marzipan I 10–1338
Marzipan II 10–1338
Mock Cream 11–1410
Orange Glaze 12–1612
Orange Marmalade Glaze 12–1612
Pastry Glazes (info) 13–1698
Piping (info) 13–1816
Plastic Icing 14–1842
Plastic Icing for Moulding 14–1842
Praline (info) 15–1961
Redcurrant Glaze 15–2080
Royal Icing 16–2175
Sour Cream Icing 18–2360
Transparent Icing 19–2537

JAMS, JELLIES AND PRESERVES

Angélique Confite (Candied Angelica) 1–32
Apple Butter 1–43
Apricot Jam 1–54
Apricot Jam with Almonds 1–56
Blackcurrant Jam 2–182
Bramble Jelly 2–232
Brandied Cherries 2–233
Cherry Jam 3–370
Chow-Chow (info) 3–419
Conserve (info) 4–441
Crab Apple Jelly 4–470
Crab Apple Preserve 4–470
Cranberry Conserve 4–476
Damson Cheese [Butter] 4–527
Damson Jam 4–528
Dundee Marmalade 5–591
Elderberry and Apple Jelly 5–640
Fig Preserve 5–690
Five Fruit Marmalade 6–718
Fruit Butter (info) 6–767
Fruit Cheese (info) 6–767
Ginger and Apple Jam 6–830
Gooseberry Curd 7–852
Gooseberry Jam 7–852
Grapefruit Marmalade 7–862
Greengage Jam 7–875
Guava Jelly 7–891
Jam (info) 8–1044
Japonica Jelly 8–1061
Jelly—Preserve (info) 8–1071
Lemon Curd 9–1226
Lemon Marmalade 9–1228
Lime Marmalade 9–1238
Loganberry Jam 9–1259
Marmalade 10–1319
Seville Orange Marmalade 10–1320
Dark Seville Marmalade 10–1320
Seville Jelly Marmalade 10–1320
Marrow [Summer Squash] and Ginger Jam 10–1328
Mincemeat I 10–1396
Mincemeat II 10–1396
Mostarda (info) 11–1425
Mulberry Jelly 11–1444
Orange Curd 12–1605
Orange Peel, Candied (info) 12–1614
Peaches in Brandy 13–1712
Peach Jam 13–1713
Pear Jam 13–1721
Pectin (info) 13–1730
Pineapple Jam 13–1806
Plum and Apple Marmalade 14–1846
Plum Jam 14–1847
Quince Jelly 15–2032
Raspberry Jam 15–2064
Redcurrant Jelly 15–2080
Rhubarb and Ginger Jam 16–2105
Rosemary Jelly 16–2167
Sloe Jelly 17–2325
Strawberry Jam 18–2419
Wine Jelly 21–2847

KEBABS

Kebabs (info) 8–1117
Agneau en Brochette (Lamb on Skewers) 1–5
Boti Kebabs (Grilled Lamb on Skewers) 2–212
Brochette (info) 2–267
Brochettes Amalfi (Kidney and Chicken Liver Brochettes) 2–267
Brochettes Italiennes (Liver and Sausage Brochettes) 2–267
Brochettes de Porc (Pork Brochettes) 2–267
Brochettes de Rognons et Foie de Mouton (Kidney and Lamb's Liver Brochettes) 2–268
Brochettes de Veau aux Champignons (Veal, Bacon and Mushroom Brochettes) 2–268
Cevapcici (Skewered Lamb and Beef Balls) 3–348
Fish Kebabs 6–710
Greek Lamb Kebabs 7–868
Kebabs American-Style 8–1118
Kebabs with Fruit 8–1118
Kebabs in Herb Marinade 8–1118
Kebabs Marinated in Yogurt 8–1118
Kebab Massalam (Minced [Ground] Beef or Lamb) 8–1120
Kebabs with Soy Sauce and Sherry 8–1120
Kebabs of Veal 8–1120
Kefta (Moroccan Minced [Ground] Lamb Kebabs) 9–1121
Moroccan Liver Kebabs 11–1422
Pakistani Chicken Tikka (Chicken Kebabs) 12–1661
Portuguese Kebabs 14–1908
Quagliette de Vitello (Veal Olives on Skewers) 15–1995
Quotban (Moroccan Kebabs) 15–2036
Raznjici (Yugoslavian Veal and Pork Kebabs) 15–2073
Scallop Kebabs 17–2264
Scampi Kebabs 17–2270
Seekh Kababs (Minced [Ground] Meat Kebabs) 17–2284
Shish Kebabs (info) 17–2303
Sosaties (South African Kebabs) 17–2350
Spiedini (Italian Kebabs) 18–2383
Tikkah Kababs (Spiced Lamb Kebabs) 18–2500
Venetian-Style Eel Kebabs 20–2667
Wecksnappspiess (Ham and Kidney Kebabs) 20–2749
Yogurtli Kebab (Lamb with Yogurt) 21–2931
Yoshida Scampi Skewers 21–2942
Zirje Island Fish Kebabs 22–3001

KITCHEN UTENSILS

Aluminium Foil 1–25
Apple Corer 1–44
Asbestos Mat 1–74
Bain-Marie 1–105
Balloon Whisk 1–108
Beater 2–141
Brander 2–233
Bulb Baster 2–278
Butter Curler 3–282
Butter Paddles 3–284
Cake Rack 3–295
Casserole 3–334
Cassolette 3–337
Chafing Dish 3–350
Chinois 3–404
Cloth Filter 4–426
Cocotte 4–430
Dariole 4–534
Deep-Frying Basket 4–552
Double Saucepan 5–574
Egg Timer 5–629
Fish Kettle 6–711
Flour Bin 6–729
Forcing Bag 6–736
Girdle 6–837
Grater 7–864
Gridiron 7–879
Hachoir 7–900

Kitchen Equipment and Utensils 9–1152
Mandolin 10–1300
Marmite 10–1322
Mortar 11–1423
Mould 11–1428
Nutcracker 11–1539
Pastry Bag 13–1694
Pastry Blender 13–1694
Pastry Cutter 13–1697
Ramekins 15–2061
Roasting Bags 16–2140
Rôtisserie 16–2168
Sieve 17–2318
Skewer 17–2323
Terrine 18–2497

MEAT

Meat (info) 10–1347
Aufschnitt (info) 1–87

Bacon

Bacon (info) 1–98
Äppel-Fläsk (Bacon Cooked with Apples and Onions 1–40
Bacon, Baked 1–102
Bacon, Boiled 1–102
Bacon Dumplings 1–102
Bacon and Egg Pie 1–102
Bacon and Liver Rolls 1–103
Bacon Whole-Wheat Scones 1–103
Bean and Bacon Soup 1–138
Egg and Bacon Bake 5–610
Egg and Bacon Scramble 5–611
Flaeskeaggekage (Danish Bacon and Egg Cake) 6–718
Gammon *see* Ham and Gammon
German Country Breakfast 6–818
Huntingdon Fidgett Pie 8–994
Kebabs, American-Style 8–1118
Kidney and Bacon Snacks 9–1134
Kidney and Bacon with Wine 9–1135
Liver with Bacon 9–1246
Mushroom Rolls 11–1456
Okra [Ladies' Fingers] with Bacon 12–1567
Olive Meat Loaf 12–1572
Olla Podriga (Meat and Vegetable Stew) 12–1574
Omelette Bonne Femme (Onion, Mushroom and Bacon Omelet) 12–1578
Omelette à la Lorraine (Bacon, Cheese and Cream Omelet) 12–1581
Pastourma (info) 13–1693
Petits Pots de Champignons (Mushrooms and Bacon Cooked in Small Pots) 13–1765
Quiche Lorraine (Cheese and Bacon Quiche) 15–2023
Zoytinyagli Pirasa (Leek and Bacon Rissoto) 22–3020

Beef

Beef (info) 2–142
Aiguillette de boeuf (info) 1–9
Albóndigas (Meatballs in Tomato Sauce) 1–9
Alouettes sans Têtes (Stuffed Beef Rolls) 1–24
Andalousian Beefsteaks 1–30
Austrian Boiled Beef 1–89
Barbecued Beef, Chinese-Style 1–117
Baron of Beef (info) 1–125
Beef and Bean Casserole 2–144
Beef Braised in Soy Sauce 2–144
Beef Brazil (Beef in Coffee and Wine Sauce) 2–146
Beef with Cabbage 2–146
Beef with Capers 2–146
Beef Casserole 2–147
Beef and Cheese Roll 2–147
Beef with Chick-Peas 2–148
Beef with Dumplings 2–148
Beef Loaf 2–149
Beef and Madeira Casserole 2–149
Beef Marjoram Ring 2–150

Beef with Olives 2–150
Beef Roll 2–150
Beef in Sour Cream Sauce 2–151
Beef with Spiced Lemon and Caper Sauce 2–152
Beefsteak and Kidney Pudding 2–152
Beef Stew I 2–153
Beef Stew II 2–154
Beef Stock 2–154
Beef Stroganov (Beef in Sour Cream Sauce) 2–154
Beef Tea 2–154
Beef and Tomato Pie 2–155
Beef Wellington (Fillet of Beef in Pastry) 2–156
Berliner Eintopf (Berlin Stew) 2–162
Bife à Portuguêsa (Portuguese Steak) 2–168
Biff à la Lindström (Swedish Hamburgers) 2–169
Biftek Haché au Vin Rouge (Minced [Ground] Beef in Red Wine Sauce) 2–169
Biftek Marchand de Vins (Sautéed Steak with Red Wine Sauce) 2–170
Biftek Sauté Bercy (Sautéed Steak with Shallot and Wine Sauce) 2–170
Biftek Sauté au Beurre (Steak Sautéed in Butter) 2–171
Bistecca alla Fiorentina (Grilled [Broiled] Marinated Steak) 2–177
Bistecca alla Pizzaiola (Pan-Grilled Steak with Tomatoes and Garlic) 2–177
Bitkis (Meat Patties in Tomato Sauce) 2–178
Bitokes (Hamburgers with Cream Sauce) 2–178
Bobotie (Spicy Minced [Ground] Beef Pie) 2–190
Boeuf Bouilli à la Diable (Devilled Boiled Beef) 2–191
Boeuf Bouilli Froid à la Parisienne (Cold Boiled Beef) 2–191
Boeuf Bourgeois (Beef with Chicken Liver Sauce) 2–193
Boeuf Bourguignonne (Beef Stewed in Red Wine with Bacon, Onions and Mushrooms) 2–193
Boeuf Braisé Prince Albert (Braised Fillet of Beef Stuffed with Pâté de Foie Gras and Truffles) 2–194
Boeuf à la Catalane (Beef Stew with Rice, Tomatoes and Herbs) 2–196
Boeuf Chinois (Beef with Chinese Mushrooms and Green Peppers) 2–197
Boeuf à la Cuiller (Chopped Braised Beef Served in a Beef Shell) 2–197
Boeuf Daniell (Beef with Corn and Tomatoes) 2–198
Boeuf en Daube (Beef Stew with Bacon, Mushrooms and Red Wine) 2–198
Boeuf en Daube Martigues (Beef Stew with Tomatoes) 2–200
Boeuf à la Mode (Braised Beef in Red Wine) 2–200
Boeuf à la Mode d'Arles (Beef Stew with Red Wine and Black Olives) 2–201
Boeuf à la Mode en Gelée (Cold Braised Beef in Red Wine in Aspic) 2–202
Boeuf Printanier (Beef with Vegetables) 2–202
Boeuf à la Russe (Beef Stuffed Cabbage Rolls) 2–203
Boeuf à la Vinaigrette (Cold Brisket of Beef with Oil and Vinegar Dressing) 2–203
Bogrács Gulyás (Hungarian Beef Goulash) 2–204
Boiled Beef and Dumplings 2–205
Bollito Misto (Italian Boiled Beef, Chicken and Sausage) 2–206
Bolognese Sauce (Italian Meat and Vegetable Pasta Sauce) 2–206
Bookmaker's Sandwich 2–209
Braciuolia di Manzo (Grilled [Broiled] Beef Rolls) 2–226
Braised Beef 2–229
Braised Ribs of Beef 2–230
Braised Round of Beef 2–230
Braised Steak 2–232
Brisket of Beef (info) 2–262
Brisket of Beef with Jelly 2–262
Bully Beef (info) 2–279

Burgers in Red Wine 2–279
Cannelloni di Manzo e Spinace (Italian Pasta Filled with a Savoury Meat and Spinach Mixture Baked in Tomato and Cream Sauces) 3–313
Carbonnade à la Flamande (Flemish Beef Stew with Beer) 3–323
Carbonnade de Boeuf à la Provençale (Casserole of Beef with Garlic) 3–324
Carpetbag Steak 3–330
Cevapcici (Skewered Lamb and Beef Balls) 3–348
Chateaubriand (info) 3–361
Chili con Carne 3–401
Ching-chiao-ch'ao niu-jou (Steak with Pepper) 3–402
Collops of Beef 4–440
Contrefilet (info) 4–443
Contrefilet Braisé Chipolata (Braised Contrefilet with Chipolata Sausages, Glazed Onions and Braised Chestnuts) 4–443
Contrefilet Rôti (Roast Upper Cut of Beef) 4–444
Corned Beef Hash 4–454
Cottage Pie 4–464
Croquettes de Pommes de Terre et Viande (Potato and Meat Croquettes) 4–505
Daube de Boeuf (French Beef Stew) 4–545
Daube de Boeuf à la Provençale (Beef Stew with Tomatoes, Mushrooms and Olives) 4–547
Dill Piroshki (Little Pies Filled with Beef, Onion and Dill) 5–565
Dolmadakia (Stuffed Vine Leaves) 5–570
Dos (Beef and Rice Stew) 5–573
Dry Beef Curry 5–579
Dutch Steak 5–594
Eggplant and Beef Balls 5–635
Egyptian Braised Steak 5–638
Empanadas (Meat-Filled Pasties) 5–644
Enchiladas (Mexican Stuffed Pancakes with Tomato Sauce) 5–645
Entrecôte (info) 5–646
Entrecôte aux Echalottes (Entrecôte Steak with Shallots) 5–647
Entrecôte à la Lyonnaise (Entrecôte Steaks in Wine and Demi-Glace Sauce) 5–648
Entrecôte Mirabeau (Entrecôte Steaks with Anchovies and Olives) 5–648
Entrecôte au Poivre (Entrecôte Steaks with Crushed Peppercorns) 5–649
Essig Flaish (Sweet and Sour Beef Stew) 5–660
Estonian Rissoles 5–662
Estouffade de Boeuf (Braised Beef) 5–662
Estouffade de Boeuf à l'Albigeoise (Braised Beef with Brandy and Wine) 5–663
Eszterhazy Steaks 5–664
Exmouth Stew 5–665
Farshmak (Meat and Pickled Herring Patties) 5–677
Faux-filet (info) 5–679
Feijoada (Brazilian Black Beans and Smoked Meats) 5–683
Fesenjen (Meatballs in Pomegranate and Walnut Sauce) 5–686
Filetgulasch mit Saurer Sahne (Entrecôte Steak with Sour Cream) 5–692
Flank (info) 6–723
Flank Steak Stew with Herbs 6–723
Fondue Bourguignonne 6–732
Fondue Orientale 6–734
Fyldt Kalvefars (Stuffed Beef Rolls) 6–778
Gaisburger Marsch (Beef Stew with Dumplings) 6–780
Gengi Tsukeyaki (Japanese Steak and Vegetables) 6–814
German Beef and Clove Casserole 6–817
Gevulde Pannekoek (Dutch Meat Pancake) 6–822
Ghost aur Aloo (Beef and Potato Curry) 6–823
Gingered Beef 6–836
Goulasch (info) 7–857
Goulasch I 7–857
Gratin de Pommes de Terre et Viande (Potato and Beef Patties with Tomato Sauce) 7–866
Groundnut Stew 7–883

Thematic

Gyuniku Teriyaki (Fillet Steaks with Soy Sauce and Sake) 7–898
Hamburgers 7–920
Hamburgers with Dill 7–920
Hamburgers with Mint 7–920
Hamburgers with Sherry 7–921
Hao Yiu Ngiu Jou Pien (Quick-Fried Sliced Beef with Oyster Sauce) 7–923
Hash with Aubergines [Eggplant] 7–933
Holstein Stew 7–957
Hot Pot 7–974
Hung Shao Ngiu Jou (Red-Cooked Beef with Star Anise) 8–986
Hungarian Beef 8–988
Hussar Meat Loaf 8–995
Hutspot (Hotpot of Beef, Carrots and Potatoes) 8–995
Indonesian Beef in Chinese Sauce 8–1022
Italian Meat Loaf 8–1037
Italian Meat and Vegetable Soup 8–1037
Ivory Coast Grill [Broil] 8–1040
Jal Farazi (Curried Meat and Potatoes) 8–1042
Jamaican Casserole 8–1050
Jarret de Boeuf en Daube (Beef and Pork Stew) 8–1061
Javanese Curry 8–1061
Javanese Steak 8–1062
Jojamba (Meat and Vegetable Stew) 8–1080
Jug Jug (Meat Mould) 8–1084
Kahklehtin (Hamburgers Cooked in Beef Stock) 8–1094
Kalops (Beef Stew) 8–1100
Kärdian Cabbage 8–1107
Kasha Cholent (Buckwheat Stew) 8–1112
Katushki and Prunes 8–1116
Kebab Massalam (Minced [Ground] Beef or Lamb Kebabs) 8–1120
Keftedes (Spiced Meatballs) 9–1122
Kerkenna Island Hotpot 9–1124
Kheema (Curried Minced [Ground] Meat) 9–1128
Khoresh Karafs (Iranian Beef Stew) 9–1130
Klops (Meat Loaf with Egg) 9–1154
Kofta-kabab Khatai (Meatballs in Yogurt Sauce) 9–1161
Kofta Kari (Meatball Curry) 9–1162
Korsakov Meat and Potato Pie 9–1168
Köttbullar (Swedish Meatballs) 9–1169
K'ou Tse Ngiu Lan (Leg of Beef in Fruit Sauce) 9–1170
Labskaus (Pickled Pork or Corned Beef Hash) 9–1186
Lihamurekepiiras (Meat Loaf in Pastry) 9–1237
London Broil with Béarnaise Sauce 10–1267
Madrid Stew 10–1286
Manzo Brasato alla Vino Blanco (Beef Braised in White Wine) 10–1305
Manzo Brasato alla Vino Rosso (Beef Braised in Red Wine) 10–1306
Marinated Pot Roast 10–1316
Marinated Salt Beef Salad 10–1316
Marinated Skirt or Flank Steak 10–1317
Marrow [Summer Squash] with Savoury Stuffing 10–1329
Matambre (Rolled and Stuffed Steak) 10–1341
Meat Loaf I 10–1352
Meat Loaf II 10–1354
Meat Loaf III 10–1354
Meat and Potato Hot Pot 10–1355
Meatballs American-Style 10–1355
Meatballs with Chutney Sauce 10–1356
Meatballs in Cream 10–1356
Meatballs with Hot Mexican Sauce 10–1356
Meatballs with Lemon Sauce 10–1357
Meatballs in Sherry Sauce 10–1359
Meatball Stew 10–1361
Meatballs Stuffed with Cream Cheese 10–1361
Meatballs in Tomato Sauce 10–1362
Mee Feng Ngiu Jou (Beef in Ground Rice) 10–1368
Mexiburgers 10–1384
Mexican Chilli con Carne 10–1385
Minced [Ground] Beef and Aubergine [Eggplant] Casserole 10–1394
Mince Casserole 10–1395

Miroton de Boeuf (Beef in Onion and Mushroom Sauce) 11–1406
Morcon (Beef Roll with Tomato Sauce) 11–1419
Mussel and Beef Pie 11–1460
Nargisi Koftas (Meatballs Stuffed with Hard-Boiled Eggs) 11–1476
Nautical Stew 11–1478
Neapolitan Beef Stew 11–1483
Neustadt Rouladen (Beef and Sauerkraut Rolls) 11–1494
New England Boiled Dinner 11–1496
New England Meat Loaf 11–1496
Ohio Meat Pie 12–1559
Oiseaux sans Têtes (Beef Rolls Stuffed with Bacon) 12–1565
Olla Podrida (Meat and Vegetable Stew) 12–1574
Oven Beef Casserole 12–1632
Oven Braised Beef with Burgundy 12–1633
Oviedo Beef Stew 12–1634
Oxrullader (Beef Rolls Stuffed with Anchovies) 12–1639
Oyster, Beef, Kidney and Mushroom Pie 12–1648
Oyster and Meat Sausages 12–1651
Pastel de Choclo (Meat and Corn Pie) 13–1692
Pastrami (info) 13–1693
Paupiette (info) 13–1704
Paupiettes de Boeuf à l'Hongroise (Beef Rolls, Hungarian-Style 13–1704
Penang Beef 13–1734
Penang Curry Puffs 13–1734
Pepper and Corned Beef Hash 13–1739
Petite Marmite (Beef Consommé with Chicken and Vegetables) 13–1758
Pikantsas Oxrullader (Beef Rolls in Piquant Sauce) 13–1793
Piquant Beef 13–1819
Piquant Meat Loaf 13–1820
Planters' Beef 14–1840
Poco Albondiga (Little Meatballs) 14–1849
Polish Meat Loaf 14–1854
Poloni (Steamed Meat Loaf) 14–1858
Port Wine Steaks 14–1904
Porterhouse Steak (info) 14–1905
Porterhouse Steak with Red Wine Sauce 14–1905
Porterhouse Steak with Roquefort Cheese 14–1906
Porterhouse Steak with Spices 14–1906
Porterhouse Steak with Watercress Butter 14–1906
Pot au Feu (info) 14–1910
Pot Roast with Brandy 14–1912
Pot Roast with Brewer's Gravy 14–1913
Pot Roast with Garlic and Wine 14–1914
Pot Roast with Peppers and Garlic 14–1914
Pot Roast with Vegetables 14–1914
Pytt i Panna (Swedish Hash) 15–1994
Quick Italian-Style Beef 15–2028
Ragoût de Boeuf aux Pois-Chiche (Beef Stew with Chick Peas) 15–2046
Red Flannel Hash 15–2081
Rendang (Curried Beef) 15–2096
Ribbons of Beef Quick-Fried with Triple Shreds 16–2108
Rice Noodles with Spicy Beef 16–2114
Rindfleisch mit Zitronensosse (Boiled Beef with Lemon Sauce) 16–2124
Roast Beef Hash 16–2142
Rollade (Rolled Braised Beef) 16–2155
Rouladen (Stuffed Beef Rolls) 16–2173
Roulades de Boeuf (Stuffed Beef Rolls) 16–2173
Roz Bi Dfeen (Rice with Meat and Chick-Peas) 16–2177
Rump Steaks with Beer and Peppers 16–2184
Rump Steaks with Coriander and Mushrooms 16–2185
Rump Steaks with Mustard and Brandy Sauce 16–2185
Salade de Boeuf Côte d'Azur (Beef, Potato and Tomato Salad) 16–2210
Salt Beef 16–2228
Salt Brisket of Beef 16–2229

Salt Pork and Beef Stew 16–2231
Sate II 17–2242
Sauerbraten I (Sweet and Sour Beef) 17–2249
Sea Pie 17–2281
Slottsstek (Royal Pot Roast) 17–2326
Spiced Beef 17–2379
Steaks with Barbecue Sauce 18–2404
Steaks with Chestnut Sauce 18–2404
Steaks Diane 18–2405
Steaks with Green Peppercorns 18–2405
Steak and Kidney Pie 18–2404
Steaks with Mixed Herbs 18–2405
Steaks with Mushrooms 18–2405
Steaks in Pastry Cases 18–2406
Steaks Raglan 18–2407
Steak Sandwiches 18–2407
Steaks Stuffed with Chicken Livers 18–2408
Steak Tartare I 18–2409
Steak Tartare II 18–2409
Stir-Fried Beef with Broccoli 18–2412
Strudel with Beef Filling 18–2426
Stufatino alla Romana (Beef Stew) 18–2427
Stufato al Vino Rosso (Beef in Red Wine) 18–2429
Sukiyaki (Quick-Braised Beef and Vegetables) 18–2440
Sussex Hot Pot 18–2446
Swedish Beef Cakes 18–2446
Swedish Meat Loaf 18–2449
Sweet and Sour Beef 18–2455
Swiss Steak 18–2459
Tabriz Meatballs 18–2464
Tamale Casserole 18–2471
Tarte à la Viande (Meat Flan) 18–2487
Teriyaki I (Marinated and Grilled [Broiled] Steaks) 18–2494
Tomaszow Roast 18–2510
Tournedos (info) 19–2529
Tournedos à la Béarnaise (Fillet Steaks with Béarnaise Sauce) 19–2529
Tournedos Chasseur (Fillet Steaks with Ham, Mushroom and White Wine Sauce) 19–2529
Tournedos à la Clamart (Fillet Steaks with Artichokes and Petits Pois) 19–2532
Tournedos Rossini (Fillet Steaks with Pâté) 19–2532
Tournedos Sautés aux Champignons (Fillet Steaks with Mushrooms and Red Wine) 19–2532
Tournedos Vert-Pré (Fillet Steaks with Potatoes and Watercress) 19–2533
Transylvanian Goulasch 19–2537
Umido di Carne (Italian Meat Stew) 19–2590
Vaca Filete con Especias (Fillet of Beef with Spices) 19–2600
Vinegared Beef and Beans 20–2700
Washington Marinated Beef 20–2738
Welfordian Steaks 20–2756
Welsh Stew 20–2760
West African Beef and Fruit Curry 20–2766
Western Burgers 20–2770
White Hatter Stew 20–2786
Wienerrostbraten (Viennese Steaks) 20–2804
Wieprza Stew 20–2807
Wild Rice Meat Loaf with Barbecue Sauce 20–2810
Windy City Beef Stew 20–2828
Wine Beef Stew 21–2844
Winter Beef Party Stew 21–2848
Woodland Picnic Sandwich 21–2863
Worcester Beef Croûte 21–2866
Wotan's Delight 21–2868
Wynns Green Beef 21–2888
Wyoming Beef Ribs 21–2889
Wyoming Devilled Steaks 21–2890
Yale Chilli 21–2905
Yankee Stuffed Corn 21–2908
Yarborough Beef Ring 21–2910
Yiddish Meatballs 21–2924
Yingkow Stuffed Pineapple 21–2925
Yorkshire Meat Pudding 21–2938
Yorkshire Pancakes 21–2938
Yorkshire Savoury Meatballs 21–2941
Yucatan Stuffed Peppers 21–2951
Yugoslavian Barbecued Beef 21–2953

Yuletide Spiced Brisket **21**–2959
Yummy Meat and Vegetable Pie **21**–2960
Zahna Meat Medley **21**–2970
Zalovnoye s Solonine (Russian Salt Beef Mould) **21**–2972
Zaria Beef **21**–2982
Zena's Sugared Steaks **21**–2990
Zhukov Boiled Beef Dinner with Horseradish Sauce **21**–2994
Zindo Vando (Meat and Fish Stew) **22**–2997
Zinfandel Beef **22**–2998
Zite with Meatballs and Tomato Mushroom Sauce **22**–3002
Znojemsky Goulasch (Hungarian Goulasch with Gherkins) **22**–3002
Zoller Pumpkin Stew **22**–3009
Zraza (Stuffed Beef Rolls in Mushroom Sauce) **22**–3021
Zrazi s Kashie (Polish Stuffed Hamburgers) **22**–3022
Zsa Zsa's Meatball Goulasch **22**–3024
Zucchini Orientali (Stuffed Courgettes) **22**–3033
Zulu Beef Pot **22**–3050
Zulu Beef Stew **22**–3050
Zwickau Stuffed Fillet of Beef **22**–3074
Zwiebelfleisch (Beef with Onions) **22**–3077
Zyman Roast Beef **22**–3079

Bone Marrow (info) **2**–209
Carcass (info) **3**–324
Chop (info) **3**–416
Cutlet (info) **4**–524
Dripping (info) **5**–578
Fillet (info) **5**–698

Frogs

Frogs (info) **6**–763
Grenouilles aux Persil (Frogs' Legs with Parsley Butter Sauce) **7**–876
Grenouilles à la Provençale (Frogs' Legs with Tomatoes and Garlic) **7**–877

General Meat Dishes

Berliner Eintoff (Berlin Stew) **2**–162
Bollita Misto (Italian Boiled Beef, Chicken and Sausage) **2**–206
Casoulet de Languedoc (Casserole of Pork and Lamb with Beans and Sausage) **3**–335
Croquettes de Pomme de Terre et Viande (Potato and Meat Croquettes) **4**–505
Farshmak (Meat and Pickled Herring Patties) **5**–677
Feijoada (Brazilian Black Beans and Smoked Meats) **5**–683
Fritto Misto (Deep-Fried Meat and Vegetables) **6**–762
Hash (info) **7**–933
Hash with Aubergine [Eggplant] **7**–933
Hash with Mushrooms and Tomato Sauce **7**–934
Hunter's Stew **8**–993
Huyman's Salad **8**–996
Olla Podrida (Meat and Vegetable Stew) **12**–1574
Pichelsteiner (Meat and Vegetable Casserole) **13**–1776
Pouding de Viande (Meat Pudding) **15**–1939
Zardov Quick Cassoulet **21**–2982

Ham and Gammon

Ham (info) **7**–910
Gammon (info) **6**–792
Apricots and Gammon or Ham **1**–57
Bouchées au Jambon (Puff Pastry Cases Filled with Ham) **2**–219
Boubon-Glazed Ham **2**–224
Cheese and Ham Soufflé **3**–365
Chicken and Ham Paste **3**–381
Chicory with Cheese and Ham **3**–400
Cornets de Jambon (Ham Cones Filled with Pâté de Fois Gras) **4**–455
Croquettes de Jambon (Ham Croquettes) **4**–503
Croûtes de Jambon (Ham Croûtes) **4**–509
Fig-Flavoured Ham **5**–688
Gammon Baked with Herbs **6**–792
Gammon with Pineapple **6**–792
Gammon with Tarragon Cream Sauce **6**–794
Gammon with Tomato Sauce **6**–794
Glazed Bacon [Ham] **6**–838
Green Peas with Ham **7**–872
Ham and Artichoke Heart Mould **7**–910
Ham Baked with Sauerkraut **7**–910
Ham Balls **7**–912
Ham Braised in Red Wine **7**–912
Ham with Cabbage and Potatoes **7**–913
Ham with Champagne Sauce **7**–913
Ham in Cider Sauce **7**–914
Ham Custard **7**–915
Ham with Figs **7**–915
Ham and Fried Rice **7**–916
Ham Fritters with Almonds **7**–916
Ham Glazed **7**–917
Ham Liscannor **7**–917
Ham and Rice Salad **7**–918
Ham Sauce **7**–918
Ham Steaks with Barbecue Sauce **7**–918
Honeyed Ham with Bean Sprouts **7**–967
Jambon Braisé au Madère (Ham Braised in Madeira) **8**–1055
Jambon Braisé au Vin Blanc (Ham Braised in White Wine) **8**–1056
Jambon en Croûte (Ham Baked in Pastry) **8**–1057
Jambon aux Echalottes (Ham with Shallots) **8**–1054
Jamon con Nabos (Spanish Ham and Turnip Stew) **8**–1058
Juleskinke (Ham Cooked in Beer) **8**–1087
Kentucky Ham (info) **9**–1124
Kromeski with Chicken and Ham **9**–1175
Mi Tse Ho-Tui (Ham in Honey Syrup) **11**–1409
Mushroom and Ham Crêpes **11**–1452
Ntroba Forowee (Ghanaian Stewed Aubergine [Eggplant] with Shrimps) **11**–1526
Oeufs Mornay (Poached Eggs and Ham with Cheese Sauce) **12**–1557
Omelette au Jambon (Ham Omelet) **12**–1581
Pain de Pommes de Terre au Jambon (Potato and Ham Loaf) **12**–1659
Pea Soup with Ham **13**–1710
Pizza al Prosciutto (Pizza with Ham) **14**–1834
Poloni (Steamed Meat Loaf) **14**–1858
Prosciutto (info) **15**–1976
Prosciutto and Chicken Rolls **15**–1978
Prosciutto with Melon **15**–1979
Prosciutto with Pear **15**–1979
Prosciutto al Piselli (Ham with Peas) **15**–1979
Putignano Ham **15**–1992
Rochester Gammon Steaks **16**–2145
Shortcake with Savoury Filling **17**–2306
Soufflé d'Epinards et Jambon (Spinach Soufflé with Ham) **17**–2354
Spinach with Ham **18**–2383
Stilton Ham Bake **18**–2412
Stuffed Onions **18**–2432
Suprêmes de Volaille au Jambon (Chicken Breasts with Ham) **18**–2444
Tagliatelle con Prosciutto (Ribbon Pasta with Ham) **18**–2465
Tamale Casserole **18**–2471
Timbale de Jambon (Ham Mould) **18**–2502
Tranches de Jambon à la Normande (Ham Slices with Apples) **19**–2534
Tranches de Jambon en Pipérade (Ham Slices with Vegetables) **19**–2536
Tranches de Jambon à la Sauce Madère (Ham Slices with Madeira Sauce) **19**–2536
Tsingshih Soup (Smoked Ham and Cucumber Soup) **19**–2557
Waffles with Ham and Cheese **20**–2724
Wecksnappspiess (Ham and Kidney Kebabs) **20**–2749
Welsh Stew **20**–2760
Wiltshire Ham with Broccoli **20**–2817
Wiltshire Ham and Celery Rolls **20**–2817
Wiltshire Ham and Cheese Snack **20**–2817
Wiltshire Ham in Crispy Baked Potatoes **20**–2817
Wisconsin Ham Casserole **21**–2855
Wrangler's Gammon Bake **21**–2870
Wrotherham Hot-Pot **21**–2874
York Ham (info) **21**–2934
York Ham Cones **21**–2934
Yorkshire Ham Pie **21**–2935
Yuletide Wessex Ham **21**–2959
Zandam Bread Bake **21**–2975
Zorrell Cheese and Ham Rolls **22**–3018
Zulcan Gammon and Gooseberries **22**–3046

Haunch (info) **7**–935
Heid (info) **7**–944
Hotch-Potch (info) **7**–978

Kid

Kid (info) **9**–1131
Kid, Italian-Style **9**–1131
Kid with Tomatoes and Courgettes [Zucchini] **9**–1132

Lamb and Mutton

Lamb (info) **9**–1191
Mutton (info) **11**–1464
Abbacchio Brodettato (Italian Braised Lamb) **1**–3
Agneau (info) **1**–4
Agneau à la Bonne Femme (Ragoût of Lamb) **1**–5
Agneau en Brochette (Lamb on Skewers) **1**–5
Agneau à la Hongroise (Lamb Sautéed with Paprika) **1**–6
Agneau aux Tomates (Lamb Sautéed with Tomatoes) **1**–6
Arabian Stewed Lamb **1**–59
Arni Psito (Roast Leg of Lamb) **1**–62
Aubergine [Eggplant] and Lamb Casserole **1**–85
Aubergine [Eggplant] and Lamb Stew **1**–85
Badami Gosht (Lamb Cooked with Almonds) **1**–104
Baghali Polo (Lamb with Rice and Dill) **1**–105
Barbecued Lamb **1**–119
Biryani (Spiced Rice with Lamb) **2**–174
Boti Kebabs (Grilled Lamb on Skewers) **2**–212
Cabbage and Lamb Hot Pot **3**–285
Calderete de Jerez (Lamb Stew with Sherry) **3**–297
Carré d'Agneau au Cidre (Lamb in Cider Sauce) **3**–331
Cassoulet du Languedoc (Casserole of Pork and Lamb with Beans and Sausage) **3**–334
Cevap (Yugoslavian Lamb Chops with Paprika) **3**–348
Cevapcici (Skewered Lamb and Beef Balls) **3**–348
Costolette di Agnello alla Milanese (Lamb Chops Coated in Breadcrumbs and Grated Parmesan Cheese) **4**–458
Côtelettes d'Agneau au Concombre (Lamb Cutlets with Cucumber and Onion) **4**–460
Couscous I **4**–468
Couscous II **4**–470
Crown Roast of Lamb **4**–511
Dala' Mahshi (Stuffed Breasts of Lamb) **4**–526
Daoud Pasha (Meat Balls with Pine Nuts and Tomato Sauce) **4**–534
Darius Casserole (Lamb and Bean Casserole) **4**–535
Daube d'Avignon (Lamb Stew with Bacon and Onions) **4**–545
Daube de Mouton (Lamb Stew with Mushrooms and Tomatoes) **4**–548
Djuvec (Serbian Lamb Stew) **5**–569
Dügün Corbari (Turkish Lamb Stew and Lemon Soup) **5**–588
Easter Lamb **5**–601
Easter Soup **5**–601
Eastern Cutlets **5**–601

Thematic

Ecuadorian Lamb Stew 5–603
Epaule d'Agneau Roulée aux Pruneaux (Shoulder of Lamb with Prunes) 5–649
Epaule de Mouton à la Boulangère (Shoulder of Lamb with Potatoes) 5–650
Epigramme (info) 5–651
Ewe (info) 5–664
Farshmak (Meat and Pickled Herring Patties) 5–677
Fata (Egyptian Lamb Soup) 5–678
Garmi Polo (Lamb Chops in Fruit Sauce with Rice) 6–801
Gigot d'Agneau à la Bretonne (Roast Leg of Lamb with Haricot Beans) 6–824
Gigot d'Agneau Farci (Stuffed Leg of Lamb) 6–826
Gigot d'Agneau à la Moutarde (Roast Leg of Lamb Coated with Mustard) 6–826
Gigot d'Agneau à la Provençale (Roast Leg of Lamb with Provençale Sauce) 6–827
Gigot d'Agneau au Vin Rouge (Leg of Lamb Marinated in Red Wine) 6–827
Giouvetsi (Roast Lamb with Macaroni) 6–837
Gormeh Sabzi (Lamb Stew with Parsley) 7–855
Greek Lamb Kebabs 7–868
Greek Lamb Stew 7–869
Guleh Kambing (Lamb Curry) 7–895
Haricot Mutton 7–928
Harira (Lamb Soup) 7–930
Hash with Mushrooms and Tomato Sauce 7–934
Huseini Kebabs (Marinated Lamb Grilled [Broiled] on Skewers) 8–995
Immos 8–1018
Irish Stew 8–1032
Jagnjeci But (Yugoslavian Leg of Lamb) 8–1042
Jal Farazi (Curried Meat and Potatoes) 8–1042
Jordanian Stuffed Lamb 8–1081
Kadu Polo (Pumpkin and Lamb Patties with Rice) 8–1092
Katsudon (Japanese Lamb or Pork Soup) 8–1116
Kebabs in Herb Marinade 8–1118
Kebabs Marinated in Yogurt 8–1118
Kebabs Massalam (Minced [Ground] Beef or Lamb Kebabs) 8–1120
Kebabs with Soy Sauce and Sherry 8–1120
Kefta (Moroccan Minced [Ground] Lamb Kebabs) 9–1121
Kemah Lamb Cubes 9–1122
Kerkenna Island Hotpot 9–1124
Kheema (Curried Mined [Ground] Meat) 9–1128
Khoresh Bademjan (Lamb with Aubergine [Eggplant] Sauce) 9–1128
Knuckle of Lamb and Tomato Soup 9–1159
Kolduny Litewskie (Lithuanian Meat-Filled Pockets) 9–1165
Korma (Rich Lamb Curry) 9–1167
Lamb with Apples 9–1192
Lamb and Apricot Pilaff 9–1192
Lamb with Artichokes 9–1193
Lamb Baked with Peppers and Cheese 9–1193
Lamb Breasts with Devil Sauce 9–1194
Lamb and Cabbage Stew 9–1194
Lamb and Cashew Nut Curry 9–1194
Lamb Chops with Rosemary 9–1195
Lamb Chops with Sweetcorn and Pimientos 9–1197
Lamb Chops with Tomatoes and Herbs 9–1197
Lamb Chops Victor Hugo 9–1197
Lamb Country-Style 9–1197
Lamb Cutlets in Aspic 9–1198
Lamb Isabella 9–1198
Lamb with Lentils 9–1198
Lamb and Mushroom Stew 9–1200
Lamb Patties, Greek-Style 9–1201
Lamb Pilaff 9–1201
Lamb with Rice 9–1201
Lamb Salad 9–1201
Lamb Shoulder with Turnips 9–1201
Lamb Stew with Vegetables 9–1202
Lancashire Hot Pot 9–1205
Languedoc Lamb Pie 9–1207
Leg of Lamb Adapazari 9–1218

Leg of Lamb with Coriander and Garlic 9–1219
Leg of Lamb English-Style 9–1219
Leg of Lamb with Savoury Rice 9–1220
Leg of Lamb with Wine and Lemon Sauce 9–1220
Loin (info) 9–1259
Loin of Lamb and Mushrooms 9–1260
Loin of Lamb with Peas and Beans 9–1260
Loin of Lamb with Tomatoes and Potatoes 10–1261
Malynka's Lamb Dumplings 10–1296
Meat and Fruit Pilau 10–1352
Meatballs with Spicy Sauce 10–1360
Moroccan Lamb and Honey Casserole 11–1422
Moussaka (info) 11–1429
Moussaka I 11–1430
Moussaka II 11–1431
Moussaka Greek-Style 11–1432
Mouton Farci (Stuffed Loin of Mutton) 11–1439
Mutton Chops Stuffed with Mushrooms and Celery 11–1464
Mutton Pies 11–1465
Nargisi Koftas (Meatballs Stuffed with Hard-Boiled Eggs) 11–1476
Navarin de Mouton (Mutton Stew) 11–1479
Navarin Printanier (Mutton Stew with Fresh Spring Vegetables) 11–1480
Neck of Lamb with Marjoram and Orange 11–1486
New Orleans Lamb Cutlets 11–1499
Noisettes d'Agneau Arlésienne (Boned Lamb Chops with Aubergine [Eggplant] and Tomato Sauce) 11–1506
Noisettes d'Agneau à la Clamart (Boned Lamb Chops in Pastry Cases with Puréed Peas) 11–1506
Noisettes d'Agneau Ismail Bayeldi (Boned Lamb Chops with Vegetables and Rice) 11–1507
Noisettes d'Agneau Milanaise (Boned Lamb Chops with Spaghetti and Tomato Sauce) 11–1507
Noisettes d'Agneau Monegasque (Boned Lamb Chops with Mushrooms and Tomato Sauce) 11–1508
Noisettes d'Agneau au Sauce Champignon (Boned Lamb Chops with Mushroom Sauce) 11–1508
Okra [Ladies' Fingers] and Lamb Casserole 12–1567
Pakistani Lamb Chops 12–1661
Peleponnesian Lamb with Noodles 13–1731
Peppers Stuffed with Lamb and Rice 13–1743
Peveragno Lamb Chops 13–1767
Pilaff with Lamb and Almonds 13–1796
Plate Pie 14–1842
Portuguese Kebabs 14–1908
Pytt i Panna (Swedish Hash) 15–1994
Quick Lamb with Mushrooms 15–2028
Quince with Lamb and Honey Stuffing 15–2032
Quotban (Moroccan Kebabs) 15–2036
Raan (Leg of Lamb Marinated in Spiced Yogurt and Roasted) 15–2037
Red Bean and Lamb Casserole 15–2076
Reform Chops 15–2089
Roghan Gosht (Curried Lamb) 16–2152
Rutabiya (Meatballs with Dates and Almonds) 16–2194
Saddle of Lamb with Mint 16–2200
Saddle of Lamb with Rosemary 16–2200
Sag Gohst (Spinach with Meat) 16–2205
Sate I 17–2242
Sauté d'Agneau (Lamb Sauté) 17–2257
Shakooti Rassa (Lamb Cooked with Coconut) 17–2293
Shao K'o Yang Jou (Steamed Lamb) 17–2296
Shashlik (Lamb Kebabs Flavoured with Lemon) 17–2297
Shepherd's Pie I 17–2298
Shepherd's Pie II 17–2299
Sosaties (South African Kebabs) 17–2350
Spiedini (Italian Kebabs) 18–2383
Stuffed Cabbage 18–2430
Swedish Lamb Stew with Dill 18–2448

Swedish Marinated Lamb 18–2449
Tajine de Mouton aux Fruits Sec (North African Lamb Stew with Dried Fruit) 18–2467
Talawa Gosht (Deep-Fried Lamb and Potatoes) 18–2468
Taraba (Meatballs enclosed in Spinach) 18–2478
Tarragon Lamb Chops 18–2480
Thayir Kari (Yogurt Curry) 18–2497
Tikkah Kabab (Spiced Lamb Kebabs) 18–2500
Transvaal Braised Lamb 19–2537
Turkari Molee (Lamb and Coconut Curry) 19–2565
Turkish Lamb Casserole 19–2577
Tuscan Meat Loaf 19–2581
Tzimmis (Lamb and Vegetable Casserole) 19–2584
Uzbeck Plov (Lamb and Rice Pilaff) 19–2598
Walnut and Lamb Bake 20–2734
Wellington Pie 20–2757
Wellington Roast Lamb 20–2759
Wensley Dale Marrow [Summer Squash] 20–2764
Wessex Lamb 20–2764
Wessex Lamb Cutlets 20–2764
West Indian Pepperpot 20–2768
Wexford Stuffed Lamb 20–2774
Wheat Germ and Lamb Casserole 20–2776
Whitsun Lamb 20–2800
Williamsburg Lamb 20–2815
Winter Lamb Stew 21–2851
Wreckin Spiced Kidneys 21–2872
Wye Valley Lamb 21–2884
Yakhni Pulao (Lamb Cooked with Rice) 21–2903
Yemeni Lamb Casserole 21–2920
Yerevan Lamb Pilaff 21–2920
Yogurtli Kebab (Lamb with Yogurt) 21–2931
Yorkshire Lamb Hot Pot 21–2938
Youngstown Lamb in Sherry Sauce 21–2944
Yugoslavian Shoulder of Lamb 21–2954
Zahna Meat Medley 21–2971
Zeera Gosht (Cumin Meat) 21–2987
Zetland Baked Lamb 21–2994
Zippy Savoury Scramble 22–3000
Zorba's Meatballs 22–3016
Zorin's Lamb with Lemon Sauce 22–3018
Zurich Lamb Delight 22–3064
Zurov Lamb 22–3066
Liver, Kidney etc. see Offal

Loin (info) 9–1259
Marrow Bone (info) 10–1328
Mince (info) 10–1394
Mixed Grill (info) 11–1409
Noisettes (info) 11–1506
Oxtail see Offal
Paupiette (info) 13–1704
Pope's Eye or Ear (info) 14–1873

Pork

Pork (info) 14–1877
Apple and Pork Casserole 1–48
Arrosto Perugina (Italian Roast Pork) 1–65
Artichokes Stuffed with Pork and Almonds 1–70
Bamboo Shoots with Pork 1–109
Barbecued Pork 1–120
Barbecued Pork Chops 1–120
Barbecued Spareribs 1–121
Bath Chap (info) 1–128
Berliner Eintopf (Berlin Stew) 2–162
Boar's Head (info) 2–189
Brochettes de Porc (Pork Brochettes) 2–267
Cantonese Roast Pork 3–314
Cassoulet du Languedoc (Casserole of Pork and Lamb with Beans and Sausage) 3–334
Cerdo a la Aragonese (Spanish Pork Casserole) 3–348
Chinese Roast Pork 3–402
Costillas a la Mexicana (Mexican Pork Chops) 4–457
Costoletta di Maiale alla Pizzaiola (Pork Chops in Tomato and Green Pepper Sauce) 4–458

Costoletta di Maiale alla Modenese (Pork Chops in White Wine with Herbs) 4–458
Côtes de Porc Braisées (Pork Chops Cooked in a Piquant Sauce) 4–461
Crackling (info) 4–475
Crown Roast of Pork with Sausage and Prune Stuffing 4–511
Cucumber and Pork Soup 4–517
Danish Pork 4–532
Devilled Pork Chops 4–560
Devilled Pork Ribs 4–560
Egg Noodles with Pork Sauce 5–623
Emincé de Porc aux Poivrons (Pork with Pimientos and Onions) 5–642
Essex Meat Layer Pudding 5–660
Estonian Rissoles 5–662
Estouffat (Pork and Bean Stew) 5–664
Feijoada (Brazilian Black Beans and Smoked Meats) 5–683
Fondue Japonais 6–733
Forcemeat of Pork 6–736
Fried Aubergines [Eggplant] with Pork and Vegetables 6–754
Frikadeller (Danish Meat Patties) 6–758
Fruit and Pork Casserole 6–772
Gelée d'Avignon (Jellied Pork Soup) 6–813
Geschmorte Schweinefleisch mit Kümmel (Braised Loin of Pork with Sour Cream and Caraway Sauce) 6–820
Ghourounaki Yemisto me Feta (Roast Suckling Pig Stuffed with Feta Cheese) 6–824
Gigot de Porc à la Crème (Roast Leg of Pork with Cream and Wine Sauce) 6–828
Green Peppers Stuffed with Pork and Veal 7–873
Griskin (info) 7–883
Hamilton Chops 7–922
Hogs Pudding 7–954
Hung Shao Chu Jo (Red-Cooked Pork in Soy Sauce) 8–986
Hungarian Layered Cabbage 8–991
Italian Meat Loaf 8–1037
Jarret de Boeuf en Daube (Beef and Pork Stew) 8–1061
Javanese Pork 8–1062
Jou Ping Hui Por-Ts'a (Fried and Baked Meat Cakes with Spinach) 8–1082
Jou Si Chow Ching Ts'ai (Shredded Pork Stir-Fried with Spring Greens) 8–1082
Jou Yuan Ts'ai Hui (Meatball Chop Suey) 8–1084
Jug Jug (Meat Mould) 8–1084
Junipered Pork Chops 8–1090
Kasseler Rippchen (Smoked Pork Chops) 8–1114
Katsudon (Japanese Lamb or Pork Soup) 8–1116
Kielbasa Loaf 9–1141
Konigsberger Klops (Meatballs in Lemon and Caper Sauce) 9–1166
Kotelett mit Pflaumen (Pork Chops with Plums) 9–1168
Köttbullar (Swedish Meatballs) 9–1169
Kuo Pa Jou Tin (Diced Pork on Crackling Rice) 9–1181
Labskaus (Pickled Pork or Corned Beef Hash) 9–1186
Liu Jou-Pien (Sliced Pork in Wine Sauce) 9–1254
Loin of Pork with Garlic and Vegetables 10–1261
Loin of Pork with Juniper Berries 10–1262
Loin of Pork with Oranges and Pineapple 10–1263
Lombo de Porco com Pimentos (Loin of Pork with Red Peppers) 10–1267
Lou Jo (Pork Simmered in Master Sauce) 10–1272
Malaysian Pork Chops 10–1292
Maple Sparerib Casserole 10–1309
Maraccas Beach Pilau 10–1310
Marinated Pork Chops 10–1314
Marinated Pork Fillets 10–1315
Martinville Soulfood Stew 10–1335
Meat Loaf II 10–1354

Meatballs in Oriental Sweet and Sour Sauce 10–1358
Meatballs in Sherry Sauce 10–1359
Mee Feng Jou (Pork in Ground Rice) 10–1368
Mein IV: Cha Chiang Mein (Noodles in Peking Meat Sauce with Shredded Vegetables) 10–1369
Melon and Cold Pork Salad 10–1372
Melton Mowbray Pie 10–1374
Mexican Pork Fillets 10–1386
Mexican Pork and Rice 10–1386
Morbrad med Aebler og Svesker (Loin of Pork Stuffed with Apple Prunes) 11–1418
Navets au Petit Salé (Turnips with Salt Pork) 11–1481
Near Eastern Pork with Peanuts and Grapes 11–1486
Netherlands Pork 11–1493
New England Meat Loaf 11–1496
New Orleans Barbequed Pork Chops 11–1499
Noisettes de Porc aux Pruneaux (Boned Pork Chops with Prunes and Cream) 11–1509
Normandy Pork 11–1516
Olive Meat Loaf 12–1572
Olive Stuffed Pork 12–1573
Olla Podrida (Meat and Vegetable Stew) 12–1574
Orange Glazed Pork Chops 12–1612
Orange and Pork Casserole 12–1615
Pai Chou Jou (White Cooked Pork) 12–1658
Paprikasertésborda (Braised Pork Chops with Paprika Sauce) 12–1674
Pastel de Choclo (Meat and Corn Pie) 13–1692
Paupiettes de Porc (Pork Fillets Stuffed with Apple Purée) 13–1706
Peruvian Pork Stew 13–1756
Pig's Head (info) 13–1792
Pig's Trotters (info) 13–1792
Pig's Trotters with Breadcrumbs 13–1792
Pineapple and Pork Casserole 13–1808
Piquant Meat Loaf 13–1820
Piquant Pork Chops 14–1821
Piquant Stew 14–1822
Planter's Pork Chops 14–1840
Pork and Apricot Salad 14–1880
Pork Balls with Ginger 14–1880
Pork Balls in Wine Sauce 14–1881
Pork Casserole with Lemon 14–1882
Pork Chilli 14–1882
Pork Chops with Apples 14–1882
Pork Chops Baked with Cabbage 14–1883
Pork Chops Baked with Cream and Tarragon 14–1884
Pork Chops Braised with Onions and Wine 14–1885
Pork Chops with Cheese 14–1885
Pork Chops with Cranberry Sauce 14–1886
Pork Chops with Morello Cherries 14–1886
Pork Chops with Mushroom and Parsley Stuffing 14–1887
Pork Chops with Mushrooms and Tomatoes 14–1888
Pork Chops with Mustard Sauce 14–1888
Pork Chops with Pistachio Nut Stuffing 14–1889
Pork Chops with Rosemary 14–1890
Pork Curry 14–1890
Pork Fillets in Cream Sauce 14–1890
Pork Fillets, Korean-Style 14–1892
Pork Fillets with Red Wine 14–1892
Pork Fried Rice 14–1893
Pork with Ginger and Pineapple 14–1894
Pork Goulasch 14–1894
Pork with Grapes 14–1895
Pork with Gruyère 14–1895
Pork Korma 14–1896
Pork with Mixed Vegetables 14–1897
Pork Pie 14–1900
Pork Ribs with Juniper Berries 14–1900
Pork with Sweet and Sour Sauce 14–1900
Pork Vindaloo (Pork Vinegar Curry) 14–1901
Pork and Walnut Casserole 14–1901
Pork with Wine and Orange Sauce 14–1901
Portuguese Kebabs 14–1908
Quick-Fried Spinach with Shredded Pork 15–2027

Ragoût Martiniquais (Chicken and Pork Stew) 15–2048
Rice Noodles with Pork and Prawns or Shrimps 16–2114
Rillettes (Potted Pork) 16–2124
Roast California Pork 16–2142
Rumanian Pork Bake 16–2182
Run Tsa Li Chi (Plain Deep-Fried Sliced Pork) 16–2187
Saddle of Pork 16–2202
Sage Pork Fillets 16–2207
Salt Pork and Beef Stew 16–2231
Sauerbraten II (Marinated Sweet and Sour Pork) 17–2250
Shao Jou I (Cantonese Roast Pork) 17–2296
Shao Jou II (Crispy Roast Pork) 17–2296
Shih-tzu-tou (Pork and Cabbage Casserole) 17–2302
Shoemaker's Pot 17–2303
Spare Rib (info) 17–2372
Spare Rib Helene 17–2372
Spare Rib Southern-Style 17–2372
Spare Rib Stuffed with Kidneys 17–2374
Spareribs with Paprika Sauce 17–2375
Spare Ribs Seville 17–2376
Spiedini (Italian Kebabs) 18–2383
Spoleto Pork Fillets 18–2392
Suckling Pig (info) 18–2436
Suckling Pig with Sausage Meat and Apricot Stuffing 18–2436
Takhing Pancakes with Pork Filling 18–2468
Tamale Casserole 18–2471
Tinga de Cerdo y Ternera (Pork and Veal Stew with Green Tomatoes) 18–2503
Tourte de Porc (French Pork Pie) 19–2534
Varkenslappen met Abricozen (Pork with Apricots) 19–2608
Vegetable and Pork Salad 19–2650
Venison and Pork Patties 20–2674
Watercress and Pork Soup 20–2743
West Indian Pilau 20–2768
Wild Boar (info) 20–2808
Wild Rice and Pork Pilaff 20–2811
Wine-Baked Pork 21–2844
Wontons with Pork 21–2859
Wontons with Pork and Prawns or Shrimps 21–2859
Wurtemburg Pork Salad 21–2880
Wylding Peppered Pork Fillets 21–2886
Wyndham Pork and Apricot Bake 21–2888
Wytcherley Pork Chops 21–2892
Yahm Chompu (Savoury Fruit Salad) 21–2901
Yanchow Noodles 21–2907
Yankee Stuffed Corn 21–2908
Yetminster Stuffed Pork 21–2921
Yewdale Pork with Peaches 21–2923
Yorkshire Meat Pudding 21–2938
Yorktown Pork Fillets 21–2941
Yoxford Crown Roast of Pork with Peaches 21–2944
Yu Hsiang Jou Si (Quick-Fried Shredded Pork with 'Fish Ingredients') 21–2948
Zahna Meat Medley 21–2970
Zardov Quick Cassoulet 21–2982
Zite with Meatballs and Tomato Mushroom Sauce 22–3002
Zooler Pumpkin Stew 22–3009
Zonza Stuffed Spare Rib 22–3013
Zoondam Pork Ratatouille 22–3014
Zsa Zsa's Meatball Goulasch 22–3024
Zubrick Pork and Spiced Plums 22–3025
Zug Pork Chops 22–3042
Zungeru Peanut Pork 22–3054
Zurich Roast Pork 22–3064
Zverovo Steamed Meat Loaf 22–3069

Rabbit

Rabbit (info) 19–2038
Daube de Lapin (Rabbit Stew) 4–547
Fried Rabbit with Hungarian Sauce 5–757
Hot Pot of Rabbit 7–974
Lapin aux Poireaux (Rabbit and Leek Casserole) 9–1208
Lapin à la Sauce Moutarde (Rabbit with

Mustard Sauce) **9**–1209
Rabbit with Apricots **15**–2038
Rabbit Broth **15**–2038
Rabbit in Cider **15**–2040
Rabbit Fried in Breadcrumbs **15**–2040
Rabbit Pie **15**–2040
Rabbit in Sweet and Sour Sauce **15**–2043
Rabbit in White Wine **15**–2043
Wimple Rabbit Casserole **20**–2821
Zingarella Stew **22**–2999
Zummah Rabbit Stew **22**–3052

Saddle (info) **16**–2200

Sausage

Sausage (info) **17**–2254
Andouille (info) **1**–31
Black Pudding (info) **2**–184
Bratwurst (info) **2**–237
Bratwurst Sausages in Sour Cream Sauce **2**–237
Cabbage and Sausage Casserole **3**–287
Cassoulet Gascogne (Casserole of Sausage and
   Beans with Garlic and Parsley Butter) **3**–336
Chipolata (info) **3**–404
Chorizo Patties **3**–416
Choucroute Garnie **3**–416
Coddle **4**–434
Egg, Sausage and Pepper Casserole **5**–625
Fabada (Spanish Bean and Sausage Soup)
Frankfurter (info) **6**–739
Frankfurters, Alabama-Style **6**–739
Frankfurter Bake **6**–739
Frankfurter Cabbage Salad **6**–739
Frankfurter Stew **6**–740
Garbure (Sausage and Cabbage Soup) **6**–796
German Country Breakfast **6**–818
German Sausage (info) **6**–819
Glamorgan Sausages **6**–838
Habas a la Catalana (Sausage and Broad Bean
   Casserole) **7**–898
Hot Dog (info) **7**–974
Kale with Onions and Italian Sausage **8**–1100
Knackwurst with Beer Sauce **9**–1156
Knackwurst and Lentil Casserole **9**–1156
Leek and Sausage Tart **9**–1216
Lesco (Sausage and Vegetable Stew) **9**–1234
Liver Sausage and Egg Spread **9**–1251
Mortadella (info) **11**–1423
Oyster and Meat Sausages **12**–1651
Paprika Vegetable and Sausage Stew **12**–1674
Peperoni (info) **13**–1746
Polish Bigos **13**–1785
Queretaro Bake **15**–2017
Reading Apples **15**–2074
Salami (info) **16**–2213
Salami Stuffed Prunes **16**–2213
Salsicce con Fagioli (Italian Sausage with
   Haricot Beans) **16**–2226
Saucisse en Croûte (Sausage in Pastry) **17**–2248
Saucisses aux Pommes (Sausages with Apples)
   17–2248
Saucisses à la Purée de Celeri Rave (Sausages
   with Puréed Celeriac) **17**–2249
Sauerkraute Casserole with Dill Cucumber
   17–2252
Sausage and Apple Cake **17**–2254
Sausage Meat (info) **17**–2255
Sausage Rolls **17**–2256
Saveloy (info) **17**–2263
Scotch Eggs **17**–2279
Talairan Rice Salad with Garlic Sausage
   18–2468
Tarte à la Viande (Meat Flan) **18**–2487
Toad in the Hole **18**–2504
Wienerwurst and Noodle Casserole **20**–2806
Wienerwurst Risotto **20**–2806
Wurst (info) **21**–2878
Wurst Ratatouille (German Sausage and Mixed
   Vegetables) **21**–2878
Wurst in Sweet and Sour Sauce **21**–2879
Wurstsalat (German Sausage Salad) **21**–2880
Wurstel Sausage in Aspic **21**–2880
Yu Savoury Toast **21**–2950
Zardov Quick Cassoulet **21**–2982

Zenda Sausage Snacks **21**–2990
Zite with Italian Sausage Sauce **22**–3001
Zoom-Zoom Sausage Toadstools **22**–3051
Zug Sausage and Leek Casserole **22**–3071
Zullah's Pasta, Sausage and Bean Salad **22**–3049
Zwartberg Mountain Cassoulet **22**–3071

Tenderloin (info) **18**–2493
Tongue *see* Offal

Veal

Veal (info) **19**–2612
Allspice Veal Roll **1**–14
Artichokes with Veal and Peppers **1**–72
Barbecued Veal Chops **1**–120
Berliner Eintopf (Berlin Stew) **2**–162
Blanquette de Veau (Veal in Cream Sauce)
   2–185
Borjúpörkölt (Veal Stew with Tomatoes,
   Paprika and Green Pepper) **2**–211
Braciuola Ripiene (Veal Stuffed Rolls) **2**–226
Brochettes de Veau aux Champignons (Veal,
   Bacon and Mushroom Brochettes) **2**–268
Côtelettes de Veau en Casserole (Veal Chops
   Casseroled with Carrots, Potatoes and
   Artichoke Hearts) **4**–461
Côtes de Veau au Genièvre (Veal Chops with
   Juniper) **4**–461
Côtes de Veau aux Herbes (Veal Chops with
   Herbs) **4**–462
Côtes de Veau en Papillote (Veal Chops Cooked
   in Paper Cases) **4**–462
Czechoslovakian Veal Ragoût **4**–525
Eminçe de Veau (Veal Strips in Wine and Cream
   Sauce) **5**–642
Epaule de Veau Farcie (Stuffed Shoulder of
   Veal) **5**–651
Escalopes de Veau Amandine (Veal Escalopes
   Coated with Ground Almonds) **5**–653
Escalopes de Veau au Calvados (Veal
   Escalopes with Calvados, Cream and Apples)
   5–653
Escalopes de Veau Cordon Bleu (Veal Escalopes
   with Ham and Cheese) **5**–654
Escalopes de Veau à la Crème (Veal Escalopes
   with Cream Sauce) **5**–654
Escalopes de Veau Holstein (Veal Escalopes
   with Anchovies and Egg) **5**–654
Escalopes de Veau à l'Hongroise (Veal
   Escalopes with Paprika and Sour Cream)
   5–655
Escalopes de Veau Perigueux (Veal Escalopes in
   Madeira and Truffle Sauce) **5**–656
Escalopes de Veau à la Provençale (Veal
   Escalopes with Wine, Tomatoes and Garlic)
   5–656
Escalopes de Veau au Vin Rouge (Veal
   Escalopes in Red Wine) **5**–656
Essex Meat Layer Pudding **5**–660
Fricadelles à la Crème (Veal Patties in Cream and
   Wine Sauce) **6**–751
Fricadelles à l'Hongroise (Veal Patties with
   Tomatoes) **6**–752
Fricadelles de Veau Smitane (Veal Patties in
   Sour Cream Sauce) **6**–752
Fricassée de Veau (Veal and Peppers Fricasee)
   6–754
Frikadeller (Danish Meat Patties) **6**–758
Galantine de Veau au Vin Blanc (Veal with
   White Wine) **6**–782
Goose with Apricot and Veal Stuffing **7**–846
Goulasch II **7**–858
Green Peppers Stuffed with Pork and Veal
   7–873
Grenadin (info) **7**–875
Hot Pot of Veal **7**–976
Involtini alla Contadino (Veal Rolls Stuffed
   with Chicken Livers and Herbs) **8**–1028
Involtini alla Marito (Veal Escalopes Stuffed
   with Cheese and Herbs) **8**–1029
Involtini alla Sophia (Veal Rolls in Wine and
   Cream Sauce) **8**–1029
Jellied Veal **8**–1070
Kaiser Cutlets (Veal Cutlets in Cream and Caper

Sauce) **8**–1095
Kalbsfrikassee mit Spargel (German Veal Stew
   with Asparagus) **8**–1098
Kalbsreisfleisch (Veal and Rice Casserole)
   8–1099
Kalveschnitzel med Sur Fløte (Scandinavian
   Veal Escalopes in Sour Cream) **8**–1101
Kalve Soubise (Veal in Onion Sauce) **8**–1102
Kalvesuppe med Madeira og Champignoner
   (Veal Soup with Madeira and Mushrooms)
   8–1102
Kalvetournedos med Asparges (Veal
   Tournedos with Asparagus) **8**–1102
Kärdia Cabbage **8**–1107
Kebabs of Veal **8**–1120
Keftedes (Spiced Meatballs) **9**–1122
Kielbasa Loaf **9**–1141
Klodnik (Iced Beetroot [Beet] and Meat Soup)
   9–1154
Knuckle of Veal with Gherkin Sauce **9**–1159
Kødboller med Sellerisauce (Danish Meatballs
   with Celery Sauce) **9**–1159
Loin of Veal with Herb Stuffing **10**–1264
Loin of Veal Vichy **10**–1264
Meatball and Onion Casserole **10**–1358
Meatballs in Sherry Sauce **10**–1359
Meatballs in Tomato Sauce **10**–1362
Mediterranean Veal Stew **10**–1365
Moscari Psito (Roast Veal) **11**–1424
Nantwinam Kyewee (Veal Chops Marinated
   in Coconut Milk) **11**–1471
Neapolitan Veal Chops **11**–1485
Neck of Veal, Braised **11**–1487
New England Meat Loaf **11**–1496
Noce di Vitello Farcito (Veal Stuffed with Meat)
   11–1502
Noix de Veau aux Fruits (Topside of Veal with
   Fruit) **11**–1510
Osso Buco (Stewed Veal Knuckle or Shank)
   12–1630
Oyster and Meat Sausages **12**–1651
Paglia e Fieno (Pasta with Veal and Mushrooms)
   12–1656
Paterson Creek Stew **13**–1702
Paupiettes de Veau (Veal Rolls Stuffed with
   Chicken Livers and Mushrooms) **13**–1708
Piroshki (Little Pies) **14**–1823
Polish Bigos **14**–1853
Quagliette di Vitello (Veal Olives on Skewers)
   14–1995
Quenelles de Viande (Meat Quenelles) **15**–2017
Ragoût de Veau (Veal Stew) **15**–2049
Rahmshnitzel (Veal Escalopes with Cream)
   15–2050
Raznjici (Yugoslavian Veal and Pork Kebabs)
   15–2073
Roulades de Veau (Stuffed Veal Rolls) **16**–2174
Scaloppine al Limone (Veal Escalopes with
   Lemon Sauce) **17**–2268
Scaloppine alla Marsala (Veal Escalopes with
   Marsala) **17**–2269
Scaloppine alla Romana (Veal Escalopes
   Roman-Style) **17**–2269
Shrimp and Veal Rolls **17**–2316
Spiced Stuffed Shoulder of Veal **18**–2381
Stufato alla Genovese (Veal Stew, Genoa-Style)
   18–2429
Stuffed Breat of Veal **18**–2429
Swedish Meat Loaf **18**–2449
Tamale Casserole **18**–2471
Tendrons de Veau aux Epinards (Breast of Veal
   with Spinach) **18**–2493
Tendrons de Veau au Jardinière (Breast of Veal
   with Vegetables) **18**–2494
Tinga de Cerdo y Ternera (Pork and Veal Stew
   with Green Tomatoes) **18**–2503
Transylvanian Goulasch·**19**–2537
Uccelli Scappati (Veal Rolls with Ham) **19**–2586
Umido di Carne (Italian Meat Stew) **19**–2590
Veal with Artichokes **19**–2612
Veal and Avocado Salad **19**–2613
Veal and Bean Stew **19**–2613
Veal Benedictine **19**–2613
Veal Bigos **19**–2613
Veal Cake **19**–2616

Veal Cheesecake **19**–2616
Veal Chops with Apple Cream Sauce **19**–2618
Veal Chops English-Style **19**–2619
Veal Chops with Olive and Tomato Sauce **19**–2619
Veal Chops with Sherry **19**–2620
Veal Escalopes with Mustard Sauce **19**–2620
Veal Escalopes Spanish-Style **19**–2631
Veal Escalopes with Tarragon Sauce **19**–2622
Veal Fasano **19**–2622
Veal Fillet with Basil **19**–2623
Veal with Ham and Cheese **19**–2623
Veal and Ham Pie **19**–2624
Veal Kidneys Braised in Port **19**–2625
Veal Kidneys with French Beans **19**–2625
Veal Kidneys with Gin **19**–2626
Veal Kidneys in Lemon Sauce **19**–2626
Veal Kidney Pasties **19**–2626
Veal with Mushroom and Liver Stuffing **19**–2628
Veal with Nut and Raisin Stuffing **19**–2629
Veal Olives **19**–2929
Veal Orloff **19**–2629
Veal, Oyster and Bacon Pie **19**–2630
Veal with Parsley Sauce **19**–2630
Veal Pâté with Calf's Brains **19**–2632
Veal Pot Roast **19**–2633
Veal Rolls with Mushrooms and Ham Stuffing **19**–2633
Veal Spanish-Style **19**–2634
Veal Stock **19**–2634
Veal Stroganov **19**–2635
Veal Stuffed with Kidneys **19**–2636
Veal Stuffed with Peppers and Sausage **19**–2637
Veal and Tongue Pies **19**–2637
Veal with Watercress **19**–2638
Veau Braisé au Vin Blanc (Veal Chops Braised in White Wine) **19**–2638
Veau à la Chinoise (Veal Chinese-Style) **19**–2639
Veau en Cocotte (Veal Casserole) **19**–2639
Veau à l'Indienne (Curried Veal Stew) **19**–2639
Veau à la Ménagère (Veal with Vegetables) **19**–2641
Veau Sauté Marengo (Veal with Mushrooms and Onions) **19**–2641
Verona Veal **20**–2681
Vitello con Melanzane (Veal Escalopes with Aubergine [Eggplant] and Tomato Sauce) **20**–2708
Vitello alla Piemontese con Tartufi (Veal Piedmont-Style with Truffles) **20**–2709
Vitello con Salvia (Loin of Veal with Sage) **20**–2709
Vitello alla Siciliana (Veal with Cream Sauce) **20**–2710
Vitello Tonnato (Cold Veal with Tuna Fish Sauce) **20**–2710
Vitello con Uova (Veal with Scrambled Egg) **20**–2711
Vitello Vincenzo (Veal Stuffed with Italian Hot Sausage) **20**–2711
Wednesday Veal **20**–2754
White Meat Casserole **20**–2788
Wienerleber (Viennese Calf's Liver) **20**–2804
Wienerschnitzel (Viennese Breaded Veal Escalopes) **20**–2804
Wild Rice Meat Loaf with Barbecue Sauce **20**–2810
Winter Warmer **21**–2853
Yugoslavian Veal Sandwiches **21**–2954
Zampa di Vitello alla Toscana (Calves' Feet Tuscan-Style) **21**–2974
Zapata Veal **21**–2979
Zardov Quick Cassoulet **21**–2982
Zogno Veal Cutlets **22**–3007
Zurich Veal and Parsnip Pie **22**–3065

MILK

Milk (info) **10**–1391
Buttermilk (info) **3**–282
Casein (info) **3**–333
Condensed Milk (info) **4**–441
Cream (info) **4**–478
Curdling (info) **4**–520
Curds (info) **4**–520
Evaporated Milk (info) **5**–664
Filled Milk (info) **5**–698
Hatted Kit (info) **7**–935
Malted Milk (info) **10**–1295
Melkeringer (Milk Curd) **10**–1370
Milkshake (info) **10**–1391
Pasteurization (info) **13**–1692
Vitalise Milk Shake **20**–2707
Whey (info) **20**–2778

NUTS

Nut (info) **11**–1531

Almond

Almond (info) **1**–18
Almond Apples **1**–20
Almond and Black Cherry Aspic Salad **1**–20
Almond Cherry Cake **1**–20
Almond Cookies **1**–21
Almond Crunchies **1**–21
Almond and Cucumber Salad Dressing **1**–22
Almond Curry Sauce **1**–22
Almond Custard Sauce **1**–23
Almond Essence (info) **1**–23
Almondine Sauce **1**–23
Bâtonnets aux Amandes (Almond Cakes) **1**–129
Blanched Almonds (info) **1**–18
Chocolate Almond Cake **3**–404
Chopped Almonds (info) **1**–18
Crêpes aux Amandes (Almond Crêpes) **4**–496
Crêpes Frangipane (Crêpes with Almond Cream and Chocolate) **4**–498
Devilled Almonds (info) **1**–18
Dutch Almond Biscuits [Cookies] **5**–592
Escravaniya (Almond Sweets [Candies]) **5**–658
Flaked Almonds (info) **1**–18
Frangipane (Almond Filling) **6**–739
Fransk Aeblekage (Apple and Almond Pudding) **6**–740
Galettes Amandines (Iced Almond Biscuits [Cookies]) **6**–784
Galettes Nantaises (Almond Biscuits [Cookies]) **6**–785
Grenadine Almond Flan **7**–876
Ground Almonds (info) **1**–18
Kelaa Almond Pastries **8**–1122
Macaroon (info) **10**–1279
Macaroons **10**–1279
Macaroon and Apricot Whip **10**–1279
Macaroons with Grand Marnier **10**–1280
Nut and Chocolate Cookies **11**–1533
Nut and Chocolate Sauce **11**–1533
Nut Princesses **11**–1537
Nutalie Flan **11**–1538
Pithiviers (Almond Pastry) **14**–1827
Polish Orange and Almond Flan **14**–1855
Praline (info) **15**–1961
Roasted Almonds (info) **1**–18
Salted Almonds **1**–18
Shredded or Slivered Almonds (info) **1**–18
Sugared Almonds **1**–18
Turron (Alomond Sweets [Candies]) **19**–2580
Velouté aux Amandes (Almond Cream Soup) **20**–2661

Areca Nut (info) **1**–61
Beech Nuts (info) **2**–142
Betel Nut (info) **2**–164

Brazil Nut

Brazil Nut (info) **2**–239
Brazil Nut Banana Cake **2**–239
Brazil Nut Cake **2**–240
Brazil Nut and Chive Spread **2**–240
Brazil Nut Piecrust **2**–240
Brazil Nut Stuffing **2**–240
Vegetarian Nut Bake **19**–2657

Cashew (info) **3**–333

Chestnut

Chestnut (info) **3**–373
Bavarois Clermont (Bavarian Cream with Marrons Glacés) **1**–135
Chamonix **3**–350
Chestnut Compôte **3**–374
Chestnut Sauce **3**–374
Chestnut and Sausage Stuffing **3**–374
Chestnut Soup **3**–375
Kirsch and Chestnut Cream **9**–1149
Marrons Braisés (Braised Chestnuts) **10**–1325
Marron Charlotte (Chestnut Mould) **10**–1327
Marrons Glacés (info) **10**–1327
Marrons Montpélier (Chestnut Dessert) **10**–1327
Marron Soufflé (Chestnut Soufflé) **10**–1327
Palissade aux Marrons (Chestnut and Chocolate Dessert) **12**–1663
Ragoût d'Oie aux Marrons (Goose Stew with Chestnuts) **15**–2048
Touraine Chestnut Pudding **19**–2529
Viennese Chestnut Cake **20**–2688

Cobnut (info) **4**–427

Coconut

Coconut (info) **4**–429
Alebele (Coconut Filled Dessert Pancakes) **1**–10
Coconut Barfi **4**–429
Coconut Cookies **4**–430
Coconut Cream Pie **4**–430
Coconut Rice **4**–430
Jam and Coconut Bars **8**–1047
Jamaican Coconut Sauce **8**–1050
Louisiana Coconut Pie **10**–1272
Shakooti Rassa (Lamb Cooked with Coconut) **17**–2293
Trinidad Coconut Ice-Cream **19**–2544
Upside-Down Coconut Cake **19**–2596

General Nut Dishes

Groundnut Stew **7**–883
Iranian Nut Bread **8**–1029
Nuss Schlagsahne (Nut Cream) **11**–1531
Nut and Apple Cream **11**–1531
Nut Apple Jellies [Gelatins] **11**–1531
Nut Clusters **11**–1533
Nut and Date Biscuits [Cookies] **11**–1535
Nut Fritters **11**–1535
Nut Meringues **11**–1535
Nut Roll **11**–1537
Nut Sauce **11**–1538
Nut and Sweet Potato Flan **11**–1538
Vegetarian Nut Roast **19**–2658

Hazelnut

Hazelnut (info) **7**–938
Chocolate Cake with Hazelnuts **3**–406
Filbert (info) **5**–692
Filbert and Chocolate Cake **5**–692
Hazelnut Cream **5**–939
Hazelnut Macaroons **5**–939
Hazelnut Sauce **5**–940
Hazelnut Soufflé **5**–940
Hazelnut Toffee **5**–940
Hazelnut Torte **5**–941
Vegetarian Nut Rissoles **19**–2657

Hickory Nut

Hickory Nut (info) **7**–952
Hickory Loaf **7**–951
Kernel (info) **9**–1125

Macadamia Nut

Macadamia Nut (info) **10**–1275
Macadamia Nut Pie **10**–1275
Nut Brittle (info) **11**–1532

Thematic

Peanut

Peanut (info) **13**–1716
Nut Croquettes **11**–1534
Peanut Biscuits [Cookies] **13**–1716
Peanut Butter **13**–1716
Peanut Butter Biscuits [Cookies] **13**–1717
Peanut Butter and Chicken Stew **13**–1717
Peanut Ice-Cream **13**–1718

Pecan

Pecan (info) **13**–1724
Macaroons with Pecans **10**–1281
Pecan Bars **13**–1724
Pecan Loaf **13**–1725
Pecan Pie **13**–1725
Pecan and Sour Cream Flan **13**–1726
Pecan Torte **13**–1727
Pine Nuts (info) **13**–1812

Pistachio Nut

Pistachio Nut (info) **14**–1824
Pistachio Ice-Cream **14**–1824

Walnut

Walnut (info) **20**–2726
Athenian Walnut Cake **1**–81
Grenadine and Walnut Soufflé **7**–876
Hermits **7**–948
Honey and Walnut Bars **7**–965
Honey and Walnut Pudding **7**–965
Jam, Date and Nut Turnovers **8**–1047
Khalva (Walnuts in Custard) **9**–1126
Nut and Cauliflower Flan **11**–1532
Nut and Cheese Dressing **11**–1533
Nut and Cream Cheese Balls **11**–1534
Nut and Cream Cheese Puffs **11**–1534
Nut and Raisin Stuffing **11**–1537
Nut Waffles **11**–1538
Onions Smothered with Walnuts **12**–1595
Onions in Sweet and Sour Sauce **12**–1597
Pickled Walnuts (info) **13**–1780
Walnut Cauliflower **20**–2726
Walnut, Cheese and Artichoke Heart Salad **20**–2728
Walnut and Cherry Buns **20**–2728
Walnut and Chicken Omelet **20**–2729
Walnut and Coffee Biscuits [Cookies] **20**–2730
Walnut and Coffee Fudge **20**–2730
Walnut and Cream Cheese Biscuits [Cookies] **20**–2731
Walnut Fruit Bread **20**–2732
Walnut Fudge Cake **20**–2732
Walnut Gingerbread **20**–2734
Walnut and Honey Sweets [Candies] **20**–2734
Walnut and Lamb Bake **20**–2734
Walnut and Liver Stuffing **20**–2734
Walnut Oil (info) **20**–2735
Walnut Pastry **20**–2735
Walnut and Rice Salad **20**–2735
Walnut and Rum Caramels **20**–2735
Walnut Soup **20**–2736
Winchester Nut Bread **20**–2821

OFFAL

Offal (info) **12**–1558
Andouillettes (info) **1**–32
Animelle (info) **1**–34

Brains

Brains (info) **2**–227
Brains Baked with Eggs **2**–227
Brains in Butter **2**–227
Brains, Breaded **2**–228
Cervelles Braisées (Braised Calf's Brains) **3**–349
German-Style Calves' Brains **6**–819
Kalbshirn in Muscheln (Calves' Brain Purée in Scallop Shells) **8**–1098
Kidney Beans and Brains in Spanish Sauce **9**–1132

Calves' Feet

Zampa di Vitello alla Toscana (Calves' Feet Tuscan-Style) **21**–2974

Caul (info) **3**–339
Chitterlings (info) **3**–404

General Offal Dishes

Brawn **2**–238
Faggots **5**–666
Haggis (info) **7**–905

Heart

Heart (info) **7**–941
Heart with Fruit Stuffing **7**–942
Hearts Stewed in Wine **7**–942
Ox Heart Stew **12**–1635

Kidney

Kidney (info) **9**–1134
Gurda Khorma (Curried Kidneys) **7**–897
Kidney and Bacon Snacks **9**–1134
Kidney and Bacon with Wine **9**–1135
Kidneys in Butter **9**–1136
Kidney Casserole **9**–1136
Kidneys Fried with Chillis **9**–1136
Kidneys in Marsala **9**–1136
Kidney and Mushroom Croûtes **9**–1136
Kidneys in Mustard Sauce **9**–1138
Kidney Ragoût **9**–1138
Kidneys with Savoury Stuffing **9**–1138
Kidneys with Sesame Sauce **9**–1138
Kidneys in Sherry **9**–1139
Kidney in Sour Cream **9**–1140
Kidneys with Sweetcorn **9**–1140
Kidneys in Their Overcoats **9**–1140
Kidney in White Wine **9**–1141
Njursaute (Swedish Sautéed Kidneys) **11**–1502
Nyrer med Karbonadepølser og Røraeg (Kidneys with Sausages and Scrambled Eggs) **11**–1540
Omelette aux Rognons (Kidney Omelet) **14**–1885
Rassolnik (Russian Kidney and Cucumber Soup) **15**–2066
Riñones al Jerez (Kidneys in Sherry Sauce) **16**–2126
Rognons à la Créole (Lambs' Kidneys Creole) **16**–2153
Rognons Sautés et Flambés (Lambs' Kidneys Sautéed and Flambéed) **16**–2153
Rognons Sautés aux Nouilles (Kidneys with Noodles) **16**–2153
Run Tsa Chin Kan (Plain Deep-Fried Liver and Kidneys) **16**–2187
Sautéed Kidneys with Chipolatas and Wine **17**–2259
Steak and Kidney Pie **18**–2404
Suet (info) **18**–2437
Veal Kidneys Braised in Port **19**–2625
Veal Kidneys with French Beans **19**–2625
Veal Kidneys with Gin **19**–2626
Veal Kidneys in Lemon Sauce **19**–2626
Veal Kidney Pasties **19**–2626
Wecksnappspiess (Ham and Kidney Kebabs) **20**–2749
Wrekin Spiced Kidneys **21**–2872
Zippy Savoury Scramble **22**–3000

Lights (info) **9**–1237

Liver

Liver (info) **9**–1246
Arnavut Cigeri (Lamb's Liver with Peppers) **1**–62
Bacon and Liver Rolls **1**–103
Calf's Liver (info) **3**–300
Calf's Liver with Apples and Onion Rings **3**–300
Calf's Liver with Mustard and Cream Sauce **3**–300
Calf's Liver Sauté **3**–301
Chicken Livers in Aspic **3**–396
Chicken Livers with Ham and Sherry **3**–396
Chicken Liver Pâté **3**–397
Chicken Liver Risotto (Chicken Liver Cooked with Mushrooms and Rice) **3**–398
Chicken Livers with Sweet and Sour Sauce **3**–398
Chicken Livers with Water Chestnuts **3**–398
Chicken Livers in Wine **3**–398
Creamed Chicken Livers **4**–486
Crêpes Fourrées Gratinées (Crêpes Stuffed with Chicken Livers and Mushrooms in a Creamy Sauce) **4**–496
Devilled Calf's Liver **4**–558
Eggs Baked with Chicken Livers and Mushrooms **5**–612
Fegatini di Pollo alla Salvia (Chicken Livers with Bacon and Sage) **5**–680
Fegato alla Veneziana (Liver with Onions) **5**–680
Fegato di Vitello alla Parmigiana (Calf's Liver with Parmesan Cheese) **5**–680
Fegato di Vitello al Pomodoro (Calf's Liver with Tomatoes, Mushrooms and Onions) **5**–680
Fegato di Vitello con Vino (Calf's Liver with Wine) **5**–681
Flan Chavette (Chicken Livers, Mushrooms and Scrambled Egg Flan) **6**–721
Foie de Porc à l'Espagnole (Pig's Liver with Tomatoes and Onion) **6**–730
Fritters Filled with Chicken Livers and Mushrooms **6**–761
Goose Liver Pilaf **7**–848
Hot Pot of Liver, Bacon and Apple **7**–974
Incanestrato Cheese with Chicken Livers and Noodles **8**–1020
Iscas (Portuguese Marinated Liver with Red Wine Sauce) **8**–1038
Kalbsleber mit Sahne (Calf's Liver with Cream Sauce) **8**–1099
Kasha and Liver Bake **8**–1112
Lamb's Liver with Cauliflower **9**–1202
Lamb's Liver with Tomato Sauce **9**–1202
Leverpostej (Liver Pâté) **9**–1235
Liver with Bacon **9**–1246
Liver Casserole **9**–1246
Liver Hors d'Oeuvre **9**–1247
Liver Italian-Style **9**–1247
Liver Mousse **9**–1248
Liver and Mushroom Omelet **9**–1249
Liver with Olives and Mushrooms **9**–1249
Liver and Olive Pâté **9**–1249
Liver and Oysters **9**–1250
Liver Pâté I **9**–1250
Liver Pâté II **9**–1251
Liver Pie **9**–1251
Liver Sausage and Egg Spread **9**–1251
Liver Stuffing **9**–1252
Liver in White Wine **9**–1252
Moroccan Liver Kebabs **11**–1422
Pakistani Spiced Liver **12**–1662
Pâté de Foie Gras (info) **13**–1701
Plön Strudel (German Liver Strudel) **14**–1846
Quenelles de Foie Gras (Liver Pâté Quenelles) **15**–2015
Run Tsa Chin Kan (Plain Deep-Fried Liver and Kidney) **16**–2187
Sautéed Liver **17**–2259
Sweet and Sour Liver **18**–2457
Tiroler Kalbsleber (Tyrolian-Style Calf's Liver) **18**–2503
Walnut and Liver Stuffing **20**–2734
Wienerleber (Viennese Calf's Liver) **20**–2804
Yiddish Chopped Liver with Green Peppers **21**–2923
Yu-Tsin Liver Pot Roast **21**–2951
Zubov Calf's Liver Stroganov **22**–3025
Zuidhorn Liver and Rice **22**–3044
Zujar Chicken Liver Casserole **22**–3044

Ox Palate

Ox Palate (info) **12**–1635
Ox Palate Fricassée **12**–1636
Ox Palate Fritters **12**–1637

Oxtail

Oxtail (*info*) **12**–1640
Braised Oxtail **2**–230
Coda di Bue Con Sedano (Braised Oxtail with Celery) **4**–432
Hochepot (Oxtail Stew) **7**–954
Oxtail, Braised **12**–1640
Oxtail Casserole **12**–1640
Oxtail, Grilled [Broiled] **12**–1642
Oxtail Ragoût **12**–1642
Oxtail Soup I **12**–1643
Oxtail Soup II **12**–1645
Queue de Boeuf au Vin (Oxtail and Wine Stew) **15**–2021
Zossen Oxtail **22**–3018

Pig's Head (*info*) **13**–1792

Pig's Trotters

Pig's Trotters (*info*) **13**–1792
Pig's Trotters with Breadcrumbs **13**–1792

Pluck (*info*) **14**–1846

Sweetbread

Sweetbread (*info*) **18**–2449
Creamed Sweetbreads **4**–487
Ris de Veau au Beurre Noir (Sweetbreads in Brown Butter Sauce) **16**–2127
Ris de Veau au Coulis de Tomates Provençale (Sweetbreads with Herb-Flavoured Tomato Sauce) **16**–2127
Ris de Veau au Fromage (Sweetbreads with Cheese Sauce) **16**–2128
Ris de Veau aux Pâtes (Sweetbreads with Pasta) **16**–2129
Sweetbreads Braised with Mushrooms and Cream **18**–2450
Sweetbreads Chinese-Style **18**–2450
Vol-au-Vent de Ris de Veau (Puff Pastry Case Filled with Sweetbreads) **20**–2720

Tongue

Tongue (*info*) **18**–2520
Kalbszunge mit Pilzen (Calf's Tongue Slices with Mushroom Sauce) **8**–1099
Lamb's Tongues in Red Wine **9**–1204
Langue de Boeuf Braisée (Braised Beef Tongue) **9**–1206
Ochsenzunge mit Madeira Sosse (Calf's Tongue with Madeira Sauce) **12**–1548
Ox Tongue (*info*) **12**–1637
Ox Tongue Braised with Bacon **12**–1637
Ox Tongue with Devil Sauce **12**–1638
Ox Tongue with Horseradish Sauce **12**–1638
Ox Tongue with Hot Raisin Sauce **12**–1638
Potted Tongue **12**–1936
Salmagundy **16**–2214
Spiced Ox Tongue **17**–2380
Tongue with Cherry Sauce **18**–2520
Tongue Salad **19**–2521
Tongue and Vegetable Aspic **19**–2521
Veal and Tongue Pies **19**–2637

Tripe

Tripe (*info*) **19**–2546
Callos Vizcainos (Tripe in Wine Sauce) **3**–301
Gras Double Provençale (Tripe in White Wine) **7**–864
Philadelphia Pepper Pot **13**–1772
Tripe and Beans **19**–2546
Tripe and Onions **19**–2546
Tripe and Tomato Casserole **19**–2548

Umbles (*info*) **19**–2590

PANCAKES AND CREPES— SAVOURY

Crêpe (*info*) **4**–494
Pancake (*info*) **12**–1668
Pancakes **12**–1668
Blinis (Russian Pancakes) **2**–186
Boxty (Irish Pancakes) **2**–225
Crêpe Batter (Savoury) **4**–494
Crêpes d'Epinards (Spinach Crêpes) **4**–496
Crêpes Fourrées Gratinées (Crêpes Stuffed with Chicken Livers and Mushrooms in a Creamy Sauce) **4**–496
Crêpes aux Fruits de Mer (Seafood Crêpes) **4**–498
Crêpes Suisses (Chicken, Ham and Mushroom Crêpes) **4**–500
Enchiladas (Mexican Stuffed Pancakes with Tomato Sauce) **5**–645
Gevulde Pannekoek (Dutch Meat Pancake) **6**–822
Käsepfannkuchen (Cheese Pancakes) **8**–1111
Latkes (Potato Pancake) **9**–1213
Mozzarella Crespoltini (Cheese and Spinach Crêpes) **11**–1441
Mushroom and Ham Crêpes **11**–1452
Nalesniki (Crêpes Stuffed with Cheese) **11**–1468
Oatmeal Pancakes **12**–1545
Pancakes with Brie Topping **13**–1669
Rolled Crêpes Stuffed with Bean Sprouts **16**–2157
Shrimp and Cress-Stuffed Crêpes **17**–2311
Spinach-Stuffed Crêpes **18**–2389
Takhing Pancakes with Pork Filling **18**–2468
Winter Fish Crêpes **21**–2851
Yorkshire Pancakes **21**–2938
Zouzou's Crêpes **22**–3020
Zucchini con Frittelle (Courgette Pancakes) **22**–3032

PANCAKES AND CREPES— SWEET

Crêpe (*info*) **4**–494
Pancake (*info*) **12**–1668
Alebele (Coconut-Filled Pancakes) **1**–10
Apple-Filled Pancakes **1**–45
Crêpe Batter (Sweet) **4**–494
Crêpes aux Amandes (Almond Crêpes) **4**–496
Crêpes à la Confiture (Jam Crêpes) **4**–496
Crêpes Frangipane (Crêpes with Almond Cream and Chocolate) **4**–498
Crêpes aux Fruits (Fruit Crêpes) **4**–498
Crêpes à l'Orange (Orange Crêpes) **4**–499
Crêpes Suzettes (Crêpes Flamed with Orange Liqueur) **4**–501
Flenjes (Dutch Crêpes) **6**–725
Ginger and Banana Crêpes **6**–830
Hungarian Layered Crêpes **8**–991
Ice-Cream Crêpes **8**–1005
Jelly Crêpes **8**–1072
Kaiserschmarrn (Emperor's Pancakes) **8**–1096
Kirschpfannkuchen (Cherry-Filled Crêpes) **9**–1150
Maine Pancakes **10**–1289
Meringue Pancakes **10**–1381
Orange Soufflé-Filled Crêpes **12**–1617
Palacsinken (Jam and Sour Cream Crêpes) **12**–1663
Pancakes with Blueberries **12**–1669
Pancakes with Maple Syrup **12**–1670
Plum-Stuffed Crêpes **14**–1848
Rolled Crêpes Stuffed with Bananas **16**–2156
Yeast Buckwheat Pancakes with Blueberries and Sour Cream **21**–2916

PASTA

Pasta (*info*) **13**–1690
Ashe Reshte (Noodle Soup) **1**–74
Bolognese Sauce (Italian Meat and Vegetable Pasta Sauce) **2**–206
Cannelloni (Italian Pasta) **3**–312
Cannelloni con Pollo e Prosciutto (Italian Pasta Filled with Chicken and Prosciutto) **3**–312
Cannelloni di Manzo e Spinace (Italian Pasta Filled with a Savoury Meat and Spinach Mixture Baked in Tomato and Cream Sauces) **3**–313
Cappelletti in Brodo (Stuffed Pasta in Broth) **3**–319
Coquilettes Farcies (Stuffed Pasta) **4**–447
Crusty Noodles **4**–514
Egg Noodles **5**–622
Egg Noodles Baked with Spinach **5**–622
Egg Noodles with Creamy Cheese Sauce **5**–623
Egg Noodles with Pork Sauce **5**–623
Farfalle (*info*) **5**–676
Fettuccine Alfredo (Fettuccine Noodles with Cheese and Cream) **5**–686
Fettuccine alla Romana (Fettucine Noodles with Tomato Sauce) **5**–687
Fox Noodles **6**–737
Fusilli Noodles with Tomatoes and Cheese **6**–777
Gnocchi (*info*) **7**–841
Gnocchi al Forno Napoletana (Baked Dumplings with Tomato Sauce) **7**–841
Gnocchi di Patate (Potato Dumplings) **7**–842
Gnocchi alla Romana (Dumplings Roman-Style) **7**–842
Gnocchi Verdi (Spinach Dumplings) **7**–842
Incanestrato Cheese with Chicken Livers and Noodles **8**–1020
Jewish Noodles **8**–1076
Käsepätzle (Egg Noodles with Cheese) **8**–1112
Kolduny Litewskie (Lithuanian Meat-Filled Pockets) **9**–1165
Kreplach (Jewish Stuffed Dumplings) **9**–1174
Lasagne (*info*) **9**–1210
Lasagne I **9**–1212
Lasagne II **9**–1212
Lasagne III **9**–1213
Macaroni Cheese **10**–1276
Macaroni and Herring Salad **10**–1276
Macaroni Neapolitan-Style **10**–1277
Macaroni with Raisins and Apricots **10**–1278
Macaroni and Ricotta Pudding **10**–1278
Manicotti with Ricotta Stuffing **10**–1303
Mein I: Chow Mein (Fried Noodles) **10**–1368
Mein II: Hui Mein (Noodles in Sauce or Gravy) **10**–1369
Mein III: Tan Mein (Soup Noodles) **10**–1369
Mein IV: Cha Chiang Mein (Noodles in Peking Meat Sauce with Shredded Vegetables) **10**–1369
Mexican Chilli Spaghetti **10**–1386
Noodles (*info*) **11**–1510
Noodles with Brown Butter **11**–1510
Noodles with Ham **11**–1510
Noodles with Mushrooms **11**–1512
Noodle Pudding with Apples **11**–1512
Nouilles au Gratin (Noodles with Breadcrumbs and Cheese) **11**–1524
Nouilles à la Lyonnaise (Noodles with Onions) **11**–1524
Nudel mit Kase (Noodle and Cheese Ring) **11**–1526
Paglia e Fieno (Pasta with Veal and Mushrooms) **12**–1656
Perciatelli ai Piselli (Pasta with Green Pea Sauce) **13**–1749
Pirogen (Polish Ravioli) **14**–1822
Quadrettini con Prosciutto (Pasta with Ham) **15**–1995
Ravioli (Italian Filled Pasta) **15**–2068
Ravioli di Manzo e Spinace (Italian Pasta Filled with Veal and Spinach with Tomato Sauce) **15**–2070
Ravioli Piedmontese (Italian Pasta Filled with Beef and Tomatoes) **15**–2072
Ravioli di Rapallo (Italian Pasta Filled with Cheese, Spinach and Egg with Walnut Sauce) **15**–2073
Romano Noodles **16**–2160
Schinken mit Makkaroni (Ham and Macaroni Casserole) **17**–2273
Spaghetti (*info*) **17**–2368

Thematic

Spaghetti con Aglio, Olio e Peperoncino
(Spaghetti with Garlic, Olive Oil and Chillis)
17–2368
Spaghetti all'Amatriciana (Spaghetti with
Bacon in Tomato Sauce) **17**–2368
Spaghetti with Butter and Cheese **17**–2368
Spaghetti alla Carbonara (Spaghetti with Bacon
and Egg Sauce) **17**–2368
Spaghetti with Fennel Sauce **17**–2369
Spaghetti with Meatballs and Tomato Sauce
17–2369
Spaghetti con Salsa Verde (Spaghetti with
Green Sauce) **17**–2369
Spaghetti alle Vongole (Spaghetti with Clam
Sauce) **17**–2370
Tagliarini con Fegatini (Thin Pasta with
Chicken Livers) **18**–2464
Tagliatelle (info) **18**–2465
Tagliatelle con Prosciutto (Ribbon Pasta with
Ham) **18**–2465
Tagliatelle Verde with Bacon and Tomatoes
18–2465
Tagliatelle Verde con Salsa di Tonno (Green
Ribbon Pasta in Tuna Fish Sauce) **18**–2466
Tortellini (Pasta Rings Filled with Chicken)
19–2524
Vermicelli (info) **20**–2678
Vermicelli Soup **20**–2678
Vermicelli and Vegetables Chinese-Style
20–2678
Wienerwurst and Noodle Casserole **20**–2806
Winter Warmer **21**–2853
Wontons (info) **21**–2858
Wonton Dough **21**–2858
Wontons with Pork **21**–2859
Wontons with Pork and Prawns or Shrimps
21–2859
Yangchow Noodles **21**–2907
Zapponetta Pasta Shells with Mussels **21**–2981
Zingari Gipsy-Style Spaghettini Omelet
22–2999
Zite with Italian Sausage Sauce **22**–3001
Zite with Meatballs and Tomato Mushroom
Sauce **22**–3002
Zite with Port **22**–3002
Zogno Vegetarian Pasta **22**–3008
Zullah's Pasta, Sausage and Bean Salad
22–3049
Zwingle Spaghetti with Crabmeat **22**–3079

PASTRY

Pastry (info) **13**–1694
Biscuit Crust (Sweet Pastry) **2**–175
Brazil Nut Piecrust **2**–240
Choux Pastry **3**–418
Croustades **4**–507
Crumb Flan Crust **4**–512
Crumble (info) **4**–512
Flan Case made with Rich Shortcrust Pastry
6–720
Flan Case made with Shortcrust Pastry **6**–720
Gougère (Cheese Pastry) **7**–857
Herb Pastry **7**–946
Hot Water Crust Pastry **7**–977
Mille-feuille (info) **10**–1392
Pastry Glazes (info) **13**–1698
Pâte (info) **13**–1698
Pâte à Pâté (Rich French Pastry) **13**–1702
Pâte Sucrée (Sweet French Pastry) **13**–1702
Patty (info) **13**–1704
Puff Pastry **15**–1984
Rough Puff Pastry **16**–2172
Shortcrust Pastry I **17**–2306
Shortcrust Pastry II **17**–2307
Strudel Pastry **18**–2425
Suetcrust Pastry **18**–2437
Turnover (info) **19**–2580
Vol-au-Vent (info) **20**–2717
Vol-au-Vent (Puff Pastry Case) **20**–2717
Walnut Pastry **20**–2735

Pastries—Savoury

Borek (info) **2**–211
Bouchées (info) **2**–218
Bouchées aux Fruits de Mer (Puff Pastry Cases
Filled with Mussels and Prawns) **2**–218
Bouchées au Jambon (Puff Pastry Cases with
Ham) **2**–219
Bouchées Newburg (Puff Pastry Cases Filled
with Lobster) **2**–219
Choux Puffs **3**–418
Cornish Pasties **4**–456
Empanadas (Meat-Filled Pasties) **5**–644
Napoleon (info) **11**–1472
Napoleon au Fromage Blanc (Puff Pastry Layers
with Cream Cheese Filling) **11**–1472
Nariel Samosas (Coconut Turnovers) **11**–1477
Petits Chaussons au Roquefort (Pastry
Turnovers with Roquefort Cheese) **13**–1758
Petits Pâtés à la Russe (Salmon and
Mushroom Patties) **13**–1762
Picnic Patties **13**–1781
Poppadum (info) **14**–1873
Profiteroles (info) **15**–1976
Rissoles de Camarâo (Portuguese Shrimp
Rissoles) **16**–2132
Samosas (Stuffed Savoury Pastries) **16**–2235
Sausage Rolls **17**–2256
Veal Kidney Pasties **19**–2626
Vol-au-Vent d'Aubergines (Puff Pastry Case
Filled with Aubergines [Eggplants])
20–2717
Vol-au-Vent d'Eté (Puff Pastry Case Filled with
Lettuce and Egg) **20**–2718
Vol-au-Vent de Pétoncles (Puff Pastry Case
Filled with Scallops) **20**–2719
Vol-au-Vent de Poulet et Champignons (Puff
Pastry Case Filled with Chicken and
Mushrooms) **20**–2719
Vol-au-Vent de Ris de Veau (Puff Pastry Case
Filled with Sweetbreads) **20**–2720
Yakutsk Choux Puffs **21**–2904

Pastries—Sweet

Alexander Torte (Iced Raspberry-Filled
Pastry Cakes) **1**–11
Apple Turnovers **1**–51
Buchteln (Viennese Jam Puffs) **2**–278
Cenci (Deep-Fried Sweet Crisp Pastries) **3**–347
Choux Puffs **3**–418
Cornet (info) **4**–454
Cornets de Crème (Cream Horns) **4**–454
Cream Puffs **4**–485
Danish Pastries **4**–530
Danish Pastries with Almond Filling **4**–531
Danish Pastries with Cinnamon Sugar Filling
4–531
Danish Pastries with Pineapple and Banana
Filling **4**–531
Dartois (Flaky Pastry with Almond Cream)
4–536
Eccles Cakes **5**–602
Eclairs (info) **5**–602
Farfallette Dolci (Sweet Pastry Bows or
Butterflies) **5**–676
Fyllda Strutar (Pastry Cones with Cream and
Fruit) **6**–778
Gâteau Mille-feuille (Layers of Puff Pastry with
Crème Chantilly and Jam) **6**–804
Imps **8**–1019
Jam, Date and Nut Turnovers **8**–1047
Jam Triangles **8**–1049
Käsestrudel (Cheese Strudel) **8**–1110
Kelaa Almond Pastries **9**–1122
Linser (Custard Tartlets) **9**–1240
Mattersburg Almond Roll **10**–1342
Mint Pastries **11**–1404
Mirlitons (Macaroon-Filled Tartlets) **11**–1405
Napoleon (info) **11**–1472
Nariel Samosas (Coconut Turnovers) **11**–1477
Nusspastete (German Nut Pastry Roll) **11**–1529
Paris-Brest (Choux Pastry Ring Filled with
Crème Pâtissière) **12**–1677
Pâtisserie (info) **13**–1703

Peach Puffs **13**–1714
Pecan Bars **13**–1724
Pithiviers (Almond Pastry) **14**–1827
Profiteroles (info) **15**–1976
Profiteroles with Ice-Cream and Chocolate
15–1976
Quesadillas (Mexican Cheese Squares) **15**–2018
Quince and Apple Turnovers **15**–2030
Recruitment Apple Pastries **15**–2074
Strudel Fruit Rolls **18**–2427
Syrian Walnut and Orange Pastries **18**–2461
Windsor Pastries **20**–2824

PATE AND TERRINE

Pâté (info) **13**–1698
Terrine (info) **18**–2497
Chicken Liver Pâté **3**–397
Cod's Roe Pâté **4**–434
Game Pâté **6**–790
Goose Pâté **7**–849
Kipper Pâté **9**–1146
Leverpostej (Liver Pâté) **9**–1235
Liver and Olive Pâté **9**–1249
Liver Pâté I **9**–1250
Liver Pâté II **9**–1251
Partridge Terrine **13**–1687
Pâté en Croûte I (Stuffed Boned Duck
Wrapped in Pastry) **13**–1698
Pâté en Croûte II (Veal and Pork Pâté Wrapped
in Pastry) **13**–1700
Pâté de Fois Gras (info) **13**–1701
Pheasant Pâté, Country-Style **13**–1770
Potted Hare **14**–1935
Potted Herrings **14**–1935
Potted Tongue **14**–1936
Smoked Trout Pâté **17**–2333
Taramasalata (Cod's Roe Paste) **18**–2479
Tarragon Pâté **18**–2480
Terrine de Canard (Terrine of Duck) **18**–2497
Terrine Maison (Chicken and Egg Terrine)
18–2497
Toulouse Spiced Pâté **19**–2527
Uppingham Pâté **19**–2593
Veal Pâté with Calf's Brains **19**–2632
Venison Pâté **20**–2674
Vintage Pâté **20**–2703
Zermatt Sardine Pâté **21**–2992

PIES—SAVOURY

Pie (info) **13**–1783
Bacon and Egg Pie **1**–102
Beef and Potato Pie **2**–155
Bobotie (Spicy Minced [Ground] Beef Pie)
2–190
Cheese and Onion Pie **3**–366
Chicken and Leek Pie **3**–382
Chicken Tamale Pie **3**–395
Cornish Pasties **4**–456
Dill Piroshki (Little Pies Filled with Beef,
Onion and Dill) **5**–565
Empanadas (Meat-Filled Pasties) **5**–644
Fish and Potato Pie **6**–713
Game Pie **6**–790
Goose Pie **7**–849
Gratin aux Fruits de Mer (Seafood Pie) **7**–865
Huntingdon Fidget Pie **8**–994
Kipper Pie **9**–1147
Korsakov Meat and Potato Pie **9**–1168
Kulebiaz Ryba (Russian Fish Pie) **9**–1178
Kurnic (Russian Chicken Pie) **9**–1183
Languedoc Lamb Pie **9**–1207
Liver Pie **9**–1251
Melton Mowbray Pie **10**–1374
Mushroom Pie **11**–1454
Mutton Pies **11**–1465
Onion Pie **12**–1593
Oyster, Beef, Kidney and Mushroom Pie
12–1648
Parsley and Fish Pie **12**–1680
Partridge Pie **13**–1685
Pastel de Choclo (Meat and Corn Pie) **13**–1692

Pigeon Pie I **13**–1791
Pigeon Pie II **13**–1791
Piroshki (Little Pies) **14**–1823
Pissaladières (Individual Savoury Tartlets) **14**–1824
Plate Pie **14**–1842
Pork Pie **14**–1900
Rabbit Pie **15**–2040
Raised Pie (info) **15**–2054
Rakott Burgonya (Hungarian Potato Pie) **15**–2060
Savoury Artichoke Pie **17**–2263
Sea Pie **17**–2281
Shepherd's Pie I **17**–2298
Shepherd's Pie II **17**–2299
Squab Pie **18**–2398
Stargazey Pie **18**–2400
Steak and Kidney Pie **18**–2404
Talmouses (Savoury Tartlets) **18**–2471
Tomato Pie **18**–2516
Tourte (info) **19**–2533
Tourte aux Champignons (Mushroom and Fish Pie) **19**–2533
Tourte de Porc (French Pork Pie) **19**–2534
Turkey and Walnut Pie **19**–2574
Veal and Ham Pie **19**–2624
Veal, Oyster and Bacon Pie **19**–2631
Veal and Tongue Pies **19**–2637
Vegetable Pie **19**–2648
Venison Pie **20**–2674
Wellington Pie **20**–2757
White Fish Pie **20**–2786
Yorkshire Giblet Pie **21**–2935
Yorkshire Ham Pie **21**–2935
Yummy Meat and Vegetable Pie **21**–2960
Zuidhorn Kipper Pie **22**–3043
Zulla Fish Pie **22**–3051
Zurich Veal and Parsnip Pie **22**–3065

PIES—SWEET

Pie (info) **13**–1783
American Apple Pie **1**–26
Äppelformar (Small Apple Pies) **1**–40
Apple Florentine **1**–46
Apple Pie **1**–48
Banana Cream Pie **1**–111
Blackberry and Apple Pie **2**–180
Black Bottom Pie **2**–182
Brandy Alexander Pie **2**–234
Buttermilk Pie **3**–283
Cherry Pie **3**–371
Chocolate Chiffon Pie **3**–407
Chocolate Cream Pie **3**–409
Coconut Cream Pie **4**–430
Cranberry Pie **4**–477
Date and Apple Pie **4**–538
Deep-Dish Peach Pie **4**–550
Double-Crust Blackcurrant and Apple Pie **5**–573
Eggnog Chiffon Pie **5**–633
Elderberry Pie **5**–640
Gooseberry Pie **7**–852
Gooseberry Steffon **7**–853
Green Grape and Apple Pie **7**–871
Grumble Pie **7**–887
Guava Pie **7**–892
Honey and Cream Cheese Pie **7**–962
Huckleberry Meringue Pie **7**–979
Hungarian Apple Pie **8**–987
Lemon Meringue Pie **9**–1228
Lime Cream Pie **9**–1238
Louisiana Coconut Pie **10**–1272
Macadamia Nut Pie **10**–1275
Maple Cream Pie **10**–1308
Marlborough Apple Pie **10**–1319
Mincemeat Pies **10**–1398
Mocha Cream Pie **11**–1410
Molasses Crumb Pie **11**–1413
Molasses Hazelnut Pie **11**–1413
Mulberry and Apple Pie **11**–1444
Nectarine Pie **11**–1488
October Cobbler **12**–1550
Pandowdy **12**–1671

Peach Cobbler **13**–1712
Pecan Pie **13**–1725
Pumpkin Pie **15**–1986
Rhubarb and Orange Pie **16**–2107
Sauterelle (Green Grasshopper Pie) **17**–2259
Shoofly Pie **17**–2304
Swedish Gooseberry Pie **18**–2447
Tyler's Custard Pie **19**–2583
Vatrushka Pie **19**–2611
Wrighton Pie **21**–2873

PIZZA

Pizza (info) **20**–1828
Neapolitan Pizzas **11**–1484
Olive Pizza **12**–1572
Pepperoni Pizza **13**–1747
Pizza alle Asciughe (Pizza with Anchovies and Tuna) **14**–1828
Pizza with Aubergine [Eggplant] **14**–1830
Pizza Canapés **14**–1831
Pizza Capri (Pizza with Tomatoes, Cheese and Capers) **14**–1832
Pizza ai Funghi (Pizza with Mushrooms) **14**–1833
Pizza al Prosciutto (Pizza with Ham) **14**–1834
Quattrostagione Pizza (Pizza with Four Toppings) **19**–2002

POULTRY

Poultry (info) **14**–1952

Chicken

Chicken (info) **3**–375
Almond Chicken **1**–20
Andalousian Chicken **1**–30
Arroz con Pollo (Chicken with Rice) **1**–65
Avocado Chicken Soup **1**–92
Avocado Chicken Supreme **1**–92
Balkan Chicken Pilaff **1**–108
Barbecued Chicken **1**–117
Bollito Misto (Italian Boiled Beef, Chicken and Sausage) **2**–206
Broiler (info) **2**–269
Brown Chicken Fricassée **2**–270
Brunswick Stew **2**–272
Caldo Tlalpeño (Mexican Chicken and Bean Soup) **3**–298
Canary Island Chicken **3**–308
Canja (Portuguese Chicken Soup with Lemon) **3**–311
Capon (info) **3**–316
Capon, Russian-Style **3**–316
Champagne Chicken **3**–353
Chicken Breasts en Papillote (Chicken Breasts Cooked in a Parcel) **3**–377
Chicken Breasts with Tarragon **3**–377
Chicken Chablis **3**–377
Chicken Chaudfroid **3**–378
Chicken Curry **3**–378
Chicken, English-Style **3**–379
Chicken Florentine (Chicken Breasts with Spinach) **3**–380
Chicken with Ginger **3**–380
Chicken and Ham Paste **3**–381
Chicken with Herbs **3**–381
Chicken Juniper **3**–381
Chicken Kiev **3**–382
Chicken à la King **3**–382
Chicken and Leek Pie **3**–382
Chicken Mayonnaise **3**–384
Chicken Mousse **3**–384
Chicken Paprikash **3**–384
Chicken Parmigiana **3**–384
Chicken Pulao **3**–385
Chicken with Rice and Cherries **3**–387
Chicken Riviera (Chicken Salad with Walnuts, Cherries and Tarragon) **3**–387
Chicken Salad with Avocados and Russian Dressing **3**–388

Chicken Salad with Bean Sprouts and Olives **3**–388
Chicken Salad with Sour Cream Dressing **3**–389
Chicken San Marino (Fried Chicken Breasts with Mushrooms and Mozzarella) **3**–390
Chicken Sauté **3**–390
Chicken Sauté Marengo **3**–390
Chicken in Sherry and Cream **3**–390
Chicken Siena **3**–391
Chicken Soufflé **3**–392
Chicken, Spanish-Style **3**–392
Chicken and Spring Vegetable Soup with Dumplings **3**–393
Chicken Stock **3**–393
Chicken Sultan **3**–393
Chicken in Sweet Red Wine **3**–394
Chicken Tamale Pie **3**–395
Chicken Tetrazzini (Casserole of Chicken and Noodles) **3**–395
Chicken Valentine **3**–396
Chicken Livers in Aspic **3**–396
Chicken Livers with Ham and Sherry **3**–396
Chicken Liver Pâté **3**–397
Chicken Liver Risotto (Chicken Livers Cooked with Mushrooms and Rice) **3**–398
Chicken Livers with Sweet and Sour Sauce **3**–398
Chicken Livers with Water Chestnuts **3**–398
Chicken Livers in Wine **3**–398
Circassian Chicken **3**–424
Cock-a-Leekie **4**–427
Coq au Vin (Chicken Cooked in Red Wine) **4**–444
Coquelets sur Canapés (Small Roast Chickens with Chicken Liver Canapés and Mushroom Garnish) **4**–446
Cream of Chicken Soup I **4**–481
Cream of Chicken Soup II **4**–482
Creamed Chicken **4**–485
Creamed Chicken Livers **4**–486
Creole Chicken **4**–492
Crêpes Suisse (Chicken, Ham and Mushroom Crêpes) **4**–500
Croquettes de Poulet (Chicken Croquettes) **4**–506
Danos Chicken **4**–532
Dansk Hönse Kasserole (Danish Chicken Casserole) **4**–533
Darioles de Volaille (Chicken Moulds) **4**–534
Devilled Chicken **4**–558
Dhansak (Chicken with Lentils and Vegetables) **5**–562
Djeja M'qalia (Chicken with Coriander and Mint) **5**–569
Dopyaza Chicken (Curried Chicken with Onions) **5**–572
Drumsticks Shanghai-Style **5**–578
Edna's Chicken **5**–604
Eggs Baked with Chicken and Tomatoes **5**–612
Eggah with Noodles and Chicken **5**–630
Fegatini di Pollo alla Salvia (Chicken Livers with Bacon and Sage) **5**–680
Foong Yin Mun Sung (Bird's Nest Soup with Chicken Cubes and Mushrooms) **6**–735
Fowl (info) **6**–736
French Roast Chicken **6**–749
Fricassée (info) **6**–752
Fricassée de Poulet (Chicken, Tomato and Mushroom Fricassée) **6**–752
Fritters Filled with Chicken Livers and Mushrooms **6**–761
Fruit and Chicken Salad **6**–767
Gallimaufry (info) **6**–787
Goan Vinegar Curry **7**–843
Grahamstown Chicken **7**–859
Grilled [Broiled] Chicken with Soy Sauce **7**–881
Hawaiian Chicken **7**–936
Hindle Wakes **7**–953
Honeyed Chicken **7**–967
Ho Tao Chi Tin (Quick Fried Chicken Cubes with Walnuts) **7**–972
Hung Shao Chi (Red-Cooked Chicken) **8**–985
Hunter's Stew **8**–993
Hyères Chicken **8**–999

Thematic

Indonesian Chicken Satay 8–1022
Jambalaya 8–1054
Jege Zeitoon (Chicken with Olives) 8–1062
Jellied Chicken Breasts 8–1065
Kaeng Chud Kai Hed (Chicken and Mushroom Soup) 8–1093
Kapaun mit Champignons und Spek (Capon with Mushrooms and Bacon) 8–1105
Karani (Russian Chicken Blinis) 8–1106
Kawasaki Chicken (Chicken in Soy Sauce and Sake) 8–1117
Khoresh Holu (Chicken with Peach Sauce) 9–1130
Knishes with Meat and Potato Filling 9–1158
Kotlety Pozharskie (Russian Chicken Patties) 9–1169
Kotopoulo Kapama (Chicken with Tomato and Cinnamon Sauce) 9–1169
Kromeski (info) 9–1174
Kromeski with Chicken and Ham 9–1175
Kuo Tieh Chi (Egg-Braised Sliced Chicken) 9–1181
Kurnic (Russian Chicken Pie) 9–1183
Kyllinger med Rejer og Asparges (Chicken with Prawns and Asparagus) 9–1185
Lin-Moun Chi (Lemon Chicken) 9–1240
Louisiana Snack 10–1272
Madras Chicken Curry 10–1286
Malaysian Grilled [Broiled] Chicken 10–1292
Maluwe Poulet (West African Chicken) 10–1296
Mango Chicken 10–1300
Maraccas Beach Pilau 10–1310
Marbled Chicken 10–1312
Marsala and Clove Chicken 10–1330
Maryland Chicken 10–1336
Matzo Chicken and Dill Casserole 10–1344
Mediterranean Chicken 10–1363
Mexican Chicken with Fruit 10–1384
Minced [Ground] Chicken 10–1395
Moroccan Chicken 11–1421
Mozzarella Chicken 11–1441
Murg Bhuna (Fried Chicken) 11–1449
Murg Kashmiri (Chicken with Almonds and Raisins) 11–1450
Murgi Dahi (Chicken Cooked in Yogurt) 11–1450
Murray Chicken 11–1451
Nabobeep Salad 11–1466
Nasi Goreng (Indonesian Rice) 11–1477
Nigerian Jollof Rice 11–1501
Nun's Salad 11–1527
Orange Chicken with Rosemary 12–1603
Orientalisk Kyckling (Oriental Fried Chicken) 12–1626
Paella (Spanish Rice with Chicken and Seafood) 12–1654
Pai Chiu Tung Chi (Long-Simmered Chicken in White Wine) 12–1656
Pai Chou Chi (White Cooked Chicken) 12–1658
Pakistani Chicken Tikka (Spicy Chicken Kebabs) 12–1661
Pakistani Pulau (Curried Rice with Chicken) 12–1661
Peanut Butter and Chicken Stew 13–1717
Penang Chicken 13–1734
Pennsylvania Dutch Chicken Corn Soup 13–1735
Picardy Rice 13–1774
Pickled Chicken 13–1778
Picnic Patties 13–1781
Picnic Salad 13–1783
Pilaff with Chicken Liver Ragoût 13–1794
Pilaff with Peppers and Chicken 13–1796
Pimiento Chicken 13–1798
Pollo alla Bolognese (Chicken Breasts with Ham and Cheese) 14–1856
Pollo alla Cacciatora (Chicken with Wine, Tomatoes and Mushrooms) 14–1856
Pollo alla Diavola (Grilled [Broiled] Chicken with Herbs) 14–1858
Pollo en Pepitoria (Chicken with Garlic and Almonds) 14–1858
Poona Pilaff 14–1872

Pot au Feu à la Béarnaise (Chicken and Vegetables in Broth) 14–1910
Poulet Brandade (Chicken with Wine and Brandy) 14–1942
Poulet en Casserole à la Bonne Femme (Casseroled Chicken with Vegetables) 14–1942
Poulet aux Cerises (Chicken in Cherry Sauce) 14–1942
Poulet aux Champignons (Chicken and Mushrooms) 14–1942
Poulet au Brocoli (Poached Chicken with Broccoli) 14–1943
Poulet aux Crevettes (Chicken with Prawns or Shrimps and Wine) 14–1944
Poulet aux Girolles à la Crème (Chicken with Mushroom and Cream Sauce) 14–1945
Poulet Grillé à la Diable (Grilled [Broiled] Devilled Chicken) 14–1945
Poulet à la Normande (Chicken with Calvados and Apple Sauce) 14–1946
Poulet aux Pêches (Chicken with Peaches and Orange-Flavoured Liqueur) 14–1946
Poulet Rôti aux Abricots (Roast Chicken with Apricots) 14–1946
Poulet Sauté à l'Archiduc (Sautéed Chicken in Madeira-Flavoured Cream Sauce) 14–1948
Poulet Sauté au Basilic (Sautéed Chicken with Basil) 14–1949
Poulet Sauté à la Bordelaise (Sautéed Chicken with Potatoes and Artichoke Hearts) 14–1950
Poulet Sauté Chasseur (Sautéed Chicken in Chasseur Sauce) 14–1950
Poulet Sauté à la Provençale (Sautéed Chicken with Tomatoes and Garlic) 14–1951
Poussin (info) 14–1956
Poussins au Gingembre (Baby Chickens with Ginger) 14–1956
Poussins Sautés au Citron (Baby Chickens Cooked with Butter and Lemon) 14–1957
Prague Chicken 14–1960
Prosciutto and Chicken Rolls 15–1978
Pullet (info) 15–1985
Queen's Flan 15–2009
Quick-Fried Chicken Cubes in White Sauce 15–2027
Ragoût Martiniquais (Chicken and Pork Stew) 15–2048
Rustom's Chicken 16–2192
Sake-Steamed Chicken 16–2209
Salade Bagration (Chicken, Macaroni and Artichoke Heart Salad) 16–2210
Salmagundy 16–2214
Sindhi Chicken 17–2320
Soy Sauce Chicken 17–2364
Spanish Chicken 17–2370
Spiced Chicken with Honey 17–2379
Spicy Chicken Casserole 18–2383
Spiedini (Italian Kebabs) 18–2383
Suprêmes (info) 18–2443
Suprêmes de Volaille Flambés (Flambéed Chicken Breasts) 18–2444
Suprêmes de Volaille au Jambon (Chicken Breasts with Ham) 18–2444
Suprêmes de Volaille Rossini (Chicken Breasts with Pâté) 18–2445
Sweetcorn and Chicken Soup 18–2452
Tabaka (Pressed Poussins, Caucasian-Style) 18–2462
Tagliarini con Fegatini (Thin Pasta with Chicken Livers) 18–2464
Taiyika Chicken 18–2467
Tandoori Murg (Marinated Spiced Chicken) 18–2474
Tarragon Pâté 18–2480
Tarte au Poulet (Chicken Flan) 18–2483
Teriyaki II (Marinated and Baked Chicken) 18–2495
Terrine Maison (Chicken and Egg Terrine) 18–2497
Tomato and Chicken Salad 18–2512
Tortellini (Pasta Rings Filled with Chicken) 19–2524
Trinidad Chicken Pilau 19–2544
Tunisian Chicken Casserole 19–2561

Tushikow Chicken 19–2581
Umabai's Spiced Almond Chicken 19–2588
Venezuelan Chicken 20–2667
Vindaloo with Chicken 20–2695
Virginia Chicken Salad 20–2704
Volaille en Escabèche (Chicken in Lemon Jelly [Gelatin]) 20–2714
Vol-au-Vent de Poulet et Champignons (Puff Pastry Case Filled with Chicken and Mushrooms) 20–2719
Walnut and Chicken Omelet 20–2729
Waterzooi de Poulet (Belgian Chicken Stew) 20–2749
West Indian Chicken Casserole 20–2768
Western Quick-Fried Chicken, Shrimps and Petits Pois 20–2770
Westphalian Chicken 20–2773
White Chicken Curry 20–2782
White Cut Chicken 20–2785
Wienerbackhendl (Viennese Breaded Chicken Pieces) 20–2804
Wild Rice Casserole 20–2810
Winter Poussins with Watercress Stuffing 21–2851
Winter Warmer 21–2853
Wladimir Chicken Breasts 21–2856
Wraby Ginger Chicken 21–2868
Wuchow Chicken Mandarin 21–2874
Wuki Chicken 21–2876
Wunnumminlake Chicken Bouilli 21–2877
Wyoming Chicken Hash 21–2889
Yiddish Chopped Liver with Green Peppers 21–2923
Yogurt Chicken 21–2926
Yogurt, Chicken and Barley Soup 21–2928
Yosenabe (Japanese Chicken and Oyster Fondue) 21–2943
Yu-Lang-Chi (Chinese Chicken and Ham) 21–2948
Yunnan Quick-Fried Prawns or Shrimps on Crackling Rice 21–2962
Yuri's Chicken Puffs 21–2963
Zafran Paella (Spanish Rice with Chicken and Seafood) 21–2969
Zagreb Chicken Casserole 21–2970
Zandar Marinated Poussins 21–2976
Zany Stuffed Drumsticks 21–2978
Zeera Murg (Cumin Chicken) 21–2989
Zinnia's Chicken with Tarragon, Whisky and Cream 22–2999
Zola Chicken 22–3008
Zoller Pumpkin Stew 22–3009
Zoltan's Chicken Breasts 22–3011
Zujar Chicken Liver Casserole 22–3044
Zuppa di Pollo (Chicken Soup) 22–3060
Zuyder Chicken Breasts with Tarragon and Sour Cream 22–3067
Zuzu Spiced Chicken Breasts 22–3067
Zwickle Capon in Pastry 22–3074

Duck

Duck (info) 5–582
Barbecued Duck 1–117
Canard Braisé avec Choucroute (Braised Duck with Sauerkraut) 3–306
Canard Braisé au Chou Rouge (Braised Duck with Red Cabbage) 3–306
Canard à l'Orange (Roast Duck in Orange Sauce) 3–306
Caneton à l'Alsacienne (Roast Duckling with Apple and Sausage Stuffing) 3–311
Caneton aux Cerises (Roast Duckling with Cherries) 3–309
Caneton aux Navets (Braised Duckling with Turnips) 3–310
Dindings Duck 5–567
Duck with Apricot and Sausage Stuffing 5–582
Duck Braised in Red Wine 5–582
Duck Curry 5–582
Duck with Figs 5–584
Duck and Grape Casserole 5–584
Duck Norman-Style 5–584
Duck with Port 5–585
Duck Provençal 5–586

Duck in a Ring **5**–586
Duck Spanish-Style **5**–587
Duckling in Sweet and Sour Sauce **5**–588
Mallard Duck (info) **10**–1294
Orlando Duck **12**–1627
Pâté en Croûte I (Stuffed Boned Duck
    Wrapped in Pastry) **13**–1698
Peking Duck (info) **13**–1731
Quetchuan Duck **15**–2021
Teal (info) **18**–2491
Terrine de Canard (Terrine of Duck) **18**–2497
Vath (Indian Roast Duck) **19**–2610
Wen Welsh Duck **20**–2760
Widdecombe Duck **20**–2803
Yorkshire Giblet Pie **21**–2935
Zuckerman Duck with Olives **22**–3041

Goose

Goose (info) **7**–846
Gaasesteg med Aebler og Svesker (Roast Goose
    with Apples and Prunes) **6**–778
Gänsebraten mit Füllsel (Roast Goose with
    Apple and Nut Stuffing) **6**–795
Goose with Apricot and Veal Stuffing **7**–846
Goose Casserole **7**–847
Goose Liver Pilaf **7**–848
Goose Pâté **7**–849
Goose Pie **7**–849
Goose Soup **7**–850
Hymettus Goose (Roast Goose with Pork and
    Olive Stuffing Glazed with Honey) **8**–999
Michaelmas Goose **10**–1388
Oca Arrosta Ripiena (Stuffed Roast Goose)
    12–1548
Oie Rôtie à l'Anglaise (Roast Goose Stuffed with
    Onion and Sage) **12**–1560
Oie Rôtie Farcie (Roast Goose with Lemon,
    Apple and Parsley Stuffing) **12**–1561
Oie Rôtie aux Marrons (Roast Goose with
    Chestnut Stuffing) **12**–1562
Oie Rôtie aux Pruneaux et Foie Gras (Roast
    Goose Stuffed with Prunes and Goose Liver
    Pâté) **12**–1562
Pecaná Husa se Zelim (Roast Goose with
    Sauerkraut Stuffing) **13**–1727
Ragoût d'Oie aux Marrons (Goose Stew with
    Chestnuts) **15**–2048
Yorkshire Giblet Pie **21**–2935

Turkey

Turkey (info) **19**–2566
Devilled Turkey Drumsticks **5**–561
Dinde aux Marrons (Turkey with Chestnuts)
    5–566
Pineapple and Turkey Salad **13**–1811
Raisin and Turkey Salad **15**–2054
Turkey American-Style **19**–2567
Turkey with Apricot Stuffing **19**–2568
Turkey with Cherry Stuffing **19**–2568
Turkey Coronation **19**–2571
Turkey with Ham and Mushrooms **19**–2571
Turkey with Ham Stuffing **19**–2571
Turkey, Lettuce and Tomato Sandwiches
    19–2572
Turkey Meat Mould **19**–2573
Turkey with Orange Sauce **19**–2573
Turkey with Veal and Rice Stuffing **19**–2574
Turkey and Walnut Pie **19**–2574
Yankee Turkey Roast **21**–2909
Yorkshire Giblet Pie **21**–2935
Zwolle Orange Turkey **22**–3079

RICE

Rice (info) **16**–2110
Azerbaijan Pilaff **1**–95
Baghali Polo (Lamb with Rice and Dill) **1**–105
Balkan Chicken Pilaff **1**–108
Biryani (Spiced Rice with Lamb) **2**–174
Brazilian Rice **2**–239
Chicken Pulao **3**–385
Chicken with Rice and Cherries **3**–387

Chicken Liver Risotto (Chicken Livers Cooked
    with Mushrooms and Rice) **3**–398
Chinese Fried Rice **3**–402
Coconut Rice **4**–430
Daurade au Riz (Bream [Porgy] with Rice)
    4–550
Feijoada (Brazilian Black Beans and Smoked
    Meats) **5**–683
Fried Rice, Chinese-Style **6**–757
Gamberi con Riso (Rice with Shrimps) **6**–787
Geelrys (Yellow Rice) **6**–811
Goose Liver Pilaf **7**–848
Green Rice **7**–874
Ham and Fried Rice **7**–916
Ham and Rice Salad **7**–918
Hawaiian Chicken **7**–936
Hoppin' John **7**–969
Indonesian Fried Rice **8**–1023
Jambalaya **8**–1054
Kadu Polo (Pumpkin and Lamb Patties with
    Rice) **8**–1092
Kalbsreisfleisch (Veal and Rice Casserole)
    8–1099
Kedgeree **9**–1121
Kedgeree of Salmon **9**–1121
Khichri (Rice with Lentils) **9**–1128
Kipper Kedgeree **9**–1146
Lamb and Apricot Pilaff **9**–1192
Lamb Pilaff **9**–1201
Lamb with Rice **9**–1201
Leg of Lamb with Savoury Rice **9**–1220
Long Island Seafood Pilau **10**–1270
Maraccas Beach Pilau **10**–1310
Mataloe Rice Cakes **10**–1340
Maze Gohan (Mixed Vegetables and Rice)
    10–1346
Meat and Fruit Pilau **10**–1352
Mee Feng Jou (Pork in Ground Rice) **10**–1368
Mee Feng Ngiu Jou (Beef in Ground Rice)
    10–1368
Mee Feng Yu Pien (Sliced Fish) **10**–1368
Mexican Pork and Rice **10**–1386
Morue à l'Americaine (Salt Cod with Rice and
    Brandy in Wine Sauce) **11**–1423
Nasi Goreng (Indonesian Rice) **11**–1477
Nigerian Jollof Rice **11**–1501
Noisettes d'Agneau Ismail Bayeldi (Boned Lamb
    Chops with Vegetables and Rice) **11**–1507
Octopus and Prawn Pilau **11**–1552
Oranges Stuffed with Prawns or Shrimps and
    Rice **12**–1618
Paella (Spanish Rice with Chicken and Seafood)
    12–1654
Pakistani Pulau (Curried Rice with Chicken)
    12–1661
Persian Fried Rice **13**–1752
Picardy Rice **13**–1774
Pilaff (info) **13**–1794
Pilaff with Chicken Liver Ragoût **13**–1794
Pilaff à la Grecque (Rice Cooked with
    Mushrooms) **13**–1795
Pilaff with Lamb and Almonds **13**–1796
Pilaff with Nuts and Fruit **13**–1796
Pilaff with Peppers and Chicken **13**–1796
Pilaff with Pineapple and Cashew Nuts
    13–1797
Poona Pilaff **14**–1872
Pork Fried Rice **14**–1893
Puntzin (Vegetable Rice) **15**–1989
Quails with Risotto **15**–2000
Quattro Formaggi con Riso (Four Cheeses with
    Rice) **15**–2002
Rice with Aubergine [Eggplant] and Potatoes
    16–2112
Rice and Beetroot [Beet] Salad **16**–2113
Rice Croquettes **16**–2113
Rice Noodles with Pork and Prawn or Shrimps
    16–2114
Rice Noodles with Spicy Beef **16**–2114
Rice Puddings *see* Desserts
Risi e Bisi (Rice with Peas) **16**–2130
Risotto (info) **16**–2130
Risotto alla Bolognese (Braised Rice with Ham
    and Bolognese Sauce) **16**–2130

Risotto con Funghi (Braised Rice with
    Mushrooms) **16**–2130
Risotto con Gamberetti (Braised Rice with
    Small Shrimps) **16**–2131
Risotto alla Milanese (Braised Saffron Rice)
    16–2132
Risotto con Zucchini (Braised Rice with
    Courgettes) **16**–2132
Riz au Citron (Boiled Rice with Lemon)
    16–2134
Riz à l'Espagnole (Spanish Rice) **16**–2135
Rizotto Corine (Rice with Chicken and
    Vegetables) **16**–2137
Rizotto aux Fruits de Mer (Rice with Shellfish)
    16–2138
Roz bi Dfeen (Rice with Meat and Chick-Peas)
    16–2177
Sabzi Pulao (Vegetable Pilaff) **16**–2198
Saffron Rice **16**–2204
Spiced Rice **18**–2381
Suppli (Stuffed Rice and Cheese Balls)
    18–2443
Talairan Rice Salad with Garlic Sausage
    18–2468
Tomato Rice I **18**–2516
Tomato Rice II **18**–2516
Trinidad Chicken Pilau **19**–2544
Uzbeck Plov (Lamb and Rice Pilaff) **19**–2598
Vegetable Kitcheri **19**–2645
Vegetable Paella **19**–2648
Vegetable Pulao with Prawns or Shrimps
    19–2651
Vulci Cheese Savoury **20**–2723
Walnut and Rice Salad **20**–2735
West Indian Pilau **20**–2768
Wienerwurst Risotto **20**–2806
Wrexham Rice Croquettes **21**–2873
Yakhni Pulao (Lamb Cooked with Rice)
    21–2903
Yellow Rice **21**–2917
Yerevan Lamb Pilaff **21**–2920
Ysa Kedgeree **21**–2944
Yueng Chow Rice **21**–2952
Yunnan Quick-Fried Prawns or Shrimps on
    Crackling Rice **21**–2962
Zafran Paella (Spanish Rice with Chicken and
    Seafood) **21**–2969
Zell Pilau **21**–2989
Zoytinyagli Pirasa (Leeks and Bacon Risotto)
    22–3020
Zuidhorn Liver and Rice **22**–3044

SALADS

Salad (info) **16**–2209
Agurkai su Rukcscia Grietne (Cucumber and
    Soured Cream Salad) **1**–6
Agurkesalat (Danish Pickled Cucumber Salad)
    1–7
Almond and Black Cherry Aspic Salad **1**–20
Apple and Cucumber Salad **1**–45
Apricot Salad **1**–56
Ardei cu Untdelemn (Marinated Pepper Salad)
    1–60
Aubergine Salad **1**–85
Avocado and Courgette [Zucchini] Salad **1**–92
Bean Salad **1**–139
Bean Sprout Salad **1**–140
Beetroot and Apple Salad **2**–158
Beetroot and Onion Salad **2**–159
Beetroot and Orange Salad **2**–159
Borani Esfanaj (Spinach and Yogurt Salad)
    2–209
Broad Beans Vinaigrette **2**–263
Broccoli Salad **2**–264
Cabbage and Pepper Salad **3**–286
Cabbage and Pineapple Salad **3**–286
Cabbage Salad **3**–287
Caesar Salad **3**–290
Cape Cod Salad **3**–315
Carrot and Radish Salad **3**–333
Cauliflower Salad **3**–340
Cauliflower Vinaigrette **3**–341
Céleri-rave Vinaigrette (Celeriac Salad) **3**–343

Thematic

Celery Vinaigrette **3**–347
Cherry Salad **3**–372
Chervil Avocado Salad **3**–373
Chicken Mayonnaise **3**–384
Chicken Riviera (Chicken Salad with Walnuts, Cherries and Tarragon) **3**–387
Chicken Salad with Avocados and Russian Dressing **3**–388
Chicken Salad with Bean Sprouts and Olives **3**–388
Chicken Salad with Sour Cream Dressing **3**–389
Chicory and Tomato Salad **3**–401
Coleslaw with Caraway **4**–438
Crabmeat Mayonnaise **4**–474
Crabmeat Salad **4**–474
Cucumber and Cheese Salad **4**–515
Cucumber and Grape Salad **4**–516
Cucumber and Onion Salad **4**–517
Cucumber and Tomato Salad **4**–518
Danish Blue Salad **4**–528
Dill Salad **5**–565
Dusseldorf Salad **5**–592
East Indian Salad **5**–596
Egg Salad **5**–624
Egg and Spinach Salad **5**–626
Egg and Yogurt Salad **5**–630
Fagioli con Tonno (White Bean and Tuna Salad) **5**–668
Fattoush (Bread Salad) **5**–678
Fennel and Cucumber Salad **5**–684
Fish and Potato Salad **6**–713
Fish Salad **6**–715
Florida Salad **6**–727
Frankfurter and Cabbage Salad **6**–739
French Bean Salad **6**–746
French Potato Salad **6**–749
Fresno Salad **6**–750
Fruit and Chicken Salad **6**–767
Fruits de Mer en Salade (Cold Seafood Salad) **6**–769
Fruit and Vegetable Salad **6**–775
Garlic Salad **6**–800
Gazpacho Salad **6**–810
Genoese Salad **6**–815
German Potato Salad **6**–819
Grape and Grapefruit Salad **7**–860
Grapefruit and Avocado Salad **7**–861
Grapefruit and Orange Salad **7**–862
Greek Salad **7**–869
Green Pepper Salad **7**–873
Green Salad (info) **7**–874
Gruyère and Mushroom Salad **7**–888
Ham and Rice Salad **7**–918
Herring Salad **7**–950
Hollandaise Salad **7**–954
Hostess Salad **7**–972
Hummersalat (Lobster Salad) **8**–984
Hungarian Apple Salad **8**–988
Huysman's Salad **8**–996
Ibadan Shrimp Salad **8**–1000
Inlagda Rödbetor (Pickled Beetroots [Beets]) **8**–1026
Insalata d'Arancia e Limone (Orange and Lemon Salad) **8**–1026
Insalata di Finocchio, Cicoria e Pomodoro (Fennel, Chicory [French or Belgian Endive] and Tomato Salad) **8**–1026
Insalata di Fontina (Fontina Cheese and Peppers Salad) **8**–1026
Insalata di Funghi (Mushroom Salad) **8**–1026
Italian Melon Salad **8**–1038
Jellied Grape and Cheese Salad **8**–1067
Jellied Melon Salad **8**–1069
Kartoffelsalat (Jewish Potato Salad) **8**–1109
Kazan Salad **8**–1117
Kokonda (Spicy Fish Salad) **9**–1164
Kopfsalat mit Apfelsinen (Lettuce and Orange Salad) **9**–1166
Kopfsalat mit Buttermilch (Lettuce Salad with Buttermilk Dressing) **9**–1166
Korean Vegetable Salad **9**–1167
Kumquat and Pineapple Salad **9**–1179
Lamb Salad **9**–1201
Lauchsalat (Leek Salad) **9**–1214

Leek and Shrimp Salad **9**–1216
Leek Vinaigrette **9**–1216
Lemon Balm and Orange Salad **9**–1224
Lettuce Heart and Fruit Salad **9**–1235
Lobster Mayonnaise **9**–1254
Lobster Salad **9**–1257
Lotus Root Salad **10**–1272
Macaroni and Herring Salad **10**–1276
Mange-Tout Salad **10**–1300
Marinated Salt Beef Salad **10**–1316
Melon and Avocado Salad **10**–1371
Melon and Cold Pork Salad **10**–1372
Millionaire Salad **10**–1394
Miranda's Salad **11**–1405
Moulded Peach Salad **11**–1428
Mushroom and Asparagus Mayonnaise **11**–1452
Mushroom and Bacon Salad **11**–1452
Mushroom and Mint Salad **11**–1454
Mushrooms with Tarragon Mayonnaise **11**–1458
Mussel Salad **11**–1462
Nabobeep Salad **11**–1466
Namasu Maguro (Tuna and Vegetable Salad) **11**–1469
Nun's Salad **11**–1527
Okra [Ladies' Fingers] Salad **12**–1567
Olive Salad **12**–1573
Onion and Mackerel Salad **12**–1592
Orange and Carrot Salad **12**–1603
Orange and Celery Salad **12**–1603
Orange and Grapefruit Salad **12**–1612
Orange Salad **12**–1616
Oslo Salad **12**–1629
Oyster and Avocado Salad **12**–1647
Palm Heart Salad **12**–1665
Parsnip Salad **13**–1682
Pear and Chicory [French or Belgian Endive] Salad **13**–1718
Pear Salad **13**–1722
Picnic Salad **13**–1783
Piedmont Salad **13**–1783
Pineapple and Cheese Salad **13**–1802
Pineapple and Lettuce Salad **13**–1806
Pineapple and Turkey Salad **13**–1811
Poireaux au Miel (Leeks with Honey Dressing) **14**–1850
Pork and Apricot Salad **14**–1880
Potato and Herring Salad **14**–1927
Potato Salad **14**–1929
Potato and Cheese Salad **14**–1929
Potato, Egg and Anchovy Salad **14**–1929
Potato Salad with Herbs **14**–1930
Prawn or Shrimp Salad **15**–1970
Pumpkin Salad **15**–1986
Radish, Celery and Cucumber Salad **15**–2045
Raisin and Turkey Salad **15**–2054
Raita I (Yogurt Salad) **15**–2059
Raita II (Yogurt Salad) **15**–2060
Red Sea Salad **15**–2086
Rice and Beetroot [Beet] Salad **16**–2113
Romaine and Orange Salad **16**–2159
Runner [Green] Bean and Bacon Salad **16**–2188
Runner [Green] Beans with Mushrooms and Sour Cream Dressing **16**–2188
Russian Herring and Beetroot [Beet] Salad **16**–2190
Russian Salad **16**–2191
Salade d'Artichauts (Artichoke Heart Salad) **16**–2210
Salade Bagration (Chicken, Macaroni and Artichoke Heart Salad) **16**–2210
Salade de Boeuf Côte d'Azur (Beef, Potato and Tomato Salad) **16**–2210
Salade Chaude Basquaise (Hot Mussel, Hake and Vegetable Salad) **16**–2210
Salade de Figues (Fresh Fig Salad) **16**–2211
Salade de Fruits à la Créole (Creole Fruit Salad) **16**–2211
Salade Mimosa (Lettuce, Celery and Watercress Salad) **16**–2212
Salad Niçoise (Potato, French Bean and Tomato Salad) **16**–2212
Salmagundi **16**–2214
Sardine Salad **16**–2241
Scallop Salad **17**–2264

Scampi Salad **17**–2270
Selleriesalat mit Obst (Celery and Fruit Salad) **17**–2286
Sesame Seed Salad **17**–2290
Shallot and Mushroom Salad **17**–2293
Smoked Fish Salad **18**–2328
Smoked Salmon Salad **18**–2332
Spinach Salad **18**–2388
Squid Salad **18**–2420
Sweetcorn Mayonnaise **18**–2452
Sweetcorn Salad **18**–2454
Tabbouleh (Wheat and Tomato Salad) **18**–2462
Talairan Rice Salad with Garlic Sausage **18**–2468
Tomato and Chicken Salad **18**–2512
Tomato and French Bean Salad **18**–2515
Tomato and Mozzarella Salad **18**–2515
Tomato and Orange Salad **18**–2516
Tomato Salad **18**–2518
Tongan Salad **18**–2519
Tongue Salad **19**–2521
Tuna Fish and Apple Salad **19**–2559
Turnip and Date Salad **19**–2578
Veal and Avocado Salad **19**–2613
Vegetable Marrow Salad **19**–2646
Vegetable and Pork Salad **19**–2650
Vellarikai Pachadi (Cucumber and Yogurt Salad) **20**–2661
Virginia Chicken Salad **20**–2704
Voedzaam Salade (Vegetable Salad) **20**–2714
Walnut, Cheese and Artichoke Heart Salad **20**–2728
Walnut and Rice Salad **20**–2735
Watercress, Fennel, Cucumber and Tomato Salad **20**–2742
Wilted Cucumber **20**–2816
Wilted Lettuce Salad **20**–2816
Windsor Salad Americana **20**–2826
Windward Island Salad **20**–2826
Wurstsalat (German Sausage Salad) **20**–2880
Wurtemburg Pork Salad **20**–2880
Wye Cottage Cheese Salad **20**–2882
Wyoming Viking Salad **21**–2892
Wyfontein Salad **21**–2893
Xato (Chicory [French or Belgian Endive] Salad) **21**–2897
Yahm Chompu (Savoury Fruit Salad) **21**–2901
Yemeni Chick-Pea Salad **21**–2919
Yogurt and Cucumber Salad **21**–2929
Yorkshire Ploughboy **21**–2938
Zabon's Salad **21**–2968
Zambesi Vegetarian Salad **21**–2973
Zihuatanejo Fish Salad **21**–2996
Zihufitanejo (Crabmeat Salad) **22**–2997
Zula Tangy Salad **22**–3047
Zullah's Pasta, Sausage and Bean Salad **22**–3049
Zute Salad **22**–3066

SANDWICHES AND FILLINGS

Sandwich (info) **16**–2238
Anchovy Butter **1**–29
Bookmaker's Sandwich **2**–209
Brazil Nut and Chive Spread **2**–240
Cheddar Spread **3**–361
Cheese and Chive Spread **3**–365
Chicken and Ham Paste **3**–381
Creamy Cheese **4**–488
Damson Cheese [Butter] **4**–527
Danish Open Sandwiches **4**–528
Double Decker Sandwiches **5**–573
Liptauer Cheese **9**–1242
Liver Sausage and Egg Spread **9**–1251
Mushroom Sandwich Filling **11**–1456
Nasturtium Spread **11**–1478
Normandy Cheese Spread **11**–1514
Onion and Egg Spread **12**–1590
Open Sandwich Gâteaux **12**–1598
Potted Cheese **14**–1935
Prawn or Shrimp and Crabmeat Spread **15**–1966
Roquefort and Brandy Spread **16**–2162

Sandwich Loaf **16**–2238
Sardine Sandwiches **17**–2242
Smorrebrod (info) **17**–2336
Tuna Fish Spread **19**–2559
Turkey, Lettuce and Tomato Sandwiches **18**–2572
West African Fish and Avocado Spread **20**–2766
Western Sandwiches **20**–2772
Woodland Picnic Sandwich **21**–2868
Yarmouth Bloater Paste **21**–2912
Zoo-Time Sandwiches **22**–3014

SAUCES AND DRESSINGS— SAVOURY

Sauce (info) **17**–2246
Alioli (info) **1**–12
Alioli Sauce **1**–12
Allemande Sauce **1**–12
Almond and Cucumber Salad Dressing **1**–22
Almond Curry Sauce **1**–22
Almondine Sauce **1**–23
Apple Sauce **1**–50
Aurore Sauce **1**–88
Avocado Herb Salad Dressing **1**–94
Barbecue Sauce **1**–117
Béarnaise Sauce **2**–141
Béchamel Sauce (White Sauce) **2**–141
Bergamot Sauce **2**–162
Beurre au Citron (Hot Lemon-Butter Sauce) **2**–164
Bolognese Sauce (Italian Meat and Vegetable Pasta Sauce) **2**–206
Bordelaise Sauce (Sauce with Red Wine, Shallots and Beef Marrow) **2**–210
Bread Sauce **2**–251
Brown-Bread Sauce (info) **2**–269
Brown Chaudfroid Sauce (Jellied Brown Sauce with Madeira) **2**–269
Brown Sauce **2**–271
Brown Sauce Diable (Spicy Brown Sauce) **2**–271
Caper Sauce **3**–316
Catsup (info) **3**–338
Chasseur Sauce (Game Sauce) **3**–360
Chaudfroid (info) **3**–361
Chaudfroid Sauce (White) **3**–361
Chestnut Sauce **3**–374
Coleslaw Dressing **4**–439
Coulis de Tomates Provençale (Tomato Sauce Flavoured with Herbs) **4**–464
Cranberry and Orange Relish **4**–477
Cranberry Sauce **4**–477
Cucumber Dressing **4**–515
Cumberland Sauce **4**–519
Demi-glace Sauce (Rich Brown Sauce) **4**–555
Devil Sauce I **4**–555
Devil Sauce II **4**–555
Egg and Caper Dressing **5**–616
Egg Sauce **5**–625
Espagnole (info) **5**–660
Fennel Cream Sauce **5**–684
Fines Herbes Sauce **5**–698
Fines Herbes Vinaigrette (Herb Dressing) **5**–700
Fish Dressing **6**–708
Fonds Blanc (info) **6**–732
Fonds Brun (info) **6**–732
Fonds Lié **6**–732
French Dressing **6**–748
Fruit Sauce (info) **6**–775
Genevoise Sauce **6**–813
Gooseberry Sauce **7**–853
Grand-Veneur Sauce (Wine and Pepper Sauce) **7**–860
Gravy (info) **7**–868
Green Goddess Sauce **7**–870
Guava Jelly **7**–891
Gurkensosse (Gherkin Sauce) **7**–897
Ham Sauce **7**–918
Hazelnut Sauce **7**–940
Herb and Lemon Sauce **7**–946
Hoisin Sauce (info) **7**–954

Hollandaise Sauce **7**–955
Hollandaise Sauce with Beaten Egg Whites **7**–956
Hollandaise Sauce with Herbs **7**–956
Hollandaise Sauce with Orange **7**–956
Holstein Sauce **7**–957
Honey and Vinegar Dressing **7**–965
Horseradish and Apricot Sauce **7**–971
Horseradish and Herb Sauce **7**–971
Horseradish Sauce (Cold) **7**–971
Horseradish Sauce (Hot) **7**–971
Horseradish and Sour Cream Sauce **7**–971
Italian Sauce **8**–1038
Jardinière, a la (info) **8**–1061
Jellied Mayonnaise **8**–1068
Lobster Sauce **9**–1258
Long Island Clam Sauce **10**–1269
Marinara Sauce **10**–1314
Mayonnaise **10**–1346
Mayonnaise Aurore **10**–1346
Melted Butter Sauce **10**–1373
Mint Dressing **11**–1402
Mint Sauce **11**–1404
Mornay Sauce **11**–1420
Mousseline Sauce **11**–1439
Mushroom Ketchup **11**–1454
Mushroom Sauce **11**–1457
Mushroom with Tarragon Mayonnaise **11**–1458
Mustard Sauce **11**–1464
Nut and Cheese Dressing **11**–1533
Nut Sauce **11**–1538
Onion and Paprika Dressing **12**–1592
Onion Sauce **12**–1594
Orange and Mint Sauce **12**–1613
Orange and Sour Cream Sauce **12**–1618
Oriental Sauce **12**–1626
Oxford Sauce **12**–1638
Oyster Sauce (info) **12**–1653
Parsley Sauce **13**–1681
Pepper Sauce **13**–1739
Pizzaiola Sauce (Italian Tomato and Garlic Sauce) **14**–1828
Plum Sauce (info) **14**–1848
Queen's Sauce **15**–2012
Quince and Apple Sauce **15**–2030
Quince Compôte **15**–2032
Quin's Sauce **15**–2035
Raisin and Celery Sauce **15**–2057
Raisin Sauce **15**–2058
Ravigote Sauce **15**–2068
Red Caviar with Radish Dressing **15**–2078
Reform Sauce **15**–2089
Rémoulade Sauce **15**–2096
Robert Sauce **16**–2144
Roquefort Dressing **16**–2163
Roquefort Mayonnaise **16**–2164
Rouennaise Sauce **16**–2169
Salad Dressing (info) **16**–2210
Sauce Bigarade (Brown Sauce with Red Wine and Shallots) **17**–2246
Sauce Gribiche (Piquant Herb Mayonnaise) **17**–2246
Sauce Hongroise (Paprika Wine Sauce) **17**–2246
Sauce à l'Indienne (Curry-Flavoured Sauce) **17**–2247
Sauce Ivoire (Cream and Butter Sauce) **17**–2247
Sauce Normande (Mushroom-Flavoured Cream Sauce) **17**–2247
Sour Pickle Sauce **17**–2361
Soy Sauce (info) **17**–2364
Tobasco (info) **18**–2462
Tamarind Sauce **18**–2473
Tamatar Sas (Indian Tomato Sauce) **18**–2474
Tarragon Sauce with Artichokes **18**–2481
Tartare Sauce **18**–2482
Thousand Island Dressing **18**–2498
Tomato Sauce **18**–2518
Vegetarian Gravy **19**–2654
Velouté (info) **20**–2681
Vermouth Salad Dressing **20**–2681
Victor's Sauce **20**–2687
Villeroy Sauce **20**–2694
Vinaigrette (info) **20**–2694

Vinegar and Egg Sauce **20**–2699
Vinegar Sauce **20**–2699
Watercress Sauce **20**–2743
White Sauce (info) **20**–2790
Wine Salad Dressing **21**–2848
Worcester Sauce **21**–2866
Worcestershire Sauce (info) **21**–2867
Yogurt Dressing **21**–2929
Zingara Sauce **22**–2998

SAUCES—SWEET

Sauce (info) **17**–2246
Brandy Butter **2**–235
Caramel Sauce **3**–320
Cardamom Honey Dressing **3**–325
Chocolate Sauce **3**–413
Cream Cheese Dressing **4**–478
Crème Chantilly (Vanilla Flavoured Whipped Cream) **4**–490
Crème à la Vanille (Vanilla Custard) **4**–492
Cumberland Rum Butter **4**–519
Custard (info) **4**–523
Flim Flam Sauce **6**–726
Fruit Sauce (info) **6**–775
Fudge Sauce **6**–776
Ginger Pear Sauce **6**–834
Ginger Sauce **6**–835
Gogol Mogol Sauce (Egg and Rum Sauce) **7**–844
Hard Sauce **7**–924
Hawaiian Sauce **7**–938
Honey Dressing **7**–963
Jam Sauce **8**–1048
Jamaican Coconut Sauce **8**–1050
Jelly Sauce **8**–1072
Juniper Berry Sauce **8**–1090
Lemon Sauce **9**–1230
Madeira Sauce **10**–1285
Maple Syrup (info) **10**–1309
Marmalade Sauce **10**–1322
Marshmallow Dressing **10**–1332
Marshmallow Sauce **10**–1332
Melba Sauce **10**–1370
Mincemeat Sauce **10**–1398
Morello Cherry Sauce **11**–1420
Nut and Chocolate Sauce **11**–1533
Nutmeg Cream **11**–1539
Orange and Honey Butter **12**–1612
Orange Sauce **12**–1616
Pineapple Sauce **13**–1808
Raspberry Sauce **15**–2064
Red Wine Sauce **15**–2089
Rum Butter **16**–2178
Rum Sauce **16**–2181
Strawberry Sauce **18**–2419
Three-Fruit Sauce **18**–2498
Toffee Sauce **18**–2509
Victoria Sauce **20**–2687
Whisky Sauce **20**–2781
White Sauce (info) **20**–2790

SCONES, MUFFINS AND WAFFLES

Bacon Whole-Wheat Scones **1**–103
Baking Powder Biscuits **1**–107
Blueberry Muffins **2**–188
Bran Nut Muffins **2**–233
Buttermilk Scones **3**–283
Crumpet (info) **4**–513
Crumpets **4**–513
Drop Scones **5**–578
Fløtevafler (Norwegian Waffles) **6**–728
Gaufres de Luxembourg (Luxembourg Waffles) **6**–809
Girdle Scones **6**–837
Muffin (info) **11**–1442
Muffin with Apples **11**–1442
Muffins with Cheese **11**–1442
Muffins with Herbs **11**–1443
Nut Waffles **11**–1538
Oatmeal Bannocks **12**–1543

Potato Scones [Biscuits] **14**–1930
Queen's Muffins **15**–2010
Scone (info) **17**–2275
Scones with Cheese **17**–2275
Scones with Dried Fruit **17**–2275
Scones with Sour Cream **17**–2278
Scones with Wholemeal [Wholewheat] Flour **17**–2278
Treacle Scones [Biscuits] **19**–2540
Trevose Barley Scones [Biscuits] **19**–2543
Waffle (info) **20**–2724
Waffles with Fruit **20**–2724
Waffles with Ham and Cheese **20**–2724
Wholemeal [Wholewheat] Muffins **20**–2802

SHELLFISH

Shellfish (info) **17**–2297

Abalone

Abalone (info) **1**–1
Abalone Chinese-Style **1**–1
Pao Yu Ts'ai Hsin (Stir-Fried Abalone and Chinese Cabbage) **12**–1672

Clam

Clam (info) **4**–426
Almejas a la Marinera (Clams in Tomato and Garlic Sauce) **1**–17
Clam Chowder **4**–426
Cream of Clam Soup **4**–482
Hamaguri Sakini (Sake-Flavoured Clams) **7**–919
Hamaguri Shigure-Ni (Sake and Soy Sauce-Flavoured Clams) **7**–919
Long Island Bake **10**–1268
Long Island Clam Sauce **10**–1269
Manhattan Clam Chowder **10**–1302
Palourdes Farcies (Stuffed Clams) **12**–1667
Palourdes Perdues (Clams Baked with Potatoes and Sweetcorn) **12**–1667
Yvetot Clam Hors d'Oeuvre **21**–2964
Zara's Turbot with Clams **21**–2982
Zuppa di Vongole e Pancotto (Clam and Bread Soup) **22**–3061

Cockle

Cockle (info) **4**–428
Cockle Soup **4**–428

Crab

Crab (info) **4**–471
Bean Curd and Crabmeat **1**–139
Canapés du Crabe (Crab Canapés) **3**–303
Crab Bake **4**–472
Crabmeat with Almonds **4**–472
Crabmeat Appetizer **4**–472
Crabmeat in White Chaudfroid Sauce **4**–472
Crabmeat Flan **4**–473
Crabmeat with Herbs **4**–474
Crabmeat Mayonnaise **4**–474
Crabmeat Mornay **4**–474
Crabmeat Salad **4**–474
Crabmeat Soup **4**–475
Feng Kuo (Dumplings Filled with Crabmeat) **5**–683
Hermit Crab (info) **7**–948
King Crab (info) **9**–1142
King Crab Louis **9**–1143
Maryland Seafood Soup **10**–1337
Mille-feuille Stuffed with Crab **10**–1392
Peebles Crab Bake **13**–1730
Prawn or Shrimp and Crabmeat Spread **15**–1966
Red Peppers Stuffed with Crabmeat **15**–2085
Velvet Crab **20**–2664
Virginia Crab Patties **20**–2707
Walter's Seafood Mousse **20**–2736
West Indian Pepperpot **20**–2768
Woosung Crabmeat Soup **21**–2865
Wuntho Crabmeat Soup **21**–2877

Zeebrugge Crabmeat and Lettuce Mould **21**–2986
Zihufitanejo (Crabmeat Salad) **22**–2997
Zwingle Spaghetti with Crabmeat **22**–3079

Crawfish (info) **4**–478

Crayfish

Crayfish (info) **4**–478
Crayfish, Scandinavian-Style **4**–478
Ecrevisses à la Nage (Crayfish Cooked in Court Bouillon) **5**–602
Zuppa di Aragosta (Crayfish Soup) **22**–3058

General Shellfish Dishes

Crêpes aux Fruits de Mer (Seafood Crêpes) **4**–498
East Coast Seafood Bake **5**–595
Fritto Mistro di Mare (Deep-Fried Fish and Shellfish) **6**–762
Fruits de Mer en Salade (Cold Seafood Salad) **6**–769
Gratin aux Fruits de Mer (Seafood Pie) **7**–865
Long Island Seafood Pilau **10**–1270
Mixed Seafood Casserole **11**–1409
Ocean Rolls **12**–1548
Paella (Spanish Rice with Chicken and Seafood) **12**–1654
Ragoût de Fruits de Mer (Seafood Stew) **15**–2047
Rizotto aux Fruits de Mer (Rice with Shellfish) **16**–2138
Zafran Paella (Spanish Rice with Chicken and Seafood) **21**–2969
Zarzuela I (Spanish Fish Stew) **21**–2984
Zarzuela II (Spanish Fish Stew) **21**–2984

Langouste (info) **9**–1206
Limpet (info) **9**–1239

Lobster

Lobster (info) **9**–1252
Aragosta Fra Diavolo (Lobster with Devilled Sauce) **1**–59
Bisque d'Homard (Lobster Bisque) **2**–176
Bouchées Newburg (Puff Pastry Cases Filled with Lobster) **2**–219
Canapés aux Ecrevisses (Lobster Canapés) **3**–304
Cape Cod Salad **3**–315
Devilled Lobster **4**–559
Fish Salad **6**–715
Homard à l'Americaine (Lobster Cooked with Garlic, Herbs, Tomatoes and Wine) **7**–958
Homard Braisé au Vin Blanc (Lobster Braised in White Wine) **7**–958
Homard à la Crème (Lobster with Cream) **7**–958
Homard à l'Ecossaise (Lobster with Whisky) **7**–958
Homard à la Parisienne (Cold Lobster Stuffed with Vegetables) **7**–960
Homard Provençale (Lobster with Tomatoes, Onion and Garlic) **7**–960
Hummer mit Dill (Lobster with Dill) **8**–982
Hummer Ragoût (Lobster Stew) **8**–983
Hummersalat (Lobster Salad) **8**–984
Lobster Bouchées **9**–1253
Lobster with Brandy Sauce **9**–1254
Lobster Butter **9**–1254
Lobster Chowder **9**–1254
Lobster in Curry Sauce **9**–1254
Lobster Mayonnaise **9**–1254
Lobster and Mushroom Mousse **9**–1257
Lobster Newburg **9**–1257
Lobster Salad **9**–1257
Lobster Sauce **9**–1258
Lobster Thermidor **9**–1258
Marsala Lobster **10**–1331
Trumps Creamed Lobster **19**–2557
Winterthur Lobster **22**–2854

Mussel

Mussel (info) **11**–1458
Bouchées aux Fruits de Mer (Puff Pastry Cases Filled with Mussels and Prawns) **2**–218
Donegal Mussel Soup **5**–572
Moules au Citron (Mussels with Lemon Sauce) **11**–1429
Moules Marinière (Mussels Mariners' Style) **11**–1429
Mussels Baked with Basil and Tomato Sauce **11**–1459
Mussel and Beef Pie **11**–1460
Mussel Chowder **11**–1460
Mussels Fried in Batter **11**–1460
Mussels with Garlic Butter **11**–1462
Mussel Salad **11**–1462
Salade Chaude Basquaise (Hot Mussel, Hake and Vegetable Salad) **16**–2210
Zaponeta Pasta Shells with Mussels **21**–2981
Zuppa di Cozze (Mussel Soup) **22**–3058

Oyster

Oyster (info) **12**–1645
East Coast Oyster Casserole **5**–595
Huîtres Gratinées à la Crème (Oysters Grilled [Broiled] with Cream and Cheese) **8**–981
Huîtres Marinées (Marinated Oysters) **8**–981
Liver and Oysters **9**–1250
Marenne (info) **10**–1312
Ostiones (Baked Large Oysters) **12**–1630
Oyster and Avocado Salad **12**–1647
Oyster, Beef, Kidney and Mushroom Pie **12**–1648
Oysters with Cheese Sauce **12**–1648
Oyster Chowder **12**–1650
Oyster Cocktail **12**–1650
Oyster Fritters **12**–1650
Oysters Kilpatrick **12**–1651
Oyster and Meat Sausages **12**–1651
Oyster Rarebit **12**–1652
Oysters Rockefeller **12**–1652
Oyster Sauce (info) **12**–1652
Oyster and Shrimp Fricassée **12**–1653
Oyster Stuffing **12**–1653
Oyster and Sweetcorn Stew **12**–1653
Pacific Oyster Soup **12**–1654
Quenelles aux Huîtres (Oyster Quenelles) **15**–2016
Yosenabe (Japanese Chicken and Oyster Fondue) **21**–2943

Periwinkle (info) **13**–1751

Prawn, Shrimp and Scampi

Prawn (info) **15**–1963
Scampi (info) **17**–2270
Shrimp (info) **17**–2310
Barbecued Prawns or Shrimps **1**–120
Bouchées aux Fruits de Mer (Puff Pastry Cases Filled with Mussels and Prawns) **2**–218
Canapés des Crevettes (Shrimp Canapés) **3**–303
Corn and Prawn Savoury **4**–453
Cream of Shrimp Soup **4**–484
Creole Shrimps **4**–493
Croquettes aux Crevettes (Shrimp Croquettes) **4**–503
Croûtes de Crevettes (Shrimps in a Bread Case) **4**–509
Dakar Shrimp **4**–526
Deep-Fried Prawns **4**–551
Dublin Bay Prawns (info) **5**–579
Dublin Bay Prawns **5**–580
Fish and Prawn Mousse **6**–713
Gamberi con Riso (Rice with Shrimps) **6**–787
Garides me Saltsa Domates (Prawns or Shrimps with Tomato Sauce) **6**–798
Gratin de Crevettes (Creamed Shrimps or Prawns) **7**–864
Guacamole Ring **7**–890
Hawaiian Soup **7**–938
Hwang Chi Hsia Ren (Prawns or Shrimps in Tomato Sauce) **8**–996

Ibadan Shrimp Salad **8**–1000
Jhinga Kari (Prawn or Shrimp Curry) **8**–1076
Jhinga Pakoras (Prawn or Shrimp and Chick-Pea Fritters) **8**–1076
Jhinga Tikka (Prawn or Shrimp Patties) **8**–1077
Kachang Bendi Goreng (Fried Mixed Green Vegetables and Prawns) **8**–1091
Kaiser Garnele mit Dillsosse (Shrimps with Dill Sauce) **8**–1096
Krabbensuppe (German Shrimp Bisque) **9**–1171
Laitues aux Crevettes (Lettuce Baked with Shrimps) **9**–1188
Langoustines (info) **9**–1206
Leek and Shrimp Salad **9**–1216
Long Island Bake **10**–1268
Maryland Seafood Soup **10**–1337
Melon and Prawn or Shrimp Cocktail **10**–1373
Merlans Farcis aux Crevettes (Whiting Stuffed with Shrimps or Prawns) **10**–1382
Mustard Mould with Prawns or Shrimps and Fruit **11**–1463
Neptune's Delight **11**–1491
Octopus and Prawn Pilau **12**–1552
Omelette aux Crevettes (Shrimp Omelet) **12**–1579
Oranges Stuffed with Prawns or Shrimps and Rice **12**–1618
Oyster and Shrimp Fricassée **13**–1653
Penang Cabbage **13**–1734
Peruvian Chowder **13**–1756
Piquant Prawns **14**–1821
Potted Shrimps or Prawns **14**–1936
Prawns or Shrimps and Avocados **15**–1963
Prawn or Shrimp and Avocado Cocktail **15**–1966
Prawn or Shrimp Chow Mein (Mixed Vegetables and Prawns or Shrimps with Noodles) **15**–1966
Prawn or Shrimp Cocktail **15**–1966
Prawn or Shrimp and Crabmeat Spread **15**–1966
Prawn or Shrimp Curry I **15**–1967
Prawn or Shrimp Curry II **15**–1967
Prawn or Shrimp Curry III **15**–1968
Prawn or Shrimp Egg Foo Yung **15**–1968
Prawn or Shrimp Fritters **15**–1969
Prawn or Shrimp Salad **15**–1970
Prawns or Shrimps in Sweet and Sour Sauce **15**–1971
Quenelles de Crustacés (Prawn or Shrimp Quenelles) **15**–2014
Quiches aux Crevettes (Shrimp Quiche) **15**–2022
Rice Noodles with Pork and Prawns or Shrimps **16**–2114
Risotto con Gamberetti (Braised Rice with Small Shrimps) **16**–2131
Rissoies de Camarão (Portuguese Shrimp Rissoles) **16**–2132
Scalloped Shrimps **17**–2265
Scampi Kebabs **17**–2270
Scampi Salad **17**–2270
Shrimp and Avocado Surprise **17**–2310
Shrimp and Cheese Mould **17**–2310
Shrimps Coralie **17**–2310
Shrimp and Cress-Stuffed Crêpes **17**–2311
Shrimps with Curried Avocados **17**–2311
Shrimp, Egg and Cucumber Ring **17**–2311
Shrimp Gilbert **17**–3211
Shrimps Provençal-Style **17**–2312
Shrimp Seviche **17**–2313
Shrimp Soufflé with Wine Sauce **17**–2313
Shrimps Stir-Fried with Ginger **17**–2314
Shrimp-Stuffed Fish **17**–2314
Shrimp and Sweetcorn Soup **17**–2314
Shrimp and Veal Rolls **17**–2316
Sondhia (Spiced Prawns or Shrimps) **17**–2349
Vatapa (Prawn or Shrimp and Coconut Stew) **19**–2609
Vegetable and Prawn or Shrimp Curry **19**–2651
Vegetable Pilao with Prawns or Shrimps **19**–2651
Yoshida Scampi Skewers **21**–2943
Yunnan Quick Fried Prawns or Shrimps on Crackling Rice **21**–2962

Zip-Zap Lunchtime Snack **22**–3000
Zucchini alla Marinara (Courgettes Stuffed with Prawns and Tomatoes) **22**–3053

Scallop

Scallop (info) **17**–2264
Cape ai Ferri (Grilled [Broiled] Scallops) **3**–315
Coquille St. Jacques (info) **4**–448
Coquilles Saint-Jacques à l'Ail (Scallops Sautéed with Garlic and Basil) **4**–448
Coquilles Saint-Jacques à la Crème (Scallops in Cream Sauce) **4**–449
Coquilles Saint-Jacques Gratinées (Scallops and Mushrooms in White Wine Sauce and Cheese) **4**–449
Coquilles Saint-Jacques aux Tomates à la Crème (Scallops in Tomato and Cream Sauce) **4**–450
Scallop Kebabs **17**–2264
Scallop Salad **17**–2264
Scallop Soup **17**–2264
Scallops with Curry Sauce **17**–2265
Scallops with Vermouth Sauce **17**–2265
Vol-au-Vent de Pétoncles (Puff Pastry Case Filled with Scallops) **20**–2719
Zumar Scallops in Port **22**–3052

Sea Urchin (info) **17**–2282
Whelk (info) **20**–2778
Winkle (info) **21**–2848

SNAILS

Snail (info) **17**–2336
Escargot (info) **5**–657
Escargots à la Bourguignonne (Snails with Garlic Butter) **5**–657
Schwabische Schnecken (Snails with Herb Butter) **17**–2274

SOUPS

Soup (info) **17**–2357
Aïgo Bouïdo (French Provençal Garlic Soup) **1**–7
Albóndigas Soup **1**–10
Ashe Reshte (Noodle Soup) **1**–74
Asparagus Cream Soup **1**–76
Augolemono Soup (Egg and Lemon Soup) **1**–88
Avocado Chicken Soup **1**–92
Avocado Soup **1**–95
Barley Country Soup **1**–123
Bauernsuppe (German Peasant Soup) **1**–133
Bean and Bacon Soup **1**–138
Beer Soup **2**–157
Bergens Fiskesuppe (Norwegian Fish Soup) **2**–162
Bird's Nest Soup **2**–172
Birnensuppe (Pear Soup) **2**–173
Bisque d'Homard (Lobster Bisque) **2**–176
Black Bean Soup **2**–179
Blumenkohlsuppe (Cauliflower Soup) **2**–188
Boerenkaas Soep (Farmers Cheese Soup) **2**–190
Borscht (Beetroot [Beet] Soup) **2**–211
Borscht Ukranian (Ukranian Beetroot Soup) **2**–211
Bouillabaisse (Fish Soup Served with Pieces of Fish) **2**–220
Bouillabaisse de Cabillaud (Cod Soup) **2**–222
Bourride (Provençal Fish Soup with Garlic Mayonnaise) **2**–225
Bramborová Polevka (Potato Soup) **2**–233
Broad Bean Soup **2**–263
Broth (info) **2**–269
Cabbage Soup **3**–287
Caldo de Congrio (Conger Eel Soup) **3**–297
Caldo Haba (White Bean Soup with Ham and Sausage) **3**–298
Caldo Tlalpeño (Mexican Chicken and Bean Soup) **3**–298
Caldo Verde (Cabbage and Potato Soup with Sausage) **3**–299

Canja (Portuguese Chicken Soup with Lemon) **3**–311
Cappelletti in Brodo (Stuffed Pasta in Broth) **3**–319
Carrot Soup **3**–333
Catalan Fish Soup **3**–337
Castilian Soup **3**–339
Cheese Soup **3**–368
Cherry Soup **3**–372
Chervil and Leek Soup **3**–373
Chestnut Soup **3**–375
Chicken and Spring Vegetable Soup with Dumplings **3**–393
Chowder (info) **3**–419
Clam Chowder **4**–426
Cock-a-Leekie **4**–427
Cockle Soup **4**–428
Consommé (info) **4**–441
Consommé Brunoise (Vegetable Consommé) **4**–442
Consommé aux Champignons (Mushroom Consommé) **4**–442
Consommé Demidoff (Vegetable Consommé with Truffle and Chicken Quenelles) **4**–442
Consommé Madrilène (Tomato Consommé) **4**–442
Corn Chowder **4**–452
Cottage Cheese Soup **4**–464
Crabmeat Soup **4**–475
Cream Soups (info) **4**–479
Cream of Avocado Soup **4**–479
Cream of Carrot Soup **4**–480
Cream of Celery Soup **4**–480
Cream of Chicken Soup I **4**–481
Cream of Chicken Soup II **4**–482
Cream of Clam Soup **4**–482
Cream of Cucumber Soup **4**–482
Cream of Green Pea Soup **4**–483
Cream of Lettuce Soup **4**–483
Cream of Mushroom Soup **4**–484
Cream of Shrimp Soup **4**–484
Cream of Tomato Soup **4**–484
Cream of Watercress Soup **4**–484
Cucumber and Beer Soup **4**–515
Cucumber and Pork Soup **4**–517
Cucumber Soup **4**–518
Curried Avocado Soup **4**–520
Donegal Mussel Soup **5**–572
Dügün Corbari (Turkish Lamb and Lemon Soup) **5**–588
Dutch Split Pea Soup **5**–592
Easter Soup **5**–601
Egg and Cheese Soup **5**–617
Egg-Drop Soup **5**–619
Erwtensoep (Pea Soup) **5**–652
Escarole Soup **5**–658
Escudilla de Cataluña (Catalan Soup) **5**–658
Eshkaneh (Persian Onion Soup) **5**–658
Fabada (Spanish Bean and Sausage Soup) **5**–666
Farm Soup **5**–676
Fata (Egyptian Lamb Soup) **5**–678
Fennel Soup **5**–684
Fish Chowder **6**–707
Fish and Mushroom Soup **6**–712
Foong Yin Mun Sung (Bird's Nest Soup with Chicken Cubes and Mushrooms) **6**–735
French Onion Soup **6**–749
Game Soup **6**–791
Garbure (Sausage and Cabbage Soup) **6**–796
Garlic Soup **6**–801
Gazpacho **6**–810
Gelée d'Avignon (Jellied Pork Soup) **6**–813
Georgian Soup **6**–816
Goose Soup **7**–850
Goulasch Soup **7**–858
Green Pea Soup **7**–872
Gumbo Soup **7**–896
Haddock Soup **7**–904
Hare Soup **7**–925
Harira (Lamb Soup) **7**–930
Hawaiian Soup **7**–938
Herb and Potato Soup **7**–946
Hollandaise Soup **7**–956
Hot and Sour Soup **7**–977
Huang Yu Tang (Yangtze Fish Soup) **7**–978

Thematic

Hungarian Apple Soup 8–988
Hungarian Apricot Soup 8–988
Hungarian Cherry Soup 8–989
Hungarian Fish Soup 8–990
Hungarian Sauerkraut and Sausage Soup 8–992
Iced Asparagus Soup 8–1007
Iced Carrot and Orange Soup 8–1007
Iced Fruit Soup 5–1009
Idma Soup 8–1014
Iranian Prune Soup 8–1030
Irish Leek and Oatmeal Broth 8–1030
Italian Meat and Vegetable Soup 8–1037
Jellied Beetroot [Beet] Soup 8–1064
Jerusalem Artichoke Soup 8–1076
Julienne Soup 8–1089
Kaeng Chud Kai Hed (Chicken and Mushroom Soup) 8–1093
Kaeng Chud Saku (Tapioca Soup) 8–1093
Kakavia (Greek Bouillabaise) 8–1096
Kaltschale (Austrian Iced Blackberry Soup) 8–1101
Kalvesuppe med Madeira og Champignoner (Veal Soup with Madeira and Mushrooms) 8–1102
Käse Bouillon Mit Ei (Cheese Soup with Egg) 8–1110
Katsudon (Japanese Lamb or Pork Soup) 8–1116
Kesäkeitto (Finnish Vegetable Soup) 9–1125
Kholodetz (Berry Soup) 9–1128
Kidney Bean Soup 9–1134
Klodnik (Iced Beetroot [Beet] and Meat Soup) 9–1154
Klyazma River Soup 9–1155
Knuckle of Lamb and Tomato Soup 9–1159
Koervelsuppe (Chervil Soup) 9–1161
Kohlrabi Soup 9–1164
Krabbensuppe (German Shrimp Bisque) 9–1171
Krupnik Polski (Barley and Vegetable Soup) 9–1176
Kuzuhiki Soup 9–1184
Leek Soup 9–1216
Linsensuppe (Lentil and Vegetable Soup) 9–1240
Lobster Chowder 9–1254
Manhattan Clam Chowder 10–1302
Marak Perot Car (Cold Fruit Soup) 10–1311
Marrow [Summer Squash] Soup 10–1330
Maryland Seafood Soup 10–1337
Mein III: Tan Mein (Soup Noodles) 10–1369
Midsummer Soup 10–1391
Minestrone 10–1400
Minorcan Vegetable Soup 11–1401
Mint and Mushroom Soup 11–1403
Mock Turtle Soup 11–1411
Mollina Soup 11–1414
Monday Soup 11–1415
Monywa Soup 11–1416
Mother's Matzo Balls with Chicken Soup 11–1426
Mulligatawny Soup (Curried Soup) 11–1449
Mushroom Soup I 11–1457
Mushroom Soup II 11–1457
Mussel Chowder 11–1460
Nettle Soup 11–1493
Norrländsk Laxsoppa 11–1516
Norwegian Cucumber and Potato Soup 11–1519
Oatmeal and Carrot Soup 12–1543
Okroshka (Beer and Vegetable Soup) 12–1568
Onion Gruel 12–1590
Onion Soup 12–1595
Ouillade (Bean and Vegetable Soup) 12–1632
Oxtail Soup I 12–1643
Oxtail Soup II 12–1645
Oyster Chowder 12–1650
Pacific Oyster Soup 12–1654
Parsnip and Tomato Soup 13–1682
Pea Soup with Ham 13–1710
Pennsylvania Dutch Chicken Corn Soup 13–1735
Persian Yogurt Soup 13–1753
Peruvian Chowder 13–1756
Petite Marmite (Beef Consommé with Chicken and Vegetables) 13–1758

Pheasant Soup 13–1772
Philadelphia Pepper Pot 13–1772
Pistou (Italian Vegetable Soup) 14–1824
Plum and Cherry Soup 14–1847
Pot au Feu (info) 14–1910
Pot au Feu à la Béarnaise (Chicken and Vegetables in Broth) 14–1910
Potage (info) 14–1916
Potage au Brocoli (Cream of Broccoli Soup) 14–1916
Potage au Chou-Fleur (Cream of Cauliflower Soup) 14–1917
Potage Crécy (Carrot Soup) 14–1918
Potage d'Hiver (Winter Vegetable Soup) 14–1918
Potage Parmentier (Potato Soup) 14–1919
Potage Paysanne (French Vegetable Soup) 14–1920
Potage de Poireaux et Cresson (Leek and Cress Soup) 14–1920
Potage de Tomate à la Paysanne (Tomato Soup Peasant-Style) 14–1921
Pottage (info) 14–1935
Pumpkin Soup I 15–1986
Pumpkin Soup II 15–1987
Quail Egg Soup 15–2001
Quebec Onion Soup 15–2005
Quebec Split Pea Soup 15–2008
Queen's Soup 15–2012
Quince Soup 15–2033
Rabbit Broth 15–2038
Rassolnik (Russian Kidney and Cucumber Soup) 15–2066
Revythia (Greek Chick-Pea Soup) 15–2098
Rose's Old-Fashioned Vegetable Soup 16–2165
Rybnaia Solianka (Fish Soup with Cucumbers and Tomatoes) 16–2195
Salt Pork and Lentil Soup 16–2231
Scallop Soup 17–2264
Scotch Broth 17–2278
Shrimp and Sweetcorn Soup 17–2314
Soupe Albigeoise (Thick Meat and Vegetable Soup) 17–2358
Soupe de Poissons (Fish Soup) 17–2358
Spinach Soup I 18–2388
Spinach Soup II 18–2389
Split Pea Soup 18–2392
Split Pea Soup with Mint and Tomatoes 18–2392
Spring Onion [Scallion] and Tomato Soup 18–2397
Sweetcorn and Chicken Soup 18–2452
Thrifty Soup 18–2499
Tomato and Courgette [Zucchini] Soup 18–2513
Tomato Soup 18–2519
Tsingshih Soup (Smoked Ham and Cucumber Soup) 19–2557
Turnip Soup 19–2579
Uncooked Fruit Soup 19–2591
Uvat Fish Soup 19–2598
Vegetable Soup 19–2653
Velouté (info) 20–2661
Velouté aux Amandes (Almond Cream Soup) 20–2661
Velouté d'Artois (Haricot Bean Cream Soup) 20–2662
Velouté aux Poissons (Fish Cream Soup) 20–2662
Vermicelli Soup 20–2678
Vichyssoise (Cold Cream of Leek and Potato Soup) 20–2685
Viennese Fresh Pea Soup 20–2690
Walnut Soup 20–2736
Watercress and Almond Soup 20–2741
Watercress and Pork Soup 20–2743
Watercress Soup 20–2744
Watermelon Soup 20–2747
Welcome Soup 20–2756
Whitstable Fish Soup 20–2799
Windermere Soup 20–2822
Windsor Cream Soup 20–2823
Windsor Soup 20–2826
Wine Consommé 21–2846
Winter Soup 21–2853

Wonton Soup 21–2860
Woosung Crabmeat Soup 21–2865
Wuntho Crabmeat Soup 21–2877
Wyoming Parsley Soup 21–2891
Xavier Consommé en Gelée (Sour Cream and Caviar Soup) 21–2897
Yablonchni Apple Soup 21–2900
Yankee Bean Soup 21–2908
Yarmouth Bloater Soup 21–2913
Yellow Lentil Soup 21–2917
Yellow Soup 21–2919
Yogurt and Avocado Soup 21–2926
Yogurt, Chicken and Barley Soup 21–2928
Yogurt Soup 21–2931
Yu-Chi-Tang (Shark's Fin Soup) 21–2947
Yulla Brown Onion Soup with Port 21–2960
Zarzar Red Pepper and Onion Soup 21–2984
Zennor's Country Parsnip Soup 21–2991
Zofe Spinach Soup 22–3007
Zonza Champagne Soup 22–3013
Zuppa (info) 22–3058
Zuppa di Anguille (Eel Soup) 22–3058
Zuppa di Aragosta (Crayfish Soup) 22–3058
Zuppa di Cozze (Mussel Soup) 22–3058
Zuppa di Fagioli Fiorentina (Bean Soup Florence-Style) 22–3059
Zuppa di Fontina (Bread and Cheese Soup) 22–3059
Zuppa di Pollo (Chicken Soup) 22–3060
Zuppa di Verdura (Green Vegetable Soup) 22–3061
Zuppa di Vongole e Pancotto (Clam and Bread Soup) 22–3061
Zuppa di Zucchini (Courgette Soup) 22–3063
Zvettl Wine Cream Soup 22–3069
Zvolen Caraway Seed Soup with Dumplings 22–3071

Spices see Herbs and Spices

STOCK

Stock (info) 18–2415
Beef Stock 2–154
Bouillon 2–222
Bouillon, Clarified 2–223
Brown Stock 2–272
Chicken Stock 3–393
Court Bouillon 4–468
Dashi (info) 4–537
Fish Stock 6–716
Fumet (info) 6–777
Game Stock 6–792
Meat Glaze 10–1352
Veal Stock 19–2634
Vegetable Stock 19–2654

STUFFING

Stuffing (info) 18–2433
Apple and Potato Stuffing 1–49
Brazil Nut Stuffing 2–240
Breadcrumb Stuffing 2–251
Chestnut and Sausage Stuffing 3–374
Duxelles (Mushroom Stuffing) 5–594
Farce Duxelles (Mushroom Stuffing) 5–676
Farce Mousseline (info) 5–676
Forcemeat (info) 6–736
Forcemeat of Pork 6–736
Godiveau (info) 7–844
Herb and Orange Stuffing 7–946
Herb Stuffing 7–947
Liver Stuffing 9–1252
Nut and Raisin Stuffing 11–1537
Oatmeal Stuffing 12–1545
Oyster Stuffing 12–1653
Parsley and Lemon Stuffing 13–1681
Pennsylvania Dutch Poultry Stuffing 13–1737
Sage and Onion Stuffing 16–2206
Tangerine Stuffing 18–2476
Thyme Stuffing 18–2500
Walnut and Liver Stuffing 20–2734
Wild Rice Stuffing 20–2812

SUGAR AND SYRUP

Sugar (info) **18**–2438
Syrup (info) **18**–2461
Aniseed Sugar **1**–35
Caramel **3**–319
Confectioners' Sugar (info) **4**–441
Corn Syrup (info) **4**–454
Demerara Sugar (info) **4**–555
Frucose (info) **6**–766
Glucose (info) **6**–840
Golden Syrup (info) **7**–846
Jaggery (info) **8**–1042
Lactose (info) **9**–1186
Molasses (info) **11**–1413
Rose Hip Syrup **16**–2164
Saccharin (info) **16**–2198
Sucrose (info) **18**–2437
Treacle (info) **19**–2538
Vanilla Sugar **19**–2608

SWEETS [CANDIES]

Barley Sugar (info) **1**–125
Butterscotch (info) **3**–284
Candied Fruits (info) **3**–306
Caramels **3**–320
Chocolate Rum Truffles **3**–413
Coconut Barfi **4**–429
Comfit (info) **4**–440
Date Fudge **4**–540
Dates Stuffed with Marzipan **4**–543
Dream Fudge **5**–576
Escravaniya (Almond Sweets [Candies]) **5**–658
Fig and Nut Sweets [Candies] **5**–689
Figos Recheados (Stuffed Figs) **5**–691
Fondant (info) **6**–731
Fondant **6**–731
Fudge (info) **6**–775
Fudge I **6**–775
Fudge II **6**–775
Fudge Fingers **6**–776
Halva (info) **7**–908
Hansom Fudge **7**–922
Hard Candy (info) **7**–924
Haroset (info) **7**–930
Haroset I **7**–930
Haroset II **7**–930
Hazelnut Toffee **7**–940
Honey Balls **7**–961
Honey and Nut Toffees **7**–964
Honey and Walnut Bars **7**–965
Honeycomb Toffee **7**–966
Humbugs **7**–982
Ingber (Ingberlach) (Carrot Sweets [Candies]) **8**–1024
Liquorice (info) **9**–1245
Maple Butterscotch **10**–1307
Marrons Glacés **10**–1327
Marshmallow (info) **10**–1331
Marshmallows **10**–1332
Marzipan (info) **10**–1337
Marzipan I **10**–1337
Marzipan II **10**–1338
Marzipan Fruits (info) **10**–1339
Marzipan Hazelnuts **10**–1339
Molasses Taffy **11**–1414
Nelusko (info) **11**–1491
Nougat (info) **11**–1521
Nougatines (info) **11**–1522
Nut Brittle (info) **11**–1532
Nut Clusters **11**–1533
Nut Princesses **11**–1537
Orange Fondants **12**–1607
Pastilles (info) **13**–1692
Pastilles Flavoured with Lemon **13**–1692
Peppermint (info) **13**–1743
Peppermint Clouds **13**–1744
Peppermint Creams **13**–1745
Peppermint Fondants **13**–1745
Petits Fours au Chocolat (Little Chocolate Balls) **13**–1760
Petits Fours aux Fruits Glacés (Glazed Fresh Fruit) **13**–1760

Praline (info) **15**–1961
Quick Crème de Menthe Turkish Delights **15**–2026
Quince Sweets [Candies] **15**–2033
Roomborstplaat (Cocoa and Hazelnut Candy) **15**–2162
Shikaree Slices **17**–2302
Teiglach (Honey Sweets [Candies]) **18**–2491
Toffee **18**–2505
Toffee with Almonds and Chocolate **18**–2505
Toffee Apples **18**–2505
Torrone di Cioccolata (Chocolate Nougat) **19**–2523
Trucial Dainties **19**–2552
Truffles, Sweets [Candies] (info) **19**–2552
Truffles with Almonds **19**–2552
Truffles with Coffee **19**–2553
Truffles with Nuts **19**–2553
Truffles with Raisins **19**–2553
Truffles with Rum **19**–2553
Truffles with Whisky **19**–2554
Tuloons (Treacle Sweets [Candies]) **19**–2557
Turkish Delight **19**–2576
Turron (Almond Sweets [Candies]) **19**–2580
Violet Creams **20**–2704
Walnut and Coffee Fudge **20**–2730
Walnut and Honey Sweets [Candies]) **20**–2734
Walnut and Rum Caramels **20**–2735
White Pumpkin Halva **20**–2790
Yellowman **21**–2917

TARTS AND FLANS— SAVOURY

Tart (info) **18**–2482
Flan (info) **6**–719
Crabmeat Flan **4**–473
Egg and Cream Cheese Tart **5**–618
Egg Tartlets **5**–628
Egg and Vegetable Flan **5**–629
Eggplant Flan **5**–636
Fish and Leek Flan **6**–711
Flan à la Bourguignonne (Flan with Leek and Bacon Filling) **6**–721
Flan de Carottes (Carrot Flan) **6**–721
Flan Case made with Shortcrust Pastry **6**–720
Flan Chavette (Chicken Livers, Mushrooms and Scrambled Egg Flan) **6**–721
Herb and Spinach Flan **7**–946
Holstein **7**–956
Jalousie (info) **8**–1043
Jalousie au Fromage (Openwork Pastry Cheese Tart) **8**–1043
Leek and Sausage Tart **9**–1216
Marquise Tartlets **10**–1324
Nut and Cauliflower Flan **11**–1532
Queen's Flan **15**–2009
Quiche (info) **15**–2022
Quiche aux Asperges (Asparagus Quiche) **15**–2022
Quiche aux Champignons (Mushroom Quiche) **15**–2022
Quiche aux Courgettes et Tomates (Courgette [Zucchini] and Tomato Quiche) **15**–2022
Quiche aux Crevettes (Shrimp Quiche) **15**–2022
Quiche Lorraine (Cheese and Bacon Quiche) **15**–2023
Quiches aux Oignons (Little Onion Quiches) **15**–2024
Quiche au Thon (Tuna Fish Quiche) **15**–2024
Quiche aux Trois Fromages (Three-Cheese Quiche) **15**–2024
Riverside Apple Flan **16**–2134
Smoked Salmon Quiche **17**–2332
Talmouses (Savoury Tartlets) **18**–2471
Tarte aux Filets de Maquereaux (Mackerel Fillet Tart) **18**–248?
Tarte au Poulet (Chicken Flan) **18**–2483
Tarte à la Viande (Meat Flan) **18**–2487
Zutian Sardine Flan **22**–3066
Zwiebelkuchen (German Onion Tart) **22**–3077

TARTS AND FLANS— SWEET

Tart (info) **18**–2482
Flan (info) **6**–719
Angelica Tart **1**–32
Apfelkuchen (German Apple and Custard Tart) **1**–38
Apricot Bourdaloue Tart **1**–52
Apricot Tart **1**–57
Bakewell Tart **1**–107
Barquettes aux Abricots (Apricot Tarts) **1**–126
Brown Sugar Tart **2**–272
Chocolate Cherry Tart **3**–406
Cream Cheese Flan **4**–478
Custard and Pear Tart **4**–524
Custard Tart **4**–524
Engadiner Nusstorte (Honey and Walnut Torte) **5**–646
Fig Tart **5**–690
Flan Case made with Rich Shortcrust Pastry
Flan Case made with Shortcrust Pastry **6**–720
Flan Case made with Sponge **6**–720
Flan d'Ananas (Pineapple Flan) **6**–721
Flan au Potiron Caramelisé (Pumpkin and Caramel Flan) **6**–722
French Peach Tarts **6**–749
Grape Tartlets **7**–860
Greengage Flan **7**–875
Grenadine Almond Flan **7**–876
Honey Pecan Flan **7**–964
Jalousie (info) **8**–1043
Jalousie à la Confiture (Openwork Pastry Jam Tart) **8**–1043
Jam Tarts **8**–1048
Jellied Cream and Strawberry Flan **8**–1065
Jelly Tart **8**–1073
Kirschkuchen (Cherry Flan) **9**–1150
Lemon and Almond Flan **9**–1223
Linser (Custard Tartlets) **9**–1240
Linzertorte (Jam Tart) **9**–1242
Manchester Tart **10**–1298
Marmalade and Tangerine Flan **10**–1322
Melktert (Custard Tart) **10**–1370
Mirlitons (Macaroon-Filled Tartlets) **11**–1405
Morello Cherry Flan **11**–1420
Nectarine Tartlets **11**–1489
Normandy Pear Tart **11**–1514
Nut and Sweet Potato Flan **11**–1538
Nutalie Flan **11**–1538
Obsttorte (Fruit Tart) **12**–1546
Peach Flan **13**–1713
Pear Tart Bourdaloue **13**–1722
Pecan and Sour Cream Flan **13**–1726
Perth Tart **13**–1755
Pineapple Flan **13**–1805
Polish Orange and Almond Flan **14**–1855
Pommes Grimaldi (Apple and Rice Flan) **14**–1864
Prune and Apple Meringue Flan **15**–1981
Quebec Butter Tarts **15**–2004
Queen Mary's Tarts **15**–2010
Queijadas de Evora (Sweet Cheese Tartlets) **15**–2013
Rauschenburg Tart **15**–2068
Redcurrant Flan **15**–2079
Regal Flan **15**–2092
Spicy Apple Flan **18**–2382
Sponge Flan with Cherry Filling **18**–2395
Sponge Flan Filled with Pineapple and Chestnut Cream **18**–2395
Strawberry Flan **18**–2419
Strawberry Tartlets **18**–2421
Sweet Potato Flan **18**–2454
Tarte aux Figues (Fig Flan) **18**–2482
Tarte à la Rhubarbe (Rhubarb Flan) **18**–2484
Tarte à la Rhubarbe Soufflé (Rhubarb Cream Flan) **18**–2484
Toucy Prune Tartlets **19**–2526
Treacle Tart I **19**–2540
Treacle Tart II **19**–2540
Turlough Tarts **19**–2577
Upside-Down Apple Tart **19**–2594
Velvet Raisin Flan **20**–2664
Yazoo Cranberry Flan **21**–2914

Thematic

York Castle Chocolate Tart **21**–2934
Yule Mincemeat and Apple Flan **21**–2958
Zulia Persimmon Flan **22**–3047
Zuki Fruit Tartlets **22**–3046
Zune Ricotta and Cherry Tartlets **22**–3053
Zwetschgenkuchen Plum Tart **22**–3072

TEA

Tea (info) **18**–2488
Orange Pekoe (info) **12**–1614
Tea Punch **18**–2490
Tea Sorbet **18**–2491
Zveno Tea Soufflé **22**–3068

VEGETABLES

Vegetable (info) **19**–2641

Artichoke

Artichoke (info) **1**–66
Artichokes, Boiled **1**–66
Artichokes Braised with Mixed Vegetables **1**–69
Artichokes with Dill Sauce **1**–69
Artichokes à la Grecque **1**–70
Artichoke Hearts **1**–68
Artichoke Hearts à l'Allemande **1**–73
Artichoke Hearts in Butter **1**–73
Artichoke Hearts with Herbs **1**–74
Artichoke Heart Soufflé **1**–68
Artichokes à la Provençale (Artichokes with
    Garlic and Tomatoes) **1**–70
Artichokes Stuffed with Pork and Almonds **1**–71
Artichokes Stuffed with Prawns and Spicy
    Mayonnaise **1**–72
Artichokes with Veal and Peppers **1**–72
Eggs in Artichokes **5**–610
Fonds d'Artichauts à la Crème (Artichoke
    Hearts with Cream) **6**–731
Fonds d'Artichauts Mirepoix (Artichoke Hearts
    with Diced Vegetables and Ham) **6**–732
Ham and Artichoke Heart Mould **7**–910
Japanese Artichokes (info) **8**–1059
Jerusalem Artichoke Casserole **8**–1074
Jerusalem Artichokes au Gratin **8**–1075
Jerusalem Artichoke Soufflé **8**–1075
Jerusalem Artichoke Soup **8**–1076
Salade Bagration (Chicken, Macaroni and
    Artichoke Heart Salad) **16**–2210
Savoury Artichoke Pie **17**–2263
Scallops with Vermouth Sauce **17**–2265
Tarragon Sauce with Artichokes **18**–2481
Yarm Stuffed Artichokes **21**–2910
Yssingeaux Marinated Artichoke Hearts
    21–2946

Asparagus

Asparagus (info) **1**–75
Asparagus au Beurre **1**–75
Asparagus Cream Soup **1**–76
Asparagus au Gratin (Asparagus with Cheese
    Sauce) **1**–76
Asparagus aux Oeufs (Asparagus with Eggs)
    1–76
Asparagus Polonaise **1**–78
Asparagus with Sour Cream **1**–78
Asparagus Timbale **1**–78
Iced Asparagus Soup **8**–1007
Mushroom and Asparagus Mayonnaise **11**–1452
Quiche aux Asperges (Asparagus Quiche)
    16–2022
Wake Island Pastry Cases with Egg and
    Asparagus **20**–2726
Warmer Malteser Spargel (Hot Asparagus with
    Orange) **20**–2736

Asparagus Pea (info) **1**–79

Aubergine [Eggplant]

Aubergine [Eggplant] (info) **1**–82
Aubergines Farcies Duxelles (Baked
    Aubergines Stuffed with Mushrooms) **1**–82
Aubergines Farcies Provençale **1**–82
Aubergine Fritters I **1**–83
Aubergine Fritters II **1**–83
Aubergines Gratinées **1**–84
Aubergines Grillées (Grilled Aubergines) **1**–84
Aubergine and Lamb Casserole **1**–85
Aubergine and Lamb Stew **1**–85
Aubergine Salad **1**–85
Aubergines Sautéed **1**–86
Aubergine Soufflés **1**–86
Aubergines à la Tunisienne **1**–87
Aubergines à la Turque **1**–87
Bharta (Curried Aubergine [Eggplant] Purée)
    2–168
Brazilian Aubergines [Eggplants] **2**–238
Caponata (Aubergines [Eggplants] in Sweet and
    Sour Sauce) **3**–318
Courgettes [Zucchini] Baked with Aubergines
    [Eggplants] **4**–466
Dulma (Stuffed Aubergines [Eggplants],
    Courgettes [Zucchini] and Tomatoes) **5**–589
Eggplant Basquaise **5**–635
Eggplant and Beef Balls **5**–635
Eggplant Boston **5**–635
Eggplant Casserole **5**–636
Eggplant Fiesta **5**–636
Eggplant Flan **5**–636
Eggplant Hungarian-Style **5**–637
Eggplant Parmesan **5**–638
Fried Aubergines [Eggplants] with Pork and
    Vegetables **6**–754
Imam Bayeldi (Aubergines [Eggplants] with
    Tomatoes and Onions) **8**–1016
Minced [Ground] Beef and Aubergine
    [Eggplant] Casserole **10**–1394
Moussaka I **11**–1430
Moussaka II **11**–1431
Moussaka with Fish **11**–1431
Moussaka Greek-Style **11**–1432
Nasu Karashi Sumiso-ae (Aubergines
    [Eggplants] with Mustard Dressing) **11**–1478
Nazkhatun (Aubergine [Eggplant] Hors
    d'Oeuvre) **11**–1482
New Haven Baked Aubergines [Eggplants]
    11–1498
Ntroba Forowee (Ghanaian Stewed Aubergine
    [Eggplant] with Shrimps) **11**–1526
Piatto Freddo di Ortaggi (Cold Mixed
    Vegetables) **13**–1773
Pizza with Aubergine [Eggplant] **14**–1830
Rice with Aubergine [Eggplant] and Potatoes
    16–2112
Roman Aubergine [Eggplant] Hors d'Oeuvre
    16–2160
Turkari Baingan (Curried Aubergines
    [Eggplants]) **19**–2564
Vol-au-Vent d'Aubergines (Puff Pastry Case
    Filled with Aubergines [Eggplants]) **20**–2717
Wengi Bhat (Aubergines [Eggplants] and Rice)
    20–2762
Wengyachen Bharit (Curried Aubergines
    [Eggplants]) **20**–2763

Avocado

Avocado (info) **1**–92
Alligator Pear (info) **1**–12
Avocado Aspic **1**–92
Avocado Chicken Soup **1**–92
Avocado Chicken Supreme **1**–92
Avocado and Courgette [Zucchini] Salad **1**–92
Avocado Dip I **1**–94
Avocado Dip II **1**–94
Avocado Herb Salad Dressing **1**–94
Avocado with Jellied Consommé **1**–94
Avocado Soup **1**–95
Chervil Avocado Salad **3**–373
Cream of Avocado Soup **4**–479
Curried Avocado Soup **4**–520
Grapefruit and Avocado Salad **7**–861
Guacamole (Avocado Dip) **7**–889
Guacamole Ring **7**–890
Melon and Avocado Salad **10**–1371
Oyster and Avocado Salad **12**–1647
Pouding d'Avocat (Avocado Ice-Cream) **14**–1936
Prawns or Shrimps and Avocados **15**–1963
Prawn or Shrimp and Avocado Cocktail **15**–1966
Shrimp and Avocado Surprise **17**–2310
Veal and Avocado Salad **19**–2613
Verity Cream **20**–2678
Volcanoes **20**–2720
Walter's Seafood Mousse **20**–2736
Watercress and Avocado Mayonnaise **20**–2742
West African Fish and Avocado Spread
    20–2766
West Indian Avocados **20**–2767
Whipped Avocado Dessert **20**–2778
Yogurt and Avocado Soup **21**–2926
Yzeron Alligator Pears **21**–2964
Zippy Avocado Hors d'Oeuvre **22**–2999
Zomba Salt Cod and Avocado **22**–3011
Zula Avocado Hors d'Oeuvre **22**–3046

Bamboo Shoot

Bamboo Shoot (info) **1**–108
Bamboo Shoots with Mushrooms **1**–108
Bamboo Shoots with Pork **1**–109

Batuto (info) **1**–133

Beans and Pulses

Bean (info) **1**–136
Pulse (info) **15**–1985
Bean and Bacon Soup **1**–138
Bean Curd (info) **1**–139
Bean Curd and Crabmeat **1**–139
Bean-Curd Skin (info) **1**–139
Bean Salad **1**–139
Black Bean Casserole **2**–178
Black Bean Soup **2**–179
Boston Baked Beans **2**–212
Broad Beans (info) **2**–263
Broad Beans à la Crème **2**–263
Broad Beans Vinaigrette **2**–263
Broad Bean Soup **2**–263
Brown Bean Soup **2**–269
Butter [Dried Lima] Beans (info) **3**–281
Butter Beans Menagère (Butter Beans in Cream
    Sauce) **3**–281
Chili Con Carne **3**–401
Dhal (info) **5**–562
Dhal Curry **5**–562
Dhansak (Chicken with Lentils and
    Vegetables) **5**–562
Egyptian Brown Beans **5**–638
Fabada (Spanish Bean and Sausage Soup) **5**–666
Fagioli al Forno (Italian-Style Baked Beans)
    5–668
Fagioli con Prosciutto (White Haricot Beans
    with Ham and Tomato Sauce) **5**–668
Fagioli con Tonno (White Bean and Tuna
    Salad) **5**–668
Faubonne (info) **5**–679
Faverolles (info) **5**–680
Feijoada (Brazilian Black Beans and Smoked
    Meats) **5**–683
French Beans (info) **6**–746
French Beans, Hungarian-Style **6**–746
French Bean Salad **6**–746
French Beans in Tomato Sauce **6**–747
Frijoles Refritos (Refried Beans) **6**–758
Habas à la Catalana (Sausage and Broad Bean
    Casserole) **7**–898
Haricot (info) **7**–928
Haricot Beans (info) **7**–928
Haricots Blancs (info) **7**–928
Haricots Rouges (info) **7**–929
Haricots Verts (info) **7**–929
Haricots Verts à la Crème **7**–929
Haricots Verts à l'Oignon et Lard (Green Beans
    with Onion and Bacon) **7**–929
Haricots Verts aux Pommes (Green Beans with
    Apples and Almonds) **7**–930

Hoppin' John 7–969
Jamaican Beans 8–1050
Judias Verdes con Salsa de Tomate (French Beans in Tomato Sauce) 8–1084
Khichri (Rice with Lentils) 9–1128
Kidney Bean (info) 9–1132
Kidney Beans and Brains in Spanish Sauce 9–1132
Kidney Bean and Herb Casserole 9–1132
Kidney Beans Mexican-Style 9–1134
Kidney Bean Soup 9–1134
Kizlyar Boby (Green Beans in Sour Cream) 9–1154
Knackwurst and Lentil Casserole 9–1156
Lentil (info) 9–1234
Lima Beans (info) 9–1237
Lima Beans with Mushrooms 9–1238
Linsensuppe (Lentil and Vegetable Soup) 9–1240
Locust Bean (info) 9–1259
Mung Bean (info) 11–1449
Ouillade (Bean and Vegetable Soup) 12–1632
Pickled French Beans 13–1780
Queretaro Bake 15–2017
Red Bean Casserole 15–2076
Red Bean and Lamb Casserole 15–2076
Runner [Green] Bean (info) 16–2187
Runner [Green] Bean and Bacon Salad 16–2188
Runner [Green] Bean Casserole 16–2188
Runner [Green] Beans with Mushrooms and Sour Cream Dressing 16–2188
Salsicce con Fagioli (Italian Sausages with Haricot Beans) 16–2226
Sambar (Lentils Cooked with Spices) 16–2234
Succotash 18–2436
Tomato and French Bean Salad 18–2515
Veal and Bean Stew 19–2613
Vegetarian Lentil Loaf 19–2654
Velouté d'Artois (Haricot Bean Cream Soup) 20–2662
Wax Beans (info) 20–2749
Winnsboro Bean Rarebit 21–2848
Yankee Bean Soup 21–2908
Yellow Lentil Soup 21–2917
Zullah's Pasta, Sausage and Bean Salad 22–3049
Zuppa di Fagioli Fiorentina (Bean Soup Florence-Style) 22–3059

Bean Sprout

Bean Sprout (info) 1–139
Bean Sprouts with Ginger 1–140
Bean Sprouts with Green Peppers 1–140
Bean Sprout Salad 1–140
Rolled Crêpes Stuffed with Bean Sprouts 16–2157

Beetroot [Beet]

Beetroot [Beet] (info) 2–158
Beetroot and Apple Salad 2–158
Beetroot, Boiled (info) 2–158
Beetroot with Cream Sauce 2–158
Beetroot and Onion Salad 2–159
Beetroot and Orange Salad 2–159
Beetroot in Orange Sauce 2–159
Beetroot Pickles 2–159
Beetroot Piquante 2–160
Beetroot in Sour Cream 2–160
Borscht (Beetroot [Beet] Soup) 2–211
Borscht Ukrainian (Ukrainian Beetroot Soup) 2–211
Dill Salad 5–565
Harvard Beets 7–932
Inlagda Rödbetor (Pickled Beetroots [Beets]) 8–1026
Jellied Beetroot [Beet] Soup 8–1064
Klodnik (Iced Beetroot [Beet] and Meat Soup) 9–1154
Pickled Beetroot [Beets] 13–1777
Polish Beetroot [Beets] 14–1853

Bredes (info) 2–253

Broccoli

Broccoli (info) 2–264
Broccoli with Almonds 2–264
Broccoli with Black Olives 2–264
Broccoli with Capers 2–264
Broccoli with Cheese Sauce 2–265
Broccoli, Chinese-Style 2–265
Broccoli with Green Peppers 2–265
Broccoli à la Polonaise (Broccoli with Fried Breadcrumbs and Chopped Egg) 2–266
Broccoli Salad 2–264
Broccoli alla Siciliana 2–264
Broccoli Soufflé 2–266
Potage au Brocoli (Cream of Broccoli Soup) 14–1916
Purée de Brocoli (Broccoli Purée) 15–1990
Zvengli's Poached Eggs 22–3068

Brussels Sprout

Brussels Sprout (info) 2–272
Brussels Sprouts with Bacon 2–273
Brussels Sprouts with Chestnuts 2–274
Brussels Sprouts Créole (Brussels Sprouts with Green Pepper and Tomatoes) 2–275
Brussels Sprouts with Grapes 2–275
Brussels Sprouts with Ham 2–275
Brussels Sprouts Mould 2–275
Brussels Sprouts Polonaise (Brussels Sprouts with Hard-Boiled Eggs, Parsley and Breadcrumbs) 2–276
Nitzanei-kruv be'dvash (Honeyed Brussels Sprouts) 11–1502

Cabbage

Cabbage (info) 3–284
Austrian Cabbage 1–89
Brèdes de Chou (Cabbage Brèdes) 2–253
Bubble and Squeak 2–277
Cabbage Braised in Stock 3–284
Cabbage in Orange Juice 3–284
Cabbage and Lamb Hot Pot 3–285
Cabbage and Pepper Salad 3–286
Cabbage and Pineapple Salad 3–286
Cabbage Rolls 3–286
Cabbage Salad 3–287
Cabbage and Sausage Casserole 3–287
Cabbage Soup 3–287
Cabbage in Sour Cream 3–288
Cabbage in White Wine 3–288
Cavolo in Agrodolce (Sour-Sweet Cabbage) 3–342
Chou au Gratin (Cabbage Cheese) 3–416
Choucroute Garni 3–416
Chou Rouge à la Flamande (Braised Red Cabbage with Apples) 3–418
Chou Rouge à la Limousine (Braised Red Cabbage with Red Wine and Chestnuts) 3–418
Colcannon (Potato and Cabbage Hash) 4–438
Coleslaw with Caraway 4–438
Dusene Zeli (Red Cabbage and Bacon Casserole) 5–592
Egg and Cabbage Pirog 5–615
Feuilles de Chou Farcies (Stuffed Cabbage Leaves) 5–687
Frankfurter and Cabbage Salad 6–739
Garbure (Sausage and Cabbage Soup) 6–796
Gevulde Kool (Stuffed Cabbage) 6–821
Golubtsy (Stuffed Cabbage Rolls with Sour Cream Sauce) 7–846
Ham Baked with Sauerkraut 7–910
Hot Slaw 7–977
Hung Shao Pai T'sai (Red Braised Cabbage) 8–986
Hungarian Layered Cabbage 8–991
Hungarian Sauerkraut and Sausage Soup 8–992
Hungarian-Style Sauerkraut 8–992
Hunter's Stew 8–993
Kärdia Cabbage 8–1107
Kim u Chi (Korean Pickled Cabbage) 9–1141
Lamb and Cabbage Stew 9–1194

Penang Cabbage 13–1734
Perdrix aux Choux (Partridges Cooked with Cabbage) 13–1751
Red Cabbage (info) 15–2077
Red Cabbage in Red Wine 15–2077
Red Cabbage Salad 15–2077
Rétes (Hungarian Strudel) 15–2098
Rødkaal (Braised Red Cabbage) 16–2150
Sauerkraut (info) 17–2252
Sauerkraut mit Aprikose (Sauerkraut with Apricots) 17–2252
Sauerkraut Casserole with Dill Cucumbers 17–2252
Sauerkraut Chocolate Cake 17–2252
Savoy Cabbage (info) 17–2263
Shih-tzu-tou (Pork and Cabbage Casserole) 17–2302
Spring Greens (info) 18–2396
Stuffed Cabbage 18–2430
Uberbackenes Sauerkraut (Sauerkraut and Potato Bake) 19–2585
Weinkraut (German Sauerkraut in Wine) 20–2755
White Cabbage in Sour Cream Sauce 20–2781
Würzsauerkraut (German Spiced Sauerkraut) 21–2882
Yorkshire Ploughboy 21–2938

Cardoon (info) 3–325

Carrot

Carrot (info) 3–331
Aniseed Carrots 1–35
Carottes à l'Algérienne (Carrots Algerian-Style) 3–327
Carottes aux Champignons (Carrots with Mushrooms) 3–328
Carottes à la Crème (Braised Carrots in Butter and Cream Sauce) 3–328
Carottes Glacées (Glazed Carrots) 3–328
Carottes à la Neige (Baked Puréed Carrots) 3–328
Carottes aux Raisins (Carrots and Onions with Raisins in Wine Sauce) 3–328
Carottes Vichy 3–329
Carrot Cake 3–332
Carrots with Onions 3–332
Carrot and Radish Salad 3–333
Carrot Soufflé 3–333
Carrot Soup 3–333
Cassolettes de Carottes au Jambon (Braised Carrots and Bacon) 3–337
Cream of Carrot Soup 4–480
Flan de Carottes (Carrot Flan) 6–721
Flemish Carrots 6–724
Gajjar Halva (Carrot Dessert) 6–781
Ingber (Ingberlach) (Carrot Sweets [Candies]) 8–1024
Orange and Carrot Salad 12–1603
Potage Crécy (Carrot Soup) 14–1918
Zanahorias Rellenas (Stuffed Carrots) 21–2975
Zenith Pear and Carrot Soufflé 21–2991

Cassava (info) 3–334

Cauliflower

Cauliflower (info) 3–339
Blumenkohlsuppe (Cauliflower Soup) 2–188
Cauliflower Cheese 3–339
Cauliflower with Italian Sauce 3–339
Cauliflower Mexicana 3–340
Cauliflower with Mustard Sauce 3–340
Cauliflower Polonaise 3–340
Cauliflower Salad 3–340
Cauliflower Vinaigrette 3–341
Chou-fleur en Casserole (Cauliflower with Tomatoes and Cheese) 3–417
Chou-fleur avec Sauce Crevette (Cauliflower with Shrimp Sauce) 3–418
Gobi Ki Sabzi (Spicy Cauliflower) 7–843
Lamb's Liver with Cauliflower 9–1202
Maine Cauliflower and Tomato Pickle 10–1289
Nut and Cauliflower Flan 11–1532

Thematic

Pain de Chou-fleur (Cauliflower Loaf) **12**–1658
Pakoras (Vegetable Fritters) **12**–1662
Paprika Vegetable and Sausage Stew **12**–1674
Piccalilli **13**–1774
Potage au Chou-fleur (Cream of Cauliflower Soup) **14**–1917
Talmouses **18**–2471
Walnut Cauliflower **20**–2726

Celeriac

Celeriac (info) **3**–342
Céleri-rave Braisé (Braised Celeriac) **3**–342
Céleri-rave à la Paysanne (Stuffed Celeriac) **3**–343
Céleri-rave Vinaigrette (Celeriac Salad) **3**–343

Celery

Celery (info) **3**–344
Céleris Amandines (Celery with Almonds) **3**–344
Céleris Braisés au Lard (Braised Celery and Bacon) **3**–344
Céleris à la Grecque (Celery, Greek-Style) **3**–344
Celery, Braised **3**–344
Celery, Creamed **3**–346
Celery Fritters **3**–346
Celery with Red Caviar **3**–346
Celery Salt (info) **3**–346
Celery Seed (info) **3**–346
Celery with Tarragon **3**–346
Celery Vinaigrette **3**–347
Cream of Celery Soup **4**–480
Far East Celery **5**–675
Jugged Celery **8**–1085
Julienne of Celery, Potatoes and Green Pepper **8**–1088
Mushrooms and Celery on Toast **11**–1452
Orange and Celery Salad **12**–1603

Chard (info) **3**–357

Chick-Pea

Chick-Pea (info) **3**–399
Channa Dhal (Curried Chick-Peas) **3**–356
Chick-Peas Catalan **3**–399
Falafel (Chick-Pea Balls) **5**–674
Garbanzos à la Mexicana (Spicy Chick-Peas) **6**–796
Hummus bi Tahina (Chick-Pea Paste) **8**–985
Jhinga Pakoras (Prawn or Shrimp and Chick-Pea Fritters) **8**–1076
Kabli Channa (Whole Chick-Peas) **8**–1091
Revythia (Greek Chick-Pea Soup) **15**–2098
Roz bi Dfeen (Rice with Meat and Chick-Peas) **16**–2177
Yemeni Chick-Pea Salad **16**–2919

Chicory

Chicory (info) **3**–399
Chicory, Braised **3**–400
Chicory with Cheese and Ham **3**–400
Chicory and Eggs **3**–401
Chicory and Tomato Salad **3**–401
Endive Farcie (Chicory [French or Belgian Endive] Leaves Stuffed with Cream Cheese) **5**–646
Xato (Chicory [French or Belgian Endive] Salad) **21**–2897

Chinese Cabbage

Chinese Cabbage (info) **3**–402
Bok Choy (info) **2**–205
Fried Chinese Cabbage **6**–755
Nai-Yu-Ts'ai-Hsin (Chinese Cabbage in Cream Sauce) **11**–1467
Pao Yu Ts'ai Hsin (Stir-Fried Abalone and Chinese Cabbage) **12**–1672

Courgette [Zucchini]

Courgette [Zucchini] (info) **4**–464
Avocado and Courgette [Zucchini] Salad **1**–92
Courgettes [Zucchini] Baked with Aubergines [Eggplants] **4**–466
Courgettes Farcies aux Amandes (Courgettes [Zucchini] Stuffed with Almonds) **4**–466
Courgettes Gratinées à la Milanaise (Courgettes [Zucchini] Baked with Cheese) **4**–467
Courgettes Grillées (Grilled Courgettes [Broiled Zucchini]) **4**–467
Courgettes à la Provençale (Courgettes [Zucchini] Cooked in Olive Oil with Garlic and Parsley) **4**–467
Courgettes Sautées Maître d'Hôtel (Courgettes [Zucchini] with Lemon, Butter and Parsley Sauce) **4**–467
Courgettes aux Tomates (Courgettes [Zucchini] and Tomato Casserole) **4**–468
Dulma (Stuffed Aubergines [Eggplants] Courgettes [Zucchini] and Tomatoes) **5**–589
Eggah with Courgettes [Zucchini] **5**–630
Elegante (Courgettes [Zucchini] and Sweetcorn with Goat's Milk Cheese) **5**–642
Quiche aux Courgettes et Tomates (Courgettes [Zucchini] and Tomato Quiche) **15**–2022
Risotto con Zucchini (Braised Rice with Courgettes [Zucchini]) **16**–2132
Tomato and Courgette [Zucchini] Soup **18**–2513
Zappellitos Rellenos (Stuffed Courgettes [Zucchini]) **21**–2979
Zucchini (info) **22**–3028
Zucchini all'Agrodolce (Courgettes in Sour-Sweet Sauce) **22**–3028
Zucchini con Aneto (Courgettes with Dill Sauce) **22**–3030
Zucchini e Cavolfiore (Courgettes and Cauliflower with Tumeric) **22**–3030
Zucchini in Dolce (Courgette Cake) **22**–3030
Zucchini con Frittelle (Courgette Pancakes) **22**–3032
Zucchini al Fromaggio (Courgettes with Cheese) **22**–3030
Zucchini con Mandorle (Courgettes with Almonds) **22**–3032
Zucchini alla Marinara (Courgettes Stuffed with Prawns or Shrimps and Tomatoes) **22**–3033
Zucchini Orientali (Oriental Stuffed Courgettes) **22**–3033
Zucchini e Peperoni (Courgettes Baked with Red Peppers) **22**–3033
Zucchini, Pomodori e Finocchio (Courgettes, Tomatoes and Fennel) **22**–3036
Zucchini Ripieni (Stuffed Courgettes) **22**–3036
Zucchini Ripieni di Salsiccie (Courgettes Stuffed with Sausages) **22**–3036
Zucchini in Stufato (Stewed Courgettes) **22**–3037
Zucchini in Sufflè (Courgette Soufflé) **22**–3037
Zuppa di Zucchini (Courgette Soup) **22**–3063

Cress (info) **4**–501

Cucumber

Cucumber (info) **4**–515
Agurkai su Rukcscia Grietne (Cucumber and Soured Cream Salad) **1**–6
Agurkesalat (Danish Pickled Cucumber Salad) **1**–7
Apple and Cucumber Salad **1**–45
Cream of Cucumber Soup **4**–482
Cucumber and Beer Soup **4**–515
Cucumber and Cheese Salad **4**–515
Cucumber in Cream **4**–515
Cucumber Dressing **4**–515
Cucumber Florentine **4**–515
Cucumber and Grape Salad **4**–516
Cucumbers and Mushrooms in Cream Sauce **4**–517
Cucumber and Onion Salad **4**–517
Cucumber and Pork Soup **4**–517
Cucumber Relish **4**–518
Cucumber Soup **4**–518
Cucumber Stuffed with Tuna **4**–518
Cucumber and Tomato Salad **4**–518
Fennel and Cucumber Salad **5**–684
Fried Pineapple and Cucumber Chinese-Style **6**–756
Gherkin (info) **6**–822
Gurkenbowle (Cucumber Punch) **7**–897
Pickled Cucumbers I **13**–1778
Pickled Cucumbers II **13**–1779
Stuffed Cucumbers **18**–2430
Tsingshih Soup (Smoked Ham and Cucumber Soup) **18**–2557
Vellerikai Pachadi (Cucumber and Yogurt Salad) **20**–2661
Wilted Cucumber **20**–2816
Yogurt and Cucumber Salad **21**–2929
Zacatecas Browned Cucumber **21**–2969
Eggplant see Aubergine

Endive (info) **5**–646

Fennel

Fennel (info) **5**–684
Fennel Cream Sauce **5**–684
Fennel and Cucumber Salad **5**–684
Fennel Soup **5**–684
Fenouils au Gratin (Fennel in Cheese Sauce) **5**–684
Fenouils à la Grecque (Fennel Greek-Style) **5**–685

Garlic

Garlic (info) **6**–798
Aïgo Bouïdo (French Provençal Garlic Soup) **1**–7
Alioli Sauce (Garlic Mayonnaise) **1**–12
Bagna Cauda (Anchovy and Garlic Dip) **1**–105
Beurre d'Ail (Garlic Butter) **2**–164
Garlic Bread **6**–798
Garlic Dip **6**–798
Garlic Mashed Potatoes **6**–799
Garlic Salad **6**–800
Garlic Soup **6**–801
Garlic Stuffed Eggs **6**–801
Garlic Toast **6**–801
Mussels with Garlic Butter **11**–1462
Omelette Provençale (Tomato, Onion and Garlic Omelet) **12**–1584

General Vegetable Dishes

Bubble and Squeak **2**–277
Crudités avec Aïoli (Raw Vegetables with Garlic Mayonnaise) **4**–512
Egg Ratatouille **5**–624
Egg and Vegetable Flan **5**–629
Fried Mixed Vegetables **6**–755
Frittata di Carne e Vegetali (Vegetable and Meat Omelet) **6**–759
Fritto Misto (Deep-Fried Meat and Vegetables) **6**–762
Fruit and Vegetable Salad **6**–775
Ghiveciu (Rumanian Vegetable Stew) **6**–823
Julienne of Celery, Potatoes and Green Pepper **8**–1088
Kachang Bendi Goreng (Fried Mixed Green Vegetables and Prawns) **8**–1091
Korean Vegetable Salad **9**–1167
Légumes à la Grecque (Marinated Vegetables) **9**–1221
Légumes Nouveaux Flambés (Mixed Fresh Vegetables with Brandy) **9**–1222
Leipziger Allerlei (Mixed Vegetables in Cream Sauce) **9**–1223
Lesco (Sausage and Vegetable Stew) **9**–1234
Olive and Vegetable Mix **12**–1574
Paprika Vegetable and Sausage Stew **12**–1674
Piatto Freddo di Ortaggi (Cold Mixed Vegetables) **13**–1773
Puntzin (Vegetable Rice) **15**–1989

Ratatouille (Mixed Vegetable Casserole) **15**–2067
Sabzi Pulao (Vegetable Pilaff) **16**–2198
Vegetable Bharta **19**–2641
Vegetable Casserole **19**–2643
Vegetable Couscous **19**–2643
Vegetable Curry **19**–2644
Vegetable Kitcheri **19**–2645
Vegetable Marrow Salad **19**–2646
Vegetable Mix **19**–2647
Vegetable Paella **19**–2648
Vegetable Patties **19**–2648
Vegetable Pie **19**–2648
Vegetable and Pork Salad **19**–2650
Vegetable and Prawn or Shrimp Curry **19**–2651
Vegetable Pulao with Prawns or Shrimps **19**–2651
Vegetable Rissoles **19**–2652
Vegetable Savoury **19**–2653
Vegetarian Moussaka **19**–2656
Voedzaam Salade (Vegetable Salad) **20**–2714
Western Fruit and Vegetable Stew **20**–2770
Zoftic Mixed Vegetables **22**–3007

Gourd (info) **7**–859

Horseradish

Horseradish (info) **7**–970
Horseradish and Apricot Sauce **7**–971
Horseradish Butter **7**–971
Horseradish and Herb Sauce **7**–971
Horseradish Sauce (Cold) **7**–971
Horseradish Sauce (Hot) **7**–971
Horseradish and Sour Cream Sauce **7**–971
Horseradish Vinegar **7**–971

Julienne (info) **8**–1088
Kail Brose (info) **8**–1095

Kale

Kale (info) **8**–1100
Kale with Cream Sauce **8**–1100
Kale with Onions and Italian Sausage **8**–1100
Sea Kale (info) **17**–2280

Kohlrabi

Kohlrabi (info) **9**–1163
Kohlrabi in Béchamel Sauce **9**–1164
Kohlrabi Soup **9**–1164
Ladies' Fingers *see* Okra

Leek

Leek (info) **9**–1215
Chicken and Leek Pie **3**–382
Cock-a-Leekie **4**–427
Flan à la Bourguignonne (Flan with Leek and Bacon Filling) **6**–721
Irish Leek and Oatmeal Broth **8**–1030
Lapin aux Poireaux (Rabbit and Leek Casserole) **9**–1208
Lauchsalat (Leek Salad) **9**–1214
Leeks in Béchamel Sauce **9**–1215
Leek and Sausage Tart **9**–1216
Leek and Shrimp Salad **9**–1216
Leek Soup **9**–1216
Leek Vinaigrette **9**–1216
Poireaux à l'Hongroise (Leeks Hungarian-Style) **14**–1849
Poireaux au Miel (Leeks with Honey Dressing) **14**–1850
Potage de Poireaux et Cresson (Leek and Cress Soup) **14**–1920
Vichyssoise (Cold Cream of Leek and Potato Soup) **20**–2685
Y Mwd Leeks **21**–2899
Zoytinyagli Pirasa (Leek and Bacon Rissotto) **22**–3020
Zug Sausage and Leek Casserole **22**–3042

Lettuce

Lettuce (info) **9**–1234
Cream of Lettuce Soup **4**–483
Eggs with Savoury Creamed Lettuce **5**–626
Iceberg (info) **8**–1000
Kopfsalat mit Buttermilch (Lettuce Salad with Buttermilk) **9**–1166
Laitues aux Crevettes (Lettuces Baked with Shrimps) **9**–1188
Laitues au Gratin (Lettuces with Cheese Sauce) **9**–1189
Lamb's Lettuce (info) **9**–1202
Lettuce Heart and Fruit Salad **9**–1235
Romaine (info) **16**–2159
Romaine and Orange Salad **16**–2159
Vol-au-Vent d'Eté (Puff Pastry Case Filled with Lettuce and Egg) **20**–2718
Wilted Lettuce Salad **20**–2817
Zeebrugge Crabmeat and Lettuce Mould **21**–2986

Lima Beans

Lima Bean (info) **9**–1237
Lima Beans with Mushrooms **9**–1238

Lotus

Lotus (info) **10**–1270
Lotus Root Salad **10**–1272

Macédoine (info) **10**–1282

Marrow [Summer Squash]

Marrow (info) **10**–1328
Custard Marrow (info) **4**–523
Fish-Stuffed Marrow [Large Summer Squash] **6**–716
Kusa (Squash Soufflé) **9**–1183
Marrow [Summer Squash] and Ginger Jam **10**–1328
Marrow [Summer Squash] Pickle **10**–1328
Marrow [Summer Squash] with Savoury Stuffing **10**–1329
Marrow [Summer Squash] Soup **10**–1330
Squash (info) **18**–2398
Squash with Bacon and Spices **18**–2399
Squash with Tomatoes **18**–2399
Tiffany Bake **18**–2500
Wensley Dale Marrow [Summer Squash] **20**–2764
Working Man's Bake **21**–2867
Xuxu (Brazilian Vegetable Marrow [Summer Squash] with Shrimps or Prawns) **21**–2898

Miso (info) **11**–1407

Mushroom

Mushroom (info) **11**–1451
Bamboo Shoots with Mushrooms **1**–108
Barley and Mushroom Casserole **1**–125
Cèpe (info) **11**–1451
Champignons au Beurre (Mushrooms Sautéed in Butter) **3**–353
Champignons à Blanc (Stewed Mushrooms) **3**–353
Champignons Farcis (Stuffed Mushrooms) **3**–354
Champignons Grillés (Grilled [Broiled] Mushroom Caps) **3**–354
Champignons au Madère (Mushrooms in Madeira Sauce) **3**–354
Champignons Pyramide (Mushrooms Baked with Cream and Sherry) **3**–355
Champignons Sautés à la Crème (Creamed Mushrooms) **3**–355
Consommé aux Champignons (Mushroom Consommé) **4**–442
Cream of Mushroom Soup **4**–484
Creamed Mushrooms **4**–486
Cucumbers and Mushrooms in Cream Sauce **4**–517

Duxelles (Mushroom Stuffing) **5**–594
Eggs Baked with Creamed Mushrooms **5**–612
Farce Duxelles (Mushroom Stuffing) **5**–676
Friar Tuck Toast **6**–750
Fungi (info) **6**–777
Gruyère and Mushroom Salad **7**–888
Insalata di Funghi (Mushroom Salad) **8**–1026
Kasha with Mushrooms and Onions **8**–1113
Kidney and Mushroom Croûtes **9**–1136
Lamb and Mushroom Stew **9**–1200
Lima Beans with Mushrooms **9**–1238
Liver and Mushroom Omelet **9**–1249
Lobster and Mushroom Mousse **9**–1257
Marinated Mushrooms **10**–1314
Morel (info) **11**–1420
Mushroom and Asparagus Mayonnaise **11**–1452
Mushroom and Bacon Salad **11**–1452
Mushroom and Celery on Toast **11**–1452
Mushrooms with Cucumber **11**–1452
Mushroom and Ham Crêpes **11**–1452
Mushrooms Hungarian-Style **11**–1453
Mushroom Ketchup **11**–1454
Mushroom and Mint Salad **11**–1454
Mushroom Pie **11**–1454
Mushroom Purée **11**–1455
Mushroom Rolls **11**–1456
Mushroom Sandwich Filling **11**–1456
Mushroom Sauce **11**–1457
Mushroom Soup I **11**–1457
Mushroom Soup II **11**–1457
Mushrooms with Tarragon Mayonnaise **11**–1458
Mushrooms in Vine Leaves **11**–1458
Omelette Bonne Femme (Onion, Mushroom and Bacon Omelet) **12**–1578
Omelette aux Champignons (Mushroom Omelet) **12**–1578
Omelette Chasseur (Omelet with Mushrooms, Shallots and Wine) **12**–1579
Paglia Fieno (Pasta with Veal and Mushrooms) **12**–1656
Petits Pots de Champignons (Mushrooms and Bacon Cooked in Small Pots) **13**–1765
Pilaff à la Grecque (Rice Cooked with Mushrooms) **13**–1795
Pizza ai Funghi (Pizza with Mushrooms) **14**–1833
Provençal-Style Mushrooms **15**–1980
Puffball (info) **15**–1984
Quiche aux Champignons (Mushroom Quiche) **15**–2022
Sardine Cups **16**–2240
Semmelknodel mit Pilzer (Dumplings with Mushroom Sauce) **17**–2286
Soufflé de Champignons (Mushroom Soufflé) **17**–2353
Tamarind-Flavoured Mushrooms **18**–2473
Tourte aux Champignons (Mushroom and Fish Pie) **19**–2533
Vine Leaves and Mushrooms **20**–2698
Wild Rice with Mushrooms **20**–2811
Wykeham Mushrooms **21**–2885

Mustard and Cress (info) **11**–1463

Nasturtium

Nasturtium (info) **11**–1477
Nasturtium Buds, Pickled **11**–1477
Nasturtium Spread **11**–1478

Nettle

Nettle (info) **11**–1493
Nettle Soup **11**–1493

Okra [Ladies' Fingers]

Okra [Ladies' Fingers] (info) **12**–1565
Gumbo (info) **7**–896
Gumbo Soup **7**–896
Ladies' Fingers (info) **9**–1187
Okra [Ladies' Fingers] with Bacon **12**–1567
Okra [Ladies' Fingers] and Lamb Casserole **12**–1567

Thematic

Okra [Ladies' Fingers] Salad **12**–1567
Okra [Ladies' Fingers] and Tomato Casserole
 12–1567
Vendai Kai Kari (Curried Okra [Ladies'
 Fingers]) **20**–2665

Olive

Olive (info) **12**–1571
Olive Meat Loaf **12**–1572
Olive Oil (info) **12**–1572
Olive Pizza **12**–1572
Olive Salad **12**–1573
Olive-Stuffed Eggs **12**–1573
Olive-Stuffed Pork **12**–1573
Olive and Vegetable Mix **12**–1574

Onion

Onion (info) **12**–1587
Cheese and Onion Pie **3**–366
Creamed Peas and Onions **4**–486
Eggs Baked with Onions **5**–613
Eshkaneh (Persian Onion Soup) **5**–659
French Onion Soup **6**–749
Glazed Onions **6**–839
Huntingdon Fidget Pie **8**–994
Imam Bayeldi (Aubergines [Eggplants] with
 Tomatoes and Onions) **8**–1016
Kasha with Mushrooms and Onions **8**–1113
Lökdolmar (Stuffed Onions) **9**–1266
Mahasha (Stuffed Onion Skins) **10**–1287
Omelette Bonne Femme (Onion, Mushroom
 and Bacon Omelet) **12**–1578
Omelette Lyonnaise (Onion Omelet) **12**–1583
Omelette Niçoise (Omelet with Anchovies,
 Olives, Tomatoes and Onion) **12**–1582
Omelette Provençale (Tomato, Onion and
 Garlic Omelet) **12**–1584
Onion Bread ·**12**–1587
Onion Dip **12**–1588
Onion, Egg and Potato Pie **12**–1588
Onion and Egg Spread **12**–1590
Onion Gruel **12**–1590
Onion Kuchen **12**–1590
Onions with Lemon and Marjoram Sauce
 12–1591
Onion and Mackerel Salad **12**–1592
Onion and Paprika Dressing **12**–1592
Onion Pie **12**–1593
Onion and Potato Hash **12**–1593
Onion and Prunes **12**–1594
Onion Ragoût **12**–1594
Onion Rings, Deep-Fried **12**–1594
Onion Sauce **12**–1594
Onions Smothered with Walnuts **12**–1595
Onion Soup **12**–1595
Onions with Sour Cream **12**–1596
Onions Stuffed and Baked **12**–1597
Onions in Sweet and Sour Sauce **12**–1597
Onion and Sweetcorn Hors d'Oeuvre **12**–1598
Piccalilli **13**–1774
Pickled Onions **13**–1780
Quebec Onion Soup **15**–2005
Quiches aux Oignons (Little Onion Quiches)
 15–2024
Scallion (info) **17**–2264
Spring Onion (info) **18**–2397
Spring Onion [Scallion] and Tomato Soup
 18–2397
Stuffed Onions **18**–2432
Succotash **18**–2436
Tzibbele Kugel (Onion Cake) **19**–2583
Welsh Onion (info) **20**–2759
Yulla Brown Onion Soup with Port **21**–2960
Zarzar Red Pepper and Onion Soup **21**–2984
Zwiebelkuchen (German Onion Tart)
 22–3077

Oseille (info) **12**–1628
Oxalis (info) **12**–1638

Palm Heart

Palm Heart (info) **12**–1664
Palm Hearts Baked with Cheese Sauce **12**–1664
Palm Heart Cocktail **12**–1664
Palm Heart Salad **12**–1665

Parsnip

Parsnip (info) **13**–1681
Parsnips, Glazed **13**–1682
Parsnips with Onions **13**–1682
Parsnips, Puréed **13**–1682
Parsnip Salad **13**–1682
Parsnip and Tomato Soup **13**–1682
Soufflé aux Panais (Parsnip Soufflé) **17**–2357
Zennor's Country Parsnip Soup **21**–2991
Zurich Veal and Parsnip Pie **22**–3065

Pea

Pea (info) **13**–1710
Cream of Green Pea Soup **4**–483
Creamed Peas and Onions **4**–486
Curried Potatoes and Peas **4**–523
Dutch Split Pea Soup **5**–592
Eggs with Peas and Corn **5**–624
Erbsenpürre (Split Pea and Vegetable Purée)
 5–652
Erwtensoep (Pea Soup) **5**–652
Green Peas with Ham **7**–872
Green Pea Soup **7**–872
Mange-tout (Snow Pea) (info) **10**–1300
Mange-tout Salad **10**–1300
Omelette Clamart (Green Pea Omelet) **12**–1579
Opiekanki z Grochu (Pea Croquettes) **12**–1598
Pea Soup with Ham **13**–1710
Pease Pudding **13**–1724
Perciatelli con Piselli (Pasta with Green Pea
 Sauce) **13**–1749
Petits Pois (info) **13**–1762
Petits Pois au Beurre (Small Garden Peas
 Cooked with Butter) **13**–1762
Petits Pois à la Bonne Femme (Small Garden
 Peas with Bacon and Onions) **13**–1763
Petits Pois à la Crème (Small Garden Peas
 Cooked with Cream) **13**–1763
Petits Pois à la Française (Small Garden Peas,
 French-Style) **13**–1764
Petits Pois aux Oignons (Small Garden Peas
 Cooked with Onions) **13**–1764
Prosciutto ai Piselli (Ham with Peas) **15**–1979
Quebec Split Pea Soup **15**–2008
Risi e Bisi (Rice with Peas) **16**–2130
Split Peas (info) **18**–2391
Split Pea Soup **18**–2392
Split Pea Soup with Mint and Tomatoes
 18–2392
Viennese Fresh Pea Soup **20**–2690
Yellow Split Pea Purée **20**–2919
Zonder Sweetcorn and Petits Pois Hors
 d'Oeuvre **22**–3012

Peppers—Green and Red

Pepper (info) **13**–1740
Ardei Umplutzi cu Orez (Stuffed Green Peppers
 and Tomato Sauce) **1**–61
Ardei cu Untdelemn (Marinated Pepper Salad)
 1–60
Bean Sprouts with Green Peppers **1**–140
Capsicum (info) **3**–319
Corn with Red Peppers **4**–454
Green Pepper Salad **7**–873
Green Peppers Stuffed with Pork and Veal
 7–873
Guido's Italian Sausage Rolls **7**–893
Neapolitan Stuffed Peppers **11**–1485
Peperonata (Red Pepper and Tomato Stew)
 13–1737
Peperoni alla Bagna Cauda (Sweet Peppers with
 Garlic and Anchovy Sauce) **13**–1738
Peperoni Ripieni (Peppers Stuffed with
 Tomatoes, Tuna, Anchovies and Olives)
 13–1738

Peperoni e Zucchini (Peppers and Courgettes
 [Zucchini] in Tomato Sauce) **13**–1739
Pepper and Corned Beef Hash **13**–1739
Pepper Sauce **13**–1739
Peppers Preserved in Vinegar **13**–1743
Peppers Stuffed with Lamb and Rice **13**–1743
Piatto Freddo di Ortaggi (Cold Mixed
 Vegetables) **13**–1773
Pilaff with Peppers and Chicken **13**–1796
Pimiento (info) **13**–1798
Pimiento Chicken **13**–1798
Pipérade (Pepper and Tomato Omelet) **13**–1815
Purée de Piments au Riz (Pimiento or Red
 Pepper Purée) **15**–1990
Stuffed Green Peppers Indian-Style **18**–2431
Stuffed Green Peppers with Rice **18**–2431
Yucatan Stuffed Peppers **21**–2951
Zarzar Red Pepper and Onion Soup **21**–2984

Potato

Potato (info) **14**–1921
Allumettes (Matchstick Potatoes) **1**–17
Apple and Potato Stuffing **1**–49
Batatas à Portuguêsa (Portuguese Fried
 Potatoes) **1**–128
Bordure de Pommes de Terre (Potato Border)
 2–210
Boxty (Irish Potato Pancakes) **2**–225
Bramborová Polevka (Potato Soup) **2**–233
Bramborové Knedliky (Potato Dumplings)
 2–233
Brown-baked Potato Slices **2**–276
Bubble and Squeak **2**–277
Champ **3**–351
Château Potatoes **3**–361
Cheeps **3**–361
Colcannon (Potato and Cabbage Hash) **4**–438
Croquettes de Pommes de Terre (Potato
 Croquettes) **4**–504
Croquettes de Pommes de Terre et Viande
 (Potato and Meat Croquettes) **4**–505
Curried Potatoes and Peas **4**–523
Duchess Potatoes **4**–581
Eggs in Baked Potatoes **5**–613
Egg and Potato Pie **5**–624
Ella's Tomato and Potato Pie **5**–642
Floddies **6**–726
French Potato Salad **6**–749
Game Chips **6**–788
Garlic Mashed Potatoes **6**–799
German Potato Salad **6**–819
Ghost aur Aloo (Beef and Potato Curry) **6**–823
Gnocchi di Patate (Potato Dumplings) **7**–842
Gratin de Pommes de Terre à la Dauphinoise
 (Potatoes Baked with Milk, Cheese and Garlic)
 7–866
Gratin de Pommes de Terre à la Savoyarde
 (Potatoes Baked with Beef Stock and Cheese)
 7–866
Gratin de Pommes de Terre et Viande (Potato
 and Beef Patties Baked with Tomato Sauce)
 7–866
Hash Brown Potatoes **7**–934
Hasselbackspotatis (Roast Potato Fans) **7**–934
Herb and Potato Soup **7**–946
Himmel und Erde (Mashed Potatoes and Apple)
 7–952
Irish Potato Cakes **8**–1031
Julienne of Celery, Potatoes and Green Pepper
 8–1088
Jumping Potatoes **8**–1089
Kartoffelmos med Aebler (Mashed Potato with
 Apple Purée) **8**–1109
Kartoffelsalat (Jewish Potato Salad) **8**–1109
Korsakov Meat and Potato Pie **9**–1168
Kümmelkartoffeln (German Caraway Potatoes)
 9–1179
Latkes **9**–1213
New Potatoes Cooked in Butter **11**–1500
New Potatoes with Sour Cream and Caviar
 11–1500
Noisette Potatoes (info) **11**–1510
Nova Scotia Potato Patties **11**–1524
O'Brien Potatoes **12**–1546

Ocopa Arequipeña (Potatoes with Peanut and Chilli Sauce) **12**–1550
Omelette Parmentier (Potato Omelet) **12**–1583
Onion and Potato Hash **12**–1593
Pain de Pommes de Terre au Jambon (Potato and Ham Loaf) **12**–1659
Palourdes Perdues (Clams Baked with Potatoes and Sweetcorn) **17**–1667
Parisian Potatoes (info) **12**–1677
Parsley Potatoes **13**–1681
Pommes de Terre Anna (Potato Slices Baked with Butter) **14**–1866
Pommes de Terre Campagnardes (Potatoes Country-Style) **14**–1866
Pommes de Terre Dauphine (Deep-Fried Potato Shapes) **14**–1868
Pommes de Terre Fondantes (Olive-Shaped Potatoes) **14**–1868
Pommes de Terre Galette (Potato Cake) **14**–1869
Pommes de Terre à la Lyonnaise (Potatoes with Onions) **14**–1869
Pommes de Terre Ménagère (Mashed Potatoes with Ham) **14**–1869
Pommes de Terre à la Provençale (Potatoes with Garlic) **14**–1869
Pommes de Terre au Roquefort (Baked Potatoes with Blue Cheese) **14**–1870
Pommes de Terre Sautées au Citron (Sautéed Potatoes Flavoured with Lemon) **14**–1870
Pommes de Terre Soufflés (Potato Puffs) **14**–1871
Portuguese Potatoes **14**–1908
Potage Parmentier (Potato Soup) **14**–1919
Potato Bread **14**–1925
Potato Casserole **14**–1925
Potato and Cheese Pie **14**–1925
Potato Croquettes **14**–1926
Potato Fritters **14**–1926
Potato and Herring Salad **14**–1927
Potato Kugel **14**–1927
Potatoes with Peppers and Olives **14**–1927
Potato Puffs **14**–1929
Potato Salad **14**–1929
Potato and Cheese Salad **14**–1929
Potato, Egg and Anchovy Salad **14**–1929
Potato Salad with Herbs **14**–1930
Potato Scones [Biscuits] **14**–1930
Potatoes with Spices and Mustard **14**–1930
Potatoes Stuffed and Baked **14**–1930
Pytt i Panna (Swedish Hash) **15**–1994
Racuchy (Polish Deep-Fried Potato Cakes) **15**–2044
Rakott Burgonya (Hungarian Potato Pie) **15**–2060
Rösti (Swiss Potato Cake) **16**–2167
Sauer Kartoffeln (Soured Potatoes) **17**–2250
Scandinavian Potato Fritters **17**–2273
Spinach with Potatoes **18**–2385
Stovies **18**–2418
Swiss Potatoes **18**–2457
Turkari Aloo (Curried Potatoes) **19**–2564
Überbackenes Sauerkraut (Sauerkraut and Potato Bake) **19**–2585
Vichyssoise (Cold Cream of Leek and Potato Soup) **20**–2685
Wiltshire Ham in Crispy Baked Potatoes **20**–2817
Yeaman's Spiced Potatoes **21**–2914
Yieldtree Potatoes with Shallots **21**–2925
Zafra Potato Crunch **21**–2969
Zuger Zee Scramble **22**–3043

Pumpkin

Pumpkin (info) **15**–1985
Flan au Potiron Caramelisé (Pumpkin and Caramel Flan) **6**–722
Hag Ha'asif Tzimmis **7**–905
Kadu Polo (Pumpkin and Lamb Patties with Rice) **8**–1092
Pumpkin Pie **15**–1986
Pumpkin Salad **15**–1986
Pumpkin Soup I **15**–1986
Pumpkin Soup II **15**–1987

White Pumpkin Halva **20**–2790
Zoller Pumpkin Stew **22**–3009
Zucca alla Parmigiana (Pumpkin Parma-Style) **22**–3027

Quelite (info) **15**–2014

Radish

Radish (info) **15**–2044
Radish, Celery and Cucumber Salad **15**–2045
Radishes in Cream **15**–2045
Radis Glacés (Glazed Radishes) **15**–2045

Rape (info) **15**–2061
Rocambole (info) **16**–2145
Root Vegetables (info) **16**–2162
Rutabaga *see* Swede

Salsify

Salsify (info) **16**–2227
Salsify Sautéed with Butter and Herbs **16**–2227
Salsify with Tarragon Sauce **16**–2228
Scallion *see* Onion
Scorzonera (info) **17**–2278

Seaweed

Seaweed (info) **17**–2283
Carrageen Moss (info) **3**–331
Irish Moss (info) **8**–1030
Irish Moss Mould **8**–1030
Laver (info) **9**–1214

Shallot

Shallot (info) **17**–2293
Omelette Chasseur (Omelet with Mushrooms, Shallots and Wine) **12**–1579

Soya Bean

Soya Bean (info) **17**–2365
Bean Curd (info) **1**–139
Bean Curd and Crab Meat **1**–139
Bean Curd Skin (info) **1**–139
Soya Protein Chilli **17**–2365
Soya Protein with Sour Cream **17**–2365
Vegetarian Moussaka **19**–2656
Vegetarian Stew, Indian-Style **19**–2658

Spinach

Spinach (info) **18**–2383
Borani Esfanaj (Spinach and Yogurt Salad) **2**–209
Canapés aux Epinards (Spinach and Cheese Canapés) **3**–304
Chicken Florentine (Chicken Breasts with Spinach) **3**–380
Creamed Spinach **4**–487
Crêpes d'Epinards (Spinach Crêpes) **4**–496
Egg Noodles Baked with Spinach **5**–622
Egg and Spinach Salad **5**–626
Eggah with Spinach **5**–632
Epinards au Gratin (Spinach with Cheese) **5**–651
Epinards à la Provençal (Spinach with Tomatoes and Garlic) **5**–652
Friar Tuck Toast **6**–750
Fritter-Coated Spinach Leaves **6**–760
Gnocchi Verdi (Spinach Dumplings) **7**–842
Herb and Spinach Flan **7**–946
Kambala s Shpinatom (Flounder Fillets Baked with Spinach) **8**–1102
Mozzarella Crespoltini (Cheese and Spinach Crêpes) **11**–1441
Nkontomire Fro (Stewed Spinach with Fish) **11**–1502
Oeufs Florentine (Eggs with Spinach) **12**–1557
Omelette Florentine (Spinach Omelet) **12**–1580
Russian Fish Bake **16**–2188
Sag Gohst (Spinach with Meat) **16**–2205

Soufflé d'Epinards et Jambon (Spinach Soufflé with Ham) **17**–2354
Spinach with Ham **18**–2383
Spinach with Potatoes **18**–2385
Spinach Ring **18**–2385
Spinach Salad **18**–2388
Spinach Soufflé **18**–2388
Spinach Soup I **18**–2388
Spinach Soup II **18**–2389
Spinach-Stuffed Crêpes **18**–2389
Taraba (Meatballs Enclosed in Spinach) **18**–2478
Timbale aux Epinards (Spinach Mould) **18**–2500
Willow Lake Spinach **20**–2815
Yarmacott Spinach and Apple Soufflé **21**–2911
Zofe Spinach Soup **22**–3007

Spring Onion *see* Onion
Squash and Summer Squash *see* Marrow

Swede

Swede (info) **18**–2446
Länttulaatikka (Swede [Rutabaga] Casserole) **9**–1208
Rutabaga (info) **16**–2192
Rutabaga [Swede] and Apple Snow **16**–2192
Rutabaga [Swede] Bake **16**–2192

Sweetcorn

Sweetcorn (info) **18**–2451
Corn (info) **4**–451
Corn Chowder **4**–452
Corn on the Cob **4**–452
Corn Oil (info) **4**–453
Corn and Prawn Savoury **4**–453
Corn with Red Peppers **4**–454
Egg and Corn Savoury **5**–617
Eggs with Peas and Corn **5**–624
Elegante (Courgettes [Zucchini] and Sweetcorn with Goat's Milk Cheese) **5**–642
Green Mealie Fritters **7**–872
Kidneys with Sweetcorn **9**–1140
Maize (info) **10**–1290
Mealie (info) **10**–1347
Mush (info) **11**–1451
Onion and Sweetcorn Hors d'Oeuvre **12**–1598
Pastel de Choclo (Meat and Corn Pie) **13**–1692
Pennsylvania Dutch Chicken Corn Soup **13**–1735
Shrimp and Sweetcorn Soup **17**–2314
Succotash **17**–2436
Sweetcorn and Chicken Soup **18**–2452
Sweetcorn Mayonnaise **18**–2452
Sweetcorn and Mushroom Croûtes **18**–2452
Sweetcorn Rarebit **18**–2452
Sweetcorn Salad **18**–2454
Timbales de Mais (Sweetcorn Moulds) **18**–2502
Torrejas de Maiz Tierno (Fresh Corn Fritters) **19**–2522
Vermont Corn Bake **20**–2680
Wyandotte Sweetcorn and Tomato Bake **21**–2882
Yankee Stuffed Corn **21**–2908
Zonder Sweetcorn and Petits Pois Hors d'Oeuvre **22**–3012

Sweet Potato

Sweet Potato (info) **18**–2454
Hag Ha'asif Tzimmis **7**–905
Sweet Potato Flan **18**–2454
Zuccotash (Sweet Potato and Marshmallow Bake) **22**–3038

Tomato

Tomato (info) **18**–2512
Basil Baked Tomatoes **1**–127
Basil and Tomato Aspic **1**–127
Chicory and Tomato Salad **3**–401
Consommé Madrilène (Tomato Consommé) **4**–442

Thematic

Cream of Tomato Soup 4–484
Cucumber and Tomato Salad 4–518
Dulma (Stuffed Aubergines [Eggplants], Courgettes [Zucchini] and Tomatoes) 5–589
Ella's Tomato and Potato Pie 5–642
Green Tomato Chutney 7–874
Imam Bayeldi (Aubergines [Eggplants] with Tomatoes and Onions) 8–1016
Kasha with Tomatoes and Parmesan Cheese 8–1113
Maine Cauliflower and Tomato Pickle 10–1289
Mussels Baked with Basil and Tomato Sauce 11–1459
Omelette Americaine 12–1574 12–1574
Omelette Niçoise (Omelet with Anchovies, Olives, Tomatoes and Onion) 12–1582
Omelette Provençale (Tomato, Onion and Garlic Omelet) 12–1584
Oriental Relish 12–1625
Ovos Duros à Portuguesa (Portuguese Eggs in Tomato Shells) 12–1635
Parsnip and Tomato Soup 12–1682
Peperonata (Red Pepper and Tomato Stew) 13–1737
Peperoni Ripieni (Peppers Stuffed with Tomatoes, Tuna, Anchovies and Olives) 13–1738
Pipérade (Pepper and Tomato Omelet) 13–1815
Pizzaiola Sauce (Italian Tomato and Garlic Sauce) 14–1828
Pizza Capri (Pizza with Tomatoes, Cheese and Capers) 14–1832
Pomodori alla Siciliana (Sicilian Stuffed Tomatoes) 14–1871
Potage de Tomate à la Paysanne (Tomato Soup Peasant-Style) 14–1921
Spring Onion [Scallion] and Tomato Soup 18–2397
Stuffed Tomatoes Indian-Style 18–2433
Tabboulch (Wheat and Tomato Salad) 18–2462
Tamatar Bharta (Puréed Tomatoes) 18–2473
Tamatar Chatni (Indian Tomato Chutney) 18–2473
Tamatar Machli (Tomato Fish) 18–2474
Tamatar Sas (Indian Tomato Sauce) 18–2474
Tomates Farcies aux Oeufs (Tomatoes Stuffed with Eggs) 18–2510
Tomates Farcies à la Provençale (Tomatoes Stuffed with Anchovies, Breadcrumbs and Garlic) 18–2510
Tomates Farcies au Riz (Tomatoes Stuffed with Rice) 18–2511
Tomato Aspic 18–2512
Tomato and Cheese Savoury 18–2512
Tomato and Chicken Salad 18–2512
Tomato Chutney 18–2513
Tomato and Courgette [Zucchini] Soup 18–2513
Tomato Curry 18–2514
Tomato-Filled Choux Pastry Ring 18–2514

Tomato and French Bean Salad 18–2515
Tomato and Mozzarella Salad 18–2515
Tomato and Orange Salad 18–2516
Tomato Pie 18–2516
Tomato Rice I 18–2516
Tomato Rice II 18–2516
Tomato Salad 18–2518
Tomato Sauce 18–2518
Tomato Soup 18–2519
Tuna-Stuffed Tomatoes 19–2560
Vine Leaves Stuffed with Tomatoes 20–2698
Wyandotte Sweetcorn and Tomato Bake 21–2882
Zujar Tomato Soufflés 22–3044

Truffle (info) 19–2552

Turnip

Turnip (info) 19–2578
Jambon con Nabos (Spinach, Ham and Turnip Soup) 8–1058
Navets Glacés (Glazed Turnips) 11–1481
Navets au Gratin (Turnips Baked with Cheese and Breadcrumbs) 11–1481
Navets au Petit Salé (Turnips with Salt Pork) 11–1481
Turnip and Date Salad 19–2578
Turnips Fried in Butter 19–2579
Turnip Pickle 19–2579
Turnip, Potato and Carrot Hash 19–2579
Turnip Soup 19–2579
Turnip Tops Creole-Style 19–2580

Vegetable Fat (info) 19–2644
Vegetable Oil (info) 19–2648
Vegetarian Diets (info) 2654

Vine Leaves

Vine Leaves (info) 20–2695
Dolmadakia (Stuffed Vine Leaves) 5–570
Mushrooms in Vine Leaves 11–1458
Vine Leaves with Apricots 20–2698
Vine Leaves and Mushrooms 20–2698
Vine Leaves Stuffed with Tomatoes 20–2698
Vine Leaf Wrapped Grey Mullet 20–2698

Water Chestnut

Water Chestnut (info) 20–2741
Chicken Liver with Water Chestnuts 3–398

Watercress

Watercress (info) 20–2741
Brèdes de Cresson (Watercress Brèdes) 2–253
Cream of Watercress Soup 4–484
Potage de Poireaux et Cresson (Leek and Cress Soup) 14–1920
Watercress and Almond Soup 20–2741
Watercress and Avocado Mayonnaise 20–2742

Watercress, Fennel, Cucumber and Tomato Salad 20–2742
Watercress and Pork Soup 20–2743
Watercress Sauce 20–2743
Watercress Soup 20–2744

Wild Rice

Wild Rice (info) 20–2810
Wild Rice Casserole 20–2810
Wild Rice Meat Loaf with Barbecue Sauce 20–2810
Wild Rice with Mushrooms 20–2811
Wild Rice and Pork Pilaff 20–2811
Wild Rice Stuffing 20–2812

Yam

Yam (info) 21–2905
Ishu Didi (Nigerian Fried Yams) 8–1034
Nakompatoa Forowee (Salted Fish Fried with Vegetables) 11–1468
Yam with Cheese Sauce 21–2905
Yam Chips 21–2905
Yam Fritters 21–2907
Yam with Oranges 21–2907
Yam with Yogurt 21–2907
Zucchini *see* Courgette

Yorkshire Pudding 21–2940

YOGURT

Yogurt (info) 21–2925
Egg and Yogurt Salad 5–630
Instant Yogurt Pudding 8–1026
Kebabs Marinated in Yogurt 8–1118
Kofta-Kabab Khatai (Meatballs in Yogurt Sauce) 9–1161
Morello Cherries with Yogurt 11–1420
Persian Yogurt Soup 13–1753
Ragenka (Rich Yogurt) 15–2046
Raita (info) 15–2059
Raita I (Yogurt Salad) 15–2059
Raita II (Yogurt Salad) 15–2060
Thayir Kari (Yogurt Curry) 18–2497
Vellarikai Pachadi (Cucumber and Yogurt Salad) 20–2661
Yogurt 21–2926
Yogurt and Avocado Soup 21–2926
Yogurt and Banana Raita 21–2926
Yogurt Chicken 21–2926
Yogurt Chicken and Barley Soup 21–2928
Yogurt Crumb Cake 21–2928
Yogurt and Cucumber Salad 21–2929
Yogurt Curd Cheese 21–2929
Yogurt Dip 21–2929
Yogurt Dressing 21–2929
Yogurt and Orange Jelly [Gelatin] 21–2929
Yogurt Soup 21–2931
Yogurtli Kebab (Lamb with Yogurt) 21–2931

International Index

A

Aberdeen

Smokies 1–3

Africa, East *see* **East Africa**
North *see* **North Africa**
South *see* **South Africa**
West *see* **West Africa**

Algeria

Carrottes à l'Algérienne 3–327

Alsace

Choucroute Garnie 3–416

America

Almond and Black Cherry Aspic Salad 1–20
    Cookies 1–21
Ambrosia 1–25
Apple Pie 1–26
Angel Cake 1–32
Baking Powder Biscuits 2–184
Banana Cream Pie 1–110
Bean Salad 1–139
Berry Torte 2–163
Black Pepper Cookies 2–184
Bloody Mary 2–186
Blueberry Crumble 2–188
    Muffin 2–188
Boston Baked Beans 2–212
    Brown Bread 2–212
Bourbon Glazed Ham 2–224
Bronx Cocktail 2–269
Brownies 2–270
Brunswick Stew 2–272
Buttermilk Pie 3–283
    Scones 3–283
Butterscotch Brownies 3–284
Caesar Salad 3–290
Cape Cod Salad 3–315
Chicken Tamale Pie 3–395
Chili con Carne 3–401
Chiopino 3–404
Chocolate Chiffon Pie 3–407
    Cream Pie 3–409
Clam Chowder 4–426
Clover Club Cocktail 4–426
Coconut Cream Pie 4–430
Collins Cocktails 4–439
Corn Bread 4–452
    Chowder 4–452
Doughnuts 5–574
Dry Martini 5–579
Early American Cookies 5–895
East Coast Oyster Casserole 5–595
    Seafood Bake 5–595
Eggnog Chiffon Pie 5–633
Eggplant Boston 5–635
Election Cake 5–641

Fish Chowder 5–707
    House Punch 5–709
Frosted Walnut Cake 6–763
Frosting 6–765
Fudge Frosting 6–776
Grilled Squab with Butter Sauce 7–882
Grumble Pie 7–887
Gumbo Soup 7–896
Hamburgers 7–920
Harvard Beets 7–932
Hermits 7–948
Highball 7–952
Homard à l'Americaine 7–958
Honey Pecan Pie 7–964
Hoppin' John 7–969
Horse's Neck 7–970
Hush Puppies 8–995
Indian Pudding 8–1020
Johnnycake 8–1080
Kebabs, American-Style 8–1120
King Crab Louis 9–1143
Lime Cream Pie 9–1238
Long Island Bake 10–1268
    Clam Sauce 10–1269
    Halibut Steaks 10–1270
    Seafood Pilau 10–1270
Louisiana Coconut Pie 10–1272
    Rice Pudding 10–1272
    Snack 10–1272
Mahogany Cake 10–1287
Maine Cauliflower and Tomato Pickle 10–1289
    Pancakes 10–1289
Mallow Brownies 10–1294
Manhattan Clam Chowder 10–1302
    Cocktail 10–1302
Maple Sparerib Casserole 10–1309
Marinated Pot Roast 10–1316
Marlborough Apple Pie 10–1319
Marshmallow So'mores 10–1332
Martha Washington Cake 10–1334
Martinville Soulfood Stew 10–1335
Maryland Chicken 10–1336
    Seafood Soup 10–1337
Meatballs American-Style 10–1356
Mint Julep 11–1402
Mocha Cream Pie 11–1410
Molasses Crumb Pie 11–1413
    Hazelnut Pie 11–1413
    Taffy 11–1414
Muffins with Apples 11–1442
    with Cheese 11–1442
    with Herbs 11–1443
Mussel and Beef Pie 11–1460
Nevada Rice Cake 11–1495
New England Boiled Dinner 11–1496
    Meat Loaf 11–1496
    Soda Bread 11–1496
    Wedding Cake 11–1496
New Haven Baked Aubergine 11–1498
New Orleans Barbequed Pork Chops 11–1499
    Lamb Cutlets 11–1499
Nut Waffles 11–1538
Ohio Meat Pie 12–1559
    Pudding 12–1560

Old Fashioned Stew 12–1569
Oregon Venison 12–1624
Oyster Stuffing 12–1653
Oysters Rockefeller 12–1652
Pacific Oyster Soup 12–1654
Pancakes 12–1668–70
Pandowdy 12–1671
Parker House Rolls 12–1678
Peach Cobbler 13–1712
Pecan Pie 13–1725
    and Sour Cream Flan 13–1726
Pennsylvania Dutch Chicken Corn Soup
    13–1735
    Mixed Chow Chow 13–1736
    Poultry Stuffing 13–1737
Pepperoni Pizza 13–1747
Philadelphia Pepper Pot 13–1772
Pineapple Upside-Down Cake 13–1811
Pound Cake 14–1952
Pumpkin Pie 14–1986
Red Flannel Hash 15–2081
Red Snapper, Almond and Walnut Sauce
    15–2087
    Oyster-Stuffed 15–2087
Rich Corn Meal Bread 16–2116
Roast Beef Hash 16–2142
San Francisco Sour Dough Bread 16–2236
Scrapple 17–2279
Screwdriver 17–2280
Shoofly Pie 17–2304
Shortcake 17–2304
Sidecar 17–2318
Spaghetti with Meatballs 17–2369
Squash with Bacon and Spices 18–2409
Succotash 18–2436
Sweetcorn and Chicken Soup 18–2452
Tain Cereal 18–2467
Thousand Island Dressing 18–2498
Turkey American-Style 19–2567
Vermont Corn Bake 20–2680
Virginia Chicken Salad 20–2704
    Crab Patties 20–2707
Waffles 20–2724
Western Burgers 20–2770
Whiskey Sour 20–2778
White Bread 2–246
    Peach Cream 20–2789
Willapa Spoon Bread 20–2815
Williamsburg Lamb 20–2815
Wilted Cucumber 20–2816
Wilted Lettuce Salad 20–2816
Winchester Bread 20–2821
Winnetka Rarebit 21–2848
Winnsboro Rarebit 21–2848
Wisconsin Ham Casserole 21–2855
Wissant Pears with Ginger 21–2855
Wyandotte Sweetcorn and Tomato Bake
    21–2882
Wyoming Cranberry Bread 21–2890
    Devilled Steaks 21–2890
    Viking Salad 21–2892
Yankee Bean Soup 19–2908
    Stuffed Corn 19–2908
Zuccotash Sweet Potato and Marshmallow Bake
    22–3038

International

Arabia

Eggah **5**–630

Argentina

Matambre **10**–1341
Queen's Soup **15**–2012

Arles

Boeuf à la Mode d'Arles **2**–201
Noisettes d'Agneau Arlésienne **11**–1506

Armenia

Kirovakan Fruit **9**–1148
Yerevan Lamb Pilaff **21**–2920

Australia

Carpetbag Steak **3**–330
Oysters Kilpatrick **12**–1651
Paterson Creek Stew **13**–1702

Austria

Bacon Dumplings **1**–102
Boiled Beef **1**–89
Buchteln **2**–278
Cabbage **1**–89
Coffee Cake **1**–89
Gugelhopf **7**–893
Jam Doughnuts **1**–89
Kaiserschmarn **8**–1096
Kalbsreisfleisch **8**–1099
Kaltschale **8**–1101
Karpion b'Paprika **8**–1108
Käsepfannkuchen **8**–1111
Kirschenstrudel **9**–1149
Linzertorte **9**–1242
Malakoff Sponge Cake **9**–1290
Nusscreme Torte **11**–1529
Orangenstangerin **12**–1623
Rococo Torte **16**–2146
Sachertorte **16**–2198
Stritzel **18**–2424
Tauchendorfer Torte **18**–2487
Tiroler Kalbsleber **18**–2503
Viennese Chestnut Cake **20**–2688
   Chocolate Dessert **20**–2689
   Fingers **20**–2690
   Fresh Pea Soup **20**–2690
   Fruit Custard **20**–2692
   Raspberry Pudding **20**–2692
Wienerbackhendl **20**–2804
Wienerleber **20**–2804
Wienerrostbraten **20**–2804
Wienerschnitzel **20**–2804
Wienerspritz **20**–2806
Wienerwurst **20**–2806
Wildbretkoteletten **20**–2808
Wildspitzer Fish Casserole **20**–2812

Avignon

Daube d'Avignon **4**–545
Gelée d'Avignon **6**–813

Azerbaijan

Pilaff **1**–95

B

Bali

Tamarind Fish **18**–2472

Balkans

Champagne Cup **1**–108
Chicken Pilff **1**–108
Yogurt Cued Cheese **21**–2929

Baltic

Agurkai su Rukcsia Grietne **1**–6

Bath

Buns **1**–128
Chap **1**–128
Oliver **1**–129

Bavaria

Apfelkuchen **1**–38
Bavarois **1**–133
Kaffeecreme **8**–1094

Belgium

Anguilles au Vert **1**–34
Carbonnade de Boeuf **3**–323
Chou Rouge à la Flamande **3**–418
Flemish Carrots **6**–724
Gâteau Flamand à la Crème **6**–802
Oiseaux sans Têtes **12**–1565
Pets de Nonnes **13**–1760
Rizotto Corine **16**–2137
Waterzooi de Brochet **20**–2747
   de Poulet **20**–2749
Wissant Pears with Ginger **21**–2855
Zoondam Pork Ratatouille **22**–3014

Berlin

Berliner Eintopf **2**–162

Bolivia

Manjar Blanco **10**–1305

Boston

Baked Beans **2**–212
Brown Bread **2**–212

Brazil

Aubergines **2**–238
Feijoada **5**–683
Macaroons **2**–236
Nut **2**–239
Rice **2**–240
Swiss Roll **2**–239
Vatapa **19**–2609
Xuxu **21**–2898

Bremen

Bremer Kuchen **2**–254

Brittany

Gigot d'Agneau à la Bretonne **6**–824

Budapest

Croissants **4**–501

Burma

Wuntho Crabmeat Soup **21**–2877

California

Chiopino **3**–404
Roast Pork **16**–2142

Cameroons

Dos **5**–57

Canada

Mallow Brownies **10**–1294
Manitoba Poppy Seed Roll **10**–1304
Quebec Butter Tarts **15**–2004
   Onion Soup **15**–2005
   Split Pea Soup **15**–2008
Wedding Salad **20**–2752
White Hatter Stew **20**–2787
Winnipeg Dipper **21**–2848
Wrangell Stuffed Halibut **21**–2870
Wunnumminlake Chicken Bouilli **21**–2877

Central Asia

Herb Fritters **7**–945

Ceylon see Sri Lanka

Chelsea

Buns **3**–369

Chile

Matambre **10**–1341
Pastel de Choclo **13**–1692

China

Abalone, Chinese-Style **1**–1
Bamboo Shoots **1**–109
Barbecued Beef **1**–117
Bean Curd **1**–139
   Sprouts **1**–140
Beef Braised in Soya Sauce **2**–144
Bird's Nest Soup **2**–172
Broccoli Chinese-Style **2**–265
Brown Bean Sauce **2**–269
Cantonese Roast Pork **3**–314
Cha Chiang Mein **10**–1369
Ching-chao-ch'ao Niu-jou **3**–402
Chow Mein **10**–1368
Deep-Fried Prawns **4**–551
Drumsticks, Shanghai-Style **5**–578
Duckling, Sweet and Sour Sauce **5**–588
Egg-Drop Soup **5**–619
   Foo Yung **5**–621
Feng Kuo **5**–683
Foong Yin Mun Sung **6**–735
Fried Chinese Cabbage **6**–755
   Mixed Vegetables **6**–755
   Pineapple and Cucumber **6**–755
   Rice **3**–402; **6**–757
Gingered Beef **6**–836
Ham and Fried Rice **7**–916
Hao Yiu Ngiu Jou Pien **7**–923
Honeyed Ham with Bean Sprouts **7**–967
Ho Tao Chi Tin **7**–972
Hot and Sour Soup **7**–977
Hui Mein **10**–1369
Huang Yu Tang **7**–978
Hung Shao Chi **8**–985
   Chu Jo **8**–986
   Ngiu Jou **8**–986
   Pai T'sai **8**–986
Hwang Chi Hsia Ren **8**–996
   Yu Pien **8**–998
Jou Ping Hui Por-Ts'ai **8**–1082
   Si Chow Ching Ts'ai **8**–1082
   Yuan Ts'a Hui **8**–1084
Kebabs with Soy Sauce and Sherry **8**–1120
Kidneys Fried with Chillis **9**–1136
   with Sesame Sauce **9**–1138
K'ou Tse Ngiu Lan **9**–1170
Kumquat Pineapple Salad **9**–1179
Kuo Pa Jou Tin **9**–1181
   Tieh Chi **9**–1181
   Tieh Yu Pien **9**–1182
Lamb's Liver with Cauliflower **9**–1202
Lin-Moun Chi **9**–1240
Liu Jou-Pien **9**–1245
   Yu-Pien **9**–1245
Lou Jo **10**–1272
Mange-Tout Salad **10**–1300
Mee Feng Jou **10**–1368
   Ngiu Jou **10**–1368

Yu Pien **10**–1368
Mein **10**–1368
Mi Tse Tui **11**–1409
Nai-yu-ts'ai hsin **11**–1467
Pai Chiu Tung Chi **12**–1656
  Chiu Tung Li Yu **12**–1656
  Chou Chi **12**–1658
  Chou Jou **12**–1658
Pork Balls with Ginger **14**–1880
  in Wine Sauce **14**–1881
Shao Jou **17**–2296
  K'o Yang Jou **17**–2296
Shih-tzu-tou **17**–2302
Shrimps Stir-Fried with Ginger **17**–2314
Sole in White Sauce **17**–2345
Spinach Soup **18**–2388
Stir-Fried Beef with Broccoli **18**–2412
Sweet and Sour Carp **18**–2456
  Liver **18**–2457
Tan Mein **10**–1369
Pork with Sweet and Sour Sauce **14**–1900
Prawn Chow Mein **15**–1966
  Egg Foo Yung **15**–1968
Quick-Fried Chicken Cubes with White Sauce
  15–2027
  Spinach with Shredded Pork **15**–2027
Roast Pork **3**–402
Run Tsa Chin Kan **16**–2187
  Li Chi **16**–2187
Takhing Pancakes with Pork Filling **18**–2468
Tsingshih Soup **19**–2557
Tushikow **19**–2581
Velvet Crab **19**–2664
Vermicelli with Vegetables **20**–2678
White Cut Chicken **20**–2785
Winter Prawns **21**–2858
Wontons **21**–2858
Wonton Soup **21**–2860
Woosung Crabmeat Soup **21**–2865
Wuchow Chicken Mandarin **21**–2874
Wuki Chicken **21**–2876
Yangchow Noodles **21**–2907
Yu-Chi-Tang **21**–2947
  Hsiand Jou **21**–2948
  -Lang-Chi **21**–2948
Yueng Chow Rice **21**–2952
Yun Yook **21**–2961
Yunnan Quick-Fried Prawns on Crackling Rice
  21–2962

Connecticut

Election Cake **5**–641

Cornwall

Heavy Cake **7**–942
Stargazey Pie **18**–2400

Cuba

Daiquiri **4**–526

Cumberland

Rum Butter **4**–519
Sauce **4**–519

Czechoslovakia

Bramborová Polevka **2**–233
Bramborové Knedliky **2**–233
Bublanina **2**–277
Dušene Zeli **5**–592
Kynute Ovocné Knedliky **9**–1185
Moravian Loaf **11**–1418
Pečana Husa se Zelim **13**–1727
Prague Apricot Loaf **14**–1958
  Chicken **14**–1960
Veal Ragoût **4**–525

D

Dakar

Shrimp **4**–526

Denmark *see also* **Scandinavia**

Agurkesalat **1**–7
Danish Pastries **4**–530
Danish Pork **4**–532
Dansk Hönse Kasserolle **4**–533
Flaeskeaeggekage **6**–718
Fyldt Kalvefars **6**–778
Gaasesteg med Aeblerog Svesker **6**–778
Havrekex **7**–935
Himmelsk Mundfeld **7**–953
Kale with Cream Sauce **8**–1100
Kalvesuppe me Madeira og Champignoner
  8–1102
Kannellagkage **8**–1102
Koervelsuppe **9**–1161
Krammerhuse **9**–1171
Kransekager **9**–1172
Kyllinger med Rejer og Asparges **9**–1185
Medaljer med Fløde **10**–1356
Morbred med Aebler og Svesker **11**–1418
Nyrer med Karbonadepølser og Roraeg **11**–1540
Potato and Herring Salad **14**–1927
Risalamande **16**–2129
Smørkage **17**–2334
Smørrebrød **4**–528
Stegt Ørred med Fløde sors **13**–1810
Veiled Country Lass **19**–2660

Devonshire

Layer Cake **5**–561
Splits **5**–562

Donegal

Mussel Soup **5**–572

Dundee

Cake **5**–590
Marmalade **5**–591

Dusseldorf

Salad **5**–592

E

East Africa

Guava Pie **7**–291
Mkate Wa Mayai **11**–1409
Mombasa Biscuits **11**–1415

Ecuador

Lamb Stew **5**–603

Egypt

Braised Steak **5**–638
Brown Beans **5**–638
Fata **5**–678
Yi'allaq Meringue Dessert **21**–2923

England

Adam and Eve Pudding **1**–4
Ale Berry **1**–10
  Posset **1**–10
Angels on Horseback **1**–32
Apple Dumplings **1**–45
  Florentine **1**–46
  Hat **1**–48
  Pie **1**–48
Bakewell Tart **1**–107

Banbury Cakes **1**–115
Bath Buns **1**–128
  Chap **1**–128
Blackberry and Apple Pie **2**–180
Bloater **2**–186
Boar's Head **2**–189
Boiled Beef and Dumplings **2**–205
Bubble and Squeak **2**–277
Chelsea Buns **3**–369
Chicken, English-Style **3**–379
Chocolate Pudding **3**–412
Christmas Pudding **4**–421
Crumpets **4**–513
Cumberland Rum Butter **4**–519
Cumberland Sauce **4**–519
Derby Biscuits **4**–555
Devonshire Layer Cake **5**–561
  Splits **5**–562
Doughnuts **5**–574
Eccles Cakes **5**–602
Essex Meat Layer Pudding **5**–660
Exeter Pudding **5**–664
Exmouth Stew **5**–665
Fish and Chips **5**–707
Flummery **6**–730
Game Pie **6**–790
Goose Pie **7**–849
Guards' Pudding **7**–891
Half Pay Pudding **7**–907
Hard Sauce **7**–924
Hasty Pudding **7**–935
Heavy Cake **7**–942
Hindle Wakes **7**–953
Hogs Pudding **7**–954
Hot Cross Buns **7**–973
Hot Pot **7**–974
Huntingdon Fidgett Pie **8**–994
Indian Pudding **8**–1020
Isle of Wight Doughnuts **8**–1034
Jugged Hare **8**–1086
Lancashire Hot Pot **9**–1205
  Tea Cakes **9**–1205
Lardy Cake **9**–1210
Leg of Lamb, Boiled **9**–1219
Lemon Posset **9**–1230
Macaroni Cheese **10**–1276
Madeira Cake **10**–1284
Maids of Honour **10**–1258
Manchester Tart **10**–1298
Marmalade Pudding **10**–1322
Melted Butter Sauce **10**–1373
Melting Moments **10**–1374
Melton Mowbray Pie **10**–1374
Mint Sauce **11**–1404
Mistress Hill's Cakes **11**–1407
Mother's Bread Pudding **11**–1426
Newcastle Potted Salmon **11**–1501
Norfolk Dumplings **11**–1513
North Country Cake **11**–1517
Northumberland Puddings **11**–1518
October Cobbler **12**–1550
Old English Cide Cup **12**–1568
  Venison Stew **12**–1569
Onion Sauce **12**–1594
Parkin **12**–1679
Pease Pudding **13**–1724
Piccalilli **13**–1774
Pork Pie **14**–1900
Potted Hare **14**–1935
  Shrimps **14**–1936
Pound Cake **14**–1952
Queen of Puddings **15**–2011
Quin's Sauce **15**–2035
Reading Apples **15**–2074
Reform Sauce **15**–2089
Rock Buns **16**–2145
Roly-Poly with Dried Fruit **16**–2159
Rutland Gooseberry Cream **16**–2194
Sage and Onion Stuffing **16**–2206
Sally Lunn **16**–2213
Salmagundy **16**–2214
Sand Cake **16**–2237
Sausage Rolls **17**–2256
Scotch Eggs **17**–2279
Sea Pie **17**–2281

International

Seed Cake 17–2283
Shrewsbury Biscuits 17–2307
Simnel Cake 17–2320
Singin' Hinny 17–2323
Solomon Grundy 17–2346
Spice and Nut Cake 17–2376
Squab Pie 18–2398
Stargazey Pie 18–2400
Steak and Kidney Pie 18–2404
Steamed Pudding 18–2409
Summer Pudding 18–2442
Sussex Hot Pot 18–2446
Syllabub 18–2459
Tansy Apple Cream 18–2477
    Cakes 18–2477
Toad in the Hole 18–2504
Treacle Layer Pudding 19–2538
    Tart 19–2540
Tripe and Onions 19–2546
Twelfth Night 19–2582
Uppingham Pâté 19–2593
Veal Cake 19–2616
    and Ham Pie 19–2624
Venison Pie 20–2687
Victoria Sandwich 20–2687
Welsh Rarebit 20–2759
Wensley Dale Marrow 20–2764
Wessex Lamb 20–2764
West Country Junket 20–2767
Widdecombe Duck 20–2803
Wigs 20–2807
Wiltshire Ham 20–2817
    Lardy Cake 20–2818
Wimple Rabbit Casserole 20–2821
Windsor Soup 20–2826
Worcester Sauce 21–2866
Wytcherley Pork Chops 21–2892
Yorkshire Cheesecakes 21–2935
    Christmas Gingerbread 21–2935
    Giblet Pie 21–2938
    Ploughboy 21–2938
    Pudding 21–2940

Estonia

Rissoles 5–662

F

Finland

Cabbage Rolls 3–286
Jänispaisti 8–1058
Kesäkeitto 9–1125

Florence

Bistecca alla Fiorentina 2–177
Zuppa di Fagioli Fiorentina 22–3059

Florida

Lime Cream Pie 9–1238

France

Agneau à la Bonne Femme 1–5
    en Brochette 1–5
Aïgo Bouido 1–7
    -Sau 1–8
Aiguillette de Boeuf 1–9
Aillade 1–9
Allemande Sauce 1–12
Allumettes 1–17
Alouettes sans Têtes 1–24
Amuse-Gueules au Fromage 1–28
Anchoyade 1–29
Apricot Condé 1–52
Artichokes à la Provençale 1–70
Aubergines Farcies 1–82
Babas 1–96–8
Barquettes aux Abricots 1–126
Bâtonnets aux Amandes 1–129

Béarnaise Sauce 2–141
Béchamel Sauce 2–141
Beignets 2–160
Beurres Composées 2–164–7
Biftek 2–169–71
Biscuit fin au Beurre 2–175
Bisque d'Homard 2–176
Blanquette de Veau 2–185
Boeuf 2–191–203
Bordelaise Sauce 2–210
Bordure de Pommes de Terre 2–210
Bouchées 2–218–9
Bouillabaisse 2–220
Boules de Neige au Chocolat 2–223
Bourride 2–224
Brèdes 2–253
Brie Cheese Croquettes 2–256
Brioche 2–258
Bûche de Noel 21–2957
Cabillaud 3–288
Café Brûlot 3–292
Cailles avec Raisin en Timbale 3–292
Carbonnade de Boeuf à la Provençale 3–324
Carpe Mâtelote 3–326
Cassoulet 3–334–6
Charlotte Russe 3–359
Chicken Sauté Marengo 3–390
Choucroute Garnie 3–416
Clafoutis 4–423
Coeur à la Crème 4–435
Coq au Vin 4–444
Coquelets sur Canapés 4–446
Coquilles St-Jacques 4–448–50
Coulis de Tomates Provençale 4–464
Coupe Jacques 4–464
Darioles de Volaille 4–534
Darne de Saumon à l'Ancienne 4–536
    Montpelier 4–537
Daube d'Avignon 4–545
    de Boeuf 4–545
    à la Provençale 4–546
Daurade au Fenouil 4–549
    aux Tomatoes 4–550
Demi-Glace Sauce 4–555
Devil Sauce 4–555
Dinde aux Marrons 5–566
Diplomate Pudding 5–568
Duck, Norman-Style 5–584
    Provençale 5–586
Duxelles 5–594
Ecrevisses à la Nage 5–602
Emincé de Porc 5–642
Entrecôte à la Lyonnaise 5–648
    Mirabeau 5–648
    au Poivre 5–649
Epinards à la Provençale 5–652
Escaloppes de Veau 5–653–6
Escargots à la Bourguignonne 5–657
Estouffat 5–664
Faisan en Chartreuse 5–670
    Normand 5–671
    en Oranges 5–671
    au Riz Basquais 5–672
    Souvaroff 5–672
    au Vin Rouge 5–673
Feuilles de Chou Farcies 5–687
Filets de Lièvre Chasseur 5–694
    de Merland Dieppoise 5–696
    de Sole Cecilia 5–697
    de Turbot Hermitage 5–697
Flamri de Semoule 6–718
Flangarde 6–722
French Dressing 6–748
Fricassée de Poulet 6–752
Galettes aux Abricots 6–783
    Amandines 6–784
    au Camembert 6–784
    de Feuilles 6–785
    au Fromage 6–785
    Nantaises 6–785
    Noisettine 6–786
    Normande 6–786
Garbure 6–796
Gâteau de Marron 6–803
    Mille-feuille 6–804

Noir 6–806
    St Honoré 6–808
Gelée d'Avignon 6–813
Genevoise Sauce 6–813
Genoise Sponge 6–816
Gigot d'Agneau à la Bretonne 6–824
Gouère aux Pommes 7–855
Gougère 7–857
Gougnettes 7–857
Grand-Veneur Sauce 7–860
Gras Double Provençale 7–864
Gratin de Pommes de Terre à la Dauphinoise 7–866
    à la Savoyarde 7–866
Grenouilles aux Persil 7–876
    à la Provençale 7–877
Harengs à la Boulangère 7–927
    à la Meunière 7–927
Haricot Mutton 7–928
Haricots Verts 7–929–30
Hochepot 7–954
Homard à l'Americaine 7–958
    à la Parisienne 7–960
    Provençale 7–960
Huîtres Gratinées à la Crème 8–981
    Marinées 8–981
Hyères Chicken 8–999
Ile Flottante 8–1016
Jambon Braisée au Madère 8–1055
Jarret de Boeuf en Daube 8–1061
Laitues aux Crevettes 9–1188
Langue de Boeuf Braisée 9–1206
Languedoc Lamb Pie 9–1207
Langues de Chats 9–1207
Lapin aux Poireaux 9–1208
    à la Sauce Moutard 9–1209
Légumes à la Grecque 9–1221
Madeleines 10–1285
Marquie Alice 10–1323
Marron Soufflé 10–1327
Marrons Montpélier 10–1327
Merlans Farcies aux Crevettes 10–1382
Mirlitons 11–1405
Mirton de Boeuf 11–1406
Moules Marinière 11–1429
Napoleon au Fromage Blanc 11–1472
Navarin de Mouton 11–1479
    Printanier 11–1480
Navets Glacés 11–1481
Neige de Pêches au Champagne 11–1490
Noisettes d'Agneau Arlésienne 11–1506
    à la Clamart 11–1506
    de Porc aux Pruneaux 11–1509
    au Sauce Champignon 11–1508
Noix de Veau aux Fruits 11–1510
Normandy Pear Tart 11–1514
    Pork 11–1516
Oeufs Mornay 12–1557
    Robert 12–1558
Oie rôtie Farcie 12–1561
    aux Marrons 12–1562
    aux Pruneaux et Foie Gras 12–1562
Omelette Americaine 12–1578
    Arnold Bennett 12–1578
    Chasseur 12–1579
    aux Fines Herbes 12–1580
    Mousseline 12–1582
    Parmentier 12–1583
    au Rhum 12–1584
    Soufflée 12–1585
Onion Soup 6–749
Oublies à la Parisienne 12–1630
Ouillade 12–1632
Pain de Choufleur 12–1658
    de Saumon 12–1660
Palissade aux Marrons 12–1663
Palmiers 12–1666
Panade 12–1668
Paris-Brest 12–1677
Pastis 13–1693
Pâté à Pâté 13–1702
    Sucrée 13–1702
Paupiettes 13–1704
Peach Tart 6–749
Pear Condé 13–1721

Pêches Cardinal **13**–1728
Perdrix aux Choux **13**–1751
Petite Marmite **13**–1758
Petits Fours **13**–1758–60
  Pois à la Française **13**–1764
Pets de Nonnes **13**–1766
Pipérade **13**–1815
Pissaladière **14**–1824
Pithiviers **14**–1827
Poires Belle Hélène **14**–1850
  au Caramel **14**–1851
Pommes et Abricots à l'ancienne **14**–1862
  à la Bourguignonne **14**–1862
  au Cognac **14**–1864
  Gratinées **14**–1864
  Grimaldi **14**–1864
  Normandes **14**–1866
Pommes de Terre Anna **14**–1866
  Dauphine **14**–1868
  Fondante **14**–1868
  Ménagère **14**–1869
  Soufflées **14**–1871
Pot au Feu à la Béarnaise **14**–1910
Potage Crecy **14**–1918
  d'Hiver **14**–1918
  Parmentier **14**–1919
  Paysanne **14**–1920
Potato Salad **6**–749
Pouding d'Avocat **14**–1936
Poulet Brandade **14**–1942
  en Casserole à la Bonne Femme **14**–1942
  aux Girolles à la Crème **14**–1948
  Sauté à L'Archiduc **14**–1948
  Sauté à la Bordelaise **14**–1950
  Sauté Chasseur Sauce **14**–1950
Profiteroles **15**–1976
Quatre Quarts **15**–2002
Quenelles **15**–2014
Queue de Boeuf au Vin **15**–2021
Quiche **15**–2022–5
Ragoût de Boeuf aux Pois-Chiche **15**–2046
Raie au Beurre Noir **15**–2050
Ratatouille **15**–2067
Ravigote Butter **15**–2068
Religieuse **15**–2095
Remoulade Sauce **15**–2096
Rillettes **16**–2124
Ris de Veau au Beurre Noir **16**–2127
Riz à l'Imperatrice **16**–2135
Roast Chicken **6**–749
Robert Sauce **16**–2144
Rouennaise Sauce **16**–2169
Sablé **16**–2197
Salade Bagration **16**–2210
  de Boeuf Côte d'Azur **16**–2210
  Chaude Basquaise **16**–2210
  Niçoise **16**–2212
Salmis de Pigeons **16**–2217
Sardines Grillées au Sauce Bresson **16**–2240
Sauce Bigarade **17**–2246
  Gribiche **27**–2246
  Ivoire **17**–2247
Saumon à la Sauce Verte **17**–2254
Savarin **17**–2260
Sole Bonne Femme **17**–2340
  Dugleré **17**–2340
  Meunière **17**–2342
  Mornay **17**–2342
  Normande **17**–2343
  Veronique **17**–2344
Soufflé au Grand Marnier **17**–2354
Soupe d'Albigeoise **16**–2358
  de Poissons **17**–2358
Suédois **18**–2437
Suprêmes de Volaille Rossini **18**–2445
Squid Stuffed with Rice **18**–2400
Talairan Rice Salad with Garlic Sausage **18**–2468
Talmouses **18**–2471
Tarragon Sauce with Artichokes **18**–2481
Tarte à la Viande **18**–2487
Terrine de Canard **18**–2497
  Maison **18**–2497
Timbale aux Epinards **18**–2500
Tomates Farcies **18**–2510

Toulouse Spiced Pâté **19**–2527
Touraine Chestnut Pudding **19**–2529
Tournedos à la Béarnaise **19**–2529
  Chasseur **19**–2529
  à la Clamart **19**–2532
  Rossini **19**–2532
Tourte aux Champignons **19**–2533
  de Porc **19**–2534
Tranches de Jambon à la Normande **19**–2534
  à la Sauce Madère **19**–2537
Truites aux Amandes **19**–2554
  Meunière **19**–2555
Turbot à Piémontaise **19**–2563
Uchaud Fish Mousse **19**–2586
Vacherin Chantilly **19**–2600
Veal Orloff **19**–2629
Veau Braisé au Vin Blanc **19**–2638
  en Cocotte **19**–2639
  Sauté Marengo **19**–2641
Velouté d'Artois **20**–2717
Vol-au-Vent **20**–2717
  d'Eté **20**–2718
  Pétoncles **20**–2719
  de Ris de Veau **20**–2720
Volaille en Escabèche **20**–2714
Whiting Colbert **20**–2794

G

Gascony

Cassoulet Gascoigne **3**–336

Genoa

Genoese Salad **6**–815
Pandolce Genovese **12**–1670
Stufato alla Genovese **18**–2429

Georgia (U.S.S.R.)

Khachapuri **9**–1126

Germany

Apfelbettelmann **1**–38
Apfelkuchen **1**–38
Apfelstrudel **1**–38
Apfelfannkuchen **1**–45
Bauernsuppe **1**–133
Bavarian Strudel **1**–133
Beef and Clove Casserole **6**–817
Beer Soup **2**–157
Berliner Eintopf **2**–162
Birnensuppe **2**–173
Black Forest Cherry Cake **2**–182
Blumenkohlsuppe **2**–188
Bratwurst **2**–237
Bremer Küchen **2**–254
Calve's Brains **6**–819
Country Breakfast **6**–818
Dattelkuchen **4**–544
Datteltorte **4**–545
Düsseldorf Salad **5**–592
Erbsenpuree **5**–562
Filetgoulasch mit Saurer Sahne **5**–692
Frankfurter Kranz **6**–739
Gaisburger Marsch **6**–780
Gänsebraten mit Füllsel **6**–795
Gefüllte Melonen **6**–812
Gefüllter Heilbutt mit Krabben **6**–812
Geschmorte Schweinefleisch mit Kümmel **6**–820
Gluhwein **6**–840
Griessklösschen **7**–879
Griesstorte **7**–880
Grüne Melone Mousse **7**–887
Gurkenbowle **7**–897
Gurkensosse **7**–897
Hasenpfeffer **7**–932
Himmel und Erde **7**–952
Holstein Flan **7**–956
Hummer mit Dill **8**–982

Hummersalat **8**–984
Hutzelbrot **8**–996
Kaffeecreme **8**–1094
Kaiser Garnele mit Dillsosse **8**–1096
Kalbsfrikassee mit Spargel **8**–1098
Kalbshirn in Muscheln **8**–1098
Kalbszunge mit Pilzen **8**–1099
Kalte Ente **8**–1100
Kapaun mit Champignon und Speck **8**–1105
Karlstadtklösse **8**–1107
Käse Bouillon mit Ei **8**–1110
Käsekuchen **8**–1111
Käsespätzle **8**–1112
Käsestrudel **8**–1110
Kasseler Rippchen **8**–1114
Katerfrühstück **8**–1114
Kinderkuchen **9**–1142
Kirschen mit Eiskrem **9**–1149
Kirschkuchen **9**–1150
Kirschpfannkuchen **9**–1151
Königsberger Klops **9**–1166
Kopfsalat **9**–1166
Kotelett mit Pflaumen **9**–1168
Krabbensuppe **9**–1171
Kuchen **9**–1177
Kümmelkartoffeln **9**–1179
Labskaus **9**–1186
Lauchsalat **9**–1214
Leipziger Allerlei **9**–1223
Linsensuppe **9**–1240
Mandel Halbmonde **10**–1298
Mandeltorte **10**–1298
Mohrschokoladedessert **11**–1412
Neustadtrouladen **11**–1495
Nudel mit Käse **11**–1526
Nuremburg Chocolate Pudding **11**–1527
  Spice Squares **11**–1528
Nuss Schlagensahne **11**–1531
Nusspastete **11**–1529
Obsttorte **12**–1546
Ochsenzunge mit Madeira Sosse **12**–1548
Pichelsteiner **13**–1776
Potato Salad **6**–819
Pretzels **15**–1974
Puttlingen Biscuits **15**–1992
Rahmschnitzel **15**–2050
Rebhühner mit Birnen **15**–2074
Rindfleisch mit Zitronensosse **16**–2124
Rollmops **16**–2158
Rouladen **16**–2173
Sauer Kartoffeln **17**–2250
Sauerbraten **17**–2249
Sauerkraut **17**–2252
Schokoladenpudding **17**–2273
Schwabische Schnecken **17**–2274
SeHeriesalat mit Obst **17**–2286
Shoemaker's Pot **17**–2303
Sour Milk Cake **17**–2360
Spice Cake **6**–819
Spitzgebäck **18**–2391
Stollen **18**–2415
Strudel Beef Rolls **18**–2427
Uberbackenes Sauerkraut **19**–2585
Urchins **19**–2596
Warmer Malteser Spargel **20**–2736
Wecksnappspiess **20**–2749
Weingelee **20**–2755
Weinkraut **20**–2755
Westphalian Chicken **20**–2773
Wotan's Delight **21**–2868
Wurst, Sweet and Sour Sauce **21**–2879
Wurstsalat **21**–2880
Zahna Meat **21**–2970
Zander im Ofen Gebäcken mit Weisswein **21**–2976
  Schnitte mit Senfbutter **21**–2977
Zwetschgenknödeln **22**–3072
Zwetschgenkuchen **22**–3072
Zwieback mit Rhabarber **22**–3076
Zwiebelfleisch **22**–3077
Zwiebelkuchen **22**–3077

Ghana

Kyenam **9**–1184

International

Ntroba Forowee 11–1526
Obuasi Peanut Stew 12–1547
Zofe Spinach Soup 22–3007

Glamorgan

Sausages 6–838

Goa

Alebele 1–10
Vinegar Curry 7–843

Grahamstown

Chicken 7–859

Greece

Arni Psito 1–62
Athenian Walnut Cake 1–81
Augolemono Soup 1–88
Celeris à la Grecque 3–344
Easter Halva Cake 5–600
    Lamb 5–600
    Soup 5–601
Escravaniya 5–658
Fennel Greek-Style 5–685
Fish Bake Greek-Style 5–704
Fritters with Honey Sauce 6–761
Garides me Saltsa Domates 6–798
Ghourounaki Yemisto me Feta 6–824
Giouvetsi 6–837
Honey and Cream Cheese Pie 7–962
Kakavia 8–1096
Kalamaria Yemista 8–1096
Kebabs Marinated in Yogurt 8–1118
Keftedes 9–1122
Kotopouto Kapama 9–1169
Kourambiedes 9–1170
Lamb Apricot Pilaff 9–1192
    Kebabs 7–868
    Patties 9–1201
    Stew 7–869
Moscari Psito 11–1424
Moussaka 11–1432
Phoenician Honey Cakes 13–1773
Revythia 15–2098
Salad 7–869
Taramasalata 18–2479
Tiraka Tiganita 18–2503
Zorba's Tipsy Cake 22–3016
Zorin's Lamb with Lemon Sauce 22–3018

H

Hamburg

Katerfrühstück 8–1114

Hawaii

Chicken 7–936
Cream 7–937
Fruit Cocktail 7–937
Macadamia Nut Pie 10–1275
Sauce 7–938
Soup 7–938
Zombie's Secret 22–3012

Holland see Netherlands

Hungary

Agneau à la Hongroise 1–6
Apple Pie 8–987
    Salad 8–988
    Soup 8–988
Apricot Soup 8–988
Aranyaluska 1–59
Beef 8–988
Bogrács Gulyás 2–204
Borjúp"ork"olt 2–211

Cheese Dip 8–988
Cherry Soup 8–989
Chicken Paprikash 3–384
Chocolate Layer Cake 8–989
Cream Cake 8–989
Doboz Torte 5–569
Eggplant 5–637
Esterhazy Steaks 5–664
Fish Soup 8–990
Goulasch 7–857–8
Karpion b'Paprika 8–1108
Layered Cabbage 8–991
    Crêpes 8–991
Lesco 9–1234
Liptauer Cheese 9–1242
Mushrooms Hungarian-Style 11–1453
Palacsinken 12–1663
Paprika and Vegetable Stew 12–1674
Paprikasertésborda 12–1674
Pork Goulasch 14–1894
Rétes 15–2098
Rigo Jancsi 16–2122
Sauerkraut 8–992
    and Sausage Soup 8–992
Tolona Baked Carp 18–2509
Töltött Csuka 18–2059
Transylvania Goulasch 19–2537
Znojemsky Goulasch 22–3002

Hyères

Chicken 8–999

I

Ibadan

Shrimp Salad 8–1000

India

Adrak Chutney 1–4
Alebele 1–10
Aviya 1–91
Badami Gosht 1–104
Bangra Masala 1–115
Bharta 2–168
Biryani 2–174
Boti Kebabs 2–212
Channa Dhal 3–356
Chapatti 3–357
Coconut Barfi 4–429
    Rice 4–430
Country Captain 8–1105
Curried Potatoes and Rice 4–523
Dhansak 5–562
Dopyaza 5–572
Dry Beef Curry 5–579
Ekuri 5–638
Gajjar Halva 6–781
Goan Vinegar Curry 7–843
Gobi Ki Sabzi 7–843
Gosht aur Aloo 6–823
Guleh Kambing 7–895
Gurda Khorma 7–897
Huseini Kebabs 8–995
Jal Farazie 8–1042
Jhinga Kari 8–1076
    Pakoras 8–1076
    Tikka 8–1077
Jumping Potatoes 8–1098
Kabli Channa 8–1091
Kebab Massalam 8–1120
Kheema 9–1128
Khichri 9–1128
Lamb Cashew Nut Curry 9–1194
Lime Pickle 8–1020
Madras Chicken Curry 10–1286
Mango Chutney 10–1300
Meat and Fruit Pilau 10–1352
Mulligatawny Soup 11–1449
Murg Bhana 11–1449
Murgi Dahi 11–1450

Nargisi Koftas 11–1476
Pakora 12–1662
Paratha 12–1675
Poona Pilaff 14–1873
Pork Korma 14–1896
    Vindaloo 14–1901
Prawn Curry 15–1967
Puris 15–1991
Raan 15–2037
Rava Kheer 15–2068
Rice with Aubergines and Potatoes 16–2112
Roghan Gosht 16–2152 ✓
Rustom's Chicken 16–2192
Sabzi Oulao 16–2198
Sag Gosht 16–2205
Sambal 16–2232
Sambar 16–2234
Samosas 16–2235
Seekh Kebabs 17–2284
Sevian 17–2290
Shakooti Rassa 17–2293
Shrikhand 17–2307
Sondhia 17–2349
Talawa Gosht 18–2468
Tali Machee 18–2470
Tamarind Sauce 18–2473
Tamatar Bharta 18–2473
    Chatni 18–2473
    Machli 18–2474
    Sas 18–2474
Tandoori Chicken 18–2474
Tenali Baked Fish 18–2493
Thayir Kari 18–2497
Tikkah Kebab 18–2500
Tomato Rice 18–2516
Umabai's Baked Spiced Fish 19–2587
    Curried Partridges 19–2588
    Spiced Almond Chicken 19–2588
Umido di Carne 19–2590
Vath 19–2610
Vegetable Bharta 19–2641
    Kitcheri 19–2645
    Pulao with Prawns 19–2651
Vendai Kai Kari 20–2665
Vindaloo with Chicken 20–2695
Wengi Bhat 20–2762
Wengyachen Bharit 20–2763
White Pumpkin Halva 20–2790
Yogurt and Banana Raita 26–2926
    Chicken 21–2926
Zarda 21–2982
Zeera Gosht 21–1987
    Murg 21–2989

Indonesia

Baked Bananas 8–1022
Beef in Cheese Sauce 8–1022
Chicken Satay 8–1022
Fried Rice 8–1022
Geelrys 6–811
Ikan Goreng 11–1477
Nasi Goreng 11–1477
Plaice, Indonesian-Style 14–1839
Serundeng 17–2289
Rendang 15–2096
Sambal 16–2233
Sate 17–2242
Soy Sauce Chicken 17–2364
Spiced Rice 18–2381
Yellow Rice 21–2917
Zell Pilau 21–2989

Iran

Ashe Reste 1–74
Baghali Polo 1–105
Borani Esfanaj 2–209
Chelo 13–1752
Chicken with Rice and Cherries 3–387
Dano Chicken 4–532
Eshkaneh 5–659
Fesenjen 5–686
Fried Rice 13–1752
Garmi Polo 6–801

Kadu Polo **8**–1092
Khoresh Bademjan **9**–1128
  Holu **9**–1130
  Karafs **9**–1130
Nut Bread **8**–1029
Onion and Aubergine **13**–1753
  Soup **5**–659
Prune Soup **8**–1030
Quince Lamb and Honey Stuffing **15**–2032
Red Bean and Lamb Casserole **15**–2076
Tabriz Meatballs **18**–2464
Yogurt Soup **13**–1753; **21**–2931

Ireland

Barm Brack **1**–125
Bookmaker's Sandwich **2**–209
Boxty **2**–225
Champ **3**–351
Cockle Soup **4**–428
Coddle **4**–434
Colcannon **4**–438
Donegal Mussel Soup **5**–572
Irish Moss Mould **8**–1030
Kidneys in their Overcoats **9**–1140
Leek and Oatmeal Broth **8**–1030
Michaelmas Goose **10**–1389
Potato Cakes **8**–1031
Soda Bread **8**–1031
Stew **8**–1032
Tipsy Pudding **8**–1032
Turlough Tarts **19**–2577
Wood Pigeons **2**–2864
Yellowman **21**–2917

Israel

Essig Flaish **5**–660
Falafel **5**–674
Hag Ha'asif Tzimmis **7**–905
Hamindas **7**–922
Haroset **7**–930
Kaklehten **8**–1094
Klops **9**–1154
Kusa **9**–1183
Marak Perot Car **10**–1311
Moussaka with Fish **11**–1431
Oznei Haman **12**–1654
Plum and Cherry Soup **14**–1847
Rollade **6**–2155
Taiyika Chicken **18**–2467

Italy

Abbachio Brodettato **1**–3
Anguilla Marinate **1**–34
Aragosta Fra Diavolo **1**–59
Arrosto Perugino **1**–65
Bagna Cauda **1**–105
Bistecca **2**–177
Bollito Misto **2**–206
Bolognese Sauce **2**–206
Braciuolia di Manzo **2**–226
  Ripiene **2**–226
Cacciucco **3**–290
Calamari Ripieni **3**–296
Cape ai Ferri **3**–315
Cappelletti in Brodo **3**–319
Cavolo in Agrodolce **3**–342
Cenci **3**–347
Cheese and Almond Pudding **8**–1036
Cherries **8**–1036
Chicken San Marino **3**–390
Chocolate Loaf **8**–1037
Coda di Bue con Sedano **4**–432
Costoletta di Maiale alla Pizzaiola **4**–458
  alla Modenese **4**–458
Costolette di Agnello alla Milanese **4**–458
Crostat di Ricotta **4**–506
Eels Neapolitan-Style **5**–606
Eggplant Casserole **5**–536
  Parmesan **5**–638
Fagioli al Forno **5**–668
  con Prosciutto **5**–668
  con Tonno **5**–668

Farfallette Dolci **5**–676
Fegatini di Pollo alla Salvia **5**–680
Fegato alla Veneziana **5**–680
  di Vitello alla Parmigiana **5**–680
  di Vitello al Pomodoro **5**–680
Fettucine alla Romana **5**–687
Filletti di Sogliole Pizzaiola **5**–692
Frittata di Carne e Vegetali **6**–759
Frittata di Ricotta con Salsa Rossa **6**–759
Fritto Misto **6**–762
  di Mare **6**–762
Fusili Noodles with Tomatoes and Cheese **6**–777
Gamberi con Riso **6**–787
Genoese Salad **6**–815
Gnocchi al Forno Napoletana **7**–841
  di Patate **7**–842
  Verdi **7**–842
Green Pea Soup **7**–872
  Peas with Ham **7**–872
  Rice **7**–874
Guido's Sausage Rolls **7**–893
Ham with Figs **7**–915
Insalata di Arancia e Limone **8**–1026
  di Finocchio, Cicoria e Pomodoro **8**–1026
  di Fontina **8**–1026
Involtini alla Contadino **8**–1028
  alla Marito **8**–1029
  alla Sophia **8**–1029
Italian Bananas **8**–1035
  Sauce **8**–1038
Kale with Onions and Italian Sausage **8**–1100
Kid, Italian-Style **9**–1131
  Tomatoes and Courgettes **9**–1132
Lasagne **9**–1212
Liver, Italian-Style **9**–1242
Manicotti with Ricotta **10**–1303
Marinara Sauce **10**–1314
Maritozzi Uso Fornaio **10**–1317
Meat Loaf **8**–1037
  Vegetable Soup **8**–1037
Melon Salad **8**–1038
Mozzarella Bread **8**–1038
  in Carozza **11**–1440
  Chicken **11**–1441
  Crespoltini **11**–1441
Negroni Cocktail **11**–1486
Noce di Vitello Farcito **11**–1502
Oca Arrosta Ripiena **12**–1548
Olive Pizza **12**–1572
Onions in Sweet and Sour Sauce **12**–1597
Osso Buco **12**–1630
Pandolce Genovese **12**–1670
Panettone **12**–1672
Peperonata **13**–1737
Peperoni all Bagna Cauda **13**–1738
  Ripieni **13**–1738
  e Zucchini **13**–1739
Pepperoni Pizza **13**–1747
Perciatelli con Piselli **13**–1749
Peveragno Lamb Chops **13**–1767
Piatto Freddi di Ortaggi **13**–1773
Piedmont Salad **13**–1783
Pistou **14**–1824
Pizza **14**–1828
Pizzaiola Sauce **14**–1828
Pollo alla Bolognese **14**–1856
  alla Cacciatora **14**–1856
  alla Diavola **14**–1858
Potato and Cheese Salad **14**–1929
  Peppers and Olives with **14**–1927
Prosciutto **15**–1978
Putignano Ham **15**–1992
Quadrettini con Prosciutto **15**–1995
Quattro Formaggi con Riso **15**–2002
Quattrostagione Pizza **15**–2002
Ravioli **15**–2068–73
Ricotta Balls **16**–2120
  al Caffè **16**–2120
Risotto alla Bolognese **16**–2130
  Alla Milanese **16**–2132
Romana Noodles **16**–2160
Salsicce con Fagioli **16**–2226
Scaloppine al Limone **17**–2268
  alla Marsala **17**–2269

  alla Romana **17**–2269
Sgombro Ripieno **17**–2290
Spaghetti con Aglio, Olio e Peperoncino **17**–2368
  all'Amatriciana **17**–2368
  alla Carbonara **17**–2369
  con Salsa Verdi **17**–2369
  alle Vongole **17**–2370
Spiedini **18**–2383
Stufatino alla Romana **18**–2487
Stufato alla Genovese **18**–2429
  al Vino Rosso **18**–2429
Suppli **18**–2443
Tagliarini con Fegatini **18**–2464
Tagliatelle con Prosciutto **18**–2465
Torrone de Cioccolata **19**–2523
Totellini **19**–2524
Trentina Dumplings **19**–2543
Trote al Pomodoro **19**–2549
  Sulla Brace **19**–2550
Turdillos **19**–2564
Tuscan Meat Loaf **19**–2581
Uccelli Scappati **19**–2586
Uova alla Cacciatora **19**–2593
Veal Fasano **19**–2622
  Stuffed with Peppers and Sausage **19**–2637
Venetian-Style Eel Kebabs **20**–2667
Verona Veal **20**–2681
Vitello con Melanzane **20**–2708
  con Piemontese con Tartufi **20**–2709
  con Salvia **20**–2709
  con Siciliana **20**–2710
  Tonnato **20**–2710
  con Uova **20**–2711
  Vincenzo **20**–2711
Zabaglione **21**–2966
Zampa di Vitello alla Toscana **21**–2974
Zapponeta Pasta Shells with Mussels **21**–2981
Zeppole **21**–2992
Zite with Italian Sausage **22**–3002
  Meatballs and Tomato Mushroom Sauce **22**–3002
  with Port **22**–3002
Zogno Veal Cutlets **22**–3007
Zucca Cheese Loaf **22**–3026
  alla Parmigiano **22**–3027
Zuccherini **22**–3028
Zucchero e Formaggio alla Crema **22**–3028
Zucchini all'Agrodolce **22**–3028
  con Aneto **22**–3030
  e Cavolfiore **22**–3030
  in Dolce **22**–3030
  al Formaggio **22**–3030
  con Fritelle **22**–3032
  con Mandorle **22**–3032
  alla Marinara **22**–3033
  Orientali **22**–3033
  e Peperoni **22**–3033
  Pomodori e Finocchio **22**–3036
  Ripieni **22**–3036
  in Stufato **22**–3037
  in Sufflé **22**–3037
Zuccotto **22**–3038
Zucutto Torone **22**–3040
Zuppa di Anguille **22**–3058
  di Cozze **22**–3058
  di Fagioli Fiorentina **22**–3059
  Inglese **22**–3059
  di Pollo **22**–3060
  di Verdura **22**–3061

Ivory Coast

Grill **8**–1040

J

Jamaica

Beans **8**–1050
Casserole **8**–1050
Coconut Sauce **8**–1050
Coffee **8**–1050

International

Pepper Wine **8**–1052
Pie **8**–1052
Plain Cake **8**–1052
Rum Pudding **8**–1052
   Punch **8**–1053
Spice Loaf **8**–1053

Japan

Fondue Japonais **6**–733
Fox Noodles **6**–737
Gengi Tsukeyaki **6**–814
Grilled Chicken with Soy Sauce **7**–881
   Fish in Japanese Wine Sauce **7**–881
Gyuniki Teriyaki **7**–898
Hamaguri Sakani **7**–919
   Shigure-Ni **7**–919
Japanese Cake **8**–1059
Katsudon **8**–1116
Kawasaki Chicken **8**–1117
Kuzuhiki Soup **9**–1184
Lotus Root Salad **10**–1272
Mackerel in Soy Sauce **10**–1282
Maze Gohan **10**–1346
Mushrooms with Cucumber **11**–1452
Namasu Marengo **11**–1469
Nasu Karashi Sumiso-ae **11**–1478
Sake Steamed Chicken **16**–2209
Sardines, Ginger and Garlic **8**–1060
Sliced Raw Fish **17**–2304
Sukiyaki **18**–2440
Tempura **18**–2491
Teriyaki **18**–2494
Yok Kai Chi Marinated Salmon **21**–2932
Yosenabe **21**–2943

Java

Curry **8**–1061
Dadar Djawa **4**–526
Fish in Soy Sauce **8**–1062
Pork **8**–1062
Steak **8**–1062

Jewry

Gebratener Pike **6**–811
Gefillte Fish **6**–811
Honey Balls **7**–961
Ingber **8**–1024
Jewish Noodles **8**–1076
Jumping Potatoes **8**–1089
Karp po Zydowsku **8**–1109
Karpion b'Paprika **8**–1108
Kartoffelsalat **8**–1109
Kasha Cholent **8**–1112
Kichlach **9**–1130
Knaidlach **9**–1157
Knishes **9**–1158
Kugel with Apples **9**–1178
Latkes **9**–1213
Lekach **9**–1223
Liver Hors d'Oeuvre **9**–1247
Matzo Brei **10**–1344
   Chicken and Dill Casserole **10**–1344
   Fry **10**–1345
   Kugel **10**–1345
Mother's Matzo Balls with Chicken Soup **11**–1426
Onion and Prunes **12**–1594
Teiglach **18**–2491
Tzibbele Kugel **19**–2583
Tzimmis **19**–2584
Yiddish Chopped Liver **21**–2923
   Meatballs **21**–2924
Yom Tov Deep Fried Fish **21**–2933

Jordan

Stuffed Lamb **8**–1080

K

Kerkenna Island

Hotpot **9**–1124

Korea

Kimi Chu **9**–1141
Pork Fillets **14**–1892
Vegetable Salad **9**–1167

L

Lancashire

Hot Pot **9**–1205
Tea Cakes **9**–1205

Languedoc

Cassoulet **3**–334
Estouffat **5**–664
Lamb Pie **9**–1207

Lapland

Loaf **9**–1209

Latin America

Empanadas **5**–644
Frijoles Refritos **6**–758
Pichones en Mole **13**–1776
Shrimp Seviche **17**–2313
Zapellitos Rellenos **21**–2979
Zihuatanejo Fish Salad **21**–2996
Zihufitanejo **22**–2997
Zoller Pumpkin Stew **22**–3009

Latvia

Alexander Torte **1**–11

Leipzig

Leipziger Allerlei **9**–1223

Lithuania

Kolduny Litewskie **9**–1165

Long Island

Bake **10**–1268
Clam Sauce **10**–1269
Halibut Steaks **10**–1270
Seafood Pilau **10**–1270

Louisiana

Coconut Pie **10**–1272
Rice Pudding **10**–1272
Snack **10**–1272

Luxembourg

Gauffres de Luxembourg **6**–809

M

Madras

Chicken Curry **10**–1286

Maine

Cauliflower and Tomato Pickle **10**–1289
Pancakes **10**–1288

Malaysia

Dindings Duck **5**–567
Fish **10**–1290
Grilled Chicken **10**–1292
Kachang Bendi Goreng **8**–1091
Omelet **10**–1292
Penang Beef **13**–1734
   Cabbage **13**–1734
   Chicken **13**–1734
   Curry Puffs **13**–1734
Pork Chops **10**–1293

Manchester

Tart **10**–1298

Martinique

Ragoût Martiniquaise **15**–2048

Maryland

Baltimore Stuffing **12**–1653
Chicken **10**–1336
Seafood Soup **10**–1337

Melton Mowbray

Pie **10**–1374

Mediterranean

Chicken **10**–1363
Fish Stew **1**–8
Morue à l'Americaine **11**–1423
Seafood Stew **10**–1365
Veal Stew **10**–1365

Mexico see also Latin America

Albondigas **1**–9
   Soup **1**–10
Caldo Tlalpeño **3**–340
Cauliflower Mexicana **3**–340
Ceviche **3**–350
Chicken with Fruit **10**–1384
Chilli con Carne **10**–1385
   Spaghetti **10**–1386
Costillas a la Mexicana **4**–457
Elegante **5**–642
Enchiladas **5**–645
Fruit Drink **10**–1386
Garbanzos a la Mexicana **6**–796
Jewfish, Mexican-Style **8**–1076
Kidney Beans, Mexican-Style **9**–1134
Meatballs with Hot Sauce **10**–1356
Ostiones **12**–1630
Pork Fillets **10**–1386
   and Rice **10**–1386
Quesadillas **15**–2018
Stuffed Eggs **10**–1388
   Peppers **10**–1388
Tamale Casserole **18**–2471
Tinga de Cerdo y Terneral **18**–2503
Yucatan Fish in Tomato Sauce **21**–2951
   Stuffed Peppers **21**–2951

Middle East

Daoud Pasha **4**–534
Dolmadakia **5**–571
Dulma **5**–589
Gormeh Sabzi **7**–855
Haroset **7**–930
Hummus bi Tahina **8**–985
Lamb Stew with Vegetables **9**–1202
Mahasha **8**–1087
Ma-Mounia **10**–1297
Muhalabia **11**–1443
Nanban Zuke **11**–1470
Nazkhatun **11**–1483
Noisettes d'Agneau Ismail Bayeldi **11**–1507
Peppers Stuffed with Lamb and Rice **13**–1743
Pita **14**–1826

Quince Sherbet **15**–2032
Rutabiya **16**–2194
Shikaree Slices **17**–2302
Turkish Delight **19**–2577
Yakhmi Pulao **21**–2903

Minorca

Vegetable Soup **11**–1401

Monaco

Noisettes d'Agneau Monegasque **11**–1508

Morocco see also North Africa

Chicken **11**–1421
Couscous **4**–468
Djeja M'qalia **5**–569
Espada Abouga **5**–659
Harira **7**–930
Jege Zeifoon **8**–1062
Kefta **9**–1121
Kelaa Almond Pastries **9**–1122
Lamb and Honey Casserole **11**–1422
Liver Kebabs **11**–1422
Quotban **15**–2036

N

Nantes

Gallettes Nantaises **6**–785
Nantais Biscuits **11**–1470
Nantes Cake **11**–1470

Naples

Beef Stew **11**–1483
Bistecca alla Pizzaiola **2**–177
Eels Neapolitan Style **5**–606
Gnocchi al Forno Napoletano **7**–841
Pizza Capri **14**–1832
Pizzas **11**–1484
Spaghetti alle Vongole **17**–2370
Stuffed Peppers **11**–1485
Veal Chops **11**–1485
Zeppole **21**–2992

Near East

Pork with Peanuts and Grapes **11**–1486

Netherlands

Boerenkaas Soep **2**–190
Delft Cake **4**–554
Dutch Almond Biscuits **5**–592
Split Pea Soup **5**–592
Steak **5**–592
Erwtensoepe **5**–652
Flensjes **6**–725
Gevulde Botterboek **6**–821
Kool **6**–821
Pannekoek **6**–822
Hutspot **8**–995
Melktert **10**–1370
Oliebollen **12**–1570
Pork **11**–1493
Roomborstplaat **16**–2162
Rotterdam Crumb Cake **16**–2169
Varkenslappen met Abrikozen **19**–2608
Voedzaam Salade **20**–2714
Zuidhorn Liver and Rice **22**–3044

Nevada

Rice Cake **11**–1495

New England

Boiled Dinner **11**–1496
Clam Chowder **4**–426

Indian Pudding **8**–1020
Maine Cauliflower and Tomato Pickle **10**–1288
Pancakes **10**–1288
Maple Sparerib Casserole **10**–1309
Marlborough Cake **10**–1319
Meat Loaf **11**–1496
New Haven Baked Aubergine **11**–1498
Parker House Rolls **12**–1678
Red Flannel Has **15**–2081
Soda Bread **11**–1496
Wedding Cake **11**–1496

New Orleans see also Southern United States

Barbequed Pork Chops **11**–1499
Lamb Cutlets **11**–1499
Oysters Rockefeller **12**–1652
White Peach Cream **20**–2789

New York

Bronx Cocktail **2**–269
Manhattan Clam Chowder **10**–1302
Cocktail **10**–1303

Nigeria see also West Africa

Fried Yams **8**–1034
Jollof Rice **11**–1502
Yam Chips **21**–2905
Zaria Beef **21**–1982

Norfolk

Dumplings **11**–1513
Fruit Chutney **11**–1513

Normandy

Duck Norman-Style **5**–584
Faisan Normand **5**–671
Galette Normande **6**–786
Omelette Normande **12**–1583
Pear Tart **11**–1514
Pommes Normandes **14**–1866
Pork **11**–1516
Poulet à la Normande **14**–1946
Sablés **16**–2197
Tranches de Jambon à la Normande **19**–2534

North Africa

Kerkenna Island Hotpot **9**–1124
Meatballs with Spicy Sauce **10**–1360
Millet Bread **10**–1392
Tajine de Mouton aux Fruits Secs **18**–2467
Vegetable Couscous **19**–2643

Northumberland

Puddings **11**–1518

Norway see also Scandinavia

Bergens Fiskesuppe **2**–162
Blotkake **2**–186
Cucumber and Potato Soup **11**–1519
Fish Pudding **11**–1519
Fløtevafler **6**–728
Juleskinke **8**–1087
Junidessert **8**–1090
Linser **9**–1240
Melkeringer **10**–1370
Oslo Eggs **12**–1628
Salad **12**–1629
Soda Bread **11**–1520
Venison Steaks **11**–1520

Nova Scotia

Potato Patties **11**–1524
Salmon Cream **11**–1524

O

Oban

Kipper Pancakes **12**–1546

Ohio

Meat Pie **12**–1559
Pudding **12**–1560

Oregon

Venison **12**–1624

Oslo

Eggs **12**–1628
Salad **12**–1629

P

Pakistan

Chicken Tikka **12**–1661
Lamb Chops **12**–1661
Pulau **12**–1661
Seekh Kebabs **17**–2284
Sevian **17**–2290
Sindhi Chicken **17**–2320
Spiced Liver **12**–1662
Zarda **21**–2982

Paris

Oublies à la Parisienne **12**–1630

Penang

Beef **13**–1734
Cabbage **13**–1734
Chicken **13**–1734
Curry Puffs **13**–1734

Pennsylvania

Dutch Chicken Corn Soup **13**–1735
Mixed Chow Chow **13**–1736
Poultry Stuffing **13**–1737
Scrapple **17**–2279
Shoofly Pie **17**–2304
Sweetcorn and Chicken Soup **18**–2452

Persia see Iran

Perth

Tart **13**–1755
Treacle Loaf **13**–1755

Peru see also Latin America

Chowder **13**–1756
Corvina a la Peruana **4**–457
Ocopa Arequipeña **12**–1550
Pork Stew **13**–1756
Quetchuan Duck **15**–2021
Seviche **13**–1756

Philadelphia

Pepper Pot **13**–1772

Philippines

Morcon **11**–1419
Piquant Stew **14**–1822

Piedmont

Insalata di Fontina **8**–1026
Ravioli Piedmontese **15**–2072
Salad **13**–1783

International

Poland

Beetroot **14**–1853
Bigos **8**–993; **14**–1853
Carp **14**–1854
Chlodnik **9**–1154
Honey Drink **9**–1176
Kromeski **9**–1175
Krupnik **9**–1176
Opiekanki z Grochu **12**–1598
Orange and Almond Flan **14**–1853
Pirogen **14**–1822
Pyrizhky **15**–1992
Racuchy **15**–2044
Tomaszow Roast **18**–2510
Vanilla Crisps **19**–2605
Warsaw Liqueur **20**–2736
Zrazi eze Ribi **22**–3022
    s Kashie **22**–3022

Portugal

Bacalhau **1**–98
Batatas à Portuguêsa **2**–169
Caldo Verde **3**–298
Canja **3**–311
Figos Recheados **5**–691
Fisherman's Lemons **6**–716
Iscas **8**–1033
Kebabs **14**–1908
Lombo di Porco Corn Pimentos **10**–1267
Ovos Duros à Portuguêsa **12**–1635
Queijadas de Evora **15**–2013
Rissoies de Camarâo **16**–2132
Xareu Portuguese **21**–2895

Prague

Apricot Loaf **14**–1958
Chicken **14**–1960

Provence

Aïgo Bouïdo **1**–7
Anchoyade **1**–29
Artichokes à la Provençale **1**–70
Bourride **2**–225
Cabillaud Provençale **3**–289
Carbonnade de Boeuf à la Provençale **3**–324
Coulis de Tomates Provençale **4**–464
Daube de Boeuf à la Provençale **4**–547
Duck Provençale **5**–586
Epinards à la Provençale **5**–652
Escalopes de Veau à la Provençale **5**–656
Gras Double Provençale **7**–864
Grenouilles à la Provençale **7**–864
Omelette Niçoise **12**–1582
    Provençale **12**–1584
Pissaladières **14**–1824
Provençale Mushrooms **15**–1980

Q

Quebec

Biscuits **15**–2004
Onion Soup **15**–2005
Split Pea Soup **15**–2008

R

Richmond (Surrey)

Maids of Honour **10**–1288

Romania

Alivenci **1**–12
Ardei cu Untdelemn **1**–60
Ghiveciu **6**–823
Moussaka **11**–1431

Pork Bake **16**–2182
Sweet Bread **16**–2183

Rome

Aubergine Hors d'Oeuvres **16**–2160
Gnocchi alla Romana **7**–842
Scallopine alla Romana **17**–2269
Spaghetti all' Amatriciana **17**–2368
Stufatino alla Roman **18**–2427

Russia

Bitkis **2**–178
Bitokes **2**–178
Blinis **2**–186
Borscht **2**–211
Capon, Russian-Style **3**–316
Chicken Kiev **3**–382
Circassian Chicken **4**–424
Dill Piroshki **5**–565
Easter Bread **5**–596
    Cake **5**–597
    Festival Bread **5**–597
Eggs **16**–2188
    and Cabbage Pirog **5**–615
Farshmak **5**–677
Fish Bake **16**–2188
Fricadelles de Veau Smitane **6**–752
Fruit Mould **16**–2190
Gogol Mogol Sauce **7**–844
Golubtsy **7**–846
Gooseberry Kissel **7**–852
Gus-Khrustalny Cream Pudding **7**–898
Herring and Beetroot Salad **16**–2190
Honey and Nut Toffee **7**–964
Hussar Meat Loaf **8**–995
Kambala s Shpinatom **8**–1102
Karani **8**–1106
Kärdia Cabbage **8**–1107
Kasha and Liver Bake **8**–1112
    with Mushrooms and Onions **8**–1113
Kazan Salad **8**–1117
Khachapuri **9**–1126
Khalva **9**–1126
Kholodetz **9**–1128
Kissel **9**–1151
Kizlyar Boby **9**–1151
Klodnik **9**–1154
Klyazma River Soup **9**–1155
Korsakov Meat and Potato **9**–1168
Koflety Pozharskie **9**–1169
Krendel **9**–1172
Kromeski **9**–1175
Kulebiak z Ryba **9**–1175
Kurnic **9**–1183
Kutya **9**–1183
Lvov Black Bread **10**–1275
Malynka's Lamb Dumpling **10**–1296
Nalesniki **11**–1468
Nesselrode Pudding **11**–1493
Okroshka **12**–1568
Pashka **13**–1689
Rassolnik **15**–2066
Rybnia Solnianka **16**–2195
Salad **16**–2191
Shashlik **17**–2297
Sour Cream Icing **17**–2360
Sturgeon, Russian-Style **18**–2433
Tabaka **18**–2462
Uvat Fish Soup **19**–2598
Uzbeck Plov **19**–2598
Vanilla Kholodetz **19**–2606
Wood Pigeons Russian-Style **21**–2865
Yablonchni Apple Soup **21**–2900
Zalovnoye s Solonine **21**–2971
Zhukov Boiled Beef Dinner **21**–2944
Zruza **22**–3021
Zvezdochki **22**–3070

Rutland

Gooseberry Cream **16**–2194

S

San Francisco

Sourdough Bread **16**–2236

Scandinavia

Almond Apples **17**–2272
Äppelformar **1**–40
Birnensuppe **2**–173
Crayfish, Scandinavian-Style **4**–478
Fiskebudding med Rejesors **6**–740
Fransk Aeblekage **6**–779
Fyllda Strutar **6**–778
Glogg **6**–840
Hasselbackpotatis **7**–934
Kalve Soubise **8**–1102
Kalveschnitzel med Sur Fløte **8**–1101
Kalvetournedos **8**–1102
Kartoffelmos **8**–1109
Kogt Torsk med Asparges **9**–1163
Krumkaker **9**–1175
Länttulaatikka **9**–1208
Leverposteij **9**–1235
Meatballs in Cream **10**–1356
Orientalisk Kyckling **12**–1626
Potato Fritters **17**–2273
Prinsessbakelser **15**–1975
Rababerkompott **15**–2037
Röding I Kapprock **16**–2147
Rødkaal **16**–2150
Rollmops **16**–2158
Sill I Kapprock **17**–2319
Söta Kakor **17**–2351
Spritsar **18**–2397
Toscakake **19**–2526
Uunissa Paistettu Hauki **19**–2597
Vatkattu Marjapuuro **19**–2611
Vetekaka med Applen **20**–2683
Veteken **20**–2684
Viking Apple Pudding **10**–2693
Vinbarsbrännin **20**–2694
Wine and Fruit Jellies **20**–2694

Scotland

Almundigoes **1**–9
Arbroath Smokies **1**–3
Atholl Brose **1**–82
Bannocks **1**–116
Baps **1**–116
Black Bun **13**–1696
Cock-a-Leekie **4**–427
Crowdie **4**–511
Cullen Skink **4**–519
Dundee Cake **5**–590
    Marmalade **5**–591
Finnan Haddie **5**–700
Het Pint **7**–945
Mince Casserole **10**–1395
Oatcakes **11**–1542
Oatmeal Bannocks **12**–1543
    Stuffing **12**–1545
Oban Kipper Pancakes **12**–1546
Peebles Crab Bake **13**–1730
Perth Tart **13**–1755
    Treacle Loaf **13**–1755
Pitcaithly Bannock **14**–1827
Poloni **14**–1902
Porridge **14**–1902
Rothesay Pudding **16**–2168
Scones **17**–2275
Scotch Broth **17**–2278
    Pancakes **5**–578
Selkirk Bannocks **17**–2284
Shortcake **17**–2304
Skirlie **17**–2323
Stovies **18**–2418
Tain Cereal **18**–2467
Uachdar Pudding **19**–2584
Wyviss Porridge Apples **21**–2893

Serbia *see* **Yugoslavia**

Shanghai

Drumsticks 5–578

Shrewsbury

Biscuits 17–2307

Sicily

Broccoli alla Siciliana 2–264
Cassata alla Siciliana 3–334
Pomodori alla Siciliana 14–1871

Singapore

Kapitan Curry 8–1105

South Africa

Asynpoeding 1–81
Bobotie 2–190
Boiled Pudding 17–2363
Edna's Chicken 5–604
Grahamstown Chicken 7–859
Honey Spice Cake 7–964
Ingelegte 8–1024
Koeksusters 9–1160
Mos-bolletjies 17–1424
Sosaties 17–2350
Transvaal Braised Lamb 19–2537
Veldt Bread 19–2660
Waterbul 20–2741
Wytfontein Salad 21–2893
Zulu Beef Stew 22–3050

South Sea Islands

Kokonda 9–1164

Southern United States

Ambrosia 1–25
Gumbo Soup 7–887
Martinville Soulfood Stew 10–1334
Mint Julep 11–1402
New Orleans Barbequed Pork Chops 11–1499
  Lamb Cutlet 11–1499
Turnip Tops Creole-Style 19–2580

Spain

Alioli Sauce 1–12
Almejas a la Marinera 1–17
Andalousian Beefsteaks 1–30
  Chicken 1–31
Arroz con Pollo 1–65
Besugo al Horno 2–164
Boeuf à la Catalan 2–196
Calamares en su Tinto 3–296
Calderete de Jerez 3–297
Caldo de Cobgrio 3–297
  de Haba 3–298
Callos Vizcainos 3–301
Catalan Fish Soup 3–337
  Omelet 3–338
Cerdo a la Aragonesa 3–348
Chicken, Spanish-Style 3–392
Chick-Peas, Catalan 3–399
Chorizo Patties 3–416
Duck, Spanish-Style 5–587
Eel Stew 5–607
Eggplant Basquaise 5–635
Escabeche 5–652
Escudilla de Cataluña 5–658
Fabada 5–666
Gazpacho 6–810
Habas à la Catalana 7–898
Hake with Ham and Egg Stuffing 7–907
Huevas à la Flamenco 7–980
Judias Verdes con Salsa de Tomate 8–1084
Kidney Beans and Brains in Spanish Sauce 9–1132
Lenguado Catalan 9–1233
Merluza à la Marinera 10–1382

Mero à la Naranja 10–1383
Mollina Soup 11–1414
Mullet Andalucian Style 11–1446
  Baked in Rock Salt 11–1447
Naranjas al Kirsch 11–1474
Oil Biscuits 12–1564
Olla Podrida 12–1574
Omelet 17–2371
Oviedo Beef Stew 12–1634
Paella 12–1654
Partridge, Catalan-Style 13–1684
Perdices Estofadas 13–1751
Pollo en Pepitoria 14–1858
Riñones al Jerez 16–2126
Torrejas de Maiz Tierno 19–2522
Torrijas 19–2523
Tortas de Aceite 19–2524
Trebujena Grapefruit Cocktail 19–2541
Turron 19–2580
Xato 21–2897
Zanahoria Rillenas 21–2975
Zarzar Red Pepper and Onion Soup 21–2984
Zarzuela 21–2984
Zujar Chicken Liver Casserole 22–3044

Sri Lanka

Dhal Curry 5–562
Tea Punch 18–2490

Sweden see also Scandinavia

Äppel-Fläsk 1–40
Beef Cakes 18–2446
Biff à la Lindström 2–169
Brown-Baked Potato Slices 2–276
Cabbage Soup 3–287
Chokladkaka 3–416
Coffee Bread 4–436
Gooseberry Pie 18–2447
Gravad Lax 7–867
Inlagda Rödbetor 8–1026
Jansson's Temptation 8–1059
Kalops 8–1100
Klenäter 9–1154
Köttbullar 9–1169
Lamb Stew with Dill 18–2448
Marinated Lamb 18–2449
Meat Loaf 18–2449
Njursaute 11–1502
Norrländsk Laxsoppa 11–1516
Oxrullader 12–1639
Pytt i Panna 15–1994
Rye Bread 2–248
Sillgratin 17–2318
Solöga 17–2346
Sommargryta 17–2347
Vortlimpor 20–2721

Switzerland

Bircher Muesli 2–172
Birnbrot 2–172
Emincé de Veau 5–642
Engadiner Nusstorte 5–646
Fondue Suisse 6–734
Poteca 14–1933
Rösti 16–2167
Winter Soup 21–2853
Zurich Hazelnut Biscuits 22–3063
  Lamb Delight 22–3064

Syria

Dala'Mahsi 4–526
Fattoush 5–678
Ma-Mounia 10–1297
Walnut and Orange Pastries 18–2462

T

Thailand

Kaeng Chud Kai Hed 8–1093
  Saku 8–1093
Rice Noodles with Pork and Shrimps 16–2114
  with Spicy Beef 16–2114
Yahm Chompu 21–2910

Tonga

Salad 18–2519

Trinidad

Chicken Pilau 19–2544
Coconut Ice-Cream 19–2544
Maraccas Beach Pilau 10–1310
Shark and Bakes 19–2544

Tunisia

Ajja 1–9
Chicken Casserole 19–2561
Kerkenna Island Hotpot 9–1124
Lamb Baked with Peppers and Cheese 9–1193

Turkey

Arnavut Cigari 1–62
Dügün Corbari 5–588
Goose Liver Pilaff 7–848
Hazelnut Sauce 7–940
Imam Bayeldi 8–1016
Lamb Casserole 19–2577
Taraba 18–2478
Yogurt, Chicken and Barley Soup 21–2928
Yogurtli Kebab 21–2931

U

Ukraine

Borscht 2–211
Lvov Black Bread 10–1275

V

Venezuela

Bien me Sabe de Coco 2–171
Chicken 20–2667

Venice

Anguilla Marinate 1–34
Eel Kebabs 20–2667

Vienna

Buchteln 2–278
Chestnut Cake 20–2688
Chocolate Dessert 20–2688
Croquettes 20–2689
Fingers 20–2690
Fresh Pea Soup 20–2690
Fruit Custard 20–2692
Raspberry Pudding 20–2693
Sachertorte 16–2198
Wienerbackhendl 20–2804
Wienerleber 20–2804
Wienerrostbraten 20–2804
Wienerschnitzel 20–2804
Wienerspritz 20–2806
Wienerwurst 20–2808
Wildbretkoteletten 20–2808

Virgin Island

Salt Cod Stew 20–2704

W

Wales

Bara Brith **1**–116
Glamorgan Sausages **6**–838
Huish Cake **7**–980
Trout and Bacon **19**–2759
Welsh Cakes **20**
    Rarebit **20**–2759
    Stew **20**–2760
Wen Welsh Duck **20**–2760
Y Mwd Leeks **21**–2899

West Africa

Beef and Fruit Curry **20**–2766
Dakar Shrimp **4**–526
Fruit and Avocado Spread **20**–2766
Groundnut Stew **7**–883
Ibadan Shrimp Salad **8**–1000
Ishu Didi **8**–1034
Ivory Coast Grill **8**–1040
Jinja Stew **8**–1078
Jojamba **8**–1080
Maluwe Poulet **10**–1296
Nakompatoa Forowee **11**–1468
Nkontomire Fro **11**–1502
Peanut Butter and Chicken Stew **13**–1717
Pepper and Corned Beef Hash **13**–1739
Puntzin **15**–1989
Red Mullets Baked with Shrimps **15**–2082
Zindo Vando **22**–2997
Zungeru Peanut Pork **22**–3054

West Indies

Avocado **20**–2767
Chicken Casserole **20**–2768
Hoppin' John **7**–969
Jug Jug **8**–1084
Pepperpot **20**–2768
Pilau **20**–2768
Ponche de Crème **14**–1872
Salt Pork and Lentil Soup **16**–2231
Tuloons **19**–2557
Virgin Island Salt Cod Stew **20**–2404

Y

Yemen

Chick-Pea Salad **21**–2919
Lamb Casserole **21**–2920

Yorkshire

Cheesecakes **21**–2935
Christmas Gingerbread **21**–2935
Giblet Pie **21**–2935
Ham Pie **21**–2935
Lamb Hot Pot **21**–2938
Meat Pudding **21**–2938
Pancakes **21**–2938
Ploughboy **21**–2938
Pudding **21**–2940
Rarebit **21**–2940
Savoury Meatballs **21**–2940

Yugoslavia

Barbecued Beef **21**–2953
Brodet Dubrovna **2**–269
Cevap **3**–348
Cevapcici **3**–348
Djuveč **5**–569
Hunter's Hare Stew **21**–2954
Jaagnjeci Beet **8**–1042
Ražnjici **15**–2073
Rice Pudding **21**–2954
Serbian Fish **17**–2288
Shoulder of Lamb **21**–2954
Veal Sandwiches **21**–2954
Zara Ice-Cream Dessert **21**–2981
Zupanja Red Snapper Bake **22**–3055

Z

Zambia

Cheese and Fish Fritters **21**–2973

Zanzibar

Salt Cod Curry **21**–2979

Zurich

Hazelnut Biscuits **22**–3063
Lamb Delight **22**–3064
Roast Pork **22**–3064
Veal and Parsnip Pie **22**–3065